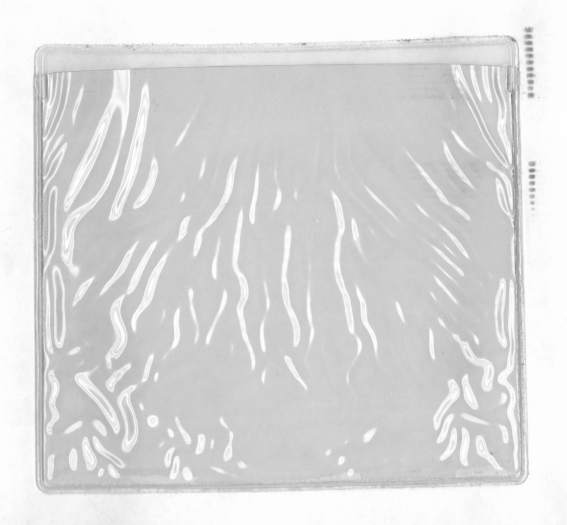

Dreamweaver UltraDev 4: The Complete Reference

About the Authors

Ray West is the Vice President and CIO of Workable Solutions, Inc., an Orlando-based company that specializes in Web-based health insurance administration. He has an extensive background in the development of data-connected Web applications including some of the first Internet Fantasy Football sites developed for NBC, HBO, and *USA Today* in 1996. Once Ray remembers what the term "spare time" means, he will likely begin practicing for his bass guitar lessons once again and maybe write a book. Ray is married and the proud father of the smartest one-year-old boy ever to grace this planet.

Tom Muck has dabbled in the computer field since 1983 but has recently turned to full-time programming. Tom works primarily in Web application development using ColdFusion and ASP, but he develops UltraDev extensions for fun. Tom has also recently been honored by Macromedia for Best UltraDev Extension at the Dreamweaver Conference in Monterey, CA.

Tom Allen is a software developer in Oviedo, Florida, and a software development consultant for medical instrument companies. His software experience includes Windows-based medical instrumentation software, Web applications, and multimedia courseware. Tom has been a frequent lecturer around the world in the field of Applied Psychophysiology and has published a number of scientific research papers in the field. He is currently working on virtual instrumentation systems for Web-based healthcare and medical research. He and his wife, Gayle, have two daughters, four grandchildren, three miniature schnauzers, and two authentic Australian Didgeridoos. In his spare time Tom enjoys playing his handmade LoPrinzi guitar and composing electronic music.

Dreamweaver UltraDev 4: The Complete Reference

Ray West
Tom Muck
and Tom Allen

Osborne/**McGraw-Hill**

New York Chicago San Francisco
Lisbon London Madrid Mexico City
Milan New Delhi San Juan
Seoul Singapore Sydney Toronto

Osborne/**McGraw-Hill**
2600 Tenth Street
Berkeley, California 94710
U.S.A.

To arrange bulk purchase discounts for sales promotions, premiums, or fund-raisers, please contact Osborne/**McGraw-Hill** at the above address. For information on translations or book distributors outside the U.S.A., please see the International Contact Information page immediately following the index of this book.

Dreamweaver UltraDev 4: The Complete Reference

234567890 DOC DOC 01987654321

Book p/n 0-07-213001-6 and CD p/n 0-07-213016-4
parts of
ISBN 0-07-213017-2

Publisher
  Brandon A. Nordin

Vice President & Associate Publisher
  Scott Rogers

Acquisitions Editor
  Jim Schachterle

Project Editor
  Jennifer Malnick

Acquisitions Coordinator
  Timothy Madrid

Technical Editor
  Massimo Foti

Copy Editors
  William McManus, Sally Engelfried,
  Lunaea Weatherstone

Proofreader
  Linda Medoff

Indexer
  Jack Lewis

Computer Designers
  Lauren McCarthy, Tara Davis

Illustrators
  Michael Mueller, Lyssa Sieben-Wald

Series Design
  Peter F. Hancik

This book was composed with Corel VENTURA™ Publisher.

Contents

Part I

Getting Started with Dreamweaver UltraDev

Part II

An Introduction to Web Scripting

Part III

Integrating Databases With UltraDev

Part IV

Building Language-Specific Data-Driven Sites

Part V

Getting The Most Out of UltraDev

Acknowledgments

It is almost too cliché to say, but writing a book like this is a scary amount of work. It only happens with the help and support of a whole lot of very talented people who work hard to make the authors look good.

First, thank you to Wendy Rinaldi at Osborne, who did so much to help this concept come together and actually make it possible for us to write this book.

We would also like to thank everyone else at Osborne for their continued support throughout the writing process, including our patient editor Jim Schachterle, Timothy Madrid, and Jennifer Malnick, who is insane but very good at what she does.

Macromedia has been very supportive of our efforts, and we'd like to thank everyone there, especially Julie Thompson, Randy Edmunds, Rob Christensen, Daniel Taborga, Noah Hoffman, Russ D. Helfand, Larry McLister, Mike Barbarelli, Scott Fegette, Matt Lerner, and Joel Huff and Leona Lapez.

Our technical editor, Massimo Foti, has been a tremendous help—both with the book and with the learning of the extensive development process. And thank you to Bruce Neiman, a truly gifted graphic artist and Dreamweaver/Fireworks monster.

Also, thanks to Drew McLellan, Joe Milicevic, Rick Crawford, and Dave George for help along the way during the first UltraDev beta.

Our thanks and appreciation goes to the folks at Senternet (www.senternet.com) and VirtualScape (www.virtualscape.com) for their JSP and ColdFusion site hosting help, respectively. Please visit them if you are in need of hosting services.

There are so many people that had to wait for me while I was working on this book. I can never tell them how much I appreciate their understanding. To my wife, Susan, who would do anything so that I could be free to work—I Love You and thank you for everything. To my boy, Caleb, who is only one but knows that Daddy always has that dang laptop going, I am so proud of you.

Thank you to Tom Muck, who continues to amaze me with the quality of the work he does, and without whom this book would not be nearly what it is. And thanks to Tom Allen for his excellent work that provides the icing on the cake.

—Ray West

I would like to thank first and foremost my life mate, Janet H. Lee, without whom I would never have been able to complete the book. She has been supportive and instrumental in helping me shape my career path, as well as helping in the day-to-day editing of the chapters. Thanks to my daughter, Amber, for her understanding of why Daddy is working all the time. Finally, thanks to my writing partner Ray West, who has shared the tremendous burden of a Complete Reference; and to Tom Allen, multimedia whiz, who put together a great tutorial.

—Tom Muck

I would like to thank my wife for her forbearance during this project. I also would like to thank Ray and Tom for their tolerance of my delays, and particularly our editors from Osborne, Jim Schachterle and Timothy Madrid, for their grace under pressure.

—Tom Allen

Introduction

Welcome to *Dreamweaver UltraDev 4: The Complete Reference*. The computer world has changed a lot over the past few years, and even more over the last several months. We went from contemplating a book on Drumbeat 2000 to a book on UltraDev 1 to this final product on UltraDev 4 in an incredibly short period of time.

There has never been a more exiting time for Web development than right now. The incredible tools that are available make professionals' jobs easier and more productive and extend the ability to produce great-looking, useful sites down to relative newcomers to programming. UltraDev has something for those people and everyone in between.

Who Should Read This Book

If you are interested in UltraDev, you should read this book. If you want to make data available on the Web, you should read this book. From beginner to professional, there is something in this book that will benefit almost anyone with an interest in Web Development with Macromedia's products.

There is a lot to cover, though. In order to be truly useful to such a broad range of users, there will be information that is either basic or very advanced to everyone who reads this book. That is a necessity we hope you understand.

How Should This Book Be Read

How you read this is up to you and what you are trying to accomplish. Some people will jump straight to the extensions section in Part 5. Others will head to the last chapter that deals with e-commerce and the shopping cart. Still others will want a general overview and may read from start to finish.

We would recommend that you read the whole thing to get a clear picture of how this software came to be and how it is intended to work. But you may have specific needs that you can pinpoint in the Table of Contents, and that is fine too. However you choose to use this resource, we hope that it makes your job easier and you sites better.

What Is In This Book

A whole lot. But seeing as that is not the answer you really want, here is how it lays out.

Part 1 is an introduction to the basic concepts that make up UltraDev, including some history and coverage of what you might call the Dreamweaver parts of the product. It takes you up through the beginnings of a site's development including much of the graphic layout.

Part 2 covers Web scripting including ASP, JSP, and ColdFusion, as well as troubleshooting and debugging.

Part 3 covers databases including their design, construction, connection, and use in the Web environment.

Part 4 continues what was started in Part 1 and adds data functionality to the sample site including the use of all three languages and several databases.

Part 5 is for the adventurous. It focuses on the extensibility layer of UltraDev and teaches you how to build and distribute your own extensions for fun and profit. The last chapter covers the UltraCart and its use in building an e-commerce site.

Conventions Used In This Book

We have used several conventions to make it easier to read the book.

You can identify code listing by their font. Here is an example:

```
<%
   Dim Text
   Text = "Hello World"
   Response.Write Text
%>
```

If a line of code needs to be split across two lines, you will see the ¬ character.

When you are supposed to press a key or a combination of keys, they will be identified like this:

CTRL+F2

Steps that you need to follow will be presented as numbered list.

Our Guarantee To You

We want you to buy this book because we think we have done a good job of presenting UltraDev to a broad audience. We know that you will find useful information here that will be worth more than the price you paid for it. But we know that we are not perfect and that we may have missed a topic that is important to you. Here is what we will do.

We have a Web site to support this book at www.basic-ultradev.com. If you buy this book and there are topics that we did not cover that you need information on, we promise to do our best to post tutorials on those topics at our site upon request. Now, we cannot solve everyone's programming problems and we can't do your projects for you, but we can add to the information in this book by covering topics in much the same manner as we would have had we covered them in the book. You may even find that we have already done so. If you have questions or problems, please visit us there and we will try to help. What more can you ask? Head for the checkout now.

Thanks, and we hope you enjoy the book.

The
Complete
Reference

UltraDev

Part I

Getting Started with
Dreamweaver UltraDev

The
Complete
Reference

UltraDev

Chapter 1

What is UltraDev and What Makes It So Ultra?

The Internet is a fast moving place. So fast, sometimes, that entire versions of software come and go without anyone ever knowing they were there. When this book was started, version 1 of Macromedia's UltraDev was just being released. By the time the book was finished, version 4 had just left San Francisco.

This was, of course, a realignment of product versions at Macromedia to bring UltraDev and its parent application, Dreamweaver, in sync. Still, the product was revised in six months and is a significantly better product.

This is a book about Dreamweaver UltraDev 4. In it, you will find a wealth of information about UltraDev and related technologies that will get you up to speed quickly with this powerful product. Before long, you will be creating Web applications that connect to databases and providing a dynamic experience for your visitors.

It seems that speed is what it's all about these days: Release the product, release a better version, make it easier and quicker to create Web sites. But there is a history here that needs to be understood; somewhere around four decades of technological revolution that put us where we are today and makes it possible for you to do the work you do.

The Internet

If you have been working with the Internet for longer than, say, a week, you have no doubt heard some permutation of the following question: "Oh yeah, the Internet—now, who exactly owns that?" Even worse are those that equate it with sex and danger or those that use the terms Internet and AOL interchangeably. It's easy to roll your eyes and snigger at those less hip than you, but it is often more difficult to clearly articulate exactly what the Internet is and where it came from.

There have been several revolutions in world history that changed the way people lived their lives permanently. But none has occurred as quickly, ubiquitously, and nonchalantly as the Internet revolution. The Internet has affected every corner of our culture in profound ways. At home, at school, and at work, our lives are different, if not better, as we move into the Information Age.

It has been said that information is power; and if that is true, then we are the most powerful we have ever been. From the theme ingredient on the next episode of Iron Chef, to last minute income tax filing forms, to the complete text of pending legislation, there is almost nothing you can't find with just a little effort and access to the World Wide Web. It is interesting that one of the most exciting uses of twenty-first century technology is the exercise of ideals hundreds of years old. Speech and the flow of ideas have never been more free.

Our businesses have changed. The bookstore isn't necessarily down the street anymore—often it is at the other end of a Uniform Resource Locator (URL) such as www.amazon.com or www.bn.com. People who could never have competed with the "big boys" now have all but equal standing and an unprecedented opportunity to market and sell their products.

We can communicate as never before. Whether it is parents to their kid in a school across the country, constituents to their representative, or a satisfied (or unsatisfied) customer to the CEO, we are more in touch with the world around us. The handwritten family letter of yesterday is today's smartly formatted electronic presentation complete with the latest pictures of the grandkids delivered instantly without a stamp. The Internet makes the world smaller than even Mr. Disney imagined.

But as with any medium with the potential of the Internet, those who choose to fill it with content bear a certain responsibility. While the Web is full of sites and pages and words of incredible utility, it is also full of poor design, bad programming, and content of dubious validity. This book aims to help you learn how to use one of the most powerful Web design tools available so that you can make a positive contribution.

The History of the Internet

Do you remember Sputnik? The sad fact is, a growing number of computer whizzes weren't around to personally remember the Bicentennial, *This Is Spinal Tap*, or the last episode of *M*A*S*H*, much less the 1957 launch of a little Russian satellite. But that little satellite was the first launched from Earth and it scared the pants off of the United States military, it being the Cold War and all.

The next year, the Department of Defense formed the Advanced Research Projects Agency (ARPA) to establish and advance U.S. dominance in military science and technology. By 1965, in its effort to establish efficient communications networks, ARPA had developed the concept of a distributed network, and it sponsored a study on networking time-shared computers. "The Experimental Network" was formed between three computers at ARPA, MIT, and System Development Corporation in California communicating over a 1,200bps phone line. This led to the initial designs of what would become the ARPANET.

Meanwhile, studies were being conducted at several locations regarding a new technology known as *packet switching*. The concept of packet switching involved the routing of information across distributed networks in small chunks called *packets*. This would allow for the efficient transfer and recovery of data with "no single outage point," as Paul Baran put it in 1964.

These two paths began to converge in 1968 when ARPA put its design out to bid. Companies were asked to propose methods by which the ARPANET could be constructed and put to use. Bolt Beranek and Newman, Inc. (BBN) was awarded the contract later that year to build Interface Message Processors (IMPs). Construction began in 1969 with 4 IMP nodes connecting computers over 50kbps phone lines.

Note

Senator Edward Kennedy got involved with the Internet very early when he sent BBN a congratulatory note for their new ARPA contract to build "Interfaith Message Processors," and expressed thanks for their ecumenical efforts.

The 1970s was an exciting decade, with progress being made on several fronts. As the ARPANET grew, other independent networks appeared that would later be connected to it. 1971 saw the first inter-machine messaging, which was expanded onto the ARPANET the following year along with the introduction of the @ symbol in the addressing scheme. Larger configurations of up to 40 machines at a time were demonstrated. In addition, other countries began to develop their own versions of the ARPANET. The Telnet specification was developed in 1972.

Two of the most significant events occurred in 1973. The first international connections were made to the ARPANET when the University of London hooked in through NORSAR. And at Harvard, Bob Metcalfe (the eventual founder of 3Com) wrote his Ph.D. thesis describing Ethernet. Ethernet was tested at the Xerox Parc laboratories (eventually responsible for the introduction of the mouse to desktop computing and the inspiration for the LISA and, eventually, the Macintosh interface). Ethernet is still the protocol of choice for thousands of LANs and the Internet in general. The specification for the File Transfer Protocol was developed in 1973.

The next several years saw the expansion of the ARPANET, along with the continued development of technologies that would become central to the Internet. In 1974, the Transmission Control Protocol (TCP) specification was published; and in 1975, the first list server was established with a science fiction lovers' list becoming one of the first mailing lists. UNIX to UNIX Copy (UUCP) was created in 1976, and 1977 saw the completion of the specification for networked mail. In 1978, TCP was divided into TCP and the Internet Protocol (IP), which remains the communications protocol of today's Internet. The decade was capped off by the invention of USENET (the system of newsgroups) in 1979 and, perhaps most importantly, the introduction of emoticons (the little emotion indicators :-) that litter our text communications to this day).

The early 1980s can be characterized as a time of rapid network creation. Across the world, networks appeared based on many of the specifications of the prior period. As many new networks developed, some of the earliest began to make a migration from independence to cooperation in what was becoming an international network.

The years 1983 and 1984 were important. Several things happened in succession during this period that spurred the growth of the Internet. First, in 1983, the Name Server concept was developed that made it possible for computers to communicate without knowing the exact path to one another across the network. This culminated in the introduction of the Domain Name Service (DNS) in 1984. Also in 1983, connectivity extended to the desktop workstation. This led to the number of Internet hosts breaking 1,000 the next year.

In 1987, the number of hosts broke 10,000. In 1988, the communications backbone was upgraded to a T1 (1.544Mbps) connection, which led to the number of hosts breaking 100,000 in 1989. During the late 1980s, there was some separation between the ARPANET and what was becoming the NSFNET, a commercially supported network. While TCP/IP was the standard, the Department of Defense decided to go with a competing protocol. By the early 1990s, ARPANET was gone and the Internet was on its way to commercial glory.

What the early 1980s were to the technical development of the Internet, the early 1990s were to its raw growth. In 1990, the first commercial dial-up server provider came online. In 1991, the communications backbone was upgraded to a T3 (45Mbps); and by 1992, the number of hosts broke 1,000,000.

In 1993, Internic was created to manage Internet services through contracts with AT&T, Network Solutions, and General Atomics. In each of the successive years, more and more countries established connections to the network, making it a truly worldwide network.

The World Wide Web

In 1991, a developer named Tim Berners Lee envisioned a means of going beyond the simple back-and-forth transfer of files over UUCP and FTP connections. He wanted a way to actually view files over remote connections in a formatted way that made scientific and technical papers available to research associates across the network. Mr. Berners Lee developed the concept of the World Wide Web, over which files could be viewed. Those files would basically be text files, but they would be marked up with a tag language (a subset of SGML called *Hypertext Markup Language*, or *HTML*) that enabled their formatting in a hierarchal way that was appropriate for the technical content he wanted to display.

The potential of this new medium was quickly realized. By the next year, the World Bank was online and the term "surfing the Internet" was coined. In 1993, Mosaic (the first real browser) experienced an unbelievable growth rate as more and more people went online for the first time.

The Web continued to expand in 1994. More commercial businesses opened for e-business, the first cyber-bank opened, and the first banner ads appeared—com became the most popular domain extension, followed by .edu for educational institutions.

Note   *If you were around to view content over the Web on pre-Mosaic browsers, you can truly appreciate the exponential growth that graphical browsers spurred. While some were awed by the ability to FTP into libraries around the world and view simple HTML files in text-based browsers, it took the eye-candy that the graphics-based browsers allowed to make the medium popular with less technically involved users.*

By 1995, use of the Web surpassed the use of FTP. For the first time, registration authorities began charging to register domain names. One of the most popular technologies became search engines, by which you could find information all over the world.

The last five years have seen a myriad of shifts and changes in the landscape of the Internet and the World Wide Web. Technologies such as Java, ASP, online stock brokerage, online banking, Internet Phones, MP3, streaming audio and video, and DSL have made the Internet more accessible and made it more worth accessing. What took 30 years to develop has become ubiquitous and universally useful in just five years. But the core of the Internet is much like electricity. While the gadgets that we plug in today are fancier that those of yesteryear, they still plug in with a three-prong plug into a copper wire outlet. The Web is certainly a fancier place today than it was even a short time ago, but it still operates on the infrastructure that was developed and introduced over the first three decades of its use.

TCP/IP

A key component of that infrastructure is the communications protocol over which the Internet operates. Actually a suite of protocols, TCP/IP is the several-tiered method by which data is packaged and sent across the wires that connect the world's computers together. It is made up of the Transmission Control Protocol and the Internet Protocol.

Internet Protocol

Although IP comes after TCP in the name of the protocol, IP is the communications core that makes the Internet work. You have likely heard of IP addresses, those sets of numbers separated by dots that are assigned to each host computer and domain on the Net. The Internet Protocol utilizes that numbering scheme to determine the path that it should take across the routers and hosts that make up the Internet to reach the destination it is intended for. When you make a connection to a computer somewhere out on the Web, you are, in reality, connecting to any number of other computers and routers that forward your request in the most efficient way they can determine, given the millisecond they have to think about it. If you are interested to see how your requests are being routed, you can use the tracert utility (for Trace Route) from a command prompt on your computer and see the connections, or *hops*, your request makes as it travels to the destination you provide (see Figure 1-1).

Now, given that this is the way that the Internet works, with each request you make being forwarded through a number of stops, consider what must happen when you download a large Web page, or even a 15MB program from a shareware site. Without the IP protocol, it might be necessary for the entire file to be copied to each node along the way until it reached your computer. That could involve as many as 30 or more copies of the same file, depending on where you and your destination site are located. But, thanks to IP, your request and the response for the computer at the other end can be split up into small packets of data that travel easily across the network, following the most efficient path each of them can find.

> **Note**   *A number of things can affect the route that a packet may take across the Internet, including bottlenecks and outages along the way. The ability of IP to dynamically route around these problems is a key factor in the stability of this kind of distributed network.*

So, consider how you might get a group of friends across town to the movies. Unless one of you owned a bus, you would probably split up into two or more cars, and head off for the theater. Perhaps one of the drivers likes the expressway, another knows a

```
MS-DOS Prompt                                                    _ 回 ×

 Auto    ▾ □ 🗐🖺 🗒 🗗🗗 A

Microsoft(R) Windows 98
    (C)Copyright Microsoft Corp 1981-1999.

C:\WINDOWS>tracert www.basic-ultradev.com

Tracing route to www.basic-ultradev.com [63.96.26.230]
over a maximum of 30 hops:

  1    32 ms    53 ms    47 ms  adsl-20-119-1.mco.bellsouth.net [66.20.119.1]
  2    12 ms    11 ms    12 ms  205.152.111.65
  3    11 ms    11 ms    12 ms  205.152.111.248
  4    10 ms    13 ms    10 ms  Serial4-1-0.GW1.ORL1.ALTER.NET [157.130.65.157]

  5    22 ms    22 ms    21 ms  504.at-2-1-0.XR2.ATL1.ALTER.NET [152.63.84.46]
  6    31 ms    31 ms    32 ms  194.ATM6-0.GW3.ORL1.ALTER.NET [146.188.233.133]

  7   176 ms   149 ms   104 ms  63.74.97.33
  8   185 ms   135 ms   158 ms  www.basic-ultradev.com [63.96.26.230]

Trace complete.

C:\WINDOWS>
```

Figure 1-1.   *Running tracert to www.basic-ultradev.com returns a number of stops along the way*

"shortcut," and a third doesn't have enough change for the tolls *and* popcorn and takes the normal route. Three cars are all taking different routes to the same destination, and each is liable to encounter things along the way that might speed their travel (such as no line at the toll booth) or slow them down (such as a wreck along the shortcut). Although each car left one after the other, there is no guarantee in what order or in what timeframe they might arrive at the theatre. One car might not even make it at all.

To make the point more clearly, suppose you ordered a book from Barnes and Noble; and, instead of shipping you the entire book at once, they sent the individual pages by different carriers with no page numbers. When and if you received all of the pages (and how would you know if you did?), you would be hard-pressed to get them back together in an order that might be useful. This is pretty close to what happens to a file that is being transmitted across to network by the IP protocol alone. IP needs some help to make sure that things end up where they belong. That help comes from the Transmission Control Protocol.

Transmission Control Protocol

The Transmission Control Protocol (TCP) is like the big stack of envelopes that the shipping clerk at Barnes and Noble would use to send you all of those pages. Each envelope would be numbered in order and would indicate the total number of envelopes in the sequence, for example, 36 of 1,008. Each envelope would also give some indication of what was on the page inside, so you could make sure that you got the right one. Using this scheme, you could receive all of the envelopes, put them back in order, and make sure that you had received what the store meant to send you. Then you could call Barnes and Noble and yell at them for sending you a book such a stupid way.

But that's the way it has to work on the Web. Each packet that is created by the IP protocol is packaged up, numbered, and labeled so the receiving computer knows what to do with it. If the receiving computer is missing any packets, it knows to send back for them from the sending computer. And the TCP information indicates what the packet should contain so that the receiving computer can identify corrupted data.

Together, the two protocols within TCP/IP provide the communications basis on which the Internet is built. But it can really only handle the connection between the computers over which the requests and responses of information are sent. Those actual messages are handled by the Hypertext Transfer Protocol.

Hypertext Transfer Protocol

There are basically four parts to any transfer of data over a client/server network (which is really what the Internet is). The first and last of these steps are the connection and disconnection of the two communicating computers, which is handled by TCP/IP. Sandwiched in between is the work of the HTTP protocol (see Figure 1-2).

You have probably noticed the "http" that begins most Web addresses. Actually, most browsers now assume the HTTP protocol is being used when you type in an address, so the http:// designation is not strictly necessary. But rest assured, that is exactly what the browser is generating when it makes a request.

Note   *Most browsers are also capable of sending ftp and news requests. If that is what is intended, the protocol must be specified or http will be assumed.*

Once a connection is made, a request for data is sent in the form of an address. This might be an IP address or it could be a fully qualified domain name such as http://www.basic-ultradev.com. That request is routed via TCP/IP to the host computer that can fulfill it, and the response is sent back as an HTTP response to the requesting

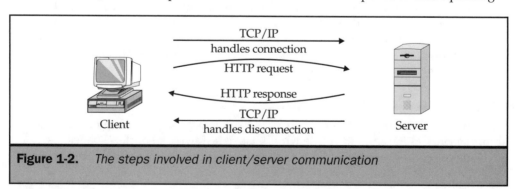

Figure 1-2.   *The steps involved in client/server communication*

computer. Once it arrives, the TCP/IP protocol again assists in putting the packets of information together so that it can be used or displayed.

How that response is used when it gets back to the requesting computer depends on the content of the information sent. For these discussions, it is assumed that you are requesting the type of content that makes up most of the World Wide Web—HTML content.

Hypertext Markup Language

Hypertext Markup Language (HTML) is the foundation of the World Wide Web. It is this set of tags that describes to the client browser how a file should be displayed, and that is the core purpose of the Web: displaying files of information.

The earliest HTML documents were just text. Often they were the text of scientific or research projects, and the way in which they were formatted was important. HTML provided a hierarchal means of organizing and displaying information so that it could be viewed in a form that emphasized its structure more than its design. It does so by providing a selection of tags that mark up the raw text in ways that the browser can understand.

For instance, you may want to display the raw text file shown in Figure 1-3, so that your fellow scientist can rip you apart for not following standard research guidelines.

This file of simple text does not really allow you to organize your content in a way that will have the maximum effect on your colleague and let him know that you really do know how to write a good outline. HTML allows you to insert indicators such as the following directly into the text that tell the browser on the other end how to display the information:

```
</html>
<head></head>
<body>
<h1>This is my research<br>

</h1>
<h2>Topic One</h2><br>

<p> This is what I found when I investigated topic one. I found that all
other scientists are idiots<br>
and I should be rich for the finding in Topic Two.</p>
<h2> Topic Two</h2><br>

<p> Topic two should really make me rich. It is where I discover a way to do
things
  that we can't<br>
   seem to get done, like counting ballots.</p>
<h2> Summary</h2><br>

<p> In summary, all other scientists are idiots. I should be rich.</p>
```

```
<p> Thank You </p>
</body>
</html>
```

To the end user, these indicators are invisible. They only see the finished product, as shown in Figure 1-4, after the browser interprets your instructions.

One of the great strengths of HTML is the ability to create and execute hyperlinks. Hyperlinks are directions built into the content itself that allow users to be sent off to related material with a click of the mouse. For instance, suppose that your document discusses material for which you relied on the writings of another author, whose work is also available on the Internet at its own document address. You could embed a portion of text referring to that work; so that when visitors clicked it, they would be whisked off to that material, where they could properly appreciate how you had interpreted and extended that information in your own research. It is this interconnected structure that led to the coining of the phrase *World Wide Web*. The Web is truly a worldwide mesh of interconnected content.

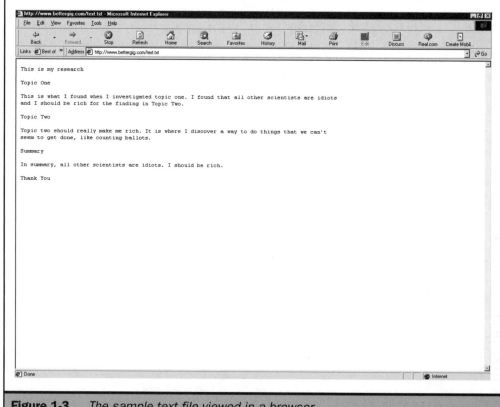

Figure 1-3.   *The sample text file viewed in a browser*

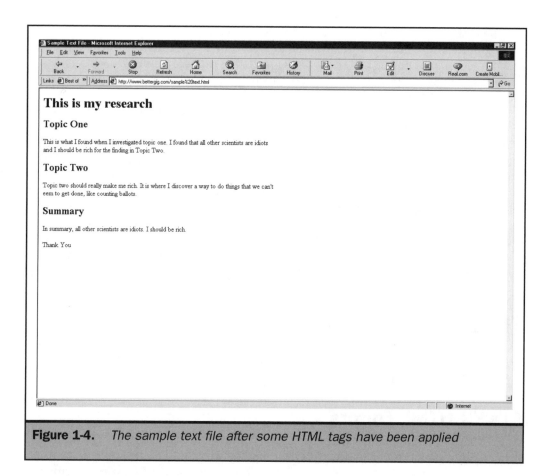

Figure 1-4.   *The sample text file after some HTML tags have been applied*

The Web Site

Everything covered so far makes up the component parts of your real interest in this book, which is the Web site. If you understand the stand-alone HTML document, you can consider the Web site to be a collection of those documents that makes up an interconnected web of information. What the entire Web is on a grand scale, the Web site is in its own little universe.

When you have a lot of content that you need to display, you have a couple of choices you can make. Believe it or not, some people actually choose to make one really long document that scrolls down forever. Although it eventually gets everything they wanted to say said, there is a more practical solution.

A Web site is formed when you bring together a collection of HTML documents that are related to one another and need to be displayed together. By organizing this content and providing logical ways to navigate it, you are turning your individual documents into a site that users can use to find and access the information they need. There are three common layouts for such a site.

The first is the Table of Contents model that provides a front-end interface to a catalog of material. For instance, if you had a book or a report that was divided into sections, you might have a table of contents page that provided links to each section. As each section is completed, users would return to the table of contents to determine the next section they wanted to access.

Second is the web structure, where content is full of cross-referencing links. On any given page, you might have a number of links to other parts of the site connecting related material. The intent of such a structure is for the user to peruse the content of the site in a sort of stream-of-consciousness way, branching off to related parts of the site at will.

Third is the Web application. In a Web application, the user is typically guided through the site in a structured way by the way the pages are designed. For instance, if you were filling out an online insurance application, it would be important to complete each section of the application in order to be sure that everything was properly filled out. The users would depend on the site designer to guide them through the specific documents that needed to be completed.

The Last Few Years

So, that 30-year history brings you up to the last few years. It is these last three or four years that a number of concurrent events have occurred that have brought us to the topic of this book: Dreamweaver UltraDev 4.

WYSIWYG HTML Editors

As HTML matured, more and more designers wanted a way to construct HTML in a fashion more similar to the desktop publishing they were used to. It should come as no surprise that people who were used to dealing in very visual media resisted having to hand-code their HTML in a text editor and run it in a browser every time they wanted to check the layout. The graphical content of HTML documents was becoming more important as the focus of new Web sites became less scientific and more commercial. Designers wanted a What You See Is What You Get (WYSIWYG) method of building Web Sites.

One of the earliest applications to offer a means of designing Web pages graphically was Microsoft's FrontPage (see Figures 1-5 and 1-6). FrontPage enables designers of all levels to construct and publish Web pages by laying them out visually rather than by hand-coding the HTML. When the pages are complete, FrontPage publishes the raw HTML file to the Web server, much as if it had been hand-coded. Browsers recognize these files as standard HTML documents and display them as expected, in most cases.

In addition, FrontPage comes with a set of server extensions that allow easy use of more advanced components. The current version of FrontPage is FrontPage 2000.

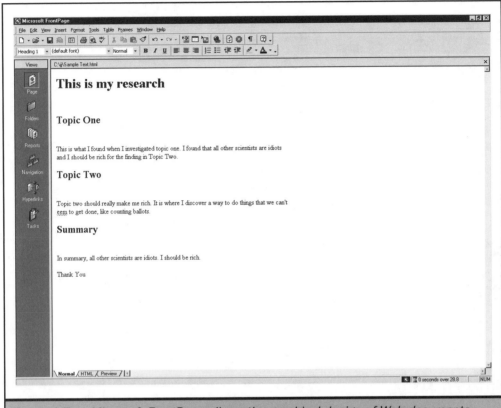

Figure 1-5.   *Microsoft FrontPage allows the graphical design of Web documents*

There have been many other WYSIWYG HTML editors along the way. Pagemill, GoLive, and a myriad of others have made their way through the market based on the same premise as FrontPage: visually designed pages are converted to their representative HTML and published as raw HTML that browsers understand.

Dreamweaver

In late 1997, Macromedia entered what was becoming a crowded HTML editor market with Dreamweaver 1. Six months later, version 1.2 was released and Dreamweaver began to gain quite a following. Version 4 has recently been released, and Dreamweaver is now the most popular HTML design tool among professional Web developers, with a user base of over 600,000. Several key concepts and features enabled Dreamweaver to make such significant inroads in a competitive market.

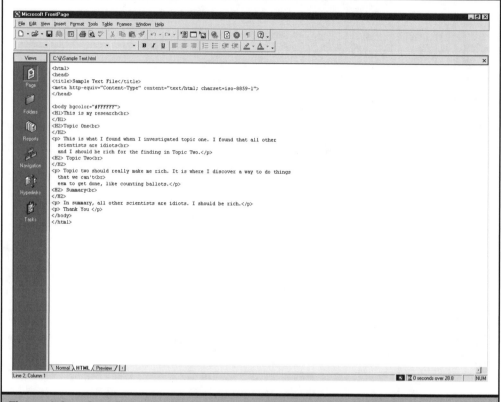

Figure 1-6. FrontPage allows users to switch back and forth between Design view and HTML view

Integration with Other Macromedia Products

There are a few companies that can drive markets just because of other product categories they already dominate. Microsoft, for instance, has enjoyed tremendous success because of the functional relationships between their operating systems and their Office suite. Perhaps more relevant is the success of Microsoft's Visual InterDev, which enjoys advanced ASP- and COM-related integration (both Microsoft technologies). This success is in spite of the fact that Visual InterDev has severely limited design capabilities, forcing its users to perform design work in another product.

Macromedia is certainly enjoying cross-pollination thanks to the development of several excellent design tools. Each of Macromedia's products stands on its own; but when a Fireworks, Freehand, Flash, or Director user goes looking for an HTML tool, the ability to integrate these products with Dreamweaver becomes an important consideration. Macromedia has paid special attention to the ways in which their products work together.

Dreamweaver 4 is particularly integrated with Fireworks, Flash, Director, and Generator. Some of their functions allow these programs' output to be included in Dreamweaver very easily. Also included are ready-made ways to determine whether a site's visitors have the necessary plug-ins installed to allow them to play special content. Some of the newest of these features, such as Flash Buttons, will be discussed in Chapter 5.

Integration with Microsoft Office

As we just indicated, Microsoft's Office is a very popular product in the business world. Many times, large portions of content that need to be placed on the Web already exist in business documents created in Microsoft Word. Word has the ability to convert its documents into HTML, but it is not a pretty thing. Word-generated HTML files are bloated, containing extraneous, unnecessary code. Often these files are four or five times larger than necessary and contain code that only works properly in Microsoft's Internet Explorer browser.

Dreamweaver contains a command call, Clean Up Word HTML, which addresses this problem. Within just a few minutes, Word-generated HTML files can be cleaned up and stripped of their Microsoft-specific code, eliminating the need to cut and paste existing content just to get usable files.

In addition, it is often important to publish data that exists in spreadsheet applications or databases to the Web. Dreamweaver contains a special version of an HTML table called Tabular Data. This advanced table allows the developer to identify a data source that is used to populate the table.

Cross-Browser Capabilities

If you have been designing for the Web for very long, you have no doubt experienced the maddening issue of cross-browser compatibility. Because of differing implementations of elements like Cascading Style Sheets and JavaScript, it can often be a difficult task to get your content to view properly in the browsers that your visitors are likely to use. And it may only get worse, with Opera's recent announcement that they will no longer charge for their browser (in the past, this highly capable browser's popularity was behind Internet Explorer and Netscape Navigator because of its $40 price tag).

Dreamweaver tries to help you deal with some of these issues by placing some indications of the design tools that are compatible with the popular browser types. For example, one of the most useful features in this regard is a built-in fix that addresses a Netscape issue. When the user resizes a Netscape browser, the page layout is often corrupted unless the page is reloaded. This included piece of script forces the reloading of the page any time the browser is resized. In Dreamweaver, it can be added or removed with one menu selection.

RoundTrip HTML and XML

An important feature to many professional Web designers is the integrity of their code. Many of the popular HTML design applications compromised this integrity by changing code. Dreamweaver was built on the concept that the designer is in charge. The program can certainly help you write HTML from your visual layout; but if you make changes to the code itself, Dreamweaver will leave it alone, representing your changes the best it can. One of the keys to Roundtrip code is that whatever is generated and published by Dreamweaver can be reopened and properly displayed. This will become an important point in the upcoming discussion of data access and Drumbeat 2000.

Templates

A key design factor for professional Web sites is a consistent look and feel across the site. It is disrupting and incongruent to radically change graphics, colors, layout, frames, and so on, each time a new page is loaded. In this sense, a designer should consider the entire site as one large design rather than a compilation of individually designed pages.

Dreamweaver's templates help you to maintain a consistent look and feel, and save you a lot of work when you add pages to your site. In creating a template in Dreamweaver, you can identify regions that will remain *locked* and, therefore, identical on every page for which the template is used. You can also identify *unlocked* regions of the page, which are the portions that you expect to change for each subsequent use of the template.

History

Professional designers and graphic artists have become used to certain features in packages like Photoshop. One of the most important features is the History function.

The History palette in Dreamweaver gives you access to the steps that you took to build your site to its current state. You use it to repeat a series of steps and even to build an executable command that will repeat those steps at will. It also enables an almost limitless undo capability.

Objects and Behaviors

Objects and behaviors will be discussed extensively later in this book, including instructions on how to create your own. But right out of the box, Dreamweaver comes with a host of prebuilt objects and behaviors that encapsulate snippets of code. Need to drop a table onto your page? There is an object that lets you do so, and it will address its properties (number of columns, for example.) in one easy step. Need to control a Shockwave or Flash movie? The simple addition of a prebuilt behavior lets you add that functionality quickly and move on to more important things.

In addition to the objects and behaviors that ship with Dreamweaver, there are tons more available for download at sites across the Web. This has become a key to Dreamweaver's popularity.

Extensibility

Closely related to the preloaded objects and behaviors is Dreamweaver's extensibility layer. Based in JavaScript, the extensibility layer provides detailed instructions for interacting with Dreamweaver at an API level. Programmers with a good JavaScript background can easily add complex functionality to Dreamweaver and distribute it to other users, making Dreamweaver a constantly maturing and evolving product.

Later chapters in the book cover Dreamweaver and UltraDev extensions in great detail.

Data Access

At the same time the HTML design application revolution was occurring, people were looking for ways to expand the concept of the World Wide Web. Static pages of graphics and text were nice, but there had to be a way to interact with Web pages, to collect information from users, and to communicate with databases of information.

One of the earliest implementations of this concept was the CGI application. Out of this (and because of its inefficiencies) grew HTML Templating—better known as ASP, JSP, and ColdFusion, to name just three examples. There are extensive discussions of these topics later in the book. Just be aware at this point that there was a crossing of the roads coming, where the users of HTML design applications would require the same ease of use for data-connected Web sites.

Drumbeat 2000

There have been several cool applications in the history of computing—applications that really pushed the limits of what you thought computers could do. Drumbeat wasn't quite one of those, but it wasn't far off.

Drumbeat 2000 (and its preceding versions) was to ASP and JSP what Dreamweaver and FrontPage are to HTML. Drumbeat actually allowed the creation of ASP code through a visual design interface.

Note *Although the latest version of Drumbeat was named Drumbeat 2000, it was actually released in 1999 and barely made it through 2000 as a supported product. More about that later in this chapter.*

If you understand how products like Dreamweaver, FrontPage, HomeSite, and others grew out of HTML, then you will understand how Drumbeat fits in. Just as Dreamweaver's main job is to convert a visual representation of a Web page into the HTML that all browsers understand, Drumbeat converts the same kind of visual representation into a combination of HTML and Active Server Pages (ASP) script.

This additional ASP capability is what gives Drumbeat the power to easily create database-driven content. Just as you can drag and drop images, lines, text, and form elements onto a page in Dreamweaver, you can drag and drop recordsets, variables, and code snippets (in the form of contracts) onto pages in Drumbeat that are interpreted by the program to generate the text that we all used to type into Notepad (see Figure 1-7).

That seems simple until you consider what a monumental task this is. ASP allows amazing power and flexibility in your Web programming. In order for Drumbeat to allow you to draw what you want on the screen and then convert it to text files that actually replicate your vision, it must be prepared to handle jobs that range from drawing a line to complex recordset manipulation.

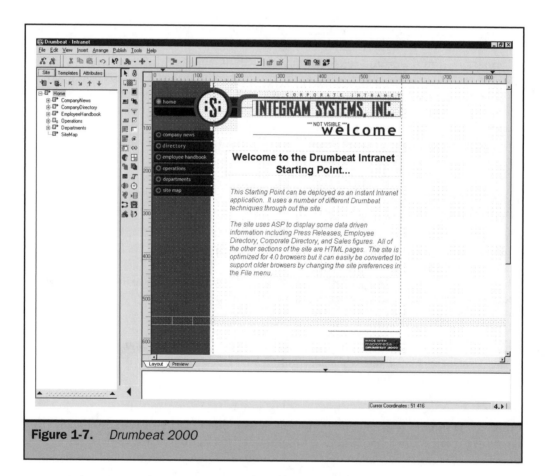

Figure 1-7.   *Drumbeat 2000*

Drumbeat did a great job of it. It did, however, have some significant limitations. Its architecture was built on a database of instructions based on the layout you created. When the file was published, those instructions were converted into ASP and uploaded to your site. While there were sophisticated ways to hand-code portions of the site, there was no access to the raw code, and this made people uncomfortable.

Also, the entire layout scheme of Drumbeat was based on Cascading Style Sheets. This made for nice, pixel-perfect design capabilities, but some simple HTML items, such as basic tables, were not even available at all.

UltraDev

In the summer of 1999, two companies had decisions to make. Elemental Software, the creators of Drumbeat, realized that they had scalability issues on their hands. They came to the decision that to take Drumbeat much father would require a rewrite, a time consuming and stiflingly expensive proposition. At the same time, Macromedia was trying to figure out a way to expand its product line into the world of data connection. Dreamweaver seemed like the place to start.

At quite a remarkably serendipitous moment, Elemental and Macromedia ended up at the table together. What ensued was Macromedia's purchase of Elemental and the migration of much of its development staff to San Francisco to head up a new project. This new project became the marriage of Drumbeat and Dreamweaver into what we now know as UltraDev.

UltraDev, and particularly version 4, is the best of both Drumbeat and Dreamweaver. Maintaining the flexibility and access to code of Dreamweaver, UltraDev has incorporated many of the best features of Drumbeat into an application that successfully advances Drumbeat's capabilities and eliminates most of the problems it had.

What Makes UltraDev So Ultra?

Well, that is what the rest of this book is about. But it's a broad question, and this is a broad topic. There are several things to keep in mind.

There is one thing you can be guaranteed of while reading this book. No matter who you are and no matter what your background, there will be content in this book that is either way above your head or very basic to you. One thing to remember about UltraDev is that it does not exist in a vacuum. Without other significant technologies, UltraDev has no purpose.

With that in mind, this book tries to address all of the topics that you need to have a grasp of in order to be productive with UltraDev quickly. Many volumes have been written on some of these topics, and the chapters here are certainly not comprehensive, but they do represent the most common issues that new users will encounter. The early chapters on the Dreamweaver functionality are intended as an overview and will not replace the excellent books that cover the stand-alone product in depth.

At the same time, this book does address some very advanced UltraDev topics, such as the extensibility APIs and detailed extension creation and distribution. The chapters on these subjects may include material that some users never need know, but an understanding of the content will certainly make you a more productive UltraDev user.

In short, this book attempts to be a one-volume solution for a variety of UltraDev users. Rather than spending hundreds of dollars for a Dreamweaver book, an SQL book, an ASP book, a JavaScript book, and this UltraDev book, it is our hope that you will be served well and become proficient very quickly with this single collection of important material.

UltraDev

Chapter 2

Configuring Your UltraDev Environment

If you are anything like us when you load a new software application, the CD-ROM drive is open before the cellophane is off the box. Manuals are set aside (or worse, left in the box), and you expect the Autorun.inf file to lead you through the setup options. You click the Typical install option and try to make sense of any of the other pop-up options to get the thing running so you can begin realizing an immediate return on the dollars you spent.

That technique may work well with your average piece of software. Standardized interfaces have made it easier to feel your way through new applications with a reasonable expectation of a somewhat productive result. But when we start talking about building something as complex as a data application that will run worldwide across a variety of platforms with an unknown number of users, there are quite a few decisions to make before we can even think of diving in:

- Will you be developing on a PC or a Macintosh?
- What kind of server will you be running and what operating system is installed?
- Where is your server located? How much control do you have over the software it runs?
- Is it local at your development site, co-located with an ISP, or co-hosted with other sites on a shared server?
- What application servers are available to you? Do you have a choice between ASP, JSP, and ColdFusion?
- Do you have access to a staging server?
- What database application will you be accessing with your site?

The answers to some of these questions will dictate the answers to others. For instance, if you will be running some flavor of UNIX on your server, then it is a pretty safe bet that you won't be running Microsoft's Internet Information Server as your HTTP server. Nor is it likely that you'll be using Microsoft Access as your database.

On the other hand, some answers will raise more questions. Just because you are running a Windows NT or Windows 2000 server does not mean you are limited to IIS and Active Server Pages. Application servers that run Java Server Pages and ColdFusion are available for a selection of operating systems, including Windows.

Let's look at some of the options you have.

Picking Your Team

While UltraDev may be the captain of your development effort, you'll need a supporting team to get something done. Seeing as the whole purpose of UltraDev is to put data applications on the Web, you will, at the very least, need a Web server, an application server, and a data store of some kind. You will also want to seriously consider a live data server and a staging server.

The Web Server

You are probably familiar with the way the World Wide Web works, but a refresher never hurts. When you create pages in UltraDev, no matter what platform you choose, you will use some kind of File Transfer Protocol (FTP) program to upload the pages to a computer that is running a Web server. The Web server program is responsible for receiving and processing HyperText Transfer Protocol (HTTP) requests that are generated when users type a Uniform Resource Locator (URL) into their browser's (see Figure 2-1).

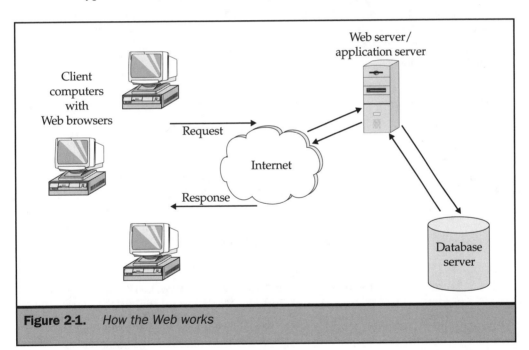

Figure 2-1.   *How the Web works*

Depending on where your host machine is located and who owns it, you may or may not have much control over which Web server you use. There are quite a number available, depending on what kind of hardware and operating system you are using. Some are free (or at least free with the operating system), like Microsoft's Internet Information Server or Apache, and others you'll need to purchase. A list of some of the more popular Web servers and the platforms they support is in Table 2-1.

The Application Server

Unless you're ignoring the good part of UltraDev, you will have pages in your site that require more processing than the Web server provides. Pages that connect to databases will have extensions such as .asp, .jsp, or .cfm. These pages require the attention of an application server that handles the code or tags in your pages that do the real work. The application server works closely with the Web server, however, to deliver pages that the user's browser can handle.

Some application servers are tightly integrated with a Web server—such as IBM's WebSphere, which can run with its own HTTP server, or with another one such as IIS or Microsoft's asp.dll, which requires IIS to run. Still others, such as ColdFusion, depend on an outside Web server. The features that you require will determine the combination that works best for you.

Web Server	Supported Platforms
Internet Information Server	Windows NT, Windows 2000
Apache	NetBSD, FreeBSD, BSDI, AIX, OS/2, SCO, HPUX, Novell NetWare, Macintosh, Be OS, Windows NT, Linux, Windows 95, Windows 98, IRIX, Solaris, Digital UNIX
Java Server	OS/2, HPUX, Windows NT, Linux, Windows 95, IRIX, Solaris
Lotus Domino Go Webserver	Digital UNIX, AIX, OS/2, HPUX, Windows NT, Windows 95, IRIX, Solaris
Stronghold Secure Web Server	NetBSD, Digital UNIX, BSDI, AIX, SCO, HPUX, Linux, FreeBSD, IRIX, Solaris
Oracle Web Application Server	HPUX, Windows NT, Windows 95, Solaris
iPlanet	HPUX, AIX, Solaris, IRIX, Windows NT

Table 2-1. *Popular Web Servers and the Platforms They Support*

The Data Store

Since you are using UltraDev, it is probably safe to assume that you have some data somewhere that you want to include in your application. Theoretically, that data can reside in a number of different kinds of files, including Excel spreadsheets and delimited text files; but as a practical matter, you will want the flexibility that a Relational Database Management System (RDBMS) provides. There are a number of database applications that qualify, from Microsoft Access, which can be had for a couple of hundred dollars, to enterprise-level server-based systems that cost thousands of dollars and require significant hardware resources.

It is important to select and plan for your database application early in the planning process. Depending on the way you build your site, changing data stores in midstream can be a frustrating, labor-intensive task.

The Staging Server

The Internet is a very public place. When you post something to it, people can and do look at it. When your company or your client depends on what the world reads about them, it is extremely important to get it right before it is made available on a live Web server. The more complex the sites you build, the more important it becomes to make use of a staging server in your development cycle.

A staging server is an interim publishing step that allows Web pages to be posted on a nonpublic server for review and quality-control purposes. Depending on the size of your organization, this staging server could be an actual computer set up to serve that purpose on an Intranet Web server, or it could be just a folder underneath the root of your Web site to which you can publish a copy of your site and any changes or maintenance items. These items can then be reviewed in a private setting within the context of the entire site. Once approved, the new pages are then copied or replicated to the live Web site.

You don't *want to be forced to put your test content up on a live site in order to debug it. Even if you just set up a hidden directory structure within your production domain, do something to allow the testing and review of your work.*

Everything from the images you use to the grammar and spelling on your Web site make a statement about your company or your client. Use of a staging server to allow comprehensive review of the information you intend to post is vital to preserving your reputation.

The Live Data Server

One of the revolutionary parts of UltraDev is its ability to "bounce" data off a live server and provide an editable design environment using actual data from your data store. While we will discuss this later, it is important at this point to consider how you will facilitate the use of this feature. For Windows users using the ASP model, it is easiest to use either Personal Web Server or a localized copy of Internet Information Server. Those using other technologies will want to identify a way to take advantage of this valuable design tool.

Server Models

UltraDev ships with three server models on which you can base your site: ASP, JSP, and ColdFusion.

The decision of which model to use may be guided by several factors and may guide other decisions that you need to make. It is important to make this decision early in your development cycle.

 You need to be careful when choosing your server technology. Once you start generating pages, it is not an easy task to switch to a different technology set. UltraDev creates code based on the preferences you have set as you work. At this time, there is no facility for converting that code.

Active Server Pages

We venture to say that the most common server language selection among UltraDev users will be ASP. Microsoft's technology is ubiquitous, easy to learn and use, and available on the many Windows-based servers currently used for Web site hosting. While some may question its speed, scalability, and ability to keep up with the needs of a growing e-commerce site, it is certainly more than capable of providing tremendous functionality to all but the largest applications.

If you are using a Windows NT or Windows 2000 server running Internet Information Server version 4.0 or 5.0 to host your site, you are all set to include ASP in your pages. IIS4 supports ASP 2. UltraDev conforms with the ASP 2 specification. IIS5 (shipped with Windows 2000) supports ASP 3. While the standard UltraDev code will not take advantage of any of the newer features found in version 3.0, you can certainly hand-code portions of your application to do so.

If you are running Windows NT 4.0 and don't have IIS installed, you will need to get a hold of the NT Option Pack. Included are several applications that you will find useful when running Web applications, but the most important at this point are Internet Information Server and Microsoft Transaction Server (both musts to run ASP). You can purchase an Option Pack CD-ROM or download it for free at www.microsoft.com/ntserver/nts/downloads/recommended/NT4OptPk/default.asp.

ASP on Non-Microsoft Servers

If you need to use a server that runs an operating system other than Windows or uses a Web server other than IIS, you can still use Active Server Pages for your site, thanks to companies who have ported ASP to other platforms through their proprietary server applications.

Chili!Soft (www.chilisoft.com) makes a program called ChiliASP. ChiliASP provides complete ASP support on AIX, HP-UX, Linux, OS/390, Solaris, and Windows NT. They are willing to consider any other platform and invite visitors to their Web site to make suggestions about the next platforms they should support.

Instant ASP from Halcyon Software (www.halcyonsoft.com) promises to provide ASP support on any Web server, application server, or OS platform. It is a Java-based port of the ASP specification and is designed to allow the ultimate in portability. Instant ASP supports an impressive list of operating systems and Web servers—too many to list here. Complete information is available at their Web site.

The most difficult thing for non-Microsoft solutions is the conversion of the COM components that make ASP so powerful. Most handle this by converting them to some sort of Java or JavaBean implementation.

ASP Scripting Languages

You'll also need to decide which scripting language to use in your ASP code. You will be writing code (or letting UltraDev write it for you) that is intended to run at the server (your Web server) and the client (your visitor's browser). Typically, the two choices are Visual Basic Script (VBScript) and JavaScript (or the Microsoft variant JScript). Which language to learn and use is an often-asked question.

VBScript   VBScript is a subset of the Visual Basic programming language. As ASP is a Microsoft technology, it is not surprising that VBScript is the preferred language for ASP development. Because of this, most ASP tutorials feature VBScript, making example code easy to find. It is relatively easy to learn because its syntax resembles English. There are tons of programmers with Visual Basic experience that find it a comfortable way to use ASP.

The downside of VBScript is that it is not practical as a client-side scripting language. Microsoft's Internet Explorer supports it for browser scripting, but Netscape's Navigator (the other major browser) does not. For this reason, some have concluded that using JavaScript for both the server and the client is a better alternative, especially for newer users who will only need to learn one language.

 If you know that your target audience will be using Internet Explorer, or if you are willing to make that a requirement, VBScript has some definite advantages as a client-side scripting language, for example, event handling is much easier.

JavaScript   Anyone who does any serious Web programming will need to learn JavaScript. While you may be most familiar with JavaScript as a client-side language used for things like form validation and DHTML effects, it is actually a robust language that allows sophisticated object-oriented programming on the server side. Since it can be used for the client side and the server side, it is a logical language choice for the new user, who can then become productive by learning just one language. And, if you plan to write extensions for UltraDev you will need to be intimately familiar with the entire JavaScript language.

However, JavaScript is more difficult to learn than VBScript. It has a less intuitive syntax, and example code is more difficult to find. It is comparable to C or Java in its format, but it must not be confused with either of these; it is its own language. Those coming from a C or Java background may suffer a bit of confusion trying to remember which command goes with which, but having a good reference handy solves this problem quite nicely.

Java Server Pages

Java Server Pages is Sun Microsystems' answer to ASP based on its popular Java programming language. While it provides a scripting environment comparable to ASP, JSP is actually a small part of the Java 2 Enterprise Edition, Sun's enterprise application development framework. Included are the most popular Java technologies like Servlets, Enterprise Java Beans (EJBs), Java Database Connectivity (JDBC), and Java Naming and Directory Interface (JNDI).

One of JSP's claims to fame is its portability. While ASP is generally limited to the Microsoft platform, JSP is available on all major Web platforms. Even better, Web servers and application servers that support JSP are available from a number of manufacturers. A list with contact information follows:

Orion	www.orionserver.com
Resin	www.caucho.com
Jrun	www.allaire.com
Tomcat	jakarta.apache.org
WebSphere	www.ibm.com
WebLogic	www.bea.com

Like ASP, JSP is script based, which means that your pages are a mix of HTML and script that is prepared at the server and delivered to the browser in a form that it can handle. The scripting in JSP is done in pure Java, so familiarity with the Java programming language and framework is helpful.

An advantage of JSP relates to its roots in the Java Servlet framework. The first time a JSP page is called, it is compiled into a servlet that accepts requests from the user and returns a response output stream. The Java Virtual Machine then translates this precompiled code.

By contrast, ASP pages are interpreted every time they are loaded. As big an advantage as this would seem to be, the interpretation of the JSP byte code and the interpretation of the ASP page take about the same amount of time; and, when properly written, ASP and JSP usually run at about the same speed.

ColdFusion

ColdFusion is a proprietary server model, produced and distributed by Allaire Corporation (www.allaire.com). Unlike ASP and JSP, ColdFusion is tag based, not script based. This fundamental difference has made ColdFusion extremely popular among Web designers and HTML authors who are used to tag-based programming. However, ColdFusion is no less capable than its competition.

Using its set of built-in tags, ColdFusion can perform any function that you can script ASP or JSP to perform. Some ColdFusion functions are even significantly easier to use because ColdFusion has encapsulated functions that require external components in other languages (such as file upload). It is a compact language that often requires fewer lines of code to accomplish tasks than its counterparts.

You will need to obtain ColdFusion Server if you plan to develop ColdFusion applications. It is available in three versions. The free Express version, which has a limited feature set, is great to get you started with ColdFusion, but its lack of support for the <cfscript> tag makes it difficult to use with UltraDev. The Professional and Enterprise editions contain more complete feature sets and run on additional platforms. A complete comparison matrix that helps decide which version is best for a particular implementation is available at the Allaire Web site.

ColdFusion Server is currently available for Windows, Sun Solaris, and Linux, making it as portable as it is powerful. For those needing to run a non-Microsoft server, ColdFusion presents a popular, scalable, very capable option.

Popular Web Servers

You are probably coming close to deciding on a combination of applications that will meet your needs. Once you begin to make a few decisions (or have them made for you by your circumstances), other things will start to fall into place. If you can reduce your potential options, your final decision will be easier. There are currently more than 35 Web server programs and, without some direction, it can become confusing.

Note *Just for the record, we know that not everyone runs Microsoft servers—indeed, most people don't. However, after careful consideration, it seemed fairly clear that most of the people who will find this section most helpful will be setting up and configuring their own Microsoft software. While we do not wish to appear Microsoft-centric in our approach to UltraDev, we have chosen to use Personal Web Server and Internet Information Server as the platform to demonstrate the configuration of new Web sites. For those of you running other setups, we hope that the principles addressed here can be applied to your situation to help you successfully use UltraDev with your project.*

You may well be one of those people who has to do all of the research yourself and make a software choice based on hours of meticulous study. However, the statistics say that there is about a 90 percent chance you will end up running a server from one of three families: Apache, Microsoft, or iPlanet (which includes the Netscape servers). While you are certainly welcome to find a way to get the most out of UltraDev using WebSitePro, WebLogic, or one of the many other servers available, we will focus our attention on these three.

Microsoft

The Microsoft family of Web servers includes three applications at this point: Personal Web Server, Internet Information Server 4.0, and Internet Information Server 5.0. Each has a specific purpose or target platform

Personal Web Server

Designed to run on the workstation versions of Windows, Personal Web Server provides a scaled down version of Microsoft's Internet Information Server. It is intended as a development test platform, but it is robust enough to act as a simple low-bandwidth server option for personal Web sites or a small corporate intranet.

Note *Personal Web Server will run on Windows NT Workstation; but Peer Web Services, an application that comes with it, offers all of the features of the Personal Web Server application and includes some security services that are useful with the NT file system. If you are using NT Workstation, it is suggested that you use Peer Web Services instead of Personal Web Server.*

Note *Internet Information Server 5.0 comes with and runs on Windows 2000 Professional, the workstation version of Windows 2000. It is a limited version, however. It allows only one Web site, one FTP site, and a maximum of ten concurrent connections. In this respect, it is more akin to Peer Web Services than the full-blown IIS server version. Those running Windows 2000 Professional with IIS5 will likely find information in this and the following section useful.*

Personal Web Server is actually a subset of Microsoft's full-fledged Web server application, Internet Information Server. It includes much of the functionality of the full package, including support for Microsoft Transaction Server (MTS), Microsoft Message Queue Server (MSMQ), Active Server Pages (ASP), and ActiveX Data Objects (ADO). Missing, however, is support for some advanced applications like Index Server, Certificate Server, and Site Server Express, which perform content indexing, security certificate management, and site reporting, respectively.

Personal Web Server is useful under any server model to test the HTML portions of your pages; but if you decide to develop an Active Server Pages application for Internet Information Server, you will definitely want to take advantage of its features. Using Personal Web Server, UltraDev allows you to view and test your pages within the design environment.

You will find the installation files you need in various places, depending on which operating system you are running, as shown in Table 2-2.

Once Personal Web Server is installed and you have rebooted your computer, there are several things to look for on your machine. First, take a look at your hard drive. On the drive on which you installed Personal Web Server, you will find a directory called InetPub and, beneath it, another directory called wwwroot. This is the default path that Personal Web Server uses to hold your Web sites. You can choose to place your pages within this path, or you can set up virtual directories that allow the server to access folders elsewhere on your computer; more about this in a bit.

If you are going to manage your Personal Web Server, you'll need to get to it, and Microsoft has made sure you won't have any problem with that. When Personal Web Server is running, an icon appears in the system tray. Double-clicking it runs the Personal Web Manager. In addition, you can run the manager from the icon on your desktop or from the Start menu. Documentation is provided on the Start menu, as well as access to the Transaction Server Manager and the Front Page Administrator. If you use Front Page extensions or Transaction Server for more than ASP support, you'll need to familiarize yourself with these programs.

The Personal Web Manager is your headquarters for administering Personal Web Server. As you can see in Figure 2-2, the manager provides several screens that help organize the tasks that Personal Web Server does for you. Let's go through them to get your server configured for use with UltraDev.

Operating System	Location of Personal Web Server Setup Files
Windows 95	With the Windows NT 4.0 Option Pack
Windows 98	On the Windows 98 Installation CD
Windows NT Workstation	With the Windows NT 4.0 Option Pack
Windows 2000 Professional	On the Windows 2000 Installation CD

Table 2-2. *Locations of Personal Web Server Installation Files*

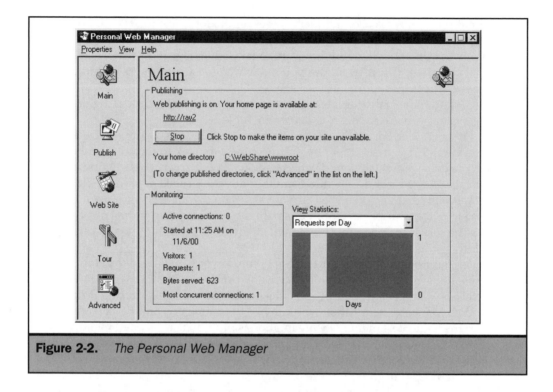

Figure 2-2.   *The Personal Web Manager*

The Main screen shown in Figure 2-2 provides basic information about your server setup and status listed as Publishing and Monitoring. The Publishing information informs you of the location of your home page. This location may look familiar; it is the name of your computer and serves as the default Web site path.

> **Note** *There are actually several ways to access the pages on your local machine. In addition to using your machine's name, you can also use either http://localhost/ or http://127.0.0.1/. 127.0.0.1 is a special reserved IP address that is used to refer only to the local machine. If your computer has a static IP address assigned to it, you can also use that address to refer to the pages housed on your computer.*

The Publishing section of the Personal Web Manager also indicates the status of Personal Web Server, whether it is running or stopped, and lets you start or stop it. Stopping and starting the server allows changes that you make to its configuration to take effect. An additional hyperlink provides quick access to the default Web directory.

The Monitoring section of the Manager gives you basic information about the use of the server, including the ability to graph common metrics. This information is most useful to you if you are actually using Personal Web Server as a server for a small-scale production Web site.

While Personal Web Server is feature-rich for a freeware application and can adequately serve small sites, it is highly recommended that you use a true server operating system and an industrial-strength Web server such as Internet Information Server to efficiently serve sites on whose reliability your client or your business will depend.

The next three sections of the Personal Web Manager are of marginal use to the UltraDev developer. The Web Site and Publish icons provide access to wizards that help you create and deploy simple HTML pages. Since you will be using UltraDev to create and deploy your pages, it is not strictly necessary for you to become familiar with these wizards. If you wish, you may use the Tour section of the Manager to learn more about how these wizards work.

The Advanced tab, however, is very important to the UltraDev developer. It is here that you will configure essential information about your sites. In the Virtual Directories list box shown in Figure 2-3, you will see several directories that have already been set up for you. Most of these are related to the way that Microsoft applications structure sites for use with Front Page and Visual Interdev and are not strictly necessary for UltraDev development. As a matter of fact, you really should not ever publish files for your sites directly into the site structure you see in this list box. If you do, you will

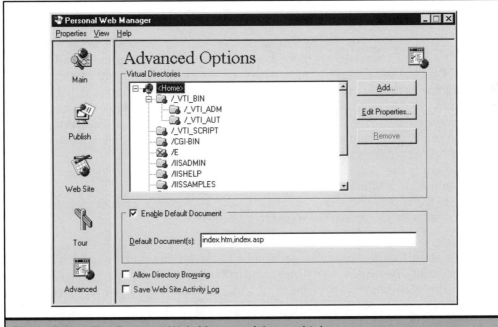

Figure 2-3.   *The Personal Web Manager Advanced tab*

quickly become disorganized. Instead, you should utilize the procedure we are about to cover.

When you load Personal Web Server, a default home page is created in the wwwroot folder. It is actually just an About Personal Web Server page; but since it is named default.asp and resides directly in the wwwroot folder (which is set as the Personal Web Server home directory), it is the page that appears if you type **http://localhost/** or one of the other local-machine referencing addresses mentioned earlier (unless you have changed your default documents, which we will discuss in a moment). To organize your local development sites, you will want to put each one in its own folder. You can do this by placing uniquely named folders underneath the wwwroot folder. For instance, you could place a folder called \GIG underneath wwwroot, place pages inside it, and reference it from a browser using http://localhost/GIG/.

Better yet, you can use the Personal Web Manager to create a virtual directory. This allows the GIG folder to reside anywhere you choose to place it, rather than being buried within the wwwroot folder. First, create a folder called GIG in Windows Explorer. Place it anywhere you can keep track of it. You will likely amass quite a collection of development folders, and a sense of organization will help you work most efficiently. After creating the folder, return to the Personal Web Manager and click the Add button next to the Virtual Directories list box. In the resulting dialog box, browse to the folder that you created. Then create an alias for this site. The alias can be anything you would like to use to refer to this site—the same as the folder name or something different. You can then refer to this site using the alias, that is, http://localhost/*aliasname*/.

The Default Documents setting will become very important as you begin to set up your site. Default Documents are those page names that will load automatically when a directory is browsed to. For instance, when you type a URL into your browser (such as **http://www.bettergig.com/**) you may not explicitly declare which page in that site you wish to view. In this instance, the Web server refers to the Default Documents list to see if there are any pages in the folder that it can display. In the order that they are listed, the server will compare the page names in your site with the default list and will show the first match it comes to.

Some people use "index" for their default page name. Others use "default," "main," or even "home." In addition, some prefer the .htm extension while others use .html or even one of the application server extensions, such as .asp, .jsp, .cfm, or .php. Create your list of default documents separated by commas.

 Use any of the page names that you might actually need in your sites, but don't go overboard. The more the server has to search through, the slower its performance will be. And make sure to use the same file extensions that will be used on the server where the site will ultimately be deployed.

The final section of the Advanced section of the Personal Web Manager is the permissions setting for the directory. Read and script access is fine for any directories except those such as cgi-bins or others that will house files that need to be executed.

Below the permissions section are two settings that are both disabled by default. Enabling the Allow Directory Browsing setting will let your site visitors see a listing of all of the pages and directories in your site if a default document does not exist—not a good thing. And if you want to save log files, enabling the Save Web Activity Log option will save NCSA formatted log files that can be viewed with a text editor.

Once Personal Web Server is set up, you are ready to test the pages you develop in UltraDev or even to deploy them for small-scale use. Personal Web Server will also figure into the use of UltraDev's Live Data feature.

Internet Information Server

Microsoft's full-featured professional-level Web server is Internet Information Server. It currently exists in two versions, 4.0 and 5.0, which run on Windows NT Server and Windows 2000, respectively. Since version 4.0 is probably still most widely used and supports ASP 2, we'll look at its implementation, which should closely match that of version 5 for our purposes.

Note   *Internet Information Server has improved over its lifetime, and version 5.0 is the best yet. Its improved support for transactions, ASP 3, and increased performance are helping solidify Windows as an enterprise-level server. While it remains well behind Apache as the most popular server, its ease of management makes it worthy of your consideration. UltraDev only requires the features of version 4.0, however, and we will focus on it.*

If you have Windows NT 4.0 Server installed, you have a good start, but IIS4 does not come with the base operating system. To get it and its related programs, you need to get a hold of the Windows NT Option Pack. The Option Pack is a separate CD that contains a number of applications that help you get your Web server set up and running. You can download all of the files from Microsoft at www.microsoft.com/ntserver/nts/downloads/recommended/NT4OptPk/default.asp. It is a large download that consists of several individual files. Once all of the files are unzipped into a directory, a setup file is run to install the Option Pack.

Tip   *If you are connected to the Internet on the server where you need to install the Option Pack, there is also an option to run the install on the Web. All of the necessary files are installed without your attending to the downloading of all of the zipped components.*

Note   *While IIS5 does not install with Windows 2000 Server by default, you will not need to download anything extra to add it. IIS5 is installable as an option from the regular Windows installation and can be added from Windows Configuration at any time.*

You will be given the option to install and configure several supporting applications along with Internet Information Server. The only one that is truly important to us at this point is the Microsoft Transaction Server (MTS). Documentation is available to explain the purpose, installation, and configuration of the additional services, such as Microsoft Message Queue Server and the Index and Certificate Servers.

Once IIS is installed, you can get to its configuration by selecting Windows NT 4 Option Pack | Microsoft Internet Information Server | Internet Service Manager from the Start button on your server. An application called the Microsoft Management Console (MMC) launches. The MMC is Microsoft's plug-in application. It is intended to provide a common interface in which to manage various pieces of your server's configuration. The MMC looks different than the Personal Web Manager (see Figure 2-4), but you will use it for the same basic functions.

As with Personal Web Server, there are certain basic functions that we expect the IIS management console to perform, such as setting up sites and starting and stopping Web services. But because a production Web server is designed to be used by a number of developers in a production environment, there are a number of additional settings that you will need to consider, including security, IP addresses, Microsoft's Collaborative Data Objects, and FTP access.

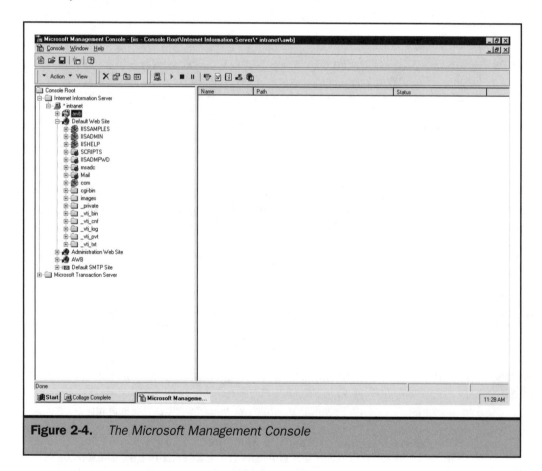

Figure 2-4.   *The Microsoft Management Console*

> **Note** *While you can certainly access an IIS server on your local network by using the machine's name in a browser, just as with Personal Web Server, it is much more likely that you will make use of Windows NT's ability to multihome its network addresses by adding additional IP addresses in Network Properties. This ability, in conjunction with a Domain Name Service (DNS) server, is what allows users to type friendly Web addresses such as http://www.bettergig.com/ into their browsers and end up at a site on your server.*

The MMC looks different from the Personal Web Manager, but you are really being given the same kinds of options in a less wizard-like fashion. Let's look at the highlights of the IIS structure without getting bogged down in services we don't have time to cover. If you have run the MMC on your server, you should be looking at a screen that closely resembles Figure 2-4.

You will see a variety of services listed under Internet Information Server. At this point, we are concerned only with the Default FTP site, the Default Web Site, and the Default SMTP site. We'll go over what each of these represents and then look at setting up a new site from scratch.

The Default FTP Site

As you might guess from its name, File Transfer Protocol (FTP) is the Internet protocol used to transfer files back and forth between machines. It is used when getting a complete file from computer A to computer B is more important than viewing the contents of the file over the Web. For instance, when you create and save Web pages as HTML files on your development computer, they are only accessible once they are placed on a server that is connected to the Internet. If that server is a machine other than your development computer, you will use an FTP program, either within UltraDev or from a third party, to transfer those complete files to the appropriate directories on the server. From there, their contents can be viewed over the Web by browsers everywhere.

The Default FTP site is the directory that has been created for this machine. Accessing FTP using this computer's name or using its default IP address will map you to this directory for uploading your files. As we will see, your machine can have many FTP sites configured for the domains that your server controls.

The Default Web Site

As with the wwwroot directory in Personal Web Server, your server has a wwwroot folder that can serve as a default Web site. Any sites that you publish to this directory are available by browsing to http://*YourMachineName*/ or this server's default IP address if browsing from a LAN, http://localhost/ or http://127.0.0.1/ (if the browser is actually on the server machine). We can set up additional sites beneath this order or by creating Virtual Directories as we did in Personal Web Server.

> **Note** *In addition to managing your IIS installation from the server itself, IIS allows you to perform many administrative tasks remotely over the Internet. See the IIS documentation for help setting up this capability.*

The Default SMTP Server

While the default SMTP server is not strictly a part of setting up IIS to work with UltraDev, sending mail within Web applications is a very popular topic of discussion. We need to discuss some preliminary setup so that we can use both this SMTP server and CDO mail in our later examples.

Simple Mail Transport Protocol (SMTP) is a very simple (as the name implies) way to send and receive mail across the Internet. With the advent of POP3 and IMAP, SMTP is not used much for mail retrieval, but it is still the standard for sending mail. The NT Option Pack installs an SMTP server along with IIS; so you can use your Web server to send mail, or you can use another mail server such as Exchange or Lotus Notes that you control. All you have to know is its IP address and security settings. We'll take the simple route and set up the local Web server to send mail for us.

Two components are necessary to get CDO mail running on your NT server: the cdonts.dll file and an SMTP server. CDO for NTS1.2 is a lightweight version of the full Collaborative Data Objects that works with Microsoft Exchange. It comes with IIS4 and should be on your server if IIS is running, but it may not be registered.

To make sure cdonts.dll is registered, use the Run dialog box from the Windows NT Start menu and type **regsvr32 c:\winnt\system32\cdonts.dll**.

Note   *You should use the path of your system folder in place of c:\winnt\system32. This is the default installation path for Windows NT.*

If the registration completes successfully, you will get a confirmation dialog box like this one:

Now that CDO is registered, follow these steps to set up IIS to send mail:

1. On your IIS computer, open the Microsoft Management Console (MMC).

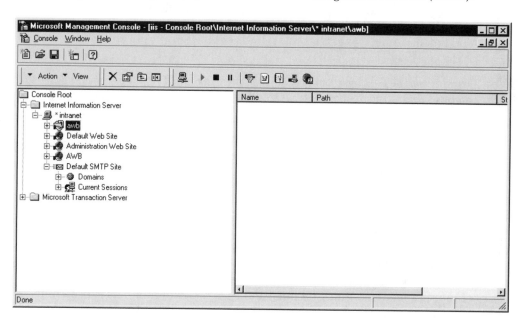

2. In the left-hand pane, expand the Internet Information Server section, and select and expand your IIS server.

3. In the right-hand pane, click Default SMTP Server and select Properties. Select the Delivery tab.

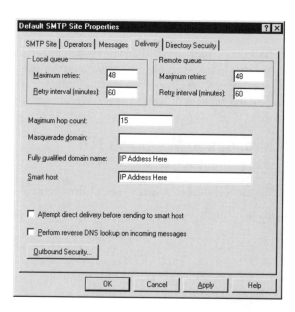

4. In the Fully Qualified Domain Name text box, enter the IIS computer name or IP address. In the Smart Host text box, enter the name or IP address. In this case, the name will be the same in both since we are using an SMTP server on the IIS server.

Whether you use the simple names of the computers in the SMTP setup or the full Internet addresses depends on whether you will be accessing these machines over a LAN or over the Web.

That should do it. Your server is now set up with a default SMTP server and the necessary CDO files. We will make use of this in later examples.

Setting Up a New Site

Since IIS is a production-level server, you can host a number of sites on the same machine. In order for your server to treat each site separately, you will need to begin by assigning an IP address for each new site. IP addresses are the numbers that are used by the Internet to identify and locate pieces of hardware. Each address is a series of four numbers separated by dots, and each series of numbers is used only once. At the highest levels of the Internet, blocks of these IP addresses are assigned through first-tier ISPs down to their customers, so a path is created that helps anyone looking for a site locate its whereabouts.

You will need to obtain a unique IP address for each piece of hardware (computer, router, and so on) you wish to put on the Internet and for each site you wish to add to your Web server. Your ISP will likely assign you a small block of numbers to use as you need them.

IP addresses are becoming scarce. Until IPv6 (IP version 6) is released, there is likely to be a shortage of available numbers due to the rapid growth of the Web. Make sure you get your ISP to assign enough numbers to carry you through a six-month period or so. A new block can take several days or weeks to get assigned.

Assigning IP Addresses in Windows NT

To assign an IP address to your NT server, follow these steps:

1. Right-click Network Neighborhood and select Properties.
2. On the Protocols tab, select TCP/IP Protocol and click Properties.

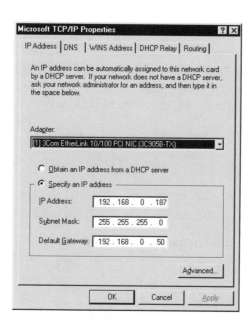

3. You will see the main IP information for this server. Since you need to add an IP address, click the Advanced button.

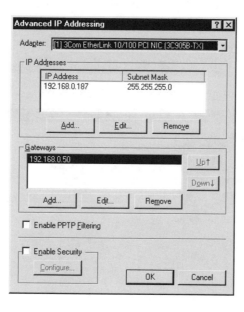

4. In the Advanced IP Addressing dialog box, you will see a list of all of the addresses that are currently assigned to this machine. Click Add.

5. In the TCP/IP Address box, type the new IP address that you want to assign for the site you are about to configure. Your ISP will have provided you with an IP address and its corresponding Subnet Mask to enter here. Click Add.

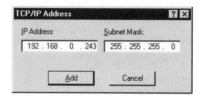

6. Click OK until you reach the Desktop again. You should reboot your machine at this point. When you do, you will have added your IP address and be ready to move on.

As with Personal Web Server, you will be storing your site in a folder on one of the hard drives of the server. In order to remain organized, this folder will be separate from the wwwroot folder. Run Windows Explorer and create a folder to hold the site. Name it whatever you like.

After your folder is set up, return to the MMC. You need to set up an FTP site and a Web site for this new project.

1. Right-click Default Web Site and choose New | Site. The New Web Site Wizard is displayed and will walk you through the setup. Choose a name for the site and click Next.

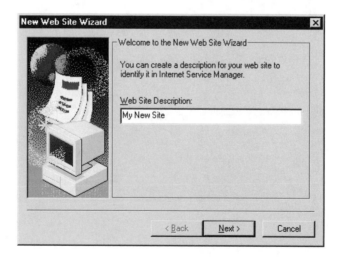

2. Select the IP address that you just added to the machine from the drop-down box, and leave the TCP port set to 80. If you have Secure Sockets installed on this machine, you can set the SSL port to use in the next box, but you should leave this as 443 for now. Click Next.

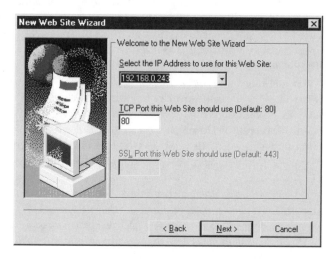

3. Select the directory to use for this site by browsing to the folder you just created. Unless you want to restrict access to this site, leave the Allow Anonymous Access option checked. Click Next.

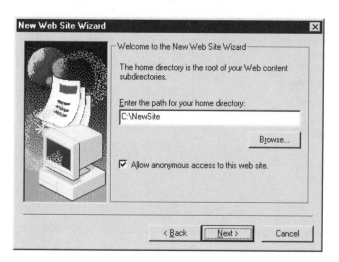

4. At the Permissions dialog box, click Finish. We will do some work with these, but not until the site is set up.

Create an FTP site by following the same steps. Select the same IP address and leave the port and permissions settings as they are. You will then return to the MMC with two new sites listed and indications that both are stopped, as in Figure 2-5. Unlike Personal Web Server, you can control the status of the Web server for each individual site in IIS.

Right-click your new Web site in the site listing in the left-hand pane. You will be presented with a tabbed dialog box that displays tons of information about your site configuration. While there are a great many things that you may want to attend to here to get your site tuned the way you want it, we really only have the time to get you set with the basics—that is, enough to get your site running. If you successfully completed the setup wizard, you just need to visit two tabs right now: Operators and Documents.

The Operators tab allows you to set security for this site by designating which registered users have access and on what level. Once you have created your users using the Windows NT User Manager for Domains, you may add them to this site, thereby giving them permission to access it as developers (see Figure 2-6). You may add individual users to groups that you have set up and already added users to.

Note   *User groups are an extremely efficient way to manage permissions on your server. By creating group accounts, you can set permissions that fit the role that a user fills, rather than creating permissions for each and every user. When permissions change or users change roles, it is then easy to make adjustments without having to do redundant work.*

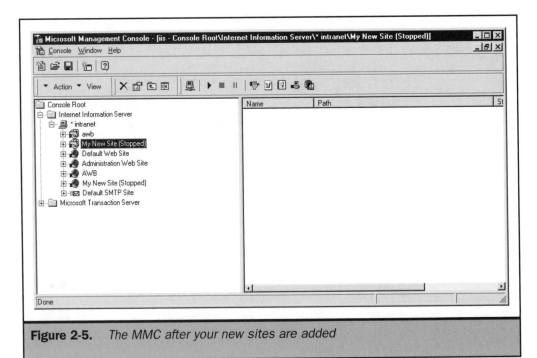

Figure 2-5.   *The MMC after your new sites are added*

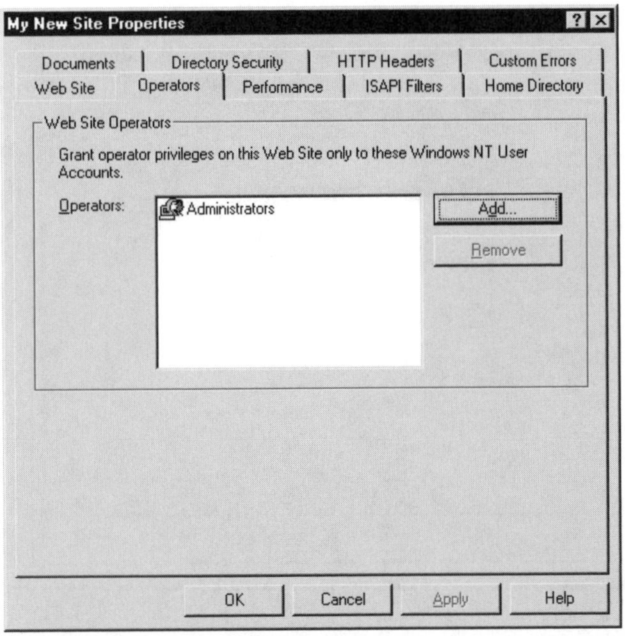

Figure 2-6.   *Set security options using the Operators tab*

The Documents tab is much like the Default Documents setting we covered in the earlier section "Personal Web Server." Set the document names in the order you are most likely to use them so that visitors browsing your site are served the proper initial document if they are unsure which page they are looking for (see Figure 2-7).

Feel free to look around at the other settings and investigate their use in the IIS documentation or a good third-party reference.

Once this is finished, your basic Web site configuration is complete. Click OK to return to the MMC, and right-click your new FTP site. Choose Properties from the menu to see the FTP configuration screen.

Again, if you have completed the wizard successfully, you should need to change only a few things. On the Security Accounts tab, deselect the Allow Anonymous Connections check box, unless you want anonymous users to use this account (see Figure 2-8). Since it is your Web site development account, that should not be the case. Also, add the user accounts or user groups that you want to have access to this account, to upload or manage site content.

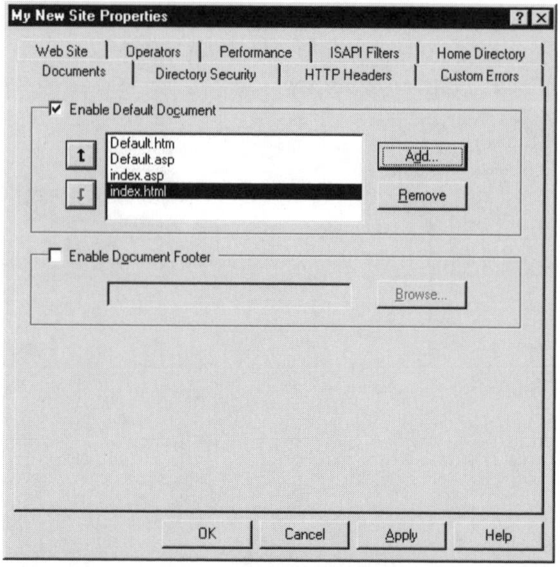

Figure 2-7. *The Documents property page*

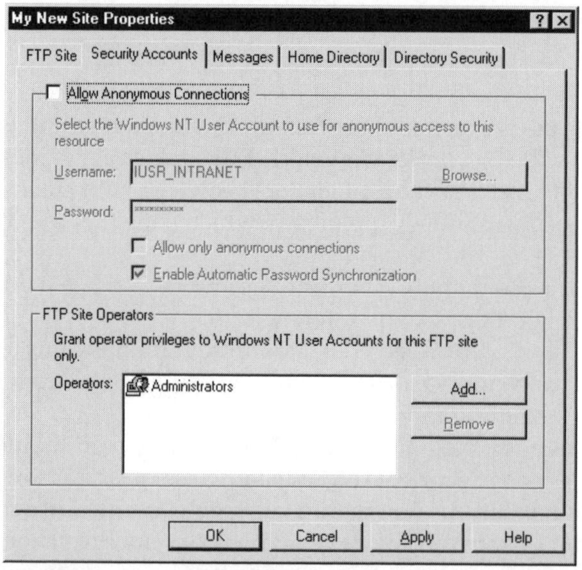

Figure 2-8. *Use the Security Accounts tab to add or delete user groups*

Note   *You may very well want to set up an anonymous FTP account that allows your users to download and even upload files to your server. This would obviously be a separate account that does not map into your site development directory. To allow users to log in anonymously, leave the Allow Anonymous Connections option checked.*

The only other change you will need to make now is on the Home Directory tab, as shown in Figure 2-9. Enable write access so that the users you have assigned can write files to this account.

As before, feel free to investigate the other options in the FTP site properties.

Right-click the FTP site and the Web site you just created, and select Start to start the services running on the server.

Congratulations! Your site is now ready to begin uploading content. Even if you are not running Microsoft servers, you should be able to identify certain topics that will be of concern to you in setting up sites on other servers. Let's look at some other options now.

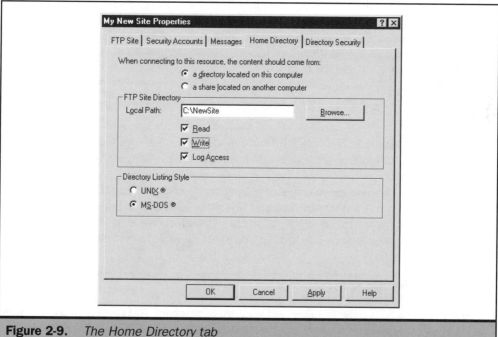

Figure 2-9.   *The Home Directory tab*

Apache

By far the most popular Web server on the net, Apache is a product of the open source movement. That means that its code is available to anyone who can download it and understand it, and it can be modified and extended to meet the disparate needs of its users. It is currently in the late 1.3 version, and an alpha release of version 2 is available.

Apache is unquestionably a robust and powerful Web server. Its huge user base assures that Apache has been tested in a wide variety of settings under innumerable configurations. It is available for all of the Unix variants, as well as Windows 95/98/NT.

But, as popular as it is, Apache is not for everyone. It doesn't have the GUI interface of an IIS or the Web administration features of many other packages. It is installed, set up, and configured from the command line; and it is often quite a complicated process to do, depending on the options you wish to employ.

Nonetheless, once you get used to the way it works, you will appreciate the power and flexibility of this package. While basic features are supported in the core application, additional modules are available to integrate things like PHP (a popular scripting language) and MySQL (a popular and free database application).

Modules allow these packages to run as processes of Apache itself—a very efficient method, to say the least. And, if you are used to working with Windows, you will be amazed at what you can accomplish remotely through a simple telnet session.

Packages and instructions are available to help you get Apache running on your server. You will need to accomplish the same kinds of tasks in Apache as you did in IIS to get sites set up. You can find directions for completing these tasks in your configuration at the Apache site (www.apache.org).

iPlanet

What was the Netscape Enterprise Edition Web server has been rolled into the iPlanet Web server. It is a full-featured server ready to play in the big leagues. iPlanet is available for Windows and Unix.

iPlanet is an expensive option (especially compared to Apache and IIS); but upcoming versions will have built-in JSP support, and iPlanet is intended to handle complex Web and data configurations with ease. Installation is straightforward, and a trial version is available to give you a look at it before you pay real money (www.iplanet.com).

Popular Databases

If you think the selection of Web servers is confusing, we are just getting started. Since you are using UltraDev, it is a safe bet that you want to put some data on the Web, and for that you will need to select a database application. From the free to the expensive and from the simple to the complex, there is a database available to meet any need.

The decision which to use is an important one that can be affected by your budget, your server platform, and several other factors. We will cover some of the more popular options and mention some others that you might want to take a look at.

No matter which database application you choose, you will need to spend some time learning a language that the database understands. Most likely this will be Structured Query Language (SQL). It is fairly easy to learn, and UltraDev will help you through as you get started. We'll cover more about SQL later.

Microsoft Access and ISAM

Perhaps the most popular database application for small sites is Microsoft Access. Access is inexpensive (it is part of Microsoft Office or can be purchased separately for just a couple of hundred dollars); is widely supported; and has a friendly user interface that makes designing your database a snap, as shown in Figure 2-10.

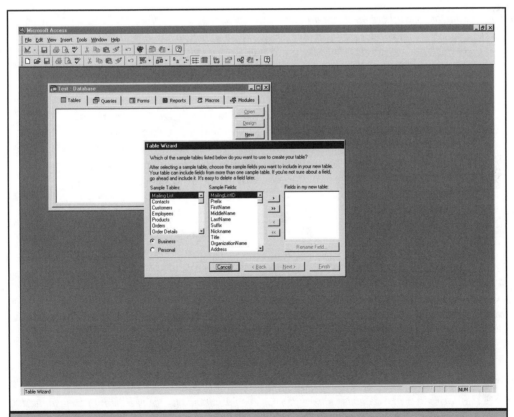

Figure 2-10.   *The Microsoft Access design environment makes creating databases easy*

Access is a member of a file-based family of databases known as ISAM (Indexed Sequential Access Method) databases. These database applications typically create a file (or sometimes a database container) that resides in a folder on your Web server. This self-contained file can be accessed through the proper driver without the actual database application being loaded on the server. For example, Access stores its table in a file with an .mdb extension. This file can be uploaded to your Web server and accessed from your Web application without Microsoft Access being loaded on the server.

> **Note** *ISAM is an older method of file access, but it's a very popular one. Databases such as Lotus Approach, Microsoft Fox Pro, FileMaker Pro, and Paradox are all file-based ISAM databases.*

Databases such as Access are a great way to get you started. They are certainly very powerful and, despite their low cost, they may have all of the features that many sites will ever need. Access can hold up to 2GB of data per table and can support up to 255 concurrent connections.

> **Note** *One of the authors once ran an Access database that had over 40 million records with more than acceptable performance. As a matter of fact, when the database was upsized to SQL Server, single connections did not perform appreciably faster than in Access. Be aware, however, that Access' performance would quickly degrade with multiple connections trying to access such a large amount of data.*

But as a practical matter, these databases are not intended to be enterprise-level solutions. The 255 connections statistic is a theoretical maximum, and you would likely experience significant performance difficulties before you got anywhere near that number. And heavy use with a large amount of data would require constant attention, as the database file would have a tendency to corrupt and would need to be repaired.

> **Caution** *It is important to remember that databases such as Access only run on Windows. If you are restricted to an operating system other than Windows, they won't even be an option for you.*

Perhaps a greater concern is the security issue surrounding the use of file-based databases. Because these files reside on the Web server machine, if your Web server is compromised, the attacker also has access to your database. This is compounded by the fact that few people bother to implement security on their database files, meaning that anyone who is able to get it off of your server will have ridiculously simple access to credit cards or whatever data you have stored in your database.

> **Caution** *There are different schools of thought on whether it is acceptable to store credit card information in a database where there is even a remote chance of it being compromised. No matter how you feel about this, it is absolutely unacceptable to store sensitive data in a file-based database without security implemented. That's just asking for trouble.*

Another issue to consider is your need for remote access to your database outside the Web application. With file-based applications such as Access, you must maintain at least two copies of your database, one on your development machine and one on the live site. If you intend to develop on more than one machine, you will need additional copies for those as well, because you will not be able to hit the database with the pages you create until they are uploaded to the live site. This means that if you have to add tables or fields, you need to pull down a copy of the database to do so, so you don't lose data, but while you are making these changes, people could be using your site and entering data that is not in the copy you have—it goes on and on. It's just a mess. It is easy to see why a site with any amount of traffic needs to look to more sophisticated means of data storage.

But there is a reason for the popularity of Microsoft Access. It is easy and inexpensive to develop in, and Microsoft provides a relatively simple upsizing tool that allows you to move your database to SQL Server at any time. SQL Server is an entirely different kind of database application, a true data server that allows enterprise deployment of your data without the performance and security issues of Access and other ISAM databases.

Database Servers

When you are more concerned about performance, security, and advanced data features than just getting your data on the Web quickly, you will need to look to products that provide true data server capabilities. Typically running on their own machines, database servers provide support for things such as record and transactional locking, stored procedures, triggers, and true security.

Record Locking

Record locking is the ability to restrict access to information that is being updated elsewhere. If two people make changes to a record at the same time, the last person to save will end up with his changes in the database—but who's to say that his is the most accurate data or that he would have made those changes had he known that another person was making changes at the same time? Record locking allows a database to lock records so that the first person to access the record has it all to himself until he's completes his work and releases it.

Most databases support some kind of locking. Some, however, implement their locks at a level that can interfere with users trying to access records other than the one that is actually being edited. Known as page-level locking, these applications restrict up to 4K of data, probably well more than is needed.

Advanced applications will implement locking at a record level, meaning that only the record that is being edited will be locked out. On busy sites, you run the very real risk that users will need to edit records that happen to be in close physical proximity to one another in the database tables. You do not want to risk the usability issue that poor locking methods would impose on your money-making venture.

Transaction Locking

Transactions allow entire sets of instructions to either completely execute or completely fail as a unit. The classic example is an online banking transaction. If you were transferring money from one of your accounts to another, two events would be required: the debiting of the first account and the crediting of the second. If the bank's computer system experienced a problem in between those two events, you would end up with money taken from one of your accounts and never put in the other. This is not good for you. A transaction guarantees that both of these events will either happen or not happen together. Once begun, a transaction either commits (writes all parts of the transaction to the database from the temporary file where it is held) or rolls back (does not write to the database and clears the temporary file, leaving your data intact as it was before the transaction was run). This is better for your checkbook.

Databases that provide transaction locking ensure that uncommitted changes are not accessible until the transaction is committed.

Stored Procedures

Stored procedures provide a means of embedding complex data manipulation in a program that is stored and run inside the database itself. When stored procedures are used, you make a simple call to the program and pass in any required parameters, rather than forcing the database to deal with your entire SQL statement every time. Stored procedures are precompiled and run quickly, improving site performance. They also provide a significant security boost, as they reduce the ability of an attacker to send malicious SQL commands to your database.

Triggers

Triggers provide the ability to teach your database how to do things that need to happen on a regular basis or when some requisite event (a trigger) occurs. For example, maybe you want to send a quick Happy Birthday e-mail to the customers in your database on their birthday, which is stored in a field of the database. You could set up a trigger to generate and send e-mails to all customers whose birthday equals today's date, and set it to run every day.

Triggers are very important when you need to respond to the data that is inserted and edited in your database. A key example is referential integrity. Maintaining referential integrity is the process of checking on a constant basis to make sure that edits to the database do not result in things like orphaned records. For example, suppose that you have a table with all of your salesmen in it. In another table, those salesmen's customers are listed. If someone were to delete a salesman's record from the first table, the database would be left with orphaned customers. They would exist in the database without a salesman. Reports of all salesmen and their customers would not show those customers, and the company would run the risk of losing them. In order to prevent this, a trigger could be set up to check for customer records whenever someone tried to delete a salesman. It would deny the ability to delete that salesman until all customers had been reassigned, thus maintaining the integrity of the database.

Security

Data servers provide a number of security benefits. For one thing, they typically reside on a separate machine from the Web server, meaning that if the Web server is compromised, the attacker does not automatically have access to the database. Typically, the server is accessed by its IP address or qualified domain name.

If you are not careful in the way you set up your site, a compromised Web server will provide access to everything on your database server, if only because the attacker can glean addresses and username/password combinations from the code on your pages.

More important, a good database server will provide a method of creating a hierarchy of passwords, accounts, and roles that allow access to certain databases and tables, and allow only certain things to be done by certain users.

Popular Database Servers

There are a number of excellent database servers available with very loyal users. Any discussion of these has to include Microsoft's SQL server. It is an excellent product with a relatively reasonable price tag, but it is limited to the Windows platform. It is a popular choice because many ISPs offer access to a SQL server account along with your hosting account for just $20 to $25 a month.

Perhaps the granddaddy of Web databases is Oracle's 8i database. It provides a truly enterprise-level database with support for many of the popular operating systems. It also offers an extensive array of development tools. It has a heavy price tag to go with it; but for a large corporation, there are certainly cost of ownership issues that reduce this as a factor.

Less popular but equally powerful are offerings from IBM (DB2), Sybase, and Informix. It is likely that your choice of which database server to use will be affected by many factors, some of them out of your control. If you have access to any of these excellent products, you should have no problem integrating them into a high-quality Web application.

Open Source

There are also a couple of Open Source options to consider. Open Source is a popular movement lately that calls upon the talents of a product's user base to assist in the improvement of the product through extensive testing and collaborative development. MySQL and PostgreSQL are two such products.

Available for free or for a low cost, these products offer very powerful features. They are both missing features of the commercial applications discussed in the preceding section, but they are nonetheless excellent products that continue to improve with each release.

Summary

Before we dig into UltraDev, you need to have a pretty good idea about the operating system, Web server, application server, and database you are going to use. If you have these chosen and installed, you are ready to discover how UltraDev brings these all together into a Web application. We'll do that in Chapter 3.

Chapter 3

Dreamweaver UltraDev Basics

As mentioned earlier, Dreamweaver UltraDev 4 is a superset of the Dreamweaver 4 product. It includes all of the functionality of Dreamweaver, plus the additional database capabilities. As such, it is impossible for this book to do justice to the Dreamweaver interface and all of it features; there are entire books dedicated to just that. Still, an overview is warranted so that the newcomer to this family of products has enough information to become productive quickly.

If you are used to Dreamweaver and its floating palette interface, you will be very comfortable when you first launch UltraDev. With only a couple of minor differences, UltraDev's default setup looks, feels, and acts just like Dreamweaver, which is a blessing or a curse, depending on your background. The good news is that UltraDev goes out of its way to allow you to customize your working environment. A little practice will allow you to make good use of UltraDev's interface; and you may even grow into one of its loyal defenders.

Working with UltraDev

UltraDev offers what is essentially a three-pronged approach to Web development. Using the tools it provides, you can enter information such as text directly onto the page, have information inserted for you with built-in objects and behaviors, and go behind the scenes to work directly in the underlying code that makes up your page. To construct a site of any substance, you will almost certainly utilize a combination of these methods.

In Chapter 2, we discussed all of the decisions you need to make in preparation to use UltraDev. Now that you are ready to start, you will first need to define a site and tell UltraDev about the decisions you made. After defining your site, you will begin to develop it by adding pages and then adding content to those pages.

When you first launch UltraDev, you are presented with several tools, as seen in Figure 3-1. This default configuration can be customized to meet your needs. We will discuss setting your preferences later in the chapter. The defaults will serve us quite nicely as we get started with UltraDev.

Locate the Launcher on your desktop. If you are familiar with Dreamweaver, you will recognize the Launcher, but it may look odd to you. While the Dreamweaver Launcher provides shortcuts to areas of the program related to page design, UltraDev opts for access to data functions such as Server Behaviors and Data Bindings. You will see that it has the Site Manager in common, though, and that's where we will begin to describe our site to UltraDev.

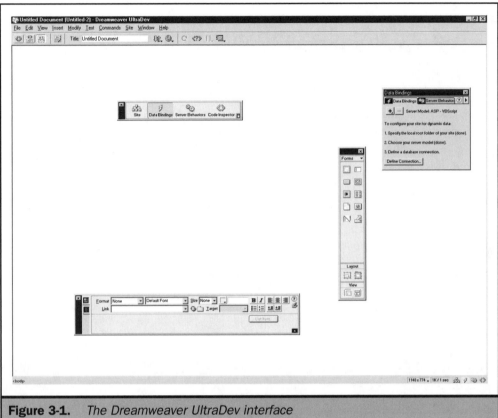

Figure 3-1. *The Dreamweaver UltraDev interface*

The Site Manager

The Site Manager, shown in Figure 3-2, provides a powerful command center from which to manage all of your Web sites. Using it, you can define the characteristics of each site so that they can be administered efficiently, even if they use different server models and reside on different servers around the Internet. You can use UltraDev's built-in FTP program to send and receive files from any of your sites. And you can manage the growth of your site by adding pages, editing pages, and structuring the directories and pages that make it up. But in order to manage a site, it must first be defined.

On the toolbar of the Site Manager is a drop-down list box that lists all of your currently defined sites. If you are using a fresh installation of UltraDev, you will have three tutorial sites in the list: one each for ASP, JSP, and ColdFusion. Selecting a site in the list makes that site active. Its directories and pages are then presented in the windows below the toolbar.

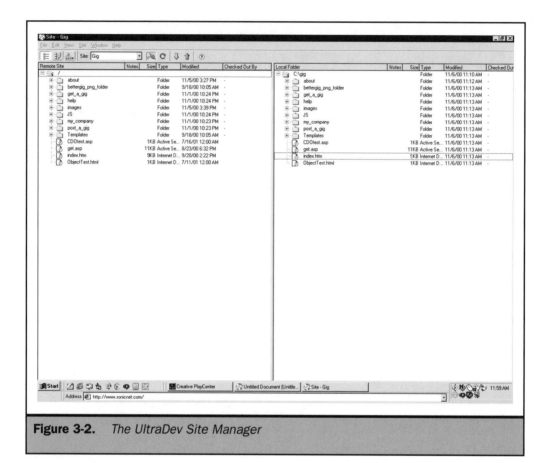

Figure 3-2. *The UltraDev Site Manager*

Defining a Site

There are a couple of ways to get to the screens that you will use to define your sites. You can double-click the site displayed in the drop-down list to edit the definition for that site. Or, you can select the Define Sites option at the bottom of the list and the following screen will appear, allowing you to select a site to edit, create a new site, or delete a site. Follow these steps to define a new site.

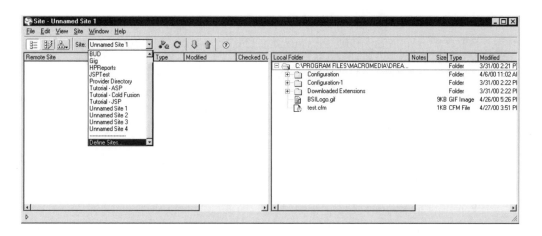

1. Select New to define a new site. The Site Definition screen will open, as shown here.

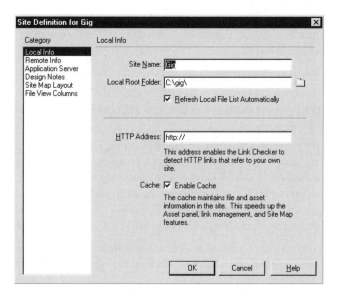

The Site Definition screen contains six categories in which you will define various parts of your site.

2. In the Local Info category, select a name for your site.

3. Select a Local Root Folder for your site. This folder will be a directory on your local hard drive. If you created a directory in Chapter 2, select this folder as your Local Root Folder. All of the HTML pages, images, media, and scripts that make up your site will be stored in this folder and its subdirectories. You can use the File icon to the right of the text box to browse your hard drive for this folder.

4. Select or deselect the Refresh Local File List Automatically checkbox. If selected, the list of files in the Site Manager will refresh automatically every time a file is added, subtracted, or edited. Deselecting this box allows UltraDev to run faster, because the screen is not refreshed every time a change is made, but you will have to refresh the file list manually from the View | Refresh Local in the Site Window menu. (SHIFT-F5)

5. In the HTTP Address field, fill in the URL that your site will use—for example, www.bettergig.com. This setting allows UltraDev to verify links within the site if you are using absolute links.

6. Check the Cache option to cause UltraDev to create a cache file that speeds up link management. If you don't select this box, UltraDev will prompt you to create a cache file later.

7. In the left pane of the Site Manager, select the Web Server Info category.

8. If you are creating pages that will not be uploaded onto a server, select None in the drop-down list box on the Remote Info category.

9. If you will be uploading your site to a local network drive or to a virtual directory on your development computer, select the Local Info option in the drop-down list box. Use the folder icon to browse to the directory where your site will be loaded. If you want the Site Manager to automatically update file listings when you make changes, check the Refresh Remote File List Automatically box. For improved performance, you can leave this unselected and refresh manually from the View menu in Windows or the Site menu on a Macintosh.

   You may also choose to use this method if you would prefer to use a third-party FTP program, such as CuteFTP or WSFTP, rather than the FTP program that's built into UltraDev.

10. UltraDev allows you to manage your local and remote site files from within the Site Manager if you select the FTP option in the Web Server Info category. Enter the URL of your FTP site in the FTP Host box. Possible entries might be

www.bettergig.com or ftp.bettergig.com. Do not include the protocol in the address, such as ftp://ftp.bettergig.com.

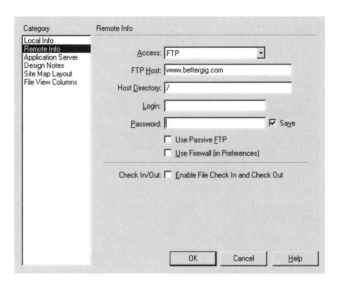

11. Enter the username and password that have been established for you at this FTP site. UltraDev will automatically save your password for future use. Deselect the Save box if you wish to be prompted for a password each time you connect to the FTP server.

12. If your network uses a firewall that you must connect through, select the Use Firewall option. Check with your network administrator to find out if your firewall requires a passive FTP connection. A passive connection requires the client machine to establish the FTP connection rather than requesting it from the FTP server.

13. Select Check In/Out in the category list at the left of the Site Manager. Check In and Check Out offers a basic level of source control within a collaborative design environment. If Check In/Out is enabled in the site definition here, the Site Manager marks local and remote files when they are opened for editing. A green checkmark indicates a file opened by you and a red one indicates a file opened by someone else. In addition, if the user has entered a name on this screen, that name is displayed next to the file; this way, if someone locks up a file that you need, you can hunt them down.

14. To use the Check In/Out feature, select the Enable File Check In and Check Out option. If you would like files to be checked out automatically when you open them, select the Check Out Files When Opening checkbox also. If you do not enable this option, you will be responsible for manually setting files as checked out as you open them. Enter a name that identifies you to other users in your group or that identifies a machine at which a file has been opened.

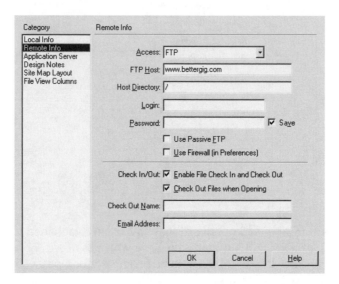

15. Select the Site Map Layout in the category list to the left.

16. Identify which page in this site is the home page in the Home Page text box. If you do not put a page name here, UltraDev will search your site for pages called index.html and index.htm. If neither exists, you will be prompted to indicate the home page when you open the site. You can either browse for your home page using the folder icon, or type a page name into the box. If the name you type doesn't exist, UltraDev will offer to create it for you.

17. The Number of Columns and Column Width options relate to how your Site Map is displayed. The Site Map is one of the options on the remote side of the Site Manager along with the Site Files listing. The Site Map is a visual

representation of the navigational layout of your site. You can control how the hierarchy is displayed by altering the Number of Columns and Column Width settings here.

18. Choose whether to display your pages by their filenames or their page titles. If you choose page titles, make sure that you actually give your pages titles, or you will end up with 100 pages called Untitled Page.

19. Two additional options allow you to choose whether hidden files and dependent files such as images, includes, and other non-HTML files are displayed.

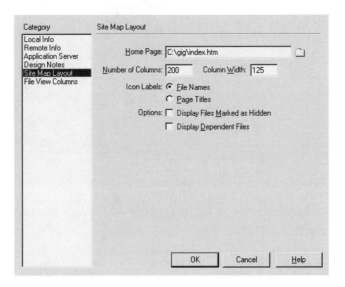

20. Next, select Design Notes in the category list in the left-hand pane of the Site Definition window. Two options on this page allow you to designate whether you want UltraDev to maintain design notes for your files and whether those notes will be uploaded along with your files to the remote site. You can add design notes to any kind of file that holds information about the file, and you can keep them for your use or share them with others on your design team. The Clean Up button will delete any design note files that are no longer associated

with a file in your site. It can be used to delete all design notes by deselecting the Maintain Design Notes Option before clicking the Clean Up button.

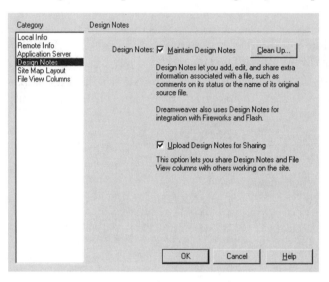

21. Click OK to complete your site definition. You will be returned to the Site Manager.

Now that you have described your preferences to UltraDev, you are ready to begin constructing your site.

Managing Site Files

You can control many high-level aspects of your site using the Site Manager. With menu options, buttons, and keyboard shortcuts you can

- Add new pages to your site
- Manage and synchronize files and folders between your local machine and your remote server
- Control changes to your site files by using UltraDev's Check In and Check Out features
- Check links
- View a graphical representation of your site using the Site Map Layout

Adding New Pages to Your Site

UltraDev offers several methods of adding pages to your site.

- From the File menu, select the New Window option. A new document window will appear. This new document window is not strictly related to your site at this point. You must select Save As from the File menu and save it in this site's folder with a unique file name.

■ From the File menu, select the New File option. A new file will appear in either the local or remote side of your site, depending on which was selected when the menu option was selected. This new filename will be highlighted, ready for you to give it a unique name.

■ From the File menu, select New from Template. This option allows you to create a new page from an existing template. This new page will inherit properties from the template, such as design elements or code. You may then add to the page according to the editable regions set in the template file. More on templates in Chapter 4.

■ In either the Local or Remote side of the Site window, right-click to display the pop-up menu. Select the New File option from the menu. This option works just like the New File option in the File menu.

Managing Your Site

In the Site Files view, the Site Manager is divided into two halves. By default, the left half of the screen displays information from your remote server. These are the files that reside in the remote folder that you specified in your site definition. The right side is the Local view and displays the files that reside in the local folder that you specified in your site definition. If everything is going well, the two sides should be pretty close to the same. It is the Site Manager's job to keep it that way.

The Connect and Disconnect Buttons

When you have created pages and are ready to upload them to your remote server, you will need to establish an FTP (File Transfer Protocol) connection. Use the Connect button to initiate a connection to the FTP server that you designated in your site definition. Once an FTP session is started, the Connect button becomes a Disconnect button that allows you to end the session whenever you wish.

You can monitor the activity in your FTP session by using the FTP Log in the Window menu.

Getting and Putting Files

The main function of an FTP program is to transfer files back and forth, as you might have guessed from the name. When you have files on your local machine that you need to transfer to your remote server, you use the Put button to place them there. When you need to receive files from the remote server, you use the Get button to get them and save them in your local folder.

To get or put specific pages or files, select them and click the Put or Get button. To get or put an entire site, select the root folder and the top of the file list, and the entire site will be transferred.

When you transfer a page, there may be dependent files such as images, Flash files, or Java applets that need to go with it. UltraDev will prompt you for whether you want those files to transfer with the Dependent Files dialog box shown next.

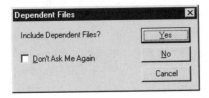

The Refresh Button

The Refresh button allows you to update your view of your site files to include the most recent changes. The Refresh button is very useful when you are working as a part of a design team. When others make changes to files, or add or delete pages to the site you are working on, you may not have the most up-to-date list in your remote view. Refreshing on a regular basis ensures that you are always aware of the changes that are happening as you work.

Synchronizing Your Site Files

If you do any work offline, or if you are away from a site while others are working on it, you will end up with copies of files in your local window that are out of synch with the versions on your remote server. You may need to place newer versions that you have created offline onto the server, or you may need to bring your local copies up to date.

To synchronize specific files, select them in the local or remote pane of the Site Manager and select the Synchronize option from the Site menu.

When you select the Synchronize menu, the dialog box in Figure 3-3 is displayed, allowing you to choose how your files are synchronized.

In this box, you can select whether to synchronize the entire site or only the files you have selected. You can also choose whether to put newer files from your local folder into the remote server, get newer files from the remote server, or do both, which generates up-to-date versions of the site in both locations.

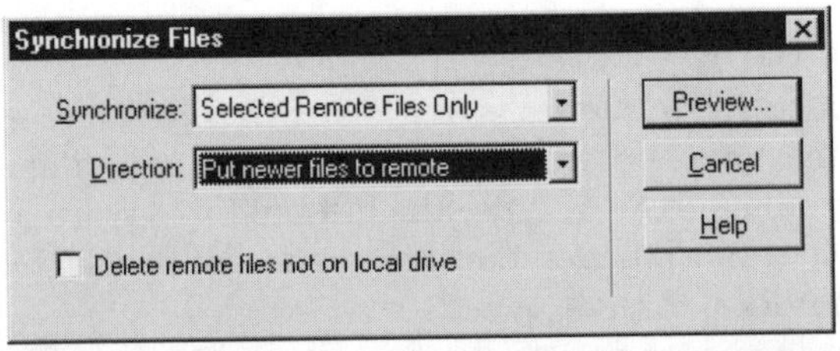

Figure 3-3.   *Synchronize Files dialog box*

If you have deleted files on your local machine, you can enable the Delete Remote Files Not on Local Drive option, and they will be deleted on the remote server also.

Be very careful when setting the Delete Remote Files Not on Local Drive option. If you are working with other developers, it is likely that someone will create a new page that would then be deleted by your synchronization because it does not yet exist on your machine.

Check In and Check Out

There is hardly anything more exciting than working on a big project with several developers. And there is hardly anything more frustrating than having your work overwritten by a careless coworker. UltraDev allows you to work safely in a collaborative environment with its Check In and Check Out features.

Checking files out is UltraDev's way of letting other developers on your team know that a file is in use and is likely being editing. It is a warning that, should they decide to edit it as well, someone's changes will get overwritten. Consider the amount of work that could be lost if you were to open a page and, while you were making major revisions to it, a coworker opened the same page to make a simple typo correction. If you saved your file, and then your coworker saved the old version on top of it, your changes would be lost and the site would be left with an old, albeit correctly spelled, version of the page.

When you check out a page, a checkmark is placed next to the page name on the remote server; and your name, or whatever identifying name you entered in the Check In/Out category of your site definition, is placed to the right of the filename. A green checkmark indicates a file that you have checked out, and a red checkmark indicates a file that someone else has checked out.

You can also use UltraDev's Check In/Out feature when you are the sole developer on a project. Many developers work from more than one computer, such as a home PC and a work PC. By selecting a name that identifies the computer that opened a file rather than the person, you can always track down the machine on which the file is opened.

UltraDev uses a small text file with an .lck extension to lock a file that is checked out. When this file is present on the server, that file is not available for others to access and edit until you check it back in. Once you have edited a file and checked it in, that file is made read-only on your local machine, forcing you to get the file from the server in order to edit it. This will keep you from editing a local copy of the file and inadvertently uploading it over a newer version of the file.

You can turn this read-only setting off in the File menu or the right-click pop-up menu by selected the Turn Off Read-Only option. You should carefully consider the consequences of doing this, however, and be careful not to overwrite newer versions of the page on your remote server.

This method of locking the remote file is not foolproof. Applications other than UltraDev with not realize the significance of the .lck file and will allow these pages to be overwritten.

Checking Links

UltraDev provides a powerful method of verifying the links within your sites. Links are those places within your pages where you offer the end user an opportunity to navigate to another page, either within your site or in another site somewhere on the Internet. If those links are broken, either because the pages they point to no longer exist or because they are mistyped, the usability of your site is severely impacted. Checking your links within UltraDev identifies broken links within your site, reports external links so you can verify them manually, and finds orphaned files.

UltraDev can verify links that point to other pages in your site. If the pages that are represented in these links do not exist or cannot be found, UltraDev reports them as broken.

Note *In order for UltraDev to be able to identify links as internal, it is important that you set the URL of your site under Link Management Options in the Local Site category of your site definition. If this value is not set, UltraDev will likely report a large number of your internal links as external links and will not verify them.*

If links to external Web sites exist on your pages, they will be reported to you so that you can verify them manually; UltraDev has no facility for verifying external links and depends on you to do it.

Orphaned files are pages within your site that have no other pages pointing links to them. Since the Web is a hyperlink environment, it is unlikely that a visitor would ever find the way to a page within your site without following a link there. Orphaned pages serve little purpose, since users will probably never see them.

You can check links in a specific page, a set of pages, or your whole site. To check a page or several pages, select them in the Site Manager and right-click to display the pop-up menu. The Check Links selection in the menu has two options: Selected Files/Folders and Entire Site. You may also check the entire site by selecting the Check Links Sitewide option from the Site menu.

After UltraDev verifies your links, a dialog box appears that reports its findings. You can use the drop-down list to filter the results that you need to view, and you can even save the report information so it is easier to refer to when making changes to the site to fix broken links and orphaned files.

The Site Map

UltraDev's Site Map offers a graphical view of your site in which you can add pages, open pages for editing, create links between pages, and change page titles. The Site Map allows you to perform many UltraDev functions in a visual manner, such as selecting a group of pages by dragging across them and adding pages to your site by dragging them from Windows Explorer. Lines between files indicate link relationships, and icons represent things such as broken links within pages.

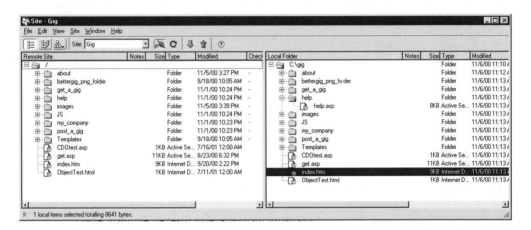

As discussed earlier, you can adjust the way the Site Map is displayed by altering the number of columns and column width in your site definition.

The Document Window

UltraDev is a WYSIWYG (What You See Is What You Get) development tool. While you can certainly build a Web page in a text editor such as Notepad and view the results after you have finished, the Web is, at its core, a presentational medium, and it's nice to actually see what you are doing while you're designing for it.

Development in UltraDev centers on the Document window, as shown in Figure 3-4.

The Document window is the graphical palette on which you will build your site. When first opened, a new window offers only a white background onto which you will place the text, images, and other elements that make up your site. The Document window also offers easy access to many of UltraDev's most powerful site creation and management tools on the status bar at the bottom of the page.

The Tag Selector

At the left side of the status bar is the Tag Selector. HTML files are made up of tags that describe the hierarchy of the content on the page. The Tag Selector provides a way to view and select that hierarchy as you edit your pages.

When a new page is created, the <body> tag is all that appears in the Tag Selector. As you add content, additional tags appear. If you place a table on the page, a <table> tag is generated. As you add rows and cells to that table, <tr> and <td> tags appear to represent those portions of the page. You can select an element on the page, and the appropriate tag becomes bold to indicate what is selected. You can also select a specific

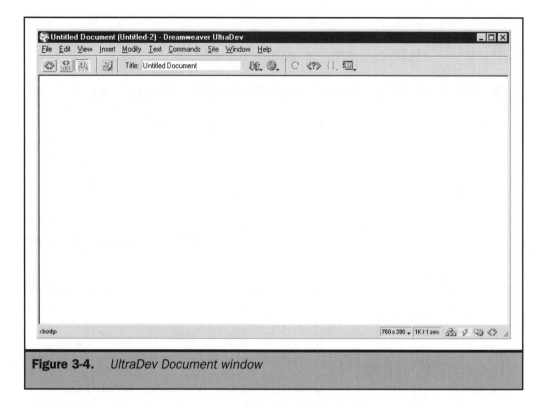

Figure 3-4.   *UltraDev Document window*

tag in the Tag Selector and that portion of the page becomes selected. Once a tag is selected, it can be easily edited or deleted. This method of selecting specific portions of a page comes in especially handy when pages grow very complex and selecting the proper portion in Design view is difficult.

Note   *The Tag Selector is dynamic, depending on what you have selected on the page. While nothing is selected, you will only see high-level tags such as the <body> and <table> tags. As you select these tags or their graphical representations on the screen, their system of child tags will appear in the Tag Selector. This method of isolating portions of the page as you navigate it makes for a very elegant way to manage complex pages.*

The Window Size Pop-Up Menu

When you are developing sites for public consumption (as opposed to a captive audience such as a corporate intranet) you must be constantly aware of the variety of client hardware and software your pages will encounter. Some users will have the latest processor with the high-resolution 21+-inch monitor that does justice to their graphical masterpieces. Others, whose attention may be just as important to you or your client, may not know how to set their video cards to a resolution greater than

640 × 480 with 256 colors. UltraDev helps you develop a variety of settings with the Window Size Pop-Up menu.

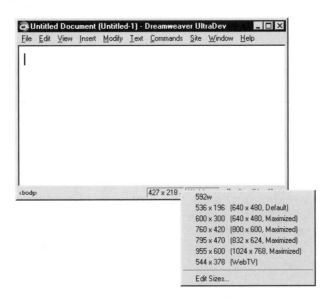

This menu lists some of the more common dimensions available to users, depending on what screen resolution they are using. By selecting an option, you can resize your screen to those dimensions and see a representation of the content area that your users will see. Some developers set their screens to a target dimension and design all of their content to conform to that size restriction. Others simply use this menu to check that their content scales gracefully on a variety of platforms.

UltraDev comes configured with several popular screen sizes. The first time you try them, you may feel quite closed in, especially in the vertical setting. Remember, though, that most browsers have chrome that you need to deal with. *Chrome* consists of the menu, button and address bars, and any advertising that may appear at the top of the interface, robbing you of screen real estate in which to place content. While these default sizes do represent a reasonable selection of the circumstances you are likely to encounter, an Edit Sizes option is available in the menu that allows you to add, delete, or edit screen sizes to suit your needs.

The Download Indicator

Just as you will encounter a variety of screen sizes and resolutions, you will also encounter a variety of bandwidth issues, including the connection speed over which your visitors view your pages. From the home user with the 28.8K modem, to the corporate users with a T1 or faster connection, you need to be prepared to serve content in a manner that keeps your audience's attention. On the Web, that generally means optimizing your content to load as quickly as possible over slower connection speeds.

Tools like this are not perfect, because they cannot take into consideration things such as line quality, bandwidth saturation, and bottlenecks in the Internet backbone itself; but the download indicator can give you a pretty good idea of the average download time your users will experience. By taking the size of all of the elements represented on your page and dividing it by the number of bits per second in the connection speed you select, the status bar gives you an indication of how long this particular configuration will take to load. Thoughts on the proper download time of the average page vary, but you should certainly keep pages with normal content within a 10 to 15–second window if you can help it. Much longer, and your visitors are going to go looking for speedier pastures.

You can alter the download speed indicated in the status bar in your Preferences, which we will cover shortly.

The download speed indicator on the status bar only takes into account the size of the actual text file you are working on. If you have images or include files that make up your page, the resulting file may be much larger than is indicated to you here. Also, Since the HTML that results from a processed ASP, JSP, or CFM page is often much smaller than the actual code file, your resulting page could be smaller and load even faster than the Status Bar shows.

The Status Bar Launcher

Actually a mini-launcher, the button area to the right on the status bar allows easy access to the Site Manager, Data Connections, Server Behaviors, and the HTML Source window. This mini-launcher makes it easy to keep your screen uncluttered by floating palettes. When you need them, they are always available from the page on which you are working.

The Floating Palettes

Floating around on your screen, as if without support, are palettes that provide access to some of UltraDev's most powerful features. The objects, behaviors, commands, and other extensions that make up the core of UltraDev's functionality are primary reasons for its popularity in the Web development world.

Note *Extensions are add-in pieces of code that allow UltraDev to perform certain tasks. An important feature of the product is the fact that the extensibility model is documented. This allows anyone with the requisite programming skills to build extensions and distribute them to others, which makes UltraDev more powerful all the time. We cover the various types of extensions and how to create them in later chapters.*

By default, UltraDev presents you with the palettes shown in Figure 3-5. Additional features are available through the Launcher or the Window menu.

A list of the available palettes is in Table 3-1.

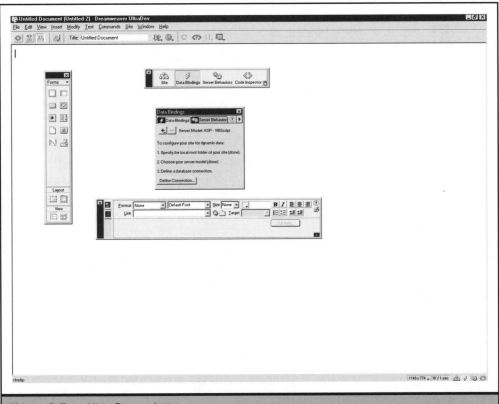

Figure 3-5. *UltraDev palettes*

Palette	Description
Objects	Objects are generally snippets of HTML code that are applied to your page. Many objects provide a user interface that allows you to set properties of the tags themselves, such as the number of rows or columns in a table. Others are simple HTML inserts such as the Horizontal Rule object.

Table 3-1. *Available Palettes in UltraDev*

Palette	Description
Properties	Property Inspectors are windows into the settings that make up objects and behaviors. When an object is selected, the Property Inspector appears to allow you to change properties and tag values without entering the HTML code itself. You can do this with Server Behaviors as well.
Launcher	Displays the Launcher, from which you can access other palettes. The Launcher is customizable in your preferences.
Data Bindings	Data Bindings are the database connections and element/ data associations that allow your page to access and display database data. A Data Connection is required before Server Behaviors such as recordsets can be applied to a page. A step-by-step outline in the Data Bindings palette walks you through the steps necessary to create Data Bindings.
Server Behaviors	Server Behaviors are combinations of head functions and body code that automate server-side functions. Server Behaviors are unique to UltraDev and make its powerful Data Access capabilities possible.
Site Files	Displays the Site Manager with the Site Files view enabled.
Site Map	The Site Map option displays the Site Manager with the Site Map view enabled.
Library	The Library is a repository for items that will be used again and again in a site. For instance, a graphic that will appear on every page could be placed in the Library and will be accessed from there each time a new page is added.
CSS Styles	Provides a list of loaded Cascading Style Sheets that can be added to content on your page. CSS Styles can be applied to any text on the page regardless of which tags control the text.
HTML Styles	Provides a list of loaded HTML Styles that can be added to content on your page. HTML Styles apply tags such as <b> for bold and <I> for italics to format selected text.
Behaviors	Behaviors are a Dreamweaver extension that are very similar to Server Behaviors, but generally concern themselves with client-side operations such as form validation and DHTML effects.

Table 3-1.   *Available Palettes in UltraDev* (continued)

Palette	Description
History	The History palette is a record of the design steps you have taken. It can be used to repeat a series of steps or even to build them into one command that can be accessed with the click of a button.
Timelines	Timelines are client-side objects that allow element manipulation based on the time it takes to occur. For instance, a timeline can be used to "fly" an element across the page in a set number of seconds.
HTML Source	The HTML Source palette allows access to the actual code that makes up the page. This is useful for tweaking a page or when you must complete an operation that is not supported by an existing extension.
Frames	The Frames palette allows you to navigate the various portions of a frameset that exists on the current page.
Layers	The Layers palette allows you to set the visibility and z-order of layers on your page, as well as modify their names.
Templates	The Templates palette provides access to the Template pages that are saved as a part of this site. Templates are pages that you can use to maintain content across pages, such as logos and design concepts. They can be marked with editable regions, allowing you to place page-specific content within the design template.

Table 3-1. *Available Palettes in UltraDev* (continued)

UltraDev's Menus

As you work in the Document window, you will access many features through the status bar and UltraDev's system of palettes. The Document window's set of menus duplicates much of this functionality, but some features can only be accessed through menu and shortcut options. Following is a description of UltraDev's default menus.

The File Menu

The File menu contains menu items that relate to file management and page-level features. Table 3-2 describes the menu choices available in the File menu.

Menu Selection	Description
New	Creates a new Document window
New from Template	Creates a new document from a saved template
Open	Allows you to browse to and open a file
Open in Frame	Opens a selected file into the current frame
Close	Closes the current window
Save	Saves the page with the current filename replacing the currently saved version
Save As	Displays a Save As dialog box
Save As Template	Saves the current page as a template file in the Templates folder for future use
Save Frameset	Saves a files that describes the current frameset
Save All Frames	Saves all component pages of the frameset
Revert	Disregards current changes and reloads the most recently saved version of the current file
Import—Import XML into Template	Creates a new page with XML data inserted inside a template
Import—Import Word HTML	Opens an HTML file generated in Word and cleans up the code
Import—Import Table Data	Imports delimited data to form a new table
Export—Export Editable Regions as XML	Saves the editable regions in the current template as an XML file
Export—Export CSS Styles	Uses the current page's style sheets to create an external style sheet file
Export—Export Table	Exports table data as a delimited file
Convert—3.0 Browser–Compatible	Converts the current page to a format that is compatible with version 3.0 browsers
Preview in Browser—Edit Browser List	Allows you to add, subtract, and configure the list of browsers loaded on your machine

Table 3-2. *The File Menu Choices*

Menu Selection	Description
Preview in Browser— Browser List	Lists the current loaded browser that UltraDev can use as preview browsers
Check Links	Verifies the integrity of the links represented on this page
Debug in Browser	Enables you to debug JavaScript within a local browser session, using any breakpoints you may have set
Check Target Browsers	Opens the Target Browsers dialog box and verifies the current page against a predetermined set of browser functionality
Design Notes	Displays the Design Notes dialog box in which you may enter notes for the current page
Previous Files List	Displays up to four recently opened files for easy access
Exit	Closes open files and exits UltraDev

Table 3-2.   *The File Menu Choices* (continued)

The Edit Menu

The Edit menu provides you with commands that make page editing easier and allow you to recover from mistakes, as shown in Table 3-3.

Menu Selection	Description
Undo	Reverses the last action taken
Redo	Re-executes a reversed action
Cut	Removes the current selection and places it on the system keyboard for use elsewhere
Copy	Copies the current selection to the system clipboard for use elsewhere

Table 3-3.   *The Edit Menu Choices*

Menu Selection	Description
Paste	Inserts clipboard date at the current cursor position
Clear	Removes the current selection
Copy HTML	Copies the current selection onto the system clipboard with the HTML tags
Paste HTML	Pastes the clipboard data to the page with the HTML tags
Select All	Highlights all of the tags and elements on the current page
Select Parent Tag	Selects the tag that surrounds the current selection
Select Child	Selects the first tag within the current selection
Find and Replace	Displays a dialog box in which you can enter the text you want to find on the page, and lets you enter text with which to replace the found instances
Find Next	Finds the next occurrence of the search string
Indent Code	Indents a selected line of code
Outdent Code	Outdents a selected line of code
Balance Braces	Checks to see that the braces that surround sections of JavaScript are balanced, that is, that each opening brace has a closing brace
Set Breakpoint	Sets a point at which execution of code will pause for debugging purposes
Remove All Breakpoints	Removes any breakpoints you have set
Edit with External Editor	Launches an instance of the text editor you have configured in your preferences
Preferences	Displays the Preferences dialog box in which you can set numerous UltraDev properties
Keyboard Shortcuts	Enables you to set, remove, and edit keyboard shortcuts that perform menu operations

Table 3-3.   *The Edit Menu Choices* (continued)

The View Menu

The View menu controls what you see on the page in the design environment, as you can see in Table 3-4. These menu items toggle page elements to allow you to customize your work environment.

Menu Selection	Description
Code	Switches your working window to Code view, where you can view your pages' underlying code
Design	Switches your working window to Design view, where you can view your page's visual layout
Code and Design	Divides your working window into two sections containing the Code view and the Design view onscreen at once
Switch Views	Switches whichever view you are currently in (Code or Design) to the other available view
Refresh Design View	Reloads the page to properly display any changes you have made
Design View on Top	When using the Code and Design option, enables you to choose whether the Code view or Design view is in the top frame of the split screen
Live Data	Toggles live data on and off
Refresh Live Data	Refreshes live data after design changes are made to the page
Live Data Settings	Displays the Live Data Server Configuration dialog
Head Content	Displays categories of information inserted into the head of the current page
Table View	Enables you to switch between Standard view and Layout view
Visual Aids	Provides a selection of layout and design aids, including whether borders are displayed on tables and layers, and whether image map overlays are visible

Table 3-4.   *The View Menu Choices*

Menu Selection	Description
Code View Options	Provides a selection of Code view options such as Word Wrap and Line Numbers
Rulers—Show	Toggles the visibility of page rulers
Rulers—Reset Origin	Resets the 0,0 coordinates to the upper left of the page
Rulers—Increments	Controls the measurement that the rulers are incremented by
Grid—Show	Toggles the visibility of the design grid on the current page
Grid—Snap To	Controls whether design elements placed on the page snap to the grid lines
Grid—Edit	Displays the Grid Settings dialog box
Tracing Image—Show	Toggles the visibility of a tracing image
Tracing Image—Align with Selection	Aligns the top-left corner of a tracing image with the top-left corner of the current selection
Tracing Image—Adjust Position	Allows a tracing image to be positioned with the cursor keys
Tracing Image—Reset Position	Places the tracing image in the upper left of the current page
Tracing Image—Load	Allows the selection of a tracing image to be placed on the page
Plug-ins—Play	Plays the currently selected plug-in
Plug-ins—Stop	Stops the currently playing plug-in
Plug-ins—Play All	Plays all plug-ins on the current page
Plug-ins—Stop All	Stops all plug-ins from playing
Hide Panels	Hides all panels and palettes except for the Design window
Toolbar	Toggles the visibility of the toolbar

Table 3-4.   *The View Menu Choices* (continued)

The Insert Menu

The Insert menu provides easy access to the wide variety of objects that are available to you in UltraDev. These objects automate the inclusion of HTML into your page using predefined modules of code. See Table 3-5 for menu choices.

Menu Selection	Description
Image	Allows the selection of an image that will be placed on the page
Interactive Images	Provides a selection of interactive images such as Flash Buttons, rollover images, and Fireworks HTML that can be inserted in the current page
Media	Provides a selection of media such as Flash files and Java applets that can be inserted in the current page
Table	Inserts an HTML table with the selected properties
Layer	Inserts a layer
Frames	Provides a selection of frame configurations to be added to the current page
Form	Inserts a form tag
Form Objects	Provides a selection of form elements such as edit boxes and Submit buttons to be added to the current form
Live Objects	Provides a selection of Live Data Objects that interact with your data connections, such as Record Inserts and Recordset Navigation
Server Side Include	Enables you to select a file to include as an SSI
E-mail Link	Inserts an e-mail link at the current selection
Date	Inserts a static client-side date at the current selection
Tabular Data	Inserts a table that connects to data files for its content
Horizontal Rule	Inserts an HTML <hr> tag

Table 3-5.   *The Insert Menu Choices*

Menu Selection	Description
Invisible Tags	Enables the insertion of a Named Anchor tag, a Script tag, or a Comment tag
Head Tags	Provides a selection of the categories of head data that can be entered for the current page
Special Characters	Provides a selection of characters such as copyright and money symbols
Get More Objects	Takes you to the Macromedia Exchange where you can download additional Objects

Table 3-5.   *The Insert Menu Choices* (continued)

The Modify Menu

The Modify menu allows you to make changes to the properties of selected elements on your pages, as you can see in Table 3-6.

Menu Selection	Description
Page Properties	Displays properties of the current page, such as Page Title, Background Image, or Link Colors
Selection Properties	Toggles the visibility of the Property Inspector
Quick Tag Editor	Toggles the visibility of the Quick Tag Editor
Make Link	Displays the file browser for selecting a file to link to
Remove Link	Deletes the currently selected link
Open Linked Page	Opens the linked page
Link Target	Sets the target of a link to the current window, a new window, or a particular frame
Table	Provides a variety of edits and properties for a selected table

Table 3-6.   *The Modify Menu Choices*

Menu Selection	Description
Frameset	Provides a variety of edits and properties for a selected frameset
Navigation Bar	Modifies properties of a Navigation bar
Arrange	Sets the z-order of a layer in relation to other layers
Align	Aligns selected layers to one another
Convert	Allows you to convert tables to layers and layers to tables
Library	Adds and updates library items
Templates	Adds, updates, and modifies template files
Timeline	Adds, updates, and modifies timelines on the current page
Connections	Displays and edits the list of currently defined connections

Table 3-6.   *The Modify Menu Choices* (continued)

The Text Menu

The Text menu provides a variety of ways to control the display of one of the most important parts of your site, as you can see in Table 3-7.

Menu Selection	Description
Indent	Indents the current selection using the <blockquote> tag
Outdent	Removes the <dir> or <blockquote> tag to cancel indentation
Paragraph Format	Provides a variety of text-formatting options

Table 3-7.   *The Text Menu Choices*

Menu Selection	Description
Font	Provides a variety of text-formatting options
List	Provides a variety of list options, such as numbered list and unordered list
Align	Provides a variety of text-alignment options
Style	Provides text style options, such as bold and italic
HTML Styles	Provides a variety of HTML styles
CSS Styles	Provides a variety of CSS styles
Size	Allows the specific sizing of text
Size Increase	Allows for relative sizing of text using +
Size Decrease	Allows for relative sizing of text using –
Color	Allows you to choose the color of the currently selected text
Check Spelling	Runs a spell checker

Table 3-7.   *The Text Menu Choices* (continued)

The Commands Menu

Commands provide streamlined ways to traverse and alter code in your site. The Commands menu provides access to loaded commands and allows you to record your own commands in a macro-like fashion, as you can see in Table 3-8.

Menu Selection	Description
Start Recording	Records a series of steps to be saved as a command
Play Recorded Command	Plays the recorded command

Table 3-8.   *The Commands Menu Choices*

Menu Selection	Description
Edit Command List	Edits the list of existing commands
Manage Exchanges	Runs the Extension Manager
Get More Commands	Navigates to the Macromedia Exchange, where you can obtain additional commands
Apply Source Formatting	Uses the Source Formatting Profile to structure the current page
Clean Up HTML	Removes HTML that does not conform to the options you select
Clean Up Word HTML	Removes HTML that does not conform to the options you select, with special emphasis on HTML added by Word
Add/Remove Netscape Resize Fix	Adds a function that forces the page to reload when a Netscape browser is resized, fixing a bug in Navigator with pages that contain frames
Optimize Image in Fireworks	Displays the Optimize Image dialog box using Fireworks 3
Create Web Photo Album	Creates a photo album site using a directory of images
Set Color Scheme	Allows you to select a color scheme for the current page
Format Table	Enables a table format to be applied to the current table
Sort Table	Displays table sorting options
Lessons	Provides a link to sample files

Table 3-8.   *The Commands Menu Choices* (continued)

The Site Menu

The Site menu provides access to features that control site-level aspects of your site, such as the Site Manager, site definitions, and FTP commands, as shown in Table 3-9.

Menu Selection	Description
Site Files	Displays the Site window
Site Map	Displays the Site window with the Site Map enabled
New Site	Opens the Site Definition window for creating a new site
Open Site	Allows you to choose a site to open
Define Sites	Opens the Site Definition window where you can create a new site or edit existing sites
Get	Gets a file or files from a remote server
Check Out	Checks out a file for editing
Put	Places a file on the remote server
Check In	Checks in a file after editing
Undo Check Out	Reverses a file check-out
Reports	Provides a series of workflow and HTML reports that contain information about your site
Check Links Sitewide	Creates a report verifying the integrity of the hypertext links in your entire site
Remove Connection Scripts	Removes data connection scripts
Locate in Local Site	Selects the current document in the Local file list
Locate in Remote Site	Selects the current document in the Remote file list

Table 3-9. *The Site Menu Choices*

The Window Menu

The Window menu provides show and hide access to all of the palettes that make up the UltraDev design environment. It is unnecessary to list them all here, but any window or palette in the program can be made visible or invisible by selecting it in this menu.

The Help Menu

The Help menu provides access to Dreamweaver help files, UltraDev help files, and a variety of online support services at Macromedia.

Preferences

As alluded to previously, UltraDev goes out of its way to allow you to customize your work environment. Selecting the Preferences option from the Edit menu presents you with 16 categories, covering everything from color schemes, to style formats, to which tag is used when you insert a layer. The preference settings are fairly self-explanatory, so we won't cover them all here. Just keep in mind that any time you wish something works a little differently in UltraDev, you can probably change it in the Preferences menu.

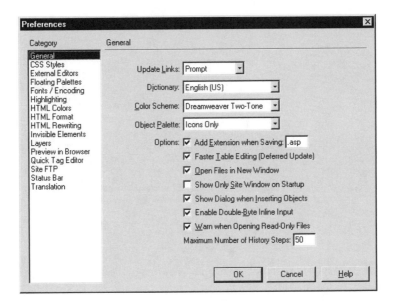

Summary

There is not the time or space to do justice to the Dreamweaver interface portion of UltraDev. The overview presented in this chapter should help you get your bearings; the next chapter should familiarize you with the way that all of these parts work together to make site design simpler, yet more powerful at the same time. In Chapter 4, we will begin to construct our first site by focusing on design elements, before moving into the data portion of our Web application.

Chapter 4

Building Your First Site

Building Web sites is a big business, and new sites are being launched at an alarming rate. Because some HTML software is available for free or only a few dollars, it is easy for the casual observer to conclude that it doesn't take a whole lot to be a Web page designer. However, in truth, designing and building quality Web applications is a difficult, time-consuming task. Tools like UltraDev make the job easier, but there are some things that no software can ever do for you. This chapter considers the importance of taking time to properly design and plan your site, and you will begin the construction of a data-driven Web application.

Note   *In the real world, Web sites cost money. While there are—and will continue to be— many people who put up sites for their own use or to promote and support their small business, the Web is becoming an increasingly important place to do business, and the sites that support this are not built in a matter of hours. A recent survey indicates that an average site with modest database interaction costs over $100,000 to build.*

Planning and Designing Your Site

When you begin to build data-driven sites, it becomes more important than ever that you take the time to plan and design your site. Too many people jump right into the construction of pages without properly considering the details of what they are doing. Not only will a lack of planning significantly impact the quality of your final product, it may also get you into a sticky situation with a client whose ideas about the site are different than yours.

Caution   *Not only is it important that you plan your site in cooperation with your client, you should also get your client to sign off on that design before you begin work. Taking this extra step will help assure that you and your client are on the same page and will help to eliminate feature creep (those persistent phone calls with neat things to add to the site while you go).*

Some of the things you need to consider when planning your site are the following:

- Purpose and goal of the site
- Target audience
- Tools and platforms available to you and your client
- Site's design
- Navigation scheme
- Development time and cost

This chapter looks at basic design considerations to help you get started with the construction of your site. It is also important to remember the data design of your site, which is discussed in Chapter 15.

The Purpose and Goal of the Site

It should go without saying that you need to understand the purpose and goal of the site you are designing; yet, too little attention is paid to this basic element of Web site creation. The following are several questions that you must answer to truly understand the purpose of the site you are creating:

- Is this an information, education, entertainment, or commerce site?
- Is the site intended to display cutting-edge technique, or to reach a broad audience?
- Will the site service a company, regional, or global community of users?
- How will the site be used?
- How will traffic be driven to the site?
- What competition is there for the niche this site will service?

If you can answer these questions, you will be well on your way to developing an understanding of the work you are about to undertake. However, it is important that your answers to these questions are the same answers as your client's. Too often, a designer has spent hours on a snazzy Flash introduction only to find that the client doesn't like Flash. Work with your client to discover the answers to these questions.

The Focus of the Site

The focus of your site will cross the lines between information, education, entertainment, and commerce. Many sites, like Pepsi's at www.pepsi.com, seek to entertain while also educating their visitors about their products and generating sales. Still, whether your site will have a single focus or a combination of purposes, you should be able to produce a statement or two that will serve as the "mission statement" under which you will work.

For instance, consider the site that you will begin to work on later in this chapter. The site is for an organization called Bettergig.com, a service that enables job seekers to search for jobs that have been posted by employers in the computer industry. It also enables them to post their resume so that employers can search them out based on the company's needs. Employers can post jobs that are available at their company or search the resumes at the site based on the requirements needed to accomplish the tasks that they have at hand.

Bettergig.com's slogan is "Get a Better Life . . . Get a Better Gig." From that slogan, you can see that this company's focus is helping its customers improve their standard of living by providing them with opportunities to improve the jobs that they perform and the compensation they receive.

You can also make some assumptions about the site. Because this will be a corporate presence for Bettergig.com, you can assume that it should be a professional presentation. "Professional" in this context refers not to quality (everything you do should be of professional quality), but to the fact that the presentation should not be artsy, cutting edge, or cutesy (using handwriting fonts, and so on). The demeanor of the site should be consistent with an appearance of experience and knowledge doing business as a job service. You may need the help of your client and some research to determine exactly what look is consistent with those things, but by making sure the presentation is "professional," you at least are on the right track.

So, to tie all of this together, the following "mission statement" might be used to guide you through the development of this site:

> The Bettergig.com Web site will be a place where our company can evolve its experience as a job placement service into a professional online meeting place for workers and the employers who need their services. It will enable employers to post jobs and search resumes, and will enable job seekers to search posted jobs and post their resumes, encouraging the ongoing involvement of both sides of the job market.

This statement may change as the site progresses, but it is a good place to start, and it provides a cogent picture of the site.

Site Content and User Community

At the same time, the mission statement tells you what the site will not be. For example, job seekers will be coming to this site to investigate opportunities for the advancement of their career. They don't care that you have the new beta of Flash that does cool new compression and that they can download your presentation three seconds faster than with the old version. It just gets in the way of their new, bigger paycheck.

This site will not be an opportunity to display cutting-edge design technique or the latest development tools. While sites like that are great and there is some truly impressive talent out there, the fact remains that most of those sites are done for the benefit of the designer and the design community. Few clients pay for content like that.

This site will seek to attract the broadest audience possible within the geographic regions that it serves. Anyone who is looking for a job in the computer industry will be welcome and will be provided unfettered access to information about the jobs and opportunities that are available to them.

How Will the Site Be Used?

Just as different sites have different purposes, different sites are used differently by their visitors. Some sites are free flowing, allowing navigation to any page from any other page. Others guide the user through a series of steps toward a goal, and allowing deviation from that series of steps would interrupt its effective use.

The Bettergig site, as with many sites, is a combination of these purposes. While the casual visitor may jump from place to place investigating the services that are available to them, a user who decides to participate will need to be walked through the steps necessary to create an online job resume or job posting.

How Will Traffic Be Driven to the Site?

It is important to consider how your audience will hear about your business and get to your site in the mangle that the Web is becoming. If your visitors will simply type in your URL or link to the home page from some outside site, then your job is pretty simple. But, if you will be running promotions or targeted advertising that makes it important to track your users and where they come from, then you may need to have a variety of entry points to your application that can make the design of your navigation more complex.

Competition

Unless you are one of the rare few who creates an industry, your site will likely have competition, and you are well advised to pay attention to it. It is entirely acceptable to offer services in a different way than your competition, but it is not acceptable to do so without a clear purpose. Learn everything you can about what is happening in your industry. It can only help you service your customer base better.

Your Target Audience

The need to understand your target audience cannot be stressed enough. In the big world of the Web, it is likely that any one site will appeal to only a small percentage of users. If you do not know who is in your percentage, you have no hope of finding them and getting them to your site. You need to know several things about your target audience before you can figure out how to reach them over the Internet:

- Does my audience have computers?
- How much time do they spend on the Web?
- What browsers do they use?
- How do they hear about new Web sites?
- How computer-savvy are they?

Two issues are especially important to the actual design of your site: the browsers your visitors use and how computer-savvy they are. A critical consideration is whether you will construct your site so that version 3 browsers (Internet Explorer and Netscape Navigator) are supported. There are different schools of thought on this issue.

One school of thought insists that sites must support version 3 browsers either in their general construction or through redirection. For the site designer, this involves constructing a site without the use of layers and dynamic HTML elements. For some applications, this presents no problem, but it can make for a less-interactive experience for your users. Although you have already established that the purpose for this site is something other than the entertainment of your visitors, it is certainly acceptable to provide an enjoyable, interactive experience.

The point of those who hold this position is that version 3 browsers are still in use by many Web users; and that even though surveys show a much higher distribution of version 4 and higher versions, the people who use version 3 browsers are not exactly the ones who find themselves in a position to take those kinds of surveys. Although it is true that newer browsers are available for free download, a few factors can hinder certain users from upgrading:

- Casual and less-knowledgeable users typically use whatever browser is preinstalled on their computer (or whatever browser their technically competent nephew loaded for them last time he visited).

- Even those who might otherwise brave the upgrade often have only 56K or even 28K connections, and 18MB downloads just aren't feasible.

The other school of thought is just as compelling. In the desktop application world, Windows 3.1 users generally are no longer considered. It has certainly become acceptable to set your program's baseline as Windows 95 or above. Given that fact, and the fact that version 4 browsers come with the operating systems above Windows 98, it is fairly safe to assume that most users have at least one version 4 browser available to them.

You will need to make decisions about the platforms you will support before you begin construction of your site. You would not want to get halfway through a site using fancy invisible-layers techniques, only to find out that your client insists on compatibility with version 3 browsers.

The Tools and Platforms Available to You

When you are working on sites for your own use, you are free to use your choice of development tools and platforms. This consideration becomes more important when you begin constructing sites for clients who already have ideas about the way they want things done. Often, you will be called upon to maintain or add to existing architecture. Convincing a client who has a considerable amount of work done in, say, Cold Fusion that they should allow you to do your part in ASP is a tough sell; and even if you can sell it, the client is often dissatisfied with the final product. While many developers work quite successfully in a number of languages, you will certainly want to build some space into your design plan if you will be working on a platform that is less than familiar to you.

The Site's Design

While you will likely begin to formulate the actual look and feel of the site only after you sit down at the computer and start fiddling with the design, the following are some decisions that you can make at this point in the process that will help you when your design comes together.

Will the site be based in HTML or in graphics? Sites based in HTML are typically made up of HTML text over a colored background or a tile or image background. This technique can be used very effectively and gives a very slim no-nonsense interface when the information is the most important thing.

Sites based in graphics often use a more intricate interface, often designed and imported from a graphics program such as Fireworks or Photoshop. The links are often graphic text overlaid with hotspots rather than text anchors.

Will you use frames? Whereas frames were all the rage for a while, they seem to have fallen into some disfavor of late. Opportunities to make good use of frames certainly exist, but you will typically find it cleaner to avoid them and the temptations they afford. Too many sites end up framing in other sites, which frame in other sites, and the result is just a big mess.

Which of the common layouts will you use? Several basic page layouts seem to work best on the Web. While designers are forever looking for ways to differentiate their pages, the most usable pages seem to adhere to two or three basic layouts: the left-hand navigation bar, the top navigation bar, and the page of links where the entire page is made up of columns that house links to other places. A few sites use a right-hand navigation bar, but users seem to have grown used to the other three layouts and find them the most easy to navigate.

Commit to avoiding the design no-nos. While you probably don't need to hear this, it is such an annoying problem that it needs to be mentioned. Text is unreadable when placed over a tiled image of your pet dog, and light-yellow text is unreadable on anything except a solid-black background. Similarly, although I'm sure the '60s were a lot of fun, tie-dyed page backgrounds are annoying.

Take care that you do not spend your time creating something that is unusable or annoying to your visitors. A quick tour around the Web will provide you with a great many examples of this. If you need help to determine an appropriate design, seek out help on the many great newsgroups or from a knowledgeable colleague.

Your Navigation Scheme

The design of your navigation scheme goes hand in hand with the site-design considerations previously discussed. But, as you begin to consider your site's navigation, it is appropriate to start sketching out the pages that you will need to create for the site. Start with the home page, and begin adding pages in your drawing and indicating links, as shown in Figure 4-1. Tools such as Microsoft's Visio and Rational Software's Rational Rose can assist in this process. You will be amazed how much more quickly your site will come together when you have planned the pages that make it up and how they connect to one another.

Development Time and Cost

It is important to carefully consider the amount of time it will take to construct a site. Only by knowing this important piece of information can you determine a fair price to charge for your work. Unfortunately, everyone works at a different pace, and no formula exists to help with this calculation. You will gain the ability to judge construction time through the experience of building sites.

There are three main ways that developers charge for site development: per page, per hour, and per project. Each has its benefits.

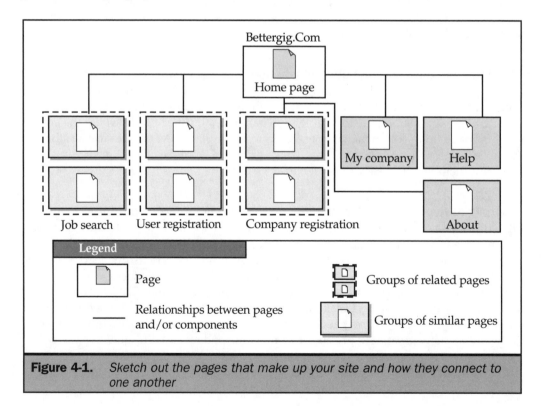

Figure 4-1. *Sketch out the pages that make up your site and how they connect to one another*

Newer developers or those used to building very small sites tend to offer a per-page pricing model. When a customer wants a simple five- or six-page presence for their small business, it is easy to budget using this method, and developers can often churn out these small sites rather quickly. This pricing model is an unwieldy method for larger sites, though.

There are two compelling reasons to insist on the per-hour method, from a developer's perspective. If you are unable to get the client to commit to a design specification and are afraid that you may be embarking on a wandering design adventure, charge a per-hour rate. As long as they are paying you per hour, you should care very little that they change their mind every couple of days. Also, if the project will entail a great deal of site maintenance, such as content rotation, an hourly rate ensures that you are fairly compensated for your work.

If, on the other hand, the client is very clear about what they want and there is a definable beginning and ending to the project, a per-project rate enables both you and the client to better budget from a time and money standpoint. Just make sure that the client signs off on what work is to be done for the price agreed upon.

If you can do this much planning before you sit down to construct your first page, you will have done far more than most developers, and you will be well on your way to a well-organized, usable site. The effort spent up front on this kind of exercise will return great dividends during the actual construction process.

Constructing Web Pages in UltraDev

One of UltraDev's key features is that it deals with HTML on HTML's terms. Simply put, this means that UltraDev allows HTML to be HTML; it does not try to turn it into a desktop publishing application.

Several years ago, when HTML began to gain popularity, many designers had difficulty coming to grips with the way it worked. The desktop publishing boom had accustomed computer graphics professionals to sophisticated software, such as PageMaker and Ventura Publisher, that allowed a true WYSIWYG design environment. When you placed things on a page, they went where you wanted them and they stayed there. Design was expressed in pixels, and precision was expected.

But HTML is not desktop publishing. HTML was designed to express the hierarchy of information, not its presentation. Remember that the first browsers were text based; and the thoughts and words themselves were the focus, not how they looked.

Much like a word processing document, HTML pages begin at the upper left of the page. To illustrate, open a project in UltraDev, and select the New Window option in the Site Manager. UltraDev will create a new page for you. Notice that the cursor is at the upper-left corner of the page. Click anywhere on the page to try and reposition it and it will not respond. While there are ways around this, discussed later, it is important to see that basic HTML pages are generally constructed from the top down.

Type a sentence into the page. Press ENTER and type another line, and then hold down the SHIFT key and press ENTER. Type a third line on the page. Now, click the HTML Source option on the launcher, and you will begin to see how UltraDev works.

The following code was generated by UltraDev after text was typed into the document window; don't worry if the words you type are different—the HTML tags are what you are interested in:

```
<html>
<head>

<title>Untitled Document</title>

<meta http-equiv="Content-Type" content="text/html; charset=iso-8859-1">

</head>

<body bgcolor="#FFFFFF">

<p>This is line one</p>

<p>This is line two<br>

  This is line three</p>

</body>

</html>
```

By default, UltraDev has created the basic framework of your HTML page, including the HTML tags, some meta information, head tags, a place to put a title, and a default background color. When you began typing on the page, UltraDev placed the words as HTML paragraph text within the <body> tags of the page (note the <p> tags). Pressing the ENTER key generated a new paragraph. Pressing the ENTER key combined with the SHIFT key inserted a break tag (<br>) and placed line three within the same paragraph.

This is the crux of how UltraDev works. The entire goal of the package is to generate an HTML file, which is really just a text file with tags that describe the information inside it. This can be accomplished in a number of ways. The simplest is what you have just caused to happen—the interpretation of keyboard input into HTML format. More complex pieces of code require other methods, such as the use of objects or Behaviors.

Objects

The previous section gave a simple example of how UltraDev interprets your input into a format that HTML can handle and display. By turning your keyboard strokes into HTML tags, UltraDev can translate the things that you are used to doing (typing on a keyboard) into things you might not be used to doing (writing HTML tags).

> **Note**   *Even if you are an HTML whiz, you have to admit that letting UltraDev handle the details for you is a real time saver.*

But, creating Web pages involves a lot more than just entering text. If this is going to be a true visual-design tool, it has to handle the more complex things that people are used to using HTML to do—things such as tables, layers, image tags, and form elements, or even inserting Flash and Shockwave files. Fortunately, UltraDev provides a feature that does those things.

It should not be a surprise to you that making UltraDev do the things listed is a bit more complicated than the simple keyboard translation reviewed earlier. To accomplish this task, UltraDev includes a method of collecting user input and turning it into HTML. This method is represented in UltraDev's objects.

When you start UltraDev, you should notice the Objects floating palette. If it is not visible, you may select Objects from the Window menu or press CTRL+F2 to make it visible. On the Objects palette, you will find several icons representing the various things you can do, as shown in Figure 4-2. These icons are divided into several categories that you can access by clicking the arrow next to the Common heading. These categories enable you to keep the objects organized by functionality or by their source, or by any other method that makes them easy for you to use. Chapter 21 looks at how you can create your own categories and move objects around within them.

In concept, objects are fairly simple. Their main purpose is to accept input from the user and place it as HTML code in the body of the page they are applied to. In practice,

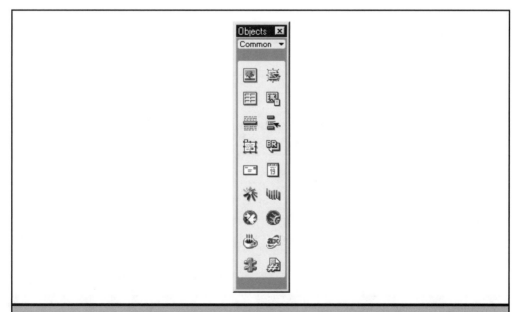

Figure 4-2.   *The UltraDev Objects palette*

every object works a little differently. With practice, you will learn what to expect from each of them. The following sections look at three objects that vary in the way they are implemented.

The Horizontal Rule Object

The simplest type of object is represented by the Horizontal Rule object on the Common tab of the Objects palette. A horizontal rule is simply a line that rules horizontally across the page. While it does have properties that can be assigned to it, a Horizontal Rule object can be represented with nothing more than an <hr> tag. At the point on the page where that tag appears, a line will be placed on the page. Place your cursor at the desired location on the page, locate the Horizontal Rule object on the Objects palette, and click it. The horizontal rule will appear on the page, as shown in Figure 4-3.

After your object is placed on the page, you may want to edit its properties to change, in the case of the Horizontal Rule object, the height or width, the color, or the alignment. When you select the Horizontal Rule object, another floating palette, the Property Inspector, will appear. The Property Inspector displays the standard

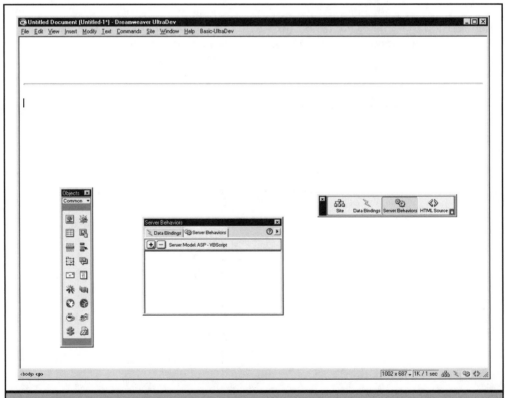

Figure 4-3. *Viewing the Horizontal Rule object*

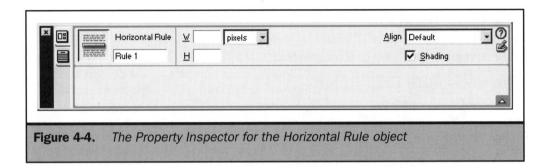

Figure 4-4.   *The Property Inspector for the Horizontal Rule object*

properties that apply to the object that is selected. For instance, when the Horizontal Rule object is selected, the Property Inspector looks like Figure 4-4.

On the Property Inspector for the Horizontal Rule object, you can set the name of the Horizontal Rule object, the width in pixels or percent, the height, the alignment, and whether the line is shaded or not. Those are the basic settings and represent the most-used attributes for this object. The Property Inspector also has an Advanced tab that enables you to set other available but less-used properties.

Near the left end of the Property Inspector, you will notice two tabs. The lower of these two takes you to the advanced properties for this object. In the advanced properties, you have access to additional attributes that can be set for the object. Click the plus (+) button to see a list from which you can select. After adding a property name, you can either enter a value or select one from the list that appears to the right of the property name.

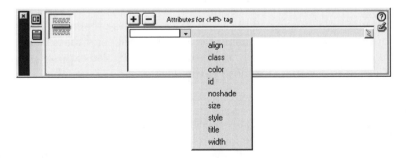

The Horizontal Rule is the simplest kind of object. It asks for no input from the user to place the basic object, and then enables you to set properties afterward.

    The Horizontal Rule object and the Table object (discussed next) are both dependent on your cursor position. They will place the object at your cursor's position.

The Table Object

If you have spent any time at all with HTML, then you are familiar with the Table object. Originally designed to allow the display of information in columns, Table objects have evolved into a primary means of allowing more complex visual designs on HTML pages. The UltraDev Table object enables you to build complex table structures to accommodate your design.

 Tables have become a popular method of display because they are lightweight and are supported by the earlier browser versions. The technically preferred method of creating pixel-perfect designs is the use of layers. Layers, however, are not supported prior to the version 4 browsers, and then not even consistently across brands. Additionally, old habits die hard, and many designers still prefer to use tables.

The Table object is much like the Horizontal Rule object in that it is dependant on your cursor's position. It will place a table on your page consistent with the properties you set; but in this case, you are asked by the Insert Table dialog box to set some of the properties up front.

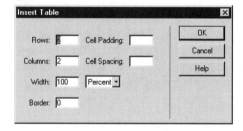

After the table is on the page, you can alter not only the properties that you set originally, but also many others by using the Property Inspector that is made available when you select the table. Selecting a particular row or cell also exposes properties such as backgrounds and fonts for those particular portions of the table.

The Layer Object

Whereas the Horizontal Rule and Table objects are dependant on the position of your cursor within the current HTML, the Layer object is a part of the newer Cascading Style Sheets (CSS) specification that allows absolute positioning of items on your page. When you select the Layer icon on the Objects palette, your cursor changes to crosshairs. Using your mouse, you may draw the layer at the position and to the size that you desire.

 Actually, drawing a layer in this fashion is only one of three ways to insert a layer into your page. You may also select Layer from the Insert menu and set it precisely using numeric settings. Or, you may use a CSS definition to set the properties of a new Layer object.

After your layer is on the page, you can use the Properties Inspector to alter any of the available Layer properties, including positioning and the HTML tag that is used to create the layer.

Note   *Four tags are available that may be used to create layers. The <div> and <span> tags are the most commonly used, and conform to the latest specifications. Netscape Navigator 4 supported the <layer> tag for absolute positioning and the <ilayer> tag for relative positioning, but they have been abandoned in version 6 for the <div> and <span> tags. It is important to know your target browser so that you know which tags to use. This will ensure that your content is presented as you intended.*

These three examples represent the diverse ways that you may be asked to interact with objects. Just remember that objects are intended to save you work by taking your input and turning it into HTML. Each object may ask for your input in a slightly different way, but you will get used to it with a little practice.

Tables 4-1 through 4-6 list the available objects in UltraDev.

Object Icon	Usage
©	Inserts a copyright character
®	Inserts a registered trademark character
TM	Inserts a trademark character
£	Inserts a English pound character
¥	Inserts a Japanese yen character
€	Inserts a Euro dollar character
—	Inserts an em dash character

Table 4-1.   *The Characters objects*

Object Icon	Usage
	Inserts a left quote
	Inserts a right quote
	Enables you to choose from a selection of other characters to insert on the page

Table 4-1. *The Characters objects* (continued)

Object Icon	Usage
	Enables you to browse for an image to insert at the cursor position on your page
	Enables you to browse for two images; one for the mouse-over state and one for the mouse-out state
	Inserts an HTML table of the dimensions that you select
	Enables you to identify a delimited file of data to be placed in a table with properties that you specify
	Inserts an HTML horizontal rule at the cursor position
	Enables you to create multistate buttons and assemble them into navigation bars
	Inserts a layer on your page that you can then size, position, and configure
	Inserts a single line break
	Inserts a mailto link

Table 4-2. *The Common objects*

Object Icon	Usage
	Inserts a client-side date based on your system clock
	Inserts a Flash animation file on your page
	Inserts a Director Shockwave file on your page
	Inserts a Generator file on your page
	Inserts a Fireworks-generated HTML file onto your page
	Enables you to browse for a Java applet to insert on your page
	Enables you to browse for an ActiveX control to place on your page
	Enables you to browse for a plug-in file to place on your page
	Enables you to browse for an include file to be inserted into your HTML source

Table 4-2.   *The Common objects* (continued)

Object Icon	Usage
	Inserts a form
	Inserts a text field
	Inserts a button

Table 4-3.   *The Form objects*

Object Icon	Usage
	Inserts a checkbox
	Inserts a radio button
	Inserts a list/menu
	Inserts a file field
	Inserts an image field
	Inserts a hidden field
	Inserts a jump menu

Table 4-3. *The Form objects* (continued)

Object Icon	Usage
	Inserts left frame
	Inserts right frame
	Inserts top frame
	Inserts bottom frame

Table 4-4. *The Frame objects*

Object Icon	Usage
	Inserts left, top-left corner, and top frames
	Inserts left and nested-top frames
	Inserts top and nested-left frame
	Inserts split-frame center

Table 4-4.   *The Frame Objects* (continued)

Object Icon	Usage
	Inserts meta tags
	Inserts keywords that describe your site
	Inserts a description of your site
	Inserts a bit of code to refresh the current page or redirect to another page in a set number of seconds
	Inserts a base URL to which your links will relate
	Inserts a link to define a relationship between the current document and another file

Table 4-5.   *The Head objects*

Object Icon	Usage
⚓	Inserts a named anchor or bookmark
💬	Inserts an HTML comment
📝	Inserts a script
📥	Inserts a nonbreaking space

Table 4-6. *The Invisibles objects*

Behaviors

Objects are designed to place code within the body of your HTML page, usually as HTML tags with a series of attributes. But, sometimes you need to do more-complex things on your page. Often, your desired effect requires the use of JavaScript functions triggered by events on the page. Behaviors are UltraDev's way of handling these issues.

By default, the Behaviors palette is turned off. To make it visible, select Behaviors from the Window menu. The palette is shown in Figure 4-5.

 Tip *You can also set the Behaviors palette to appear on the Launcher for quicker access in the Floating Palettes section of the Preferences dialog box.*

Behaviors are used for client-side events. Because of this, and because different browser brands and versions implement client-side code differently, it is important to apply Behaviors that are meant to work in your target browser.

A successful Behavior has three parts: an object, an event, and an action. The object is the part of your page that the event will occur against. For instance, you may have a button that will trigger an action when it is clicked. The button is the object, the click is the event, and the response is the action.

To illustrate, follow this example. On a new UltraDev page, place a Form button from the Forms tab of the Objects palette. Make sure the Behaviors palette is visible, and select the button. The title bar of the palette will indicate the object to which you are about to apply your Behavior. This indication actually shows the tag that is selected. By default, the Form button is created as a Submit button, so you will notice that the Behaviors palette

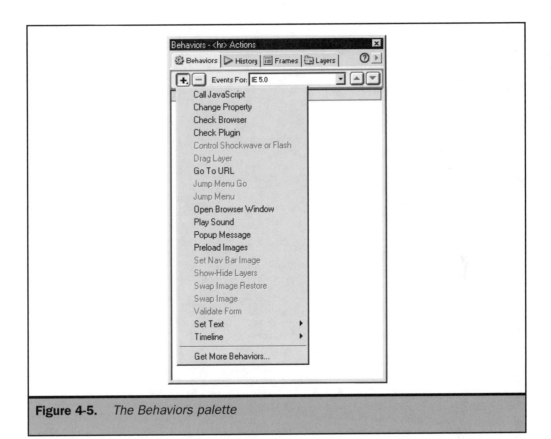

Figure 4-5. *The Behaviors palette*

title says <submit> actions. If you change the button type to Reset, the title bar will read <reset> actions; and if you change it to None, it will read <button> actions.

Click the plus (+) button on the Behaviors palette to view a list of available Behaviors. Select the Go To URL Behavior. In the resulting dialog box, set the URL that you want to go to. Now, whenever this button is selected, your Go To URL Behavior will appear in the list of Behaviors on the palette.

Next, select an event by selecting it in the list and clicking the down arrow. A list of available events is presented. Select the onClick event to cause your action to be followed when the button is clicked.

Now, take a look at the HTML source window to see what this behavior did in your code:

```
<html>

<head>
```

```
<title>Untitled Document</title>

<meta http-equiv="Content-Type" content="text/html; charset=iso-8859-1">

<script language="JavaScript">

<!--

function MM_goToURL() { //v3.0

  var i, args=MM_goToURL.arguments; document.MM_returnValue = false; _

  for (i=0; i<(args.length-1); i+=2) eval(args[i]+".location='"+args[i+1]+"'");

}

//-->

</script>

</head>


<body bgcolor="#FFFFFF">

<form name="form1" method="post" action="">

  <input type="button" name="Submit" value="Submit"
onClick="MM_goToURL('parent','www.bettergig.com');return document.MM_returnValue">

</form>

</body>

</html>
```

Note that the Behavior did two things in the preceding code, one in the body of the page and one above the body. To the basic button tag, the Behavior added the onClick event and the parameters you set within a call to a function called MM_goToURL. That function was also inserted above the body, ready to be called by the click of the Submit button.

Table 4-7 lists the Behaviors that are available in UltraDev.

Behavior	Associated Action
Call JavaScript	Enables you to define a JavaScript routine that will be run when the associated event occurs
Change Property	Enables you to dynamically alter the properties of several high-level HTML tags, such as Span, Form, and Layer
Check Browser	Allows the determination of a visitor's browser type and subsequent redirection to suitable content
Check Plugin	Checks for the existence of a required plug-in (such as a Flash Player) on a visitor's computer
Control Shockwave or Flash	Supplies external controls to allow the control of Flash and Shockwave files
Drag Layer	Allows the creation of a variety of effects based on a user dragging and dropping layers and their content
Go To URL	Allows the variety of events available to trigger redirection to a URL
Jump Menu Go	Adds a Go button to an existing jump menu
Jump Menu	Enables you to edit an existing jump menu
Open Browser Window	Opens a new, customized browser window when the associated event is triggered
Play Sound	Plays a sound file of a variety of types when the associated event is triggered
Popup Message	Triggers a JavaScript alert (a pop-up message box) to display a message to your user
Preload Images	Causes all images to be preloaded when the page loads; especially useful for rollover buttons and images that are initially hidden
Set Nav Bar Image	Enables you to edit an existing navigation bar
Show-Hide Layers	Gives you control over the visibility of layers based on the triggering of certain events
Swap Image Restore	Restores an image to its original state after an event has triggered a Swap Image

Table 4-7.   *The UltraDev Behaviors*

Behavior	Associated Action
Swap Image	Swaps an original image for another image when an event occurs
Validate Form	Validates to contents of form fields before submission
Set Text	Sets the text property of the status bar, a layer, a text field, or a frame
Timeline	Provides a variety of controls to manipulate an existing timeline

Table 4-7. *The UltraDev Behaviors* (continued)

You now have reviewed the basics of creating Web pages in UltraDev. By using a combination of keyboard input, objects, and Behaviors, your actions construct a file of HTML suitable for display in your local browser. But no matter what the history of HTML, today's Web is all about design and presentation, which is where Dreamweaver UltraDev shines.

Design Concepts

It's all about packaging really. The days of single-color or tiled backgrounds with simple text on them are not gone, as a quick tour around the Web will show, but they are going. Your competition has great-looking sites, and if you want to be competitive, you need a great-looking site, too.

If I could teach you in a few paragraphs how to become a world-class graphic artist, I would be rich, and this book would be worth its weight in gold. However, this book can teach you a few things that will be very valuable to you as you design Web sites.

Navigation

Navigation is the means by which you enable users to get around your site. As stated earlier, sometimes you will want to allow users to move freely to and from any page that strikes their fancy, while other times you'll need them to remain on a set path in order to complete the task they have set about. Both forms of navigation will be used in the Bettergig Web site.

The basic motto that applies to navigation in general is to keep it clear, keep it simple, and don't overdo it.

Keep It Clear

When users look at your site, they should be able to tell two things rather quickly: where the navigation links are (how to get around) and where those links will take them. There is a trend in Web development that has been dubbed "mystery meat navigation," which refers to when the designer presents you with image-based links with little if any indication of where they lead. At best, you can hover over the image link (if you can find it) and get a tooltip with a hint as to where you might end up if you were to click on it. While this kind of navigation might lend itself to the look and feel of the art you are trying to create, it is frustrating to the user and is more likely to prompt visitors to move on to a site that clearly presents the information they are seeking than to stay and fawn over your design sense.

Keep in mind that most Web sites are for the purpose of communicating with visitors. Use links that are text based (either HTML or graphic text) or images along with text that identify the links. While it may offend your design sense, it will keep visitors at your site longer because they can clearly see how to get around.

Keep It Simple

Your site may be 200 pages. There may be something very interesting on each and every page that you are excited about sharing with everyone who drops by. But 200 links on your home page is going to overwhelm them and drive them away in frustration.

Keep your navigation simple. Design a hierarchy of concepts within your site that leads visitors to areas of interest, and then offer additional pages that fall within that area. Keep the number of links on your home page reasonable. What is reasonable? That is for you to decide. But if you are feeling the need to put much more than ten navigational links on the home page, you may want to rethink your site structure. If every one of those pages is so unrelated to the other pages around it that it has to have its own link from the home page, then you have a maze on your hands that few people will want to wade through.

Note *These "rules" are generalizations. They are good generalizations, but they may not apply to your specific circumstance. If you are designing a site, perhaps a portal site like www.yahoo.com or www.cnet.com, there may be a good reason to make your home page a mass of links. As always, rules are made to be broken, but you must know what rules you are breaking and why.*

Don't Overdo It

Another disturbing trend in page design is repeating links. Almost as a means of filling space, designers will put identical links in the left-hand navigation bar, as an image in the body of the page or at the top, and as a text link at the bottom of the page. Unless your pages are extremely long and you are concerned that users will get lost in them, you don't need to provide duplicate links all over the place.

Usability

It can't be said enough: Web sites are for the communication of information to your visitors. It does not matter whether you are tired of making sites with left-hand navigation, if that is what your visitors expect to see; if that is what will keep them at your site, then that is what you need to give them.

The following are a few more rules that are fairly accepted usability practices:

■ Keep your page load times to 15–20 seconds on a 56K modem.

■ Don't pop up new windows on your visitors.

■ Frames are not the best idea. If you do use them, don't frame in other sites. It is annoying to your users and to the people whose site you are framing in.

■ Always provide a link back to your home page.

■ Make sure that your site's features work in the available browsers. Make sure you know going into a project what browsers you are targeting so that you can test for degradation, especially if you plan to use CSS styles.

Media

Media is a pretty broad term. It can relate to anything from the images on your site, to sound files, to extravagant Flash files. Here is a list of things to remember when choosing and using media on your site:

■ **Use the appropriate file type for images**   JPEG files are often preferred for photographs, but they are *lossy*—meaning that the compression used to make the file smaller can affect the quality of the resulting image, and the files can be larger if you are not careful. GIFs are good for graphics and graphic text.

■ **Only use transparency when it is needed**   Don't make part of an image transparent and then stick it on a white background. It bloats the file unnecessarily.

■ **Use an appropriate number of colors in your image files**   A product like Fireworks enables you to optimize your files by selecting different numbers of colors and observing how the change affects the picture quality.

■ **Size your images properly before putting them on your page**   Resizing in HTML takes a long time and produces questionable quality.

■ **Use Flash cautiously**   While the Flash player is becoming ubiquitous, bandwidth that can handle the files is not. If you do use it, give your visitors a way out—a way to skip the file or never start viewing it in the first place.

■ **Do not load with your home page MIDI files that start playing as soon as the page loads**   They usually sound terrible. If you are forced to use one, provide a prominent Off button.

The Home Page

Armed with some basic information about your site and some good design rules to follow, you're prepared to turn to the creation of your home page. By reviewing the description of the Bettergig site from earlier, you can get a pretty good idea of the structure the home page needs to take, including what links it needs to provide.

Bettergig.com Mission Statement

Bettergig.com is a service that enables job seekers to search for jobs that have been posted by employers in the computer industry. It also enables them to post their resume so that employers can search them out based on the company's needs. Employers can post jobs that are available at their company or search the resumes at the site based on the requirements needed to accomplish the tasks that they have at hand.

Because this is a simple site, you don't have a whole lot to link to, but the following links are pretty important:

- **Home** This will become a template for the rest of the site, and you always want a link back to the home page.
- **Get a Gig** A place for job seekers to search for jobs and post their resumes.
- **Post a Gig** A place for employers to post new job opportunities.
- **My Company** A place for employers to manage the jobs they have posted.
- **Help** To provide assistance with the site.
- **About** To provide company information and sales contacts for Bettergig.com.

You also need a logo, a design theme, and a place to put content. You'll handle these items in your actual design session, which you can complete using Macromedia Fireworks.

Fireworks

While you can do your site layout and data integration with UltraDev, you need a means of creating and editing the graphical elements that will make up your pages. Macromedia has developed the Fireworks application for high-end graphics manipulation. As with most Macromedia products, it is designed to work well with the rest of the product line.

One of the great things about designing Web sites with Dreamweaver or UltraDev is the way in which you can integrate Fireworks with them to produce high-quality graphics. Fireworks has whole books written about it, and whole sections of those books describe all the things you can do with Dreamweaver and Fireworks together. This section focuses on creating a design, slicing it, and exporting it to be used in your UltraDev site.

The actual design that you use is up to you. The design chosen for this book is shown in Figure 4-6. Notice that, just as described in the previous section, this design includes a logo, a links section, a design theme, and space to place content. A 750 by 500–pixel palette was used to work on, to target an 800×600 screen resolution. That may work for you, or you or your client may feel that it is important to capture 640×480

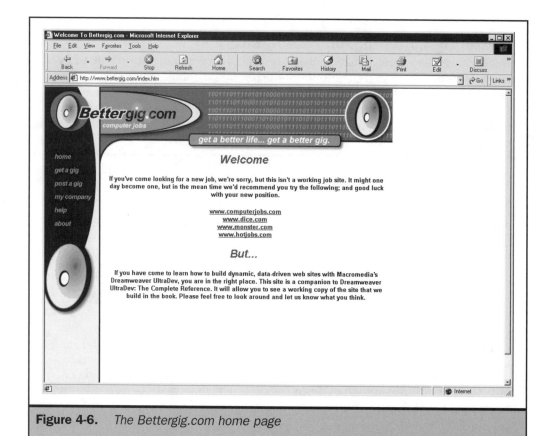

Figure 4-6.   *The Bettergig.com home page*

users. Either way, use your best design skills to create a page that looks professional, incorporates the required features, and presents the site in the manner you desire.

Using the layers feature of Fireworks to build your site from the background up is suggested. Any background graphics, or anything that you are sure will remain static, should go on the bottom layer. When you are through with that layer, lock it in the Layers palette and create a new layer from the Insert | Layer menu. This second layer should contain things like text, button text or graphics, or anything that may change as the site evolves. Later, you will see how to use this configuration to allow the replacement of portions of the graphic without having to replace the whole thing on your page. When the initial components of this second layer are complete, lock it also, to make sure that nothing gets moved. Then, create a third layer on which you will build your slices and prepare the page for export to UltraDev.

Slicing the Image

Depending on your background, slicing graphics may or may not be familiar to you. The concept is simple, and is, in some fashion, an outgrowth of the very earliest use of HTML. Back even before the introduction of tables to the HTML specification, navigation was often accomplished through the use of server-side image maps. Image files, which often were very large image files, were downloaded along with hotspot coordinates that identified areas of the image to the server. The server would redirect based on which hotspot was clicked. It was a slow, cumbersome system, but it got designers used to using graphics files as navigation.

Slicing takes advantage of HTML tables to allow an image to be split into smaller images, which load faster. Instead of one big image, the graphic is divided into several pieces. Those pieces are then loaded into table cells that put them back together so that they appear as one graphic to the end user. You can do this manually, but I would not recommend it when you have a tool as powerful as Fireworks available.

Start with the graphic you have created. You should have the bottom two layers locked so that you do not inadvertently move something. You will be working on the top layer (WebLayer, in the example file). Look carefully at your design. You should be able to identify some natural boundaries within it where slicing the image would make sense. Try to keep logos and message areas together. Be as neat as possible or else the table that is created by this process will be a mess.

Locate the slice tool, as shown in Figure 4-7. Selecting it will turn your cursor into a crosshair with which you will draw your slices onto the graphic.

On the Bettergig home page, I started slicing at the top left, and already I ran into a problem. There is no way to capture the entire logo without encroaching on the slogan area. This is where you will have to start making decisions about how your site is most likely to evolve. On the Bettergig site, it is possible that the slogan area could change or that the tagline in the logo could change, so I chose the compromise seen in Figure 4-8. It splits up some of the graphic, but preserves the parts that I may need to change in the future. You will see how important this is a little later. Use these same ideas to guide you through the slicing of the remainder of your graphic.

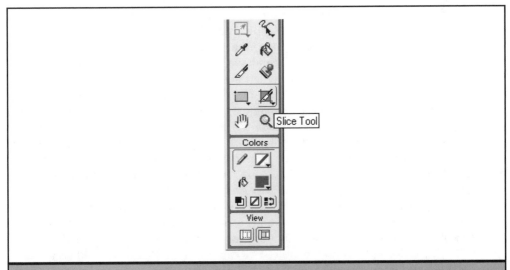

Figure 4-7.   *The Fireworks Slice tool*

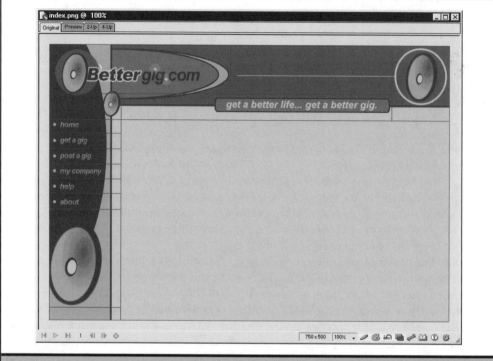

Figure 4-8.   *Completed slices on the Bettergig home page*

The next area you need to pay special attention to is the text that will become your navigational links. After you get your graphic into UltraDev, you'll want to turn these text links into *rollover buttons*. Rollover buttons are areas that react visually when the user's mouse interacts with them. They can have up to four states, with a different look for when there is no mouse activity, for when the mouse hovers over them, for when the button is depressed, and for when the mouse hovers over a depressed button. The present example will use a simpler form that just uses the up state (no mouse interaction) and the over state (when a mouse hovers over the button). This means that you need two graphics for each of these buttons, each with a slightly different appearance. For now, just make sure that the slices that make up each text area are as equal as possible. Make liberal use of the magnifier to make sure your slices' lines are exactly where you intend them to be. You can even select a slice and use the Modify menu to transform its dimensions numerically or by a percentage. These topics are covered in a moment.

Complete your slices so that the entire graphic is included. Make sure that you include a slice that encompasses the content area of your page. This ensures that this area will be included as a cell in the table. You can set that cell as an editable region in the template that you will create later.

GETTING STARTED
WITH DREAMWEAVER
ULTRADEV

 This procedure has an awful lot of overlap. You really have to plan ahead as you work so that the decisions you make work with the steps you take later. I hope you are able to follow this description. It will make sense the first time you try it, or maybe the second time.

Hopefully, you are starting to understand what is going to happen when you move this graphic to UltraDev. When you export the graphic in the next step, Fireworks will actually create an HTML page with a table on it that mirrors the slices you created, with a table cell for each slice. So, you will end up with a table with a bunch of image references and a directory of images that fit in those table cells. If you have 14 slices, as in the example page, you will have 14 images, and that means 14 filenames. Fireworks will automatically name your images by using the Fireworks filename and appending a number to it. That is very convenient, but makes later identification of the parts of your page very difficult. Luckily, Fireworks will let you rename the slices to names that are more meaningful to you.

One at a time, select each slice and go to the Object panel. At the bottom of the panel, deselect the Auto-Name Slices checkbox and type a new name into the text box that appears. For the text images that will become your buttons, use "up" in the name to indicate that these are the up-state images. Later, you will create your over-state buttons and name them with "over" in the name so that you may easily identify them.

Exporting the Fireworks Graphic

After you have all of your slices in place and have renamed them, it is time to export the graphic so that you can use it in UltraDev. Select File | Export. In the Export dialog box, shown in Figure 4-9, select a directory in which to save your HTML page and image files. Set the base name of the export. If left as the default, the base filename will be the name of the Fireworks file, as will the name of your HTML page. You can leave it that way or change it to "index" or "default" or any other name you choose. In the Slices drop-down list, select Use Slices.

In the HTML section of the dialog box, you can choose the Style you wish to export. Choose Dreamweaver 3, choose the Same Directory option of the Location drop-down list, and click Save.

 You can set many of the options that control how slices are exported by clicking the Setup button in the HTML section of the Export dialog box.

Go to UltraDev and open the HTML file that was just created during your export. You should see your graphic reappear, formatted in a table on the UltraDev page. It doesn't get much easier than that, but those buttons still need to be addressed.

Creating Rollover Buttons

You are getting ready to see the real power of handling your graphics in this fashion. Return to your file in Fireworks. You should be looking at a picture that is obscured by the green glow of your slices. It is very important that those slices do not get moved

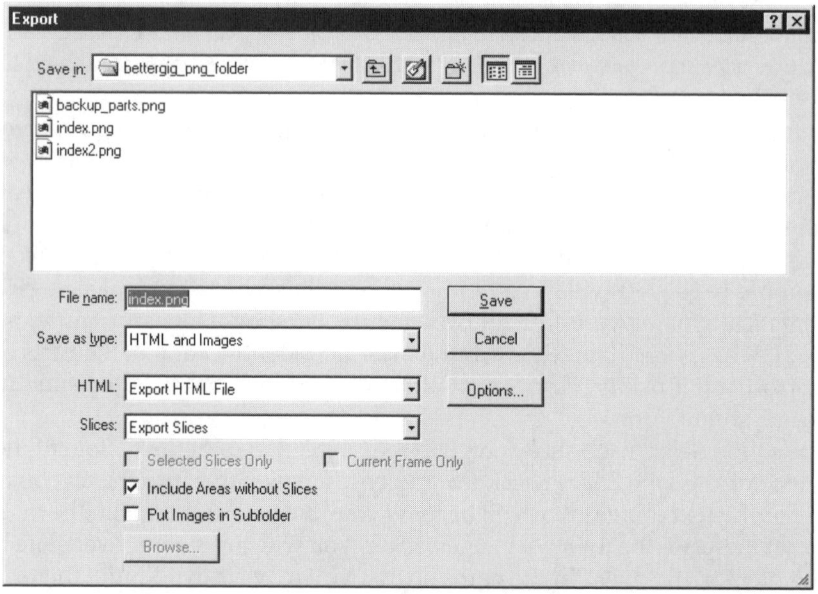

Figure 4-9.   *The Export dialog box*

or resized. Lock the WebLayer in the Layers panel. Then, click the eye next to the lock to make the WebLayer, and the green glow, invisible.

You can now make any changes you would like to the graphic by unlocking the layer on which you want to work. Because, for this example, you want to work on the text links, unlock Layer 2. I made two changes to the text. First, I selected it, and went to the Effects panel and altered the bevel slightly. I then placed a dot next to each word.

After those changes are made, relock Layer 2 so that nothing gets changed by accident. Now, turn the WebLayer back on, making the slices visible. Select each of the slices and use the Object panel again to rename them, changing "up" to "over." You are now going to export just the slices that have changed.

Select each slice one at a time and select File | Export Special | Selected Slice. Export the slice to the same directory in which you exported the entire graphic.

Next, return to the UltraDev page that you opened earlier. Now that you have your over-state button available, you need to replace the static graphics with a rollover button. Select one of the text links and delete the graphic from the table cell. Select Insert | Rollover Image. You will be presented with the dialog box shown in Figure 4-10.

Choose a descriptive name for this image, in case you need to reference it in your code. In the Original Image box, select the up-state button graphic. In the Rollover Image box, select the over-state button graphic. Leave the Preload option checked and set the URL hyperlink to follow when this button is clicked.

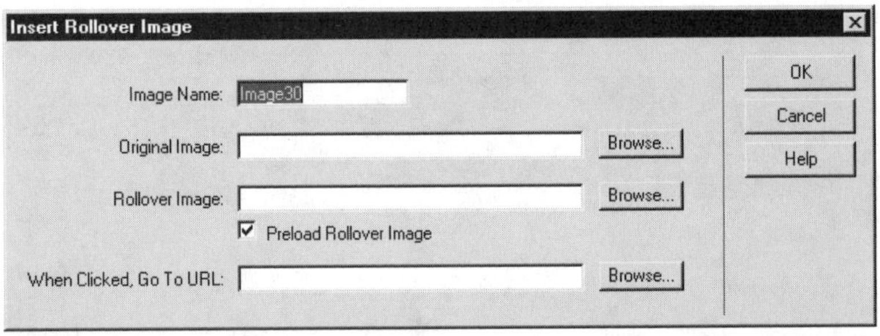

Figure 4-10.   *Creating Rollover buttons*

Note

The Preload Rollover Image option causes both graphics to load when the page initially opens. If you deselect it, your users will likely notice a slight delay the first time they move over the link as the over-state image loads from the server.

This procedure represents only a fraction of the power you have available when using UltraDev with Fireworks. You now have a home page with rollover buttons ready to use in your site.

Templates

Because you decided earlier that your site would utilize a consistent design that is represented in the home page, it makes sense to use an UltraDev template to build your pages. *Templates* are files that maintain specific portions of a page to which you can add content. By using a template in this case, your graphics and navigational links will remain consistent across your pages while the information in the content section of the page changes.

UltraDev templates work by locking the regions of the site that you want to remain consistent. Actually, all the areas of a template file are locked except for the areas that you mark as editable regions. On your page, you want everything but the content area to remain locked.

Select the content area of the page. The Fireworks export routine has placed a filler object that you don't need. Press DELETE to remove the graphic. You will be left with an empty table cell the size of the original content area. Right-click the content area and choose Editable Regions | New. Give it the name **Content**. UltraDev will place a text filler with the name of the region, as shown in Figure 4-11.

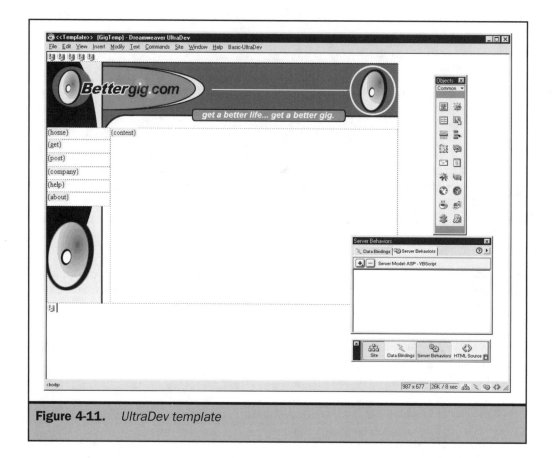

Figure 4-11.   *UltraDev template*

Select File | Save As Template. Select the site that you wish to save the template in and then name the file. You have created a template that you will use to build the remainder of your pages.

Now that you have designed your site and built a template on which to base your pages, you are ready to begin the actual construction of the site by adding the pages you decided on earlier. Using the information in this chapter, you should be able to begin the very important task of designing your site by identifying its purpose, its audience, and an outline of its content. By using other tools that integrate with UltraDev, you can begin the graphic construction of your site and use templates to define its look and feel. Chapter 5 shows you how to use your template file to build HTML pages that will lead you toward your data-driven site.

Chapter 5

Adding Pages to Your Site

hapter 4 looked at basic site design and created a template that can be used to add pages to your site while maintaining an overall graphic and navigational theme. Most of the functionality of the Bettergig site will be built in later chapters where database connectivity is discussed, but there is no telling what design elements you may want to use in your site; so this chapter will cover page design using many of UltraDev's most popular features, as well as some of the new tools that are available in version 4.

Creating Pages from Templates

Once you have one or more templates defined and saved as a part of your site, creating new pages based on them is simple. From the File menu on either an existing page or the Site window, select the New from Template option.

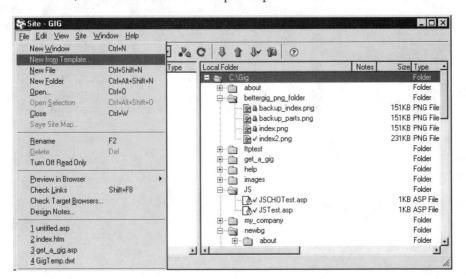

You will be prompted to select a template on which to base this new page. You may, of course, have more than one template in any particular site, and sets of pages can be based on those templates to give areas of your site different looks and navigational content.

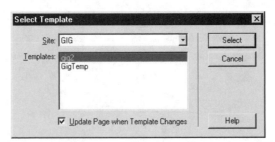

Once you select a template for your new page, a new document window is opened. That new document is an instance of the template you close, and contains the same locked regions and editable regions as the template. Locked regions are those parts of the page that you want to remain untouched. The only place that new content can be added to the page is in those areas that you have defined as editable.

When the page first opens, you can identify those editable regions by the default text that is placed in each one when the template is created. In Figure 5-1, you can see the one page-level editable region in the Bettergig template, called Content.

Note   *The small tag in the upper-right corner of the page indicates the template that this page is based on. This tag will only appear at design time.*

The content region is not really the only editable region on the page, though. To see all of a page's editable regions listed by name, select Modify | Templates from the menu bar (see Figure 5-2). The bottom portion of the Templates submenu lists all the

Figure 5-1.   *A new page created from the Bettergig template*

Figure 5-2. *The Templates section of the Modify menu*

editable regions on the page. The checkmark indicates the active region, and you can select the region that you want to make active by selecting one from this menu.

In addition to the content region, this page has an editable region called doctitle. This is a default region that allows the title of each page that is based on a template to be unique. A look at the code behind a templated page will help you understand why this is important.

Take a look at line 5 of the code in Figure 5-3. This line is the comment tag that signals the beginning of an UltraDev template. From that point on, this page is considered locked. It is only by explicitly unlocking an area that a region can be made editable. For example, look at line 42 of the code in Figure 5-4. Two tags are used here to identify an area of the page that is editable. The BeginEditable tag also contains the name of the editable region ("content," in this case). The EndEditable tag signals the end of the editable region. Within those tags is that area to which new content can be added. Notice that the default text is all that is there right now.

Now look back at Figure 5-3 and notice that the <title> HTML tag comes after the BeginTemplate tag. By the rules previously described, that would mean that the title of

Figure 5-3. *An UltraDev template is defined by the BeginTemplate tag*

each page would remain locked and, therefore, the same for every page based on the template. Making this section of the code an editable region by default ensures that you will always have access to the Title tag of your pages.

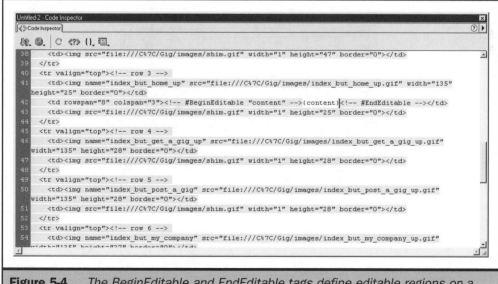

Figure 5-4. *The BeginEditable and EndEditable tags define editable regions on a template*

Using the Asset Panel to Create Templated Pages

You can also create pages based on templates by using the Templates section of the Asset panel. The Assets panel is a centralized place where pieces of content, or *assets*, are available to you. These might be images, or templates, or specialized content such as Flash and Director files. The Asset panel will be covered in more detail later in this chapter, but you will get a good idea of how it works right here.

Applying a template to a page from the Asset panel is as easy as dragging and dropping the template. With any new document window open, you can simply select a template file from the Templates section of the Asset panel, shown in Figure 5-5, and drag it onto the document window. That template is immediately applied to the page just as if you had used the New from Template command.

Adding Templates to Existing Pages

You can add a template to an existing page, even if there is already content on the page. Figure 5-6 is a new page with a little bit of text on it to represent existing content.

Select a template file from the Asset panel and drag it onto the document. The dialog box in Figure 5-7 is displayed.

This dialog box appears because there is content that the template is not sure what to do with. You are given the choice of all the page-level editable regions. The existing content will be placed into the region you choose, as shown in Figure 5-8. You can only select one region into which all of the existing content will be combined. If you select None from the dialog box shown in Figure 5-7, the existing content will be deleted.

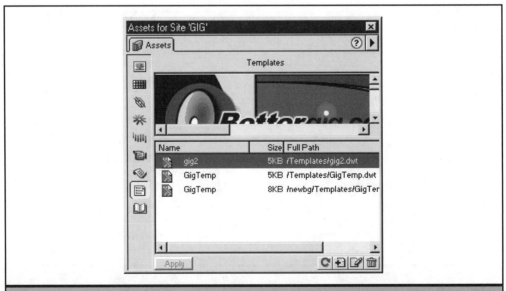

Figure 5-5.   *The Templates section of the Asset panel*

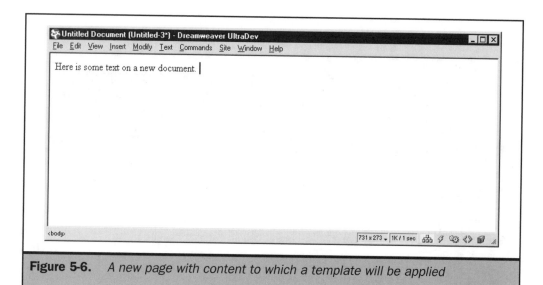

Figure 5-6.   *A new page with content to which a template will be applied*

Applying Templates to Templated Pages

The same principle from the previous section applies if you apply a template to a page that is already based on a template. UltraDev locates all the content in the existing page's editable regions and tries to find a place to put it within the new template. It does this by first matching the editable regions in the old and new templates by name. Any matching regions have their content transferred to the new template, to the region of the same name.

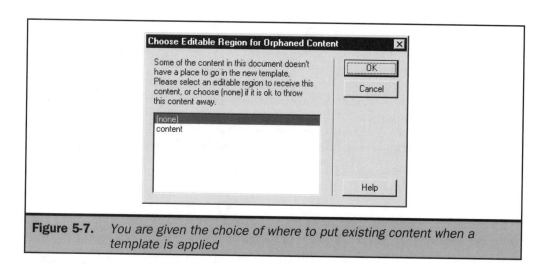

Figure 5-7.   *You are given the choice of where to put existing content when a template is applied*

Figure 5-8. *Existing content is placed into the editable region that you choose*

If there is content in regions of the old template that do not have matching regions in the new template, the same kind of dialog box shown in Figure 5-7 is displayed, giving you the opportunity to select a region in the new template to house that content. Once again, you can select only one region into which all the orphaned content will be combined. If you are unsure as to why content is being orphaned, you can cancel the application of the new template at this point and reexamine your work. You may find that a region you meant to include in the new template is missing or misnamed. Selecting None from the dialog box causes the orphaned content to be deleted from the page.

Managing Templates

Looking back at Figure 5-2, you will see many of the functions that you can perform to manage your templates and the pages that are based on them. In addition to applying templates from this page, you can also detach a page from its template. Doing this will cause the link to the template to be broken, but the existing content of the page will remain in place. The primary effect of detaching a template from a page is that the page will no longer be updated when changes are made to the template.

Updating Templates

So what do you do when you have a whole site full of pages built on a template and then one of the links changes, or a logo changes, or pages are added that need navigational presence on the home page? Luckily, that is one of the beauties of templates, and is the reason you went to the trouble of creating one in the first place. When you edit a template, either by opening the template file directly or from the Modify | Templates menu (refer to Figure 5-2) with the Open Attached Template command, any changes you make can be cascaded down through all the pages that are based on the template. When your changes are saved, you will be prompted to cascade the changes. You can also update your attached pages either one at a time or sitewide with the Modify | Templates menu selections.

Templates can be a powerful way to manage the look and feel of your site. They can also make maintenance of your site much easier by cascading changes down throughout all the pages that are attached to them.

Basic Page Elements

When it comes down to it, constructing pages is just the process of combining page elements in a fashion that meets your design goals. Once you know what you want your page to do and how you want it to look, it's simply a matter of choosing the right combination of elements. This section provides instruction on the use of the basic page elements available in UltraDev. Some page elements will be demonstrated within the content region of the Bettergig page, while others are better shown on their own on a blank document.

Tables

Since you are likely to want to use other page elements along with tables, tables will be covered first. Tables are a lightweight, widely supported means of positioning elements on the page. UltraDev supports the creation of everything from simple tables to complex row and column spans that permit precise positioning of your layout.

Simple Tables

A *simple* table is defined as one that is created by selecting a number of rows and columns, without any fancy alteration of the basic table structure. These tables generally have a number of columns that extend the entire length of the table, and a number of rows that span its entire width. These tables are useful for displaying text or images in a columnar format.

To place a table on your page, select the table object from the Objects palette. When the table object button is clicked, the dialog box in Figure 5-9 is displayed.

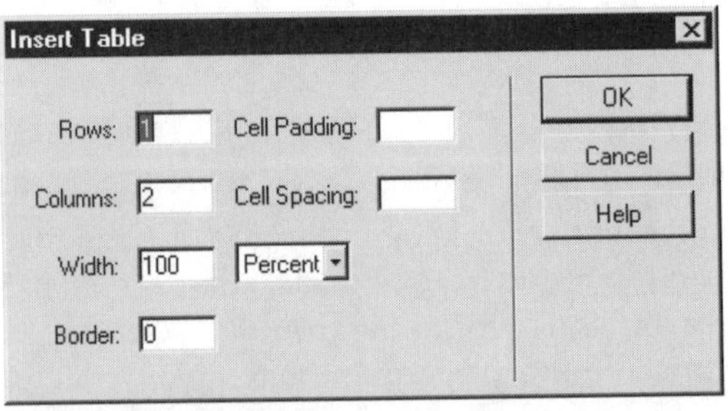

Figure 5-9.   *The Insert Table dialog box*

In this dialog box, you can select the number of rows and columns you want the table to start out with. You are not limited to the choices that you make here, because you can always add or subtract rows and columns at any time. It simply provides a starting point for your new table.

Also in this dialog box, you can set the width of the overall table in pixels or percent, the border width, cell spacing, and cell padding. Figure 5-10 shows the content region of the Bettergig template with a table inserted that is three rows by ten rows. This table has no border, meaning that the individual cells will not be separated by lines when the page is viewed in a browser. In the design window, dashed lines indicate where the cells are so that you can identify your position within the table.

After your table is inserted into the page, you still have access to all of its properties through the Property Inspector, a palette that adjusts dynamically to the element that is active on the page. Selecting the table you inserted will cause the Property Inspector for tables to appear (see Figure 5-11) with the particular data of that table populating its field. You can change the properties of the table in the Property Inspector, and the table on the page will immediately respond to your changes.

More Complex Table Structures

Using the Property Inspector, you can manipulate the cells in your table to create more complex table structures. Use your mouse to select any adjacent rows or columns. Click the Merge Selected Cells button in the Table Property Inspector. A span will be created that combines the selected cells into a single cell. Figure 5-12 shows the original table with a column span across the top and a row span down the left side.

By starting with a simple table and combining cells, you can create structures that allow even more precise placement of your content.

Layout View

All the tables you have been creating up to this point have been done in standard view. Standard view is the default working mode, but there is a new mode available in

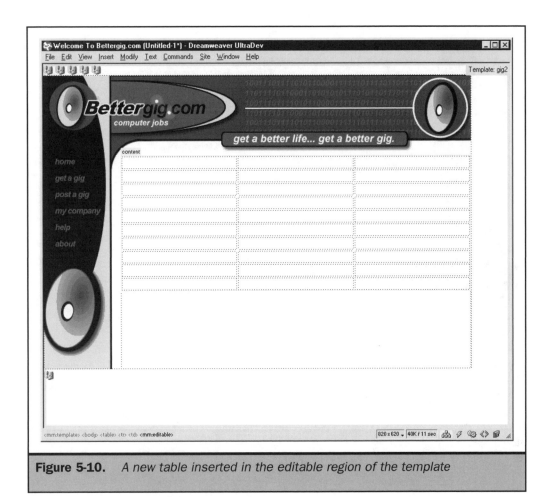

Figure 5-10. *A new table inserted in the editable region of the template*

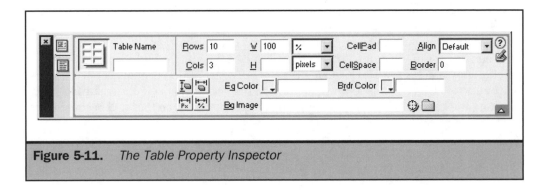

Figure 5-11. *The Table Property Inspector*

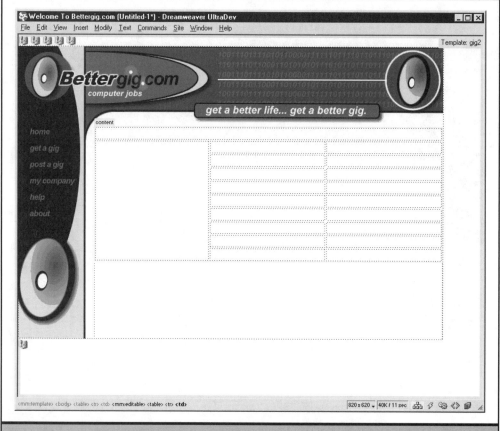

Figure 5-12. *The table with column and row spans applied*

UltraDev 4 called Layout view. Layout view allows you to draw tables and table cells on the page anywhere you want them. UltraDev then creates the table structure that is necessary to house what you have created on the page.

You can control the mode you are in with the buttons at the bottom of the Objects palette, shown in Figure 5-13. Clicking the Layout View option enables you to choose one of the two Layout tools to draw regions on the document. You can create a table by selecting the Layout Table tool and drawing a box on the screen that will become your table (see Figure 5-14).

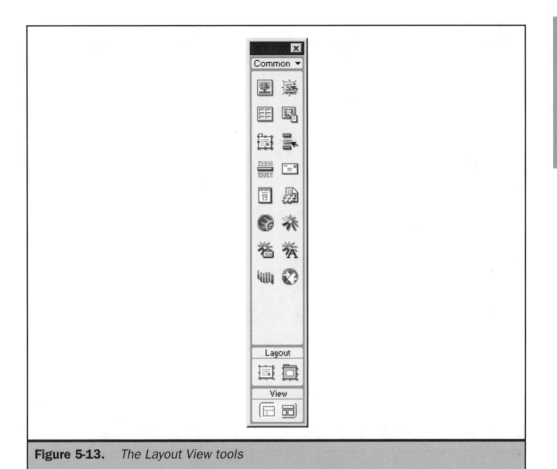

Figure 5-13. *The Layout View tools*

When you create a table in Layout view, you are restricted to the rules of HTML, which means that a new table that you draw snaps to the most upper-left section of the page that is available. You can then draw cells within the table with the Layout Cells tool. To create multiple cells at once, hold down the CTRL key while you draw the cells; otherwise, you will need to reselect the tool for each cell you create. You can see in Figure 5-15 that a cell drawn in a layout table caused UltraDev to create a table structure around the cell to permit its placement to remain where you specified. This image shows two cells drawn separately from one another to demonstrate how UltraDev compensates for your design.

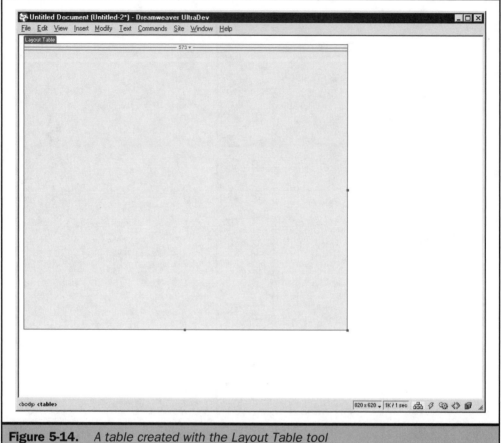

Figure 5-14. *A table created with the Layout Table tool*

It is not necessary to create a layout table before you create layout cells. You can draw cells on the page at any position, and a layout table of sufficient size to contain them will be created at the most upper-left position available. Inside the table will be your cells and sufficient additional structure to maintain the positioning of those cells. Figure 5-16 shows the result of randomly drawing cells on a blank page.

As long as you remain in Layout view, your cells are highlighted within the structure created to contain them. You can place content in your cells, but not in the UltraDev-created cells. They remain "locked" because they are really just there to accommodate the cells you created. If you find yourself needing to place something in a grayed-out structure cell, then you can just create a new layout cell with the Cell tool at that position.

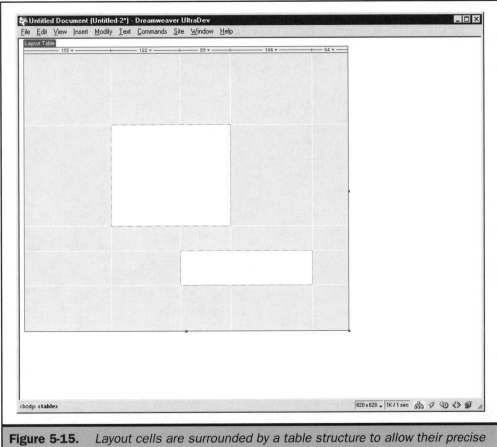

Figure 5-15.   *Layout cells are surrounded by a table structure to allow their precise placement*

Once you return to standard view, your cells are still there and available to you, but the structure cells are no longer locked and can be filled with content. You can go back and forth between the two views "locking" and "unlocking" the structure cells. If you place content in a structure cell while in standard view, that cell will become a layout cell when you return to Layout view, "unlocked" and available for content. But, if you delete that content, the cell will return to "locked" status.

Layers

While tables have become a popular way to position content on your pages, there is another method that is actually more in line with an important principle of Web design, that of the separation of content from design structure. While tables and other

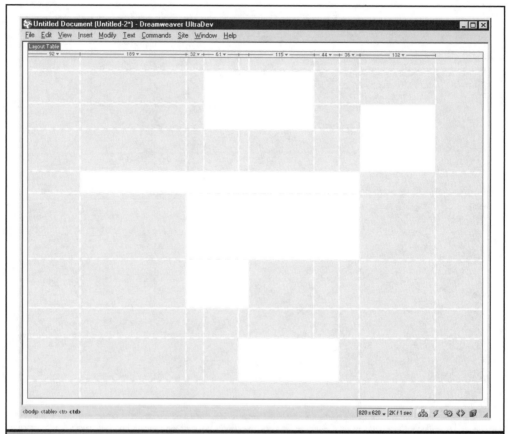

Figure 5-16. *Drawing layout cells on a page causes UltraDev to create the structure to contain them*

HTML tricks are effective to a degree, the elements of Cascading Style Sheets (CSS) allow precise control over the display of your content without littering it with display instructions.

Layers are the CSS method for allowing precise content placement on your pages. Rather than treating a page like a top-down word processor page, as HTML does, CSS treats the page as an X-Y grid on which elements can be placed. A *layer* is defined as an area of some number of pixels across and some number of pixels down that begins at a certain X-Y coordinate. This allows a more "desktop publishing" style of page layout.

Note *Even though CSS is gaining better cross-browser support and is technically the superior choice for page layout, tables are so popular that Macromedia went to great efforts to incorporate the Layout view discussed in the previous section. Even those who use layers to design their pages will often utilize the UltraDev command that converts layers to tables for their final output.*

Placing a layer on a page is as simple as choosing the layer tool from the Objects palette and drawing the layer where you want it. Unlike the tables and layout tables in the previous section, layer placement is not dependent on HTML rules that force content up and to the left. Figure 5-17 shows a layer drawn in the middle of the page.

Note *You must be in standard view for layers to work. Once layers are drawn, you can switch to layout view and draw tables, but your layer will be ignored in the construction of the table structure. When you return to standard view, you will have a z-order situation with your layer and table cells overlaying one another, as shown in Figure 5-18.*

Once you have layers on your page, each one acts as its own little HTML page, meaning that within a layer, the rules of top-left HTML apply. For instance, if you place an image within a layer, it will snap to the upper left of the layer. To place

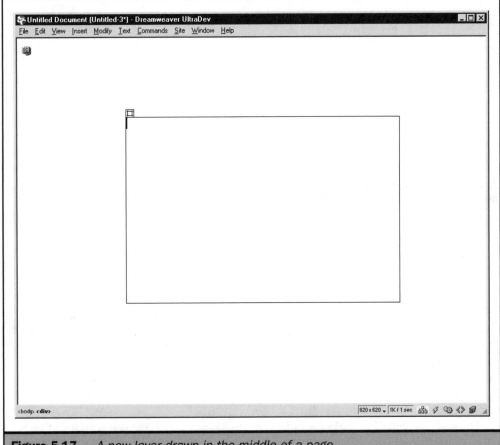

Figure 5-17.   *A new layer drawn in the middle of a page*

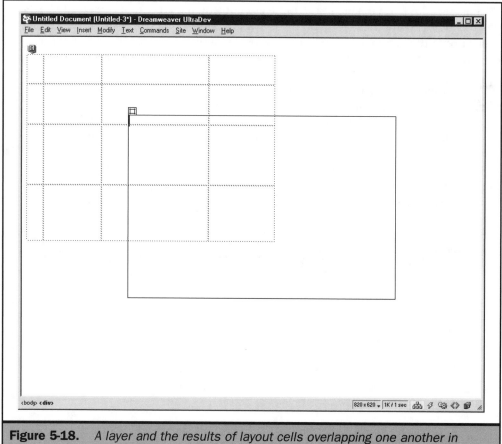

Figure 5-18. *A layer and the results of layout cells overlapping one another in standard view*

content within a layer more precisely, you can build a table (not in Layout view) within the layer and place content within the cells of the table.

Many times, designers need to precisely place their content but need to target version 3 browsers (or have some other reason that they are reluctant to publish with layers). You could spend the time to meticulously create a table structure that meets your needs, or you can let UltraDev do that for you. Once your site is created using layers, you can tell UltraDev to convert those layers to tables. The Modify | Convert menu offers two options: Layers to Tables, and Tables to Layers. The Tables to Layers option allows you to switch back to layers if you find that you need to make changes after you have converted to tables.

Once you have either tables or layers on your page, you have the structure that will allow your content to be displayed with the look you have designed. You need only to begin placing that content using the other tools that are available to you.

Images

Images are a key part of the modern Web site, whether they are a part of your page design, pictures of products you are selling, or even pictures of your kids on your personal Web page. Images and graphics are, in large part, what differentiates modern sites from the text-laden sites of a few years ago.

As with most things, adding images to your site is a simple matter. Once you have the structure of the site completed, as discussed in the previous section, placing images on the page is just a matter of inserting or dropping them on the page in the correct table cell or layer.

Locate your cursor at the spot where you want to place an image. This example uses the random layout cell example demonstrated earlier just to show that you can put an image anywhere that you have created a spot to hold it.

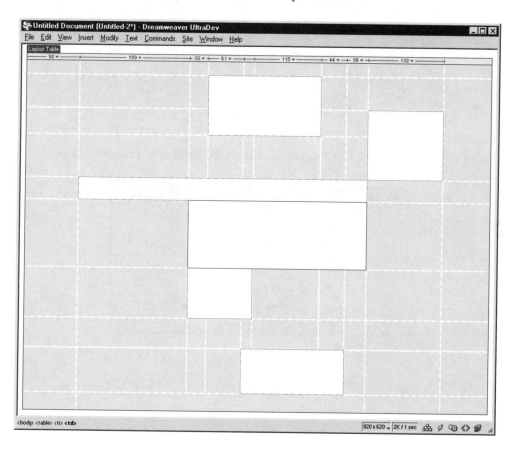

A dialog box will appear asking you to locate the image that you want to use. Browse to the location on your computer where the file resides and select it. You can see a preview of the file you have selected to the right of the box.

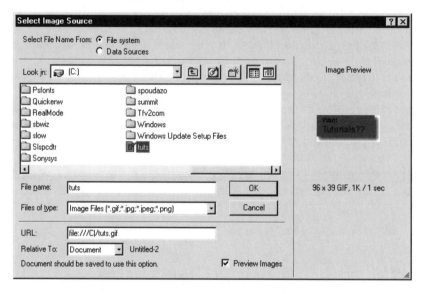

You will be warned that a relative path cannot be used until you save the page.

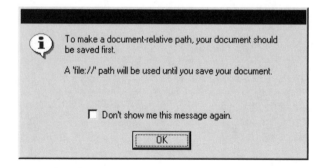

If the file you have chosen resides outside the file structure of the current site, you will be notified and given the opportunity to copy it into the current site so that it will be available when the site is published.

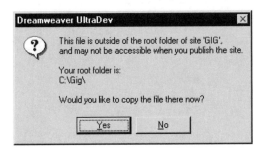

If you choose Yes, you will be asked to choose the directory you want the file saved to. Choose whichever directory you are saving your images to.

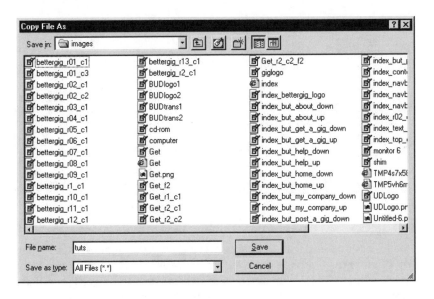

When you have finished, the image is a part of your page.

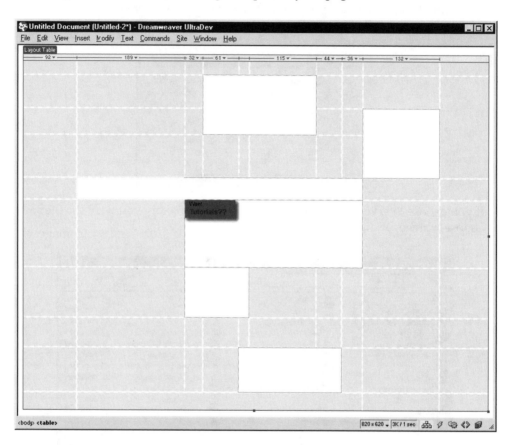

Rollover Images

Rollover images operate under the same principle as regular images, except that they are made up of more than one image so that they are able to react to mouse activity. Basic UltraDev rollover images have two states: an *out* state that is visible when a mouse pointer is not over the image, and an *over* state that is visible when a mouse pointer is hovering over the image. Thus, you have to create two images in advance to fulfill these two states. At this point, you are just adding them to the page. A way to create these images with Fireworks and UltraDev was covered in Chapter 4.

Note   *Rollover buttons can have up to four states: the two states previously mentioned, as well as an up and down state indicating whether or not a button has been pressed. To create these kinds of buttons, you will need to use a program such as Fireworks and import the packaged button into UltraDev as Fireworks HTML.*

Select the spot where you want a rollover image inserted and click the rollover image button on the Objects palette.

Because you will be using more than one image, each with its own name, to build this rollover, name the rollover so that you can refer to it if need be. You will need to browse to your images twice to select the out state image and the over state image.

Note *Make sure when you create your images that will be used for rollovers to name them so that they are easily identified when you look for them. For instance, name the out state image with the image name plus _out and the over state image with the image name plus _over.*

The two additional settings for a rollover image are the URL and Preload options. Selecting the Preload Rollover Image checkbox will cause all of the images that make up the various image states to load into the browser when the page loads. It takes a fraction longer for the page to load when this option is selected, but that is better than the browser having to make additional trips to the server each time one of the images is engaged for the first time.

The URL setting allows you to select a URL to send the user to when the image is clicked.

When you have finished with the dialog box, the new image displays in your page.

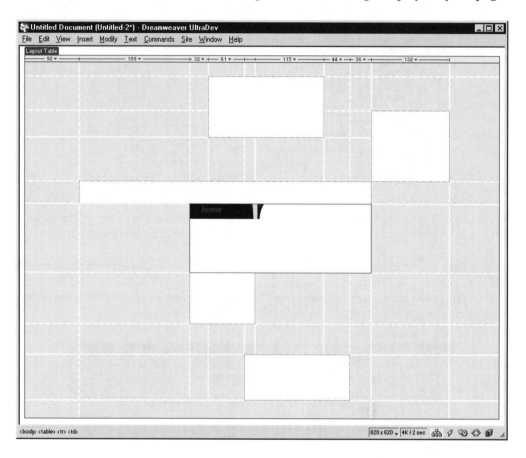

Forms

So far, there has been a lot of discussion about providing an interactive experience for your site's visitors. One of the more basic ways for a user to communicate with a Web application is through forms. A form is an HTML element that uses a variety of field types to collect information from a user and pass it along, usually to a CGI application or ASP, JSP, or CF page that takes the data and does something with it. There will be a lot of discussion of forms in the later database chapters, but this section will cover the basics of adding forms and form fields to your pages.

A form is kind of a self-enclosed element that contains the pieces that collect information. Everything that makes up the form is housed within the HTML form tags <form> and </form>. Whatever form elements you choose to place within those tags are affected by the form's buttons.

There are typically two form buttons associated with a form. One is a Submit button that is responsible for taking the information that has been entered and sending it off to the destination you have specified for the form. The second button is a Reset button that clears all of the form fields.

To place a form on your page, switch to the Forms tab of the Objects palette.

With your cursor positioned where you want the form inserted, click the form button on the palette. A form will be inserted on the page. The base form is invisible, and is indicated in the design window by broken lines.

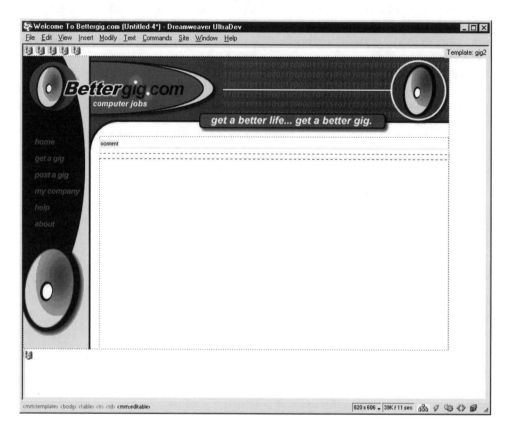

When you select the form by clicking it, the form's Property Inspector is displayed.

In the Property Inspector, you will see three important properties that need to be set for your form:

- **Name**   The form name is a means of referring to the entire form. It is especially important to name your form if you will be using more than one form on a page.

- **Method**   There are two options for the Method parameter. The Get method attaches the form information to the URL. There are size limitations associated with the use of the Get method that make it less practical to use than the other method, Post. The Post method passes the form's information behind the scenes directly to the target pages or application. There is no size restriction on the Post method.

- **Action**   The action of a form is the target to which the form will be posted. The action could be a Perl script, a CGI application, or an ASP page. It could even be the same page that the form resides on, as covered in Chapter 11.

Form Elements

There are nine basic form elements available on the Objects palette, which are discussed in the following sections.

Text Field

The text field is used to collect text information, such as names and addresses. It has several properties that can be set in the Property Inspector.

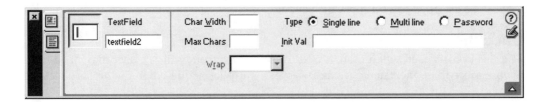

You can set a name for the field, which is very important to do so that you have a way of referring to the field in the application or on the page that handles its data. UltraDev sets a default value for the name, but you will be well served to assign meaningful names to these fields so that you can refer to them easily.

There are three choices for the format of the field. Single Line is the standard one-line text box. Multi Line allows you to set the box up as a memo field. When Multi Line is chosen, you can also set how text within the field wraps. The Password option causes asterisks to be displayed for the characters that are entered in the field so that they cannot be viewed by casual observers.

You can also set a width in characters for the box, a maximum length to do some data validation, and an initial value that can serve as a default.

Button

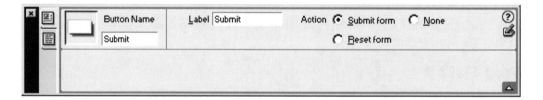

The Form button can be used for three different purposes. Its properties can be set in the Property Inspector.

Set a Name for the button so that you can refer to it in your code. You can set a Label that is separate from its name. Submit is the default, but it could be Go! or Send, or anything you would like. The three Actions that can be set are Submit, which submits the form; Reset, which resets the form; and None, which creates a disconnected button that you can reference in your code to call a piece of code or perform any other action that can be assigned to a button's click event.

Checkbox

The checkbox is used when there is a list of selections from which a user may need to choose more than one. Each checkbox passes a supplied value when the box is checked.

The checkbox has three properties that can be set from the Property Inspector.

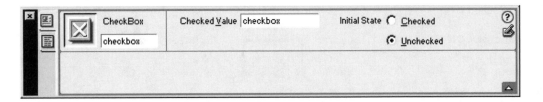

The name of the checkbox can be used to refer to it. You can also set a checked value, which is the value that is passed when the box is in a Checked state, and you can select whether or not the box is checked when the page loads.

Radio Button

Radio buttons can be used when there is a list of selections from which a user can select only one.

The radio button's properties can be set in the Property Inspector.

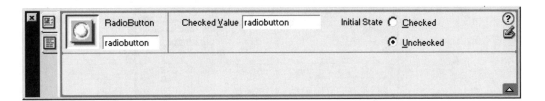

You can make a set of radio buttons by setting the name of more than one button to the same name. Then, set the checked value of each to a distinct value. You can then check the value of the base radio button name for which checked value was passed. You can also set the initial position of each button to Checked or Unchecked.

List/Menu

The list/menu field provides a drop-down list or menu list of selections that the user can select from.

You can set several properties in the Property Inspector.

In addition to the name of the field, you can select whether it will be a drop-down list or a menu box. If you choose a menu box, you can set the height in rows and whether multiple selections are allowed. Use the List Values button to display the List Values dialog box.

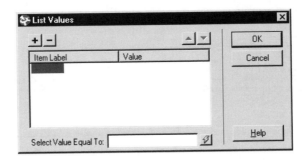

In the List Values dialog box, you can set the display values that will appear in the menu, and the associated values that will be passed when each of the display values is selected. Back in the main Property Inspector, you can select which of these values is initially selected.

File Field

The file field provides the functionality to browse for a file on the local client computer. This field can be used in conjunction with file upload code to collect a file from your user, such as an image or a resume.

The properties for the file field are very simple.

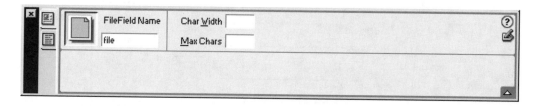

You can set a name, a character width for the field, and a maximum number of characters.

Image Field

The image field provides a means for placing images within a form. When you select the image fields, you are prompted to select an image from the directories on your computer, much like the insertion of a regular image. From the Property Inspector, you can name the image field and edit the source of the image that fills it.

Hidden Field

A hidden field is a text field that posts with the form but is not displayed on the page. You can set the value of a hidden field programmatically and use it to pass information that you don't want seen. Keep in mind, though, that the value of a hidden form field can be seen in the source of the page, which is viewable in most browsers.

Jump Menu

A jump menu is a drop-down box that provides navigation for a user. By selecting a topic in the menu, the user is immediately redirected to an associated URL. When you select the jump menu button on the Objects palette, you are presented with the following dialog box.

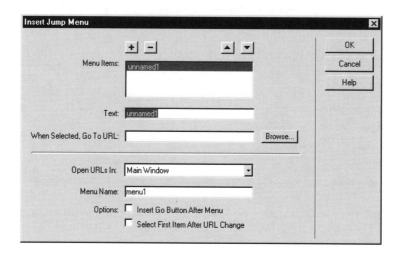

In this dialog box, you can set display items for your jump menu; and for each display item, you can set a URL to which users will be directed when they choose that menu item. You can also select a target for the new page to open into.

Frames

It is not necessary to have just one HTML page on a Web page. A method known as *framing* allows you to put two, three, or more totally independent pages within a frameset. While these independent pages, called *frames*, can work together, they are really separate pages that are constructed and tied together in the frameset.

UltraDev takes a lot of the complexity out of creating frames by providing prebuilt framesets that can be dragged onto your page. Once the frameset is added, you can construct each of the frame pages in the design window.

UltraDev Features

In addition to the basic page elements, UltraDev provides other features that you can use to make your pages more interesting and functional.

Behaviors

Behaviors are page-level JavaScript that have been prewritten and packaged for use within UltraDev. Behaviors are typically made up of an event and an action. In other words, to make use of a behavior, you first identify an event, such as a button click, that will trigger an action, such as the calling of a piece of code or the playing of a Flash file. UltraDev's built-in behaviors are available on the Behaviors palette.

 Note *Behaviors are different than Server Behaviors. Server Behaviors typically involve server-side code that does things such as interact with databases and send e-mail. Behaviors are limited to client-side code for things such as DHTML effects.*

To illustrate, the following example creates a button that displays a message when it is clicked:

1. Drag a form button to the page. When UltraDev asks if you want to create a form tag, select No.

2. Change the name of the button to Message in the Property Inspector.

3. Change the Action of the button to none.

4. Select the button by clicking it.

5. Make sure that the Behaviors palette is displayed by selecting it from the Windows menu.

6. From the (+) button on the Behaviors palette, select the Popup Message behavior.

7. A dialog box is displayed in which you can type the message that you want to be displayed.

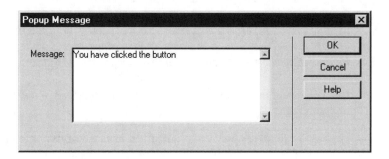

8. When the behavior is applied, it appears in the Behaviors palette. You can edit it by double-clicking the listing in the palette.

9. When the page is published and a visitor clicks the button, a JavaScript pop-up menu appears with your message.

You can apply many different behaviors to different events involving a variety of elements on your page. Many of the best behaviors have been written by third-party authors and do ship with UltraDev. You can get information about these at the Macromedia Exchange or around the Web.

Reference Materials

Version 4 of UltraDev ships with O'Reilly HTML, JavaScript, and CSS references built in. You can also download extensions from the Macromedia Web site that provide excellent ASP references. You can access these from the References palette. They provide a convenient way to search for information on the languages you are using to build your site.

Assets Palette

The Assets Palette is also new to version 4 of UltraDev. Inspired by the Asset Center in Drumbeat 2000, the Assets palette provides easy access to all of the individual pieces of your site. The Assets palette has nine categories represented by the icons to the left of the palette:

- Images
- Colors
- Links
- Flash Content
- Shockwave Content
- Movie Files
- Scripts
- Templates
- Library

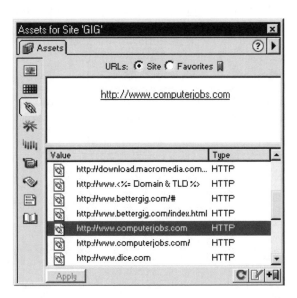

Not a lot can be said about the Assets palette except that it makes the management of site content extremely easy. Any content that is placed within the directory structure of the site is automatically available and can be added to your site by dragging and dropping it straight from the palette. This makes the continual browsing for files unnecessary and saves time by making your actions more accurate and purposeful.

Library

One particularly useful part of the Assets palette is the Library. Much like templates, Library files are linked files. That means that changes to files in the Library can be cascaded down through the pages that use them. For instance, your site may utilize a graphic that changes on a periodic basis. If this graphic is added to the Library and placed onto pages from the Library, it could be updated on all of the pages that use it just by updating it in the Library. The same could be done with pieces of code or server-side includes.

History

The History file contains a list of all the steps you have taken in the construction of your pages. The History palette provides almost unlimited undos. You can also select series of steps from the History palette and create commands out of them so that they can be repeated with one menu selection.

Flash Buttons

You know that you can add Flash and Director content to your pages by using the Objects palette or by dragging the files from the Assets palette. UltraDev 4 includes a new item called a Flash Button. Flash Buttons are animated buttons based on Flash files. UltraDev comes with a selection of Flash Button bases that you can use to build your buttons. To build a Flash Button, follow these steps.

1. Place your cursor on the page where you want a Flash Button inserted. Click the Flash Button button on the Objects palette.

2. Select one of the premade Flash Button templates.

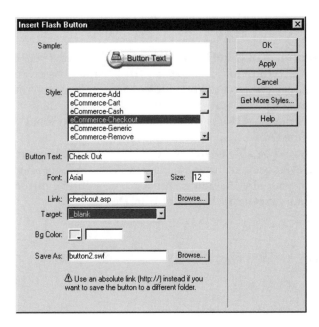

3. You can set custom text for the button. In addition, you can select the URL link and target for the button click, as well as the font and background color.

4. Finally, you can save this button in your site for use later. The button is saved in a Flash format. If you want to add it to another part of your site, you can do so from the Assets palette or by inserting Flash content from the Objects palette.

5. When the site is published, the Flash Button will appear as an animated button on the page. It requires the Flash plug-in to play, but provides a more capable option that includes full animation, rather than simple rollover buttons.

Summary

The Dreamweaver portion of UltraDev, as it is called, provides a very capable and feature-rich WYSIWYG editor for HTML pages. This chapter has given you an overview of the tools that are available to you. You will see many of these tools in action in later chapters as you continue the construction of your data-driven site. For more in-depth coverage of these client-side features, you are encouraged to seek out one of the good volumes that cover the Dreamweaver 4 features specifically.

By now, you should be able to add basic HTML features to your site and use some of the UltraDev-specific features such as the Assets palette and behaviors to add content and code to your site. As you go forward, you will be introduced to Web scripting and the data-driven capabilities of UltraDev 4.

The Complete Reference

Chapter 6

Publishing Your Site to the Internet

N ow that you have completed the beginnings of your site, you will likely turn your attention to getting it published to the Internet. After all, as cool as your site may be, no one else will know about it, much less praise it or nominate you for designer of the year, until they can see it in their browsers. You are likely have a domain name, or at least an IP address, attached to a set of directories on a Web server, as discussed in Chapter 2. In order to make your site available on the Web, you will need to transfer the files from your local development computer to that set of directories.

You have some options as to how you accomplish this. UltraDev has the built-in capability to publish your files, and there are several third-party options, if you prefer. Let's look at the technologies involved in publishing your site to the Internet and some of the options you have.

FTP

One of the oldest Internet protocols is still one of the most popular for publishing Web sites to your remote server. File Transfer Protocol (FTP) is a well-named protocol. Its purpose is just that, to transfer files from one place to another. As a means of viewing and interacting with content, it is very limited, which is why HTTP replaced it as the protocol of the Web. But as a means of moving files around, it remains an efficient tool.

Remember that your Web application is really just a collection of individual files. They may be HTML pages, ASP pages, CFM pages, GIF images, or any of a number of file types. But they are still just a series of files that work together as they call each other and pass data back and forth. Publishing a site to the Web involves the transfer of that collection of files to an Internet-connected server. Once that is completed, maintenance of your application can be accomplished by editing and replacing only those files that require changes.

> **Note**   *In order to use an FTP program on your computer (called an FTP client) to upload files to a remote computer, that remote machine must be running an FTP server program that allows you to connect and deposit files in its directories. Chapter 2 discusses the steps necessary to set up an FTP server.*

There are many FTP programs available; for example, you can access FTP from the command line in UNIX or Windows. For our purposes, let's look at FTP from the Windows command line. The greater understanding you gain of FTP's commands and capabilities, the easier it will be to master whichever FTP client you choose to use.

> **Note**   *Although the following examples use the Windows command prompt to illustrate the use of FTP, you may use the command-line functionality of whichever operating system you use on your development computer.*

FTP from the Command Line

While there are as many as 60 FTP commands available, the core of what you will want to accomplish can be summed up in the following list:

1. Connect to an FTP server.

2. Use a username and password to log in.

3. Figure out where you are in the directory structure.

4. Change to the remote directory you want to communicate with (after creating it, if necessary).

5. Get a listing of the files in that directory.

6. Upload or download files.

7. Disconnect from the FTP server.

To begin the preceding process, open a DOS prompt on your Windows computer by selecting MS-DOS Prompt from your Start menu.

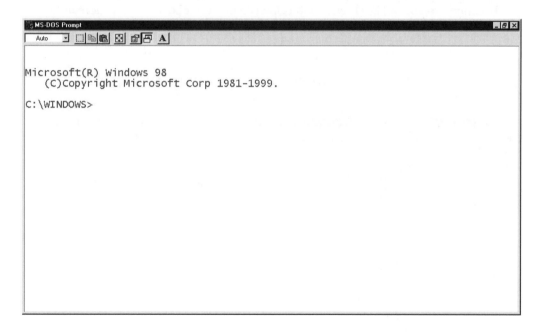

Type **FTP** to start the FTP client. You will be presented with an FTP prompt at which you will enter your FTP commands.

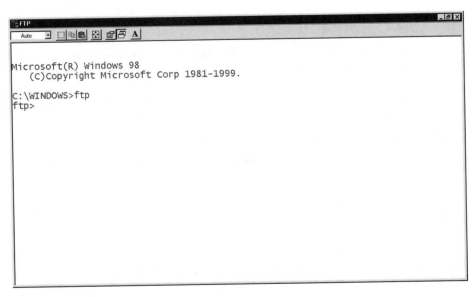

To connect to your FTP server, use the Open command followed by the domain or IP address of your remote computer. For the Bettergig site, you would type the following:

```
open www.bettergig.com
```

You will then be presented with a prompt for your username and password to log in to the site.

Once logged in, you are still only at an FTP prompt. To see where you are in the directory structure, use the pwd command to print the working directory. You may be deposited in the root of the site (the highest directory in the structure), or your administrator may have assigned your login a default directory in which you will begin. Depending on your security settings, you may or may not be able to see and navigate to directories about your default location. The dir command will show you the files and directories that are immediately available to you.

```
FTP                                                                    _ 8 X
 Auto   ⏷ ☐ ▤ ▦ ▨ ▤▤ A
Password:
230 User ray logged in.
ftp> pwd
257 "/" is current directory.
ftp> dir
200 PORT command successful.
150 Opening ASCII mode data connection for /bin/ls.
drwxrwxrwx  1 owner    group            0 Nov  5 15:27 about
drwxrwxrwx  1 owner    group            0 Sep 18 10:05 bettergig_png_folder
-rwxrwxrwx  1 owner    group          686 Jul 16  2001 CDOtest.asp
-rwxrwxrwx  1 owner    group           41 Nov  5 15:23 CDOtest.asp.LCK
-rwxrwxrwx  1 owner    group        11257 Aug 23 18:32 get.asp
-rwxrwxrwx  1 owner    group            9 Aug 22 22:17 get.asp.LCK
drwxrwxrwx  1 owner    group            0 Nov  1 22:24 get_a_gig
drwxrwxrwx  1 owner    group            0 Nov  1 22:24 help
drwxrwxrwx  1 owner    group            0 Nov  5 15:39 images
-rwxrwxrwx  1 owner    group         8641 Sep 20 14:22 index.htm
drwxrwxrwx  1 owner    group            0 Nov  1 22:24 JS
drwxrwxrwx  1 owner    group            0 Nov  1 22:23 my_company
-rwxrwxrwx  1 owner    group          279 Jul 11  2001 ObjectTest.html
drwxrwxrwx  1 owner    group            0 Nov  1 22:23 post_a_gig
drwxrwxrwx  1 owner    group            0 Sep 18 10:05 Templates
226 Transfer complete.
ftp: 1058 bytes received in 0.06Seconds 17.63Kbytes/sec.
ftp>
```

You may want to work in this default directory, or you may need access to another directory, which may or may not exist at this point. To create a new directory inside the directory in which you currently reside, use the mkdir command followed by the name of the directory you wish to create.

```
FTP                                                                        _ 8 X
[ Auto  ▾ ]
drwxrwxrwx   1  owner      group           0 Sep 18 10:05 bettergig_png_folder
-rwxrwxrwx   1  owner      group         686 Jul 16  2001 CDOtest.asp
-rwxrwxrwx   1  owner      group          41 Nov  5 15:23 CDOtest.asp.LCK
-rwxrwxrwx   1  owner      group       11257 Aug 23 18:32 get.asp
-rwxrwxrwx   1  owner      group           9 Aug 22 22:17 get.asp.LCK
drwxrwxrwx   1  owner      group           0 Nov  1 22:24 get_a_gig
drwxrwxrwx   1  owner      group           0 Nov  1 22:24 help
drwxrwxrwx   1  owner      group           0 Nov  5 15:39 images
-rwxrwxrwx   1  owner      group        8641 Sep 20 14:22 index.htm
drwxrwxrwx   1  owner      group           0 Nov  1 22:24 JS
drwxrwxrwx   1  owner      group           0 Nov  1 22:23 my_company
-rwxrwxrwx   1  owner      group         279 Jul 11  2001 ObjectTest.html
drwxrwxrwx   1  owner      group           0 Nov  1 22:23 post_a_gig
drwxrwxrwx   1  owner      group           0 Sep 18 10:05 Templates
226 Transfer complete.
ftp: 1058 bytes received in 0.06Seconds 17.63Kbytes/sec.
ftp> mkdir ftptest
257 MKD command successful.
ftp> cd ftptest
250 CWD command successful.
ftp> dir
200 PORT command successful.
150 Opening ASCII mode data connection for /bin/ls.
226 Transfer complete.
ftp> _
```

This example created an ftptest directory. The server responded that the command was successful. The cd command was then used to change to the new directory, and the dir command listed the files within the directory (none, of course, since it was just created).

As in the example, you can use the mkdir and the rmdir commands to make and remove directories, and the cd command to move around within the directory structure you have created.

Once you have created or moved to the directory in which you need to place or download files, you can use the get and put commands to do just that. The put command enables you to specify a directory and file on your local machine to be uploaded. The get command enables you to specify which file in the current remote working directory you want to download to your local computer.

```
FTP                                                                    _ 🗗 ✕
  Auto    ▼  🔲 🖻 🖬  🔲 🖆 🖵  A
226 Transfer complete.
ftp: 1058 bytes received in 0.06Seconds 17.63Kbytes/sec.
ftp> mkdir ftptest
257 MKD command successful.
ftp> cd ftptest
250 CWD command successful.
ftp> dir
200 PORT command successful.
150 Opening ASCII mode data connection for /bin/ls.
226 Transfer complete.
ftp> put c:\mydocu~1\ftptest.txt
200 PORT command successful.
150 Opening ASCII mode data connection for ftptest.txt.
226 Transfer complete.
ftp> dir
200 PORT command successful.
150 Opening ASCII mode data connection for /bin/ls.
-rwxrwxrwx   1 owner     group              0 Nov 14 23:12 ftptest.txt
226 Transfer complete.
ftp: 72 bytes received in 0.00Seconds 72000.00Kbytes/sec.
ftp> get ftptest.txt
200 PORT command successful.
150 Opening ASCII mode data connection for ftptest.txt(0 bytes).
226 Transfer complete.
ftp>
```

The close command will close the connection; the bye command closes the connection and exits FTP.

This is certainly not the easiest way to use FTP; but it is good to know, because it works great in a pinch and should help you understand a bit about the mechanics of the protocol. Table 6-1 contains a more complete listing of the available FTP commands (some on Windows and some on UNIX) and their meanings.

FTP Command	Meaning
!	Escape to shell
ascii	Set the file transfer mode to ascii
bell	Sound a beep when complete
binary	Set the file transfer mode to binary
bye	Close the FTP connection and exit the FTP program

Table 6-1.   *FTP Commands*

FTP Command	Meaning
cd	Change to a specified directory
cdup	Move up one directory in the current structure
close	Close the FTP connection
delete	Delete a file
dir	List the files in the current directory
disconnect	Terminate the FTP session
get	Get a file from the remote computer
help	Get help on a listed command
lcd	Change the local current directory
ls	List the file in the current directory
mdelete	Delete multiple files
mdir	List the contents of multiple remote directories
mget	Get multiple files
mkdir	Create a new directory
mls	List the contents of multiple remote directories
mput	Put multiple files
open	Open an FTP connection
prompt	Force interactive prompting on multiple commands
put	Put a file on the remote computer
pwd	Print working directory
quit	Close the connection and exit FTP
recv	Receive a file
rename	Rename a file
rmdir	Remove a directory
send	Send one file
status	Show current status
?	Print local help information

Table 6-1.   *FTP Commands* (continued)

Good FTP clients are readily available, including the one in UltraDev, which allows you to interact with your FTP server in a more visual way.

FTP in UltraDev

FTP in UltraDev offers this functionality in a visual interface that makes it easy to use and navigate. For almost every command in Table 6-1, there is a corresponding UltraDev action that accomplishes the same thing. FTP is accessed directly in the site files window, as shown in Figure 6-1.

If you set up your FTP access in UltraDev as discussed in Chapter 3, you have already told UltraDev how to contact and log in to your FTP server. Figure 6-2 reviews that procedure.

Just as in the earlier example, there is a set of goals to accomplish with UltraDev's FTP client implementation. You need to connect to the site, log in, move around, and upload and download files. Depending on whether you are using UltraDev 1 or UltraDev 4, your buttons may look a little different, but their general placement and effect are the same.

To connect to your FTP server, click the Connect button in the Site window. Figure 6-3 shows the toolbar from UltraDev 4 with the Connect button pressed. Since you have identified your server, the remote directory, and your username and password in your site definition, a lot of work is done for you when you press the Connect button. The server is located, initial contact is made, the request for a username and password is received and responded to automatically, and you are deposited into the remote

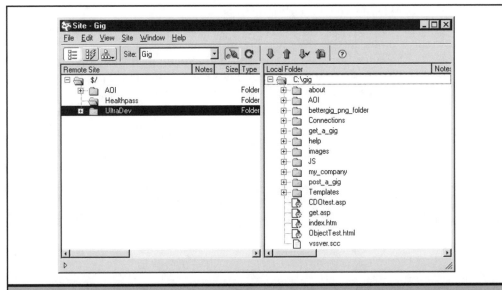

Figure 6-1.   *The Site window in UltraDev provides access to FTP functionality*

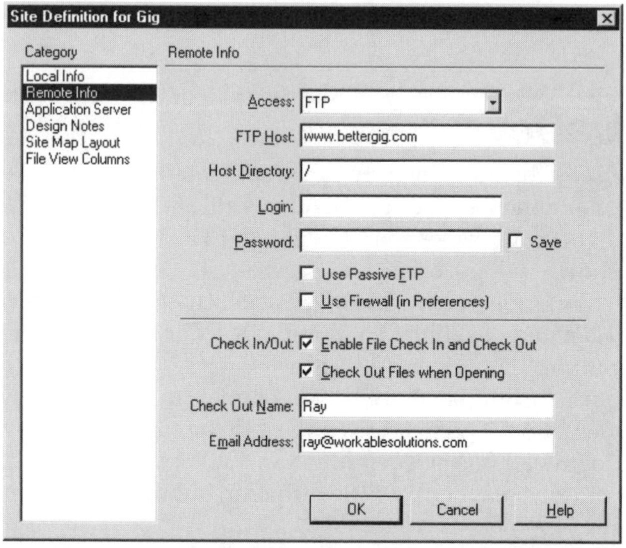

Figure 6-2. *Use the Remote Info section of your Site Definition to identify your FTP server, username, and password*

directory that you have requested. You have already selected your site on your local computer, and it has a local working directory assigned to it. So, one button press has taken the place of at least five manual commands.

Once connected, your local site structure is displayed on the right (by default) and your remote site is on the left, as shown in Figure 6-4.

Now, instead of having to type in commands to navigate your directory structure, you can treat the two site structures just as you work the Windows Explorer, selecting and opening directories by clicking and double-clicking them.

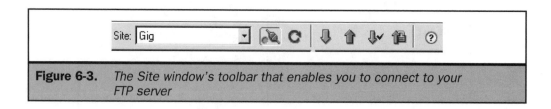

Figure 6-3. *The Site window's toolbar that enables you to connect to your FTP server*

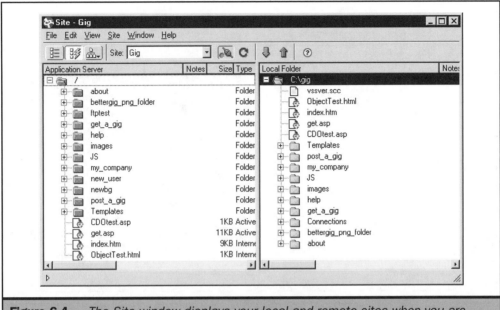

Figure 6-4. *The Site window displays your local and remote sites when you are connected to the FTP server*

Getting and Putting Files

Once you are connected and can navigate around the site, you can begin to publish your site. If you have developed your site completely within UltraDev, publishing can be as easy as the click of a button. If, however, you have files and images scattered throughout the hard drive on your development computer, you may need to publish by piecemeal to get all of the files in the correct place.

If you have been following along, you probably have a single directory on your hard drive that contains your entire site, including images, templates, and any additional support files that you may need for the site to operate. The first time you log in to your FTP server to publish your site, you will likely encounter an empty directory that you, your system administrator, or ISP created and tied to your domain name. This directory will serve as the repository for your site files.

During this first visit, you may need to publish the entirety of your site (or at least what you have completed up to this point). To do so, highlight the root directory in your local site tree, as shown in Figure 6-5.

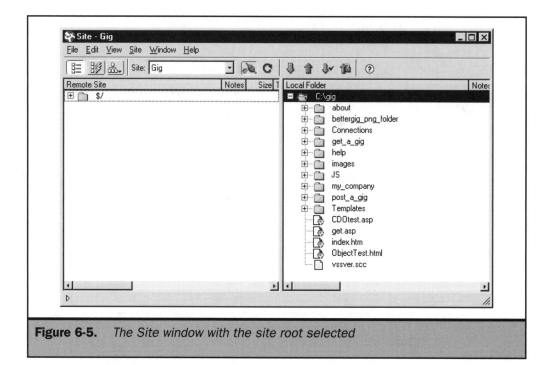

Figure 6-5.   *The Site window with the site root selected*

With the root highlighted, click the Put button indicated previously in Figure 6-3. UltraDev will ask you to confirm that you want to upload the entire site. When you acknowledge that you do, it will upload the site to the remote server.

You can follow the same procedure to upload a single directory of files or a single file. Just keep in mind that whatever you select, as well as anything beneath it in the file structure (meaning any files with a selected directory), will be uploaded. Navigate to and highlight whatever it is that you want to move, click the Put button, and the procedure will be complete.

As a shortcut, you can often double-click the file that you want to transfer. If you do so on the local side, the file will be uploaded; if you do so on the remote side, the file will be downloaded to your local machine.

Getting files from the remote location works just as easily. Highlight a file or directory on the remote side of the Site window and click the Get button indicated in Figure 6-3. The items you have selected will be downloaded to your local computer.

Synchronizing Files

If you are working on more than one development computer, you may get into a situation in which you have site files spread over more locations than just a development machine and your server. In these cases, it is very important that you keep all of the site files synchronized. Imagine the wasted effort if you spend hours on modifications at your office computer and then overwrite them with an older file on your home computer.

UltraDev has a Synchronize function that you can access from the Site | Synchronize menu to help you keep your files up to date. When you select this menu option, you are presented with the dialog box shown in Figure 6-6.

In the dialog box, you can choose to synchronize the entire site you are working on or only the files you have selected. You can also choose how you want to synchronize by filling in the Direction text box with one of the following:

- Put newer files to remote
- Get newer files from remote
- Get and put newer files

The last of these options (Get and put newer files) ensures that both locations have the newest and most updated files.

The last option in the dialog box asks if you want to delete files from the remote site that have been deleted locally. While this can keep your remote site clean and free of extraneous files, make sure you only use it when your local site contains a full and complete copy of the site as it should exist.

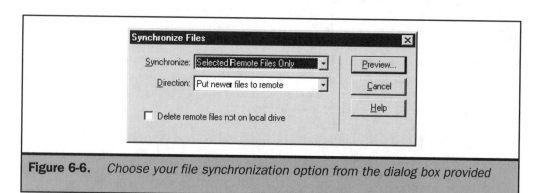

Figure 6-6.   *Choose your file synchronization option from the dialog box provided*

Versioning and Source Control

Two facts regarding Web development are indisputable:

- Sites are getting larger and more complex.
- Because of this, they are increasingly developed and maintained by teams of programmers and designers rather than lone-person operations.

These facts raise a number of issues for the development team:

- How to make sure that files are not edited by more than one programmer at a time
- How to make sure the latest, most accurate versions of your files are published to the Web
- How to allow centralized access to files by all team members

UltraDev 4 offers three ways to answer these questions:

- Check in/check out
- Microsoft SourceSafe
- WebDAV

Check In/Check Out

When you define your site in UltraDev, you have the opportunity to enable its check in/check out functionality. Checking files in and out protects their integrity by making sure that only one person can edit them at a time. A file that is checked into the system is available to be opened, edited, and saved by any developer with access to the site. A checked out file is locked from other developers until the person who checked it out is finished and checks it back in. When you consider the disaster that would occur if two people were editing a file at the same time and overwriting each other's changes, the benefit of being able to check out files is obvious.

To enable File Check In and Check Out, check the appropriate box at the bottom of the Remote Info tab of the Site Definition window, shown in Figure 6-7.

You will be asked to enter a name and an e-mail address. The name will be attached to any files you have checked out so that other users can identify who is working on the file. The e-mail address is also indicated next to the checked-out file and can be used to contact you regarding the file.

When File Check In/Out is enabled, the status of the remote file is checked each time you try to open a file. Rather than simply opening the file from the local site, UltraDev connects to the remote server and checks the availability of the file. If it is not being edited by another user, you will be able to open the file and the remote file will be marked with a lock file that indicates who has it checked out. When you've finished working with the file, you can check it back in and it will be available to other users.

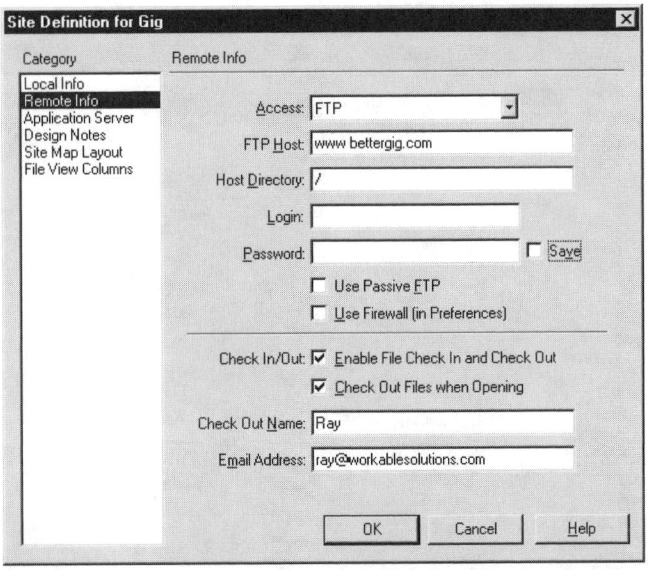

Figure 6-7.   *The Remote Info section with File Check In enabled*

It is important to note that UltraDev does not make the remote file read-only in any real, universal sense. Another FTP application could easily overwrite the file since it does not understand the instructions given to it by the UltraDev lock file. To implement more stringent source control, you must migrate to a product designed to enforce file integrity, such as Microsoft's SourceSafe.

Microsoft Visual SourceSafe

Microsoft SourceSafe is a true source control environment that ships with Microsoft Visual Studio. It has both client and server components that manage user accounts and enforce file integrity during the development process. UltraDev 4 integrates with SourceSafe through its Remote Info section of the Site Definition window.

Note   *In order to use Microsoft SourceSafe, you must have its components installed on a server and your client machine. The SourceSafe administrator will set up a working directory, username, and password so that you can access and utilize the features of the system. Make sure that this is done and that you have that information available to you before attempting to set UltraDev to use SourceSafe.*

In the Remote Info section of the Site Definition window, where you set FTP as your access point before, set the Access to SourceSafe database, as shown in Figure 6-8.
Click the Settings button to display the dialog box shown in Figure 6-9.

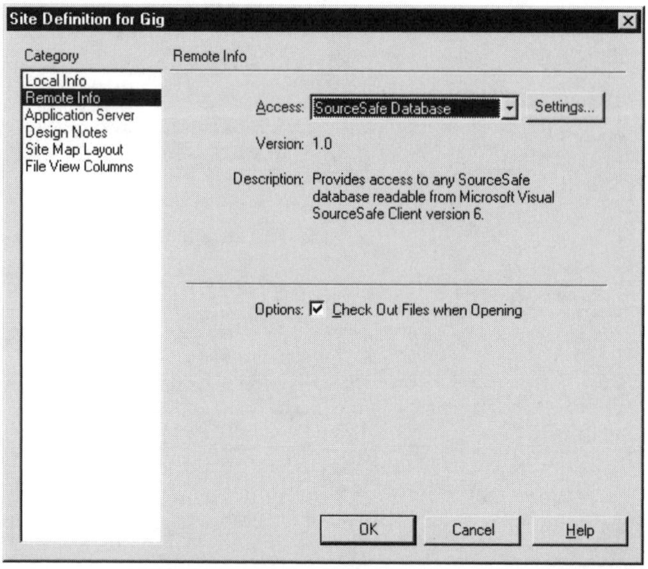

Figure 6-8. *Set SourceSafe as your access point in the Site Definition window*

You may browse your network to locate the SourceSafe database you wish to use. Ask your system administrator if you are unsure about its location. Enter the project name that was assigned in SourceSafe, and the username and password that was assigned to you, and click OK to save.

When you connect to your remote site at this point, you are connecting to the SourceSafe project that you specified, not to a remote FTP site. When you open files, they are checked out of the SourceSafe database and are not available to any other

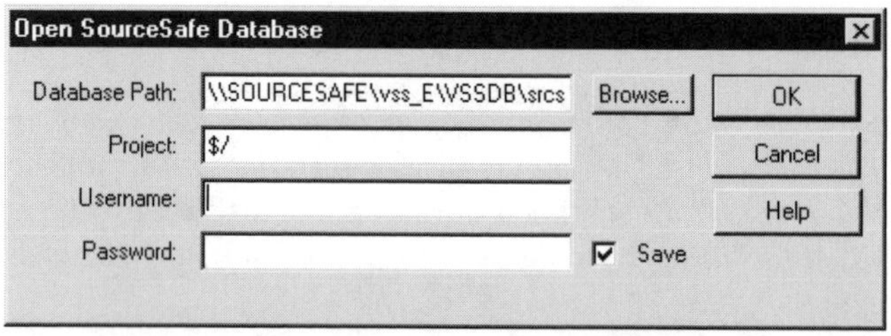

Figure 6-9. *The SourceSafe Settings dialog box*

users until you check them back in. When you are ready to publish your site to the FTP server, you will need to change your settings to allow FTP access or use a third-party FTP client application.

WebDAV

WebDAV stands for Web-based Distributed Authoring and Versioning. It is a set of HTTP extensions that allows you to establish a source control directory that is available from anywhere over the Web. There are open-source WebDAV implementations available at www.webdav.org.

Once you (or an administrator) have established a WebDAV site and you have been assigned a username and password, setup is much like the SourceSafe setup covered earlier. Select WebDAV in the Access portion of the Remote Info section of the Site Definition window, as seen in Figure 6-10.

Click Settings, and the dialog box in Figure 6-11 appears.

Enter the URL of the WebDAV server, your username and password, and an e-mail address. This e-mail address will be displayed in conjunction with your checked-out files so that you can be contacted by other users.

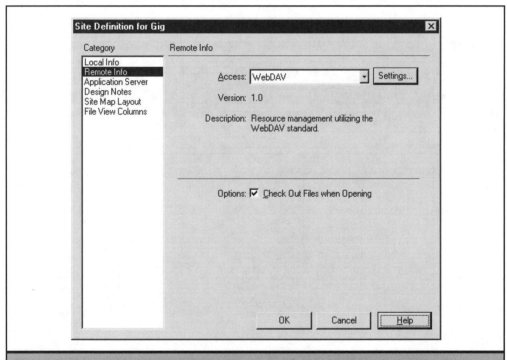

Figure 6-10.   *Select the WebDAV option in the Remote Info section of the Site Definition window*

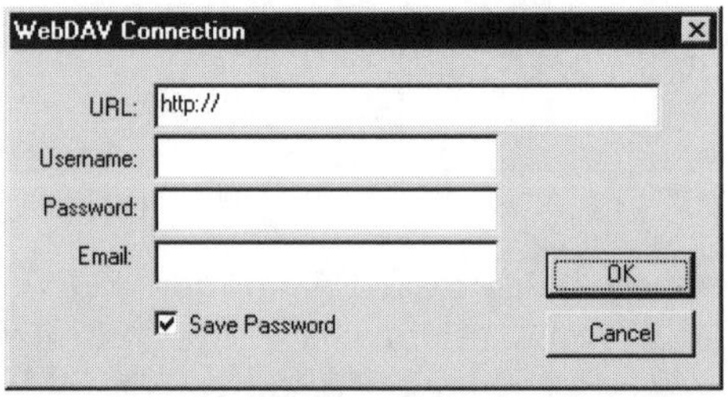

Figure 6-11. *The Settings dialog box for WebDAV*

Other FTP Clients

While UltraDev's FTP access is convenient and powerful, some people prefer to use a third-party FTP application for any number of personal reasons. You have several choices, many of which can be seen and evaluated at sites like www.tucows.com. A couple of popular options include WSFTP and CuteFTP, as shown in Figure 6-12.

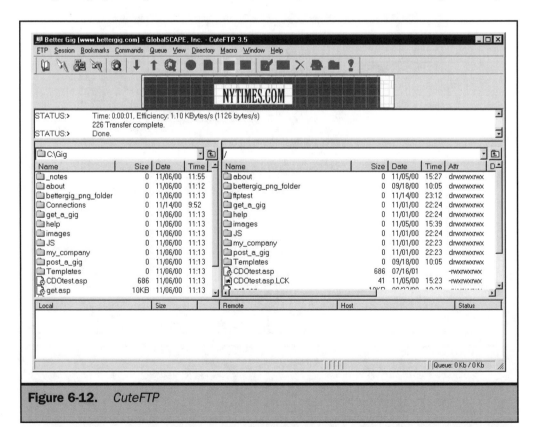

Figure 6-12. *CuteFTP*

Most of these work in a very similar fashion to UltraDev's FTP client, and you should have no trouble getting up to speed with whatever you select.

Summary

In this chapter, we covered many options related to site management and publishing, including the basics of FTP, the UltraDev FTP client functionality, and source and versioning control. By now, you have completed the basic design of your site and a few of the pages that will make up your site. As we move forward, we will discuss the addition of data access to the work that you have completed, and guide you through the languages and technologies you have selected to use for your site.

The
Complete
Reference

UltraDev

Part II

An Introduction to Web Scripting

The Complete Reference

UltraDev

Chapter 7

Developing a Web Application

Up to this point, you've been able to do some rather powerful things without a lot of programming. Even without knowing much HTML, you can use the objects and Behaviors in UltraDev to build sophisticated Web sites. But static HTML is not why you bought UltraDev, and it's not the state of the Web today.

Today's Internet is a dynamic, interactive, happening place to be. On the Web, you can plan and book your next vacation, download and listen to music, buy gifts for your favorite UltraDev author, and get information about just about anything you need to know. Try sitting in front of the television with your laptop in your lap, acting like you're working, while "Who Wants to Be a Millionaire" is on. Your family will be quite impressed when you correctly answer each and every question thanks to a quick search on Hotbot.

But the Web was not always such a dynamic place. The earliest uses were really just for information sharing between workers and researchers, and were based around protocols such as UNIX to UNIX Copy (UUCP) and File Transfer Protocol (FTP). The idea was simply to get a file of information from one place to another so that someone else could open and use it and then send it back to you.

HTML

Eventually, the idea of actually being able to display the information upon request led to the development of the HTML tag language. HTML was intended as a hierarchical organization method, which explains the entire <H1> <H2> structure. This is an important point to grasp. HTML was never intended to be a display language capable of the intricate graphical product that Web users have grown used to. Its purpose was to allow the viewing of information in an outline form based on the hierarchy that was described in the tags.

Note *Consider the importance of this point as the Web stretches its boundaries into appliances and platforms that are not strictly display based. For instance, how do you imagine that a Web browser that converts the text of a Web site into speech for a visually impaired user would handle a <bold> or <italics> tag? The original HTML specifications, as primitive as they may seem, are actually better suited to these applications. The <strong> directive of the earlier specifications likely would be more meaningful to a speech converter than would <bold>. Although you could certainly program your new-age application to respond to the <bold> tag however you would like, the word "bold" has a specific connotation in the publishing world—that of a heavier typeface. The word "strong," on the other hand, has a more universal connotation—that of additional emphasis that could be handled by a color change on a simple terminal or increased volume on a speech interpreter.*

Remember that the birth of HTML was coming about at a time when desktop publishing was gaining popularity. Programs such as PageMaker and Ventura

Publisher made it possible to create pixel-perfect designs for advertising or publishing. While the Web offered a tremendous opportunity for distributing content to a wide audience, HTML just didn't provide the control that many designers required.

For a long time, the graphical wizards of Web design were forced to find workarounds to enable them the design control they needed to make the Internet interesting to look at. Perhaps the most popular "hack" that gave them that control was the way in which tables have been used over the past several years.

Tables were originally intended as a means of viewing related data in a logical columnar format. Using the <table> tags, you can define a table and its properties, such as the width of the border and whether is takes up a set number of pixels in width or takes up a certain percentage of the screen. Within the table, the <tr> (table row tag) controls the creation of rows, and the <td> tag controls the creation and population of table cells within a row. The following code sets up a table that lists the positions within a company, and the people who fill those positions:

```
<html>
<head>

<title>Table Example</title>
<meta http-equiv="Content-Type" content="text/html; charset=iso-8859-1">

</head>

<body bgcolor="#FFFFFF">

<table width="75%" border="1">

  <tr>
    <td>President</td>
    <td>Jim Wagner</td>
  </tr>

  <tr>
    <td>Vice President</td>
    <td>Jane Grier</td>
  </tr>

  <tr>
    <td>Secretary</td>
    <td>Albert Luffman</td>
```

```
    </tr>

    <tr>
      <td>Treasurer</td>
      <td>Roy Thompson</td>
    </tr>

    <tr>
      <td>Manager</td>
      <td>Theresa Franklin</td>
    </tr>

  </table>

  </body>

  </html>
```

When displayed in a browser, the previous code looks like Figure 7-1.

Not very exciting, but certainly functional. You can, of course, set additional properties within the tags of the table to adjust for background colors, fonts, typefaces, and so forth. You can even set specific widths for cells within the table, which prompted the idea that if you could set specific pixel widths, you could use tables to approximate a page's layout— especially because you can set the border attribute to 0, making the

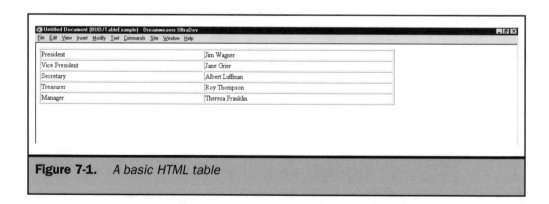

Figure 7-1.   *A basic HTML table*

table's borders invisible. Use of tables as a layout tool grew from there. More recent HTML specifications have included such tags as <colspan> and <rowspan> to allow individual cells to spread out over multiple rows and columns.

Even with the advent of Cascading Style Sheets (CSS) as a presentation language, which will be covered shortly, HTML tables remain a popular method of designing a page layout because they are supported by earlier browser implementations and are relatively lightweight in the bytes they add to a file. UltraDev enables you to either develop in tables or do your layout in CSS layers and then convert it to tables. But these fancy uses make for quite convoluted table layouts, which are nothing like the simple example provided earlier. Figure 7-2 shows the table structure that is required to properly display the Bettergig.com home page.

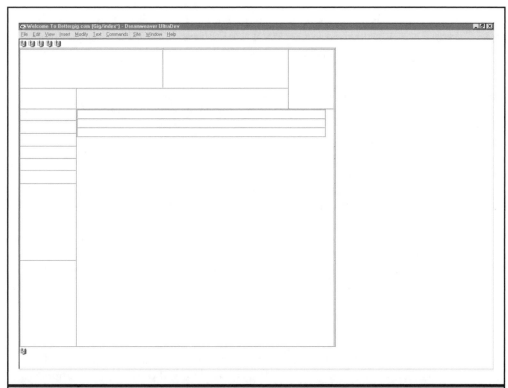

Figure 7-2.   *The complicated table structure used to display the Bettergig.com home page*

Cascading Style Sheets

Everything that HTML is not from a presentation standpoint, CSS tries to be. CSS gives the designer the power to control design in a manner that is impossible using just HTML. From precise margins to pixel-perfect spacing to fonts and typefaces, CSS is becoming the layout method of choice for today's designers.

As important as the power that CSSs provide is the fact that they separate the organization of Web content from its presentation. Instead of having to embed presentational commands within the actual HTML script, the CSS commands that control the layout of the content exist more as wrappers, allowing content developers and designers to work independently, and allowing the same content to be displayed differently in different contexts.

The concept of separating content from presentation is an important one. It is the same idea that spawned the separation of static content from data and led developers out of the difficult world of CGI scripts. More on that shortly.

CSSs also restore some control over the final display of pages, which developers had lost with HTML. Often, the final output of a page was dependent on settings in the end user's browser, including the type size selection and available fonts. The fact that CSSs "cascade" is an important aspect of their power. CSSs can be set as "global" to a site, meaning that they cascade down the site tree to the pages below. Those pages can, however, have local style sheets that override the global settings. Also, in certain circumstances, a developer's settings can override the end user's preferences, allowing for a more faithful presentation of the intended look and feel of the site.

As powerful as all of this technology is, though, it's still only static Web content. The real excitement is dynamic content—specifically, content that responds to a user's actions and involves content fed by databases. As with the presentational side of the Web, the generation of dynamic content has undergone an evolution that began with the CGI script.

CGI Scripts

One of the first attempts to make Web content dynamic came in the form of CGI programming. CGI stands for *Common Gateway Interface* and describes a method by which a browser can request information from an executed program rather than a simple HTML text file. Typically, a Web server has a directory usually called cgi-bin, which means that the directory holds CGI programs. Its permissions are set so that programs within the directory can be executed. These programs can be written in a number of different languages.

For instance, consider a very simple example that outputs a message to the screen. In HTML, it might be as simple as the following:

```
<html>

<body>

<h1>The browser sees this as HTML.</h1>

</body>

</html>
```

If you wanted to re-create this output from a CGI script, you might use one of several languages, discussed next.

C

One of the earliest CGI programming languages was C. It is powerful and widely used, and is a compiled language, which adds to its speed of execution. To get the same output from a C program, it might look like this:

```
#include <stdio.h>

int main()
{

  printf("Content-type: text/html\n\n");

  printf("<html>\n");

  printf("<body>\n");

  printf("<h1>The browser sees this as HTML</h1>\n");

  printf("</body>\n");

  printf("</html>\n");

  return 0;

}
```

That is too complicated a way to do simple HTML output, but remember that this is just an example. What it does illustrate clearly is how wrapped up in the logical the content becomes when you program this way. Any change to the text would require the editing and recompiling of the C program. As quick as C is, that is a lot of maintenance overhead. The search for an easier way led to script languages that can also be executed from a CGI directory.

Perl

One of the first scripting languages used in CGI programming was Perl. Perl was developed by a man named Larry Wall, whose goal was to include everything from other languages that was cool, and to exclude everything that was not. The same script in Perl looks like this:

```
#! /usr/bin/perl

print "Content-type: text/html\n\n";

print "<html><body><h1>The browser sees this as HTML.";

print "</h1></body></html>\n";
```

Easier to write, edit, and maintain, Perl improves upon the CGI concept. Perl, however, is an interpreted language, You will notice the first line of the script, which is a pointer to the Perl interpreter that resides on the server. What Perl gains in manageability, it gives up in processing speed compared to a compiled C program. Still, it is a worthwhile tradeoff when the name of the game is keeping your code up to date in the simplest way possible.

Other Scripting Languages

Since the introduction of Perl, other scripting languages have emerged as popular CGI scripting languages, such as Tcl and Python. While the syntax is often different, the concept of the easily maintained script at the core of the CGI program remains intact with these other implementations.

The real usefulness of CGI scripting is seen in its ability to handle all the dynamic things that you might want a site to do: handling forms, sending e-mail, and interacting with databases. CGI was one of the first ways that these things became possible. But CGI has its limitations.

The Problem with CGI

CGI programs are executed in response to a request by a browser. They do their work and then go away. Each time a new request comes in, a new program is spawned, and then it goes away when its job is completed. What's more, a CGI program's definition of "its job" is much narrower than you would like it to be. For instance, regular CGI scripts have no way to maintain the state of a visitor. So, if you are using CGI to implement a shopping cart, the program does not know from page to page what the shopper has done or seen or purchased earlier in the visit, without some help. Usually, the script uses information stored in a database or text table of some sort to keep track of visitors. By placing a cookie on the user's computer, the script can track that user as he or she moves through the system. The overhead of this continuous database access is stifling, though, and can easily impact your Web server.

Attempts have been made to improve on CGI, specifically through a process known as *Fast CGI*. Fast CGI overcame some of the issues discussed by creating programs that run continuously (more like a service responding to multiple requests), rather than shutting down after every job. Fast CGI is more difficult to maintain, however, because the program has to be shut down and restarted to implement any changes.

One of the most pressing problems with CGI was mentioned a bit earlier. Examine the previous script examples and notice how the actual HTML is embedded within the program code. Now, think about how most Web teams work. Very often, a team is made up of programmers and designers, each of whom has a task to perform that is complementary to, but very different from, one another. In most shops, designers complete the look and feel of sites and then pass them on for inclusion of the code that makes them work by the programmers. In real life, the transfer is not quite that clean; but in concept, it is an efficient way to work. How would a designer and a programmer work together if they were required to construct a program like these CGI examples? The programmer would have to sit down and type until he or she came to a design part, and then would have to trade off while the designer added some lines, and this process would continue back and forth until they finished the page. Not very efficient.

An easier way was needed, one that provides for the power of CGI with the flexibility of scripting and the separation of content from design seen in the relationship of CSS to HTML. HTML templating provides just such a method.

HTML Templating

Consider what is meant by a "template." If you need to fill out some legal paperwork, such as a simple will or a bill of sale, you might go to the office-supply store and buy a book of legal templates. These forms contain the basic language of the page, with blanks for you to fill in the specific details that pertain to your situation. HTML pages that use a templating method are very much the same.

From user to user, most of an HTML page remains the same. The basic content, the menus, the graphics—all of these elements are preset by the designer so that all visitors have a uniform experience. It is the details that differ from user to user, such as the specific account information, the package shipment detail, or the merchandise order. Given that fact, it is easy to see how a designer might build the structure of a page and then pass it to the programmer to implement the details.

For instance, if the designer wants to greet a user by name on a certain page, the designer might enter the following:

```
Hello <enter name here>
```

The programmer would then be instructed to look for all the bracketed references inserted by the designer and to implement the requested data. So, depending on the languages and methods of data access in use on the particular site, the programmer would enter the code necessary to obtain and display that user's name at that point on the page. Everything on the page remains the same for every user, except for their names. That is an HTML template.

Several languages exist that allow for the implementation of HTML templates, and three of them that make up the core of UltraDev are discussed next. A forth, PHP, is becoming as popular and may be included at some time.

ASP

Microsoft's Active Server Pages was one of the first implementations of the templating concept. ASP uses VBScript and JavaScript (or JScript, as Microsoft's implementation is known) as its scripting languages. ASP has gained wide popularity as a result of the large Visual Basic user base that exists. ASP's true power is seen in its integration with Microsoft's COM architecture. ASP is covered in detail in Chapter 8.

JSP

A newer templating implementation is Sun's Java Server Pages. JSP is built upon the Java programming language. As such, it is very secure, because its components are intended to run in *sandboxes* (secure memory spaces separated from the core of the computer so that they cannot affect its internal workings). Integral to JSP are all the components of the Java 2 Enterprise architecture, including Servlets and Beans. JSP is covered in depth in Chapter 9.

ColdFusion

Although ColdFusion is not strictly a scripting language, it takes advantage of the same concepts being discussed here. ColdFusion is really more of a tag language. Its custom tag structure defines functions that take developers many lines of code to implement in other languages. Its tag-based nature has made it extremely popular with HTML authors who are used to using tags to develop. ColdFusion is covered in Chapter 10.

PHP

As open source software such as Linux grows in popularity, open source implementations of technologies other than OSs are appearing. PHP is an open source implementation of a hypertext preprocessor that fulfills the same role as these other languages. It is available for free and is extremely popular among users of Linux, Apache, and MySQL, which has spawned the term *LAMP*—meaning a computer configured with Linux, Apache, MySQL, and PHP.

Summary

The Web has come a long way in its structure, both from a presentation perspective and a dynamic content perspective. As with any technology, it began with methods that were useful for their time, and that have been improved upon as the medium has evolved. The early roots of CGI programming have largely been supplanted by the more modern techniques, such as ASP, JSP, ColdFusion, and PHP. But without that history based in CGI, Web design would not be where it is today, and advances undoubtedly are around the corner that will make these techniques appear primitive. But you can do a lot with the languages that already are available. The next chapter examines the details of these languages and how they can be used to create and manage dynamic content on your sites.

The
Complete
Reference

Chapter 8

Active Server Pages in the UltraDev Environment

197

ince you have decided to learn how to use UltraDev, it is a pretty safe bet that you realize the incredible benefits of connecting your site to a database. While you have several options for doing so, the most popular is certainly Microsoft's Active Server Pages (ASP).

For some time, Web designers have recognized the benefits of dynamically altering their pages. For Web pages to take into account the input of a user or the data from a database table, there must be some means of changing the static HTML that makes them up. One of the first methods of doing so involved the use of Common Gateway Interface (CGI) applications. Often known as CGI scripts, these programs were written in languages such as Perl or C, and were stored in directories within your site and invoked from the URL. But, there were limitations, especially performance limitations, because of the way that CGI scripts were run.

Active Server Pages

Active Server Pages are part of a newer breed of methodologies known as *HTML templating*. An HTML template actually embeds the dynamic portions of the page within the static HTML. The static portions make up a template that is then customized by the embedded code. For instance, consider the following:

```
<html>
<head>
<title>Hello</title>
<meta http-equiv="Content-Type" content="text/html; charset=iso-8859-1">
</head>

<body bgcolor="#FFFFFF">

Hello George

</body>
</html>
```

This very simple ASP page will print "Hello George" in the Browser when run from a Web server. You can begin to make this page dynamic by removing the name "George" that is hard-coded into the page. Suppose that you want to address your visitor at several places throughout the page. Changes are good that only a very few of the visitors will actually be named "George," so you need to prepare to handle other names as well. Your first attempt might look something like this:

```
<html>

<%

Dim name

name = "George"

%>
<head>
<title>Hello</title>
<meta http-equiv="Content-Type" content="text/html; charset=iso-8859-1">
</head>

<body bgcolor="#FFFFFF">

Hello <%Response.Write name%>

</body>
</html>
```

This file will result in exactly the same browser output as the previous one. If you were to view the source of each of these pages, they would be identical. But, more certainly is going on in the second version.

The first thing you may notice is little bits of code that don't make any sense as far as HTML is concerned. What makes them work is the fact that they are enclosed in pairs of tags like these: <% %>. These tags notify the server that it has some work to do before it can send this page to the browser.

Client/Server Architecture

Everything that happens on the Web is based on a client/server architecture. The process begins when a browser (the client) requests a page from a Web server (the server). The server then returns a block of text that is interpreted and displayed by the browser. When the page is simple HTML, the contents are returned to the browser, which knows how to handle the commands and functions contained in it. When the page contains extra code like the preceding second example file, the server must perform some additional processing before the file can be returned to the browser.

Your Microsoft Web server includes a file called asp.dll, which is a dynamic link library that handles the processing of the dynamic portions of an Active Server Page. Whenever the Web server is parsing a page and comes across the <% %> tags, it calls the asp.dll file to help it interpret the enclosed code. The code enclosed in the ASP tags can do anything from complex database manipulation to the simple text handling in the previous example.

Note   *The code within the ASP tags can be a combination of ASP objects, VisualBasicScript (VBScript), and JScript. Each of these is covered in turn later in this chapter.*

So, when your page loads, the Web server takes a look at the page before sending it to the requesting browser. When it notices the ASP tags, it calls the asp.dll file to help it interpret portions of the page that the browser will not understand. Within the first pair of tags, the server comes across these directives:

```
dim name

name = "George"
```

Dim is a VBScript command that causes the dimensioning of a variable; in this case, a variable called *name*. The next line sets the string value "George" to that variable. At this point, the page has set a variable and assigned it a value, and is holding it to see what it will be asked to do with it.

Note   *In ASP, all variables are set as variants. A* variant *is a data type that can hold any type of value and manipulate it in the most logical way based on your instructions. For instance, if you were to set two variables, i and j, to the values 1 and 2, those values are stored not as integers or as strings, but as variants. If you then try to concatenate the two variables as strings (i & j), the result will be consistent with string concatenation (the string 12). If you then try to add them as integers (i + j), you would get the result that you expect (3). Variants can be very convenient to use, but can also cause trouble when dealing with databases, and whenever the specific data type and format are important to your procedure.*

The next few lines of the file won't cause any trouble for the browser, so they are sent as is in the response stream. Then, after the word "Hello", another set of tags surrounds this line:

```
Response.Write name
```

Response is an ASP object that is responsible for sending things out in the response stream. It has a Write method that causes HTML to be written to the browser.

That HTML can be defined literally as a string or expression result, or it can be defined as a variable, as it is here in the example code. The variable name holds the string value "George", so this line of code will result in the text "Hello George." The rest of the file is just HTML that the browser can parse itself, so it is sent in the response stream as is.

Note   *Response is just one of several objects in the ASP object model, all of which are discussed later in this chapter.*

Getting User Input

The page discussed in the preceding section was a little fancier, but it could still cause a problem for any site except onlygeorgesallowed.com. At the very least, you will probably want to ask your user what his name is and then address him by it. If you place a form on your page with a place for your user to enter his name, and then post that form to the following page, you will get this resulting HTML:

```
<html>
<head>
<title>Hello</title>
<meta http-equiv="Content-Type" content="text/html; charset=iso-8859-1">
</head>

<body bgcolor="#FFFFFF">

Hello George

</body>
</html>
```

This very simple ASP page will print "Hello George" in the browser when run from a Web server. You can begin to make this page dynamic by removing the name "George" that is hard-coded into the page. Suppose that you want to address your visitor at several places throughout the page. Chances are good that only a very few of the visitors will actually be named "George", so you need to prepare to handle other names as well. Your first attempt might look something like this:

```
<html
<%
Dim name

name = Request.Form("name")
%>
```

```
<head>
<title>Hello</title>
<meta http-equiv="Content-Type" content="text/html; charset=iso-8859-1">
</head>

<body bgcolor="#FFFFFF">

Hello <%Response.Write name%>

</body>
</html>
```

Notice the one small change where the value of the variable name is set. Instead of setting a literal string value, the page looks for a form element called "name" in the form that is posted to it. The value of that form element is set to the variable and is then returned later in the code.

Note *This time, another of the ASP objects was used, called Request. Whereas the Response object sends things out, the Request object is responsible for taking things in from a form, query string, cookie, or some other source. The Response object is discussed at greater length later in this chapter.*

Although ASP is often spoken of as an entity unto itself, it is actually a combination of technologies that work together to deliver dynamic page content. At the base is the HTML that serves as the static framework of the page. To that is added a series of ASP objects that can be manipulated by scripting languages such as VBScript and JScript. Finally, ASP can include a number of Active Server Components from Microsoft's ActiveX Data Objects (ADO) for data access to custom COM components that you develop in-house or get from third parties.

The ASP Object Model

Integral to the process are the ASP objects that tie together the client and the server. The following are the six ASP objects:

- Request
- Response
- Session
- Application
- Server
- ObjectContext

Because UltraDev supports the ASP 2 specification, this discussion focuses on that version. Version 3 is available with Internet Information Server on Windows 2000 Server.

The Request Object

When a browser makes a call to a server to retrieve a Web page, it is making a *request.* In addition to the name of the page it wants, the browser sends a variety of other information to the server. The added information may be intentional, such as a form post or a query string, or it may be the standard information that is passed in by the browser behind the scenes whenever it communicates with a server. Either way, the ASP Request object grabs all of that information and makes it readily available to the server.

The Request object has five collections from which it gathers all of this information:

- The QueryString collection
- The Form collection
- The ServerVariables collection
- The Cookies collection
- The ClientCertificate collection

The QueryString Collection

You are no doubt familiar with the Uniform Resource Locator (URL) used to direct your browser to the site you wish to visit. A URL contains a protocol (such as http://) and a fully qualified domain name (for example, www.macromedia.com). It may also contain a reference to the specific page that you are looking for.

A QueryString is additional information that is passed to the page you request. The information is passed in name/value pairs following a question mark. For example, a page called login.asp at the Basic-UltraDev site would be accessed with the following URL:

    http://www.basic-ultradev.com/login.asp

That page might expect a username and password to be passed in so that your visit can be validated. That username and password could be passed in a QueryString like this:

    http://www.basic-ultradev.com/login.asp?name=jim&pass=huffy

Notice the extra information in this version of the URL. Following the ? are two name/value pairs. The parameter names "name" and "pass" are assigned the values "jim" and "huffy," respectively. Each pair is separated by an ampersand (&).

You can pass parameters into any page like this. If the page doesn't expect them, they are ignored. But if the page knows what to do with this information (or even requires it to work properly), it can make use of it within the page's code. The Request object enables you to retrieve and manipulate these parameters.

To retrieve the value of a name/value pair, you can simply place the following line within ASP tags on your page:

```
Request.QueryString("name")
```

This creates a direct reference to the value for "name" ("jim," in this case). You can set this to a variable to use later, like this:

```
dim user

user = Request.QueryString("name")
```

Note *It is not strictly necessary to use the .QueryString indication in the previous example. The Request object will search through its collections to find the parameter name that you ask for. If only one instance of that parameter name exists (meaning that a form doesn't try to post a duplicate value or there is not a cookie with the same name), then a simple Request("name") will do just fine. If a duplicate value exists, the QueryString is searched first and will be used. Although not required, explicitly declaring where you expect your page to find its parameter is still more accurate and a better practice.*

You can also set multiple values to a QueryString parameter, as follows:

```
?name="jim","bob","billy"
```

You can then get a count of parameter values,

```
Request.QueryString("name").Count
```

and reference them by index:

```
Request.QueryString("name")(2)
```

The QueryString is a convenient way to pass information between pages. It enables you to use a single page destination for multiple purposes by passing in a parameter that indicates where a user came from or where the user wants to go. Remember, though, that the QueryString is available to users in the address bar of their browsers. They can see what you are passing, and can even fiddle with it by changing parameter values and resubmitting the page. This can cause a security nightmare if you do not consider ways to make sure that visitors only see information that should be available to them.

There are ways to hide the QueryString from your user by passing it in an internal page of a frameset or by opening a custom browser with no address bar. A savvy user can circumvent these efforts, though, and these techniques should not be considered a substitute for adequate security planning.

The Form Collection

The Form collection works much like the QueryString collection, except that its name/value pairs come from the elements of a form that is posted to the ASP page. While the QueryString is a great way to pass parameters that you can control, a form is much more suited to collecting input from your user and capturing it for manipulation within your code.

The form in the following illustration will be posted to a page that expects to receive values for each of its fields.

On the resulting page, you can capture all of this information into variables, as follows:

```
Dim name, address, city, state, zip, email

name = Request.Form("name")

address = Request.Form("address")

city = Request.Form("city")

state = Request.Form("state")

zip = Request.Form("zip")

email = Request.Form("email")
```

Note *Bear in mind that the parameter names that you will reference in the Forms collection refer to the names of the actual form elements on the previous page, not to the field labels. For example, you may choose to label a text field "Street Address" for your users' benefit, but name the actual text field associated with that label "StAddress." To reference this value, you would use Request.Form("StAddress").*

The ServerVariables Collection

Each time a request is sent by a client to your Web site, a wealth of information is sent along with it. You can think of this information as freebies, because you don't have to do anything extra to get it; it comes by default each time someone views one of your pages. Some of the information is supplied by the client, and some of it is supplied by the server on which the application is running. Server variables contain information about things such as the client's browser, the page that referred to your page, and even the location of your pages on the server. You can access all of this information through the Request object; and although some of it is of dubious use to the average user, some can be quite helpful to you.

Table 8-1 lists the available server variables and a description of each one.

Server Variable	Description
ALL_HTTP	All the HTTP headers sent by the client request formatted with HTTP_ in front of each capitalized header name

Table 8-1.   *The List of Server Variables Sent with Each HTTP Request*

Server Variable	Description
ALL_RAW	All of the HTTP headers sent by the client in raw form, exactly as they are sent
APPL_MD_PATH	Retrieves the metabase path for the application for the ISAPI DLL
APPL_PHYSICAL_PATH	Retrieves the actual physical path of the application by converting the metabase path to the physical directory where the application resides
AUTH_PASSWORD	The value entered into the client's authorization dialog box if Basic Authentication is used
AUTH_TYPE	The authentication type used by the client when accessing a protected area
AUTH_USER	The raw authenticated username
CERT_COOKIE	The unique ID of the client certificate
CERT_FLAGS	A 2-bit header that indicates the presence and validity of a client certificate: bit 0 set to 1 if the client certificate is present, and bit 1 set to 1 if the client certificate's certificate authority (CA) is not in the list of recognized CAs on the server (indicating that it may be invalid)
CERT_ISSUER	Issuer of the client certificate
CERT_KEYSIZE	Number of bits in the Secure Sockets Layer key, e.g., 128 for 128-bit encryption
CERT_SECRETKEYSIZE	Number of bits in the server certificate private key
CERT_SERIALNUMBER	The serial number of the client certificate
CERT_SERVER_ISSUER	Issuer of the server certificate
CERT_SERVER_SUBJECT	Subject of the server certificate
CERT_SUBJECT	Subject of the client certificate
CONTENT_LENGTH	The content length as given by the client

Table 8-1. *The List of Server Variables Sent with Each HTTP Request* (continued)

Server Variable	Description
CONTENT_TYPE	The type of data that makes up the content, such as GET, POST, or PUT
GATEWAY_INTERFACE	The revision of the CGI specification used by the server
HTTP_ACCEPT	The value of the ACCEPT header
HTTP_ACCEPT_LANGUAGE	The language used for displaying content
HTTP_USER_AGENT	Information concerning the browser that sent the request
HTTP_COOKIE	The cookie string that was sent with the request
HTTP_REFERER	The URL of the original request when a redirect has occurred
HTTPS	ON if the request came through SSL (a secure channel) or OFF if it came through a nonsecure channel
HTTPS_KEYSIZE	Number of bits in the SSL layer connection key
HTTPS_SECRETKEYSIZE	Number of bits in the server certificate private key
HTTPS_SERVER_ISSUER	Issuer of the server certificate
HTTPS_SERVER_SUBJECT	Subject field of the server certificate
INSTANCE_ID	The ID of the IIS instance to which the request belongs
INSTANCE_META_PATH	The metabase path of the IIS instance that will respond to the request
LOCAL_ADDR	The server address to which the request came
LOGON_USER	The Windows account that the user is logged in to
PATH_INFO	Any extra path information sent by the client
PATH_TRANSLATED	The translated path after any virtual-to-physical mapping is completed

Table 8-1.   *The List of Server Variables Sent with Each HTTP Request* (continued)

Server Variable	Description
QUERY_STRING	Information following the ? in the HTTP request
REMOTE_ADDR	The IP address of the remote host that sent the request
REMOTE_HOST	The name of the remote host that sent the request
REMOTE_USER	The username string sent by the user unmodified by authentication filters
REQUEST_METHOD	The method used to make the request, i.e., GET, HEAD, or POST
SCRIPT_NAME	The virtual path to the script being executed
SERVER_NAME	The server's name or IP address used in self-referencing URLs
SERVER_PORT	The port number to which the request was sent
SERVER_PORT_SECURE	Returns 1 if the request is being handled on a secure port, or 0 if being handled on a nonsecure port
SERVER_PROTOCOL	The name and revision of the request information protocol
SERVER_SOFTWARE	The name and version number of the server software that answers the request
URL	The base portion of the URL

Table 8-1. *The List of Server Variables Sent with Each HTTP Request* (continued)

Perhaps it would be useful if you could view a listing of the actual HTTP headers that are generated by a request to one of your pages. The following script can be saved as an ASP page and loaded onto your server. Open a browser and navigate to the page, and you will see a list of server variables and the values they hold live from your site.

```
<!DOCTYPE HTML PUBLIC "-//W3C//DTD HTML 4.0 Transitional//EN">

<HTML>
```

```
<HEAD>

<TITLE> The ServerVariables Collection </TITLE>

</HEAD>

<BODY BGCOLOR="#FFFFFF">

<TABLE BORDER = 1>
<TR><TD><B>Variable Name</B></TD> <TD><B>Value</B></TD></TR>
<% for each key in Request.ServerVariables %>
<TR>
<TD><% = key %></TD>
<TD>
<% if Request.ServerVariables(key) = " " then
     Response.Write "No Information"
     else
     Response.Write Request.ServerVariables(key)
end if
%>

</TD>

</TR>

<% next %>

</BODY>
</HTML>
```

Similar to the way in which you access information with other collections, you can access ServerVariable collection information as follows:

```
Request.ServerVariables("header")
```

where "header" is the name of the variable you want to access. Some server variables just supply you with information. It may even be information you already know. For instance, you could access the Server_Software variable like this:

```
Request.ServerVariables("SERVER_SOFTWARE")
```

This would return information about the name and version of the software on the server that was receiving the request. For instance, IIS 5 might return "Microsoft-IIS/5.0." But, you probably already knew what software your server was running; and even if you didn't, you could easily find out without checking the server variables each time.

Your visitor's browser, however, is something that is likely to change with each new user. Depending on what features your site uses, it may be important for you to be aware of the capabilities of the browser that is trying to view your site. Information like this enables you to redirect visitors with browsers that do not conform to certain specifications either to a site that is friendly to their browser or to a message informing them that their visit will be hampered by the software they are using.

The information you need to do this is in the USER_AGENT variable, which you access like this:

```
Request.ServerVariables("USER_AGENT")
```

This will return information like the following:

Mozilla/4.0 (compatible; MSIE 5.0; Windows 98; DigExt)

indicating that Microsoft Internet Explorer is being used on a Windows 98 computer. By checking the contents of this variable in your server-side code, your initial page can make decisions about how to handle requests coming from a variety of browsers.

For now, it is mainly important that you understand what kind of information is available to you in the ServerVariables collection. As you become a proficient ASP programmer, you will come across uses for this information, and it will be good that you are aware of what is available to you.

The Cookies Collection

The use of cookies has created much hoopla over the past several years. Apparently, people want a highly interactive Web experience, but object to the tiny files called "cookies" that help make that possible. However, cookies play an important role in a site's ability to offer a personalized experience for its users. They make the Web more interesting and more convenient for most users. The risk of a security breach is overblown, which becomes obvious when you understand how cookies work.

Cookies are nothing but small text files that reside in a directory on your user's computer. Each browser has a special directory in which it keeps cookies. As a result, a computer may have more than one directory of files, each associated with a particular brand of browser. These files store information about a user that relates to the site that creates the cookie. It could be a username and password, or the user's choice of a colored background that he prefers when visiting the site. Anything that can be expressed as a name/value pair in a small text file can be written to a cookie by an application and later retrieved.

Note *You may have seen sites with a "Remember Me" check box near the username and password entry fields. If you select this box when you log in, you will likely not need to use your password to gain access next time. Your user information is written to a cookie on your computer, and the site simply queries for your identity the next time you visit. This is very convenient, but it can also risk revealing information or allowing access to private information if others use your computer. If they were to visit the same site, the cookie information would still be read and they would be permitted to use the site as if they were you.*

The number and size of cookies on a user's computer have limits. An individual cookie cannot be larger than 4K, and no more than 300 cookies can be on the computer at a time. Each cookie over 300 knocks one off the list at the other end, so that you end up with a rolling directory of the most recently set cookies. A little math will tell you that the most space cookies can take is a little over a megabyte, but it is extremely rare that a single cookie reaches anywhere near the 4K limit, so the actual impact is much smaller.

Note *The fact that cookies are stored on a user's computer, and are stored separately for each browser that the user may use, means that cookies are not universal to a visitor's use of your site. If they use a different computer or even a different browser, the information you store about them will not be accessible to your application. It is important that you consider how you can gracefully handle a user's visit regardless of whether information is available about them.*

An important point to remember is that a Web application can read only the cookies that it wrote itself. So, a rogue application cannot read the information on the user's computer and glean password information for another site.

Cookies are read using the Request object, much like the other collections. Use the following format to read a cookie that was set previously:

```
Request.Cookies("cookiename")
```

The section on the Response object will look at how to set cookies.

The ClientCertificate Collection

You may have heard of Secure Sockets Layer (SSL), the protocol that allows for secure, encrypted communication across the Internet. SSL uses certificates to verify the legitimacy of the client and the server and to encrypt and decrypt information as it is sent back and forth. For the client computer to identify itself to a secure server application, it sends a client certificate along with its ASP page request. The particulars of this certificate can be accessed with the Request object.

Table 8-2 lists information that is sent with each client certificate.

Field	Description
Certificate	The entire set of certificate information in one stream
Flags	Additional information about the certificate, such as whether the issuer is recognized
Issuer	A string of values about the issuer listed in subfields— primarily, names and locations of the certificate issuers
SerialNumber	A string representation of the certificate's serial number
Subject	A string of subfields that lists information about the subject of a certificate
ValidFrom	A date that the certificate becomes valid
ValidUntil	A date until which the certificate is valid

Table 8-2.   *The Properties of the ClientCertificate Collection*

You can access portions of the ClientCertificates collection in the same manner as you access the other collections. For instance,

```
Request.ClientCertificate("SerialNumber")
```

would return the serial number of the certificate sent with the Request object.

An interactive Web site is all about communication with the users. The Request object helps make that communication effective by giving you a means of retrieving information from their computers, their input, and their requests. But good communication must be two-way. The Response object helps you complete the loop by providing ways to talk back to your users that make for a satisfying experience.

The Response Object

What the Request object is to receiving information, the Response object is to sending it out. Whether you simply need to write information into the user's browser or direct them off to another location, you can send information and commands back to your visitor's browser by using the Response object. This section covers four main methods of the Response object:

- Buffer
- Write
- Redirect
- Content Expiration

The Buffer Method

The Buffer method of the Response object controls how content is sent back to the browser. You can think of the data that is sent by a Web server in response to a request by a browser as a stream of information. Like a stream of water, the information that is sent out first reaches the destination before information that is sent after it; often just milliseconds before, but still before. After some data has been sent back to the browser and a page has begun construction, you no longer can do some things. For instance, consider the following code:

```
<!DOCTYPE HTML PUBLIC "-//W3C//DTD HTML 4.0 Transitional//EN">
<HTML>
<%

Dim X

X=53

%>

<HEAD>
<TITLE> Buffer Example </TITLE>
</HEAD>

<BODY BGCOLOR="#FFFFFF">

This is a test page to show how the HTML stream can be affected by your ASP code

<%

If x = 53 Then

Response.Redirect ("SomeOtherPage.asp")

End If
```

```
%>

</BODY>
</HTML>
```

Note   *The Redirect method of the Response object and the If ...Then constructor are covered later in this chapter in the section "Conditional Statements."*

This code will cause your application to fail with an error to the user that headers have already been written to the page. Basically, this means that since some information has already been sent out the HTML stream to the browser, the page is no longer able to obey the Response.Redirect directive, which tells it to send the user to another Web page altogether as long as X = 53. After a page has been started, a command like that is not allowed.

The problem is that you may well encounter times when you need to get into the processing of the ASP page itself before you will know whether a condition exists that requires the user to be redirected. The key is to complete all the necessary processing before sending the HTML stream to the browser. This can be accomplished by the use of the Buffer property of the Response object.

The following is the same code with one minor alteration:

```
<!DOCTYPE HTML PUBLIC "-//W3C//DTD HTML 4.0 Transitional//EN">
<html>
<%
Response.Buffer = true
Dim X

X=53

%>

<head>
<title> Buffer Example </title>
</head>

<body BGCOLOR="#FFFFFF">

This is a test page to show how the HTML stream can be affected by your ASP code

<%

If x = 53 Then

Response.Redirect ("SomeOtherPage.asp")
```

```
End If

%>

</body>
</html>
```

Notice, two lines after the <HTML> tag, the following line:

```
Response.Buffer = true
```

This line tells the ASP page that no information should be sent to the browser until the entire page has been processed. It holds the entire HTML stream in a buffer until all the code is run and all the decisions have been made. Then, it sends the entire thing at once. This allows for the interruption of processing by things such as a redirect command that causes the early parts of the response to be ignored in favor of sending the user to an alternate page for some reason.

Under normal circumstances, the pages would then be buffered until the code was completed, and then the result would be released to the browser and displayed. Sometimes, however, you may want portions of the buffer released prior to the completion of the code. If, for instance, a particular operation is time-consuming, you may want to first send a message to the browser indicating that code is running and that the user should stand by. Then, the intensive portion will be processed into the buffer so that it will be delivered all at once, and not piecemeal. You can precisely control at what points during your page's processing buffered information is released to the browser by using the Flush method, as follows:

```
Response.Flush
```

When this command is encountered, all buffered information is sent out the HTML stream and subsequent processing is buffered until the page completes or another Flush is encountered. If you want to flush the buffer and stop processing the page at that point, you can use the following:

```
Response.End
```

The only difference is that the page ceases processing at the point at which the End method is called.

You may also have occasion to clear a portion of the buffer if, for example, some condition exists that means a subset of a page's processing should not be released to the browser. Response.Clear will clear any portion of the buffer since the last flush was called, but it will clear body information only, not header information.

The Write Method

Now that you know how the HTML stream works, you will be interested to know how you can use ASP to insert items into it based on the processing of your page. The Write method of the Response object can be used to insert information into your pages. For instance,

```
Response.Write variable
```

will write the value of the variable into the text stream wherever it occurs. The following is a slight alteration of the example previously being used:

```
<!DOCTYPE HTML PUBLIC "-//W3C//DTD HTML 4.0 Transitional//EN">
<html>
<%

Dim X

X=53

%>

<head>
<title> Write Example </title>
</head>

<body BGCOLOR="#FFFFFF">

This is a test page to show how the Write method works.
<br><br>

<%

Response.Write "The value of X is " & x

%>

</body>
</html>
```

This code shows four ways to get information written back to the browser. The first is the straight HTML at the beginning of the <body> tag. You should be familiar with HTML text at this point.

The other three ways are within the Response.Write just before the closing <body> tag. You can use the Write method to return a literal string by enclosing that string in double quotes. You can also get the Write method to return the value of a variable by referencing that variable's name, as was done with the variable X in the preceding code. Last, you can concatenate the two methods as the following does to end up with an actual line of text:

The value of X is 53

In this method, any portion of the string that is a literal value or that you want interpreted as HTML must be enclosed in strings. For example,

Response.Write

would return an error. To get an HTML break within a Response.Write call, the <br> tag must be in quotes, like this:

Response.Write "<br>"

Because VBScript is being used here, the & character is used to concatenate the strings. In JScript or JavaScript, you can do the same thing by using the + operator.

You can also use a shortcut method to write the value of a variable, like this:

```
<% = X %>
```

This line would simply write "53" to the browser. This method is best used when the data you are writing is self-explanatory, such as <% = Now %> to write the time, or when it is in conjunction with other formatting that makes the values that you are displaying meaningful.

The Redirect Method

Often, you'll need to send users to other pages within your application based on their input or the processing of the data that they submit. The Redirect method of the Response object enables you to do server-side redirection to the page of your choice.

A good example of this would be a username and password verification that you might use to secure portions of your site. Consider the following code:

```
<!DOCTYPE HTML PUBLIC "-//W3C//DTD HTML 4.0 Transitional//EN">
<html>
<%

Dim username, password
```

```
username = Request.Form("user")
password = Request.Form("pass")

If username = "tommy" AND password = "3245" Then

Response.Redirect ("success.asp")

Else

Response.Redirect ("fail.asp")

%>

<head>
<title> Redirect Example </title>
</head>

<body BGCOLOR="#FFFFFF">

</body>
</html>
```

This is a very simple login routine insofar as it does not even rely on a database; it simply checks that the values entered on the preceding page match the hard-coded values selected. The point is that if they do match, the user is sent to a "Success" page called success.asp, and if they do not match, they are sent to a "Fail" page called fail.asp.

Anything that happens on the pages after a redirect occurs is abandoned. The user is gone and is no longer available to accept output from the page that redirected him. Make sure that no critical information processing occurs after your user has been redirected.

Content Expiration

If you have spent any time at all on the Web, you know what a cache is. Intended as a means to save strain on servers and to speed up the surfing experience, a browser's cache saves recently viewed pages and graphics so that they can be viewed again quickly. That is great when the page's content is static. When it is dynamic, however, you need a way to make sure that each time a visitor tries to view a page, the user gets it directly from the server. That way, you can make sure that the user is viewing the latest data.

The Response object provides two properties that enable you to limit the amount of time that a page is cached in your visitor's browser. The Expires property enables you to set a number of minutes for which the existing content is valid. After that time passes, subsequent views must come from the server. A value of 0 ensures that each page view comes from a hit to the server. You can set the Expires property for a page as follows:

```
Response.Expires = minutes
```

You can also set an absolute day and time at which content will expire. This is helpful if content is updated on your site on a periodic schedule, and you want to make sure that any page view after the next update cycle comes from the server itself, and not from the cache. You can set the ExpiresAbsolute property like this:

```
Response.ExpiresAbsolute = #DateTime#
```

The Session Object

Essentially, the Internet operates on what are known as *stateless* protocols. This means that the basic HTTP protocol does not maintain a record of who is currently connected to it. Each request is handled by the server as if it were the only time that particular client had asked for something.

Contrast that to the way in which LANs work. If you have ever rebooted your computer in a networked setting, you may have seen a warning message stating that a certain number of computers are currently connected to your computer and that shutting down will disconnect them. Your local network protocols are maintaining the state of those users connected to your computer.

Your Web server, however, treats each request it receives as totally independent of other requests. That means that the server must have some way of reconstructing where the user is in the flow of the application each time it responds. It is especially important for a secure application to keep track of the following pieces of information:

- Who is making the request
- Whether they have been validated
- Whether they have placed anything in their shopping cart

You can pass a lot of this kind of information in the QueryString. As discussed earlier, you can then use the Request object to access that information on each page. This method has several problems, though:

- It makes for long, confusing QueryStrings.
- It is insecure, because all the information in the QueryString is open for examination and alteration by a user who has only a little knowledge about how they work.
- Complicated QueryStrings must be reconstructed each time a user changes pages, to pass the correct information to the next page.

You can also keep a lot of this kind of information in cookies. Again, though, a user could open the cookie's text file and play around with the name/value pairs that make it up.

ASP provides a quite elegant solution to the problem of maintaining state in Web applications. The Session object can hold information about your user in a way that is unique, secure, and easy to use. The Session object is actually a set of variables that you define that are stored on the server. As long as your visitor remains connected to your site (meaning that he or she continues to make requests without pausing longer than the timeout value set for the Session object), those variables persist and can be used to identify and track them.

Note *The Session object uses a unique session ID for each user. This ID is written to a cookie on the client computer and serves to identify which set of session variables should be associated with that user. So, if the user has cookies disabled in his or her browser, the Session object will fail.*

A session variable can have just about any name you choose, and can hold any type of data in a variant data type. For instance, to create a session variable called ID and assign a value of 25 to it, you would simply use the following:

```
<% Session("ID") = 25 %>
```

To recall the value of the session variable, simply call it by name, like so:

```
<% = Session("ID") %>
```

or

```
<% Response.Write Session("ID") %>
```

or

```
<%
Dim userid
userid = Session("ID")
Response.Write userid
%>
```

Note *Technically, the correct way to write these references is Session.Content("ID"), but it is regularly abbreviated Session("ID").*

Because session variables are stored on the server, you have total control over how they are set and what values are allowed in them. This is a much more secure way of maintaining sensitive pieces of data away from the access of your users.

You need to consider some issues as your sites start to scale up in size. Sessions are dependant on the server on which they were created. In a load-balancing scenario in which several servers are used to serve identical content while spreading the user load over several CPUs, there is no way to guarantee that each hit to the server will reach the server where that user's session information is stored. Special third-party software is necessary for session management in these situations.

Session Properties

The Session object has several properties that you can set. The two most important to you will be the SessionID property and the Timeout property.

The SessionID property will return the unique session ID that is assigned to visitors when they first begin using your application. You can access it as follows:

```
<% = Session.SessionID %>
```

The Timeout property is used to set the length of time that a session persists without activity from the user. For instance, you can set the timeout value to 30 minutes like this:

```
<% Session.Timeout = 30 %>
```

Session Variables

Much debate has occured about the expediency of session variables because of the drain they place on server resources. Each time a session is begun (when a user hits an ASP page in your application), a session is created to service that user. That takes 2K of server memory right off the bat. The only way around that is to turn off sessions on the server, in a global.asa file or at the page level. Most people don't do that, especially in a cohosted environment, so each user has 2K set aside for them. If you then store an integer UserID in the session, that takes 8 more bytes, for a total of around 2,008 bytes; 2,000 bytes if you don't use session variables, and 2,008 bytes if you do. At this point, the difference between using and not using session variables is really all about the delta; the 8-byte difference between 2,000 and 2,008. For the incredible convenience they provide, and the relatively low server resources they take, session variables are a tremendous asset to the Web developer. Passing around recordsets in them isn't recommended; but for storing IDs and user group settings that facilitate site security, session variables are ideal.

The trick is coming up with the correct value for your site. Too short a session timeout value will abandon the information you are storing on users too often, perhaps while they take the time to read information that is presented to them on the site. They will be constantly required to log back in, which will hamper their use of the site. Too long a value opens the security risk of someone coming up behind a user and gaining access to the user's session, and also ties up server resources longer than necessary.

Session Methods

The one method of the Session object is the Abandon method, which releases all the variables in a session ID and frees the server resources associated with them. Calling Session.Abandon when your user logs out destroys that user's session variables, requiring the user to log in again if he or she wishes to continue using the site; and it frees the related server resources immediately when your visitor has completed the application, rather than waiting for the timeout period to elapse.

The Application Object

What the Session object does for the individual user, the Application object does for the entire site. Variables can be set in much the same way:

```
<% Application("users") = Application("users")+1 %>
```

The difference is that this variable is accessible by any user at any time. Any page within your application can then access the "users" variable and display the number of people currently logged in.

 A script that can be used to track users is discussed later in this chapter in the section "Global.asa." file.

Because any user can access the application variables and modify them, it is important to manage your users' access with the Lock and Unlock methods of the Application object. Calling Application.Lock before allowing the manipulation of a variable ensures that two concurrent applications will not affect one another. Application.Unlock will then release the variable to other users within the site.

The Server Object

The Server object is a low-level object that can be used to perform several tasks within ASP. The most common use is to create instances of server-side components using the following syntax:

```
Set InstanceName = Server.CreateObject("ClassName.ComponentName")
```

So, to create an instance of the CDO Newmail object to send e-mail from your page, you might use the following:

```
Set Email = Server.CreateObject("CDONTS.NewMail")
```

The object reference Email can then be manipulated as the class itself, adding properties and calling methods.

The ObjectContext Object

The ObjectContext object relates to ASP's use of Microsoft Transaction Server. It enables you to access the MTS component management system from within ASP. For more information on this object, see a reference on programming using MTS.

global.asa

This is a file, core to the ASP Object model, that is left out of the basic UltraDev implementation. While it is not strictly necessary to have this file in your application, it can be a powerful addition, enabling you to do things on a site-wide basis that make your site more responsive to your user's needs and your own. The global.asa file is a site-wide file that lives in the root directory of your domain. It contains just four functions by default:

- Application_OnStart
- Application_OnEnd
- Session_OnStart
- Session_OnEnd

You will recognize the names of these functions from the previous discussion of Application and Session objects. The functions in the global.asa file take advantage of ASP's ability to know when sessions and applications begin and end, and they can react to those events with code that you specify.

You can do anything from setting up recordset connections to tracking users with the global.asa file, and that's what you will do here. After you launch your new site, you will no doubt be sitting back waiting for the thousands of concurrent connections that forced you to shell out the big bucks for SQL Server. Sitting there looking at your home page, you will wonder who else is looking at it right that minute. Will it look different while experiencing the adoring stares of users across the globe? How can you tell how many people have visited?

Some people like those speedometer-looking graphic numbers that pronounce the number of times your home page has been visited since some date in the past. Prominent hit counters too often just confirm the fact that, in the scheme of things, no one has visited your site much at all in the months since it was last updated (and if you're not going to update it, don't put a date on there that proves it); and, other than the occasional snicker, no one really much cares anyway. Except for you. That's why you need an accurate, discreet way to track how many people have visited your site and how many are there right now. The following is global.asa code to allow you to do just that.

```
Sub Application_OnStart
Application("visits") = 0
Application("Active") = 0
End Sub

Sub Application_OnEnd

End Sub

Sub Session_OnStart
Application.lock
Application("visits") = Application("visits") + 1
Application.unlock
Application.lock
Application("Active") = Application("Active") + 1
Application.unlock
End Sub

Sub Session_OnEnd
Application.lock
Application("Active") = Application("active") - 1
Application.unlock
End Sub
```

Understanding the use of the Application and Session objects in the global.asa file is helpful, and thus is the focus of the rest of this section. The Application object is accessible and writable from your entire site, meaning that all the users of your site can read and write to the same variables. The Session object is unique to each user and is only accessible by that user.

As is implied by their names, these functions are triggered when your application begins or ends, and when an individual session begins or ends. The global.asa file sees these events automatically, so you don't need to do anything extra to cause the events that you place in these functions to occur.

The Application_OnStart function will really only trigger once, unless you shut down your site or have some special functionality that restarts the application. You will use it to initialize and store variables that are available to everyone at the site. This allows the beginning of each session to increment your visits counter and your active counter and allows a counter page to display these figures for you. The following is the code:

```
Sub Application_OnStart
Application("visits") = 0
Application("Active") = 0
End Sub
```

That's all you need. Because the site starts only once, you initialize the two variables you are interested in: how many total visits have you had and how many active users are there.

The Application_OnEnd function has no code in this context. You are not explicitly calling the end of the application; and an accidental crash of the site would not allow OnEnd code to run anyway, so there is no need for it.

The Session_OnStart function triggers each time a new user visits your site. This function increments both counters to add a visit and a new active user to your application variables. Here is the code:

```
Sub Session_OnStart
Application.lock
Application("visits") = Application("visits") + 1
Application.unlock

Application.lock
Application("Active") = Application("Active") + 1
Application.unlock
End Sub
```

Notice that you call an Application.Lock and Application.Unlock each time you write to a variable. This ensures that two users don't try to overwrite each other and mess things up. Each variable that you initialized in the Application_OnStart function is incremented to update the counters with this current user.

All that is left is the Session_OnEnd function:

```
Sub Session_OnEnd
Application.lock
Application("Active") = Application("active") - 1
Application.unlock
End Sub
```

When a session ends (either explicitly, by calling the session.abandon event, or by timing out), this code runs and decrements the active users variable. Notice that the visits variable is not decremented and contains a complete history of the number of session ever started in the application.

Keep in mind that few sites even try to coax users into logging out of a site, and even fewer are successful. Therefore, most sessions end with a timeout. Remember, too, that your count of active users will be off slightly, because some users who have left your site still have active sessions as far as the server is concerned. But, over time, you will receive an accurate average of the momentary usage of your site.

Now, all you need is code in an ASP page to read the application variables and present your counters to you:

```
<%
Response.write Application("Active") & " active users<BR>"
Response.Write Application("visits") & " total visits"

%>
```

As you become more comfortable with the way ASP works, you will recognize the power of the global.asa. file. While UltraDev currently focuses on development at the session level, you can certainly add site-wide code that extends the abilities of your site.

The Languages

All the intricacies of languages as powerful as VBScript and JScript (or JavaScript) cannot be covered in this space, but a review of the following few things will help you with some light-duty scripting:

- Variables
- Conditional statements
- Loops

Variables

Variables are simply representations of other things to your computer program. You no doubt can remember a time when you grabbed a few rocks to draw out the battle plan for storming the neighbor kids' tree fort, or even when you played Monopoly and each chose a die-cast token to represent you on the board. You didn't actually become the car or the shoe, but everyone knew what space you occupied on the board by locating the token you had selected. Every time they saw your playing piece, they saw you within the scope of the game. The next time the game was played, someone else might have chosen the same token, and thus it represented them that time around. The tokens are variable in their representation, taking on the value of whomever selected it in the minds of the players.

Program variables are the same, except you are not limited to eight or ten little pieces of metal to hold your values. You can make up pretty much whatever character combination you'd like to represent other things to the computer. For instance, you could select the letter *i* to represent the age of your user. A 25-year-old user who visited your site would then have the value 25 assigned to the letter *i*. Then, every time the computer came across the letter *i* in your code, it would really see the number 25. You could add 1 to *i* and the computer would respond with 26. Or you could add *i* to another *i* and get the answer 50.

But, if a new user were to come along who is 40 years old, his instance of the application would assign the number 40 to *i* and all of his calculations would be altered accordingly. That is the power of variables. One set of code can be reused regardless of the actual values that need to be manipulated, because the representation, the variable itself, is always the same. You just tell the computer what to see when it comes across the variable by assigning a value to it.

This concept is consistent in both VBScript and JavaScript, but the implementation is slightly different.

VBScript

Here is a sample VBScript that you can examine:

```
<%
Dim name
Dim address, city, state, zip
name = "Joe"
address = Request.Form("address")
city = "Florida"
zip = 32811
Response.Write "Your name is " & name & ".<BR>"
Response.Write "You live in " & city & ", " & state & ".<br>"
%>
```

The first two lines take care of a process known as *declaring* variables. Although declaring your variables is not absolutely necessary, it is a good practice that will save innumerable debugging headaches down the road. Get into the habit of declaring your variables.

In VBScript, this is known as *dimensioning* variables and uses the Dim keyword. The previous example does this on two lines to illustrates the ways that it can be done. The first line dims one variable, and the second line dims three separate variables. The commas indicate that you are describing three different variables that you will be using, and VBScript treats these just as if you had dimmed them on three separate lines.

Because all variables in ASP are variants (meaning that they can hold any data type), there is no need to specify that one is an integer or another is a string. VBScript assigns the variable the most logical way that it can and manipulates it according to its best interpretation of the instruction you give it.

The rules for variable names are as follows:

- They must begin with an alpha character.
- They cannot contain embedded periods.
- They should be unique within the page or function in which they are used (or you risk overwriting information unintentionally).
- They cannot be more than 255 characters long.

Next, you assign values to the variables. The previous example assigned hard-coded string values to some and used a Request for another. You likely won't have such a combination on your page, but it illustrates the point that you can assign variables from a number of places. Notice also that VBScript accepts both string values and numerical values into the variable because all variables in ASP are variants.

When you are ready to output your variable values, it is most meaningful to the end user if they are displayed within the context of how they are being used. You can concatenate (string together) literal string output without variable values by using the & operator. When used with string values, the & operator tells VBScript to put the values together into the output string.

JavaScript

The script for JavaScript is much the same. Only slight differences exist in how the variables are declared and then concatenated with the string output:

```
<%
var name
var address, city, state, zip
name = "Joe"
address = Request.Form("address")
city = "Florida"
zip = 32811
Response.Write "Your name is " + name + ".<BR>"
Response.Write "You live in " + city + ", " + state + ".<br>"
%>
```

You will notice two changes. First, the keyword var is used to declare the variables instead of Dim. Second, the + operator is used to concatenate the string values. Otherwise, the VBScript code and the JScript code are the same.

Note   *The + operator has different uses in JavaScript. When used with numerical values, it does addition, as you would expect. If any of the values are strings, however, it concatenates instead.*

Conditional Statements

Conditional statements are ways of testing what is going on in your application, and responding differently to the variety of situations you may encounter. For instance, you may want to send your visitors to one site if they live in the North, to another if they are from the South, and yet another if they are from the West. You could use a conditional statement to gather information and determine what action to take. Consider this VBScript code:

```
<%
Dim region
region = Request.Form("region")

If region = "North" Then
     Response.Redirect("North.asp")
ElseIf region = "South" Then
     Response.Redirect("South.asp")
Else Response.Redirect("West.asp")
End If

%>
```

In this script, a variable is dimensioned to hold the region, and then a value is assigned to it that is gleaned from a form submitted by the user. A conditional statement is then entered that tests the value of the region variable and sends the user off accordingly.

The If keyword begins by checking to see whether the value is North. If it is, then the redirect to the North.asp page occurs. If it is not, the next line is invoked, which asks again whether the value is South by using Else If. Else If begins another test for the value of region. If the value if neither North nor South, then your script assumes it must be West and uses the Else keyword to invoke the only remaining option, which is to send the user to the West.asp page. The End If statement is required to demarcate the entire conditional statement so that the script knows when to stop testing conditions and return to regular code.

The JavaScript version of this script is somewhat different:

```
<%
var region
region = Request.Form("region")

If (region = "North") {
     Response.Redirect("North.asp")}
Else if (region = "South") {
```

```
      Response.Redirect("South.asp")}
Else {
      Response.Redirect("West.asp") }

%>
```

Each If conditional in JavaScript is contained within parentheses, and the response to a true response for that condition is then enclosed in brackets beneath it. This is really just a syntactical difference, and the concept of conditionals remains the same in the two languages.

Loops

Loops are places in your code where you will want to run a set of instructions a number of times. It may be a set number of times, such as 100; or it may depend on some criteria that you won't even determine until the program runs, such as once for every record in a recordset. Although several different ways to manipulate a for. . . next loop are available, the basic idea is that you determine a starting number, an ending number, and an increment.

So, suppose that you want to perform an operation on all the even numbers from 1 to 100. The first even number is 2, so the starting number is 2. The last even number is 100, so the ending number is 100. Even numbers occur every two numbers, so you want to increment by two at each pass. Consider the following VBScript code:

```
<%
Dim I
For I = 2 to 100 step 2
Response.Write I * I
Next
%>
```

Here, the variable *I* is dimensioned to hold where you are in your loop. You then begin the loop in the next line, which says that you want to run the code that is coming up once for each value of *I* that is between 2 and 100, stepping up two each time. The code then outputs the current value of *I* times itself and calls the Next keyword to begin the process again with the next value of *I*.

The concept is the same in JavaScript, with a bit of a syntactical difference:

```
<%
var I
for (I=2;I<=100;I=I+2){
      Response.Write I * I
}
```

The JavaScript code in this case uses the same parentheses and bracket construct that you saw earlier. After the for statement, the three portions of the statement in parentheses establish the starting, ending, and incremental value of the variable, and then the code within the brackets runs until the ending conditional is no longer true.

Summary

Thus concludes a quick overview of Active Server Pages as they are used in UltraDev. With this information, you should have a better handle on how UltraDev uses ASP to do the following:

- Get user input with the Request object.
- Output information and browser commands with the Response object.
- Maintain state with the Application and Session objects.
- Script logic with VBScript and JavaScript.

The limited space devoted here to ASP cannot do justice to all of its features and associated technologies. Hopefully, the information presented will help you be more productive with UltraDev as you begin learning your way around the details of what the program does. Numerous excellent tutorials, both in book form and on the Web, are available that can teach you more advanced features of ASP, when you are ready.

The
Complete
Reference

Chapter 9

Java Server Pages in the UltraDev Environment

One of the most popular programming languages that emerged from the Web era of the late 1990s is Java. While Java has been around for several years, it is only in the last few years that JSP has come into prominence. JSP was built upon some of the same ideas as its predecessor, ASP, but was able to avoid some of its shortcomings by taking the "best" ideas of ASP one step further.

JSP is a mixture of Java code within the constructs of an HTML page. The Java code is enclosed in <% %> server tags, like ASP code, but the code is compiled into *servlets* on the Web server when the page is browsed for the first time. Upon each successive hit, the code doesn't have to be compiled again—the compiled version remains on the server. In fact, the entire page is compiled, not merely the code that is between the server tags.

Java is a language that is based in part on the C language. It started as a small language that could be used in a wide variety of appliance hardware. It quickly grew, however, into a robust, platform-independent language that enabled Web developers to include *applets* in their Web pages. Applets are mini applications that exist client side and can be executed from a browser by invoking the Java of that browser. Applets can exist server side as well.

From applets, to servlets, to JSPs and Enterprise JavaBeans (EJBs), Java has steadily evolved over its short lifetime. Applets have been considered somewhat of a failure to most Web developers, because the technology never really took off as anticipated. JSP, however, now has a solid foundation and a large user base.

The JSP Server

Although Java was developed by Sun Microsystems, JSP is not strictly a Sun technology. Indeed, JSP servers are produced by some of the top names in the computer software industry today—IBM, Allaire, Sun, and Apache all have implementations of a JSP server. Some, like IBM's Websphere and Allaire's JRun, are available in Enterprise editions at a substantial cost. Others, like Apache Tomcat, are available as downloads from the Internet. Whichever implementation you choose, there are enough similarities among them to allow a general discussion of JSP.

UltraDev ships with the Standard edition of IBM's Websphere Application Server for Windows NT on the CD-ROM. If you have Windows NT, you might consider installing this server on your machine for local development. In addition, nearly all of the companies that market a JSP server have a development version that you can use for little or no charge. These versions are typically scaled-down versions of the full server, which may limit simultaneous connections. Allaire's JRun is also available on the UltraDev CD-ROM, and is an excellent choice for a JSP server.

JSP servers aren't limited to Windows and are available for most of the major operating systems. Versions of Tomcat and JRun for Linux are extremely popular. Web sites designed on UltraDev, on the PC or on the Mac, should be compatible with most of the major JSP servers and operating systems.

The Java Programming Language in JSP

The underlying language of JSP is Java. If you are familiar with Java, you should have no trouble transferring your skills to the arena of Web programming with JSP. If you have a C, C++, or JavaScript background, much of the syntax will be familiar to you.

Java offers many advantages compared to other programming languages. For starters, it's an object-oriented programming language, and offers a full set of standard classes for most tasks. Java is also portable, having the ability to run on most platforms using the same code. One advantage it has over C++ is automatic garbage collection. C++ programmers have to take care of their own memory management. In addition, Java is multithreaded, which allows the programmer to run different tasks at the same time.

JSP pages are HTML pages with a .jsp file extension and Java server-side code mixed in. There are three types of scripting contained in JSP pages—scriptlets, expressions, and declarations. Java snippets, called *scriptlets*, are contained inside <% and %> tags. The code inside the tags is compiled and run on the server, and the resulting HTML code is sent to the browser. A Java scriptlet in a JSP page might look like this:

```
<% out.println("Greetings " + request.getParameter("firstname"));%>
```

Another type of JSP expression is called, simply, an *expression*. A JSP expression looks like the shorthand Response.Write expression in ASP but is, in fact, a member of the *out* object rather than the response object. The out object is another name for the JSPWriter, which writes directly to the output stream. For instance, the following code displays the session variable "Username":

```
<%=(session.getValue("Username"))%>
```

When the JSP server sees the =, it's telling the server that the following expression is to be evaluated and sent to the browser as text to be displayed. Additionally, if the parameter inside the expression isn't a string, the JSP server converts it to a string to allow it to be displayed. If you look at the code that UltraDev generates for the same type of expression, it looks something like this (all on one line):

```
<%=((session.getValue("Username")!=null)? ¬
    session.getValue("Username"):"")%>
```

UltraDev adds error checking to most of the code it generates to prevent the occurrence of error messages. UltraDev uses the *ternary* expression in the preceding expression, which you can consider as a shorthand if/else statement (explained in more detail in the section "Control Structures in Java," later in this chapter). If the session variable is not null, the server will pass the value to the browser. If it is null, the server will pass an empty string to the browser. This prevents unwanted errors and allows the user to concentrate on the functionality of the site and spend less time on "bullet-proofing" the code.

Another type of JSP tag that you might see is the *declaration*. The declaration is used to declare a method, variable, or field. A declaration tag will have *page* scope, meaning that anything declared within the tag will be available to the whole page. A JSP declaration looks like this:

```
<%! int i = 1000; %>
```

One thing that you must be mindful of when writing Java code is that everything is case-sensitive. The following might look the same to someone not familiar with Java, but the first is correct and the second will cause an error:

Correct:

```
<%=(session.getValue("Username"))%>
```

Incorrect:

```
<%=(session.GetValue("Username"))%>
```

The latter code snippet will cause the JSP server to throw an error message that "No method named GetValue was found." Java developers must pay strict attention to the case of the code they write. This applies to functions, variables, properties, methods, events—in short, the whole of the language has to be thought of as being 100 percent case-sensitive.

Variables in Java

Java is strictly *typed* when it comes to variables. Type, in the case of variables, refers to the kind of data that the variable will contain. In ASP—both JavaScript and VBScript—you can get away with declaring variables without worrying about the type. The ASP variable type is a *variant*, which can hold any kind of data. In Java—and in JSP—you have to declare the variable type when you declare its name, as in these examples:

```
<%
boolean myFlag = (session.getValue("Username")!=null);
String myFirstName = "Tom";
int myCounter = 0;
%>
```

Note   String *is a special Java class, and not a variable type per se.*

If you try to use a variable before it's declared, the JSP server will throw an error. Also, if you try to put a value into a variable of the wrong type, the JSP server will throw an error. This forces the programmer to maintain strict coding practices. Java developers consider the nontyped ASP languages to be "lazy" languages, allowing the programmer to develop bad programming habits by not typing the variables.

In addition to declaring the variables with the proper type, you can't change types or mix two variables of different types in the same expression without first *casting* the variable. Casting refers to "changing" the variable type for the expression. The actual variable isn't changed, but the way that the server "sees" the variable is changed. For instance, to cast a session variable as an integer, you might use an expression like this:

```
<% int myUserID = (int)session.getValue("UserID");%>
```

The rules for casting variables are described in the Java API or any good Java reference. For example, a Boolean value can't be cast into another type. If you are planning to do any JSP development, you should have a good Java reference handy at all times. Table 9-1 shows the different variable types that are available to the Java developer.

INTRODUCTION TO
WEB SCRIPTING

Type	Range of Values	Description
byte	−128 to 127	Byte-length integer (8-bit)
short	−32768 to 32767	Short integer (16-bit)
int	−2147483648 to 2147483647	Integer (32-bit)
long	−9223372036854775808 to 9223372036854775807	Long integer (64-bit)
float	+/−3.40282347e38 to +/−1.40239846e−45	Single-precision floating-point number (32-bit)
double	+/−1.79769313486231570e308 to +/−4.94065645841246544e−324	Double-precision floating-point number (64-bit)
char	Single character	A single 16-bit Unicode character

Table 9-1.   *Variable Types and Their Ranges in Java*

You can also declare more than one variable on a line of code, as in this example:

```
<%
int i=1, j=100, k=1000;
boolean isAllowed, isNewUser, isAdmin = false;
char newLine = '\n', answerYes = 'y', quoteChar = '\u0022';
%>
```

Variables must be named according to Java conventions, which also apply to functions, classes, and packages. They may contain upper- or lowercase letters, digits, underscore characters, and the $ character. Although upper- and lowercase letters are allowed, Java is case-sensitive. For instance, the variables "myCounter" and "MyCounter" would be completely different variables.

Expressions

Java is an expression-based language, like C. Java expressions represent computations, declarations, and flow of control. The simplest of Java expressions is a variable declaration, as in the following:

```
int i = 0;
```

A more complicated expression would be a computation, which can use any of the Java operators listed in Table 9-2.

The following statements are examples of legal expressions in Java:

```
int a = 1 + 2;
total += subtotal;
boolean c;
c = a > b;
```

This example illustrates a Boolean value being assigned to the boolean variable c as the result of a comparison between a and b. In Java, unlike some other languages such as C and JavaScript, a comparison yields a true or false (Boolean) value, rather than a one or a zero.

Integers have another set of operators available to them, outlined in Table 9-3.

In addition to the integer operators shown in Table 9-3, the binary operators can be used as compound operators. Also, the integer types (int, long, short, and byte) can be operated on in combinations—type casting is automatic, and the result is always type-cast into the higher of the values. For instance, if you add a byte variable to an int type variable, the result would be an int type. This allows you to work with

Operator	Type	Function
+	Arithmetic	Add
–	Arithmetic	Subtract
*	Arithmetic	Multiply
/	Arithmetic	Divide
<	Relational	Less than
>	Relational	Greater than
<=	Relational	Less than or equal to
>=	Relational	Greater than or equal to
==	Relational	Equal to
!=	Relational	Not equal to
+=,–=, *=, and so on	Compound assignment	Uses the right-hand expression double-duty as the first operand

Table 9-2.   *Operators in Java*

Operator	Function
+	Arithmetic constant
–	Arithmetic negation
~	Bitwise complement
++	Increment
——	Decrement
%	Modulus (remainder)
&, | , ^	Bitwise AND, OR, and XOR
<<	Left bit shift
>>	Right bit shift with sign fill
>>>	Right bit shift with zero fill

Table 9-3.   *Integer Operators*

different integer data types without worrying about casting the variables into the same type beforehand.

Strings can also be operated on with a plus sign (+), which effectively concatenates the variables, as in this example:

```
<%
String myFirst = "Fred";
String myLast = "Periwinkle";
String myName = myFirst + ' ' + myLast;
out.println(myName);//the result would be "Fred Periwinkle"
%>
```

Strings also allow the use of compound concatenation, as in this example:

```
theCode += '\n';  //add a line feed to the end of the code
```

Control Structures in Java

Java uses control structures that are similar to C or JavaScript. The most common control structure would have to be the if/else structure, but there are others that may be more suitable for certain tasks. The basic structures are outlined next. Note that some of the control structures evaluate an expression inside a set of parentheses that returns a Boolean value, and then act upon the result of the value.

if/else

```
<%
if (username == "Jim") {
    out.println("Hello, Jim");
    }else{
    out.println("Hello");
    }
%>
```

switch/case

```
<%
switch (whichPage) {
case 1: response.sendRedirect("Page1.jsp");
    break;
case 2: response.sendRedirect("Page2.jsp");
    break;
```

```
default: response.sendRedirect("Home.jsp");
}
%>
```

The Ternary Operator: Shorthand if/else

```
<%
(userid!=null)?out.println("Goodbye"):out.println("Welcome")
%>
//The ternary operator deserves a little explanation.  The first
//expression is evaluated (userid!=null) to true or false.
//If true, the next expression is executed and if false, the third
//expression is executed. The statement above could have been
//written as:
<%if(userid!=null) {
    out.println("Goodbye");
}else{
    out.println("Welcome");
}
%>
```

| Tip | *UltraDev uses the shorthand version of the if/else construct in code that displays a data source on the page.* |

Looping Construct Using for

```
<%
for(i=0; i<totalRows; i++) {
    out.println("<tr><td>" + cookies[i].getName() + "</td></tr>");
    }
%>
```

while Statements

```
<%
while (i<10) {
    spaceString += ' ';
    i++;
    }
%>
```

do/while Statements

```
<%
do {
    out.println("<li>" + myList[i] + "</li>");
    i++;
    }
while (i < 10);
%>
```

JSP Objects

If you're an ASP programmer looking to expand your knowledge by learning Java, learning JSP is an excellent way to start. If you are new to the language and server-side technologies in general, JSP is a good, but difficult, way to learn this complex technology. JSP contains many of the same server-side features and objects that an ASP developer might be familiar with. If you've skipped the ASP chapter, you are advised to go back and read it, because it contains explanations of most of the basic server-side functionality that is common to ASP and JSP.

This section provides a brief rundown of the eight built-in variables, or *implicit objects*, that a JSP developer can use. They are request, response, out, session, application, config, page, pageContext, and exception.

The request Object

This object gives the Web developer access to the incoming HTTP headers, request parameters, and request type (GET, POST, and so on). Similar to ASP and ColdFusion, these request objects can be any of the following types (also called *collections*):

- Form
- QueryString
- Cookies
- ServerVariables

The Form and QueryString parameters can be retrieved from the client by using the following syntax:

```
request.getParameter("myFormElement")
```

or

```
request.getParameter("queryStringVariable")
```

Since Java is case-sensitive, it expects the request object to be in lowercase. The getParameter() method covers both GET and POST processes of form submission. To display the contents of a Form or QueryString variable, you can use the shorthand version of JSP expression evaluation, which displays the result in the browser, similar to the Response.Write object in ASP:

```
<%=request.getParameter("myVariable")%>
```

Cookies in JSP

JSP has its own method for retrieving cookies that differs considerably from the other server environments. You can't retrieve a cookie by name in JSP. You have to retrieve the entire Cookies collection and loop through the results looking for your particular cookie. First, you create a new Cookie object, and then you retrieve the Cookies collection using the request object:

```
Cookie[] myCookies = request.getCookies();
```

Then, you must loop through the collection to look for the cookie that you are interested in (in this case, a cookie named "username"):

```
for (int i=0; i<myCookies.length; i++) {
    if (myCookies[i].getName().equals("username")) {
        String strUsername = myCookies[i].getValue();
        break;
        }
    }
```

 Looping through the Cookies collection is a frequently used method and could be made into an Enterprise JavaBean (EJB) for reuse.

The ServerVariables Collection

The request object can also retrieve the ServerVariables collection, as in ASP and ColdFusion. The server variables are retrieved one by one, by using methods of the request object that roughly correspond to the names of the server variables. The list of available methods for retrieving server variables is as follows:

- **request.getAuthType()** The authentication type (generally not used)
- **request.getContentLength()** Indicates the number of bytes in the response
- **request.getContentType()** MIME type of the response document
- **request.getHeader("User-Agent")** The client browser being used
- **request.getMethod()** The method of the response, usually GET or POST

- **request.getPathInfo()**   Path from the site root
- **request.getPathTranslated()**   Full physical path to the page
- **request.getProtocol()**   The HTTP protocol being used
- **request.getQueryString()**   The entire QueryString following the question mark
- **request.getRemoteAddr()**   The IP address of the client
- **request.getRemoteHost()**   If remote user has DNS entry, might be returned in this value
- **request.getRemoteUser()**   Possibly contains username of user, but generally not used
- **request.getRequestURI()**   Section of the path to the page, usually from the site root
- **request.getServerName()**   Name of the server, useful for building links
- **request.getServerPort()**   Port number of the JSP server, usually 80
- **request.getServletPath()**   Path to the page, usually from site root

The response Object

This object is the HTTPServletResponse for sending responses back to the client, such as status codes and response headers. As in ASP, the response is buffered and is not legal to send to the browser once the HTML headers have been sent.

There are various methods of the response object, including the following:

response.setHeader(), response.setDateHeader(), and response.setIntHeader()

These methods are useful for setting the header of the Web page, as in the following statement, which instructs the user's browser to never cache the page:

```
response.setHeader("Cache-Control","no-cache");
```

response.sendRedirect()

This statement is similar to the Response.Redirect in ASP or the CFLOCATION in ColdFusion. Provided the headers haven't been sent to the browser yet, this method will redirect the user to a page specified in the string, as in this example:

```
String strErrorMessage = "Unknown%20user";
response.sendRedirect("error.jsp?error=" + strErrorMessage);
```

response.setContentType( )

This is a widely used method to set the content type of the response output sent to the browser. The *type* attribute is a standard MIME type that the browser recognizes, such as text/html or image/jpeg. For example, to display the contents of a shopping cart variable in the browser, you could use something like this:

```
<%
response.setContentType("text/html");
out.println("<table>");
for (i=0;i<cart.length;i++) {
    out.println("<tr><td>" + cart.productName[i] + "</td></tr>");
    }
out.println("</table>");
%>
```

response.setContentLength( )

This method is useful for setting up persistent connections to the browser, among other things. Rather than open and close connections for a large number of items, such as text files or images, you can use this method to set the content length and then use the output stream to send the files as one large stream.

response.addCookie( )

Use this method for adding a new cookie to the client's machine. Generally, when you set a cookie, you'll want to give it a name, a value, and an expiration time, as in the following example:

```
<%
String strUsername = request.getParameter("username");
Cookie ckUsername = new Cookie("ckUsername",strUsername);
response.addCookie(ckUsername);
ckUsername.setMaxAge(24*60*60*30);//set age to thirty days
%>
```

The out Object

Also known as the JSPWriter (the buffered form of the PrintWriter), this object sends a stream of output to the client's browser. This object is used in scriptlets and is usually accessed by using the println method, as in the following example:

```
<%
out.println("Your book is " + request.getParameter("title"));
%>
```

The JSP expression syntax (<% = %>) rarely uses the out object, because the equal sign (=) automatically places the expression in the output stream.

The session Object

The session object enables you to store *state* information regarding a client/server session, and is created even if you don't explicitly reference the session object. Since the Web is a stateless environment, Web servers must use other methods to maintain state in an application. Creating a unique session ID number for every user is one way. The session ID is stored on the user's computer in a cookie. Each time the user requests another page, the cookie is read and the value of the session ID is compared against the active sessions to determine whether the user has an active session. Just like ASP, if the client has cookies turned off, you can't use the session object. The only way the session object isn't created is if you specifically turn sessions off with the following:

```
<%@ page session="false" %>
```

To access the session object, you have to set a name and a value to a variable. In JSP, the session variable name is referred to as a session *attribute*. You have to explicitly set the attribute and the value when you create a session variable, as in this example that uses the setAttribute() method of the session object:

```
<%
session.setAttribute("Username",request.getParameter("Username"));
%>
```

In the example, you are setting a session variable named "Username" to the value retrieved in either a QueryString or a Form variable (recall that the getParameter method of the request object can take either type). You could also have used the putValue method of the session object, as in this example:

```
<%
session.putValue("Password",request.getParameter("Password"));
%>
```

You can retrieve the values by using the getAttribute (*variable name*) method of the session object, as in this example:

```
<input type="text" value="<%=session.getAttribute("Username")%>">
```

The previous example combines HTML with a JSP expression that will put the value of the session variable named "Username" into the text field before it is sent to the browser.

 While simple expressions are being used to demonstrate some of the methods of JSP, note that all variables should be checked for their existence before using them in an expression, as was demonstrated earlier, to avoid compiler errors.

To remove a session variable from the session object, you can use the following method:

```
<%
session.removeAttribute("Username");
%>
```

The removeAttribute method effectively removes not only the value, but also the reference to the session variable.

To list all session variable names (attributes) in the session object and their corresponding values, you can use the following method:

```
<%
Enumeration mySession = session.getAttributeNames();
while(mySession.hasMoreElements()) {
    String mySessionVarName = (String)mySession.nextElement();
    String myValue = (String)session.getValue(mySessionVarName);
    out.println(mySessionVarName + "=" + myValue + "<br>");
    }
%>
```

The previous example will display all current session variables and their values. To use this scriptlet, you need to include the java.util.* library to be able to use the Enumeration class. The object returned by the getAttributeNames() method of the session is an Enumeration object. The Enumeration class has two methods—hasMoreElements() and nextElement(). These methods should be self-explanatory. One of the nice features of Java is the plain-language syntax of many of the classes. The Enumeration type has to be converted explicitly to a String type upon each iteration of the loop, as you can see in the example. You then use the out object to print the session variable name and value to the browser.

Caution *The session object will only be created if session tracking is enabled. It is enabled by default, but can be turned off with a page directive of session="false". Also, a session object is maintained only if the user has cookies enabled on his or her system.*

The application Object

The same way that you can track a variable in the session of one individual user, you can track a variable that is available to all users in the application. These application variables can be defined and retrieved anywhere in the site, but are usually placed somewhere at the entry point of your application, such as in the Home.jsp or Index.jsp file. Most of the methods that are available for the session are also available for the application object, such as getAttribute(*string name*) for the retrieval of a variable, and setAttribute(*string name*, *value*) for setting the variable's value.

The following code will count the hits to the page and store the count in an application variable named "counter":

```
<%
Integer hits = (Integer)application.getAttribute("counter");
if(hits==null) {
     hits = new Integer(0);
}else{
     hits = new Integer(hits.intValue() + 1);
}
application.setAttribute("counter",hits);
%>
```

Then, you can display the result on the page with this expression:

```
<% =application.getAttribute("counter")%>
```

Note that this is a page-hit counter, not an application-hit counter.

If you are familiar with ASP, you may have used the global.asa file in your ASP applications. Some JSP servers have adopted a global.jsa file that works in a similar fashion, with application start and end events, as well as session start and end events. As of this writing, it's a nonstandard file, so its details won't be examined here. Allaire's JRun allows the use of the global.jsa file.

The config Object

This is an instance of the javax.servlet.ServletConfig class and represents the servlet configuration. This object is not typically used; but it will give you information about the configuration, such as the current servlet name, with the getServletName() method, as in this example:

```
<% = config.getServletName()%>
```

The page Object

The page object is also a rarely used object, and is mentioned here for the sake of completeness. It has page scope and can be accessed as *this*.

The pageContext Object

The pageContext object was created for JSP as an easy way to get information about the page. Each JSP page has a pageContext object that is created when a user visits the page, and is destroyed after the page is executed. Some of the methods of the pageContext object are as follows:

- findAttribute(String *name*)
- getAttribute(String *name*)
- getAttributesScope(String *name*)
- setAttribute(String *name*, Object *obj*, int *scope*)
- findAttribute(String *name*)
- removeAttribute(String *name*)

The exception Object

The exception object will allow the programmer to have access to the errors that are thrown on a JSP page. The exception object has three methods that are available to the programmer:

- **getMessage()**   Returns the error message
- **printStackTrace()**   Returns the entire stack trace
- **toString()**   Returns a string that describes the exception object

You would generally use the exception object on an error page, which you can define with the page directive

```
<%@ page isErrorPage="true"%>
```

 The exception object is only enabled if you have defined an error page with the method just outlined.

The Directives

Directives are used in JSP to set certain properties of the page, scripting language, tag libraries, and include files for the page. The three possible directives are *page, include,* and *taglib*. Some directives are placed at the beginning of the file, and occur before any processing is done on the page; but they can be placed where needed. The JSP server parses the page before any evaluation of expressions on the page. As such, the directives can't contain variables or expressions. The directives also don't produce any output for the client, because they aren't evaluated—they are simply there to give instructions to the server.

The page Directive

The page directive has several possible attributes to tell the server various things about the current JSP page. These attributes are discussed next.

The language Attribute

By default, the language of the page will be Java, using the language attribute of the page directive as shown in this example:

```
<%@ page language="java" %>
```

You'll find in UltraDev-generated pages that the program will insert this directive by default into your page when you add server-side code in the form of data sources or Server Behaviors. You could conceivably set the language to be something other than Java, such as JavaScript, as in this example:

```
<%@ page language="javascript" %>
```

When working with a JavaScript page, all of the standard objects of JSP will be available to your server-side JavaScript. The following example shows the use of JavaScript in a JSP page:

```
<%
var a=1;
var b = "Hello, World";
session.setAttribute("c",2 + a + b);
%>
<%=a%>              <!--prints "1.0" to the screen-->
<%=b%>              <!--prints "Hello, World" -->
<%=session.getAttribute("c")%> <!--   prints "3Hello, World" -->
```

As you can see, in JavaScript, the variables are all treated as variants, and type-casting isn't an issue. The session variable "c" contains the addition of the literal value 2 to the value of variable a, which is "1.0", and the result is concatenated as a string to the contents of variable b, "Hello, World". Not all servers support languages other than Java. Allaire's JRun supports JavaScript as well as Java. In the future, other servers may support JavaScript or other languages.

The import Attribute

This attribute will tell the JSP server which class packages it needs to include on the page. Generally, several packages are included by default (if the language is Java) and don't need to be explicitly declared:

- java.lang.*
- java.servlet.*
- java.servlet.jsp.*
- java.servlet.http.*

You can explicitly declare other packages that your page might need by adding an import attribute to the page directive, or by including a comma-delimited list of packages if the import attribute already exists, as in this example:

```
<%@ page import = "java.io.*, java.sql.*, java.util.*"%>
```

When you use the built-in UltraDev Server Behaviors and data sources, the page directives are included as needed and don't need to be added by hand. For instance, when you add a recordset to the page, the java.sql.* package is included in the import attribute.

The contentType Attribute

This attribute specifies the MIME type and character set (charset) of the page. The default MIME type is text/html unless you specify a different MIME type with this attribute, as in this example:

```
<%@ page contentType = "text/plain; charset=us-ascii" %>
```

The contentType attribute can be used to great effect for allowing the dynamic generation of different file types. For instance, a content type of "application/ unknown" will cause the output stream to be downloadable as an unknown file. A content type of "application/vnd.ms-excel" will cause the resulting page to be output to Microsoft Excel, if the user has it on his or her computer.

The contentType can also be specified using the setContentType() method of the response object, as in <%response.setContentType("text/plain");%>.

The session Attribute

The session attribute is true by default—allowing the use of session tracking and session variables. You can turn off sessions by specifying "false", as in this example:

```
<%@ page session="false" %>
```

The buffer Attribute

The buffer attribute is the size of the buffer before it is flushed to the client. If you specify a size, you have to use "kb" in the string, as in this example:

```
<%@ page buffer ="32kb" %>
```

The default buffer size is 8K unless specified otherwise. You can also specify buffer="none", which will cause the output stream to go right to the browser instead of being buffered.

The autoFlush Attribute

By default, the buffer will flush automatically when it fills up. You can override this behavior by specifying the following:

```
<%@ page autoFlush = "false" %>
```

This setting will cause an exception to be thrown when the buffer reaches capacity. Note that you can't set the autoFlush attribute to "false" when the buffer is set to "none," because there is no buffer to flush.

The isThreadSafe Attribute

This attribute sets the thread safety level of the page, and will cause the server to create multiple instances of the page if the attribute is set to "false". This will cause the servlet to use the SingleThreadModel. By default, the isThreadSafe attribute is set to "true".

Generally, when the user accesses a page, multiple threads can access a single instance of the servlet, sometimes causing overlap. In most cases, this isn't a problem; but if you have critical or private data, such as user information or ID numbers that you don't want to be accessed by more than one person, you should set this attribute to "false", as in the following example:

```
<%@ page isThreadSafe = "false" %>
```

The info Attribute

The info attribute defines a string that can be retrieved later with the getServletInfo() method. It's used like this:

```
<%@ page info="Some info about this page, last updated 10-20-00" %>
```

You can display the info attribute at some point by using the following:

```
<%=getServletInfo()%>
```

The errorPage Attribute

This attribute will allow you to set an error page to catch any exceptions that are thrown on the current page. The exception object of the current page will be available to the error page specified. The attribute is used like this:

```
<%@ page errorPage="error.jsp" %>
```

The isErrorPage Attribute

For the errorPage attribute to work, you need to have an error page set up in your application. This is accomplished with the isErrorPage attribute of the page directive. The attribute is placed on the error page itself, as in the following:

```
<%@ page isErrorPage = "true" %>
```

After the error page is defined, you can use the exception object to report the error of the page that caused the error, or use it to perform some predefined action depending upon what type of error is encountered.

The extends Attribute

This attribute allows you to specify a fully qualified class name that the servlet produced by the JSP page extends. The attribute is usually not used. The servlet engine generally has a specific class that adds functionality to the server that would be circumvented by using this attribute. Avoid it, unless you have a specific reason for using it. It is implemented like this:

```
<%@ page extends = "com.myCustomClass.MyServletImplementation" %>
```

The include Directive

Just as in ASP and ColdFusion, in JSP, you can include files at translation time that will be inserted directly into the place where the include directive is placed in the page. For instance, if you have a page footer that is on every page, it makes sense to make an include file out of it, so that if it changes, you only have to change it in one place. The directive is used like this:

```
<%@ include file="myfooter.jsp" %>
```

The file path is considered to be relative to the current page unless it has a leading /, in which case the file path is relative to the application.

The taglib Directive

You can use this directive to declare a tag library to be used in the JSP page, but UltraDev doesn't yet support tag libraries. UltraDev added JavaBean support in version 4, but tag libraries were left behind. Hopefully, support will be added in future versions, because some people feel that tag libraries are the preferred method to access EJBs in JSP pages.

Tag libraries enable you to create your own custom tags that can be called within the JSP page. The tag library is called with the taglib directive like this:

```
<%@ taglib uri="/myTagLib" prefix="myTagLib" %>
```

After adding the directive to the page, you can call your custom tags with XML syntax like this:

```
<myTagLib:tagname id="obj1" attribute="value" />
```

Tag libraries are an important part of JSP development, and something that should be learned if you intend to pursue a path as a JSP developer.

Serving the JSP Page

When a JSP page is browsed for the first time, the JSP server will compile the Java and HTML code into servlets that are then stored in the default servlet directory for the server. The first time the page is visited, there is additional overhead to the compile time; but after that, the pages will execute more quickly because the code is already translated into Java bytecode. You can avoid this delay by always testing the page one time after the page is deployed. Depending on which JSP server you are using, the actual source code of the servlet can be accessed as well. The following is a typical JSP page, which is followed by the servlet source code that is generated by the server in the next section:

```
<%@page language="java" %>
<html>
<head>
<title>Test JSP</title>
<meta http-equiv="Content-Type" content="text/html;¬
charset=iso-8859-1">
</head>
<body bgcolor="#FFFFFF">
<table border="1">
<%
int x = 10;
while (x > 0){
%>
  <tr>
    <td><%= x-- %></td>
  </tr>
 <% } %>
</table>
</body>
</html>
```

This simple page sets a variable "x" to the value of 10, and then counts down to 1 using a while loop and displaying the countdown in a table. Note that the variable declaration is inside a scriptlet. The JSP tags are closed to allow the table row tags, <tr>, and the table cell tags, <td>, to be sent to the browser, after which a JSP expression of <%= x--%> is placed in the page. This expression displays the variable and also decrements the value by one. Then, the table cell and table row tags are closed, and once again a JSP scriptlet is used to close out the while loop with a simple bracket. Then, the <table>, <body>, and <html> tags are closed.

In ASP, when you open and close the server-side tags like this, the server executes each tag set individually, so you actually lose a little bit of execution time by opening and closing the tags. In JSP, as you'll soon see, the entire page is translated into Java as the page is executed for the first time. If you open the *.java file that is generated by the JSP server (in this case, it's a JRun 3 server), you'll see the actual Java code:

```
// Generated by JRun, do not edit
import javax.servlet.*;
import javax.servlet.http.*;
import javax.servlet.jsp.*;
```

```java
import javax.servlet.jsp.tagext.*;
import allaire.jrun.jsp.JRunJSPStaticHelpers;
public class jrun__TestJSP2ejspc extends
allaire.jrun.jsp.HttpJSPServlet
implements allaire.jrun.jsp.JRunJspPage
{
    private ServletConfig config;
    private ServletContext application;
    private Object page = this;
    private JspFactory __jspFactory =
JspFactory.getDefaultFactory();
    public void _jspService(HttpServletRequest request,
HttpServletResponse response)
        throws ServletException, java.io.IOException
    {
        if(config == null) {
            config = getServletConfig();
            application = config.getServletContext();
        }
        response.setContentType("text/html; charset=ISO-8859-1");
        PageContext pageContext = __jspFactory.getPageContext(this,
request, response, null, true, 8192, true);
        JspWriter out = pageContext.getOut();
        HttpSession session = pageContext.getSession();
        try {
    out.print(" \r\n<html>\r\n<head>\r\n<title>Test JSP</title>
\r\n<meta http-equiv=\"Content-Type\" content=\"text/html;
charset=iso-8859-1\">\r\n</head>\r\n<body bgcolor=\"#FFFFFF\">\r\n
<table border=\"1\">\r\n");
int x = 10;
while (x > 0){
    out.print(" \r\n   <tr> \r\n     <td>");
out.print(x--);
out.print("</td>\r\n   </tr>\r\n ");
}
    out.print(" \r\n</table>\r\n</body>\r\n</html>\r\n\r\n");
    } catch(Throwable t) {
            if(t instanceof ServletException)
                throw (ServletException) t;
            if(t instanceof java.io.IOException)
                throw (java.io.IOException) t;
            if(t instanceof RuntimeException)
```

```
            throw (RuntimeException) t;
            throw JRunJSPStaticHelpers.handleException(t,
pageContext);
        } finally {
            __jspFactory.releasePageContext(pageContext);
        }
    }
      private static final String[] __dependencies__ =
{"/TestJSP.jsp",null};
    private static final long[] __times__ = {972008391139L,0L};
    public String[] __getDependencies()
    {
        return __dependencies__;
    }
    public long[] __getLastModifiedTimes()
    {
        return __times__;
    }
    public int __getTranslationVersion()
    {
        return 14;
    }
}
```

Several things should be immediately apparent from the code:

- The JSP server has translated everything into Java—the JSP tags are gone.
- The HTML code is enclosed in quotes inside of out.println statements.
- The entire while loop is enclosed in a try/catch block to catch any errors that might occur.
- Carriage return and line feed characters are explicitly written to the out stream.
- All servlet classes and helper classes that are needed by the page are included.
- It's a lot of code!

If you happen to be using the JRun server, these Java files are located in the Allaire\JRun\servers\default\default-app\WEB-INF\jrun folder. In the Tomcat 3 server, you have to specifically set the isWorkDirPersistent attribute in the Install_dir/server.xml file to "true" (it's set to "false" by default). The files are located in the install_dir/work/port-number directory. If you have another JSP server, consult your documentation to locate the source files.

These files should never be edited, but looking at them can give you some insight into what's going on behind the scenes in the JSP server. Along with the *.java files, which are the source code, the compiled files that the JSP server uses when a page is served are stored. As long as the original page isn't edited, it won't be translated again, and serves simply as a "pointer" to the actual compiled code. The first time the page is browsed, the code is translated into a servlet. You'll notice a definite speed improvement the second time you browse the page, because the servlet has already been compiled.

Using JSP with UltraDev

UltraDev supports ASP, JSP, and ColdFusion using the same interface. This is previously unheard of in the world of Web development, but it's not without its price. As the first-generation product, UltraDev 1 came up a little short in its JSP implementation. The original release in June of 2000 had many problems with JSP. A patch was soon released that fixed a few of the issues, but many features were still lacking, such as EJB and tag library support. If you are using UltraDev 1 with JSP, make sure you have the patch installed as well.

The JSP patch for UltraDev 1 can be downloaded from the Macromedia site at http://download.macromedia.com/pub/ultradev/jsp_update.mxp. UltraDev 4 doesn't need the patch.

Also, the vast majority of UltraDev users seem to be focused on ASP. This is due to many factors, but the primary reason is that the ASP server is available for free for Windows computers. Also, Macromedia is partly responsible, because it didn't support JSP in the UltraDev 1 release to the same extent as it supported ASP. In any event, the version 4 release is much better overall and is now a viable solution for the JSP developer.

Note *A company named Unify has created a set of J2EE 1.2 extensions for UltraDev 1 and has also pledged support for UltraDev 4. The extensions implement a completely new server model and offer support for JavaBeans, RowSets, RowSets returned by a Bean method, and connection pooling, which substantially increase the JSP power of UltraDev. You can get a trial version at www.unifyewave.com/products/ udextensions.htm.*

The following sections go through some of the key features of UltraDev that relate to the JSP implementation.

The Data Bindings Palette

UltraDev is based on Dreamweaver, as you know by now. Dreamweaver uses a floating menu interface with dockable menus called *floaters* or *palettes*. The main distinction of

UltraDev is the addition of two new floaters—the Data Bindings palette and the Server Behavior palette. Data Bindings are so-called because they "bind" the data on your page to a server-side construct, such as a recordset or a variable. The elements that reside on the Data Bindings palette are called *data sources*, and vary in complexity from the simple (sessions and requests) to the complex (stored procedures and recordsets).

The Recordset Data Source

Recordsets are the key element to the dynamic Web page—the back-end database gives the static HTML page dynamic content. To create a new recordset, you need to first define a JDBC connection (connections are described in Chapter 12). In UltraDev 1, the connection was defined right on the page; but in UltraDev 4, the connection is placed into an include file, and the connection information is placed into variables that are then used on the page.

After the connection exists, you can name your recordset and then write a SQL statement to retrieve data from the database (see Figure 9-1).

INTRODUCTION TO
WEB SCRIPTING

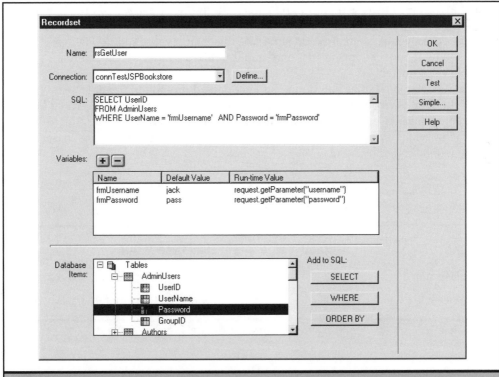

Figure 9-1.   *The Recordset definition dialog box for JSP*

To define a basic SQL statement, you can the Simple dialog box or the Advanced dialog box. For most SQL statements, you'll probably want to stay with the Advanced dialog box, in which you can define variables and attach them to other data sources, such as request objects and session objects. A typical SQL statement might read like this:

```
SELECT UserID
FROM AdminUsers
WHERE Username = 'frmUsername'
AND Password = 'frmPassword'
```

UltraDev doesn't allow you to insert your parameters directly into the SQL statement, but instead gives you a box in which you can enter the variable names, default values, and run-time values that will substitute the variables in the SQL with the correct parameters. For example, in the preceding SQL statement, the two variables frmUsername and frmPassword have to be declared using values similar to those shown in Table 9-4.

Note that the Default Value is a value that will be inserted in the page as a default in the event there is no incoming value. In a testing situation, you might want to include a default value that is in your database so that you can see the data on the finished page; but in a real-world situation, the default value should always be something that won't appear in your database, such as a special character or sequence of characters.

The SQL statement that you define will get passed directly to the database—both in the UltraDev environment and in the deployed Web application. The syntax of the statement should be legal to your particular database. Also note that the SQL builder in UltraDev will only build simple SQL statements. Anything but the most basic SQL will have to be coded by hand.

Name	Default Value	Run-Time Value
frmUsername	jack	request.getParameter("username")
frmPassword	pass	request.getParameter("password")

Table 9-4.   *Declaring Variables in the Recordset Definition Dialog Box*

The JavaBean and JavaBean Collection Data Sources

JavaBeans are reusable classes that bring portability to JSP applications. The JavaBean API allows Beans to be created that conform to a standard interface. The basic structure of the Bean is this:

- It must contain a constructor that names the Bean and has no parameters or attributes.
- Private variables in the Bean can be made accessible to the programmer through the getMyBeanProperty and setMyBeanProperty methods, where myBeanProperty is the name of the property.
- The Bean should have no public variables.

UltraDev 4 added JavaBean support, much to the delight of JSP programmers. The JavaBean data source that appears in both the Data Bindings palette and the Server Behaviors palette allows the programmer to access the methods of the Bean through a visual interface, with UltraDev generating the appropriate code in the background.

To get UltraDev to recognize your Bean, you have to first put the compiled Bean CLASS file, or the archived JAR or ZIP file, into the Classes folder under the Configuration folder in the UltraDev root program folder. The class has to be accessible to UltraDev using the same structure of the package. In other words, if the JavaBean has the structure of com.MyPackage.MyBean, then you can put the MyBean.class file into the Configuration>Classes>com>MyPackage folder or put your package MyBean.class directly into the Classes folder. After doing this, UltraDev will be able to recognize the Bean for use in the program.

The following is an example of a very simple Bean that accepts a message and then returns it. First, you need to create the Bean in your Java IDE and create a class file. The Bean class is called MessageBean, and the Java class file is called MessageBean.class. Here's the MessageBean.java file before compilation:

```java
public class MessageBean {
  private String message = "No message";
  public MessageBean(){
  }
  public String getMessage() {
    return(message);
  }
  public void setMessage(String newMessage) {
   this.message = newMessage;
   }
}
```

The MessageBean class constructor is empty, as required, and there is a getMessage method that returns a property named message, and a method for setting the message, named setMessage, that has a String parameter named newMessage. This is the complete Bean, and can be compiled into a class file and dropped into the Classes folder in UltraDev. In addition, it will have to be copied to the appropriate directory for your JSP server to be able to access it.

The following page has been created in UltraDev:

```
<%@page language="java" %>
<BODY>
<CENTER>
  <TABLE BORDER=2 align="center" size="80%" width="328">
    <TR>
      <TD bgcolor="#FF9900">
        <center>
          <b>Type a message to try out the Bean</b>
        </center>
      </td>
    </tr>
    <form name="theForm" method="post">
      <tr>
        <td align="center">
          <input type="text" name="message" size="60">
        </td>
      </tr>
      <tr>
        <td align="center">
          <input type="submit">
        </td>
      </tr>
    </form>
  </TABLE>
  <H1>Message: <I> (bean goes here)</I></H1>
</CENTER>
</BODY>
</HTML>
```

The page has a heading that states "Type a message to try out the Bean," a text field to accept the message that the user types in, and a Submit button. To apply the Bean to the page, you have to choose the JavaBean data source from the Data Bindings palette and bring up the JavaBean dialog box (see Figure 9-2). If you've placed your CLASS, JAR, or ZIP file in the Classes folder, the Bean should appear on the drop-down list.

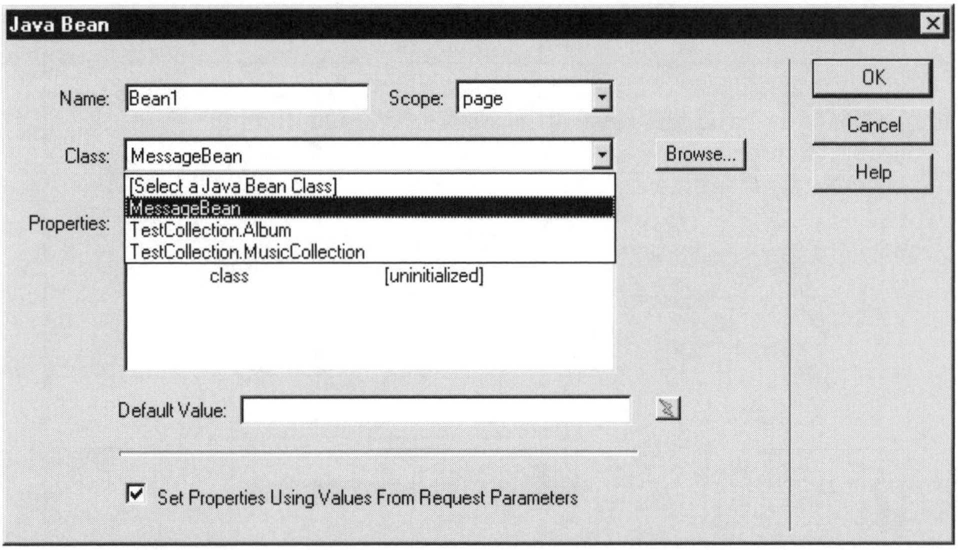

Figure 9-2. *The JavaBean dialog box in UltraDev 4*

Check the box at the bottom of the dialog box that says Set Properties Using Values From Request Parameters. Leave the Scope attribute set to Page for this particular example; the other possible values in the drop-down list are Request, Session, and Application.

After clicking OK, the Bean class should appear in the Data Bindings palette, with the properties of the class accessible by clicking the plus sign (+) next to the JavaBean in the window. You can highlight the "(bean goes here)" placeholder text and drag the message property from the Data Bindings palette to the placeholder and drop it. Your screen should now look like Figure 9-3.

The code inserted by UltraDev is XML scripting, which the JSP server recognizes. The code looks like this:

```
<jsp:setProperty name="Bean1" id="Bean1" class="MessageBean"
scope="page"/> <jsp:setProperty name="Bean1" property="*"/>
```

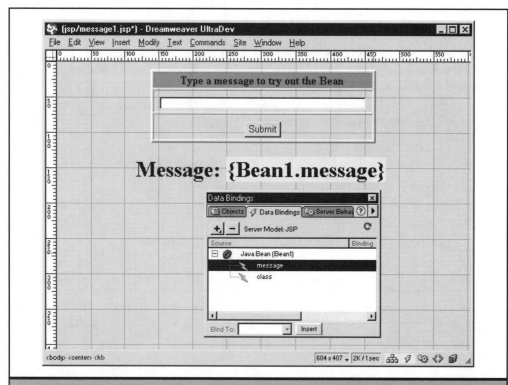

Figure 9-3. *The Data Bindings palette with a newly registered Bean, which has also been placed on the page by dragging and dropping it*

That's the code for the Bean instantiation, and the code to set the Bean property to the incoming request variable. The code that allows the Bean to be viewed on the page is this:

```
<jsp:getProperty name="Bean1" property="message"/>
```

Tip *The use of the asterisk allows for the Bean properties to assume all of the incoming form fields with form field names that match the properties. For example, if form fields named firstname, lastname, and message were submitted to the page, the Bean would attempt to match up each of the incoming form field names as Bean properties. By checking the Set Properties Using Values From Request Parameters box in the JavaBean dialog box, UltraDev automatically writes this shorthand version.*

Callable (Stored Procedure) Data Source

The Callable data source enables you to insert a callable statement to access a stored procedure from your database. Stored procedures will be addressed in Chapter 19.

Session and Request Variables

The session and request data sources simply give you a place to store the names of session and request variables that you might use on your page. You simply insert a name for the variable, and it will show up on the Data Sources palette. Once it's in the palette, you can drag it to the page, or use it in JavaBeans, form elements, or other constructs. Session variables that are set up in this way on one page will be available for use in the entire site.

The Server Behaviors Palette

Server Behaviors are the main server-side code generators of UltraDev. These Server Behaviors insert code into your documents to perform a variety of functions. Most of these functions are related to the display of the recordset on the page and the recordset navigation. The use of Server Behaviors will be covered in Chapters 18 and 19, but here's a brief introduction to some of these Behaviors.

Repeat Region

The Repeat Region Server Behavior enables you to loop through a resultset with a simple point-and-click interface. The Repeat Region uses a while loop to iterate through a resultset. One of the advantages to using the Repeat Region rather than hand-coding is that it is a way to set up the Move to Server Behaviors. When you apply a Repeat Region to the page, there are variables that go with the Behavior that allow interaction with the other Server Behaviors. Like the recordset Server Behavior, the Repeat Region has to be inserted for many of the other Server Behaviors to work with your code.

Hide/Show Region

UltraDev 1 had a Server Behavior called Hide Region. This was changed to the exact opposite in UltraDev 4—Show Region. The Behavior works similarly for both implementations. The Behavior allows you to hide or show a specific region on the page based on a specific condition that you can set up in the Behavior. The available choices are to Hide/Show Selected Region:

- If Recordset is Empty
- If First Record
- If Last Record

- If Recordset Is Not Empty
- If Not First Record
- If Not Last Record

Move to Record

This is a group of Server Behaviors that interact with a recordset and a Repeat Region Server Behavior. They allow you to move to the First, Previous, Next, Last, and Specific records.

Dynamic Elements

The Data Bindings palette allows you to apply dynamic text items to the page, and also allows you to insert values into other objects, such as form objects. Another way to do this is to use the Dynamic Elements menu entry in the Server Behaviors palette and click one of the five items:

- **Dynamic Text**   A text item, such as a recordset column or a session variable that's on the page
- **Dynamic List/Menu**   A list/menu form element that gets its values from a data source
- **Dynamic Text Field**   A text field form element that gets its value from a data source
- **Dynamic Check Box**   A checkbox form element that gets its checked value based on a data source
- **Dynamic Radio Buttons**   A set of radio buttons that get their value from a data source

Summary

This chapter was intended as a general introduction to JSP and the Java language. The Java language is a vast and powerful language with a rich history. Also, JavaBeans allow you to encapsulate code for reuse and move your business logic out of the pages and into the Beans. UltraDev started off slowly with its JSP support in version 1, but has become a full-fledged JSP power tool with version 4.

The
Complete
Reference

Chapter 10

ColdFusion

UltraDev comes in three flavors of server models, the tastiest of which is ColdFusion. The other two flavors are Active Server Pages (ASP, which was discussed in Chapter 8) and Java Server Pages (JSP, which was discussed in Chapter 9). ASP offers unparalleled support, compatibility, and ease of use for a Microsoft-based solution. JSP, on the other hand, offers tremendous power for a variety of server types and operating systems. ColdFusion offers the best qualities of JSP and ASP, but also offers the accessibility of HTML.

ColdFusion is a tag-based language, like HTML, but offers a rich set of over 70 tags that are executed on the server—unlike HTML, which is executed on the client. When you execute the CFQUERY tag, for example, the server interprets the tag and executes a connection to the database and a return of information from the database. A single CFQUERY tag offers the same functionality as eight to ten lines of ASP or JSP code.

Tip	*ColdFusion tags use name/value pairs, just as HTML tags do.*

In addition, ColdFusion has just about everything you need built right into the language, including such functionality as database manipulation, e-mail distribution and retrieval, file manipulation, directory manipulation, and anything else you might need to get your site up and running. In ASP and JSP, much of this functionality involves add-on components or hand-coding of complex scripts, beans, applets, and objects. ColdFusion programmers can realize the complexity of a data-driven site by implementing tags that are similar in style to HTML tags.

The ColdFusion Server

In addition to the ease of programming, ColdFusion offers a powerful server that is able to scale to the most demanding of Web applications. It offers load balancing, just-in-time compiling, security, dynamic caching, and failover. The server is robust and capable of high volume using multithreaded processing. Also, it is easily integrated with other programming technologies—such as ASP, XML, COM, CORBA, EJB, Java, and C++—and with application technologies, such as databases, mail servers, file systems, and a host of others. The server is also easily clustered and offers unparalleled server administration features that enable you to administer the server remotely—including your database connections and DSNs.

In addition to its Windows functionality, ColdFusion can be deployed on Solaris, HP-UX, and Linux, making it quite versatile as an option for a non-Windows system. The Linux version of ColdFusion has become quite popular since its release in late 2000.

UltraDev is shipped with a single-user license of the ColdFusion Server Enterprise version. The server will run on Windows 95, 98, NT, or 2000. Different levels of the

ColdFusion server are available, with the Enterprise version being the top of the line. The version that ships with UltraDev contains all the advanced features of the Enterprise edition, but can be accessed only locally—that is, through http://localhost or through the default 127.0.0.1 IP address.

The Enterprise version has all the features that a high-end Web application demands—clustering; load balancing; server failover; and native database drivers to Sybase, Informix, DB2, and Oracle. In addition, the security features are top-notch, including the "sandbox" security, which allows multiple applications to have their own security features.

The Professional version of ColdFusion is a much–lower-cost alternative to the Enterprise version, and has most of the key features. Where the Professional version fails, however, is that it doesn't allow the use of native database drivers, and also isn't available for the HP-UX or Solaris platform. Also, it doesn't offer the load balancing or server failover that the Enterprise version offers. If you don't specifically need this functionality, you might well consider this version, which is available at a substantially lower cost than the Enterprise version. This is the ideal application server to run in a one-server environment.

ColdFusion also comes as a free version—ColdFusion Express. ColdFusion Express has 19 of the most popular tags, including CFQUERY and CFOUTPUT. Although Express is certainly a viable option to run your data-driven site, it doesn't contain certain key features to make it usable with UltraDev-generated code. UltraDev uses CFScript in many of its Server Behaviors, and CFScript isn't included with the ColdFusion Express server. The Express version also doesn't include CFMAIL, CFFILE, or CFPOP, among other tags. Nonetheless, an application developed to run on ColdFusion Express will be 100-percent compatible with the Professional or Enterprise versions.

CFML: The ColdFusion Programming Language

ColdFusion Markup Language (CFML) isn't a traditional programming language, per se. CFML is a tag-based language, which is somewhat different than the script-based ASP languages and the object-oriented Java language. ColdFusion has a script language built into it—CFScript—but the majority of ColdFusion programming involves the use of tags. A page that contains CFML is saved with a .cfm or .cfml file extension. Any page with a .cfm or .cfml extension that is requested from the Web server will be parsed by the ColdFusion server before being sent to the browser.

A tag is nothing more than a command that is flanked by the < > symbols, like the HTML tags that Web developers are used to seeing. A typical ColdFusion statement might look like this:

```
<CFOUTPUT>#form1.Username#</CFOUTPUT>
```

The CFOUTPUT statement is similar to Response.Write() in ASP or out.print() in JSP. The pound signs (#) are signals to the ColdFusion server that the code contained within the signs is to be evaluated by the server. In this particular case, a Form variable named "Username" will be evaluated and directed to the browser. Specific rules apply to using the pound signs, and these are covered in an upcoming section; but in general, the pound signs imply that the code contained within is a variable or an expression. Also, they must exist inside of a ColdFusion tag or tag set. In other words, the server won't interpret the pound signs if they aren't contained within a valid ColdFusion tag.

ColdFusion tags all begin with the <CF prefix. Those three characters act as a signal to the server that the current tag is to be executed by the ColdFusion server. It's similar to the <% prefix found in ASP and JSP. Some of these tags come as a "set," with an open tag and a close tag, such as the preceding CFOUTPUT tag. Others, such as the CFFILE tag, exist as one tag. A complete list of the available ColdFusion tags is shown in Table 10-1. Generally speaking, a ColdFusion tag contains a series of name/value pairs that provide the server with the information needed to execute the tag. The following CFFILE tag is an example:

```
<CFFILE ACTION="Delete"
        FILE="c:\inetpub\wwwroot\images\#form.filename#">
```

The ACTION attribute of the tag is set to Delete, the FILE attribute is set to the c:\inetpub\wwwroot\images directory, and the filename is set to an incoming Form variable named "filename." When the ColdFusion server reads this tag, it will execute the tag—which, in this case, will cause a file named in the form element to be deleted from the server. Using the same CFFILE tag, you can create a file upload by setting the ACTION attribute to Upload:

```
<CFFILE ACTION="Upload"
        FILEFIELD="Filename"
        DESTINATION="c:\inetpub\wwwroot\images\"
        NAMECONFLICT="Overwrite">
```

In this case, a FILEFIELD attribute of Filename is specified, which will be the name of the incoming Form variable. The DESTINATION attribute is the folder on the server in which the file will be stored, and the NAMECONFLICT attribute instructs the server what to do if the name happens to conflict with a file that already exists on the server.

As with most ColdFusion tags, the CFFILE tag has some required attributes and some optional attributes. The NAMECONFLICT attribute in the preceding CFFILE tag is optional. Whenever an optional attribute is included, the server follows a default behavior if the attribute isn't contained in the tag. In this case, if the NAMECONFLICT attribute isn't defined, the default behavior is to throw an error if a file already exists.

ColdFusion tags all behave differently and all have different degrees of complexity. For instance, a CFABORT tag exists by itself, and has an optional attribute of SHOWERROR. You can put it on the page like this:

```
<CFABORT>
```

If the ColdFusion server encounters this tag, it will simply stop processing the page. If you give it a SHOWERROR attribute, as in this example,

```
<CFABORT SHOWERROR="You have to be more careful!!!">
```

the page will execute and the error page will display the message (see Figure 10-1). A CFABORT tag is useful in a conditional statement to stop processing the page if a certain condition exists.

ColdFusion Functions

In addition to the 70 ColdFusion tags that are available, over 200 functions are available. These functions consist of everything from basic string-handling functions—such as Len(string), which returns the length of a string—to complex functions, such as QuotedValueList, which will convert a column returned from a database into a

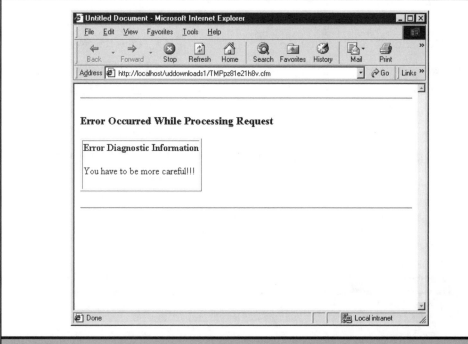

Figure 10-1. *A custom error message is displayed that was defined in the CFABORT tag*

CFABORT	CFAPPLET	CFAPPLICATION
CFASSOCIATE	CFAUTHENTICATE	CFBREAK
CFCACHE	CFCOL	CFCOLLECTION
CFCONTENT	CFCOOKIE	CFDIRECTORY
CFERROR	CFEXECUTE	CFEXIT
CFFILE	CFFORM	CFFTP
CFGRID	CFGRIDCOLUMN	CFGRIDROW
CFGRIDUPDATE	CFHEADER	CFHTMLHEAD
CFHTTP	CFHTTPPARAM	CFIF/CFELSEIF/CFELSE
CFIMPERSONATE	CFINCLUDE	CFINDEX
CFINPUT	CFINSERT	CFLDAP
CFLOCATION	CFLOCK	CFLOOP
CFMAIL	CFMAILPARAM	CFMODULE
CFOBJECT	CFOUTPUT	CFPARAM
CFPOP	CFPROCESSINGDIRECTIVE	CFPROCPARAM
CFPROCRESULT	CFQUERY	CFQUERYPARAM
CFREGISTRY	CFREPORT	CFRETHROW
CFSCHEDULE	CFSCRIPT	CFSEARCH
CFSELECT	CFSERVLET	CFSERVLETPARAM
CFSET	CFSETTING	CFSILENT
CFSLIDER	CFSTOREDPROC	CFSWITCH/CFCASE/ CFDEFAULTCASE
CFTABLE	CFTEXTINPUT	CFTHROW
CFTRANSACTION	CFTREE	CFTREEITEM
CFTRY/CFCATCH	CFUPDATE	CFWDDX

Table 10-1.   *Complete List of ColdFusion Tags Available in ColdFusion 4.5*

comma-separated list with the values enclosed in single quotes. The functions are grouped into these categories:

- Array functions
- Authentication functions
- Date and time functions
- Decision functions
- Display and formatting functions
- Dynamic evaluation functions
- International functions
- List functions
- Mathematical functions
- Query functions
- String functions
- Structure functions
- System functions
- Other functions

The functions have to be contained within a ColdFusion tag to be recognized. Also, in some instances, they will be contained within the pound signs. These functions don't begin with <CF like the ColdFusion tags—they are simply descriptive names of the functions they represent. When the ColdFusion server sees a function, the code is executed on the server and the result of the function is returned. In this example, the RepeatString function returns a string of 20 nonbreaking spaces:

```
<cfoutput>#RepeatString(" ",20)#</cfoutput>
```

ColdFusion functions can be combined and nested, also, creating some pretty complex statements:

```
<CFLOCATION URL="#IIF(ListFind(ValueList(
     myquery.username),form.username),'Page1.cfm','Page2.cfm')#
</CFLOCATION>
```

This statement uses a query named "myquery" that contains a *resultset*. The resultset is transformed into a list with the ValueList function; then, the form.username is checked against that list with the ListFind function. Finally, the IIF function performs an if/else statement, depending on whether or not the username is found in the list returned by the query. The CFLOCATION tag only sees the result of the function— either Page1.cfm or Page2.cfm.

 All the ColdFusion functions are available to the built-in scripting language as well—CFScript.

ColdFusion contains some truly powerful functions that make the development process much quicker. For instance, some list and array functions are available that make working with lists and variable arrays much easier. Some system functions also are available, such as the DirectoryExists function, which determines whether a given directory exists on the server; and the GetCurrentTemplatePath function, which returns the path on the server to the current page that's being served.

ColdFusion Variable Types

Like other languages, ColdFusion uses some specific types of variables, and each type has its own unique uses. Variables can be named with alphanumeric characters or underscores, and must begin with a letter. The type, or *scope,* of the variable is generally appended to the beginning of the variable with dot notation, as in *form.username*. However, a variable can be addressed without using the prefix. The following statement, for instance, is legal:

```
<CFOUTPUT>Hello #username#</CFOUTPUT>
```

Whenever a variable doesn't have its variable scope specified, the ColdFusion server checks all possible scopes for the existence of the variable. Obviously, this is going to slow the execution time, because the server will run through each possible scope; but in some cases, the vague reference to the variable is desirable, as in the case in which a username could be coming from a form, a database, or a cookie. In this case, if you were to specify form.username, the page wouldn't work with a URL variable named "username."

The following is a list of all the variables used in ColdFusion:

- **Local** A variable that has page scope and that doesn't use a prefix. You can also use the name "LocalVariable" as a prefix.
- **Session** A variable that's available for the entire session of the user.
- **Application** A variable that is available to all users of an application.
- **Client** Special variables that are stored in a cookie on the client's machine, and also in the registry or an ODBC data source on the server, used to identify the user to the server.
- **Form** A form element from the previous page that has been submitted to the current page is treated as a variable with Form scope.

- **URL**   A variable that is attached to the URL from the previous page or from a link.
- **Server**   Variables used by the server.
- **Cookie**   Variables written to the client's machine as cookies.

Caution   *ColdFusion expects a variable to be defined before it is used, and it will throw an error if it finds a variable that hasn't been defined. Always set a default value with a CFPARAM tag if a variable is expected but not defined with a CFSET, like a Form, Session, or URL variable.*

ColdFusion allows the use of arrays and lists, as well, and has a whole slew of functions for dealing with them and converting between the two types. A *list* is simply a comma-separated list (or a list separated by a user-defined character) of values that can be stored in a single variable and manipulated with the various list functions that are available.

Table 10-2 shows a list of the different object and variable types that are permitted in ColdFusion. In general, these types can be assigned to variables and passed in any of the variable types previously described.

Object Type	Object Description
Arrays	Arrays of values or objects.
Boolean	The result of an expression—TRUE or FALSE; converting to numerical gives you 1 and 0, and converting to a string gives you "yes" and "no."
COM	Component Object Model objects can be assigned to variables; and the properties, methods, and events can be addressed with DOT notation.
Date	Date and time values.
Integers	Numbers with no decimal point.
Lists	Strings consisting of any number of elements separated by a delimiter, such as a comma.
Queries	Any resultsets returned from a CFQUERY tag can be treated as an object.
Real Numbers	Floating-point numbers (numbers with a decimal point).
Strings	Text values enclosed by single or double quotes; because of a bug in UltraDev, it is wise to always use single quotes.
Structures	A grouping of elements that enables you to refer to them by name (as in Employee.LastName, if the structure were named Employee).

Table 10-2.   *Object Types in ColdFusion*

The Pound Signs in ColdFusion

If you're unfamiliar with the CFML language, then you're probably wondering about the use of the pound signs (#) around certain expressions. A lot of rules apply to the use of pound signs; but in general, they are used when something is to be evaluated before being sent to the browser, and they are placed around an expression that the ColdFusion server is to differentiate from regular text. For instance, in the following expression, the pound signs signify to the server that the name "username" should be replaced by the value that's stored in the variable named "username":

```
<CFOUTPUT>Welcome #username#!</CFOUTPUT>
```

The pound signs aren't limited to use in text that is to be written to the Web page, however. They can be used inside of any ColdFusion tag to allow a value to be replaced by the current value of the variable:

```
<CFQUERY NAME="myQuery" STARTROW="#startrow#" DATASOURCE="#myDSN#">
```

In this case, assume that two variables have been set up in advance: startrow and myDSN. The startrow variable holds the data that the STARTROW attribute of the CFQUERY tag needs in order to process the tag. The myDSN variable holds the name of a system DSN that was set up in advance as a variable. What the ColdFusion server is doing, in essence, is evaluating the areas in between the pound signs first, then substituting the results of the evaluation in the expression, and then evaluating the expression.

If you are using a function, you have to place the pound signs around the entire expression, as in this example—which simply converts the value in the variable username to uppercase:

```
<CFOUTPUT>Welcome <b>#Ucase(username)#<b></CFOUTPUT>
```

This example also shows that you can put HTML tags inside of a CFOUTPUT statement. Whatever is inside of the CFOUTPUT statement will be sent to the browser.

The pound signs aren't always used, however, which may be confusing to some people. In this expression, for instance, the variable name is enclosed in quotes:

```
<CFIF IsDefined("Form.username")>
```

Here, you are verifying that the Form variable named username exists—you aren't interested in the value. In general, when you are using the variable itself in the expression, and not the value, you don't use the pound signs.

Installing the ColdFusion Server

The ColdFusion server shipped with UltraDev is a single-user version of the ColdFusion Server 4.5.1 Enterprise version, which can be installed on a Windows 95, 98, NT, or 2000 machine. On the Windows NT and Windows 2000 Server OSs, the CF server will run as a service. On the Windows 95 and Windows 98 OSs, the CF server will start as an application and remain running in the background, using a small amount of the system's resources.

Having the server installed on your local machine enables you to test CFM pages locally. You will also have access to the ColdFusion Administrator and the ability to administer your sites and database connections, as well as debug your pages with CF's debugging options.

The installation requires that you have a Web server running on the machine—ColdFusion requires an outside Web server to operate. That server can be Microsoft Internet Information Server (IIS), Microsoft Personal Web Server, the Apache Web server, or Netscape Enterprise Server, among others.

To install the server, you'll need to follow these steps:

1. If you're on a Windows NT or Windows 2000 Server machine, you should install from an account with full administrator privileges. Double-click the Installer icon to run the Installer. Enter your name, company name, and serial number (see Figure 10-2). The serial number should be on your UltraDev jacket sleeve.

2. The wizard will ask you for your Web server type (see Figure 10-3). On a Windows machine, this most likely is the default IIS, Peer Web Server, or Personal Web Server.

3. You are asked to provide the location of a Web server directory (see Figure 10-4). The installation program will default to the root folder of your Web server. All of the Web content of the server will be unpacked to subdirectories under this directory, such as the documentation, examples, and HTML components.

4. You have to decide which components you want to install (see Figure 10-5). Installing everything is recommended. The documentation and examples are invaluable while you are programming your pages.

5. You are asked to provide a program folder name to which to install the Start menu (see Figure 10-6). By default, it will be installed to ColdFusion Server 4.5.1 Enterprise.

6. A confirmation screen shows the selected settings (see Figure 10-7). You have the option of going back and making changes if you so desire, or clicking Next to proceed with the installation.

7. The installation program proceeds to copy the files and folders to the hard drive, and make the necessary changes in the system registry (see Figure 10-8). After the installation is completed, you are asked to restart the computer. When you restart, you will have a fully functional ColdFusion server on your machine.

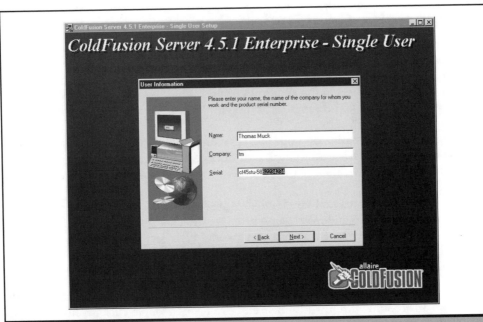

Figure 10-2.   Enter your name, company name, and serial number to begin the ColdFusion server installation

Figure 10-3.   The installation next asks you for your Web server type

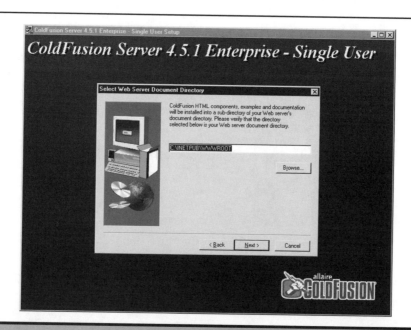

Figure 10-4. *Browse to a folder under your Web directory; the installation program will create subfolders for each of the components it installs*

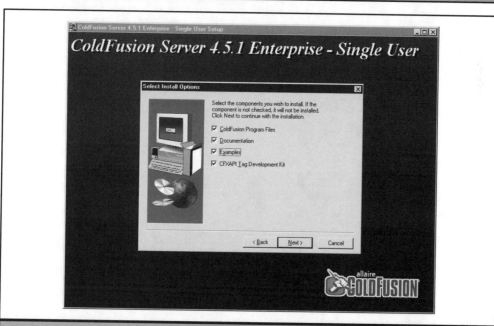

Figure 10-5. *Choose the features you want to install; it's a good idea to check all the features*

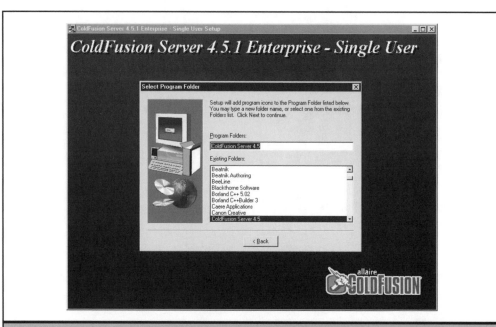

Figure 10-6.   *The Start Menu program folder is chosen next*

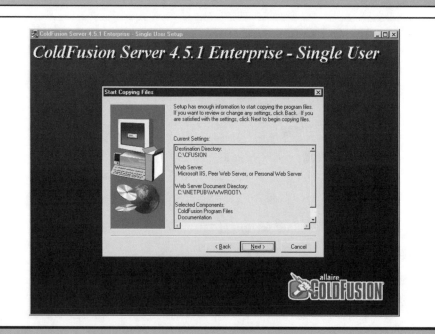

Figure 10-7.   *The installation confirmation page—click Next to continue*

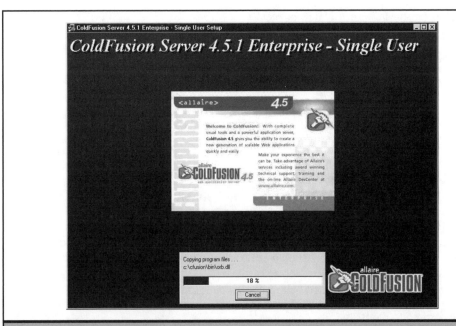

Figure 10-8. *Installing the files necessary for ColdFusion*

ColdFusion Documentation

The best place to start with the server is the ColdFusion Documentation item in the Start menu. The documentation that comes with ColdFusion is fairly extensive and offers examples of each function and tag that is available with the server. The documentation has four sections, and each is broken down into chapters.

Administering the ColdFusion Server

This section of the documentation demonstrates the installation process, as well as some of the basic administration features that you may want to use. Pay particularly close attention to the database administration features of the server. The ColdFusion Administrator enables you to create or modify your system DSNs from the Web interface.

The chapters in this section are broken down as follows:

- Welcome to ColdFusion
- Chapter 1: Installing and Configuring ColdFusion
- Chapter 2: Introduction to ColdFusion Server
- Chapter 3: Configuring ColdFusion Server

- Chapter 4: Managing Data Sources
- Chapter 5: Scheduling and Static Page Generation
- Chapter 6: Creating Scalable and Highly Available Web Sites
- Chapter 7: Using CGI with ColdFusion
- Chapter 8: ColdFusion Security
- Chapter 9: Configuring Basic Security
- Chapter 10: Configuring Advanced Security

Developing Web Applications with ColdFusion

This section of the documentation describes the language and demonstrates how to create Web applications in CFML using step-by-step tutorials. This language is very robust, and the tutorial starts off with the basics and ends up with more advanced topics, such as accessing the registry through ColdFusion. There is a section dealing with the CFAPPLICATION tag, which enables you to create an Application.cfm file that acts as a "global" file in your Web application.

The section is broken down into the following chapters:

- Welcome to ColdFusion
- Chapter 1: Introduction to ColdFusion
- Chapter 2: Writing Your First ColdFusion Application
- Chapter 3: Querying a Database
- Chapter 4: Retrieving and Formatting the Data You Want
- Chapter 5: Making Variables Dynamic
- Chapter 6: Updating Your Data
- Chapter 7: Reusing Code
- Chapter 8: Debugging and Error Handling
- Chapter 9: Handling Complex Data with Structures
- Chapter 10: Building Dynamic Forms
- Chapter 11: Indexing and Searching Data
- Chapter 12: Using the Application Framework
- Chapter 13: Sending and Receiving Email
- Chapter 14: Managing Files on the Server
- Chapter 15: Interacting with Remote Servers
- Chapter 16: Connecting to LDAP Directories
- Chapter 17: Application Security
- Chapter 18: Building Custom CFAPI Tags

- Chapter 19: Using CFOBJECT to Invoke Component Objects
- Chapter 20: Extending ColdFusion Pages with CFML Scripting
- Chapter 21: Accessing the Windows NT Registry

CFML Language Reference

This section of the documentation is the reference that you'll be using most: every tag, function, and expression that is available in ColdFusion is described in detail (see Figure 10-9) within this section. In addition, each tag and function has a corresponding example that runs from the live server using sample databases that are installed with the ColdFusion server. You'll find that you can copy and paste code from the Language Reference into your programs to give you an extra boost when you don't understand a particular syntax.

The chapters available in this section are as follows:

- Contents
- Welcome To ColdFusion
- Chapter 1: ColdFusion Tags

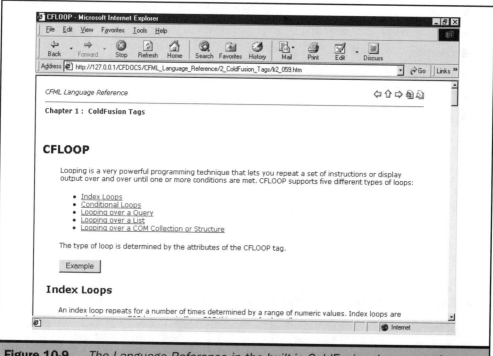

Figure 10-9.   *The Language Reference in the built-in ColdFusion documentation contains information on all tags and functions*

- Chapter 2: ColdFusion Functions
- Chapter 3: WDDX JavaScript Objects
- Chapter 4: ColdFusion Expressions: Operators and Other Constructs

Using ColdFusion Studio

In addition to the server documentation, documentation is provided for ColdFusion Studio, which is available for purchase from Allaire. ColdFusion Studio is based on Homesite, which is also included in the UltraDev package; however, it goes a few steps further. With ColdFusion Studio, you have access to the Remote Data Services, which enables you to access any database connections that you have residing on a remote server. Also, it contains complete support for all the ColdFusion tags.

ColdFusion Studio is a program that works well hand in hand with UltraDev. You can set it up as your default editor for UltraDev and use it to tweak your code after you design the pages inside the UltraDev environment. Trial versions of ColdFusion Studio are available from the Allaire Web site. If you have a slow connection to the Internet, you may request a trial CD-ROM from the Alliare Web site.

The section dealing with CF Studio is broken down into the following chapters:

- Welcome to ColdFusion Studio
- Chapter 1: Installing and Configuring ColdFusion Studio
- Chapter 2: Getting Started
- Chapter 3: Learning HTML and CSS
- Chapter 4: Getting the Most from the Help System
- Chapter 5: Creating Pages
- Chapter 6: Best Practices for Coding HTML and CFML
- Chapter 7: Accessing ColdFusion Data Sources
- Chapter 8: Editing Pages
- Chapter 9: Debugging CFML Applications from Studio
- Chapter 10: Using Projects for Site Management
- Chapter 11: Deploying Projects
- Chapter 12: Testing and Maintaining Web Pages

The ColdFusion Administrator

The ColdFusion Administrator is the interface that enables you to administer the ColdFusion application server (see Figure 10-10). In the Administrator you'll find the functionality to change security settings, add database connections, administer log

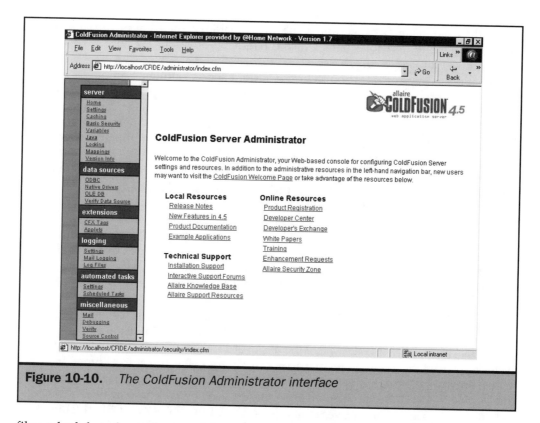

Figure 10-10. *The ColdFusion Administrator interface*

files, schedule tasks, and set up debugging, among other things. If you have a full version of the server installed (not the single-user version), you can administer the server from a remote location through a Web browser.

Accessing the Functionality of the Administrator

When you first install the ColdFusion server, you provide a password for the Administrator. This password is needed to log in to the Administrator. You can override this password setting and allow your Web server to handle the security by protecting the folders that the Administrator pages reside in. You can do this from the Basic Security settings in the Administrator interface.

The server functionality is provided through links in a navigation bar in the left frame of the Administrator interface. This section goes through the various pages that the links point to and gives a short description of some of the things that they do.

The Server Settings

Several functions are listed under the Server heading. The Home page contains links to a wide variety of resources for ColdFusion. Some of these resources were installed as part of the ColdFusion package, and some are available on the Allaire Web site. You can also find the release notes here, which is handy if you apply a service pack to the server and want to know which issues are addressed in the service pack.

The Settings page enables you to assign various server settings. You can set up the limits of simultaneous requests, among other things, which will improve your system's performance. Also, this is where you can define a site-wide error page, and also a site-wide missing template handler. This would be a default page to go to if the user requests a page that doesn't exist. By creating a site-wide error-handling page, you can define how an error will appear to an end user.

The Caching page is where you can set up the size of the Template cache for your machine. If you have plentiful memory, this figure can be set to a fairly high level to allow for faster execution of pages. The pages are stored in cache as they execute, and get removed from cache in a last-in, first-out scenario. Obviously, if the pages are in memory and don't have to be accessed on the hard drive, they will execute more quickly. Also on this page, you can set up the query cache maximum. ColdFusion gives you the opportunity to cache a query in memory, which means that the entire resultset of a query remains in memory. Obviously, this can be overused if you're not careful, but it has definite advantages in certain situations.

The Basic Security page is where you can change the passwords for the Administrator, and also for the ColdFusion Studio. Users of ColdFusion Studio can access the Administrator if they have the password that is defined here. Also on this page, you'll find the ability to restrict access to certain powerful tags. At times, in a shared environment, certain tags should be disabled because of the power behind them. These particular ColdFusion tags should be used only by responsible individuals, to prevent any server meltdowns. The CFREGISTRY and CFFILE tags are especially powerful, and can give a user the ability to take down the server. There is, however, an Unsecured Tags directory that you can set up here to allow access to the forbidden tags by a trusted user.

In the Enterprise version on an NT or Windows 2000 Server, there is also a page for Advanced Security. These settings override the Basic Security settings and allow more advanced security settings to be implemented. Security Contexts can be set up here, which act as "access groups" to allow access to certain pages to certain individuals.

The Variables page enables you to specify where you want your Client variables to be stored. These are special variables that enable you to keep track of users through ID numbers, and that are stored in cookies on a user's machine. By default, these variables are stored in the registry; but they can be stored in an ODBC datasource if you specify a datasource here. Additionally, this page allows you to enable/disable Session and Application variables, or set the default timeout values of these variables.

The Java page allows configuration of the Java settings that might be used by ColdFusion. For instance, if you have custom CF tags written in Java you can store the classpath here so that CF will have a way to access it.

The Locking page gives you the opportunity to lock Session, Application, and Server variables by default, or allow only single-threaded access to variables by one user.

The Mappings page allows you to set up virtual directories that the ColdFusion server will recognize. By default, the only directory listed here is the root directory that you specified upon installation.

The Version Info page gives you the information about the build that you have installed on your machine. Here you will find the version number, edition, serial number, and operating system information.

Data Sources

ODBC is a page on its own that gives you a complete list of system Data Source Names (DSNs) that are available on the machine. You can also verify the connection from this interface. In addition, it acts as the interface to actually create DSNs or modify existing DSNs, eliminating the need to use the ODBC Control Panel.

If you have the Enterprise version, or the Single-User Enterprise Edition, there is a page for Native Drivers. These are native connections to certain high-end databases, such as Oracle, DB2, Informix, and Sybase. You can add, modify, or delete native connections from this page.

The OLE DB page enables you to create OLE DB connections. By default, it has settings for SQLOLEDB and Microsoft.Jet.OLEDB.3.51. On this page, you can add, modify, or delete OLE DB connections.

Finally, the Verify Data Source page lists all connections available to ColdFusion, with the ability to verify the data source. The page also has a button that enables the administrator to release all cached connections.

Extensions

ColdFusion is extensible through C++ or Java and the use of CFX_ tags. These tags can be registered on the machine through the CFX Tags page. Custom tags can be an extremely powerful addition to the server, and they can be found on the Allaire site or on many other ColdFusion support sites all over the Internet.

The Applets page enables you to register Java applets for use by the ColdFusion server. After naming the applet and clicking Register New Applet, you are taken to a form in which you can enter all of its parameters.

Logging

On the Settings page, you can define a default directory for all ColdFusion logs. Also, the system administrator's e-mail address is stored on this page. If you insert an e-mail address here, it will appear on error pages. There's also a handy option here to log which pages take longer than a specified number of seconds to execute, to help you pinpoint where bottlenecks exist.

The Mail Logging page gives you the option to log all messages sent by ColdFusion.

The Log Files page is a handy access to the log files through hyperlinks to the actual log files on your server. You can view the log as a text file in your browser or choose to download the file.

INTRODUCTION TO WEB SCRIPTING

Automated Tasks

The Settings page enables you to specify how often to check for new scheduled tasks; also, it allows you to enable the logging of scheduled tasks.

Scheduled tasks can be a great time saver for repetitive tasks, and they have the full arsenal of ColdFusion tags available to them, such as CFFILE and CFMAIL.

The Scheduled Tasks page enables you to automatically execute a ColdFusion page. You could, for instance, schedule a page to automate creation of reports for logging or click-through information (see Figure 10-11).

Miscellaneous

The Miscellaneous heading has a few server options that don't fit well into any other category.

The Mail page enables you to set up the default mail server for ColdFusion.

The Debugging page enables you to set up debugging for your ColdFusion development. By default, it's disabled; but you can allow debugging information to be accessible to certain IP addresses. The debugging information available includes such

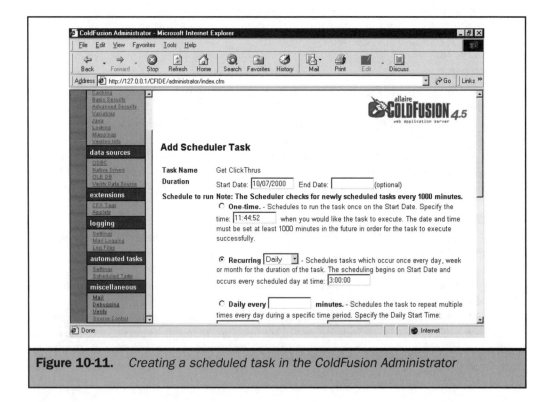

Figure 10-11. *Creating a scheduled task in the ColdFusion Administrator*

things as processing time; variable names and values; query record count, time, and SQL statement; and all server variables.

The Verity page enables you to set up verity collections for allowing searches on your site. One verity collection is already set up when you install the server—the cfdocumentation collection, which allows fast searches of the ColdFusion documentation that resides on your Web server.

The Source Control page allows the administrator to set up Microsoft Visual SourceSafe for use by ColdFusion Studio. The SourceSafe network installation must be on the same server as the CF server in order to use this feature.

Learning the CFML Language

It is not required that the ColdFusion server be installed on your local machine to use UltraDev with ColdFusion, but it makes life easier. In general, you'll be able to debug your pages more quickly locally if you don't have to upload them to the server each time and maintain a connection to the remote server.

Furthermore, you don't have to know the language of ColdFusion to use UltraDev—but it surely helps. This section goes through some of the basic (and later through some of the advanced) functionality of ColdFusion and how it relates in the UltraDev environment. This discussion assumes the reader has a little general programming knowledge.

The Core ColdFusion Tags

These are the tags that are considered "required" for any ColdFusion developer. Coincidentally, all of these tags are included in the ColdFusion Express package.

CFSET and CFPARAM

These two tags enable you to set variables and parameters in ColdFusion. What's the difference between them? With a CFSET tag, you are simply assigning a value to a variable, as in the following expression:

```
<CFSET Session.UserID = myQuery.userID>
```

Here, you are assigning the userID value from a query to the Session variable UserID.

With CFPARAM, you have three choices. You can check for a parameter's existence by using the NAME attribute, check to make sure that a variable is of a specific type by using the TYPE attribute, or set a DEFAULT value for a possible variable:

```
<CFPARAM NAME="form.username" DEFAULT="newuser">
```

In this instance, you have a Form variable of "username" that is expected on the page. But what if the user types in the link by hand and doesn't use the login form? In that case, there is a risk of errors on the page, because your ColdFusion functions are expecting a Form variable named "username." If the Form variable doesn't exist, it's given a default value. If the variable *does* exist, the CFPARAM statement doesn't do anything. It's only there as a safeguard to give a value to a parameter that may or may not exist. It can be used with any of the variable types, as in this statement:

```
<CFPARAM NAME="url.userid" DEFAULT="baddata">
```

In this case, you're expecting that a URL variable contains the value for userid. If, for some reason, the URL variable doesn't come through, the default value of "baddata" is assigned to the URL variable.

 When addressing variables on the ColdFusion page, an error will be thrown if the variable is referred to and it doesn't exist. You can either check for the variable's existence before using it, or you can set up a CFPARAM to give it a default value.

You can also use ColdFusion functions within a CFSET or CFPARAM declaration. The CFSET in that statement will assign a date that is seven days ago from the current server date to the variable named "Lastweek":

```
<CFSET Lastweek=DateFormat((Now()) - 7)>
```

The following statement sets a variable equal to the filename of the current page without the file extension such as *mypage* if the path was c:/inetpub/wwwroot/bettergig/mypage.cfm:

```
<CFSET CurrentPage = GetFileFromPath(GetCurrentTemplatePath())>
<CFSET CurrentPage = Left(CurrentPage,Len(CurrentPage)-4)>
```

Variables can also be declared in CFSCRIPT, which is discussed in the next section.

CFOUTPUT

The CFOUTPUT tag is the multipurpose bull worker of ColdFusion. It does many things besides display text, which you've seen in a few examples. In general, it's used to interpret ColdFusion functions and expressions so that the result can be output to the browser. It also acts as a loop when you specify the QUERY attribute. The QUERY attribute can be the result of a database query, or it can be the name of a CFPOP tag or a CFDIRECTORY tag. It can be used in the body of the document to display text in the browser, or to dynamically apply a value to an HTML element. Here are a few examples. The following simply displays the current server time in the browser:

```
<CFOUTPUT>The time is now #TimeFormat(Now())#</CFOUTPUT>
```

This example shows the CFOUTPUT tag used to insert a value returned from a query into a hidden form element:

```
<input type="hidden" name="hiddenAccessCode"
value="<CFOUTPUT>#UserAccessQuery.AccessCode#</CFOUTPUT>">
```

The next example will populate an unordered list (bulleted list) with the results of a CFQUERY tag, which can be one row or a thousand rows. The results are limited only by the capacity of the browser. In actual practice, you'll break up the queries with the MAXROWS attribute:

```
<ul>
<CFOUTPUT QUERY="myQuery"><li>#FirstName# #LastName#</li></CFOUTPUT>
</ul>
```

> **Tip** *The CFOUTPUT QUERY acts as a loop by itself and does not need any other programming to construct a loop, such as a for/next or do/while construct.*

The next example will dynamically populate the title of the page with the filename of the current file without the path. In other words, the browser will see <title>*mypage*</title>:

```
<title><CFOUTPUT>
#Replace(GetFileFromPath(GetCurrentTemplatePath()),".cfm","")#
</CFOUTPUT></title>
```

CFIF/CFELSE/CFELSEIF

These tags are used in ColdFusion to implement conditional logic. The CFIF tag enables you to check for a condition before executing a statement. The CFIF tag has a corresponding closing tag that must be used. Here's an example:

```
<CFIF form.password NEQ rsCustomers.password>
    <CFLOCATION URL="FailedLogin.cfm">
</CFIF>
```

> **Note** *The NEQ statement means "not equal to" and is the same as <> in VBScript or != in Java and JavaScript. ColdFusion uses EQ for "equal to" in comparisons.*

The CFELSE and CFELSEIF tags can be used in the conditional statements to construct more complex conditions. They must be used within a CFIF code block. Here's an example using both:

```
<CFIF form.location EQ "Buffalo">
    <CFSET session.location = "NY">
<CFELSEIF form.location EQ "Rochester">
    <CFSET session.location = "NY">
<CFELSE>
    <CFSET session.location = "not valid location">
</CFIF>
```

There are many functions available to ColdFusion users that increase the efficiency of the conditional logic. Here are a few examples. The first one uses the ColdFusion function IsDate to determine whether the user has entered a date value:

```
<CFIF form.dateofbirth EQ "">
    You didn't enter a date!
<CFELSEIF IsDate(form.dateofbirth) is TRUE>
    You were born
<CFOUTPUT>#DateDiff('yyyy',form.dateofbirth,Now())#
    </CFOUTPUT> years ago.
<CFELSE>
    Your entry was invalid.  Please go back and try again.
</CFIF>
```

The next example checks a variable to make sure it's an array, using the ColdFusion function IsArray. If it isn't an array, the user hasn't reached the minimum of two purchases. If it is an array, the shipping cost is set using the number of elements in the session.ShoppingCart variable:

```
<CFIF Not(IsArray(session.ShoppingCart)) is TRUE>
    <CFLOCATION URL="Error.cfm?error=LessThan2Items">
<CFELSEIF IsArray(session.ShoppingCart,2) is TRUE>
    <CFSET session.shipping = 7.50>
<CFELSEIF IsArray(session.ShoppingCart,3) is TRUE>
    <CFSET session.shipping = 8.50>
<CFELSE>
    <CFSET session.shipping = 9.50>
</CFIF>
```

CFQUERY

If you are familiar with ASP or JSP, you know that you must create a recordset object to retrieve a *resultset*. In ColdFusion, you don't create a recordset, per se—you define a CFQUERY tag giving a datasource and a Select statement, and the ColdFusion server does the rest. Here's an example that simply retrieves all columns and all records from the Customers table of the Orders database:

```
<CFQUERY NAME="rsCustomers" DATASOURCE="Orders">
Select * from Customers
</CFQUERY>
```

The only two required parameters for the tag are NAME and DATASOURCE. The query needs a name so that it can be referred to on the page when displaying the information. For instance, a FirstName column can be referred to like this:

```
<CFOUTPUT>#rsCustomers.FirstName#</CFOUTPUT>
```

The DATASOURCE parameter is simply a system DSN that has been previously established in the ODBC Administrator on the machine, or in the ColdFusion Administrator interface.

The CFQUERY tag can pass commands to your database in the form of valid Structured Query Language (SQL). These commands can be simple Select statements, as in the previous example, or they can be Insert, Update, or Delete statements—or even stored procedures. The CFQUERY tag can be thought of as an interface to the database.

> **Tip** *Although the CFQUERY tag will perform all the required database interactions, other ColdFusion tags are targeted for inserts, updates, and stored procedures.*

Another powerful construct of the CFQUERY tag is that you can use any valid ColdFusion statements within the text of the query. Here's an example that checks for the existence of an optional search attribute; and if it exists, it then checks for a null value before assigning a WHERE clause to the query:

```
<CFQUERY NAME="rsProducts" DATASOURCE="Orders">
SELECT * from Products
<CFIF IsDefined("form.product")>
    <CFIF form.product NEQ "">
        WHERE Product Like '%form.product%'
    </CFIF>
</CFIF>
</CFQUERY>
```

By using conditional logic inside of a ColdFusion query, you can save server resources by passing only the statements that are needed for the current task.

Other attributes are available to CFQUERY, such as STARTROW and MAXROWS, which make it easy to set up pages that show partial resultsets. Consult the ColdFusion documentation for a full explanation of the CFQUERY tag.

CFLOCATION

The CFLOCATION tag is similar to the Response.Redirect statement in ASP or the response.sendRedirect statement in JSP. When the ColdFusion server finds this tag, the processing of the page stops and the user is redirected to another page. The tag has only two parameters: URL and Addtoken. The URL parameter is simply the location that the user will be redirected to. It can be a relative or an absolute URL. The Addtoken parameter adds the user's Client variable information to the URL and takes a "yes" or "no" value (which is assumed to be "no" if it's not specified). In this example, the user is redirected to an error page, with Client variables not being sent:

```
<CFIF Not IsDefined("form.username")>
<CFLOCATION URL="error.htm">
</CFIF>
```

CFCOOKIE

The CFCOOKIE tag sets a cookie on the user's machine. The parameters are NAME, VALUE, EXPIRES, SECURE, PATH, and DOMAIN. The NAME parameter is the only required parameter of the tag. The VALUE parameter enables you to set a value to the cookie. The EXPIRES parameter can be used with an absolute date, as in 12/31/2000, or a number of days, as in 10, 30, or 100. Two other values can be used in the EXPIRES parameter: Now and Never. If you set the attribute to Now, you are effectively deleting the cookie from the client's browser. If you set it to Never, the cookie never expires.

Here's an example of a cookie being set depending on the status of a "Remember Me" check box on the previous page:

```
<CFIF IsDefined("chkRememberMe") is TRUE>
    <CFCOOKIE NAME="RememberMe" VALUE="TRUE" EXPIRES="Never">
<CFELSE>
    <CFCOOKIE NAME="RememberMe" EXPIRES="Now">
</CFIF>
```

For a full explanation of the use of the CFCOOKIE tag, see the Allaire ColdFusion documentation.

CFINCLUDE

The CFINCLUDE tag takes only one parameter: Template. Recall that a template is the ColdFusion term for a .cfm or .cfml page. The CFINCLUDE statement enables the user to insert a separate ColdFusion page into the current page. This is useful for such things as headers, footers, login screens, welcome statements, and a host of other uses. In addition, any variables declared in a ColdFusion page can be referenced from the included file, and vice versa. When you use the CFINCLUDE tag, it's as if the code were directly inserted into your page. Here's an example of a CFINCLUDE tag being used conditionally in a login page:

```
<CFLOCK SCOPE="Session" TYPE="ReadOnly">
<CFIF (Not IsDefined("session.login") is TRUE)
      AND (session.login NEQ "loggedIn")>
    <CFSET NotLogged = "true">
</CFIF>
</CFLOCK>
<CFIF NotLogged EQ "true">
    <CFINCLUDE Template="LoginForm.cfm">
<CFELSE>
    <CFINCLUDE Template="WelcomePage.cfm">
</CFIF>
```

ColdFusion Comment Tags

You can comment your code in ColdFusion using the special comment tags that look similar to HTML comment tags, except that they have an extra dash character, as in the following example:

```
<!---This is a ColdFusion Comment--->
```

The comments that you create using this syntax won't be viewable in the browser—the server strips them out when the page is processed. They also don't add significantly to the processing time, so it's wise to use comments liberally so that the code can be more easily deciphered.

CFSCRIPT and Its Use in UltraDev

CFScript, introduced to ColdFusion in version 4, allows the use of a JavaScript-like syntax to write code on a ColdFusion page. Although CFScript is similar to JavaScript, it's not interchangeable. Many features of JavaScript aren't available to CFScript. One advantage of CFScript over JavaScript is the use of ColdFusion functions within the script language—all ColdFusion functions are available to the script language as well.

Caution *Although ColdFusion functions are available to CFScript, the tags are not.*

The creators of UltraDev used CFScript extensively in all of the Server Behaviors that work with ColdFusion. This was done primarily to keep the Server Behaviors consistent between server models, and also because of the way in which the Server

Behavior API works. In any event, when you start to look at the code that UltraDev generates, you'll notice a large amount of CFScript as opposed to ColdFusion tags.

CFScript has some great features, but also some major limitations:

- You can't create a user-defined function, as you can in JavaScript, although the upcoming ColdFusion 5 promises to add user-defined functions.

- You can't create "local" variables—all variables are accessible to the whole page.

- It provides no access to the Document Object Model (DOM) of the Web page. This is a client-side technology, and CFScript is executed only on the server.

- The JavaScript functions, methods, and operators aren't carried over, such as the string manipulation methods and the comparison operators.

Here is an example of a CFScript code block and the equivalent code using ColdFusion tags:

Using CFScript

```
<CFSCRIPT>
Customers = StructNew();
  Customers.Name = form.name;
  Customers.CustID = Session.UserID;
  Customers.email = form.email;
  Customers.state = form.state;
  Customers.LastAccessDate = Now();
</CFSCRIPT>
```

Using ColdFusion Tags

```
<CFSET Customers = StructNew()>
<CFSET Customers.Name = form.name>
<CFSET Customers.CustID = Session.UserID>
<CFSET Customers.email = form.email>
<CFSET Customers.state = form.state>
<CFSET Customers.LastAccessDate = Now()>
```

The key advantage to using CFScript in this example is to avoid the redundant use of CFSET tags to declare the variables. In general, if you have three or more variables in a row to declare, you might consider enclosing the declarations within a CFScript block.

There's not much documentation on CFScript, but you can use what you know about JavaScript and make notes of the changes between JavaScript and CFScript. Table 10-3 shows the comparison operators in JavaScript and the equivalent CFScript operators. Note that the comparison operators are also valid in CFML.

Comparison Operators	JavaScript	CFScript
Equal to	==	EQ or IS
Not equal to	!=	NEQ or IS NOT
Greater than	>	GT
Less than	<	LT
Greater than or equal to	>=	GTE
Less than or equal to	<=	LTE
Contains	indexOf method	Contains
Doesn't contain	indexOf method	Does Not Contain

Table 10-3.   *Comparison Operators in JavaScript and the Equivalent CFScript Operators*

Advanced ColdFusion Tags

You've seen some of the simple tags and examples that make up ColdFusion, but you may have been wondering how to do more advanced programming using the CFML tags. Some of the more advanced server-side functionality is built right into the ColdFusion language.

Sending E-Mail with ColdFusion

One of the features of ColdFusion that is widely used is the CFMAIL tag, which enables you to send e-mail from the Web page. You need to have access to a mail server to use this feature, but most Web servers nowadays include this functionality. To use the tag, you have to put it on the page with a few parameters, and you're all set. The next example assumes that you've submitted a form from the previous page with text fields named txtFrom, txtTo, txtSubject, and txtBody:

```
<CFMAIL TO="#form.txtTo#"
    FROM="#form.txtFrom#"
    SUBJECT="#form.subject#"
    SERVER="mail.mysite.com"
    >
#form.message#
</CFMAIL>
```

The CFMAIL tag also has other optional attributes. You can find the full list in the ColdFusion documentation. An easy method to send bulk e-mail to a list of e-mail addresses in a database is also available. You simply have to use a CFQUERY tag to get the e-mail addresses, like this:

```
<CFQUERY NAME="emailQuery" DATASOURCE="Customers">
SELECT email FROM customers
</CFQUERY>
```

Then, you can use this query name in the CFMAIL tag by using the QUERY attribute of the CFMAIL tag:

```
<CFMAIL TO="#emailQuery.txtTo#"
     QUERY="emailQuery"
     FROM="info@bettergig.com"
     SUBJECT="Monthly News from Bettergig"
     SERVER="mail.mysite.com"
     TYPE="HTML"
     >
<CFINCLUDE TEMPLATE="ThisMonthNewsletter.htm">
</CFMAIL>
```

Notice that the FROM and SUBJECT attributes were specified this time, and TYPE, which enables you to send HTML e-mail, and QUERY, which causes the CFMAIL tag to loop through all rows returned by the query, were added. Then, the emailQuery.email column of the database is referenced in the TO attribute to cause the tag to send out an e-mail to everyone in the database. Also, the body of the e-mail wasn't hard-coded— instead, the CFINCLUDE tag was used to include an HTML file as the body of the e-mail.

Retrieving E-Mail with ColdFusion

In addition to the CFMAIL tag for sending e-mail, ColdFusion comes with a tag to retrieve e-mail from a POP e-mail server. The CFPOP tag enables you to get the messages from the server, or the headers only, and also offers the option to delete the messages. Here's a basic CFPOP implementation that checks an e-mail box that a user has specified in a form on the previous page, and returns the messages, displaying them on the page using a CFOUTPUT tag:

```
<CFPOP SERVER="#form.servername#"
     USERNAME="#form.username#"
     PASSWORD="#form.password#"
     ACTION="GetAll"
     NAME="exampleMessages">
<!---at this point, all messages have been retrieved
     The Cfoutput tag will display the entire list--->
```

```
<CFOUTPUT>
<b>You have #exampleMessages.RecordCount# messages</b><br>
</CFOUTPUT>
<table>
<CFOUTPUT QUERY="exampleMessages">
<tr><td>#From#</td><td>#subject#</td><td>#date#</td></tr>
<tr><td colspan=3>#body#</td></tr>
<tr><td colspan=3><hr></td></tr>
</CFOUTPUT>
</table>
```

First, the CFPOP tag retrieves all the messages. There are also optional attributes for STARTROW and MAXROWS that make it possible to page through the resultset as if it were a resultset of rows from a query. A CFOUTPUT tag is used to display the number of messages, stored in the RecordCount property that is referenced by the name of the CFPOP instance using dot notation. Then, a CFOUTPUT tag is used to display the results in a table. The table has three rows; with the From, Subject, and Date fields of the e-mail displayed in the first row, the Body of the e-mail in the second row; and a horizontal rule tag (<hr>) in the third row to act as a divider between rows. The page can be seen in Figure 10-12. As you saw in the earlier CFOUTPUT examples, the tag serves as a loop if a QUERY attribute is specified. In this case, the query name is the name of the CFPOP instance, specified by the NAME attribute of the CFPOP tag.

Other attributes for the CFPOP tag make it usable for attachments. Consult the ColdFusion documentation for a full explanation of this powerful tag.

File Manipulation in ColdFusion

The CFFILE tag is a multipurpose tag for file manipulation. It's a powerful tag that has access to the entire server, so many Web-hosting companies have the tag disabled in the ColdFusion Administrator. The ACTION attribute specifies the type of action that you want to take with the file. The ACTION attribute can take any one of the following parameters:

- Upload
- Move
- Rename
- Copy
- Delete
- Read
- ReadBinary
- Append

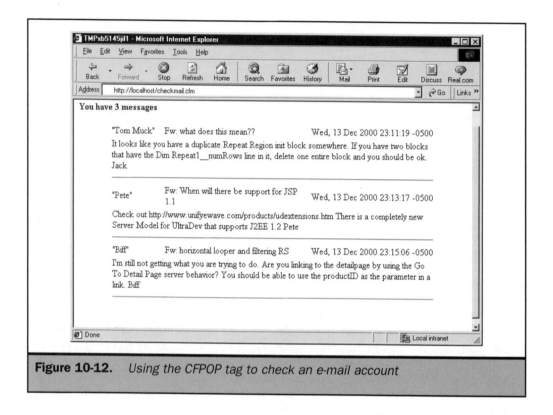

Figure 10-12. *Using the CFPOP tag to check an e-mail account*

The following is an example of a CFFILE tag used with an action of Upload, to allow a user to upload files to the server:

```
<CFFILE ACTION="Upload"
    FILEFIELD="txtFilename"
    DESTINATION="c:\inetpub\wwwroot\uploads\"
    NAMECONFLICT="MakeUnique"
    ACCEPT="image/gif,image/jpg">
```

This example assumes that a user has entered a filename in the txtFilename text field on the previous page. This should be a text field with a type of file, and includes the Browse button for the user to browse to a file on the user's hard drive. The destination in this case is set to the uploads directory under c:\inetpub\wwwroot; and the NameConflict attribute is set to MakeUnique, which will ensure that the filename is unique when it is saved to the hard drive.

> **Note**
>
> *Other NameConflict values are Overwrite, Skip, and Error. Overwrite is
> self-explanatory, but the Skip and Error values need further explanation. The Error
> value enables you to write custom code to handle conditions of the upload in the event
> of an error—i.e. you can display your own error message and redirect the user to try
> another filename if the file already exists. The Skip attribute enables you to write custom
> code to handle conditions of the upload depending upon the value of the FILE attribute
> that is returned when the CFFILE executes.*

In the next example, a file named GuestBook.txt is written to by the user;
the example assumes that the user has filled out a txtComment text field on the
previous page:

```
<CFFILE ACTION="Append"
    FILE="c:\inetpub\wwwroot\comments\GuestBook.txt"
    OUTPUT="#form.txtComment#">
```

Using CFFILE in Combination with CFDIRECTORY

Finally, the next example
is of a CFFILE tag using an action of Delete. This example also illustrates the use of
a CFDIRECTORY tag, which will display the contents of a given Web directory. This
page will display a list of files in the current directory as a list of links to download the
file, and also display a Delete link that enables you to delete the file from the server
(see Figure 10-13). The file is named Home.cfm. As you can see, the CFFILE tag is
capable of some pretty powerful functions.

```
<!---First, set up a url parameter named "file" --->
<CFPARAM Name="url.file" default="">
<!---Next, check for a value in url.file, and create a variable
    named DeleteFile containing the path to the file--->
<CFIF url.file NEQ "">
    <CFSET DeleteFile = ¬
        Replace(GetTemplatePath(),"home.cfm","") & Url.file>
<!---Next, the CFFILE tag has two parameters: Action, and File--->
    <CFFILE ACTION="Delete"
        FILE="#DeleteFile#">
</CFIF>
<!---Next, the CFDIRECTORY tag displays the whole directory,
    using a filter of *.gif to only display GIF files--->
<CFDIRECTORY DIRECTORY="c:\inetpub\wwwroot\testingCFFILE"
    NAME="FileCleanup"
    FILTER="*.gif"
```

```
     SORT="name ASC, size DESC">
<!---Lastly, we set up a table using the CFOUTPUT tag to loop thru
     the list of names in the directory by specifying a Query
     attribute.  Variables are defined for "link" and "deletelink"
     upon each iteration of the loop.  The "deletelink" contains
     the URL variable for the current filename--->
<table>
<CFOUTPUT QUERY="FileCleanup">
<CFSET link='<a href=' & chr(34) & #FileCleanup.Name# ¬
    & chr(34) & '>#FileCleanup.Name#</a>'>
<CFSET deleteLink = '<a href=' & chr(34) & ¬
'home.cfm?file=#FileCleanup.Name#' & chr(34) & '>Delete</a>'>
<tr>
    <td>#link#</td>
    <td>#deleteLink#</td>
</tr>
</CFOUTPUT>
</table>
```

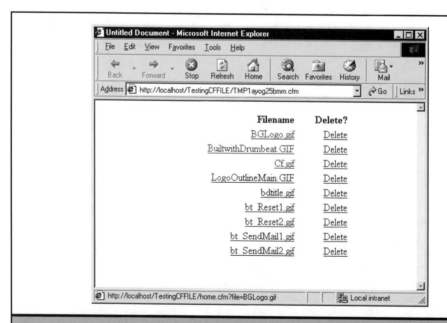

Figure 10-13.   *Using a CFDIRECTORY tag in combination with a CFFILE tag using a Delete action*

Using CFTRY and CFCATCH

One of the more powerful features of ColdFusion is the error-handling ability using CFTRY and CFCATCH. The way these tags are utilized is to put a CFTRY tag around a block of code on which you want to enable error handling. For instance, you could place the CFTRY block around a database insert, and then handle any resulting database errors using your custom code rather than by letting ColdFusion display an error message.

CFTRY requires that you have at least one CFCATCH block within the CFTRY block. CFCATCH encloses the code that you want to execute if an error occurs within the CFTRY block. The CFCATCH tag enables you to use the TYPE attribute to pinpoint the types of errors that are encountered. This way, you can customize the error handling of the page depending upon what type of error is encountered. The types that are allowed are as follows:

- Application (default)
- Database
- Template
- Security
- Object
- MissingInclude
- Expression
- Lock
- Custom_type
- Any (default)

Here's an example of a CFTRY/CFCATCH block that traps the database errors that might occur when the CFQUERY tag executes:

```
<CFTRY>
<CFQUERY NAME='rsCustomers' DATASOURCE='Orders'>
INSERT into Customers(FirstName, LastName, CurrentDate)
VALUES ('#form.Firstname#','#form.lastname#',#Now()#)
</CFQUERY>
<CFCATCH TYPE='Database'>
    <CFLOCATION URL='Error.cfm?error=database'>
</CFCATCH>
<CFCATCH>
    <CFLOCATION URL='Home.cfm?error=1'>
</CFCATCH>
</CFTRY>
```

The example is a CFQUERY using an Insert statement inside of a CFTRY block. The first CFCATCH statement checks for database errors and redirects the user to the Error.cfm page with an error parameter set to "Database." The second CFCATCH block catches all other errors and redirects the user to the Home.cfm page, with an error flag set as well.

The use of CFTRY/CFCATCH is useful for debugging, as well, with options for error messages, exception type, stack trace, SQLSTATE from the database, and a host of other informative properties. Check the ColdFusion documentation for a full explanation of the error-handling capabilities of ColdFusion.

Creating a ColdFusion Application with the CFAPPLICATION Tag

The Application.cfm file and the CFAPPLICATION tag that is associated with the page require mention. For those familiar with ASP, the Application.cfm page is similar in concept to the global.asa file. Session and Application variables are enabled in this file (you can't use the variables without first enabling them from this file), and timeout values for the Application and Session variables are set.

When a page is requested with a .cfm extension, the ColdFusion server first checks whether an Application.cfm file exists. If it does, the server executes the Application.cfm page first. The Application.cfm page, in many cases, will contain the authentication code for a user. If the user is logged in, the page that was requested will execute; if the user is not logged in, the login form in the Application.cfm page will be displayed.

The CFAPPLICATION tag is declared on the page as follows:

```
<CFAPPLICATION NAME="myApplication"
     SESSIONMANAGEMENT="Yes"
     CLIENTMANAGEMENT="Yes"
     APPLICATIONTIMEOUT="#CreateTimeSpan(2,0,0,0)#"
     SESSIONTIMEOUT="#CreateTimeSpan(0,0,5,0)#"
>
```

The SESSIONMANAGEMENT attribute assumes a Yes or No value. If the value is Yes, then Session variables can be used in the pages of the application. The CreateTimeSpan function is a built-in ColdFusion function that enables you to specify days, hours, minutes, and seconds as a comma-delimited list and have the list automatically converted to a date/time object that can be manipulated by the ColdFusion server.

Also, application-level variables can be defined on this page. These are variables that can be used by all users of the application. These variables are usually locked with a CFLOCK tag, as in the following example:

```
<CFLOCK SCOPE="Application" TIMEOUT="30" TYPE="Exclusive">
<CFIF Not IsDefined("application.States")>
     <CFQUERY NAME="getStates" DATASOURCE="Orders">
     SELECT States from StateTable
     </CFQUERY>
          <CFSET application.States = ValueList(getStates.States)>
</CFIF>
</CFLOCK>
```

The example first locks the Application variable from all access. Then, it checks whether the Application variable named "States" has been defined. If it has, nothing is executed; but if it hasn't, a CFQUERY tag is executed. The query returns a list of U.S. States, which is then stored as a list in an Application variable named "States." The access of the variable inside of a CFLOCK ensures that no access is permitted to the variable by any other user while it is being written to by this page. This block of code is executed only once when the page is hit for the first time, and then again after the application times out. Application timeouts are usually set pretty high—several days—whereas Session timeouts are usually set between 5 and 20 minutes.

ColdFusion and UltraDev

ColdFusion has been around for a while and has developed a core following of loyal users. ColdFusion developers did not have a visual tool for developing Web sites until UltraDev came along. ColdFusion Studio is an impressive package for the programmer, but offers little in the way of a visual design environment. UltraDev, in its first-generation release, is the strong beginning of a powerful visual environment for designers and programmers. Also, because it is multiplatform, many of the same techniques can be applied to ASP, JSP, and ColdFusion pages from within the same environment.

The ColdFusion Data Bindings Palette

When you click the Window menu and select Data Bindings, the Data Bindings Inspector pops up, which is side by side with the Server Behaviors Inspector in a default "out of the box" environment. The palette contains the various data sources that are available to the ColdFusion developer:

■ **Recordset**   This is where the CFQUERY tag is generated. It can be a Select, Insert, or Delete statement.

■ **Stored Procedure**   This data source writes a CFSTOREDPROC tag to the page.

■ **Form Variable**   Displays the contents of a Form variable on the page.

- **URL Variable**   Displays the contents of a URL variable on the page.
- **Session Variable**   Displays the contents of a Session variable on the page.
- **Client Variable**   Displays the contents of a Client variable on the page.
- **Application Variable**   Displays the contents of an Application variable on the page.
- **Cookie Variable***   Displays the contents of a cookie.
- **CGI Variable***   Displays the contents of a CGI variable.
- **Server Variable***   Displays the contents of a Server variable.
- **Local Variable***   Displays the contents of a Local variable.

*Introduced in UltraDev 4

Defining a recordset on a ColdFusion page causes UltraDev to generate a CFQUERY tag with a DATASOURCE attribute that matches the datasource that was established when you defined your connection. If you've coded ColdFusion queries in the past, you may have used a Select statement similar to this:

```
SELECT UserID, Username, Password, GroupID
FROM AdminUsers
WHERE Username = '#form.username#'
AND Password = '#form.password#'
```

In UltraDev, the run-time values for the query have to be defined as variables before using the query (see Figure 10-14). This is done by defining a variable Name, a Default Value, and a Run-time Value. The Name entry can be any valid variable name, but it's a good idea to use something that won't be mistaken for something else or cause a conflict. It's also a good idea to append a prefix to your variables to distinguish them from other variables. The Default Value entry should be something that won't be in the database, although for testing, you can use a value here that you know *is* in the database. The Run-time Value column is where you put the incoming data that you want in your query—in this case, form.username and form.password.

The following is the code that UltraDev 1 will produce for this query:

```
<cfparam name="form.username" default="%">
<cfparam name="form.password" default="%">
<cfparam name="rsUsers__TM_username" default="#form.username#">
<cfparam name="rsUsers__TM_password" default="#form.password#">
<cfquery name="rsUsers" datasource="db2000_bookstore"  >
SELECT UserID, UserName, Password, GroupID
FROM AdminUsers WHERE UserName =
```

```
#rsUsers__TM_username#'
AND Password = '#rsUsers__TM_password#'
</cfquery>
<cfset rsUsers_NumRows = 0>
<cfset rsUsers_Index = 1>
```

Note *ColdFusion programmers generally like to use uppercase letters when referencing tags. However, UltraDev generates lowercase tags for most of its ColdFusion code.*

The code is fairly clean, but contains an extra set of variables that UltraDev has generated for the query—rsUsers__TM_username and rsUsers__TM_password. These variables take the place of the run-time values that you inserted when the recordset was created. You can also see from the listing that UltraDev has set up the CFPARAM statements to assign default values to the variables used. Last, two more variables are set up after the query is executed—rsUsers_NumRows and rsUsers_Index. These variables are used by the Repeat Region Server Behavior and also by a few of the "Move to" Server Behaviors. UltraDev 4 uses the same principle, but shifts the actual

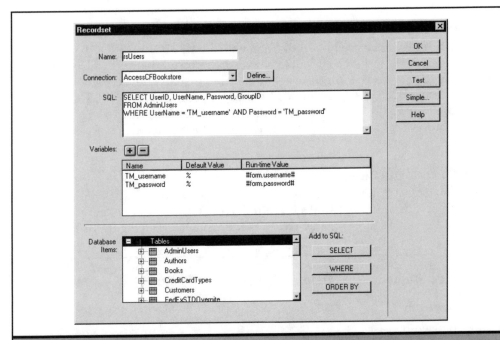

Figure 10-14.   *Setting up a CFQUERY in UltraDev using the recordset datasource*

datasource name, username, and password to an external connections file that it includes with a CFINCLUDE tag, and uses variables to reference the connection.

 If you hand-code a CFQUERY tag on your page instead of using the Data Bindings interface, these extra variables normally created by UltraDev won't be in place and you won't be able to use certain Server Behaviors.

The Recordset dialog box also enables you to create Insert, Update, and Delete statements by hand-coding the SQL in the dialog box; but the resulting CFQUERY doesn't show up in the Data Bindings palette, because it doesn't return a resultset. It will, however, show up in the Server Behaviors palette. There are also Server Behaviors that enable you to create Insert, Update, and Delete statements in a more "wizard-like" manner. The following SQL statement inserted in the SQL box of the Recordset dialog box will insert the values of two form fields—username and password—into the Employers table. The variables that take the place of the form fields in the SQL statement are shown in Table 10-4:

```
INSERT INTO Employers (EmpUsername, EmpPassword) VALUES
('emp_username','emp_password')
```

Stored Procedures

Stored procedures can be used in ColdFusion with the CFSTOREDPROC tag, and offer significant power over single SQL statements. Stored procedures are available from the Data Bindings palette. The interface enables you to visually develop your stored procedure code, which is then generated by UltraDev as a CFSTOREDPROC tag and inserted into the page.

Stored procedures are described in Chapter 19, which deals with more advanced database interactions.

Other Data Sources

The remaining Data Bindings menu items are the Session, Form, URL, Application, and Client variables. In addition, UltraDev 4 introduced CGI, Server, Cookie, and Local variables. These data sources enable you to specify a name, as in Figure 10-15, but not

Variables: Name	Default Value	Run-Time Value
emp_username	%	#form.username#
emp_password	%	#form.password#

Table 10-4. *Variables Defined for the Insert Statement*

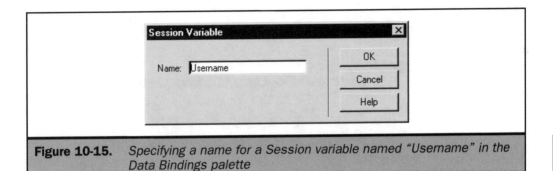

Figure 10-15. *Specifying a name for a Session variable named "Username" in the Data Bindings palette*

a value. To declare variables in your code, you have to hand-code them or find a third-party Server Behavior that writes the code for you. The data sources available here, however, make it easy to drag and drop the variables on the page so that you can edit the visual appearance of the variables on the page. Here's an example of a Session variable that's been defined as Username:

```
<cfoutput>#Session.Username#</cfoutput>
```

After defining the variable in the palette, you can drag it to the page and apply a Server Format to the displayed value by clicking the down-arrow on the selected variable and choosing one from the drop-down menu (see Figure 10-16). There are many Server Formats available to the UltraDev ColdFusion developer—and most of them insert standard ColdFusion functions "around" your code. For instance, when you choose Trim > Both from the Server Formats menu, the Session variable code from the preceding example now looks like this:

```
<cfoutput># Trim(Session.Username) #</cfoutput>
```

The Server Behaviors Palette

Server Behaviors are the core server-side code builders of UltraDev. These Behaviors generate code to insert into your documents to perform a variety of server-side functions. Many of these functions are related to the recordset, or CFQUERY tag. The use of Server Behaviors is covered in the coming chapters, but here's a brief introduction to some of these Behaviors.

The Repeat Region

This is the granddaddy of Server Behaviors. It enables you to loop through a resultset with a simple point-and-click interface. This is of greater significance to ASP and JSP developers, because they have no built-in structure that accomplishes this. However, with ColdFusion, this Behavior is less of a time saver, because ColdFusion has the CFOUTPUT statement that contains automatic looping behavior.

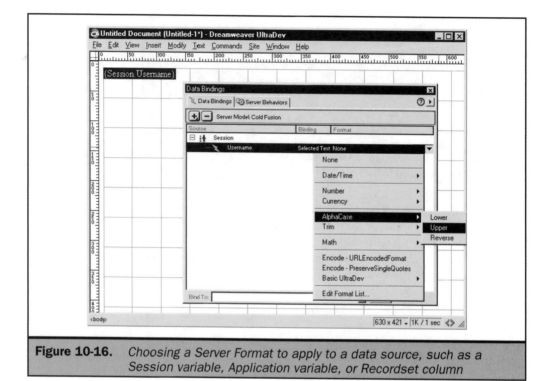

Figure 10-16.   Choosing a Server Format to apply to a data source, such as a Session variable, Application variable, or Recordset column

One of the advantages of using the Repeat Region rather than hand-coding ColdFusion is that it is a way to set up the "Move to" Server Behaviors. When you apply a Repeat Region to the page, variables are written to the page with the Behavior that allow interaction with the other Server Behaviors. Like the Recordset Behavior, the Repeat Region has to be inserted for many of the other Server Behaviors to work with your code. For example, if you insert your own CFOUTPUT statement to loop through a recordset, you can't use the Move to Next Record Server Behavior.

Show Region (was Hide Region in UltraDev 1)

This Behavior enables you to show a specific region on the page based on a specific condition that you can set up in the Behavior. The available choices for conditions are to Show Selected Region:

- If Recordset is Empty
- If First Record
- If Last Record
- If Recordset Is Not Empty

■ If Not First Record

■ If Not Last Record

This Behavior generates code that uses the ColdFusion CFIF tag and tests the values of certain variables. The following example shows the ColdFusion code written by the Show If Recordset Is Not Empty Behavior:

```
<cfif rsProducts.recordCount GT 0>#rsProducts.Name#</cfif>
```

Tip   *The Show Server Behaviors can be applied to a single item or to a whole block of code—HTML or ColdFusion code.*

Move To Record

This is a group of Server Behaviors that interacts with a recordset and a Repeat Region Server Behavior. All of these Behaviors share a fairly substantial set of code blocks made up of CFScript tags. This code is pretested and optimized, although it appears quite large. A careful study of this code is a good introduction to the CFScript language, and also enables you to create your own interactions using the variables that have been predefined by the built-in code.

These Behaviors will be detailed in the coming chapters as you build the Bettergig.com Web site.

Dynamic Elements

The Data Bindings palette enables you to apply dynamic text items to the page, and also enables you to insert values into other objects, such as form objects. Another way to do this is to use the Dynamic Elements menu entry in the Server Behaviors palette and click one of the five items:

■ **Dynamic Text**   A text item, such as a Recordset column or a Session variable that's on the page.

■ **Dynamic List/Menu**   A list/menu form element that gets its values from a data source.

■ **Dynamic Text Field**   A text field form element that gets its value from a data source.

■ **Dynamic Check Box**   A check box form element that gets its checked value based on a data source.

■ **Dynamic Radio Buttons**   A set of radio buttons that get their values from a data source.

The Dynamic Elements have to be applied to an existing element on the page. For instance, if you have a basic list/menu on the page, you can apply the Dynamic List/Menu Server Behavior to the page, and define the values for the element (see

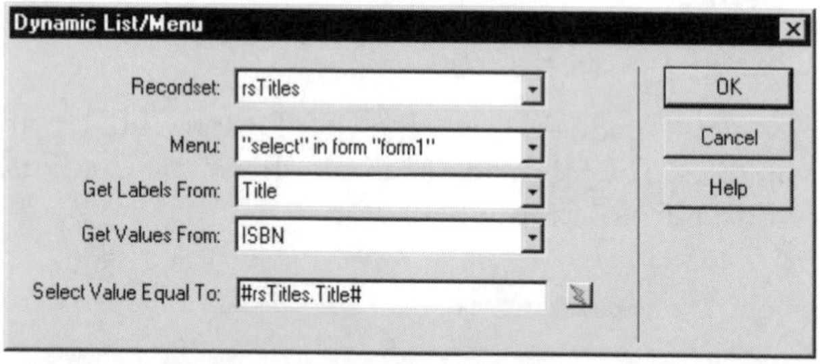

Figure 10-17. *A dynamic list/menu dialog box prompts for a number of values*

Figure 10-17). The following is sample code written by the Behavior, and it is what you would expect if you had hand-coded a list/menu using ColdFusion:

```
<select name="select">
<cfloop query="rsTitles">
    <option value="<cfoutput>#rsTitles.ISBN#</cfoutput>"
    <cfif (#rsTitles.ISBN# EQ #rsTitles.Title#)>SELECTED</cfif>>
    <cfoutput>#rsTitles.Title#</cfoutput></option>
</cfloop>
</select>
```

User Authentication Server Behaviors

UltraDev 4 introduced some new Server Behaviors that offer user login and authentication features. The Login User Behavior enables you to check a database for an existing user and redirect the user to a page if the login is successful, and redirect to a "failed" page if the login is unsuccessful.

The Restrict Access Behavior enables you to set an access level on the page. This Behavior depends on the Log in User Behavior being applied to a login page. In this Behavior, you can define access levels that will be available to the site.

The Logout Server Behavior enables you to set a link on your page to allow a user to log out from the site and be redirected to another page.

Last, the Check New Username Server Behavior enables you to check the database for an existing username before inserting the user data into the database. This Behavior requires that an Insert Server Behavior already exists on the page.

Live Objects

UltraDev 4 introduced some new objects to the Objects palette—Live Objects. These are basically combinations of various Objects and Server Behaviors into "wizard-like" forms that enable you to insert several things at once into a page. These Live Objects include the following:

- **Insert Master-Detail Page Set**   Enables you to define a standard Master/Detail page combination.
- **Insert Recordset Navigation Bar**   Inserts a set of recordset navigation links, such as First Previous Next Last, inside a small table.
- **Insert Recordset Navigation Status**   Inserts a set of recordset status numbers, such as Records 1 to 5 of 20.
- **Insert Record Insertion Form**   Automates the process of creating an Insert Record Server Behavior, and also will insert all form fields and form information to the page.
- **Insert Record Update Form**   Similar to the Insert Record Object, but works with an Update Behavior and also inserts all form fields to the page.

Note   *Live Objects will be covered in detail in Chapter 18.*

Inconsistencies in UltraDev with ColdFusion

If you decide to use UltraDev with ColdFusion, note that several problems exist with UltraDev 1. UltraDev 4 fixed most of the problems with the ColdFusion implementation, but some still remain, including:

- Certain hand-coding will result in Server Behaviors showing up as "partial" on the Server Behavior menu.
- Certain combinations of quote characters, pound signs, and various special characters in your hand-coding will cause UltraDev to "URL Encode" the characters as "%22" and "%23". A common workaround is to use single quotes instead of double quotes. This was fixed in UltraDev 4.
- Queries containing ColdFusion syntax may cease to show up in the Data Bindings palette, or may show up there but not allow you to work with the recordset columns.
- "Unbalanced" ColdFusion tags show up as invalid HTML tags, even though it's perfectly legal, because the ColdFusion will be stripped out by the server before the page is executed. An example of "unbalanced" tags is shown in Figure 10-18. Many of these problems were fixed in UltraDev 4.
- ColdFusion tags that allow the use of a CFOUTPUT tag with a QUERY attribute, such as CFPOP and CFDIRECTORY, may cause a Repeat Region to show up with an error, because no recordset is defined. This was also fixed for UltraDev 4.

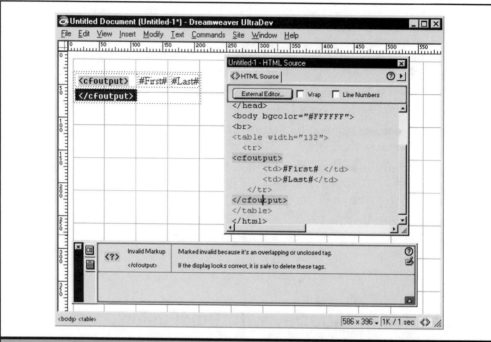

Figure 10-18. An "Invalid Markup" error shows up if you "unbalance" your ColdFusion and HTML tags—in this case, the </tr> tag was closed before closing the </cfoutput> tag

■ Use of an OLE DB connection or native database connection is not supported in UltraDev. UltraDev 1 was friendlier toward a hand-coded connection—it shows up as a broken connection in the Data Bindings palette. In UltraDev 4, the connection doesn't even show up. However, UltraDev 4 added the ability to use RDS. If your connection is defined in the CF Administrator, it will show up in UltraDev 4.

A few inconsistencies are to be expected in a version 1 product, and we look forward to the coming versions and the bug fixes that they promise. The best thing to do if you find a bug, whether it's a known bug or not, is to forward as much information as possible to Macromedia at wish-ultradev@macromedia.com so that the issue can be addressed. Although a large number of the ColdFusion bugs were fixed for version 4, many were not addressed and several new ones surfaced as well.

ColdFusion Resources

A tremendous amount of support is available from the Web and in user groups around the world. The Allaire Web site is the best place to start when you need assistance. Numerous technical documents and white papers are available, as well as the complete set of documentation that ships with ColdFusion. Also, most of Allaire's products are available as trial downloads from the site, including ColdFusion server and ColdFusion Studio. The Allaire Developer Forums are also a good place to get your questions answered. In addition, any patches or updates to Allaire products are available for download from the site.

The Allaire Partners program is a good way for a developer to get developer versions of Allaire software. If you have a ColdFusion-related product to sell and are interested in the program, go to the Allaire site and look for the Partners link.

ColdFusion User Groups (CFUGs) are popping up all over the world, and may number in the hundreds by now. Most of these groups have monthly or bimonthly meetings that you can attend to hear lectures, see demonstrations, or bring some code that you need some help with. The ColdFusion community is a close-knit group of people who are usually willing to help out.

Several ColdFusion books also are available on the market. The most popular of these are *The Allaire ColdFusion 4 Web Application Construction Kit* and *Advanced ColdFusion 4 Application Development,* both written by Ben Forta (Que Publications), highly regarded as one of the top ColdFusion experts in the world. Ben Forta also hosts one of the top ColdFusion Web sites, at www.forta.com, with examples, articles, links, and custom tags.

ColdFusion Developer's Journal is another resource. It is a monthly magazine available from your local newsstand or directly from the publisher, Sys-Con Media. The company also publishes *Java Developer's Journal* and *The XML Journal,* among other magazines. For more information on these periodicals, consult the Sys-Con Web site at www.sys-con.com/coldfusion.

The mailing lists at www.houseoffusion.com have some of the top ColdFusion experts in the country among their members. Literally hundreds of posts per day occur on the various lists. Chances are good that if you have a ColdFusion-related question, you can get it answered here.

Dreamweaver users have enjoyed the ColdFusion Objects that allow the use of ColdFusion tags within the Dreamweaver framework. These can be used with UltraDev, too, although much of the functionality is duplicated in the Server Behaviors. The ColdFusion Objects for Dreamweaver can be found on the Macromedia Exchange, at www.macromedia.com/exchange. In addition, many ColdFusion Server Behaviors are popping up on the Exchange, including some by the authors and the technical editor of this book.

A list of ColdFusion resources is provided in Appendix B.

Summary

This chapter was intended as a general introduction to ColdFusion and the CFML language. CFML is a robust language, and is relatively easy to use—especially for the Web developer who is already familiar with HTML. The ease of use, however, doesn't imply that the language is any less powerful than ASP or JSP. In fact, many consider it more powerful because of all the built-in functionality. Whatever your background, ColdFusion is a viable way to get your data-driven site to the Web, and UltraDev is the perfect way to combine the designer-friendly environment of Dreamweaver with the server-side functionality of ColdFusion.

Chapter 11

Advanced
Scripting Topics

This chapter will cover some scripting topics that are more advanced than regular page design but don't really belong in the database section either. These items represent things that many UltraDev users ask about. Some are ASP specific, and others have additional platform information provided.

E-mail

Sending e-mail is an important part of many data-driven Web sites. The ability to respond to users by e-mail can be used to confirm orders, provide usernames and passwords, or notify users that a site's content has changed.

There are several basic parts of an e-mail message, listed here:

- **From** The name or e-mail address the message is sent from
- **To** The e-mail address that the mail is intended for
- **Subject** The subject of the e-mail
- **Body** The text of the e-mail message
- **CC** An address to which you want to send a carbon copy of the e-mail
- **BCC** An address to which you want to send a blind carbon copy (a copy that the primary recipient has no knowledge of)
- **Attachment** A file that is attached to the e-mail
- **Priority** The priority setting of the e-mail

No matter which method you choose to create and send your e-mail, you will be setting some or all of these properties in your code and then calling a method that sends the e-mail.

CDO Mail

CDO mail is a Windows/ASP method of creating and sending e-mail. It relies on the cdonts.dll file that is a subset of Windows Collaborative Data Objects. Setting up the cdonts.dll component was covered in Chapter 2.

Once your server is configured to use CDO, constructing and sending an e-mail is as easy as typing a few lines of code.

```
<%
Dim CDOMail
Set CDOMail = Server.CreateObject("CDONTS.NewMail")

CDOMail.From = "ray@workablesolutions.com"
CDOMail.To = Request("customeremail")
```

```
CDOMail.Subject = txtSubject
CDOMail.Body = "Thank you for writing. Attached is a file that explains our
order process. Please let us know if you have any questions"
CDOMail.CC = "ray@workablesolutions.com"
CDOMail.AttachFile = ("d:\files\orders.txt")
CDOMail.Send

Set CDOMail = nothing
%>
```

An explanation of the preceding code follows.

```
Dim CDOMail
```

Here, a variable is created. In ASP, all variables are variants, meaning that they can hold any kind of data. The variable will be used to hold an object, assigned in the next step.

```
Set CDOMail = Server.CreateObject("CDONTS.NewMail")
```

This line assigns an object to the variable CDOMail based on the NewMail class of the CDONTS object. If you have set up CDO mail as covered in Chapter 2, this step should complete itself without incident.

```
CDOMail.From = "ray@workablesolutions.com"
CDOMail.To = Request.Form("customeremail")
CDOMail.Subject = txtSubject
CDOMail.Body = "Thank you for writing. Attached is a file that explains our
order process. Please let us know if you have any questions"
CDOMail.CC = "ray@workablesolutions.com"
```

This code illustrates several ways to assign values to the properties of the CDOMail object. The From line assigns a static string value that is hard-coded. The To line uses an ASP request object to get a value from a form field named customername and assign it to the To property of the object. The Subject line uses a variable (that must have been defined and assigned a value earlier in the code) called txtSubject to assign a subject value. You can see that you can use any of a number of common programming methods to collect data and assign it to the properties of the CDOMail object.

```
CDOMail.AttachFile = ("d:\files\orders.txt")
```

The AttachFile property is used to attach a file to the e-mail, much as you might attach a file to an e-mail you send from Outlook or Eudora. Keep in mind that the path described here is to a physical file on the Web server from which this e-mail is being sent.

```
CDOMail.Send
```

The Send method is used to complete the assignment of properties and send the e-mail.

```
Set CDOMail = nothing
```

As with any ASP object, it is important that you set the variable reference to nothing in order to free unneeded server resources.

JMail

JMail is an alternative to CDO mail available from dimac.net. Its syntax is a little different, but it works basically the same as CDO. Following is an example of a JMail e-mail.

```
<%
Set JMail = Server.CreateObject("JMail.SMTPMail")
JMail.ServerAddress = "exchange.emailserver.com"
JMail.Sender = "ray@workablesolutions.com"
JMail.Subject = "txtSubject"

JMail.AddRecipient Request.Form("customeremail")
JMail.Body = "Thank you for writing. Attached is a file that explains our
order process. Please let us know if you have any questions"
JMail.Priority = 1

JMail.AppendBodyFromFile "d:\email\email_footer.txt"

JMail.AddAttachment " d:\files\orders.txt "

JMail.Execute

Set Jmail = nothing

%>
```

Other ASP E-mail Programs

There are several other e-mail components available for little or no cost. You may find one that you like better, or you may be forced by your ISP to use a particular version.

Just keep in mind that most operate in the same fashion as the preceding examples, and follow these steps:

- Dimension (Dim in VBScript) a variable to hold an object.
- Set the object as an instance of the component class.
- Set static text, ASP objects, or variables to each of the component's properties that you want to make use of.
- Call a method of the component to send or execute the e-mail.
- Set the object equal to nothing to free server resources.

No matter what program you choose to use, there will be some documentation or examples that explain the properties and methods of the component. Referencing these, you should be able to make quick work of the implementation of any component.

ColdFusion Mail

ColdFusion mail was discussed briefly in Chapter 10. Sending an e-mail in ColdFusion is simply a matter of including a <CFMAIL> tag on your page:

```
<CFMAIL TO="#myToVariable#"
FROM="#myFromVariable#"
SUBJECT="Your order was received">
Thank you for submitting your order!
</CFMAIL>
```

While that is all you need to send a simple e-mail, other attributes of the tag allow you to add other options to the e-mail:

- CC="copy_to"   Specify a CC address.
- BCC="blind_copy_to"   Specify your BCC address.
- TYPE="msg_type"   This can be set to html for an HTML e-mail.
- MAXROWS="max_msgs"   If your e-mail is coming from a query, you can specify the maximum number to send.
- MIMEATTACH="path"   Specify an attachment. Other attachments can be specified with a <CFMAILPARAM> tag.
- QUERY="query_name"   Used if you want to send an e-mail to every name in a database, or if you want to send a series of e-mails to one person based on the results of the query. One e-mail is sent for every row returned by the <CFQUERY> tag.
- GROUP="query_column"   Use this feature if you want to group the output within one e-mail, such as an Order Details result within an e-mail to a customer.

- GROUPCASESENSITIVE="yes/no".

- STARTROW="query_row"   Start the e-mails at this row of the recordset.

- SERVER="servername"   This will override the default mail server setting in the CF Administrator or specify a server if there isn't one previously defined in the Administrator.

- PORT="port_ID"   Overrides the default port of 25.

- MAILERID="headerid"   You can specify a mailer ID to be passed in the X-Mailer SMTP header. This header identifies the mailer application, which is set to Allaire ColdFusion Application Server by default.

- TIMEOUT="seconds"   Specify a timeout in seconds to stop waiting for the e-mail server.

To demonstrate a slightly more advanced use of the <CFMAIL> tag, assume you have an e-mail statement that is personalized for customers in your database as they order something online. A generic e-mail is stored as an HTML page in your Web folder (GenericOrderPage.htm), and the customer's account information is stored in the database along with the other customer information, such as name, address, and the orders placed. For the sake of this example, assume that all information is coming from the getOrderDetails view that is stored in the database. The view retrieves related information from the Customers, Orders, OrderDetails, and Products tables, but that's not important for the understanding of this example and will be covered later.

Note   *Chapters 13–19 cover database design, SQL, and database implementation within the UltraDev environment.*

This is what the page would look like:

```
<CFQUERY Name="rsOrders" DSN="#mydsn#">
Select * from getOrderDetails where OrderID = #OrderID#
</CFQUERY>
<CFMAIL TO="#rsOrders.emailaddress#"
    FROM="sales@acmedatabases.com"
    SUBJECT="Your order number #Order ID# is on its way!"
    TYPE="HTML">
<CFINCLUDE TEMPLATE="GenericOrderPage.htm">
<table><CFLOOP QUERY="rsOrders">
    <tr>
        <td>#rsOrders.ProductID#</td>
        <td>#rsOrders.ProductName#</td>
        <td>#rsOrders.Price#</td>
        <td>#rsOrders.Quantity#</td>
<CFSET TotalLineItem = rsOrders.Price * rsOrders.Quantity>
        <td><b>TOTAL:</b> #TotalLineItem#</td>
```

```
    </tr>
</CFLOOP>
</table>
Total Order cost = #rsOrders.TotalPrice#
<CFINCLUDE TEMPLATE="ThankYou.htm">
</CFMAIL>
```

The small amount of code in this example performs the following tasks:

- Retrieves the order information from the database, including the customer's information.
- Includes a generic HTML e-mail text that is stored on the server (GenericOrderPage.htm) for the first part of the e-mail.
- Loops through all the orders, adding up the line items as it goes and formatting the order details into a table.
- Includes another include file that has the closing thank you information.

You can see that by using a combination of include files, looping constructs, and HTML tags, you can create truly dynamic e-mails with ColdFusion. You can even include variables in the included HTML page. They can be embedded into the HTML include file like this:

```
Hello #rsQuery.FirstName#.  Thank you for your order of #rsQuery.TotalPrice#.
```

The ColdFusion server reads through and evaluates everything sequentially up to the closing </CFMAIL> tag.

The <CFQUERY> tag in this example doesn't affect the number of e-mails sent, since you didn't specify a Query attribute in the <CFMAIL> tag. The example in Chapter 10 demonstrated the use of bulk e-mails using a Query attribute.

Please make sure to check the documentation for whichever e-mail method you choose so that you'll know all the properties and methods that are available to you.

Controlling Where Script Is Run

Traditionally, scripts have been run in the normal course of page execution, meaning that a script that appears at the top of the page is going to run when the form loads. The pages that come before it are responsible for gathering information that the script needs so that when the scripted page loads, the code is ready to go. This is still a very valid and useful way to do many things, but there is a different method of placing scripts and their predicate requirements on the same page. This can also be a very efficient means of handling traffic through your application.

This method may have been in use elsewhere, but it was really introduced, it seems, with Drumbeat 2000. The idea is that code can be placed on a page that expects data that is also collected in a form on that page. The invocation of the script code is then made dependent on the value of the button that posts the form.

If you have done much work with forms, you may know that the Submit button also has a value that can be gleaned from the post. When the Submit button has been clicked, that value is available on the page that the form posts to in the request object. Thus, when a page loads, you can determine whether it is a result of the click of a certain button by checking for that button's value in the post. If it has no value (it equals "") or it is null, the page loaded because of a call from a different page and no information is available for the script. If, however, the value of the button is set, then you know that the page loaded as the result of the form being submitted to it, and values are available for the script to execute.

Note *For this method to work, you must set the form on the page to post back to the same page. For instance, if the page you are working on is called CDOTest.asp, then the form on that page should post to CDOTest.asp.*

Very often when the page reloads from the form post, the display part of the page is never reached the second time through. The purpose of this method is to process the form data into the necessary code and then send the user off to the proper place with a redirect statement. The following code illustrates using a CDO e-mail component this way.

```
<%@LANGUAGE="VBSCRIPT"%><% if (cStr(Request("Submit")) <> "") Then
Dim objCDO
Set objCDO = Server.CreateObject("CDONTS.NewMail")
objCDO.From = "ray@workablesolutions.com"
objCDO.To = Request("to")
objCDO.CC = ""
objCDO.Subject = "Test"
objCDO.Body = "test"
objCDO.Send()
Set objCDO = Nothing
Response.Redirect("mailsent.asp")
End If
%>
```

If the Submit button in this example has been clicked, the If statement is invoked, the e-mail is constructed and sent, and the user is redirected to the mailsent.asp page. If the button has not been clicked, this code is skipped and the HTML beneath it displays an HTML form to collect the information to send the e-mail.

This method can be very efficient because it eliminates the need for processor ASP pages that handle code and direct the user but serve no display purpose. Many of the functions and behaviors in UltraDev use this method. The code that you see generated by UltraDev will be easier to understand once you have a handle on this way of doing things.

The FileSystemObject Object

The FileSystemObject (FSO) object provides a means for your ASP pages to access the file and drive systems of the server on which they are running. There are four objects in the FSO collection, listed in Table 11-1.

Using the FSO object, you can do pretty much anything you need to regarding the file system of the computer your pages are running on. You can create files and write to them, delete files, move files around, and even create databases and search files.

The FSO model is available in a Microsoft-provided dynamic link library called scrrun.dll. You can access the functionality of this DLL from any application that provides access to objects, such as Visual Basic or Access. To access it from ASP, you must create an object, much as we did with the CDOMail object earlier.

```
<%
Dim fso
Set fso = Server.CreateObject("Scripting.FileSystemObject")
%>
```

The FileSystemObject object has several methods available to it by which you can perform your tasks. The most commonly used are listed in Table 11-2.

FSO Object	Description
Drive object	Enables access to physical and network drives
FileSystemObject object	Enables access to the computer's file system
Folder object	Enables access to folders and their properties
TextStream object	Enables access to a file's contents

Table 11-1.   *The FileSystemObject Objects*

INTRODUCTION TO WEB SCRIPTING

FSO Method	Description
CopyFile	Copies files from one place to another.
CreateTextFile	Creates a text file and returns a TextStream object so that you can write to the file.
DeleteFile	Deletes a file.
OpenTextFile	Opens a file and creates a TextStream object that you can use to read from the file or append to the file. This method can also create the file if it does not exist, if you have set its parameter to allow it to do so.

Table 11-2. *Popular Methods of the FSO*

Once you have created a FileSystemObject object in your code, you can call these methods to perform operations on your file system. For instance, suppose that you have collected information about a person from a form and you want to write that information to a text file for later use (say as a guest book). You can use the information you have collected to write to a file.

```
<%
Dim fso, file
Dim name, zipcode, emaile
name = Request("name")
zipcode = Request"(zip")
email = Request("email")

path = "c:\guestbook\book.txt"

set fso = Server.CreateObject(Scripting.FileSystemObject")

set file = fso.opentextfile(path, 3, TRUE)

file.write(name) & vbcrlf

file.write(zipcode) & vbcrlf

file.write(email) & vbcrlf
```

```
file.close

set file = nothing
set fso = nothing
%>
```

The preceding code gathers information from a preceding form into a collection of variables. It then sets a path to the file that will be written. The path is a file on the server computer and must be an actual file path. It does not affect the file system of the client computer that is viewing these pages.

Once the FSO is created, the opentextfile method is called to open a file. This method takes three parameters: the path to the file (provided here by a variable), an indication of the purpose for which you will use the file (represented by a 1 here; see Table 11-3), and a true or false setting that tells the method whether or not to create the file referenced in the path if it does not already exist.

After the file is opened, you can use the methods of the TextStream object that is created by the OpenTextFile method to write to the open file. In the preceding code, the values of the variables were written to the file using the write method. The vbcrlf command was used to place a carriage return after each line.

Note   *VBCRLF is a VBScript command that stands for Visual Basic Carriage Return Line Feed. It is used to place a carriage return (return to the far left of the line) and a line feed (go to the next line on the page) in the output of your code.*

Once this is complete, the file is closed and the File object and the FSO object are set to nothing to free server resources.

The TextStream object also has methods such as Readline and Skipline that allow you to navigate through the contents of a file. See Microsoft's documentation or the MCDN Web site for a more complete description of the FileSystemObject object and the tasks you can accomplish with it.

File Use Integer	Description
1	The file is opened for reading.
2	The file is opened for writing.
3	The file is opened for appending.

Table 11-3.   *The File Use Parameter of the OpenTextFile Method*

Debugging and Troubleshooting Common Errors

No matter how careful you are, some problems are likely to pop up that you will need to resolve to get your pages working. If you are working with Internet Information Server and ASP, the errors that you will receive can be rather confusing and not at all indicative of the true nature of the problem. Here are some of the more common errors that occur and their possible remedies.

Microsoft OLE DB Provider for ODBC Drivers error '80004005' [Microsoft][ODBC Microsoft Access Driver] Operation must use an updateable query

This is usually because of the write permissions on the NT directories. You can read from databases anywhere on the drive, but to write to them they have to be in a directory to which the IUSR_ user has write permissions. The IUSR_ user is the default user that your visitors access your site under. Speak to your ISP or network administrator about the proper permission to allow users to write to the database on your server; this will usually fix the error.

   If this doesn't help, check to make sure you are not using joins in your query. Queries with joins are not updateable.

Error 0156: 80004005 The HTTP headers have already been written to the browser. Changes in HTTP headers should occur before page is written

Your ASP page is most likely trying to redirect to another location after data has already been written into the HTML response stream. This can occur if programmatic decisions in the body of your page try to send the user to another page after elements of the current page are already on the way to the browser. To prevent this problem, put the following code at the top of your ASP page:

```
Response.Buffer = true
```

   The Response object, including the Buffer property, is covered in Chapter 8.

Microsoft OLE DB Provider for ODBC Drivers error '80004005' Data source name not found and no default driver specified

This error indicates that a Data Source Name (DSN) has not been set up on the server. It is most commonly encountered the first time you upload a site to your remote server.

You may have been developing and testing on a computer that has the DSN set up correctly, but you must also set one up on the server machine that maps the correct path to the database (or have your ISP do it for you).

Keep in mind that if you are using an Access database, the database file (.mdb file) must also be uploaded to a directory on the server. This directory might end up being different from the one on your development machine, and the server's DSN will need to be mapped appropriately. The directory needs to have read and write permissions set for the IUSR_<machine_name> user, or you will end up getting the 80004005 error.

Note

The IUSR_<machine_name> user is a special user that IIS sets up to accommodate visitors to your Web site. It represents the default user account that anonymous users will access to be allowed privileges on your server. The actual name of this user depends on the name you have given your computer. For instance, if the computer's name were WWW, this account would be IUSR_WWW.

Microsoft OLE DB Provider for ODBC Drivers error '80040e14' [Microsoft][ODBC Microsoft Access 97 Driver] Syntax error in INSERT INTO statement

This error is often caused by a reserved word used as a column name. Make sure that you do not have a column named "date" or some other reserved word.

Microsoft OLE DB Provider for ODBC Drivers error '80040e10' [Microsoft][ODBC Microsoft Access 97 Driver] Too few parameters. Expected 1

This error usually occurs when a column name in your query does not exist. Make sure that you are using the actual column names rather than alias names and that you have spelled all of your column names properly.

My script is showing up in the browser window instead of being run by the server

There are a couple of possible causes for this problem, which are illustrated in Figure 11-1.

First, you may have created an ASP page but given it an .html or .htm extension. This can be a common problem in UltraDev if you set .html as you default page extension and then save pages without specifying the .asp extension. This can be a stealthy problem because it may cause your page to display correctly in the browser, but your ASP code is viewable in the source view of the page, exposing what should be secure information. Check the page you are trying to access to see that it has the proper extension.

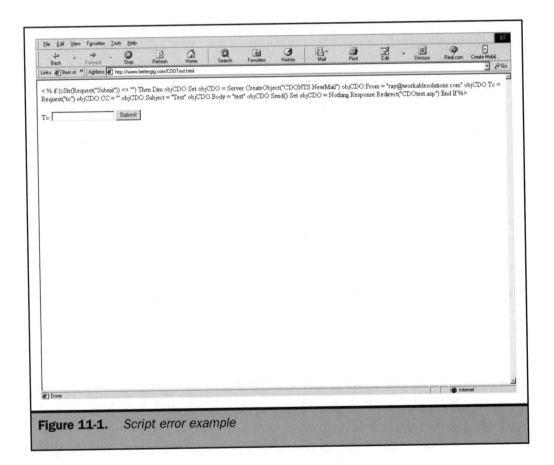

Figure 11-1. *Script error example*

Tip *It is sometimes wise to set the default extension to .html in your site definition. Many times, a site has only a few pages that contain code that needs to be processed by the ASP, JSP, or CF engine. Those pages, if given an .asp, .jsp, or .cfm extension, will access the engine and slow performance even though there is no code on them to run. Setting your default to .html in UltraDev can help you save regular Web pages as HTML files. This processes more quickly, but you will have to remember to save your coded pages with the appropriate extension.*

Second, you may have hand-written code that is not properly delineated with script tags (<% %>, etc.). If you have missed tags, or mistyped them, portions of your code will be treated as text rather than being sent through the processing engine, and the code will display as text in the user's browser.

Third, it is possible that the mapping in your Web server that tells the server where to run script code has been corrupted. For example, when running ASP on Internet Information Server, the server knows from the .asp file extension that the file needs special handling. It gets instructions on how to process the file from the Applications Settings dialog box in the Web sites properties in IIS. In Figure 11-2, you will see that IIS holds a list of file extensions and the processing libraries that are needed to interpret them. If this list becomes corrupted, or the dynamic link library (DLL) that is referenced is missing or corrupted, the server may either display the ASP file or try to download it to the user's computer. Either one is bad.

To repair this problem, it is usually necessary to reload IIS or PWS on the problem computer. The ASP DLLs will be replaced with the reload, and the files should interpret properly.

Debugging Server-Side ASP

Internet Information Server provides a means for debugging server-side VBScript or JScript. To do this, you must enable debugging for the Web site in the Microsoft Management Console. In the properties for the site, choose Configuration on the Home Directory tab (see Figure 11-3) and enable ASP server-side debugging on the App Debugging tab (see Figure 11-4).

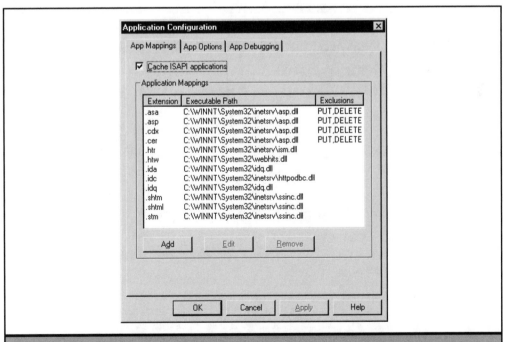

Figure 11-2.   *IIS file extension application mapping window*

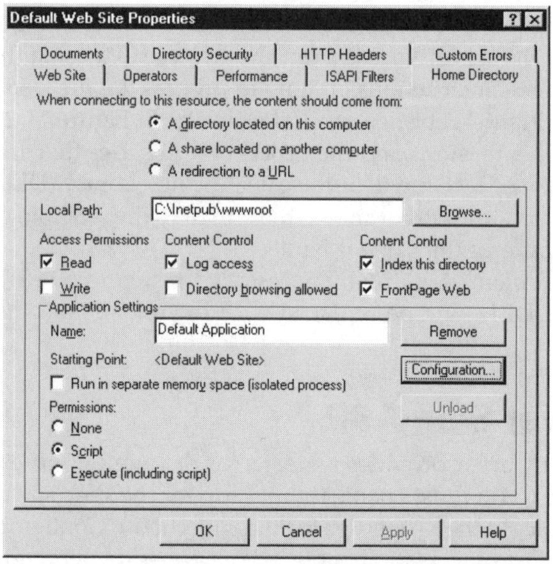

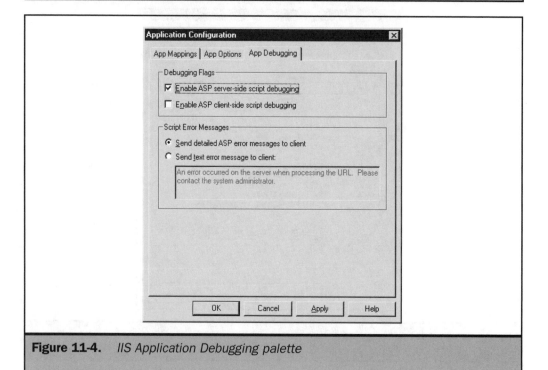

Figure 11-3. *IIS Home Directory Configuration palette*

Figure 11-4. *IIS Application Debugging palette*

In your ASP script, include the debugging keyword appropriate to your server-side language choice immediately before the line where you want the debugger to pause. For VBScript, the keyword is Stop.

```
<%
    Response.Write "The debugger will start right after this line"
    Stop
    Response.Write "The debugger has paused the page"
%>
```

For JScript, use the debugger keyword.

```
<%
    Response.Write "The debugger will start right after this line"
    debugger
    Response.Write "The debugger has paused the page"
%>
```

When viewed in a browser, the page will pause and allow you to inspect assigned variables before they are passed on.

Those are just a view tips for troubleshooting and debugging script problems. Even if you are not using ASP, these issues should give you some idea of where to look to find what your problem might be. Remember to check permissions for your database, your file extensions, your database connection strings or DSN, and your tags and syntax, and you will eliminate most of the common errors that people encounter.

Summary

There are so many great things you can do with Web scripting. This chapter has given you some basics that should help you understand how to work with components, e-mail, script positioning, and the FileSystemObject object. Once you understand these basics, you should be able to create ways to accomplish the tasks you need to perform—or at least have a base upon which you can build when seeking out further training and information.

INTRODUCTION TO
WEB SCRIPTING

The Complete Reference

UltraDev

Part III

Integrating Databases With UltraDev

Chapter 12

Making a Database
Connection in UltraDev

UltraDev is designed to work with many configurations of server languages, Web servers, and databases. One of the primary reasons for choosing to use a dynamic Web authoring environment such as UltraDev is to connect your Web application to a database. There are more ways to connect to a database than there are databases.

UltraDev is capable of connecting to your database in a variety of ways, depending on the configuration on your machine and on the server that you are deploying your site from. Whether you are running an ASP site from your local Winows 95 machine, or a JSP site running on a UNIX server, or connecting to a ColdFusion server from a Macintosh, UltraDev has a connection method that will work with your machine.

The connection interface changed considerably from version 1 to version 4 of UltraDev. UltraDev 1 offered both design-time and run-time connections; so you could easily build a ColdFusion site, for instance, that depended on a ColdFusion connection, and not even have ColdFusion installed on your system. In the Macintosh version of UltraDev 1, all the design-time database connections were done through Java Database Connectivity (JDBC) on a remote Windows machine, connecting a JDBC:ODBC bridge to an ODBC connection. This created all sorts of problems for Mac users who couldn't find a host who would install the JDBC driver. Starting with UltraDev 4, all users connect to the remote server through HTTP using server-side scripts.

Beginning with UltraDev 4, the database connections are defined for Windows users as one of two options:

- Using a connection on the local machine
- Using a connection on the application server

Note *Macintosh users connect through the application server.*

In addition, ColdFusion developers can use a JDBC connection on the local machine using the Data Source Name – Advanced dialog box. The design-time and run-time connections that were in UltraDev 1 don't exist per se in UltraDev 4, but the functionality remains consistent by choosing either a local machine data source or an Application Server data source. You can, for instance, name your connection "connBettergig" and use an Access database on your local machine, and then later change the data source to point to a SQL server database on the Web server.

The connection information is saved in an include file that resides in the Connections folder of your site. By changing the connection information in this one file, all pages in your site that depend on the connection will reflect the changes. In the first version of UltraDev, the connection information was written to each individual page, making it more difficult to make a simple change in connection information. Also, you could keep a separate connection file on your local machine that is different from the connection file on your server, allowing you to have a different connection method for files that reside on the local machine.

As mentioned earlier, UltraDev 4 gave Macintosh users the same methods for connecting to databases that Windows users can enjoy. All of the following sections apply to Macintosh machines as well as Windows machines. The only limitations for Macintosh users are that you have to connect to your application server to get the design-time database connections. Considering that you need an application server to be able to implement a data-driven site, this is hardly a limitation.

UltraDev connects to your database on the application server through an HTTP request. This is very similar to what happens when a browser requests a page from the Web server. The server receives the request and sends the page back to the browser. In this case, the database information is sent back to UltraDev. There is a special file that UltraDev writes to the server that takes care of the connection and communication with the program during the design phase. On an ASP server, this is an ASP file; on a JSP server, it's a JSP file; and on a ColdFusion server, it's a ColdFusion file. The file connects to the database on the server as it is called, and sends the information back to UltraDev in the form of XML. All of this is invisible to the user.

> **Tip** *If you upgrade from UltraDev 1 to UltraDev 4, you can convert the recordsets you created in UltraDev 1. Simply open the recordset from Data Bindings palette, and then click OK.*

This chapter reviews a few of the more popular methods for connecting UltraDev to a database.

ADO Connection Using ODBC

ODBC, or Open Database Connectivity, is probably the most widely used connection method, given the number of Microsoft Windows machines out there. ODBC drivers come preinstalled with Windows and provide a standard way to connect to most databases. The vast majority of databases that run on Windows are ODBC compliant.

ODBC was developed as an answer to the ever-present problem of compatibility between different machines, different operating systems, and different software. When you connect to an ODBC data source, you are connecting to the ODBC driver for that database, not to the actual database. The driver does the job of translating your commands into something that the database can understand—similar to speaking through an interpreter. You communicate to the driver with a SQL statement that complies with a limited generic subset of the SQL language. By translating the statements through ODBC, a small performance penalty occurs, but nothing significant in the grand scheme of things in Web time.

> *UltraDev needs the MDAC version 2.1 at the very minimum; so if you have version 1.5 or 2 installed, you need to upgrade. It is advisable that you upgrade to version 2.5 to avoid any potential problems.*

When using ODBC, the Web page doesn't need to know where the database is located on the machine. In fact, it doesn't even have to be on the same machine, and is often located on a machine that is specifically set up as a database server and accessed through a network. You give the connection to the database a *data source name (DSN)* that enables you to refer to the connection by name in your program (or Web application). As long as the DSN points to the database in the ODBC Data Source Administrator interface, the Web page will be able to communicate with the database.

If you are developing ASP, JSP, or ColdFusion pages, you can connect to the database through ODBC. In JSP, JDBC:ODBC bridge drivers can be used to connect via JDBC to an ODBC data source, making it necessary to define your data sources in both the ODBC administrator and the JSP server administration page. In ColdFusion, all the system DSNs appear in the ColdFusion Administrator and are accessible by all ColdFusion pages. In addition, if you have direct access to the ColdFusion Administrator, it allows you to remotely create and edit DSNs.

Note *Depending on which database you are using, the drivers may or may not be preinstalled with the MDAC. If you are running Microsoft Access, FoxPro, or SQL Server, the drivers are preinstalled and ready to run. Other preinstalled drivers include dBase, Oracle, Paradox, and Visual FoxPro. Drivers for MySQL and other databases are available on the Web, or from the database manufacturer.*

The first thing you need to do is define an ODBC connection in the ODBC Data Source Administrator, shown in Figure 12-1, which is located in the Control Panel folder. Each ODBC driver interface is a little different, but the principles of each are the same. As an example, an Access database will be used. UltraDev requires a System DSN to recognize the database. A System DSN is available to all users and all services (on Windows NT)—as opposed to a User DSN, which is available only to the current user, or a File DSN, which has the DSN stored in a file (independent of users).

Note *If you are using a Web-hosting company, it will set up the data source for you. You simply need to upload the database to the Web site to a folder on the server (preferably a cgi-bin or a similarly secured directory for safety) and give the Web-hosting company the information about the directory, database name, and DSN it should use. An administrator from your ISP can then set up the connection on the computer that your database resides on. Also, many Web-hosting companies allow the user to interact with the DSN administrator through a Web-based user interface.*

Click the Add button in the ODBC Data Source Administrator. This brings up the Create New Data Source dialog box, shown in Figure 12-2, which enables you to create a new data source.

After choosing the appropriate driver for your database, click the Finish button. This takes you directly to the ODBC setup for the particular driver that you are adding.

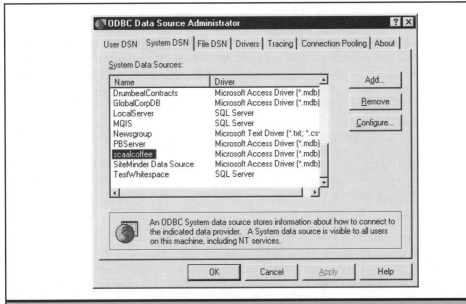

Figure 12-1. *The ODBC Data Source Administrator in Microsoft Windows*

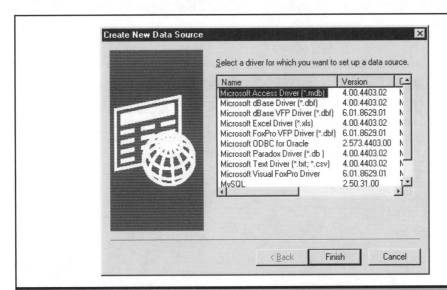

Figure 12-2. *Select the database driver for your database in the Create New Data Source dialog box*

Again, each driver has its own unique interface, but the result is the same. Figure 12-3 shows the ODBC Microsoft Access Setup screen.

Insert a DSN and a description (if you like, although the description is not mandatory), and then select the database. By going into the Advanced tab, you can also set a login name and password. Other databases, such as MySQL, might have all of their options on one screen; and some databases, such as Microsoft SQL Server, use the wizard metaphor. The bottom line is that you are assigning a DSN to a database, enabling you to refer to that database by name from this point forward.

The ODBC Microsoft Access Setup screen also offers options for repairing and compacting databases—these come in handy if you don't have a copy of MS Access on that particular machine.

Connecting through ODBC is a simple process, and connecting with UltraDev is even simpler. You need to define a connection either by selecting Modify | Connections (see Figure 12-4), or by going to the Data Bindings palette and choosing Recordset, which brings up the Recordset dialog box (see Figure 12-5), and then clicking the Define button.

That opens the Connections dialog box (see Figure 12-6), in which you can choose to edit an existing connection or create a new connection by clicking the New button. An option for Duplicate also exists, in case you want to copy a connection under a different name.

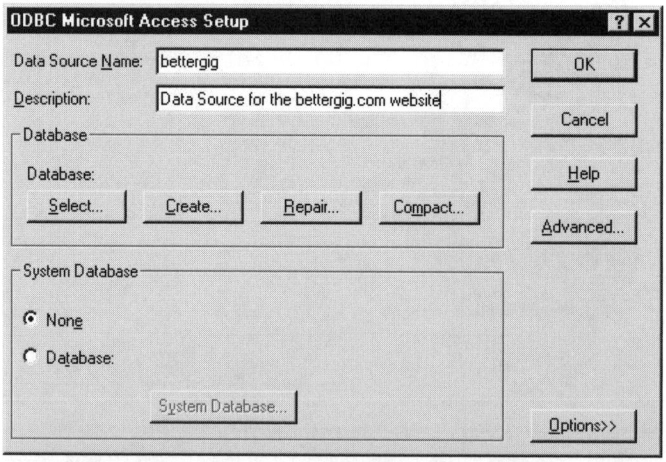

Figure 12-3. *Setting up a DSN for Microsoft Access*

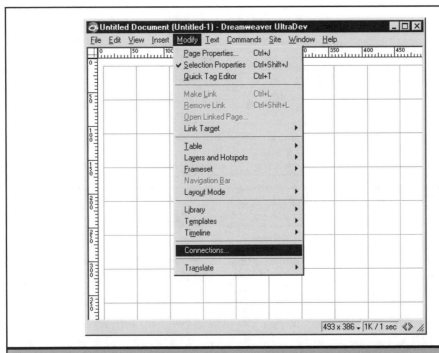

Figure 12-4. *You can define a connection selecting Modify | Connections*

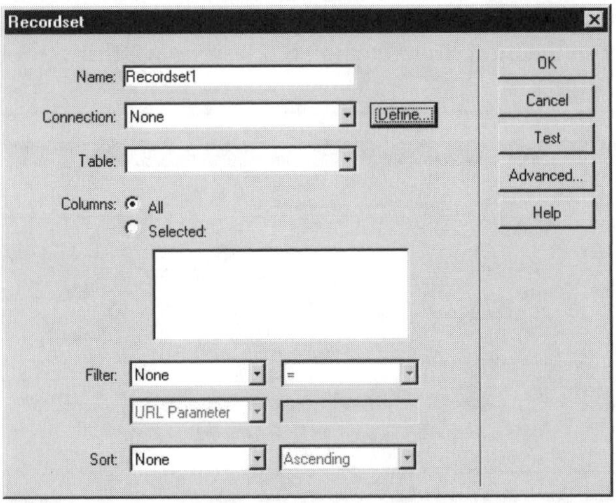

Figure 12-5. *You also can define a connection directly from the Recordset dialog box by clicking the Define button*

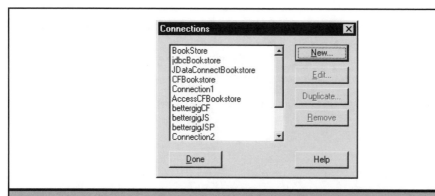

Figure 12-6. *The Connections dialog box, in which you can edit existing UltraDev database connections or create new ones*

UltraDev 1 uses a design-time connection that usually indicates your local machine. The run-time connection in UltraDev 1 is the actual production server from which your Web site will be deployed.

To define a ColdFusion ODBC data source in UltraDev 1, you must fill in the CF ODBC DSN (which is usually identical to the system ODBC DSN) for the run-time connection, and then use an ADO ODBC data source for the design-time connection. This is a limitation with UltraDev 1 that is eliminated in UltraDev 4.

When you click either New or Edit, the Data Source Name dialog box opens (see Figure 12-7). This box has two radio buttons: one for a local machine and one for an application server connection (the Macintosh doesn't have this option).

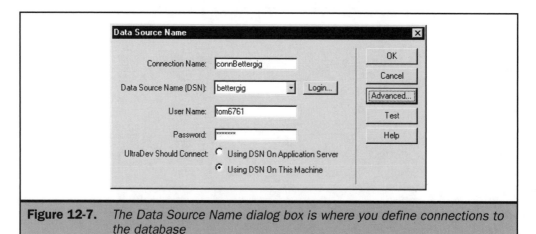

Figure 12-7. *The Data Source Name dialog box is where you define connections to the database*

You can also fill in the username and password in this dialog box, if you've implemented them in your database. It's always a good idea to set a username and password on any database that might be accessible to others. Even if you are not worried about malicious attack, it's good to keep the database secured—if only to prevent possible corruption of data from somebody opening the database by mistake.

If you've made a successful connection, after you click Done, you should see a drop-down list of all the tables in your database (if you are in Simple view) or a tree view showing all of your tables (if you are in Advanced view).

Caution	*If you are using a Web hosting company, there is a security issue with ODBC data sources. You might find that you can access all of the data sources on the server— including data sources of other customers of the Web host. There is a tech note on the Macromedia Web site that addresses this security issue.*

ADO Connection String

If you are using ASP, several other methods are at your disposal with which to connect to a database. UltraDev gives the option to use a connection string, if you choose Custom Connection String (ADO Connection String in UltraDev 1) as your connection type. Connection strings are also varied, so only some of the more popular types will be presented here.

OLE DB

OLE DB (object linking and embedding database) is the preferred method for connecting to a database in Windows. When you define an ODBC connection, you are putting a wrapper around an OLE DB connection to the database, and adding another step to the connection process. By connecting directly to OLE DB, you eliminate the middleman, so to speak, and create a connection that is a little speedier and a little more stable. OLE DB connections are not as universally compatible as ODBC connections, but their use has become fairly widespread. Also, many Web-hosting companies require a DSN-less connection or an OLE DB connection, because these require no intervention on the company's part and have fewer security issues.

Instead of using the ODBC DSN, as in the previous examples, you use the *provider*, which is specific to the database that you are working with. When you install the MDAC, several OLE DB providers are installed, including an ODBC provider that enables you to access any ODBC-compliant database through an OLE DB connection. You have the option to access the database through the native provider or through the ODBC provider, which is not the same as accessing the database through the ODBC DSN connection. The following is a typical Microsoft Access connection string using the native provider.

```
Provider=Microsoft.Jet.OLEDB.4.0;¬
Data Source=C:\inetpub\wwwroot\cgi-bin\bettergig.mdb;¬
User ID=username;Password=password;
```

Caution *Although the connection strings appear broken in print, they should be entered all in one line in the UltraDev environment.*

Here, note also that you are connecting directly to the database by using a path to that database. This speeds up the connection, because your system doesn't have to access the Registry to look up the DSN—it goes directly to the database. This method is not to be confused with a DSN-less connection, which is outlined next.

The way to enter the OLE DB connection string into UltraDev is to first bring up the Data Connection dialog box by choosing Modify | Connections, and then create a new connection. This time, instead of choosing Data Source Name, choose Custom Connection String. This opens the Custom Connection String dialog box, shown in Figure 12-8.

In the empty box for Connection String, you can put the previous Access connection string, if you are using the Access database, or use the following string for SQL Server:

```
Provider=SQLOLEDB;Data Source=myMachineName;¬
Initial Catalog=bettergig;User ID=username;Password=password;
```

If you enter the correct string and click the Test button, you should see the dialog box shown in Figure 12-9. Note that Initial Catalog refers to the actual database name in SQL Server, and Data Source refers to the actual machine name that the SQL Server resides on. Keep in mind that you must substitute your own username and password, as well as the server name, the database path for Access databases, and the Initial Catalog for SQL Server.

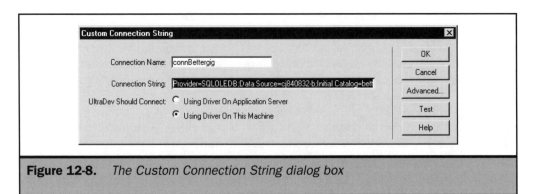

Figure 12-8. *The Custom Connection String dialog box*

Figure 12-9. *The test of a successful connection—this box appears after you click the Test button in a Define Connection session*

ODBC DSN-less Connections

Another form of connection is available to the ASP developer—a DSN-less connection. This connection is often preferable to the ODBC connection, because you don't need to have a system DSN set up to use it. The DSN-less connection is available for most of the databases that are ODBC compliant, and it uses the ODBC driver to connect to the database. The following string is in the format for an Access database:

```
Provider=MSDASQL; Driver={Microsoft Access Driver (*.mdb)};¬
Dbq=c:\inetpub\wwwroot\cgi-bin\bettergig.mdb;¬
UID=username;PWD=password
```

 The driver name inside the curly braces {} is the exact driver name as it appears in the ODBC Data Source Administrator. You can look at the Drivers tab of the Administrator to see which drivers are available and what the correct syntax is.

The Provider attribute is the default ODBC provider and is sometimes omitted from the string. ADO assumes that you are using the MSDASQL provider (the default ODBC provider) if you don't specify otherwise. It's a good idea to specify the provider directly.

Using the Microsoft Text Driver

One of the little-known features of ADO is the ability to define a connection to a text file. The text file can have an extension of .txt, .csv, .asc, or .tab. You can set up an ODBC DSN for a text driver connection, or you can use a DSN-less connection. Using the DSN-less connection, you must fill in the ADO connection string, as follows:

```
Driver={Microsoft Text Driver (*.txt; *.csv)};¬
Dbq=c:\somepath\;Extensions=asc,csv,tab,txt;¬
Persist Security Info=False;
```

Of course, all of this should be placed on one line. The driver works a little differently than the standard database drivers insofar as you define a *directory* instead of a path to a physical database or a physical file. After defining the connection, you should be able to click the Test button and make a successful connection. In defining the recordset, you'll see a list of text files in the directory specified by the connection string, instead of a list of tables. When you define your SQL statement, you'll be using the filename of the text file instead of a column name. A typical SQL statement using the text driver might look like this:

```
SELECT * FROM C:\inetpub\wwwroot\cgi-bin\addresses.txt
```

Make sure that the backslashes are all in the proper place in the file path. Some limitations may exist when using the text driver, but being able to display data in an organized fashion directly from a text file has many benefits.

Sample ADO Connection Strings

Note that in the Connection dialog box, the connection strings will be placed on one line in the ADO Connection String text field.

- Access ODBC DSN-less Connection

```
Driver={Microsoft Access Driver (*.mdb)};¬
Dbq=c:\somepath\dbname.mdb;Uid=Admin;Pwd=pass;
```

- dBase ODBC DSN-less Connection

```
Driver={Microsoft dBASE Driver (*.dbf)};¬
DriverID=277;Dbq=c:\somepath\dbname.dbf;
```

- Oracle ODBC DSN-less Connection

```
Driver={Microsoft ODBC for Oracle};¬
Server=OracleServer.world;Uid=admin;Pwd=pass;
```

- SQL Server DSN-less Connection

```
Driver={SQL Server};Server=servername;¬
Database=dbname;Uid=sa;Pwd=pass;
```

- Text Driver DSN-less Connection

```
Driver={Microsoft Text Driver (*.txt; *.csv)};Dbq=c:\somepath\;¬
Extensions=asc,csv,tab,txt;Persist Security Info=False;
```

- Visual FoxPro DSN-less Connection

```
Driver={Microsoft Visual FoxPro Driver};¬
SourceType=DBC;SourceDB=c:\somepath\dbname.dbc;Exclusive=No;
```

- Access OLE DB Connection

```
Provider=Microsoft.Jet.OLEDB.4.0;¬
Data Source=c:\somepath\dbname.mdb;User Id=admin;Password=pass;
```

- Oracle OLE DB Connection

```
Provider=OraOLEDB.Oracle;Data Source=dbname;¬
User Id=admin;Password=pass;
```

- SQL Server OLE DB Connection

```
Provider=SQLOLEDB;Data Source=machineName;¬
Initial Catalog=dbname;User ID=sa;Password=pass;
```

Using Server.Mappath in a Connection String

Many ASP developers prefer to use the server function Server.Mappath in the connection string when using a file-based database such as Microsoft Access. What this function does is to map the path to the database on the server if you supply the relative path to the database. For instance, if your database resides at e:\inetpub\wwwroot\ bettergig\cgi-bin\bettergig.mdb, you could use the following connection string (all on one line):

```
"Provider=Microsoft.Jet.OLEDB.4.0;Data Source=" &
Server.Mappath("\bettergig\cgi-bin\bettergig.mdb")
```

This option allows greater flexibility when you have a Web hosting company and you may not know the directory path to your Web site or your database. UltraDev 4 introduced the ability to use this type of path: Simply choose Using Driver on Application

Server as your connection method and supply a Custom Connection String like the preceding example. This method works with both OLE DB and DSN-less connections. The path has to be the relative path of the database to the site root, including a preceding backslash (\), as outlined.

Closing an ADO Connection

If you are using UltraDev 1, you may have noticed that UltraDev does not close recordset connections explicitly, but rather relies on the server to close the database connection. Some controversy exists over this, because it is a general rule of programming to destroy any object explicitly. You can add the following lines to the bottom of your ASP file (or anywhere in the file after you have finished with the recordset) to make sure that the database connection is closed and destroyed properly:

```
//VBScript
<%
Recordsetname.close
set Recordsetname = nothing
%>

//JavaScript
<%
Recordsetname.close();
Recordsetname = null;
%>
```

UltraDev 4 has made many improvements in the implementation of server-side code, and closing recordsets is one of those improvements. If you are using UltraDev 4 with ASP, recordsets are closed automatically at the bottom of the page. Also, when you access a recordset created in UltraDev 1 within UltraDev 4 by double-clicking it in the Data Bindings palette, the recordset will be converted to UltraDev 4 specifications upon clicking the OK button.

 Included on the CD-ROM is a Server Behavior that you can apply to a page containing a recordset that will automatically insert these lines into your ASP file. Note that you should use this Server Behavior only if you are still using version 1 of UltraDev.

ColdFusion Database Connections

ColdFusion allows the user to connect to a database using a system DSN much like the ASP method previously outlined. In fact, if you go to the ColdFusion Administrator contained within ColdFusion Server and click ODBC in the Data Sources menu, you are taken to a screen that shows you all the ODBC DSNs available on that particular machine. Not only can you access the data sources from the Administrator, but you also can edit, add, or delete data sources right from the Web interface. Defining ODBC and OLE DB data sources remotely is one of the great features of ColdFusion.

Note *Defining a data source using the CF Administrator is just like using the Control Panel. In other words, the data source created in the ColdFusion Administrator will show up as a system data source within the Control Panel.*

To be able to access a database in UltraDev for a ColdFusion site, you need to have a data source set up in the ODBC administrator as a system DSN (setting up an ODBC data source was outlined earlier under the section "ADO Connection using ODBC"). To create the connection, go to the Modify menu and click Modify I Connections or click the Define button on the recordset declaration dialog box to bring up the dialog box shown in Figure 12-10. Next, do the following:

1. Give the connection a name.
2. Click the Login button to log in to the ColdFusion RDS server. Use your CF Administrator password here. In most cases, the CF Administrator doesn't have a username, so you can leave the Username field blank.
3. Choose the ColdFusion Data Source Name from the drop-down box.
4. Fill in your username and password (if they are implemented).
5. Choose either Use DSN on This Machine or Use DSN on Application Server.

The code for the connection is automatically written to a *connName*.cfm file in the Connections folder after you create the connection, where *connName* refers to the actual name that you give the connection. All you have to worry about when you define your

INTEGRATING DATABASES WITH ULTRADEV

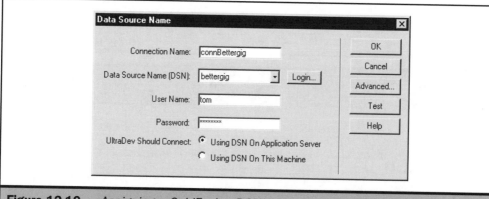

Figure 12-10. *Assigning a ColdFusion DSN name in the Data Source Name dialog box for a database connection*

connection is that you are using a valid DSN, username, and password. UltraDev will do the rest.

The Data Source Name – Advanced dialog box (shown in Figure 12-11) is available to ColdFusion users to allow the use of a JDBC driver to connect to a local database. This is provided for Macintosh users who can't run a local copy of ColdFusion, but still works with UltraDev by using a JDBC driver to connect to a local database at design time. The functionality is also available in the Windows version to allow for collaborative development in a situation in which one user has a Macintosh and another user has a Windows PC. The next section, "JDBC Connections," explains the JDBC driver connection method for UltraDev.

UltraDev supports a standard ColdFusion OLE DB connection and the native database driver connection for Oracle, Sybase, DB2, or Informix, if they are defined in the CF Administrator as data sources. Because UltraDev is fairly new software, many features have not been implemented yet, such as the ability to define an OLE DB connection in

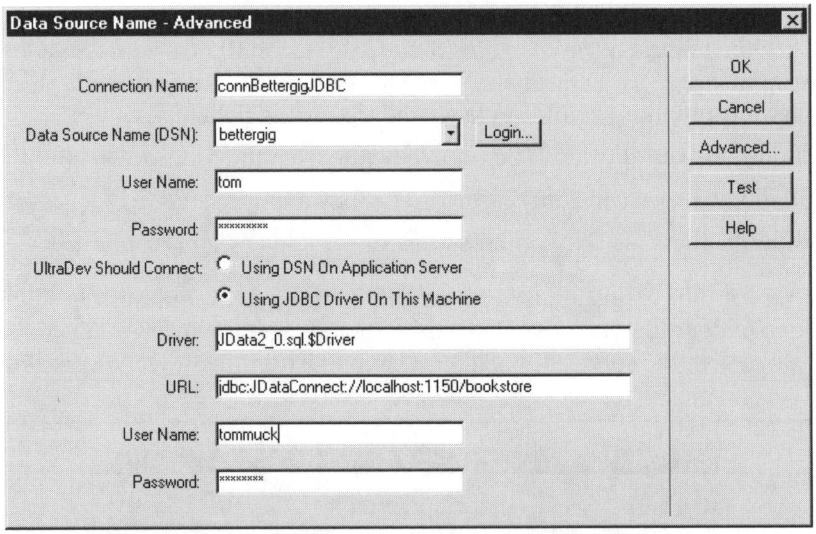

Figure 12-11. *The Data Source Name – Advanced dialog box for ColdFusion developers allows a local JDBC connection to be used*

the CF Administrator and override the default database setting with a DBNAME attribute in your CFQUERY tag. Hopefully, additions to upcoming releases will address these needs. Until then, if you are a ColdFusion developer, you have to stick to the standard database connections that are set up in the CF Administrator, or edit your connections manually after you have finished designing the page in UltraDev.

Note   *If you change the connections on the page, you will no longer be able to edit the connections from within the UltraDev environment, and the Data Bindings palette will no longer show your recordset columns. Possibly the best workaround for this is to have a local database with a DSN set up for it that mimics your final database.*

Caution   *For ColdFusion users, UltraDev doesn't allow for stored procedures in databases other than Microsoft SQL Server 7 using the Application Server option of the connection method. If you want to use a stored procedure in a database other than MS SQL Server, use the Local Machine data source option and connect to it with ODBC.*

JDBC Connections

JDBC is the standard for connecting a Java application or Web page to a database, much like ODBC is the standard for ADO. The JDBC technology is central to the Java platform, and is the primary method to connect a JSP page to a database. The JDBC classes are located in the java.sql package. As with the ASP and ColdFusion connections, the UltraDev JSP connection requires the data source to be specified in a connection string. Those familiar with JSP will note that you need only to provide the driver, username, password, and URL string in the connection definition dialog box. UltraDev takes care of writing the code to actually connect to the database, manipulate the recordset, and then disconnect with a recordset.close() method and a connection.close() method.

JDBC, like ODBC, uses a generic SQL implementation rather than trying to cater to one specific database. Java was designed as a cross-platform language, and JDBC was designed as a cross-database connection to provide a Java application with the ability to talk to a database in an independent fashion.

Four basic classifications of JDBC drivers exist for JSP and Java, as outlined in Table 12-1.

Driver Type	Description
Type 1	The first JDBC drivers to come along were bridges to ODBC. Because this driver type had to "bridge the gap" to the ODBC driver, it wasn't a pure Java driver. Drivers such as the Sun JDBC:ODBC bridge are Type 1 drivers.
Type 2	Type 2 drivers were the next step. These drivers connect to native database drivers without relying on the ODBC interface. Again, this driver type isn't 100 percent Java, and requires binary code on the client machine.
Type 3	This driver type generally is a 100 percent Java implementation that still requires server middleware to connect to the database.
Type 4	This driver type is a true Java implementation that connects to the database directly through a native network protocol. This is the latest and best type of driver to use for your database connection, and generally is proprietary for each individual database.

Table 12-1.   *The Four Basic Classifications of JDBC Drivers Available for JSP Pages*

UltraDev is ready to run with the Sun JDBC:ODBC Bridge, provided you are accessing a server with ODBC data source availability. To use the Bridge connection, you need to do the following:

1. Open the Connections dialog box by clicking Modify | Connections.

2. Click New to bring up a drop-down list of available drivers (see Figure 12-12).

3. Choose the Sun JDBC:ODBC Driver from the drop-down list, or choose Custom JDBC Driver to type it in manually (see Figure 12-13).

4. Give the data source a name (such as "connBettergig").

5. Choose a username and password, if you've defined them for your database.

6. Fill in the URL field, or substitute your own database information for the variable that might be in a preformatted URL field, such as [odbc dsn]. This, again, is specific to the driver that you use. In the case of the Sun driver, replace the jdbc:odbc:[odbc dsn] in the URL field with the following:

   ```
   jdbc:odbc:yourdsnName (replacing the jdbc:odbc:[odbc dsn])
   ```

7. Choose either Use Driver on This Machine or Use Driver on Application Server.

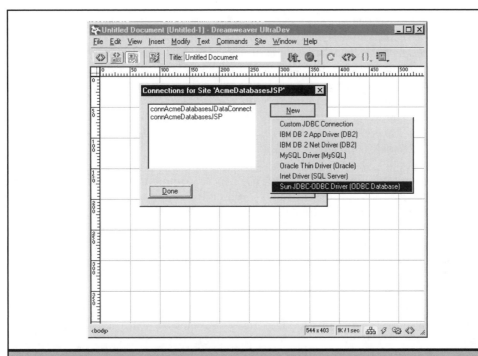

Figure 12-12. *A drop-down list of JDBC drivers is provided, or you can add your own with the Custom JDBC Connection*

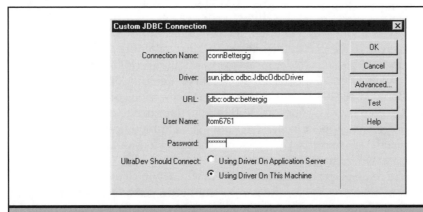

Figure 12-13. *Using the Custom JDBC Connection dialog box for a JDBC data source*

> **Note** *UltraDev 1 had a design-time connection that depended on the machine on which you were working to supply a design-time connection. You could use a local ADO ODBC DSN to connect to a replica of the actual database using a local DSN. The code you see while editing your page is your run-time code, with all connections and related code being JSP specific. The actual fields that appeared in your Data Bindings tab were courtesy of the UltraDev design environment, and effectively enabled you to edit your JSP page without having JSP on your machine. Unfortunately, this feature didn't work very well, and thus was removed in UltraDev 4 to prevent the confusion of the design-time and run-time connections. UltraDev 4 connects through the application server.*

The Sun driver, although fairly easy to use, isn't recommended for anything other than testing. It's actually very unreliable on certain JSP servers, such as the JRun Server from Allaire, as documented on the Allaire Web site. We recommend a Type 4 JDBC driver that's tailored specifically for the database that you plan to implement. A comprehensive list of the available JDBC drivers is available at the Sun Web site, at /java.sun.com/products/jdbc/driverdesc.html. IBM DB2 comes with its own JDBC drivers, as does Oracle. If you are implementing an Access or MS SQL Server database, you'll have to find a third-party driver.

Generally, third-party JDBC drivers don't come cheap, but "trial" versions of these drivers often are available for download. In many cases, the software vendors will allow you to use the driver indefinitely as a developer, and only prohibit you from using the driver in a production environment. In any case, it is wise to test a driver fully before deciding to purchase it.

Getting the JDBC Drivers into UltraDev

The process of installing a third-party JDBC driver and having UltraDev recognize it isn't a straightforward process. After installing the driver into your machine, per the software vendor's instructions, you still must perform a few additional steps to have UltraDev recognize your driver. First, the JAR or ZIP file containing the Java classes has to be copied to the JDBCDrivers folder inside the Configuration folder. By performing this step, UltraDev will recognize the driver when you choose Use Driver on This Machine. Then, when you click the New button in the Connections dialog box, you can choose to use Custom JDBC Connection and type in your driver information.

If you want the driver to appear in the drop-down box automatically, additional steps are involved. You have to create your own connection extension, which is a simple HTML file in this case. Open the Configuration | Connections | JSP folder—and then open the Mac or Win folder—depending on which machine you're using. In that folder are the interface files (dialog boxes) for the various connections that are implemented in UltraDev. If your driver isn't here, you'll have to create your own interface for the driver. The following are the general steps you must follow to create the driver interface:

1. Copy one of the other driver files, such as the db2app_jdbc_conn.htm file, and open it in Notepad or your text editor of choice.

2. Change the <title> tag to reflect your new driver name. In this example, the JDataConnect driver from NetDirect is used:

```
<title>JDataConnect JDBC Driver</title>
```

3. Find the global variables section and replace the individual variables with your own driver information:

```
//Global Variables
var DEFAULT_DRIVER = "JData2_0.sql.$Driver";
var DEFAULT_TEMPLATE="jdbc:JDataConnect://[hostname:port]/[odbc]";
var MSG_DriverNotFound = "JDataConnect Driver not found!";
var FILENAME = "JDataConnect_jdbc_conn.htm";
```

4. Save the file with the filename used in the FILENAME variable in the proper folder (Win or Mac).

5. Restart UltraDev and create a new connection by clicking Modify | Connections and clicking the New button. Your new driver should appear (see Figure 12-14).

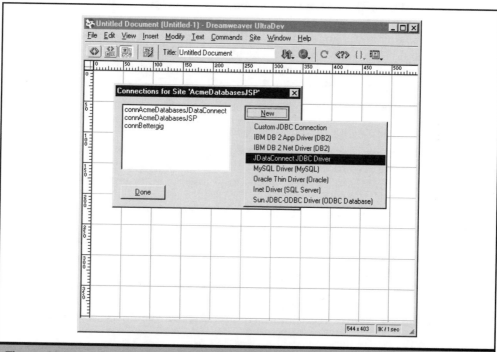

Figure 12-14. *Confirmation that the new driver has been successfully installed*

UltraDev 1 JDBC Connections

The method for getting your drivers to be recognized by UltraDev is a little different for UltraDev 1. You still have to put the classes into the JDBCConnections folder, but the step to get the driver to appear in the drop-down box is a little different. If you open the Connections.xml file that's in the Connections folder, you'll see several <driverinfo> tags at the bottom of the file. These are the drivers that UltraDev will recognize, providing a drop-down box in the Define Connection dialog box.

If your driver isn't listed here, you can still get it to appear in the drop-down box. One method is to manually type your driver name in the Driver box in the Define Connection dialog box. The next time you need to access the driver, it will be there. In fact, you will even notice an entry for it in the Connections.xml file. The connection, however, will still lack the built-in URL template. Again, you can either type this manually, or edit the Connections.xml file yourself and include it.

To edit the Connections.xml file, you must open the file in your favorite text editor (WordPad in Windows or BBEdit on the Mac are good choices for editing the internal UltraDev XML files). The XML files used by UltraDev are not *true* XML files, so it is necessary to use a plain text editor when viewing or making changes to them. UltraDev's XML is not well formed, so a real XML editor will recognize the XML as invalid.

Before making any changes, however, it is always a good idea to back up the file. This should be common practice whenever you edit a menu or any other file that is integral to UltraDev's operation. You can then add your own <driverinfo> tag, containing complete information about your driver.

A few sample <driverinfo> lines are shown here:

- Oracle Thin Driver

```
<driverinfo name="oracle.jdbc.driver.OracleDriver"
urltemplate="jdbc:oracle:thin:@[hostname]:[port]:[sid]" />
```

- IBM DB2 Driver

```
<driverinfo name="COM.ibm.db2.jdbc.net.DB2Driver"
urltemplate="jdbc:db2://[database name]" />
```

- Sun JDBC:ODBC Bridge

```
<driverinfo name="sun.jdbc.odbc.JdbcOdbcDriver"
urltemplate="jdbc:odbc:[odbc dsn]" />
```

- RmiJdbc Driver (for Macintosh connections to a Windows server)

```
<driverinfo name="RmiJdbc.RJDriver"
urltemplate="jdbc:rmi://[hostname]/jdbc:odbc:[odbc dsn]" />
```

- JDataConnect JDBC driver (for Access and SQL Server)

```
<driverinfo name="JData2_0.sql.$Driver"
urltemplate="jdbc:JDataConnect://[hostname][:port]/[odbc dsn]" />
```

- MySQL Driver

```
<driverinfo name="org.gjt.mm.mysql.Driver"
urltemplate="jdbc:mysql://[hostname][:port]/[dbname]" />
```

The *name* attribute will show up in your Driver drop-down box the next time you start UltraDev, and the *urltemplate* attribute will show up in your URL text field as a template that you can use to format your own URL. These are just examples, and you should use the driver name and URL that are specified in the documentation for the particular driver that you are using.

The DEFAULT_DRIVER variable is the driver name that will appear in the Driver text field when you create the new connection. The DEFAULT_TEMPLATE variable is the URL of the driver that acts as a template, with brackets surrounding information that the user can supply. The MSG_DriverNotFound variable is the error message that will be displayed if an error occurs. The FILENAME variable is the present connection file's name. The extensibility chapters (Chapters 20 to 23) cover the various methods for extending UltraDev by creating your own extensions such as this one.

Caution   *A patch needs to be applied to UltraDev 1, available on the Macromedia Web site at http://download.macromedia.com/pub/ultradev/jsp_update.mxp, that fixes a few problems with the JSP implementation. Many users are not able to get a database connection without applying the patch. UltraDev 4 doesn't require this patch.*

Macintosh Database Connections

The Apple Macintosh has long been a favorite with graphic artists and Web designers. With the advent of the iMacs and the newer G4 Macintoshes, Apple is once again a viable alternative to Windows as a tool for professional Web developers. Until now, however, Macintosh Web developers didn't have access to the same types of dynamic Web page creation using database connections to ADO, JSP, and ColdFusion. UltraDev bridges that gap by providing a *design-time* connection to a live database that resides on the application server.

Before discussing the implementation of database connections for Macintosh users, you should know some history behind the UltraDev Macintosh version. The first version of UltraDev had a fairly complex setup procedure. Local connections were maintained through a Java JDBC driver named RmiJdbc that resided on the Mac, but they also had to communicate with an RmiJdbc driver that resided on a Windows server. One of the problems that faced many Mac users was the simple fact that many Web-hosting companies were reluctant to have the JDBC driver running on their servers. It had to be run from a command line, and didn't work as a service on NT machines.

Also, no method was in place for having a local Mac database used for the design of a site. This alienated users of Filemaker Pro and other Macintosh databases who wanted to work exclusively on a Mac. In addition, Linux and UNIX servers were out, too, because the RmiJdbc driver required by UltraDev only ran on a Windows server.

Connecting to the Database Server from a Macintosh

The key to a successful database connection from a Macintosh to a remote server is the Site Definition dialog box. Beginning with UltraDev 4, all database connections are achieved through HTTP, allowing Macintosh and PC users to enjoy the same types of connections. To set up a connection, you have to be connected to the Internet and have access to your application server.

When defining your site, the Application Server dialog box has to be filled out properly to connect to your server. You need to define the following items assuming you are connecting through FTP:

- **Server Model**   This can be ASP, JSP, or ColdFusion.
- **Default Scripting Language**   For ASP developers, this can be VBScript or JavaScript (JScript).
- **Default Page Extension**   This should reflect your server model (.asp, .jsp, or .cfm).
- **Server Access**   This should be set to FTP (Local Network could be used as well).
- **Host Directory**   The directory on the application server that hosts the Web site.
- **Login**   Your username for the FTP setting.
- **Password**   Your password.
- **URL Prefix**   The IP address and path to your site; this is the key ingredient to a successful connection.

If you have defined your site correctly and are able to view your pages by previewing (using F12), then the database connections should work as well. The URL prefix will be the determining factor in getting the connection to work. If your site is located at http://24.10.235.158/mysite, then that's exactly where the URL prefix should be pointing.

Upgrading from UltraDev 1 to UltraDev 4

UltraDev 4 introduced a new method of connecting to the database, as was previously discussed in this chapter. If you are upgrading from UltraDev 1, all of your connections from UltraDev 1 are included in each site that you define. This may be what you want, but it may be something that's not desired. These extra connection files can be deleted from your site Connections folder each time you create a site. The only files that should remain inside the Connections folder of a completed site are the actual connections that the site is going to use.

You can edit the connection information that appears in each site by editing one of the UltraDev XML files that reside in the Configuration folder. If you go to Configuration I Connections, you'll see a Connections.xml file that contains all connection information imported from UltraDev 1. You can safely delete any lines that apply to connections that you don't want to have imported into each site, or remove the file completely. The connections.xml file is created the first time you start up UltraDev 4.

Also, any recordsets that were created with UltraDev 1 will be treated differently when you open the page up in UltraDev 4. The recordset name will have #prior version# tacked on to the end of it in the Data Bindings palette. By double-clicking the recordset name in the palette, you are prompted to convert the recordset to the new format. You should only do this if you don't intend to edit the page in UltraDev 1 again, as the connection information will not be understood by UltraDev 1.

Converting recordsets from the UltraDev 1 version is a process that needs to be done on a page by page basis. It is not strictly necessesary to convert the pages, but it is a good idea if you plan to maintain your sites in the future with UltraDev 4.

Summary

This chapter has reviewed a few of the connection methods available to the Web developer in UltraDev. Not all possible connection methods are available in UltraDev, but chances are good that they will be implemented in future versions. In addition, the connection methods are extensible, as are most features in UltraDev, so that third parties can create new connection methods. Chapters 20 to 23 cover the Dreamweaver UltraDev extensibility API.

After the connection is made, the next step is to retrieve the data from the database that you want to display on the page. The next few chapters will detail designing and implementing a database for use in an UltraDev site, and accessing the data to be displayed on the page.

Chapter 13

Designing a
Relational Database

If you are going to store something, especially a lot of something, then it is a pretty good idea to have a system for storing it that lets you find it and get it back out of storage when you need it. Filing cabinets have alphabetical folders, the library has the Dewey Decimal System, and databases have the Relational Design Model.

In 1970, E. F. Codd, then a researcher at IBM, published a paper that was the first conception of what we now know as the Relational Database Design Model. Codd was concerned with the mechanics of storing and retrieving data in large database applications. His model stood in contrast to the models that were in use at the time, which were more reliant on the physical storage of the data and were significantly less flexible than Codd's vision.

Note *Many people think that Codd's design model is called "relational" because of the way that tables are "related" to one another when querying a database. Actually, Codd's terminology was somewhat different than today's. What we call a "table," Codd called a "relation" because, by definition, that table should hold information about individual items that are in some way related to one another. What we call "columns" and "rows," Codd called "attributes" and "tuples."*

Since that time, Codd has revised and expanded the rules that govern relational database design. The last 30 years have proven the validity of the relational concept, and it is the model on which all modern databases are built. In order for you to access data from an application built with UltraDev, you are going to need to design that data store.

The design of a data store is really a separate issue from how you connect to the database or how you query data from it. While closely related to your overall goal, database design is a discipline all to itself. In this chapter, we will cover the points that you need to know to design a database that will be flexible and powerful enough to serve your application well.

What Is a Database?

Perhaps the best way to think of a database is like a big filing cabinet that you have squeezed onto the hard drive of your computer. In that filing cabinet, you have file folders. In those folders, there is paper; and on that paper is information. If you think carefully about how you set up your filing cabinet, it can be a quick-and-easy way to put your hands on the data you need.

Suppose that you need to collect information about all of the players in a golf tournament that you have started. For the most part, you need the same information about each player. You might want to collect the following information:

- Name
- Address
- Phone number

- Payment method
- Handicap (a method of tracking average score related to par, and thereby skill level)
- Team number (which team of four players this person is assigned to)
- Score (this team's score for the tournament)
- Ranking (the ranking of this team in relation to other teams in the tournament based on their score)
- Notes (any miscellaneous information you may need to store about this player)

In order to collect this information, you might whip up a quick form in your favorite word processor and print off a copy for each player you expect to register. Once you have filled out the form (which, keep in mind, is identical for every player) with each player's individual information (which is obviously different for each player), you can store those forms in a file folder for future reference. To make sure that you can always find this information, you place this folder in a drawer in your filing cabinet.

So, in the current example, there are five items that are necessary to collect and store information about the players in your golf tournament: a filing cabinet, a filing drawer in the cabinet, a file folder, a basic form design, and an individual form for each player. These physical items relate directly to the basic parts of a modern database system. They are as follows:

- Database management system
- Individual database
- Tables
- Columns
- Rows

Note *There are other parts of a database, such as stored procedures and triggers, that are discussed later in this chapter. These elements represent the basics and are sufficient for this discussion.*

The Database Management System

The database management system is the overall application framework within which you design, house, and manage all of the databases you create for your individual projects. Figure 13-1 shows the SQL Server Enterprise Manager. The Enterprise Manager is a centralized place where you can view, open, interact with, and maintain your databases.

Smaller, file-based database applications, such as Access, don't provide the same level of database management as their server-based big brothers, but you can think of

Figure 13-1. *The SQL Server Enterprise Manager*

the basic Access program as a place where you can quickly manage the individual database files that you have created. The principal difference is that you will use Access to find and open an individual file on your computer rather than having all of the files located and displayed for you within a management system (see Figure 13-2).

In the current example, the database application or management system represents the filing cabinet in which your filing drawers are kept. You may have several drawers within the cabinet, but they are all available to you right there in the filing cabinet along with the rest of the data.

In a filing cabinet, you only have so many drawers, usually two or four. One of the great things about a database management system is the ability to keep adding drawers (databases) as you need them to hold more data.

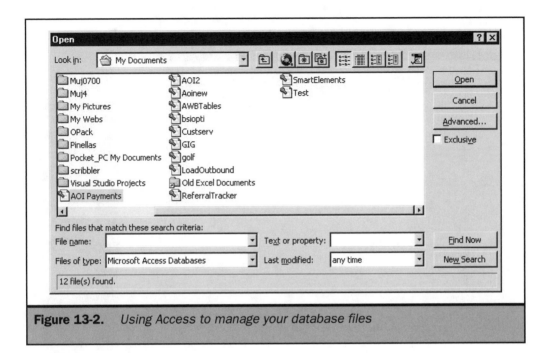

Figure 13-2. *Using Access to manage your database files*

The Individual Database

Within your database management system are individual databases that you have created. An individual database is a set of components and data that serve a particular purpose for a particular project. While it is possible to keep shoving data into one expanding database to serve multiple purposes, such a database will quickly become unorganized and useless. It is highly advisable to create separate databases for each project—and sometimes even more than one for a project if the project is of sufficient size and scope to require it.

Note *The decision of how many databases are required to service a project is a many-faceted consideration. Topics such as security, performance, maintenance, and data compatibility need to be investigated in the design stage in order to make a reasonable determination.*

In the current example, the individual database is represented by the file drawer. The file drawer is housed within the filing cabinet, just as the database is housed within the database application. Just as you might designate a drawer in your file cabinet for financial information, contracts, or golf tournament participation, you would create and populate individual databases for each type of data you need to store (see Figure 13-3).

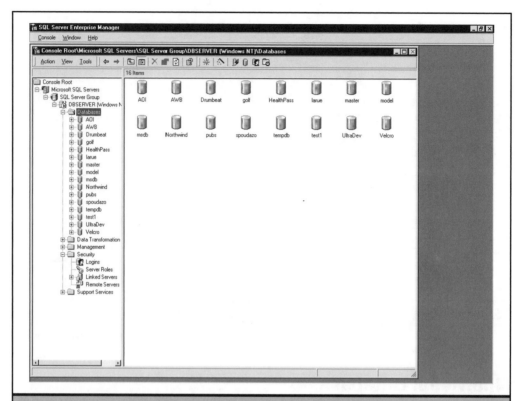

Figure 13-3.   *A selection of databases within the SQL Server Enterprise Manager*

Tables

Just as you have organized the places in which you will store data by selecting a
database application and creating an individual database to segregate related data,
you must organize the data being stored within each database. In addition to the
players in your golf tournament, you may need to store information about sponsors,
advertisers, judges, golf courses, and prizes. It would be a mistake to try and store
all of this information within the same file folder, just as it would be a mistake to jumble
it all together within your database.

Tables are the components of your database that are responsible for holding your
data for you. Typically, you will have a table for each set of related data you need
to store; in the present example, you would create a different form on which to write
information about the participants, advertisers, and golf courses if you were doing
this on paper. There are a couple of reasons for this.

First, different forms for each type of contact make it easier to identify the data that the form holds. Each player has at least one thing in common: each is a player in this golf tournament. Likewise, each advertiser has in common an advertisement at the tournament. It is logical to keep those groups of contacts segregated by the thing they have in common—their type of participation in the event

Second, you are likely to need different kinds of information about different kinds of contacts. The information you might need about the players was discussed at the beginning of this section. It would be silly to put a place to store the team assignment or score of an advertiser, but you would need a place to put the type of advertisement, the rate they paid, and their billing information—information that you do not need to collect about your players. When the specific information that you need to collect and store differs to this degree, it is a strong indication that it should be stored on two different forms, or in two different database tables.

Note	*Looking back up the chain of data constructs you are creating, you can clearly see the relation that each has to the other. No matter how many tables you create, they all relate to your golf tournament, and hence belong in your golf tournament database. That golf tournament database, in turn, is one of your projects; and, therefore, it belongs in the database management system that houses your projects.*

Figure 13-4 illustrates the tables that you might create within your golf tournament database.

Columns

On the form that was created in this example to hold information about the players in the golf tournament, there were several pieces of information identified that needed to be collected about each player. This information represents attributes of the individual players. These translate to your database table as the columns of the table. While these attributes are not always represented as columns, the datasheet view, a common way of looking at data, looks much like a spreadsheet with the *attribute*, or *field*, names listed across the top. You can see this in Figure 13-5, which makes it clear why *columns* is the common name for this part of the table.

In essence, each column represents a question about the topic of the table. For instance, in the players table, each column relates to one of the attributes of the player. In filling out each column for each player, you are, in effect, answering a question about that player that represents information you have decided your database needs to know about the players in order to manage the tournament effectively.

Rows

Closely related to the columns of the database are the *rows* that make up the left-hand axis of the datasheet in Figure 13-5. These rows are represented in the current example

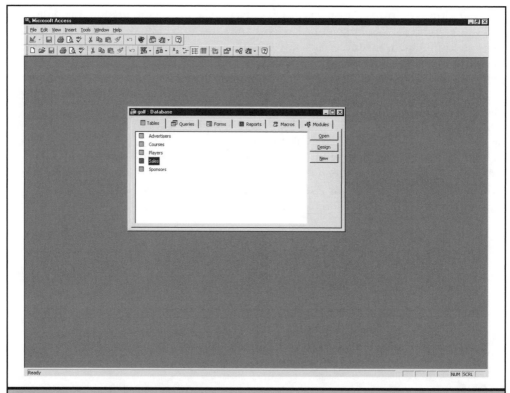

Figure 13-4.   *The tables of the Golf Tournament database*

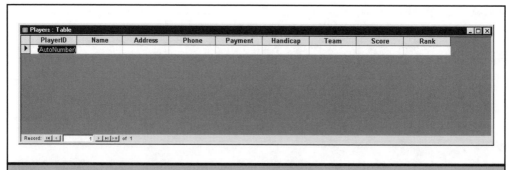

Figure 13-5.   *A database table showing the column names across the top*

by the individual copies of your form that hold the information about the individual players in your tournament. In the database table, each player is entered on his or her own row of the table. That row holds information about that player and only that player. On each row, a field is available for each column in which you can enter information about that player that answers the question represented by the column, such as what the player's name is, or which team the player is assigned to.

Designing a Relational Database

Some people's filing cabinets are nothing but collecting spots for excess paper they can't decide what to do with. The drawers barely open and close and they quickly become useless space wasters. If you are not careful and organized, your database will end up the same way: overstuffed, useless, and difficult to open and close.

Despite all that computers can do for you, sometimes it is a good idea to set them aside and start with a pencil and a piece of paper. When you first begin to sketch out the functionality of a computer project, and especially a database schema, it is often best to get out a good number 2 pencil and a legal pad and try to get your thoughts organized so that the job of actually implementing the database can be done right the first time.

If you are new to programming, the importance of doing things right the first time cannot be overemphasized. True, you will almost always have bugs that need to be fixed and maintenance to perform, but you can significantly reduce these and eliminate more major problems by spending the time to design your application properly.

There are several questions that you need to answer before you can begin constructing your database:

- What kind of data will you be storing?
- How will the database be accessed?
- Will your users need to add and change things in the database or just look things up?
- What kind of special functionality might you need access to?
- What changes might you need to make in the future?

Your Data

What kind of data you will store in your database is an important consideration, both in selecting the database management system (or application) you will use and how its structure in defined. If, for instance, you will only be storing text information, such as names and addresses of clients and simple product information, you are pretty safe in assuming that any modern system can accommodate your needs. If, however, you need the ability to store things like BLOBS (Binary Large Objects), such as images and sounds directly in the database tables (rather than just storing references to them), you will need to do some extra research to make sure that your database selection supports them and find out whether they require any special considerations.

An important point in this day and age is the security level of the information you will be storing. Financial, medical, and other personal information is stored in databases all over the world. If you will be handling information of this nature, you will need to pay special attention to the security scheme that you implement to ensure that the data remains secure.

Database Access

Determining how your database will be accessed is also an important consideration. For instance, will this database service only a Web site, and only one Web site? Or will it need to be accessed by multiple applications such as a sales site, an administration site, and an internal office application written in another language such as Visual Basic so your sales staff can query information and maintain the site's data?

Think also about how the different uses of the database might affect your security needs. It is unlikely that a stand-alone Access database that lets users look up ZIP code information, for instance, would pose the same security risk as a large database management system operating at a financial institution. Likewise, a database that only allows office users to access it may not need the same level of security planning as one that makes data available over the Web. Since you are contemplating data access over the Internet with UltraDev, it is likely that you will need to spend some time in this important area.

 It is not possible here to adequately cover database security. Security is a complex matter with different implementations, depending on the software you need to use. If you are unsure as to the steps required to successfully secure you data, please seek competent help before you attempt to place sensitive information in a Web-connected database.

Use of the Database

The purpose for which your database will be used is also an important point to consider. In the preceding section, a ZIP code lookup function was mentioned. In such an application, the user would most likely be providing some simple information on which a database query would be constructed. The database would return to the user information based on the input the user had provided. For example, if the user supplied a ZIP code, the application might tell him or her for which cities that ZIP code was valid. The functionality could likely be accomplished with only a table or two of data. Such a database would be used to query data from the tables, but it is unlikely that you would ever allow a user to add or change ZIP code information. That kind of information is updated by official sources on a periodic basis, and your own maintenance procedures are all that should be allowed to alter any data within the tables.

However, the golf tournament database discussed in the previous section required several tables to store all of the data. In addition, not only will you and visitors to your site need to query data out of this database, but some of these tables will need regular updating as new players and advertisers sign on and team assignments and scores are updated. Designing a database of even moderate complexity like this can take careful consideration.

For example, it is important to keep data that needs to be updated separated from static or private data, so that users don't inadvertently change something that they shouldn't. In addition, you can save a significant amount of space and simplify maintenance of your site if you use properly normalized data, which will be discussed shortly.

Database Functionality

If you are new to databases, it may seem strange to talk about a database doing anything besides storing data in tables. In reality, there are several additional functions that can be performed inside the database itself that can increase or improve the performance of your overall application. Some of the most useful functions are listed here:

- Stored procedures
- Triggers
- Views
- Security
- Relationship management

Stored Procedures

Stored procedures are a method of storing the code you use to interact with your database within the database itself. Instead of passing a series of commands into the database every time you need to perform an action, you can create stored procedures that are callable from your application.

Stored procedures enable you to create database code in a modular format that you can reference each time you need to perform a particular task. They can accept input parameters, execute complex series of code, and return recordsets and values to the calling application.

In addition, stored procedures provide the following enhancements:

- **Increased execution speed**   Because they are precompiled by the database, stored procedures execute more quickly than the same code passed in from your application.

- **Reduced network traffic**   Calling a stored procedure that is already stored in the database takes fewer commands, and, therefore, less traffic is sent across the network.

- **Increased security**   A user can be given permission to execute stored procedures that execute code that the user would not be authorized to run on his own. You can, therefore, better control the combinations of commands that users can execute, increasing the control you have over access to your data.

INTEGRATING DATABASES WITH ULTRADEV

Triggers

Triggers are a special kind of stored procedure that you can set to run in reaction to changes in your database's data. When an Insert, Update, or Delete command runs, a trigger can be set to run and enforce sets of business rules that you describe.

For example, referential integrity is a very important consideration for your database. Maintaining referential integrity in your database requires that you set up rules so that data cannot be altered with impunity in your tables. The triggers that you set up will be responsible for checking to see that any modification of your data conforms to the rules you have described.

For example, in one table you may store information about an employer that will be posting job opportunities to the Bettergig Web site. In another table, you may store information about each of those jobs. If an employer in the first table terminated their relationship with Bettergig.com, you might choose to delete them from the database. If you stopped there, what would you be left with? The answer is a bunch of job opportunities in another table with no information about the company that is offering the jobs. These records are known as *orphan records* because the parent information that makes them meaningful is gone. Without the employer information, the job information is useless and needs to be deleted from the database at the same time as the employer record. You can set up a trigger on the table that runs each time an employer is deleted. When you delete an employer, that trigger can be set to check the jobs table for job opportunities that were offered by that employer, and it will delete them at the same time.

Likewise, you can set triggers to run when records are added or updated in your database. Combinations of triggers can be run in response to single events to allow for complex data manipulation when data is modified in your tables.

Views

A view is a virtual table. That means that its contents are defined by a query, not by an actual physical table that contains data. When a view is created, it is really defined as a query that is run when the view is called from an application or another query. Each time it is called, the query is re-executed so that the data you receive remains current.

In one way, a view is like a stored procedure in that it is a predefined query that can be called when needed. But a view is intended to return data just as a call to a table would; it doesn't perform complicated manipulations and return values as a stored procedure does.

An interesting use of views is the combination of similarly structured data that exists across servers, perhaps in different departments or different divisions of a company. With a view, you can combine, for instance, sales numbers from a variety of departments that all store their data on separate database servers.

In addition, data can be updated through the use of views as long as the view follows these rules:

■ There is at least one table in the From clause, meaning that the view is not based entirely on tableless calculations.

■ There are no aggregate functions in the view. (See Chapter 14 for a discussion of aggregate functions.)

■ Each field in the view must be based on a simple column expression, meaning that no functions or mathematics can have been applied.

Security

As mentioned earlier, security is a major concern for any database that you will be placing on the Web. Most database management systems provide a means of defining users and setting security options for individual users or groups of users. Make sure that you understand how your database authenticates users and their appropriate roles before you put data of a sensitive or personal nature anywhere near a Web site.

Relationship Management

When you are setting up your tables in a new database, it is important to identify relationships among the data that is stored in the tables. Once again, this relates to database normalization, and relationships will no doubt make more sense after the normalization discussion coming up in this chapter. But a quick example here should help you get started.

When you set up the data for the Bettergig.com Web site in Chapter 16, you will see that this database stores information about employers and the jobs they are offering on the site. In one table of the database, information about the participating employers is stored. Information about the jobs they are offering is stored in a different table. How do you know what jobs belong to what employers? Good question.

You could store the name and other information about the employer that is offering a particular job in the table alongside the job details. But this is impractical and unnecessary when you are working within the relational database model. Instead, information about the employer can be stored once in a different table. In that table, each employer is assigned a unique identifying piece of information, usually an integer or small piece of text that you can use to reference that specific employer wherever you need its information. In the jobs table, all you need to do is supply a field in which you can store the identifier of the employer that is offering the job. Then, whenever you reference that job, you can look in this field of the table and identify the employer.

But that little identifier will quickly become useless to you by itself, because you cannot possibly remember all of the employers and their identifiers as the database gets larger. By defining a relationship between the jobs table that holds the identifier and the employers table that tells you which employer that identifier belongs to, you can be sure you always have access to all of the information you need about a job offering.

A database of any size will likely have a number of relationships defined. Figure 13-6 shows a database diagram with several table relationships defined.

In addition to helping you identify your data, relationships can help you make sure that your data remains meaningful. For instance, in this example, suppose that someone tried to assign an identifier to a job for which there was no employer defined in the employers table. The database would throw an error warning you that you were about to corrupt the integrity of your data by assigning a nonexistent employer to a job. In this way, the database can help you enforce the fact that it is proper to set up an employer before entering jobs that they have to offer.

There are several different kinds of relationships between database tables. These are discussed in the upcoming section "Table Relationships."

Database Maintenance

The last item on the list of considerations when designing a database is the methods you will use to perform maintenance. Ideally, there will be as little maintenance as

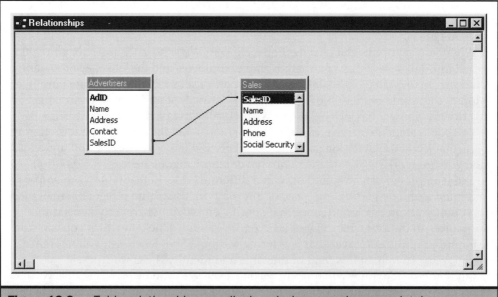

Figure 13-6. *Table relationships are displayed when you view your database diagram*

possible; but the real-world facts are that you will end up performing some maintenance on your database as you go. Careful planning will help minimize the number of alterations you need to make, but the sheer complexity of some sites means you are bound to either miss something or experience an honest to goodness change in how you need the database to work.

One of the primary concerns about altering databases once they are in use is what happens when you find yourself needing to add or change fields (or columns) in a table. In either case, you will likely have existing data that will be affected by the change, and you will need to carefully consider how your changes will impact that data. Give special notice to how existing data will react if you need to change data type—meaning changing a field from a text data type to an integer, for instance. Think also about existing records if you must add a field to a table. What will it mean that all of the existing records have had no data inserted into that new field, and how can you best address collecting and inserting the appropriate values for each existing record?

Uniqueness and Keys

Suppose that you had several bills of U.S. currency of different denominations in front of you, from a $1 bill up to a $100 bill. If someone asked you to hand him a particular bill that had a U.S. president's picture on it, how would you know which one he meant? Not all U.S. currency has presidents on it (Benjamin Franklin was never president), but certainly more than one denomination has a president on it.

Luckily, there is unique information on the bills. Each has a different denomination that can identify the bill uniquely when compared to other bills. But even that would not be sufficient in, say, a stack of $10 bills. In that case, you would need to look at the serial number on each bill to be sure that you could identify each bill uniquely.

The records in your database are much the same. Many of them may have information in common. Just as many U.S. bills have presidents on them, many of the players in your golf tournament may live in Georgia. You can go a level deeper and look only for the players from Atlanta. That may work, just as you may only have had a single $10 bill, but it is just as likely that you could have multiple players from Atlanta. In order to be sure that you can identify a single player without question, it is necessary to have information that is unique to that player. Although we are not collecting this information, you might think of something like a social security number, which is guaranteed by an outside source to be unique to each person. While it may be inappropriate to demand players' social security numbers just so they can play golf, you can approximate the role of the social security number by telling your database to assign a unique identifier to each entry in the database.

Think about why table uniqueness is so important. First, from a common-sense standpoint, how much sense does it make to store multiple copies of identical data in your table? If there is nothing different about a second or third record, then there is no reason to waste space storing them.

Second and more important, when you attempt to update or delete a database record, the database must be able to identify exactly which record you are trying to operate on. If it can't do so, the database will likely throw an error rather than risk corrupting your data by altering the incorrect record. Records can be identified by the use of three kinds of keys:

- Candidate keys
- Primary keys
- Foreign keys

Candidate Keys

A candidate key is a set of one or more columns in your database that are unique across all occurrences. For instance, consider the following table of data:

ZIP Code	City
32811	Orlando
32835	Orlando
34749	Ocoee
32789	Winter Park
32790	Winter Park

In the preceding sample, there are two possible candidate keys based on their uniqueness. The first is the ZIP Code column. Because no value repeats, it can be considered a candidate key. In addition, although the city names in the City column do repeat on occasion, the combination of the ZIP Code and City columns together never repeat, providing another possible candidate key. Because the City column does repeat, it has no value by itself for identifying unique records.

> **Note** *Just because the values in these columns do not repeat in the sample data does not necessarily mean that they never will. The designation of a candidate key is based upon your knowledge of the data that will be placed in your tables and your knowledge that certain combinations of columns will remain unique. Once designated, this decision will be enforced in your database to call attention to attempts to duplicate data that you have identified as a candidate key.*

Another consideration when identifying a candidate key is where it is possible for a particular record to be null for a key column. Because null values cannot be guaranteed to be unique, no candidate key can contain nulls.

Primary Keys

A primary key differs from a candidate key only in that it has been arbitrarily designated as the primary key from the selection of candidate keys already defined. Although primary keys, in the current thinking, are not strictly necessary in your tables, they are quite useful—especially because of their minimalist nature.

Note	*There is another kind of relational key called an alternate key. An* alternate key *is any candidate key that has not been designated as the primary key for a table.*

While a given candidate key may be up to several columns in complexity, a primary key is often designated as a single column that uniquely defines a row in the database. Sometimes this single column has no real relationship to the actual data that is being stored, other than the fact that you have designated it as an arbitrary identifier. Developers will often use an autonumber or Identity function to have the database itself create a random or incremental integer or whole number that is used as the primary key. In many cases, you can construct the database so that the number becomes meaningful for the data in question, such as making the generated number a group or account number, but this is not strictly necessary. Primary keys are of the greatest use when used to refer to table data being referenced from a foreign key.

Foreign Keys

Foreign keys are not strictly keys at all, in that they do not typically have any impact on the uniqueness of a particular record. The job of a foreign key is to refer to the primary key (or candidate key, to be proper) of a table that holds more detailed information about some topic that is related to the current record.

For example, let's return to the golf tournament database. In that database, a table was created to hold information about advertisers at the golf tournament. Suppose that this year, the tournament is becoming quite an event, and you must hire some sales people to handle the transactions with your advertisers. You have promised those sales people a commission, so you must, of course, track the sales they have made. To do this, you will need to add a table to hold data about your sales staff. Consider Table 13-1.

Note that the SalesID column is designated as a primary key (PK) for the table. The SalesID is a unique value that is automatically assigned by the database when a new

PK	SalesID	Integer
	Name	Text
	Address	Text
	Phone	Text
	Social Security	Text
	Commission Rate	Integer

Table 13-1.   *The Sales Table*

sales rep is entered. As mentioned earlier, this autonumber field has been given significance by making it the sales representative's identification number.

Now look at the structure of the advertisers in Table 13-2.

The advertisers table also has a primary key assigned. In addition, the SalesID field has been designated as a foreign key (FK). When you enter a new advertiser into the table, the ID of the sales rep who sold the transaction is entered in the SalesID column. By relating the SalesID foreign-key column from the advertisers table to the SalesID primary-key column in the sales table, you gain a couple of distinct advantages. First, information about your sales staff only has to be stored once and then can be referenced by a simple integer from wherever else in your database you need this information. This saves space in the database, as well as data entry time. Second, you can very easily assign multiple accounts in the advertisers table to the same sales rep, creating a one-to-many relationship between the tables. Table relationships are discussed next.

PK	AdID	Integer
	Name	Text
	Address	Text
	Contact	Text
FK	SalesID	Integer

Table 13-2.   *The Advertisers Table*

Table Relationships

There are three types of relationships between database tables:

- One to one
- One to many
- Many to many

One-to-One Relationships

A one-to-one relationship between two tables means that for each record in the first table, there can be one and only one related record in the second table. This type of relationship is rarely used; and when it is, it is usually because of some limitation of the database application that requires a piece of information unique to one record to be stored separately, perhaps because of its size.

One-to-Many Relationships

One-to-many relationships are by far the most common in relational databases. A one-to-many relationship means that one record in the first table may have multiple related records in the second table, usually identified by a foreign key. The golf tournament database is a good example of this. In it, there is one record for each sales representative. The sales representative's ID, however, might show up in multiple records in the advertisers table if one sales rep sold advertisements to many different companies. The one-to-many relationship is the most useful type of relationship and is a core component of the relational database model.

Many-to-Many Relationships

A many-to-many relationship exists when there are many records in one table related to many records in a second table. In reality, this relationship cannot be properly illustrated using the relational database model. To do so would require the use of several overlapping one-to-many relationships. Thus, it is unlikely that this relationship would be used in a well-designed database.

Database Normalization

An in-depth discussion of database normalization could take many chapters, and, indeed, it has in some books. For our purposes, it is important that you understand that normalization is the process of organizing data to reduce duplication. This is most often accomplished by separating data into two or more related tables. When done properly, advantages are more storage space, better performance, ease of use, and easier maintenance.

There are at least five normal forms that can define how data is laid out in a database. The most common form through which databases are normalized is the third normal form.

The third normal form represents a good compromise between performance and design considerations, and the total eradication of data duplication. When you get beyond the third form, the recommendations for how data can be organized get rather absurd and unworkable in the modern environment.

The First Normal Form

The first normal form holds that each field in a database table must contain different data. For instance, in the golf tournament players table, you could only have one field in which the score was entered.

The Second Normal Form

The second normal form says that no field of data may be derived from another field. For example, if in the players table you were storing the date of birth of the players, it would be improper to have a second field that stored the year of birth alone because that data would be redundant.

The Third Normal Form

The third normal form says that duplicate information is not allowed in the database. The third normal form is what was achieved in the golf tournament foreign-key example. Instead of storing information about the sales rep for an account directly in the advertisers table each time the sales rep sold a new account, a sales table was created to hold that information, which was then referenced by a foreign key in the advertisers table.

Summary

When you are getting ready to design a database for use on the Web, there are several aspects to take into account, including performance, security, data layout, and functionality. Fortunately, you can take advantage of years of research and save yourself the trouble of determining an efficient means by which to implement your data needs by applying the principles set forth in the relational database model, such as relationships, keys, and normalization. There are volumes written on database design, and you are encouraged to learn as much as you can; it is an important topic that is often overlooked. If this is the job that you have chosen to do, you are well served to learn as much as you can about the mechanics of constructing a well-designed database.

The Complete Reference

Chapter 14

An Overview of the Structured Query Language

Once you have a database set up for your site, you will need to turn your attention to getting data in and out of it. The kind of site you are planning to build will, in some ways, dictate how familiar you will need to be with the language of data access. If you just need to provide your users with access to existing data and to allow them to search and view what is already there, you may be able to get by with just a small portion of the capabilities of your database system. If, however, you will be collecting and deploying information in a true dynamic environment, you will want to become very familiar with the subject of this chapter.

In this chapter, we will cover the language of the modern database. Structured Query Language (SQL, pronounced "sequel") began life in the IBM labs of the late '70s. As the relational model of database design took hold, a need evolved for a structured way to interact with the individual tables that make them up. Utilizing fewer than 30 keywords, SQL is a simple yet powerful means of performing a variety of operations on your chosen database.

Note *There are at least two SQL standards proffered by ISO and ANSI, plus the variants that are implemented by the manufacturers of the different database programs. This chapter will attempt to adhere to the ANSI standard. When you select the database application you will use for your site, you will do well to obtain a SQL reference that is specific to the brand and version you have chosen.*

The individual commands that you construct using the SQL language are known as *statements*. SQL statements range from very simple, with as few as four words, to very complex, with intricate joins and subqueries. There are entire books written on the topic, and this chapter cannot hope to adequately cover everything you might want to know about it, but an overview will be very helpful as you get started with UltraDev. This chapter will serve as an excellent jumping off point for further study as your needs develop.

Basic SQL

A vault full of money is no good if you don't have the combination. A book full of knowledge is no good if you can't read. And a database full of information is no good if you don't have a way to get it out. SQL provides a means of getting information out of your database through the use of a query. Although they are not written like questions, the purpose of the SQL query is to ask for information from your tables.

Note *The name Structured Query Language can be misleading. SQL can actually do much more than just ask for information from your database. It can create tables and modify their structure. It can insert, update, and delete data. The term "query" is simplistic compared to the actual power of the language.*

The questions you can ask are limited only by the data that you have chosen to store in your tables. For instance, your database may have a table that holds information about architects. You can write a SQL query to ask that table for a listing of all of the left-handed, commercial architects that live in Orlando. As long as you store the city where each architect lives, their specialty, and whether they are right-handed or left-handed, your database will respond with a list of architects that meet the criteria you have specified. If, on the other hand, you have never established dexterity as a field of data to be collected, your database will not know how to handle a query that uses it as criteria.

So, it is very important that you consider the kinds of questions that you will need to ask your tables when you are setting them up. You don't want to collect a bunch of data, only to find out that you missed an important component that makes it useless for your intended purpose. Since the tables in the BetterGig database are a little too big to illustrate easily, let's create a new table to work with that tracks the receipt of payments.

Consider the things that you need to know about a payment that you have received in order to store it in a meaningful way. You need to know what account to credit the payment to, the date it was received, the check number, and the amount. You might also want to set up a field to serve as a unique identifier for a particular transaction. This field would be a numeric field that automatically increments each time a new record is added to the table.

Note *A concept of a unique identifier for each record is an important one to grasp. Most databases offer some means of automatically creating an incremented counter for each record as it is added to the table. In Access, it is called an* autonumber data type; *in SQL Server, it is an* Identity field.

The database structure for the Payments table is shown next.

Field Name	Data Type	Width
Transaction	Autonumber	4
Account	Text	5
CheckNumber	Text	10
Amount	Money	8
DateReceived	Date	8

Next, the table needs some data that you can work with.

Transaction	Account	CheckNumber	Amount	DateReceived
1	12345	301	200.53	10/25/00
2	47638	1245	100.00	10/26/00

Transaction	Account	CheckNumber	Amount	DateReceived
3	75892	746	503.42	10/30/00
4	12345	321	150.04	11/03/00
5	75892	803	400.00	11/05/00
6	12345	340	623.00	11/10/00

The Select Statement

The foundation on which the SQL language is built is the Select statement. Just as its name implies, the Select statement is used to select a row or rows of data from a table or tables that meet the set of criteria that you provide. While a Select statement can be very complex, the simplest form provides two pieces of information for the database to act upon: what you want to see and where it comes from. For instance, the following Select statement retrieves all of the fields from all of the records in the Payments table:

```
Select * From Payments
```

The asterisk is shorthand for "show me all of the fields," so the preceding statement produces identical results to the following statement:

```
Select Transaction, Account, CheckNumber, Amount, DateReceived From Payments
```

This simple query is actually providing a number of pieces of information to the database.

- **Select**   The Select keyword is used to identify the statement that follows as a query to the database for information. Other keywords such as Update, Insert, or Delete might be used in this position to implement other actions that will be covered later.
- *** or Field Names**   The asterisk or list of field names tells the database which fields you want to see and in what order.
- **From**   The From keyword is required for all Select statements and identifies in which table or tables the requested data is found.
- **Table Names**   The listed table or tables are used to fulfill the request.

There is also another piece of information provided because this SQL statement ends where it does. The lack of any additional information beyond the Table Name indicates that you want to see all of the records in the specified table. You can, of course, filter your results by any number of criteria, which will be covered shortly.

Returning to the original query, it becomes clear what data will be returned.

```
Select * From Payments
```

or

```
Select Transaction, Account, CheckNumber, Amount, DateReceived From Payments
```

returns the following resultset:

Transaction	Account	CheckNumber	Amount	DateReceived
1	12345	301	200.53	10/25/00
2	47638	1245	100.00	10/26/00
3	75892	746	503.42	10/30/00
4	12345	321	150.04	11/03/00
5	75892	803	400.00	11/05/00
6	12345	340	623.00	11/10/00

Selecting Specific Fields

You can select only specific fields from the table by identifying them in your query as in the following:

```
Select Account, Amount From Payments
```

which returns the following:

Account	Amount
12345	200.53
47638	100.00
75892	503.42
12345	150.04
75892	400.00
12345	623.00

Changing the Order of the Returned Fields

You can also change the order in which fields are returned by specifying in your statement the order you want:

```
Select Transaction, Account, DateReceived, Amount, CheckNumber From Payments
```

which returns:

Transaction	Account	DateReceived	Amount	CheckNumber
1	12345	10/25/00	200.53	301
2	47638	10/26/00	100.00	1245
3	75892	10/30/00	503.42	746
4	12345	11/03/00	150.04	321
5	75892	11/05/00	400.00	803
6	12345	11/10/00	623.00	340

Selecting Only Unique Records

Suppose that you need to find out which accounts are represented in your Payments table. You might execute a SQL query like this:

```
Select Account From Payments
```

which would, of course, return

Account

12345

47638

75892

12345

75892

12345

This result does show you all of the accounts that are represented on your Payments table, but it gives every instance of each Account number, which can be unwieldy in a larger table. SQL provides a means of identifying and displaying only unique values in your table. You still get a resultset that contains all of the individual Account values that are represented in your database, but you get each value only once. This is accomplished with the Distinct keyword as follows:

```
Select Distinct Account From Payments
```

which returns

Account

12345

47638

75892

Expressions and Conditions

As stated earlier, a SQL statement can do much more than just ask for a listing of all of the records in a database table. This section will cover manipulating data with expressions and filtering data with conditions.

Expressions

You may be familiar with expressions from other programming that you have done. An expression is anything that returns a value, such as $2 + 2$ or variable1 + variable2. Expressions can also be used within SQL statements to perform operations on the values in your tables and return a result in your query. To help illustrate this, add a new Accounts table that will go along with the Payments table from the earlier example. The structure of the table is shown next.

Field Name	Data Type	Width
Account	Text	5
FirstName	Text	20
LastName	Text	20
City	Text	25
State	Text	2
ZipCode	Text	5

This table simply holds information about the accounts that will be sending payments. There is a first name, a last name, a city, a state, and a ZIP code for each account. These tables will help illustrate many of the powerful capabilities of expressions in SQL statements.

 Note *You will likely want to capture much more information about an account holder than just their name, city, state, and zip code, but this amount of information will serve to demonstrate the point without introducing extraneous detail that would only be confusing.*

Since there are three accounts that are making payments (as seen in the previous example), you need to make sure that those three accounts are represented in the Accounts table. Here is some sample data:

Account	FirstName	LastName	City	State	ZipCode
12345	Jim	Randolph	Orlando	FL	32886
47638	Susan	Tudor	New York	NY	10011
75892	Trevor	Patrick	El Paso	TX	79925

You can certainly get information out of this table using the same kinds of queries we used earlier.

```
Select * From Accounts
```

This would return the following:

Account	FirstName	LastName	City	State	ZipCode
12345	Jim	Randolph	Orlando	FL	32886
47638	Susan	Tudor	New York	NY	10011
75892	Trevor	Patrick	El Paso	TX	79925

But what if you needed the account holder's full name to display on a screen or on a letter or a bill? If you have had any experience with databases before, you know that it is impossible to get two separate fields such as FirstName and LastName to line up together for every record. You need a way to put the FirstName and LastName fields together so that they display properly. You can use an expression for that.

The expression that we will use will join two strings (pieces of text) together. This is known as *concatenation*. Depending on what brand of database you are using, this may be done in a slightly different way. Following are the two most common methods of concatenation.

The idea behind concatenating two strings in a SQL query is to combine the field values together, possibly with some literal text that makes it display properly. To combine the field values, you will use either the & operator or the + operator, depending on your database version.

Note *The + operator is often used to concatenate strings, but you can get unpredictable results if you are not sure of your data types. When a + operator is used on two numbers, they will be added together. When it is used on two strings or one string and one number, the two values will be concatenated.*

Consider the following SQL query:

```
Select Account, FirstName, LastName from Accounts
```

This statement returns the following:

Account	FirstName	LastName
12345	Jim	Randolph
47638	Susan	Tudor
75892	Trevor	Patrick

But you need the first name and last name together, so you might try this:

```
Select Account, FirstName & LastName As Name From Accounts
```

Notice that the & operator was used. Your statement may need to read like this:

```
Select Account, FirstName + LastName As Name From Accounts
```

Also notice the As keyword. This keyword is used when an expression is entered to provide a name by which the results will be referenced. It creates a kind of virtual field name that can be referenced just like a real table field once the result set is generated. This query will return a field called Name, which is not really a field at all, just a title that you have given to the results of your expression.

You might think that you are in good shape with this query. Look at the results:

Account	Name
12345	JimRandolph
47638	SusanTudor
75892	TrevorPatrick

The database has taken your instructions quite literally and has concatenated the string values right next to each other. As mentioned earlier, you must often combine field values with some literal string values to get the proper display values from the query. Try this:

```
Select Account, FirstName & ' ' & LastName As Name From Accounts
```

which returns

Account	Name
12345	Jim Randolph
47638	Susan Tudor
75892	Trevor Patrick

The previous statement concatenates not only the two database fields but also a literal space to result in the logical display of the first name and last name. The following query takes this concept one step further:

```
Select Account, FirstName & ' ' & LastName As Name, City & ', ' & State & ' ' & ¬
ZipCode As Address From Accounts
```

which returns this:

Account	Name	Address
12345	Jim Randolph	Orlando, FL 32886
47638	Susan Tudor	New York, NY 10011
75892	Trevor Patrick	El Paso, TX 79925

This statement concatenates the City, State, and ZipCode fields together with a comma and a space between the City and State and a space between the State and ZipCode fields to result in the expected display format for the address of the account holder.

You can use expressions to do any number of additional manipulations on your data. You can multiply a unit price times a number of units to get a subtotal, or you can multiply a subtotal times a sales tax figure to get the sales tax. Expressions are a powerful way to manipulate your data against itself or against external values that you introduce.

Conditions

So far, you have had practice retrieving data from your database in blocks that include everything that is available in the tables. Chances are, however, that you will need to filter the results of your data so that only certain records are retrieved. Data can be filtered by the use of conditional clauses such as the Where clause. The Where clause enables you to specify criteria against which the data in your tables will be compared. Only those records that meet your criteria will be returned in the resultset. Consider the following SQL statement:

```
Select * From Payments Where Account = '12345'
```

Depending on your brand of database, this query may need to read

```
Select * From Payments Where Account Like '12345'
```

| **Note** | *In this example, the account number is enclosed in quotes since the field was defined as a text field. Had this field been identified as a numeric field, the quotes would not be necessary.* |

The previous statement returns these records:

Transaction	Account	DateReceived	Amount	CheckNumber
1	12345	10/25/00	200.53	301
4	12345	11/03/00	150.04	321
6	12345	11/10/00	623.00	340

Notice that only records with the account number 12345 were returned, because that is the criteria you specified in the query. The Where clause can also be used in the Accounts query used earlier.

```
Select Account, FirstName & ' ' & LastName As Name, City & ', ' & State & ' ' & ¬
ZipCode As Address From Accounts Where LastName = 'Randolph'
```

This returns

Account	Name	Address
12345	Jim Randolph	Orlando, FL 32886

Additional Operators

In addition to the equal (=) operator, several other operators are available for you to use as part of expressions and conditions. Table 14-1 lists many of the operators and their intended use.

Operator	Use
*	The multiplication operator; multiplies field values by one another or by literal values that you provide
/	The division operator; divides field values by one another or by literal values that you provide
−	The minus operator; subtracts field values from one another or to perform subtraction with field values and literal values that you provide
>	The greater than operator; used in conditional Where clauses such as: Select * From Payments Where Amount > 300.00
<	The less than operator; used in conditional Where clauses, such as Select * From Payments Where Amount < 300.00
>=	The greater than or equal to operator; used in conditional Where clauses
<=	The less than or equal to operator; used in conditional Where clauses
<>, !=	Not equal to operators; used in conditional Where clauses
AND	The logical And operator; used in conditional Where clauses, such as Select * From Payments Where Account = 100.00 AND Amount > 400.00

Table 14-1.   *Common SQL Operators and Their Uses*

Operator	Use
OR	The logical Or operator; used in conditional Where clauses, such as Select * From Payments Where Amount < 100.00 OR Amount > 400.00
LIKE	The Like operator; used in conditional Where clauses when a wildcard is necessary. For example, Select * From Accounts Where LastName Like 'Ran%' would return any record in which the LastName starts with Ran
NOT	The Not operator; used in conditional Where clauses such as Select * From Accounts Where LastName Not Like 'Ran%'
_	The single character wildcard operator; used when you don't know a single character. For example, Select * From Accounts Where State Like 'C_' would return any record where the State field contained CA, CO, CT, or C plus any other one character
%	The multiple character wildcard operator; used like the _ operator except that it allows for multiple characters

Table 14-1. *Common SQL Operators and Their Uses* (continued)

Functions

While you can choose to implement certain operators within expressions that you construct to manipulate your data, there is also a selection of functions available for you to use. Functions are, in essence, prewritten snippets of code that perform an operation and return a value. The code snippets are available to you by simply calling the function and providing the value or values on which it will operate. This section will cover common SQL functions and their uses.

Note   *Again, you will need to reference the language guide for your brand of database to see the full range of functions that are available to you. Some of the functions discussed here may not be available; others may be specific to your implementation.*

Date and Time Functions

Data and Time functions enable you to perform manipulations on dates and times that you have stored in your database. Much like expressions, these functions are called within the Select statement. You can use the As clause to give the resulting value a unique name with which to refer to the results.

Since there is a Date field in the Payments table, try the following examples using that data.

```
Select * From Payments Where DateReceived Like '10/25/00'
```

This would return

Transaction	Account	DateReceived	Amount	CheckNumber
1	12345	10/25/00	200.53	301

But suppose you want to find all of the accounts for which you have received a payment in the last 30 days. Try this:

```
Select * From Payments Where DateReceived > DateAdd(m,-1,Date())
```

The results that this query return depend on the date that you run it. If the date is 12/1/2000 when the query is run, it will return

Transaction	Account	DateReceived	Amount	CheckNumber
4	12345	11/03/00	150.04	321
5	75892	11/05/00	400.00	803
6	12345	11/10/00	623.00	340

This query makes use of two functions (both of which are Microsoft database functions, but there will be equivalents for the product you are using). The Date() functions get today's date. The DateAdd function adds a variety of date parts to a supplied date to get a result. This query uses DateAdd and passes in three values:

- The unit of time that will be added to the supplied Date (in this case, m for month; it can also be d for day, w for week, or other available values)

- The number of units to add (in this case, –1, so one month will be subtracted)

- The supplied Date (in this case, the result of the Date() function, or 12/01/2000 if that is the current date)

So the result of the DateAdd function (if the date is 12/01/2000) is 11/01/2000. To the database, this query looks like this:

```
Select * from Payments Where DateReceived > '11/01/2000'
```

This returns the records in which the DateReceived field is greater than November 1.

> **Caution**   *The Date() function gets the system date on the machine where the code is being run. If the database resides on your local machine, its system date will be used. If the database is on a Web server or its own database server machine, then that computer's system date and time will be used for these functions. To get the most consistent results, make sure that your remote computers are synchronized with your development machine. This can be difficult if your ISP's server is in a different time zone or a different country. You may have to make systematic adjustments for the time difference between your local site and your ISP's location.*

Other Date and Time functions are available for your use, depending on the database you choose to use. If you can define in prose the end result you need to obtain, there is most likely a function or combination of functions that will allow you to manipulate your dates and times to return the proper set of records.

Aggregate Functions

Aggregate functions allow you to retrieve results that are based on the combined data of records in your table. For instance, you might need to determine the amount of the largest payment you have ever received or the average of the payments made during a particular period of time. Aggregate functions allow you to do this.

The following five Aggregate functions will be covered in this section:

- Count
- Sum
- Avg
- Min
- Max

You may have others available to you.

The Count Function

The Count function is used, obviously, when you need to count something, such as the number of account holders who live in Wyoming or the number of payments received during a specific period of time. Suppose you need to determine the number of payments received during the month of November 2000. There may be a couple of ways to do this, but here is one way using the Count function:

```
Select Count(Transaction) As Payments From Payments Where DateReceived >=
'11/01/00' and DateReceived <= '11/30/00'
```

This query returns

Payments

3

In the query, a unique identifier (the transaction number) was selected as the field value to count. The database then selected all of the records in which the payment was received in November, counted the number of unique transaction numbers, and returned 3. You can use the Count function to count any unique set of values in your tables.

The Sum Function

The Sum function returns a sum of a collection of fields. Suppose, in addition to the number of payments received in November, you also need to know the sum of those payments. The Sum function will select the records what match the criteria in your Where clause, add them up, and return the value to you.

```
Select Sum(Amount) As Total From Payments Where DateReceived >=
'11/01/00' and DateReceived <= '11/30/00'
```

This returns

Total

1033.01

The Avg Function

The Avg function returns the average of the values in the field that you select for the records that meet your criteria. If you need to know the average payment received in the month of November, you can just run the two queries previous and then divide the Sum result by the Count result. Or, you can do this:

```
Select Avg(Amount) As Average From Payments Where DateReceived >=
'11/01/00' and DateReceived <= '11/30/00'
```

which returns

Average

344.34666

The Min and Max functions

Keeping with the November payments theme, you may also need to know the amount of the smallest and largest payments received during November. To get the smallest, use the following:

```
Select Min(Amount) As Minimum From Payments Where DateReceived >=
'11/01/00' and DateReceived <= '11/30/00'
```

This returns

Minimum

150.04

To get the largest payments, use this:

```
Select Max(Amount) As Maximum From Payments Where DateReceived >=
'11/01/00' and DateReceived <= '11/30/00'
```

which returns

Maximum

623.00

Arithmetic Functions

A number of Arithmetic functions are available to you. Their uses are similar to the other functions. Table 14-2 lists some common arithmetic functions and their uses.

Arithmetic Function	Use
ABS	Returns the absolute value of the value operated on
CEIL	Returns the smallest integer greater than or equal to the value operated on
FLOOR	Returns the largest integer less than or equal to the value operated on
COS	Returns the cosine of the value where the value is the radians (not degrees)
COSH	Returns the hyperbolic cosine of the value where the value is the radians
SIN	Returns the sine of the value where the value is the radians (not degrees)
SINH	Returns the hyperbolic sine of the value where the value is the radians
TAN	Returns the tangent of the value where the value is the radians (not degrees)
TANH	Returns the hyperbolic tangent of the value where the value is the radians
EXP	Raises the mathematical constant e by the provided value
MOD	Returns the modulus (remainder) of two provided values
SIGN	Returns a –1 if the value provided is less than 0, a 1 if it is greater than 0, or a 0 if the value is 0

Table 14-2.   *Common SQL Arithmetic Functions and Their Uses*

Arithmetic Function	Use
SQRT	Returns the square root of the value provided
POWER	Raises one value to the power of a second value
LN	Returns the natural logarithm of the value
LOG	Returns the logarithm of one value in the base of a second value

Table 14-2.   *Common SQL Arithmetic Functions and Their Uses* (continued)

String Functions

String functions operate on text values. They work in a similar fashion to other functions, with a value or values (either literals or field references) being provided. Table 14-3 lists common String functions and their uses.

String Function	Use
CHR	Converts an ASCII value to its string equivalent
CONCAT	Concatenates (splices together) two values
INITCAP	Capitalizes the first character of each word and makes all of the remaining characters lowercase
UPPER	Capitalizes all of the characters in the string
LOWER	Makes all of the characters in the string lowercase
LPAD	Pads the left of a provided string with a provided character with as many spaces as you indicate

Table 14-3.   *String Functions and Their Uses*

String Function	Use
RPAD	Pads the right of a provided string with a provided character with as many spaces as you indicate
LTRIM	Trims all spaces from the left of a string value
RTRIM	Trims all spaces from the right of a string value
REPLACE	Takes three values: the string to be searched for, the string within the searched string, and what to replace each occurrence of the string with. If the third value is omitted, the found characters are deleted and replaced with NULL.
SUBSTR	Returns a piece of a string value starting at the character position you provide and continuing for as many characters as you specify
LENGTH	Returns the length of a provided string value

Table 14-3.   *String Functions and Their Uses* (continued)

There will likely be additional string functions available to you in your database application.

Clauses

Clauses are optional parts of a SQL statement that specify additional criteria for the query or additional work that needs to be done before the results are returned. The Where clause was covered earlier in this chapter. There are two other clauses that you need to be aware of:

- The Order By clause
- The Group By clause

The Order By Clause

The Order By clause provides a means by which you can sort your data in either ascending or descending order. Depending on the type of application you are developing and the specific use of the query you are working on, you may want to sort account holders by their last names or payments by the date they were received. The Order By clause lets you specify which field or fields are used to sort your data.

 Note   *One of the premises of the relational database is that physical storage is of little importance. Depending on how data is entered and what indexes operate on it, you may well find that the most recently entered records in a particular table do not appear at or near the end of the table. If it is at all possible that the sorting will matter when the data is used or displayed, it is wise to specify how you want data ordered.*

An unordered query on the Accounts table like this

```
Select * From Accounts
```

returns this:

Account	FirstName	LastName	City	State	ZipCode
12345	Jim	Randolph	Orlando	FL	32886
47638	Susan	Tudor	New York	NY	10011
75892	Trevor	Patrick	El Paso	TX	79925

But it may be important for you to have the data sorted by the account holders' last names. You can add an Order By clause as in the following:

```
Select * From Account Order By LastName
```

which would return

Account	FirstName	LastName	City	State	ZipCode
75892	Trevor	Patrick	El Paso	TX	79925
12345	Jim	Randolph	Orlando	FL	32886
47638	Susan	Tudor	New York	NY	10011

You can also add the ASC designation for ascending, making the records sort from A to Z. This is the default option, though, so it is not necessary. If you want them in Z to A order, however, you need to specify the descending option, as in the following:

```
Select * From Account Order By LastName DESC
```

which would return:

Account	FirstName	LastName	City	State	ZipCode
47638	Susan	Tudor	New York	NY	10011
12345	Jim	Randolph	Orlando	FL	32886
75892	Trevor	Patrick	El Paso	TX	79925

Ordering by More Than One Column

You can also order by more than one column at a time. Say, for instance, that you want to order by the account number in the Payments table and then by the amount, so that you will get a result ordered by the account number in which the payment amounts are ordered from smallest to largest.

```
Select * From Payments Order By Account, Amount
```

This would return

Transaction	Account	DateReceived	Amount	CheckNumber
4	12345	11/03/00	150.04	321
1	12345	10/25/00	200.53	301
6	12345	11/10/00	623.00	340
2	47638	10/26/00	100.00	1245
5	75892	11/05/00	400.00	803
3	75892	10/30/00	503.42	746

The Group By Clause

The Group By clause enables you to perform aggregate functions on groups of records and display them by group rather than operating on the entire table. For instance, if you want to find out how many payments were received into the Payments table, you can run the following query:

```
Select Count(Transaction) As NumberOfPayments From Payments
```

which would return:

NumberOfPayments

6

But you may need to see how many payments each account has made and group the payments by account number, so that you get a list of each account and the number of payments made to that account. The Group By clause lets you do this.

```
Select Account, Count(Transaction) As NumberOfPayments From
Payments Group By Account
```

This returns

Account	NumberOfPayments
12345	3
75892	2
47638	1

The Having Clause

Closely related to the Group By clause and other aggregate functions is the Having clause. If you are using the Group By clause and need to set criteria to be applied to the data, you cannot use a Where clause because of the order in which the various parts of the statement are processed. In this case, you need to use the Having clause, as in the following:

```
Select Account, Count(Transaction) As NumberOfPayments From
Payments Group By Account Having Account Like '12345'
```

which would return

Account	NumberOfPayments
12345	3

You can also apply an aggregate function in the Having clause.

```
Select Account, Avg(Amount) AS AveragePayment From Payments Having
Avg(Amount) > 400.00
```

This would return

Account	AveragePayment
75892	451.71

Joins

So far, all of these examples have pulled data from only one table at a time. It is very likely, however, that you will spend a great deal of your time mixing the data from more than one table into your results. To do so, you will need to use *joins* to identify the ways in which tables relate to one another. There are several kinds of joins; two basic types will be covered.

- Inner joins
- Outer joins (left and right)

There is also a type of outer join known as a full join, *or* Cartesian Product, *in which all records from both tables are returned regardless of whether they relate to records in the other table. While there is some limited use for these, they will not be covered here.*

Inner Joins

Inner joins are the most common type of join. They are used when you want to see all of the records in two tables that have a direct relation to each other. For instance, review the records in the Accounts and Payments tables used in the prior examples. You will notice that each record in the Accounts table (identified by the Account Number) has related records in the Payments table. In other words, every account in the Accounts table has made at least one payment.

Each time a query was run in the previous sections, it was run on only one table. But suppose you want to return information that spans both tables? Maybe you need to see not only the account numbers and payment amounts, but also the names of the account holders that made those payments. When you want to see only the records that are related in the two tables, you can use an inner join, as in the following:

```
Select Acccounts.Account, Accounts.FirstName, Accounts.LastName,
Payments.Amount From Accounts Inner Join Payments on
Accounts.Account = Payments.Account
```

This returns

Account	FirstName	LastName	Amount
12345	Jim	Randolph	150.04
12345	Jim	Randolph	200.53
12345	Jim	Randolph	623.00
47638	Susan	Tudor	100.00
47638	Susan	Tudor	400.00
75892	Trevor	Patrick	503.42

Outer Joins

There will likely be times when you need to query data from tables in which you know or suspect that unrelated records exist. For instance, it is entirely possible that you have an account holder set up in the Accounts table that has not made any payments yet. To help illustrate, add a fourth account holder to the Accounts table.

Account	FirstName	LastName	City	State	ZipCode
12345	Jim	Randolph	Orlando	FL	32886
47638	Susan	Tudor	New York	NY	10011
75892	Trevor	Patrick	El Paso	TX	79925
98734	Victor	Patitucci	Atlanta	GA	30305

If you were to run the inner join query that you just ran on the two tables now, you might be surprised to see the exact same results as you did before you added your new account holder. Since there are no related records in the Payments table, the new account is ignored by an inner join query. To see the new account in the results, you must use an outer join.

There are three types of outer joins: left, right, and full. The types relate to which tables are given the special attention that an outer join provides. If you think about the tables that you join being next to one another on a board or a data environment display, then the first one referenced in the join expression is on the left and the second is on the right. As mentioned earlier, the full outer join (or Cartesian Product) is of dubious use and will not be covered here.

So, using the previous example, say you want to make sure that all of your account holders are listed, whether or not they have made a payment. The Accounts table will be on the left, so you will get a listing of all accounts and their related payments in addition to a listing of the accounts that have no payments.

```
Select Acccounts.Account, Accounts.FirstName, Accounts.LastName,
Payments.Amount From Accounts Left Outer Join Payments on Accounts.Account =
Payments.Account
```

This returns

Account	FirstName	LastName	Amount
12345	Jim	Randolph	150.04
12345	Jim	Randolph	200.53
12345	Jim	Randolph	623.00
47638	Susan	Tudor	100.00
47638	Susan	Tudor	400.00
75892	Trevor	Patrick	503.42
98734	Victor	Patitucci	

The right outer join is used when you suspect that there are records in the right-hand (payments) table that have no account holder. The need for right outer joins can indicate a data integrity problem in your tables. While it is perfectly acceptable to have an account holder who has made no payments (to your database, if not to your accounting department), it is problematic to have payments that have no account holder. Nonetheless, right outer joins can be used to display records in your related table that have no corresponding records in the main table.

Note Notice the dot notation *in the preceding query. When you are using tables that have the same field name in each of them, you must identify from which table you intend the data to come. Use the format* table_name.field_name *to clearly identify your intentions to the database. There is also a method in which each table is given an alias within the query, making it simpler to reference.*

Subqueries

Subqueries are queries within another query. Sometimes it is not possible to construct a resultset directly from the data in your raw tables. It may be necessary to do some "preprocessing" in order to develop a subset of data that you wish to query. If you are familiar with Access queries, then you may have queried a query before and will have a good idea of the concept. In some other languages, such as FoxPro, you can actually select data into a cursor and then query that cursor directly. SQL itself does not have a way to do that, but you can include queries within your queries to simulate the same thing.

Some databases do not support subqueries, but there are often ways to get around using them by using complex Where clauses instead. Subqueries can be handy, however, if you have access to them.

There are two types of subqueries covered in this section:

- The In statement
- The embedded Select statement

The In Statement

The In statement is used with the Where clause of a SQL query to identify a list of values to be used as criteria for the primary query. For a simple example, suppose you want to select all of your account holders who live in New York or Florida. Using the In statement you can create the following query:

```
Select * From Accounts Where state In ("NY", "FL")
```

The In statement allows you to specify a list of criteria against which the primary query will be tested. Any record in which the state is NY or FL will be pulled in the preceding query. You can also use an embedded Select statement within the In statement.

The Embedded Select Statement

An embedded SQL statement is a complete query, including any legal portion of a Select statement that is contained within the Where clause of the primary query used, along with the In statement. Suppose you want to see a list of account holders who have made payments on their accounts. Consider this statement:

```
Select * From Accounts Where Account In (Select Distinct Account From Payments)
```

Notice how the various elements of the SQL statement begin to come together as the queries get more complex. In this statement, a distinct (or unique) list of account numbers that appear in the Payments table is created. Then the primary query pulls the records from the Accounts table that have account numbers that appear in the subquery list.

If you want to see the opposite, those account holders who have not made payments, you can insert the Not operator as follows:

```
Select * From Accounts Where Account Not In (Select Distinct Account From Payments)
```

You may find it interesting to know that an embedded Select statement can also be used within the From clause of the primary query. Queries this complex are beyond the scope of this chapter; but as you become more proficient with the SQL language, you will likely find a use for the capabilities that this structure provides.

Action Queries

In addition to Select queries, there are queries that perform some action on your database. This section will cover three types of Action queries:

- Insert queries
- Update queries
- Delete queries

Insert Queries

If you are planning to collect information from your users, the time will quickly come when you need to insert information into a table. The Insert statement lets you do just that. There are two ways to use the Insert statement.

The first way is the direct insertion of values into the fields of the database. Used this way, the Insert statement enables you to identify the fields that you wish to populate and the values you wish to place in those fields. Suppose that you need to add an account holder to the Accounts table.

```
Insert Into Accounts (Account, FirstName, LastName, City, State, ZipCode)
Values ('73647', 'Theresa', 'Andrews', 'Chicago', 'IL', '60606')
```

Running this statement causes a new record to be added with the specified values.

It is also possible to use a Select statement to provide the insertion values for your Insert statement. Suppose that you have a backup Accounts table with the same structure as the Accounts table, and you want to copy the Accounts table data into it.

```
Insert Into BackupAccounts (Account, FirstName, LastName, City, State, ZipCode)
Select * From Accounts.
```

The Select statement used in place of the Values clause provides the insertion values. This statement can be any legal SQL statement that provides the correct number of fields in the correct order with the correct data types to insert data into the indicated table.

Update Queries

If data never changed, you would not need the Update statement, which enables you to change data in your tables. However, it does change. For instance, suppose that one of your account holders got married and changed her last name.

```
Update Accounts Set LastName = "Thomas" Where Account = '73647'
```

This query locates the record for account number 73547 and changes the LastName field to Thomas.

Delete Queries

Delete queries delete records from your tables when provided criteria are met. If you want to delete all records (much like selecting all records), then no criteria are supplied.

```
Delete From Accounts
```

This statement deletes all records from the Accounts table, ruining your data and, probably, your job. To be selective in what is deleted, provide criteria that uniquely identifies the record or records you want to delete.

```
Delete From Accounts Where Account = '73647'
```

This statement deletes only the record for Theresa Andrews that was created and altered in earlier sections.

You can also delete multiple records at once. Suppose you needed to purge all payments received before a certain date from the Payments table.

```
Delete From Payments Where DateReceived < '01/01/1990'
```

This statement deletes all records that contain payments received before 1990.

Variables

Within your use of UltraDev, you will likely need to use variables in your SQL statements to dynamically filter data. While the specifics of this operation will be covered in a later chapter, it is important that you understand the concept here.

Each of the queries performed in this chapter so far have been based on hard-coded criteria, where you specified a date or series of dates to search for, or specified the last name of the account holder you wanted to find. In most real-life cases, however, you will not know this information until your user begins to interact with your application and tell you the things they need to find. Within your ASP, JSP, or CF code, you will allow for the capture of this data into variables that you can insert into your SQL statements, thus dynamically creating a query that is customized to the visitor's needs.

Remember that a SQL statement is really just a line of text. It does not get parsed out and take on meaning until it arrives at the database as a query. Until the statement is sent to the database, you can perform a number of common programming techniques on it to construct it as you see fit. One of the most common procedures is to use variables in the Where or Having clause.

Suppose that you know that a certain portion of your application will need to pull payments from a particular account number. Maybe account holders can sign in and view the payments posted to their accounts. But you won't know which account holder's information to pull until an account holder logs in and tells you she wants to see her payment history. By capturing account numbers at log in, you can be prepared to show account holders their payments by setting up your SQL statement as follows.

You can begin by writing your SQL statement as if you knew the account number you wanted to view, like the following:

```
Select * From Payments Where Account Like '12345'
```

Then go back and take the hard-coded value out and prepare the statement to accept a variable. In this case, the variable name will be *acct*.

```
Select * From Payments Where Account Like & acct
```

Note   *Depending on your database implementation, you may need to use the + operator instead of the & operator.*

This code will actually be processed by the code in your page, and UltraDev helps you set this up without having to code it by hand. By the time the query gets to the database, it is fully formed and in a format that the database expects to see. If the visitor logged in with a username that indicated an account number of 12345, the SQL statement with the variable in the preceding code would look exactly like the one before it to the database. This method allows you to put off the designation of the account number until run time when it can be determined by the user's information.

Summary

Structured Query Language (SQL) and its various permutations is a powerful programming language. Part of its power lies in its ability to use a relatively simple set of commands and keywords in a variety of combinations that build on one another and provide a means of manipulating data in almost any way you can imagine. Using SQL in a programming environment increases the kinds of manipulations you can perform on your data so that you can query, display, and use it in any way your application might require.

This chapter introduced you to the language, functions, and uses of SQL in a general fashion. It is intended to help you get started with UltraDev's data access capabilities and provide you with an idea of SQL's structure, so that you will be able to determine your needs and know in what direction you are likely to find help for the problems you face. Since UltraDev is so helpful in constructing, implementing, and manipulating your SQL statements, this information should allow you to successfully build a number of different kinds of sites.

However, there is not room enough to cover other significant topics—such as Referential Integrity, Stored Procedures, and Triggers—all of which are very important to a development effort of any size. If this chapter enables you to get started and prepares you to expand into these topics, then it has served its purpose.

INTEGRATING DATABASES
WITH ULTRADEV

The Complete Reference

Part IV

Building Language-Specific Data-Driven Sites

The Complete Reference

Chapter 15

Designing and Planning Your Site

C hances are good that if you've purchased UltraDev, or are planning to purchase it, you need a Web application. Web applications are simply a series of Web pages that are linked together to perform some function defined by the end user, which could be as simple as displaying text, or as complex as a dedicated e-store selling a product or a series of products. Whatever your requirements may be, UltraDev is up to the task. The page-design tools of Dreamweaver are second to none in the arena of Web-design software. UltraDev adds tools to the underlying architecture of Dreamweaver to make the task of adding database features to your site easy as well.

Planning Your Web Application

Building a Web page is easy, but building a Web application with a database back end is no trivial task, and proper planning is a necessity. From the server type to the database type to the language you are going to use—these are all considerations when planning your Web site. You might have a background in Visual Basic but decide that the features of a ColdFusion site make it more cost-effective. Or, maybe you have access to JSP and MySQL but only know ASP. UltraDev makes the transition from one server model to another much easier. This one tool works with three different server models, and makes the transition between them almost invisible. Applying a Server Behavior to a JSP page is identical to applying the same behavior to an ASP page or a ColdFusion page.

After you decide on a course of action, however, you can't change midstream easily. UltraDev doesn't have any built-in functionality for changing or converting from one server model to another or from one language to another while constructing the site. Planning your site in minute detail before actually committing yourself with the pages that you've built is always a good idea. Although the techniques for building the pages are the same, the code that's used in creating the functionality is completely different.

Intranets and Extranets

In addition to UltraDev's application as an Internet development tool, it is also a powerful tool for designing an *intranet* or *extranet*. These are simply Internet-like applications that reside on a local area network (LAN) or wide area network (WAN). These applications are also served from a dedicated Web server, and in the case of extranets, are often linked to the Internet as well. An extranet can be described as an intranet that generally is connected via the Internet to external clients, and can be deployed from various locations.

The benefit of using an intranet over a conventional application is the universal nature of the Web browser. In the old days of sharing software on a network, the interfaces didn't allow for consistent communication, nor were they always compatible with the different types of data to be accessed. Today, anyone with a browser can view an application and interact with it as if it were an application on his or her own machine. Also, any data that is necessary for that application can be contained on a central server, in a central database, so that everyone accessing the intranet is accessing the same data.

These applications require some sort of security, such as a username and password system, or encryption. Things such as employee databases, cost analysis applications, stock inventories, sales applications, company calendars, and other internal company information all are valid candidates for an intranet.

A company intranet could also be deployed as an addition to the company Internet (Web site). The Internet Web application could have a "back door" for employees to gain entry to the Intranet upon supplying their username and password. The site can be deployed from the same server using the same resources as the Web site, but have added security to keep unwanted visitors out of the site.

Access to Legacy Data and Applications

A Web browser is a quick and easy interface for developing applications—especially if the data and the logic already exist. A *legacy* application is simply an application that was created a few years ago or an application that was created by someone who no longer is with your company. Many computer applications were created years ago and have not been updated because of the tremendous cost to build new applications. With the advent of the Internet and intranets, it's much easier to put a new face on an old application. The data can be exported to a modern database, and new Web pages can be designed to display, insert, update, and delete data from that database. A complete application can be created in a fraction of the time, and made to be more versatile because of the universal nature of the browser. An application that used to require dedicated servers and network connections can now be relayed over the Internet to locations all over the world and be viewed by anyone with a Web browser.

In designing a "Web version" of your application, many of the functionality decisions are already in place. You should go through the application as an end user and create an outline of what the application currently accomplishes. Then, figure out how it will translate to the Web. In other words, determine how you can implement the application's functionality within a browser. For example, the entry point to the application might ask for a username and password—this would be one page in your Web application. The screen to which you are directed upon a successful login would be another Web page. This page could be a menu of some sort that enables you to branch off into other areas of the application (the menus options would become *links* in Internet terminology). All of these pages should be plotted out on paper, with details for each individual page—what it does, what its prerequisites are, and what is passed to and from the page.

New Applications

With a Web browser working as the universal interface, it's fairly easy to come up with new and often unique uses of the Web. Do you have family pictures you would like to have online so that family members all over the country can see them? Put them up on the Web. Do you need a company-wide calendar program for corporate dates and events? Put it on the Web. Need a place to buy and sell your antiques? Put them on the Web. Do you own a restaurant and want people to be able to see what's on the menu?

Put it on the Web. There are as many uses for the Web as there are Web sites. Every site is unique in some way, whether it's the product of a professional Web designer or someone doing it for fun. With the advent of the versatile Web-design software that's available today, people with little or no experience are putting attractive, functional sites on the Web.

Outlining Your Site

All the site's pages should be diagrammed or plotted out, as in a flowchart, and the functionality of the pages should be outlined. Questions should be answered for each page, such as:

What does each page do? What is required to be in place when a user is taken to the page?

- A login name/password or user access level?
- Information from a previous page?

What is the outcome when the user clicks OK on that page?

- Is information passed to the next page?
- Is any information from the previous page included?

For example, a page that asks a user to fill in a name and address form might have the following information available to it upon entering the page:

- A cookie that has been set previously with the person's name.
- If coming from a "new customer" page, a flag that is set to perform an insert to the database.
- If coming from a "change user information" page, a flag that is set to perform an update, and all form fields filled in with existing information from the database.

Next, you have to outline the tasks that this particular page will perform:

- If no cookie has yet been set, the user hasn't come to the page from the proper "lead-in" page. Send the user there.
- If the user is a "new user," create a new unique ID for that person, or design the functionality for the database to do it.
- If the user is changing the data, the information has to be pulled from the database using the unique ID of the user and displayed in the form fields on the page.
- When the user clicks Submit, all data needs to be checked for accuracy using client-side JavaScript validation routines.

- Name, Address, City, State, and ZIP are required fields, so they must be checked for a value. The nonrequired fields should be checked for *valid* data, but *no* data also should be allowed.

- If everything passes the validation checks, the data is either updated or inserted, and the user is directed to another page.

- If the data *isn't* valid, a message is displayed and the page is redisplayed to the user.

- The user ID is put into a URL variable.

Now that you know the prerequisites upon entering the page, and you know the duties that the page performs, you also need to know what is passed to the next page, if anything:

- The user ID is passed to the next page as a URL variable, or set as a session variable.

- On an error, an error message is passed to the Error page.

This was only an example, but if you plot your whole site out in this way, all that remains is to decide which Server Behaviors to apply to each page to achieve the functionality. If the functionality can't be achieved with built-in Server Behaviors, you may have to look for one on the Web that may be available, or hand-code the functionality yourself. Additionally, you may decide that the hand-coded functionality would be better served as a custom Server Behavior, either because it needs to be included in several pages or because it may be something that you will use frequently in your sites. Chapters 20 to 23 go through the process of creating your own extensions, including Server Behaviors.

By outlining your functionality in this fashion, collaborative development is easier, because each page has a specific function in the overall scheme of the application. Each individual page has a specific requirement for how it is called, and what is returned upon completion. Each page acts as a *black box*—that is, you know what goes *in* to the page and what comes *out* of the page, but aren't concerned with how it's accomplished. An individual developer can work on one page while another developer works on another page, and the pages will mesh together in the completed application.

Collaboration

In addition to the physical specifications of the Web site, such as server type, database type, and server language, you must make other decisions as well. If more than one person is involved with the site design and implementation, you need to decide on the workflow and who handles the different aspects of the site. If different people are doing the design and server-side programming, UltraDev makes it easy to work side by side and not interfere with each other's workflow.

UltraDev offers the ability to have more than one designer or programmer working on a site by using "check in" and "check out" features, and by including design notes in the site. By selecting the Enable File Check In And Check Out in the Site Definition the check box (see Figure 15-1), you can implement this feature in your site. When a page is "checked out" by a user, it is marked as such in the site tree, and it will be locked from editing by another user.

UltraDev 4 introduced the integration with Microsoft Visual SourceSafe and WebDAV (Web-based Distributed Authoring and Versioning) to further enhance the collaboration features. SourceSafe is Microsoft's version-control program that is fully integrated with Visual Studio. WebDAV is a set of extensions to the HTTP protocol that enables Web developers to collaboratively edit and manage files on remote Web servers.

In addition to the collaboration features, another UltraDev feature that makes it easier for programmers and designers to work together is that they can both work from the same program. This is a feature unique to UltraDev. The server-side code will be unobtrusive to the designer, because most of the code has *translators* that make the design environment easy to work with.

A translator *is a Dreamweaver or UltraDev extension that is able to take a section of code and translate it into something that's meaningful to the developer. For instance, a translator for a recordset column translates the code into a readable* {Recordsetname.columnname} *that shows up in the design environment.*

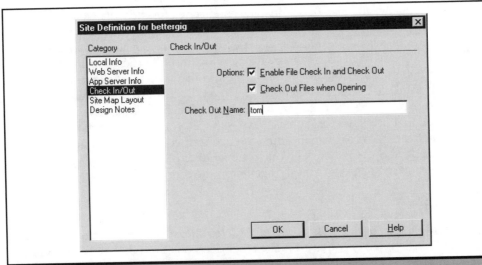

Figure 15-1. The Site Definition dialog box enables you to set up the File Check In/Check Out features of UltraDev

Choosing the Server Model

UltraDev works with three major server models, and in the case of ASP, with two choices of language. This may or may not be a consideration for you, but you shouldn't make the decision without a little background information. There isn't a "better" or "best" server model in the world of Web development. Each server model has strengths and weaknesses, and often the one you may be most familiar with isn't the best choice for the task at hand.

ColdFusion

ColdFusion has a definite advantage with Web developers who already know HTML. It is a tag-based language, and offers a substantial set of tags and functions to handle everything from database interaction to file manipulation. Pop e-mail retrieval and sending e-mail through an SMTP server are also powerful options. Things like Java-based grids for data display and tags for registry manipulation make it an extremely flexible and powerful environment. There's even a built-in scripting language—Cfscript—that's similar to JavaScript.

ColdFusion is available for Red Hat Linux and Sun Solaris servers in addition to Windows servers, so you have a little flexibility in the OSs and databases that ColdFusion will work with. Also, ColdFusion will work with a variety of databases on each of the platforms.

One of the disadvantages of ColdFusion is the relatively high cost of a dedicated server. If you're planning to set your Web site up with a Web host somewhere, this isn't an issue, unless the Web host happens to charge more on a per-month basis for use of the ColdFusion server. Many of them do, but many also offer ColdFusion at the same price as ASP. It's important to find out all the costs of a Web host before deciding which route to take.

ColdFusion Server includes an Administrator interface (shown in Figure 15-2), from which you can set most of the settings that your site needs, such as datasources, variable storage, security, logs, and so forth. The Administrator can also be accessed from any Web browser.

Using the ColdFusion Administrator remotely, you can set up your own system DSNs and datasources right from the Web.

Allaire offers 30-day trials of all of its products, so a test-drive of ColdFusion is within everyone's reach. A complete tutorial on how to use ColdFusion and how to program in the tag-based language is included with the trial, and may be a real eye-opening experience. Many of the most powerful features can be accessed with just a few lines of code. Chapter 10 offers a brief introduction to the ColdFusion language.

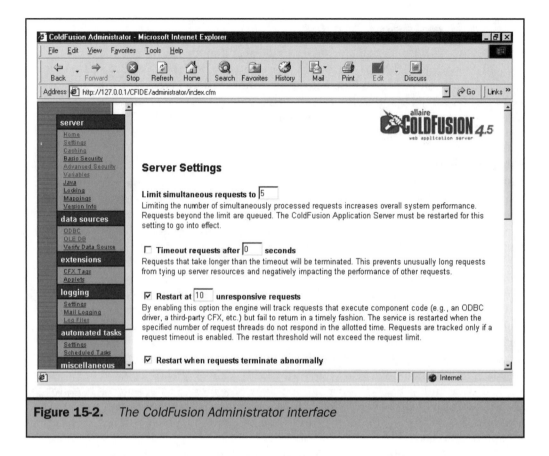

Figure 15-2. *The ColdFusion Administrator interface*

UltraDev makes a lot of the language-specific advantages irrelevant, but learning the underlying language of your Web application should be one of your prime concerns. ColdFusion is certainly the easiest of the three server models to learn.

 ColdFusion, like HTML, is a tag-based language; so many HTML developers feel right at home with its syntax, and make the transition easily.

ASP

The popularity of ASP has a lot to do with the mass popularity of Microsoft Windows, and the fact that anyone with Windows can set up a Web server that runs ASP for free. Even Windows 95 users have access to the Personal Web Server that is capable of deploying ASP pages. If you have a cable-modem or DSL line, you can have a Web site running from your basement in no time.

Also, ASP pages in UltraDev can be written in either JScript or VBScript, so if you have knowledge of either language, learning ASP is a snap. JScript is Microsoft's version of ECMAScript, which is a standardized form of JavaScript that was implemented in 1997. The terms JScript and JavaScript are used interchangeably in the book, but when referring to server-side ASP code, JScript is the language being used. Many Web developers have a basic knowledge of JavaScript, so following the UltraDev-generated code in JavaScript flattens the learning curve. Also, VBScript has a basis in Visual Basic, which many programmers learn in school or use in corporations all over the world. With a little knowledge of either language, ASP might be right up your alley.

Note *The VBScript programmer has a distinct advantage over the JavaScript programmer in ASP. If you look at the various books, magazine articles, and Web sites devoted to ASP, most of them show you the examples in VBScript. Also, VBScript has a lot of built-in language features that make it a good choice for developing your site.*

Of course, if your site isn't on a Windows server, ASP might not even be an option. You can run ASP on UNIX, Solaris, HP, and other servers using a third-party ASP product such as Chili!Soft (see Figure 15-3), but you always risk incompatibilities when you use third-party components. These are things to consider, and a full test of the environment should be performed before committing to it. Chili!Soft offers trial versions of its software for the various configurations of servers that it supports.

One of the disadvantages of using ASP is that it doesn't support some of the advanced features, such as e-mail and file manipulation, without configuring server components or purchasing third-party server components. Most Web-hosting companies have one of the popular server components installed, but you should find out all the details and specifications for what's provided. For instance, to send an e-mail, you could use CDONTS, ASPMail, JMail, or SA-SMTPMail. Whichever component your ISP is using, you will have to learn the syntax for hand-coding the necessary code, or find a Server Behavior that works with the component, if you want to use such a feature.

Caution *Many Web hosts won't set up special third-party components for you, so make sure you find out what the Web host is using before you commit yourself to that particular host. E-mail components and file-upload components are a necessity in today's Web applications.*

JSP

JSP may be the most powerful and versatile of the three server models, but it is also the most difficult to use and program for. The language for JSP is Java, and is much more complex than the tag-based ColdFusion Markup Language or the scripting languages, VBScript and JavaScript. JSP developers have at their disposal the whole of the Java language. With the added complexity of the language comes added power, but not without a cost: JSP pages also need proprietary servers to run them.

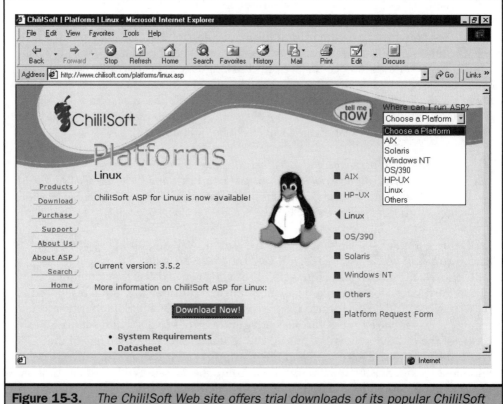

Figure 15-3. The Chili!Soft Web site offers trial downloads of its popular Chili!Soft ASP software

JSP servers come in various shapes and sizes, from Allaire's JRun (see Figure 15-4) to IBM's WebSphere (see Figure 15-5), to Apache Tomcat. Each one has different requirements, so you're going to need to do some research to find out the advantages and disadvantages of each. Most JSP servers are available as trial versions, so a test-drive of the server environment is always an option. Configuring a JSP server can be something of a nightmare, so it's not something that should be taken lightly. Also, JSP-based Web hosts are a little harder to find and generally don't come cheaply.

In addition to the server, most databases need specific drivers in order to be accessible to the JSP server, so you're going to need to find a driver that meets your needs. Many drivers are available, and all are of varying degrees of quality and cost. Again, trial versions of most of these are available as well. UltraDev ships with the Sun JDBC:ODBC Bridge, but it should be used only in a test environment and not on a production server.

The UltraDev implementation of JSP can't really be described as a "full" implementation of the environment. Servlets, Taglibs, and Beans weren't given much support in UltraDev 1. With UltraDev 1, if you were content to program with JSP using

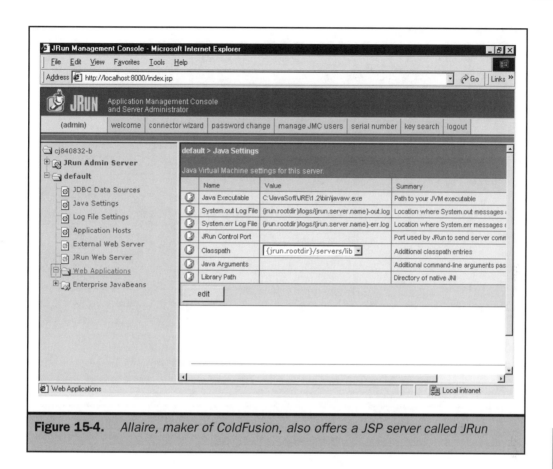

Figure 15-4.   *Allaire, maker of ColdFusion, also offers a JSP server called JRun*

the script-like syntax of the UltraDev code, then UltraDev provided a viable solution for you. UltraDev 4 added support for Beans, making the whole package much more JSP friendly.

Choosing Your Database

Each of the server models that you can work with in UltraDev—ASP, JSP, and ColdFusion—has specific databases that it works well with. Although you may be fully committed to one database or another in your day-to-day workflow, putting that same data up on the Web is another matter entirely. Most databases have an export facility of some sort, so changing databases in many cases may be a viable option. The following sections cover some of the pluses and minuses of the different databases available to you.

Microsoft Access

Access is one of the cornerstones of Web development because of its ease of use and universal appeal. Databases can be designed easily on Access, and can be integrated

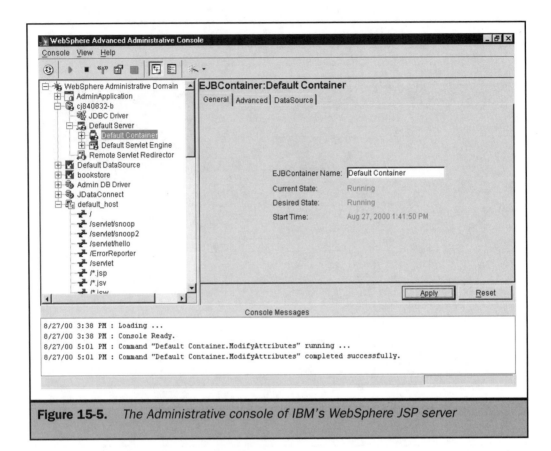

Figure 15-5. *The Administrative console of IBM's WebSphere JSP server*

into your Web site easily as well. It is almost certainly the best database for the job of a design-time connection, because it will run on Windows and exist even without having Access installed on the system. All you need is the MDB file that contains the data, and you will be able to connect to it via ODBC or an ADO Connection String, or even through the Sun ODBC:JDBC driver if you are using JSP.

Access comes as part of Microsoft Office Professional or Premium versions, and is also available as a stand-alone product. You can get a special competitive upgrade price on Access from a variety of different databases. Having Access installed on your system is considered a "must" for the Web developer, because it allows easy manipulation of tables and queries in the design environment, before actually deploying your data to the server. Access can be used on a Macintosh also, if you have FWB SoftWindows or Connectix Virtual PC installed on the system. For a Macintosh user, it's a much more suitable alternative to the various Macintosh-only databases. Keep in mind, however, that you can't use the Access database within UltraDev from the SoftWindows or Virtual PC environment. The database has to reside on an actual Windows server to be able to access it from UltraDev. The advantage to using SoftWindows or Virtual PC is the fact that you can design and configure your database on the Mac before deploying it to a server.

In addition, Access contains a query builder that enables you to test your queries in a controlled environment before deploying from your Web page. An Access query can be copied/pasted into the UltraDev environment with minor changes. Access databases also contain a *Compact* command that decreases the size of the data, and also optimizes the data for quicker access. The Compact command can be accessed right from the ODBC administrator as well.

If Access sounds too good to be true, it is. While we wholeheartedly recommend Access for use in the design environment, we can't recommend its use on a live database, unless you expect that your Web site will never have more than a few simultaneous users. Although the specifications of Access claim more users, many people have found that slow access and data corruption can result when used in a real-world environment. Also, if the machine that hosts your Web site isn't a Windows machine, Access might not even be an option.

Tip　*Microsoft Access 2000 can be used as a front end to a Microsoft SQL Server–like database by using Microsoft Data Engine (MSDE). MSDE is an actual client/server data engine, which makes it much more scalable than the Jet engine of a typical file-based Access database. Access 97 doesn't have this option.*

Microsoft SQL Server

If you plan to deploy your Web site from a Windows-based server, Microsoft SQL Server would have to be the number one choice for the database. Beginning with SQL Server 7, Microsoft began implementing some of the ease-of-use features of Access. Enterprise Manager (see Figure 15-6) allows quick access to tables, views, and stored procedures that make using SQL Server a snap. In addition, upsizing from Microsoft Access is a simple process.

Whereas Microsoft Access is a file-based database, SQL Server is a full-fledged server. Making simultaneous connections in SQL Server is no problem, and SQL Server can maintain hundreds of connections without corruption of data. In addition, SQL Server has more security than the file-based Access.

SQL Server also offers the use of stored procedures, which not only speed up the data transfer, but also allow the use of *transactions*, which enable you to execute several queries at once, thereby making it possible to do batch updates or deletes from your Web site.

Note　*One possible scenario to illustrate stored procedures and transactions is a bank transfer. In that scenario, the first account is debited and the second account credited. When using a transaction, the two actions always occur together. If you were to execute them as separate queries, the possibility would always exist that one would execute and the other one would have some sort of error, which would have serious consequences!*

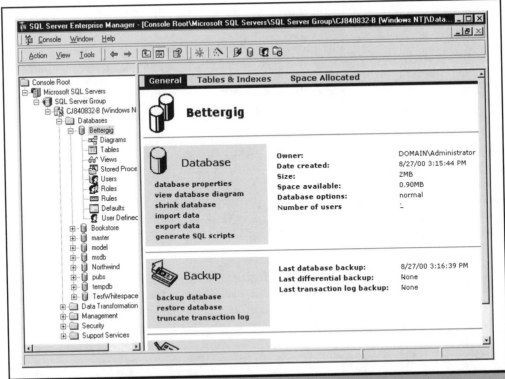

Figure 15-6.   *Microsoft SQL Server Enterprise Manager enables you to easily create tables, views, and stored procedures and administer your databases*

In addition, stored procedures give you the capability to retrieve return values from your database. Suppose you are adding a new customer to an e-store, and the user has entered all of his personal information. Some sort of *primary key* in the database would be necessary to enable you to access that particular user in the future. When the data is being inserted, the primary key could be returned via the stored procedure, to enable you to continue to access the database from within the Web application.

Microsoft SQL Server is an expensive proposition if you are deploying your site from a dedicated server. On the other hand, if you are deploying your Web application from an ISP, it's certainly a viable option. Most ISPs charge a small surcharge of $20 to $40 a month for the use of SQL Server, but it's well worth it if you plan to run a professional Web site.

If you have a Windows server, trial versions of SQL Server are available from Microsoft that will give you an opportunity to try out the advanced features of this database.

Oracle

Oracle is an option for a Windows-based server, and also is available for most other servers, making it the best choice for a Web site deployed from a non-Windows-based server. Many would argue that it is the best choice for a Windows-based server as well. Oracle has all the advanced features of Microsoft SQL Server, and many more, and it also runs on a Linux or Sun Solaris server.

Oracle also has advanced security and encryption features for maintaining secure access to sensitive data. Also, auditing features enable you to track users and the way that the data is accessed, for even greater security.

Oracle has a tight integration with JSP servers, and has native drivers available for OLE DB using ColdFusion or ASP. ColdFusion also allows native connections to the Oracle server, making the connection faster and more reliable than an ODBC connection. Note, however, that native connections to an Oracle database from ColdFusion aren't easily programmed with UltraDev. UltraDev 1 offered no support for native drivers, and UltraDev 4 enables you to use native connections only if they are defined in the ColdFusion administrator.

Trial versions of Oracle databases can be ordered from the Oracle Web site at www.oracle.com, and a Lite version is also available for download.

MySQL

MySQL and mSQL have become immensely popular in this day of open-source software. Despite being lightweight, they are sophisticated, efficient, and powerful database applications. On top of that, the price can't be beat, because they can be downloaded from various sources for free or for a small licensing fee. Of the two, MySQL has built up the most momentum over the last few years, and is now a viable choice for a professional Web application.

MySQL is available in many shapes and sizes, and is available for most configurations of servers. Whether you decide on a JSP, ASP, or ColdFusion site, you can probably find a MySQL implementation to meet your needs. The latest builds can usually be found on the MySQL Web site, at www.mysql.com. In addition, ODBC drivers are generally available for MySQL, to make connections quick and painless in the design-time environment. The MyODBC driver also is available from the MySQL Web site. For JSP, several JDBC drivers are available for MySQL.

One of the disadvantages of the open source databases is that they lack an "administrator" or GUI, thus making the design and implementation of the database a little tricky for beginners. An option here is to design your database in Microsoft Access and then convert your data to MySQL format using one of the utilities that are freely available from the Web. Also, front ends for MySQL are becoming more commonplace. One of the best of the GUIs for MySQL is the urSQL utility, available at www.urbanresearch.com/software/utils/urbsql/.

MySQL is highly optimized for Web applications, and is one of the fastest and most lightweight databases around. Reading from the database is very fast with MySQL, although it's slower with insert, modify, and delete tasks. Also, it doesn't offer some of the advanced features of its rivals, such as stored procedures and nested Select statements.

DB2

DB2 is IBM's answer to Oracle and SQL Server. It is an enterprise-level database, much like Oracle and SQL Server, and is very well integrated with IBM's WebSphere JSP server. If you plan to implement a JSP site on a WebSphere server, DB2 certainly is a good choice for the database. It also has ODBC drivers for simple connections, and even has a native OLE DB driver, if you happen to be using ASP. ColdFusion Enterprise Server contains native database drivers for DB2. DB2 will run on a variety of systems, such as Windows, OS/2, Linux, Sun Solaris, and HP-UX.

The DB2 Control Center, shown in Figure 15-7, is reminiscent of SQL Server Enterprise Manager. Databases can be created here from scratch or from built-in templates. Database creation is a simple process with the Control Center. Views and stored procedures can also be created easily.

In addition, DB2 has a highly optimized in-memory search engine, making text searching one of its strong points. It was designed from the ground up with the Internet in mind, according to in-house blurbs.

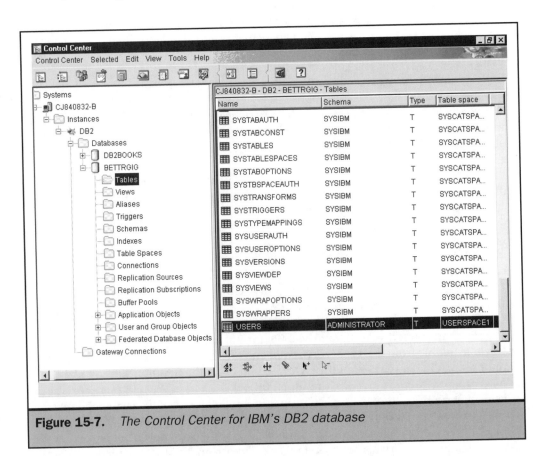

Figure 15-7. *The Control Center for IBM's DB2 database*

IBM usually has free downloads of this enterprise-level database for developers available from its Web site, but the commercial version is pricey. Still, in terms of functionality, it's right up there with Oracle and SQL Server.

Other Databases

Although this chapter has covered the major databases, several others are available that you might be tempted to use. Filemaker Pro, for example, is a popular Macintosh database, but it's not a viable option for an UltraDev Web site. The Macintosh version isn't usable, because no Mac server configuration is supported at this time; furthermore, the Windows version seems to have ODBC driver difficulties. Other possibilities include dBASE, FoxPro, Paradox, PostgreSQL, Sybase, and Informix, but these databases don't offer the robust environment of Microsoft SQL Server, Oracle, or IBM's DB2. Above all, real-world testing will give you the best indication of whether or not one of these other databases will do the job for you and your planned site. You can even use a text or CSV file for a database, using Microsoft's text ODBC driver, as long as you are aware of the limitations.

The next chapter starts the actual database implementation and explores how it relates to the Bettergig.com Web site you are going to develop.

Chapter 16

Setting Up Your Data

Preceding chapters have reviewed some of the preliminaries of database design, database connections, and writing SQL. Now, it's time to put together the actual database that will drive your Bettergig.com Web site. Several sample databases have been included on the CD-ROM. We'll be using a Microsoft Access database for our design-time connection, but you can use whatever database is available to you. The principles are the same. This database will reside on the local Windows machine that we're working on. The run-time connection will be a Microsoft SQL Server database located on the Web server. Connections are covered in Chapter 12, and the differences in the connections between UltraDev 1 and UltraDev 4 should be noted.

Before getting to that, however, you need to design the database.

OLTP and OLAP Databases

The database you'll be designing will be an *online transaction processing (OLTP)* database. Most databases these days are of this variety. OLTP databases are designed with transaction processing in mind. This does not refer to a monetary transaction; rather, by our definition, a *transaction* simply means that the database will be capable of *interaction* with a user through the Web interface you design, and will allow data to be inserted, updated, and deleted. A typical transaction might be a user changing his contact information, such as his or her e-mail address. OLTP databases try to eliminate redundancy for both performance and data integrity.

The other type of database is an *online analytical processing (OLAP)* database. These databases typically are used to report information and rarely have updates to them. In these kinds of databases, redundancy isn't really an issue, and can even help the performance. A typical OLAP database might be a U.S. ZIP code database, in which the data doesn't change very often and needs to be searched quickly.

The Data

The purpose of this database is to hold the data that drives the Bettergig.com Web site. Because the site is a job-search tool, the database has to hold data about available jobs. It also has to hold personal data about the people who are looking for jobs, as well as their resume information. Finally, it must hold data about the employing companies.

Proper planning in advance is key to a successful database design. Start with the data that you need and organize it into logical tables. Each table should hold data that belongs to one unit/object/entity. After the data is organized in a logical fashion, you'll go through the *normalization* procedure to eliminate redundant data and to avoid problems with inserting, updating, and deleting data, which you may run into later. Start with these four tables:

- **Seekers** Holds personal data about the people who are looking for jobs
- **Employers** Holds data about the employing companies that have jobs available
- **Jobs** Holds a list of current jobs available
- **Resumes** Holds current resumes of the job seekers

These tables will simply hold your raw data. The data doesn't have to be in any particular order, and is generally ordered "as entered." When a new row is added, the data typically gets added to the end of the table, but it could also be inserted somewhere else. The tables are simply storage facilities for the data.

> **Caution**   *Avoid the use of terms that might be reserved words for the database. Because all databases have different reserved words, it's beyond the scope of this book to give a complete list. However, words such as date, data, time, name, table, field, or any other generic word that might be used inside of the functionality of the database or SQL should be avoided.*

Each table holds all the data for one *specific* entity. In the case of the Seekers table, that entity is the personal information of the job seekers. One thing you want to avoid is to combine different entities in one table. For instance, at first glance, the Seekers and Resumes could have been contained together in one table. Each job seeker will have a corresponding resume. Upon closer inspection, though, the job seekers and the resumes are two distinct entities, so it's logical to split them into two tables. By clearly separating distinct entities, you are able to keep your logic easy to understand.

Most tables will have a *plural* name, because they are *collections* of individual rows of data. The fields generally have a *singular* name, because a field should hold only one item of data. This section looks at the fields for the four main tables and how the tables relate to each other. Note that you aren't actually working with the database at this point. You'll map out your tables and columns on paper and then figure out the relationships before moving on to the normalization phase.

The preliminary field lists for the database tables are given in Tables 16-1 through 16-4.

> **Caution**   *The data types are listed for Microsoft Access. Look at the Data Type Comparison Chart for different databases (see Table 16-5). The primary key columns are integers, and could be MS Access autonumber types or SQL Server Identity columns.*

Name	Type	Size	Special Characteristics
SeekID	Number (Long)	4	Primary key
SeekFirstName	Text	50	
SeekLastName	Text	50	
SeekAddress	Text	60	
SeekCity	Text	50	
SeekState	Text	2	
SeekZip	Text	10	
SeekPhone	Text	20	
SeekFax	Text	20	
SeekEmail	Text	50	
SeekUsername	Text	12	
SeekPassword	Text	12	
SeekAccessGroup	Text	20	Default value "Seekers"

Table 16-1. *Seekers Table, for Job Seeker Personal Information*

Name	Type	Size	Special Characteristics
EmpID	Number (Long)	4	Primary key
EmpName	Text	50	
EmpAddress	Text	60	
EmpAddress2	Text	60	
EmpCity	Text	50	
EmpState	Text	2	
EmpZip	Text	10	

Table 16-2. *Employers Table, to Hold Company Data*

Name	Type	Size	Special Characteristics
EmpContact	Text	50	
EmpPhone	Text	20	
EmpFax	Text	20	
EmpEmail	Text	50	
EmpUsername	Text	12	
EmpPassword	Text	12	
EmpAccessGroup	Text	20	Default value "Employer"

Table 16-2. *Employers Table, to Hold Company Data* (continued)

Name	Type	Size	Special Characteristics
JobID	Number (Long)	4	Primary key
EmpID	Number (Long)	4	Foreign key to Employers
JobCategory	Text	50	
JobSubCategory	Text	50	
JobLocation	Text	50	
JobStatus	Number (Long)	4	
JobSalary	Text	50	
JobEducation	Text	50	
JobDescription	Text	255	
JobStartDate	Text	50	
JobTerm	Text	50	
JobCitizenship	Text	50	

Table 16-3. *Jobs Table, to Hold Job Information, Including Links to Employers Table*

Name	Type	Size	Special Characteristics
ResID	Number (Long)	4	Primary key
SeekID	Number (Long)	4	Foreign key to Seekers table
ResGoal	Text	255	
ResEducation	Text	255	
ResExperience	Text	255	
ResCitizenship	Text	50	
ResAvailable	Text	50	
ResStatus	Text	50	
ResSalary	Text	50	
ResContact	Text	50	

Table 16-4. *Resumes Table, to Hold Data About Individual Resumes*

Access	SQL Server/MSDE	Oracle	DB2
AutoNumber (Long)	int (w/ IDENTITY property)	Number(38)	Integer
Byte	smallint	Number(38)	smallint
Currency	money	Number(p,s)	
Date/Time	datetime	date	date or time
Hyperlink	ntext (hyperlinks inactive)	-	-
Memo	ntext	clob	clob
Number (Decimal)	decimal	Number(p,s)	Decimal
Number (Double)	float	Float	Double

Table 16-5. *Data Types Comparison Chart for Several Leading Databases*

Access	SQL Server/MSDE	Oracle	DB2
Number (Integer)	smallint	Number(38)	integer
Number (Long)	int	Number(38)	bigint
Number (ReplicationID)	uniqueidentifier	rowid	-
Number (Single)	real	Number(p,s)	real
OLE Object	image	blob	blob
Text	nvarchar	nvarchar	varchar
Yes/No	bit	-	-

Table 16-5. *Data Types Comparison Chart for Several Leading Databases (continued)*

An identifying prefix is prepended on each field in the table so that the field can be identified as a member of that table. For instance, SeekFirstName is used in the Seekers table (refer to Table 16-1) for the first name of a job seeker. This keeps things more organized when you start writing your SQL statements with joins in them, and also helps you keep track of foreign keys in other tables. For instance, the SeekId field is the primary key of the Seekers table, but it can be found as a foreign key in the Resumes table, identifying the individual job seeker by his or her unique identifier.

Tip *Several methods exist for making your field names unique. Spaces are not permissible in naming conventions, nor are special characters. You can use a prefix in small letters, such as seekFirstName, or simply capitalize the first name of every word, as done in this book. Another typical naming convention uses underscores, as in Seek_First_Name.*

Starting with the Seekers table, note that it contains all the personal information about the job seeker, such as name and address, a username and password, and an AccessGroup level. The SeekId field will be the primary key of the table. You can use this field now as a foreign key in another table to reference a particular job hunter. Most of the fields will correspond directly to the form fields that the job seeker will fill out in the Web application.

Note *Primary keys, foreign keys, and other database terms were introduced in Chapter 13.*

The AccessGroup field is a special field that automatically inserts a value of Seeker into the field every time a new row is added to the table. There are other ways of doing this, but this is a quick way to make sure that everyone in this table has an AccessGroup level of Seeker. This way, you don't have to complicate your Web application with any of the details of logic—simply selecting the row with the Seeker information will automatically give you the AccessGroup level.

The Employers table is similar to the Seekers table in design, but it will hold the data about each particular employer who may use the site. The employers will be the group responsible for posting the jobs and the job information. Also, they will be the group that is able to search the resumes for likely candidates for the jobs. The EmpId field is the primary key for the table, and will be used to reference a particular employer in other tables as a foreign key. Like the Seekers table, an AccessGroup field exists for the access level of the employer. This field also has a default value—Employer. Employers will have access only to those areas of the site that have an access level of Employer.

The Jobs table is the job listing provided by the employer. The primary key is the JobID field, which is used as a unique identifier to be able to refer to any particular job. The EmpId field is a foreign key from the Employers table. Each job will be supplied by one particular employer, and this field will reference that employer. This provides a one-to-many relationship from the Employers table to the Jobs table. Although each job has a specific employer that it references, each employer could have many jobs being offered.

The Jobs table also contains fields for job categories, job location, salary, description, and education requirements, among other things. In short—all the data about a particular job will be held in this table. The fields will correspond directly to the form fields that the employer will use to insert the job into the database from the Web application.

The Resumes table will hold individual resumes of the job seekers. We've elected to pull the resume information from form fields entered into a Web form, so the fields in this table will represent the results of those Web forms. The other option was to have the user upload an actual resume to the server, but that presents other problems and complicates the issue at hand. For one thing, you would need an upload component if you were to have an ASP or JSP site. Also, the information wouldn't be readily available to the database for searches. The file would have to be broken down into a text-only file, and the keywords would have to be extracted from it. We'll leave that for the next version.

The fields in the Resumes table contain all the information that a person would generally enter on a resume, such as work experience, education experience, and so forth. The ResId field is the primary key for the table. The SeekId field is a foreign key from the Seekers table, because the resumes will be submitted by the job seekers.

The four tables comprise all the information that you need to complete your application, but there are some scenarios that you need to think about before you commit to this design.

The JobCategory field in the Jobs table, for instance, could come from a predefined list of categories. This prevents redundant information from being entered, and also prevents cases of people entering two similar values, such as S/W Design and Software Design. The JobSubCategories field is also a candidate for a separate data table. The two new tables, Table 16-6 and 16-7, are shown next.

Name	Type	Size
CatID	Number (Long)	4
CatDesc	Text	50

Table 16-6. *The New Categories Table Is a Reference for Categories for the Jobs Table*

Tables such as the Categories and SubCategories tables that simply list some unchanging data are frequently used to feed list menus on Web pages. If the user has to update or insert some information into a table, it's best that the choices also come from the database, rather than being hard-coded in the page.

The process that you're going through is called *normalization,* as discussed in Chapter 13. Now that you've created these data tables, you have to go back to the Jobs table and change the plan for the JobCategory and JobSubCategory fields. Instead of Text, change these to Number (Long) types, and use the field as a foreign key to the primary keys just created in the two new tables.

You also have to consider other information that you might need. People generally think of a database in terms of *information;* but a database, in fact, holds only raw *data.* After that data is processed by an application, it becomes information. All the data that you need is already in the database, but now you must think in terms of the end user, and what sorts of information the user will want from the database.

Typical Bettergig.com Uses

A typical user of the Bettergig.com Web site will be a job seeker who will come to the site, enter personal information, and compose his or her resume. The following are some other things a job seeker might want to do:

- Search the job database
- View a list of employers
- View the job database by category

Name	Type	Size
SubCatID	Number (Long)	4
SubCatDesc	Text	50

Table 16-7. *The New SubCategories Table Is a Reference for Subcategories for the Jobs Table*

- Check the status of his or her resume to see whether anyone has looked at it
- Update personal information
- Update his or her resume
- Delete his or her account
- Apply for jobs

As you go through the functionality, you'll see that several of these functions can already be performed using the data previously entered. Searching the job database or viewing by category will entail setting up a search form and searching the Jobs table. Viewing a list of employers is also easy, by displaying information from the Employers table. What about checking the status of the resume? Right now, no way exists to keep track of this information, although the data is already in place. You need to use the ResId field from the Resume table to keep track of which resume is being looked at, and the EmpId field from the Employers table to see who has viewed it. A new table called ResumesViewed is created to hold these two pieces of data, as shown in Table 16-8; this table contains a new field to hold a unique ID number for the row.

The ResumesViewedId field is the primary key, and is an Access Autonumber field (or an equivalent field in the database of your choice). The ResID field is the primary key of the Resumes table, and it acts as a foreign key here. A one-to-many relationship exists between the Resumes table and the ResumesViewed table, because one resume may be viewed any number of times. The EmpID field is the primary key of the Employers table and acts as a foreign key in this table. A one-to-many relationship exists here as well, since one employer can view many resumes.

In your Web application, you have to add the functionality to achieve these results, but now you have a table to hold the data. With this information, you can offer the job seeker a count of how many times his or her resume has been viewed, or even give information about the various employers that may have viewed the resume. This is probably *too* much information to give the job seeker, but the data is there if you need it. By the same token, this table will give employers information about the number of resumes they've viewed.

Name	Type	Size
ResumesViewedId	Number (Long)	4
ResId	Number (Long)	4
EmpId	Number (Long)	4

Table 16-8.   *The ResumesViewed Table, Containing Two Foreign Keys Referencing the Resumes Table and Employers Table*

Next, you know that you need to include the capability for job seekers to update their personal information and resumes. This is a straightforward process, as well, and doesn't require any additional database functionality. One thing that you could consider is a date field to keep track of updates, for your own use, in case you want to purge the database of older entries—but that will be left for the next version!

Deleting the data is another gray area. When a job seeker deletes his or her resume or personal information, do you purge it from the database or simply mark his or her data as "inactive" with a Boolean value (yes/no or bit data type)? In this case, you should allow a purge of the record. This is always an option when you design your own database. By allowing the user to delete an entry, rather than simply marking the user as "inactive," you eliminate all traces that the user ever existed! That's fine for this demonstration, but in your own real-world database, you might want to keep track of the deleted entries as well.

To ensure referential integrity (described in Chapter 13), you need to make sure that if a job seeker decides to delete his personal data, any entries in the Resumes table will be deleted as well. This can be done at the application level or at the database level. In Access, when you are building your relationships, you can specify to "ensure referential integrity."

The last item on the list for the job seeker is the ability to apply for jobs. Currently, no way exists to keep track of jobs that are applied for in the database. Thus, Table 16-9 is created (called JobsAppliedFor) to hold the SeekId field for the job seeker and the JobId field for the job, as well as a new field to hold a unique identifier for the row.

Again, the table doesn't add any new data to the mix, but provides a new relationship: jobs to seekers. The JobsAppliedForId field is the primary key, and is an Access Autonumber field (or an equivalent field in the database of your choice). The Jobs table has a one-to-many relationship to the JobsAppliedFor table, because one job could have many applicants. The Seekers table also has a one-to-many relationship to the JobsAppiedFor table, because the job seeker could have applied to many jobs.

If you look at a diagram of the relationships, you can see the entire database as it stands now. The database diagram is shown in Figure 16-1. The little "keys" signify the primary key of a certain table, linked to an "infinity" sign, showing the one-to-many relationship. The built-in diagram editor of Microsoft SQL Server 7 was used to generate

Name	Type	Size
JobsAppliedID	Number (Long)	4
SeekId	Number (Long)	4
JobId	Number (Long)	4

Table 16-9. *The JobsAppliedFor Table Tracks Which Jobs Have Been Applied For*

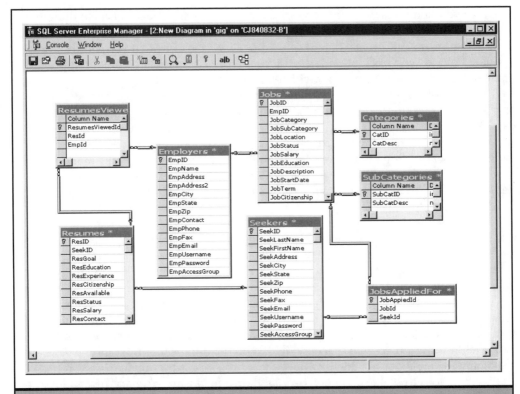

Figure 16-1.   *A diagram of the physical structure of the database*

this diagram. A diagram like this should be drawn by hand before starting on the actual implementation. It's important to spend the time in the design phase of the database before committing it to your server. It's the same principle as building a house. You wouldn't give the carpenters a pile of wood and tell them to start building without first committing the design of the house to a set of blueprints. This database diagram is the blueprint for the database, and exists on paper before the first table is created in your database.

Implementing the Database

Now that the design is complete, you can implement the database. You have the choice of using one database or two for design-time and run-time connections in UltraDev 1. If you are using UltraDev 4, then you have to physically change the connection information in the Connections folder to switch from a design-time database to the actual run-time database. The connection methods were outlined in Chapter 12. The run-time connection is the connection to the database that resides on your Web server. The server could be a computer at your shop or an unknown computer located at a remote location at an Internet service provider (ISP) somewhere.

> **Note**
> *The concept of design-time and run-time connections is confusing to some people, which is why Macromedia omitted the feature in UltraDev 4. When you look at the code on a page that has a connection on it, the actual code shows your run-time connection. UltraDev uses the design-time connection internally, and you'll never see the code on the page for it. UtlraDev keeps track of it for you.*

You may decide to make the design-time and run-time connections to the remote Web server and not even implement a local database. While it's certainly an option, you'll find that having a local copy of the database makes your Web site creation much less painful. A process that is popular is to use a local copy of Microsoft Access and upsize the database to a remote copy of Microsoft SQL Server for your run-time connection. If you are using UltraDev 4, you simply have to redefine the connection in the Connections folder for the remote Web server.

> **Caution**
> *While you may be tempted to use the same database and connection for your design-time and run-time connections, it's not a good idea to work with critical live data while you are in the design phase. At the very least, you should be working from a "copy" of the original database, and not the actual database.*

If you are working on a local copy of Access, SQL Server, or any other database, then creating the database and tables will be easy. In Access, you simply choose New from the File menu and give the database a name. After creating a "new" database, you can create the tables simply by typing the information into the table design interface (see Figure 16-2). Most RDBMS software has a user interface of some kind that makes creating databases and tables easy.

You'll be assigning the field names and data types, as well as the maximum length for the individual fields. This is often a gray area. You don't want to use too much space for your fields, but you also don't want to take the chance that the data won't fit into the field. Use your own discretion when deciding on your field lengths.

Access has a special Autonumber field that typically is used for the primary key. Access will automatically increment the previous number for any new row that is being inserted. Keep in mind, however, that after Access starts to autonumber a field, there's no turning back. You can't turn the numbers back and start at one again. In fact, if you delete all the rows in your table, Access will still start numbering any new rows from where it left off. Microsoft SQL Server has a similar structure when using the int data type—the Identity column. You choose the Identity column by checking "Identity" in the table design interface (see Figure 16-3) and giving a value of 1 to both the Identity Seed and the Identity Increment.

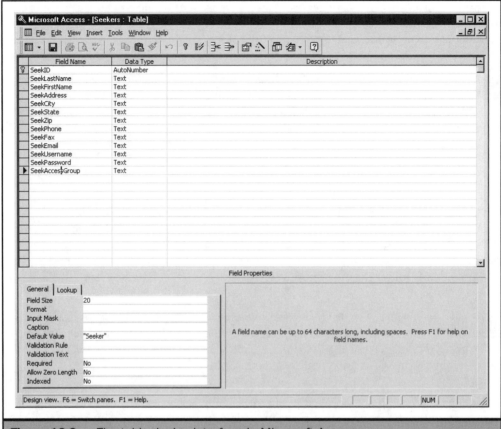

Figure 16-2. The table design interface in Microsoft Access

If you don't have access to the Administrator console or database interface, you'll have to write the SQL code to create the database; create the tables; and then create the views and stored procedures, if any. This procedure varies from manufacturer to manufacturer, so you'll have to consult the documentation from your Web-hosting company to determine the procedure you need to use to create and implement databases on its server. Some Web-hosting companies may create your databases for you, so that all you need to do is create the tables and fill them with data. A typical SQL statement to create a table is shown here:

```
if exists (select * from sysobjects where id =
object_id(N'[dbo].[Seekers]') and
OBJECTPROPERTY(id, N'IsUserTable') = 1)
```

```
drop table [dbo].[Seekers]
CREATE TABLE [dbo].[Seekers] (
     [SeekID] [int] IDENTITY (1, 1) NOT NULL ,
     [SeekFirstName] [nvarchar] (50) NULL ,
     [SeekLastName] [nvarchar] (50) NULL ,
     [SeekAddress] [nvarchar] (60) NULL ,
     [SeekCity] [nvarchar] (50),
     [SeekState] [nvarchar] (2)NULL ,
     [SeekZip] [nvarchar] (10) NULL ,
     [SeekPhone] (20)NULL ,
     [SeekFax] [nvarchar] (20) NULL ,
     [SeekEmail] [nvarchar] (50)NULL ,
     [SeekUsername] [nvarchar] (50) NULL ,
     [SeekPassword] [nvarchar] (50) NULL ,
     [SeekAccessGroup] [nvarchar] (50)NULL
) ON [PRIMARY] TEXTIMAGE_ON [PRIMARY]
```

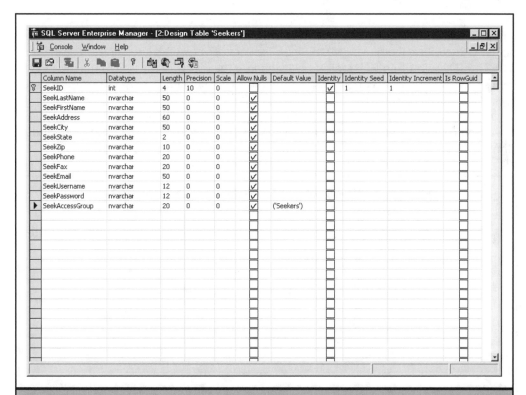

Figure 16-3.   *The table design interface in Microsoft SQL Server 7*

This statement creates the Seekers table in Microsoft SQL Server, after first deleting an existing table of the same name if it already exists. This is where a thorough knowledge of SQL is going to pay off. You'll need to become completely familiar with the implementation of SQL for your particular database if this is the route you intend to take. Databases such as MySQL often aren't implemented with a GUI, and table creation can be something of a nightmare—especially from a remote location.

Figures 16-4 and 16-5 show the design-time and run-time connections for the Bettergig database that you just created, as they appear on our machine in UltraDev 1. We've implemented the database as a local Access database running on Windows 98 on the local machine for the design-time connection. We used an ODBC DSN for the connection. The run-time connection will connect via an OLE DB connection string to a Microsoft SQL Server database running on Windows NT Server. Notice that we've named the connection with a prefix of "conn." This is a typical prefix used to show a connection. You can, of course, use whatever naming convention you're comfortable with. In UltraDev 4, the connection will be stored in the Connections folder at your site root.

Deploying Your Database

Deploying a database on the Web server is going to vary depending on what database you're using. An Access database, for instance, is a file-based database, so it's simply a matter of including the Access MDB file in the root of your Web site and uploading it with UltraDev's built-in FTP tools. Simply choose the file from the Site Manager and then either use the "put" command or drag and drop the database into the appropriate Web folder on the server.

You'll find that as you deploy databases on the server, a Web-hosting company with good customer service is essential. There are permission issues, DSN issues, and a host of possible problems that will need personal attention from a representative

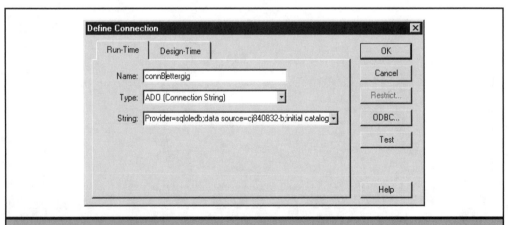

Figure 16-4. *The run-time connection for the Bettergig database, using an OLE DB connection string to a Microsoft SQL Server database*

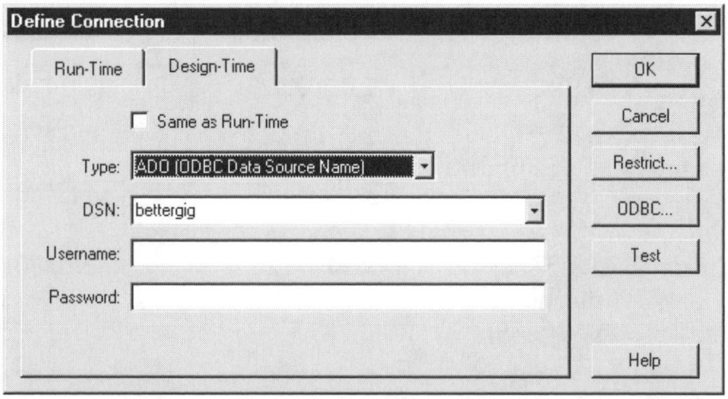

Figure 16-5. *The design-time connection for the Bettergig database is a local copy of Access 97 running on Windows 98. The connection is an ODBC DSN*

from your Web-hosting company. If you find that you can't reach them by phone or e-mail, and can't get your service set up with a database connection, then it's probably time to switch Web-hosting companies.

Remote Access Databases on Windows NT

One of the most popular databases for small- to medium-sized Web sites is Microsoft Access. It is also the database with the most potential problems, if you don't configure it correctly.

The server needs to have the Microsoft Data Access Components (MDAC) version 2.1 or later installed, which includes the Microsoft Jet Database Engine 4. We recommend nothing less than MDAC 2.5, because version 2.1 has been known to become corrupt and cause the database connections to stop working until the MDAC is reinstalled. Table 16-10 shows the different versions of the DLL files that indicate which version of the MDAC you have installed. If you aren't sure of your version number, find either the Msdadc.dll or the Oledb32.dll file (usually in a shared folder under Program Files), and check its version number by right-clicking and viewing its Properties page.

MDAC	Version	Msdadc.dll	Oledb32.dll
MDAC	1.5c	1.50.3506.0	N/A
MDAC	2.0	2.0.3002.4	2.0.1706.0

Table 16-10. *MDAC Version Numbers and Their Respective DLL Version Numbers*

MDAC	Version	Msdadc.dll	Oledb32.dll
MDAC	2.0 SP1	2.0.3002.23	2.0.1706.0
MDAC	2.0 SP2	2.0.3002.23	2.0.1706.0
MDAC	2.1.0.3513.2 (SQL)	2.10.3513.0	2.10.3513.0
MDAC	2.1.1.3711.6 (Internet Explorer 5)	2.10.3711.2	2.10.3711.2
MDAC	2.1.1.3711.11 (GA)	2.10.3711.2	2.10.3711.9
MDAC	2.5	RTM	(2.50.4403.12)

Table 16-10.   *MDAC Version Numbers and Their Respective DLL Version Numbers (continued)*

MDAC 2.5 comes preinstalled with Windows 2000 and doesn't have to be installed separately. Version 2.1 comes with Office 2000 and Microsoft SQL Server 7. Microsoft has also released a version 2.6 of the MDAC, but it should be avoided, because it doesn't contain OLE DB providers for the Jet database engine (MS Access), although these components can be added separately.

Caution   *Some programs will write over the MDAC with an older version. If things stop working for you, this is one of the potential problem areas to check first. You can download the latest MDAC from Microsoft's Web site. Information and downloads are at www.microsoft.com/data.*

In the best possible scenario, the database should reside in a folder that's apart from the root of your site. For instance, if the site is located at e:\inetpub\wwwroot\mysite, your database could be at e:\databases. If you have a Web-hosting company, that might not be an option for you. It is important, however, for your database to reside in a folder that is not available to Internet Information Server (IIS) to read from. Typically, there is a cgi-bin directory on the server located in the root of the site. That folder is protected from within IIS from prying eyes by having its read permission turned off. This is not the Windows NT read permission, but rather the IIS read permission, which is accessible through the IIS Administrator interface, shown in Figure 16-6.

Tip   *You can check whether the read permission is set correctly by trying to browse to the database from your local machine. Simply put the known path in the Web browser, such as www.mysite.com/cgi-bin/mydatabase.mdb, and you should see an error page. If the File Download dialog box pops up, you know the permissions are set incorrectly!*

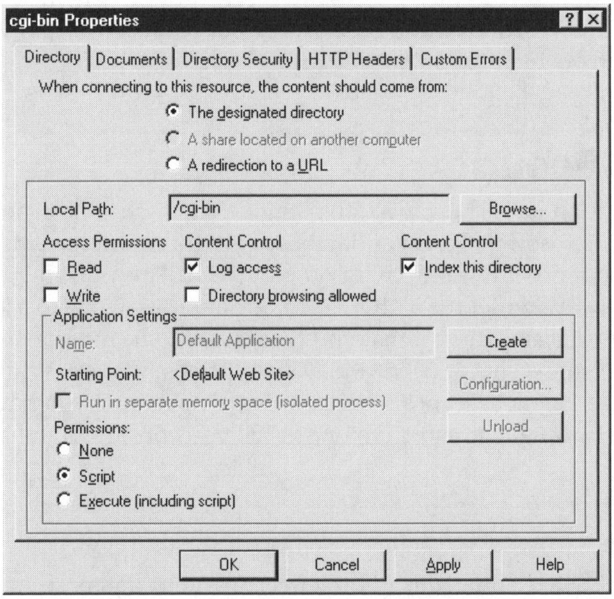

Figure 16-6. *The Properties window of the cgi-bin directory from within IIS 4*

Also, the actual folder needs to have full IUSR_MACHINENAME permissions set up on it under Windows NT. When IIS is installed, a user account is created in Windows NT, which can be viewed by going to Start | Programs | Administrative Tools (common) | User Manager For Domains. Again, if your database is on a remote server owned by the Web-hosting company, they will have to make sure the proper permissions are set.

In addition to the folder having full access to the IUSR account, the database must have it as well. Frequently, the database is uploaded to the folder, or copied from another location, and doesn't inherit the permissions from the folder. You should explicitly check the permissions for the database. One of the most common errors for Access database users in ASP is the following:

```
Microsoft OLE DB Provider for ODBC Drivers error '80004005'
[Microsoft][ODBC Microsoft Access 97 Driver] Operation must use an updateable query.
```

This error message actually usually has nothing to do with the query. The error will occur if the database isn't in a folder with IUSR permissions, or if the database itself doesn't have these permissions. Just another example of a cryptic Microsoft error message. Luckily, Microsoft has a very good Knowledge Base in which errors like this can be tracked down easily. In many cases, if you copy and paste the entire error message into a Microsoft Knowledge Base search query, you will find white papers dealing with the errors in question.

Database Security

Database security is an important, and often neglected, issue. One estimate says that 25 percent of the Microsoft SQL Server databases out there still have the default "sa" system administrator account set up with no password. This is asking for trouble. Your database should always be set up with a username and password to access it. If your database has some critical data on it that you don't want to be made available to hackers, you might consider some sort of encryption/decryption software. While the server-based databases are the most secure, your data is only secure if you have complete trust in your Web-hosting company. No one is 100 percent safe from hackers.

Summary

By now, you should have some idea of how to create your database, and how to deploy one. Whichever database you decide to use, you need to become familiar with the intricacies of that particular database. Creating tables remotely, or even creating the whole database remotely, is sometimes a necessity. Knowing only the basics is going to get you into trouble.

These days, becoming a Web developer means you have to wear many hats. UltraDev makes the hats fit a little better by giving you some powerful tools to ease the whole process, and hide some of the complexities of the underlying code.

Chapter 17

Defining Your Site

The Site window in UltraDev allows you to see the site laid out in a Windows Explorer–like view (see Figure 17-1). By default, your Application Server pages are on the left-hand side and the local pages are on the right-hand side. This can be changed through a Preference menu item. The Site window also acts as if it's a separate application. That is, if you minimize UltraDev, the Site window will stay in place, and vice versa. This can be annoying if you're accustomed to the standard Windows interface that minimizes and maximizes as a unit. What some people do is to give up a portion of the screen to the Site window and keep it open as a small window (see Figure 17-2). The advantage to having it open is that you can drag a page out of the Site window and drop it onto your current document, and it will effectively change the page you are working on.

The Site window is also the FTP interface to the remote server, acting as an effective FTP program that allows you to keep track of all of your sites and keep site notes and even individual page notes. Indeed, you can even "check out" and "check in" pages in a team environment, so that two people aren't working on a page at the same time.

Let's go over the features of the UltraDev site window in more detail.

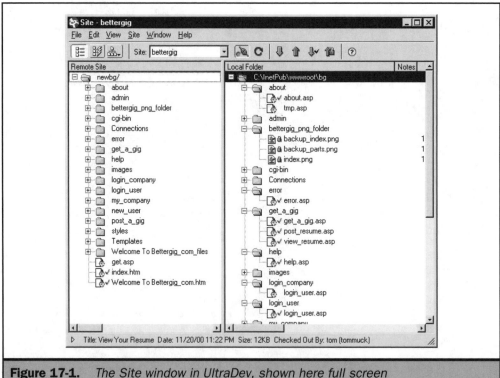

Figure 17-1. *The Site window in UltraDev, shown here full screen*

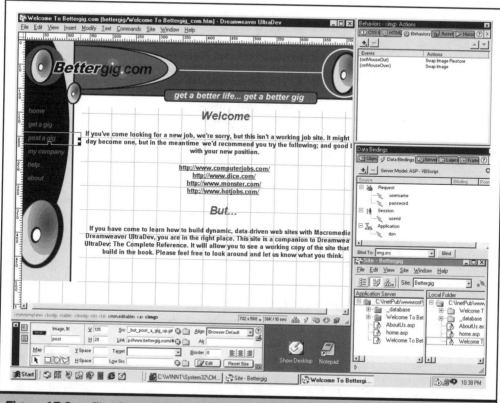

Figure 17-2. *The Site window can be left open and made smaller while you design your pages, and it gives you easy access to the pages in your site*

Defining a New Site

To define your new site, select New Site from the Site menu in either the main UltraDev window or the Site window (see Figure 17-3). In addition, if you choose Define Sites from either of those menus, you will have the option to define a new site from that menu as well. As is true with many of the UltraDev features, there are a number of ways to do this specific thing.

After choosing New Site, you will be presented with the dialog box shown in Figure 17-4. There are six dialog screens that you have to fill out for the site; each one deals with one aspect of the site definition.

Local Info

The first screen that you see (see Figure 17-4) allows you to enter the basic information for your site. The Site Name text box allows you to give the site a name. The name

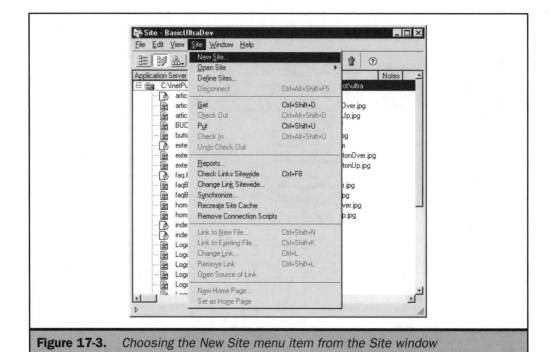

Figure 17-3. *Choosing the New Site menu item from the Site window*

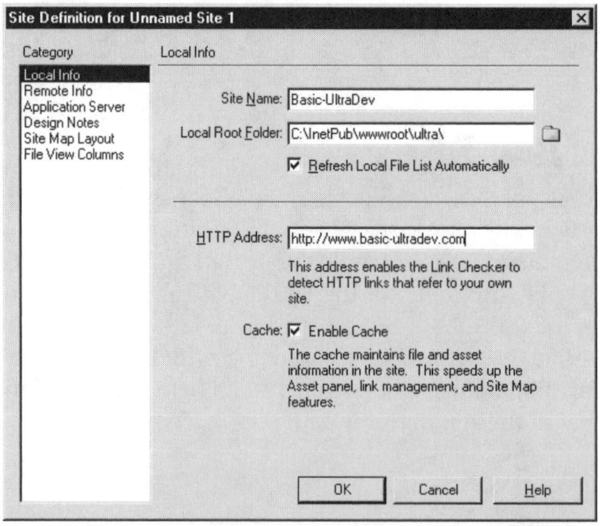

Figure 17-4. *The Site Definition dialog box has six screens; the first one is for Local Info*

should follow general naming conventions (alphanumeric characters) and should be descriptive of the site that you are about to work on.

The Local Root Folder text box allows you to either type in the local path to your site (for example, **c:\inetpub\wwwroot\myrootfolder**) or click the folder icon, which brings up the Choose Local Folder dialog box. The Choose Local Folder dialog box will allow you to browse to a folder on your hard drive or create a new folder, if necessary.

Underneath the Local Root Folder box is the Refresh Local File List Automatically check box. Checking it will cause the site files in the local window to be refreshed if any changes are made to the site. Whether or not you check this box is personal preference, as you may find that it slows down the program if your site tree is refreshed too often. You can refresh files manually by clicking the Refresh icon in the taskbar of the Site window.

The HTTP Address text box should be filled out with the actual Web address of your site. This is optional and is only there to help the Link Checker detect links in your site that might reference pages by the full URL, rather than a relative file path.

Checking the Enable Cache check box causes UltraDev to write a cache file to the hard drive that allows most link management, Asset Panel, and Site Map features. The cache file is stored in the SiteCache folder under Configuration.

Remote Info

The Remote Info dialog screen (see Figure 17-5), formerly known as Web Server Info in UltraDev 1 and Dreamweaver 3, is where you enter information about the remote Web

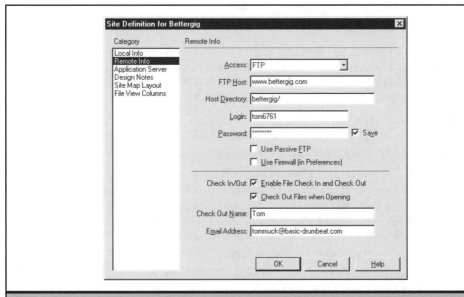

Figure 17-5. *The Remote Info dialog box allows you to set up the method of remote access to the site*

server if it differs from the local environment. The choices for the Access drop-down box are listed in the following sections.

None

No other user input is required for this option. This assumes that the local and remote hosts are the same.

FTP

This option assumes that you will have FTP access to your remote host. With this option you will have to input the following information:

- **FTP Host** This is the actual address of your FTP site, such as ftp.bettergig.com or 24.10.235.158. A common mistake here is to use the protocol name as a prefix—it's not needed and will cause errors.

- **Host Directory** This is the physical directory on the server where your files are located. If, for example, you log in and have to browse to the bettergig directory to get to your site, you would enter **bettergig/** in the box. If you log in directly to your site root, all you need in this box is a forward slash (/).

- **Login** This is your FTP username.

- **Password** This is your FTP password, which is shown as asterisks for security. You can check the Save checkbox next to the password so that you don't have to enter the password each time, or you can leave it unchecked.

In addition to the above information, you will also need to decide whether you want to check the following check boxes:

- **Use Passive FTP** Checking this allows the FTP connection through a passive connection (through your local software rather than the remote server) that is required in certain firewall situations. Check with your Web host if you are unsure whether you need to check this option.

- **Use Firewall** Again, you should check with your Web site administrator or Web host if you are unsure whether you need this option. If checked, the firewall options have to be defined in the Preferences menu.

- **Enable File Check In and Check Out** Check this option if you want to be able to use UltraDev's built-in check-in/check-out features for accessing pages. If you decide to check the box, there are a few other items that have to be filled in: the checkbox for Check Out Files When Opening and Check Out Name and E-mail Address fields. These items are to identify you to your coworkers as the person who has checked out a given page.

- **Refresh Remote File List Automatically** Check this box to allow the automatic refresh of the left side of the site window (the remote files).

When setting the FTP host, it is a common mistake to include the full address of the host, such as ftp://ftp.bettergig.com, http://24.10.235.158, or http://www.bettergig.com. This will cause errors. All you need to put in this box is the address without the prefix, as in ftp.bettergig.com, 24.10.235.158, or www.bettergig.com.

Local/Network

This option can be used if your Web server resides on the same physical network as your local machine. You can type in the path to the folder on the network drive, or you can click the folder icon to browse to the folder. The path will show up as a network path, as in \\machine2\inetpub\wwwroot\bettergig.

As with the FTP option, the Local/Network option allows you to select Refresh Remote File List Automatically to refresh the files, and the file check-in/check-out options also apply.

SourceSafe Database

This feature was introduced in UltraDev 4 and allows you to use Microsoft's Visual SourceSafe 6 on a Windows machine or MetroWerks Visual SourceSafe version 1.1.0 on a Macintosh to allow for version control of your files. The options available when you click the Settings button are as follows:

- **Database Path**   This is the SourceSafe database name that you are using. This can be set up in the Visual SourceSafe Administrator interface.

- **Project**   This is the name of the project as it is set up in the Visual SourceSafe Explorer.

- **Username**   This is the username that is set up for you by the SourceSafe Administrator.

- **Password**   Your SourceSafe password, which is also set up from the SourceSafe Administrator.

- **Check Out Files When Opening**   This option allows you to check out the files so that others can't access them while you work on them.

 To use the SourceSafe Database option, you have to have Microsoft's Visual SourceSafe 6.0 installed on the server and a SourceSafe client such as MetroWerks Visual SourceSafe 1.1.0 (Macintosh) or Microsoft Visual SourceSafe 6.0 (Windows PC).

If you try to check out a page that's been checked out by another user when using SourceSafe, you'll get an error message (see Figure 17-6). You will also be able to use the built-in features of SourceSafe for version control, allowing you to track and view different versions of your pages so that you can see all the changes that were made on each version (see Figure 17-7).

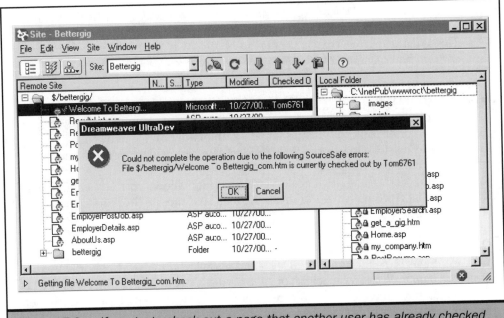

Figure 17-6.   *If you try to check out a page that another user has already checked out, you'll get an error message*

WebDAV

WebDAV is the Web-based Distributed Authoring and Versioning standard and is a set of extensions to the HTTP protocol. It was developed as an easy way for developers to share files. When a Web folder is set up with WebDAV, it acts as a virtual drive that you can access via HTTP. You can check out files and lock them to keep others from making changes while you are working on the file. Information about WebDAV can be found at www.Webdav.org. There are currently several open source WebDAV servers available.

To connect to your remote site through a WebDAV server, choose the WebDAV option, and then click the Settings button that will bring up a dialog box for the following attributes:

- **URL**   This is the URL that you will use to access the remote server.
- **Username**   Your WebDAV username.
- **Password**   Your WebDAV password.
- **E-mail**   Your e-mail address to identify you to other WebDAV users of your site.

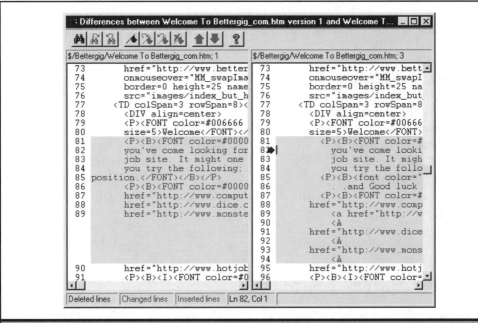

Figure 17-7.   *Microsoft's Visual SourceSafe allows you to view changes made between different versions of a file*

Application Server

The third page of Site Definition options allows you to define the settings for the Application server. This page was labeled App Server Info in UltraDev 1.0, and the settings that are defined are a little different, but the functionality remains the same. In UltraDev 1.0, there was a Live Data Server that could be set to Local Web Server or Remote Web Server. In addition, there was a Live Data Prefix option that confused many people. Macromedia changed these features to avoid potential confusion.

The new settings allow you to define the application server and specify whether it's a local/network drive, FTP site, or no access, which effectively shuts off the Live Data feature. The parameters that you need to enter for the Application Server are listed in the following sections.

Server Model

This can be one of four choices at this point: ASP 2.0, ColdFusion 4.0, JSP 1.0, and None. If you choose none, you will only be able to edit and browse HTML and other nondynamic files. In the future, these choices could be extended to include ASP 3.0, ColdFusion 4.5, PHP 4.0, or other server models.

The First server model developed by a third party was released in December 2000 by Unify Corporation for J2EE 1.2 for UltraDev 1, with a forthcoming UltraDev 4 in the works. The extension is available at www.unifyewave.com/products/vdextensions.htm.

Scripting Language

For ASP 2.0, you are allowed to choose between VBScript and JavaScript in this setting. ColdFusion only allows CFML at this point, and JSP only allows Java. At a future date, these scripting languages could be expanded on, or an extension could be developed to allow for other languages, such as Perl, JavaScript in a JSP site, or PHP.

Page Extension

This is the default file extension given to your pages when you save them. The defaults are as follows:

- **ASP**   .asp, .htm, and .html
- **JSP**   .jsp, .htm, and .html
- **Cold Fusion**   .cfm, .htm, and .html

Access

This is how you set up the access to the Application server (or Live Data server, as it was known in UltraDev 1.0). Your three choices are as follows:

- **None**   This option means no server is required for the pages, which basically means that you are defining a static site. If you choose None for this option, you have to make sure that the option for Preview Using Application Server in the preferences section Preview in Browser is unchecked.

- **FTP**   The FTP option brings up options for FTP Host, Host Directory, Login, Password, and the other options that were also available for the Remote Info page, as described earlier. Use this option if you are using a database and Web pages located on the remote server with no local previewing. You have to also set up a URL prefix, which would be the URL used to access your site, such as www.bettergig.com.

- **Local/Network**   With this option, you have to browse to a local or network folder and then set up the proper URL prefix to be used for the site. A typical prefix would be http://localhost/bettergig/ for a Web site located in the bettergig folder at the root of the local site.

Design Notes

This page (see Figure 17-8) allows you to use Design Notes in the site, which are stored in the _notes folder under your site root. The actual Note file is an XML file with an *.mno extension that UltraDev will read internally. Each page that has a note attached

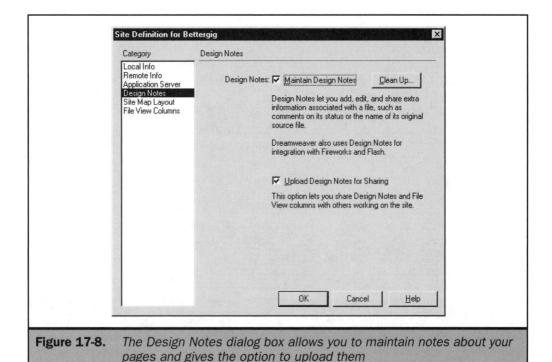

Figure 17-8. *The Design Notes dialog box allows you to maintain notes about your pages and gives the option to upload them*

to it will cause a file to be generated in the _notes folder on the remote site (and the local site). A typical note is shown in Figure 17-9.

There are two checkbox options in the dialog box:

- **Maintain Design Notes**   This option effectively turns the feature on.
- **Upload Design Notes for Sharing**   This feature will cause your notes to be uploaded to the remote server for other people who are working on the site to have access to.

Design Notes are a great way to log changes to a page so that other people working on the site can follow what is going on. If everyone is religious about adding notes every time they make a change, the design process can be a lot smoother.

In addition, there is a Clean Up button that will cause all orphan notes to be deleted (notes not associated with a file).

Site Map Layout

The site map is a visual representation of the linking in your site. For instance, if you have a home page with links to six pages, the site map will show the home page with six arrows pointing to the six files that the home page links to. Each link in those six

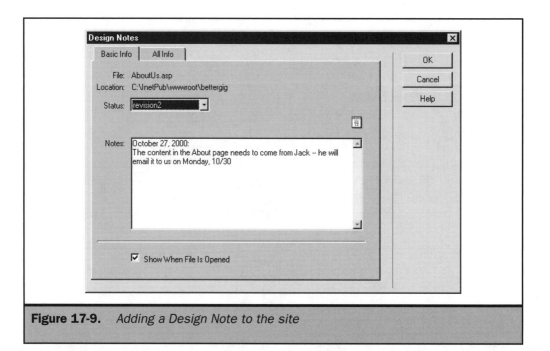

Figure 17-9.   *Adding a Design Note to the site*

pages will have a corresponding arrow pointing to pages that the link points to. The
Site Map Layout dialog box contains the following attributes to help define the site map:

- **Home Page**   This is your site's home page. You can either fill in the complete
  path or browse to it by clicking the folder icon.

- **Number of Columns**   This is the number of columns in the top level of the site
  map. For instance, if you have a home page that links to five pages under it,
  you might set up the number 5 for Number of Columns.

- **Column Width**   This is a number between 70 and 1000 to define the width of
  each column in the site map. If you make your columns wider, you will be able
  to fit more items in each group, but you may have to scroll left and right to see
  the whole map.

- **Icon Labels**   These two radio buttons are labeled File Names and Page Titles.
  You can choose one or the other for the label of the page on the site map.

- **Options**   These two check boxes allow the following:

  - **Display Files Marked as Hidden**   Allows you to display pages such as
    template files, which are generally hidden from view.

■ **Display Dependent Files**   These are files that may not be linked to a page, but they are dependent on the page via a form action or some other means. This box allows these pages to be shown as well.

File View Columns

The last dialog box in the Site Definition window allows you to configure the look of the site window by allowing you to pick, choose, and even define the columns that you are going to show (see Figure 17-10). For instance, you could have a Programmer column to show the name of the person responsible for a given page, or you could have a Date Due column listing specific due dates for pages. An Important Message column could allow you to place a short message that will be seen by everyone on your team when they open up the site. You can use your imagination and create columns that pertain to your own situation and add the appropriate design notes to each page. The way this is done is to define your column with a column name and then associate it

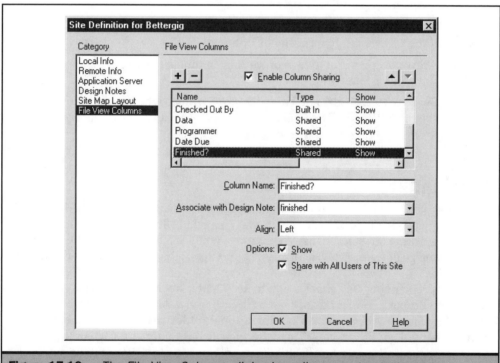

Figure 17-10.   *The File View Columns dialog box allows you to create custom columns that appear in the Site window*

with a design note. When you create a design note, you can give the note a name/value pair that will cause it to show up in the column.

You can add a new column by clicking the plus (+) button above the column list, or you can take one away by clicking the minus (–) button. The up arrow and down arrow buttons allow you to arrange the columns in a particular order. The attributes associated with the File View Columns window are as follows:

- **Enable Column Sharing**   This check box enables the columns to be shared between users. In other words, the columns that you see are the same columns that the rest of your design team will see.

- **Column Name**   A unique name that will be the column heading in the Site window.

- **Associate with Design Note**   The name of the design note that the column will get its information from. For instance, if you have a design note named Important Message, every page that has an Important Message note attached to it will show the actual contents of the message in the column whenever someone opens up the Site window.

- **Align**   The alignment of the data in the column (left, right, or center).

- **Options**   There are two check box options:

  - **Show**   Allows you to turn off certain columns if you don't want them to show in the Site window.

  - **Share with All Users of This Site**   Determines whether the column is something that will be stored on the server for all users to see, or if it's only to be seen on your particular computer.

Preplanning

Preplanning your site is the most important aspect of the creation of your site. This holds true for any site, but is especially true with sites created in UltraDev and Dreamweaver. By planning the site out beforehand, you can save yourself a lot of work in the long run by taking advantage of features like templates, library items, the Asset center, and site-wide link checking.

Proper preplanning also enables you to keep better track of your files. A typical Web site could have thousands of files in it—from graphics to hit counters, to the actual Web pages themselves. An organizational folder structure is something to decide on early on in the process. The Bettergig site has folders for each of the main navigation links the home page. Each folder contains the files that are required for the specific page that the link points to. For example, the Get a Gig link has a corresponding get_a_gig folder name containing the get_a_gig.asp file and other files that are required by that page.

Images typically will have their own folder as well—depending on the size of your site, you may decide you need subfolders for different categories of images. Perhaps you have a graphical menu that has a set of images that go with it—this could have its own folder. However you decide to organize your site, it's important that the organization is easy for you and your fellow developers to follow. In addition, the folder structure should be identical on your local site and the remote site.

Site Reporting

The site reporting functionality is accessed by using the Site menu in the Site window and clicking Reports. You'll see the dialog box shown in Figure 17-11. The options are as follows:

- Current Document
- Entire Local Site
- Selected Files in Site
- Folder

The report will tell you the current state of the site—who has the files checked out and all the design notes of the site. In addition, it will allow you to check for certain HTML aspects, such as font tag nesting, untitled documents, and removable empty tags. The report can be viewed or saved to an XML file. In addition, there is an Open

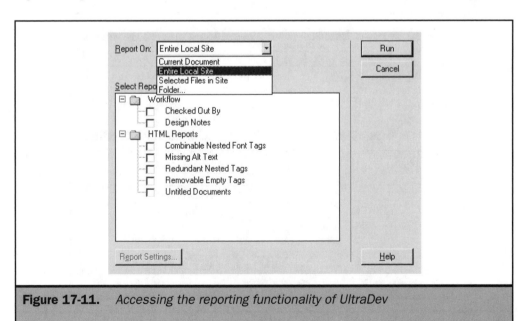

Figure 17-11.   *Accessing the reporting functionality of UltraDev*

File button (see Figure 17-12) that allows you to open the file in question and edit the line in question. For example, if your file has a default title (Untitled Document), clicking the Open Document button will open up the document in question, and the title tag of the file will be selected in HTML source view

Synchronizing the Site

When more than one person works on a site, there is often a need to make sure you have the most recent files on your own machine. That's where the Synchronize feature comes into play. Clicking Synchronize in the Site menu of the Site window updates the site with the most recent files. This feature works with selected files or an entire site. There are three options to choose from when you are ready to synchronize:

- Put Newer Files to Remote
- Get Newer Files from Remote
- Get and Put Newer Files

After clicking the Preview button, the synchronization begins, and a list of files is built. You can then choose which files you want updated, or choose to update all of them.

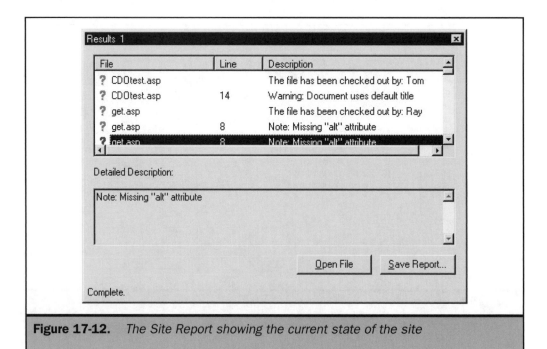

Figure 17-12.   *The Site Report showing the current state of the site*

Adding a Database to the Site

Obviously, if you are using a server-based database such as IBM's DB2 or Microsoft SQL Server, the choice of database location won't be necessary. However, if you're using a file-based database, such as Microsoft Access, you'll have to decide where to put it.

The database should always be stored in a location that is inaccessible to the Web browser. A location outside of the site root is preferable, but you can store it in a protected folder within the site, also. The best possible location would be in a folder that is not even accessible to the Web server.

In many cases, such as a situation in which a hosting company hosts your site, you may only have access to the site root. If this is the case, you might be able to put your database in a protected folder on the root and place your site in another folder within the root, as well. For instance, if your site root were located at the location e:\inetpub\wwwroot\yoursite, you could place the database in the folder e:\inetpub\wwwroot\yoursite\cgi-bin, and put your actual Web site into the folder e:\inetpub\wwwroot\yoursite\sitefiles. Then you can point your domain name to the sitefiles folder.

Obviously, if the file-based database is stored somewhere other than your site root folder, you will need to set up a way to get the database uploaded to the server. You could use a third-party FTP program, or you could use UltraDev's FTP capabilities and simply set up a new "site" that would contain only the database. The purpose of this dummy site is only to get your database to and from the server. Obviously, if you are testing your site, you should be working with a duplicate of the live database. Never use the actual live data for testing purposes.

Database Permissions

If you've stored your database on the server, the folder that it is in must have certain permissions set up for it, or you may not be able to write to the database. On a Windows server, simply setting the permissions to Everyone within Windows NT is not good enough. The folder needs to have the *IUSR_machinename* permissions set for full control (or read/write) so that the Web server can access the database. Then, within IIS or the Web server of your choice, you can set up the permissions so that the Read permission is turned off for the folder (see Figure 17-13). Browsing the folder won't be permitted, but the Web pages will be able to access the database through scripting.

You should also check to make sure that the database itself has IUSR permissions set up for it. If you happen to be copying the database from another location, the database might not automatically pick up the permissions from the folder that you are putting it in. Many times you'll have to explicitly set up the permissions for the database itself within Windows NT. Again, this applies only to the file-based databases such as Microsoft Access.

Setting Up Data Sources for the Site

We know that the database is the key data source for the site, and Chapter 12 went into the various connection methods for the database. Once a connection is made to the database by defining the connection within UltraDev, it is available to all pages in

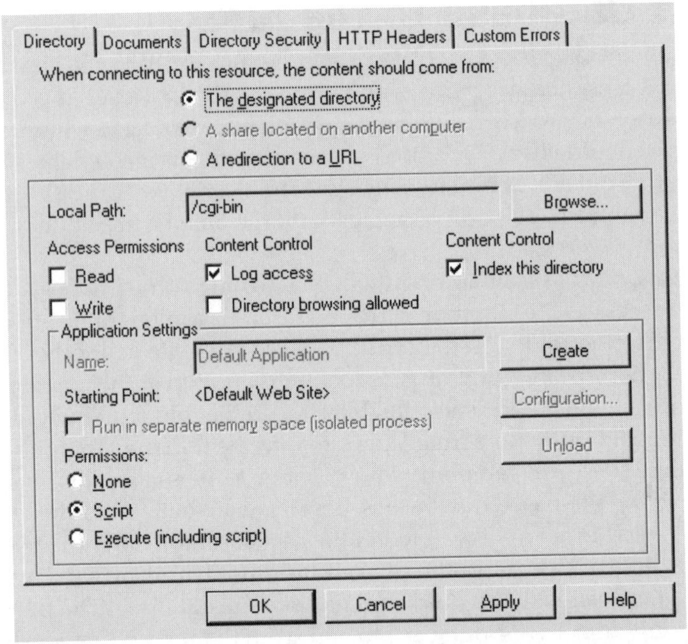

Figure 17-13. *The Microsoft Internet Information Server properties dialog box allows you to set permissions for folders*

the site. Beginning with UltraDev 4, the connection information is stored in a central Connections folder within your site. All pages have access to and can include this one file to get the connection information. Also, by changing this one connection file, the connection is effectively changed on all pages.

The database connection information is stored in a file that is named after your connection. For example, if you named your connection "connBettergig" in a ColdFusion site, your connection file would be connBettergig.cfm. The file is kept in the Connections folder in your site root. Every connection that you define for your site will be stored in this folder. Also, when you first install UltraDev, you might find that all of your connections from UltraDev 1 (which were machine-wide connections) are migrated to the Connections folders for each site.

You can safely delete any connection file in your Connections folder in your site that doesn't pertain to the current site. UltraDev 4 migrates all connections from UltraDev 1 to this folder. To keep UltraDev from adding these connections to future sites, you can edit the connections.xml file in the Dreamweaver UltraDev>Configuration>Connections folder and remove the connections that you don't want copied into every new site.

The pages that you use the connection on will use an include file that will dynamically include the connection file when a user browses the page. Having the connection stored in an external file like this allows you to make site-wide connection changes and have the changes reflected on every page.

Another possible application of this is to define a connection that resides on your remote machine and then redefine the connection to store it on your local machine for a local database. To do this, you have to follow these steps:

1. Define your connection using the remote database information.

2. "Put" the site (upload all files to the remote site).

3. Redefine your connection using a local database.

Caution   *If you use this method, make sure you don't write over your remote connection file when uploading your site. This is easy to do if you Put your entire site. Always choose to Put only selected files.*

With this method, it is possible to view your remote files using your remote database; it is also possible to view the local files using a local database. This is handy for people with laptops who don't always have a connection available to the remote machine. Note that this only works if you can define a local connection on your particular machine. If you have a Macintosh, you will be strictly limited to connections available to your particular Mac, such as a JDBC connection if you're running a JSP server from the Mac.

Other Data Sources

One thing that you may not realize is that other data sources, such as Session or Application variables, can be set up and accessed by all pages in the site. By defining a Session variable on one page, it will appear in the Data Bindings palette in other pages in your site. By planning out your session variable usage at the beginning, you can save yourself some time by having the variable available when you need it. There is also less margin for error when you drag and drop a data source on the page rather than typing it in by hand each time you need it. This is especially true of JSP pages, in which upper- and lowercase letters are treated as different entities. To define a site-wide Session or Application variable, follow these steps:

1. Open up the Data Bindings palette.

2. Click the plus (+) sign to create a new data source.

3. Click Session Variable (or Application Variable).

4. Give the variable a name and click OK.

5. The variable is now available as a data source on all pages in the site.

Defining data sources in this way allows you to easily display variables, but there is no built-in method to assign values to variables. This can be done by hand or with a Server Behavior.

Site-wide Find/Replace

One feature that you may find very handy is the site-wide Find and Replace dialog box. Find/Replace has become a standard feature in most computer programs—and it's one of the most often used features, as well. One thing that you might not be aware of, however, is that in UltraDev you can do the searches on a site-wide basis. This makes it especially handy for changing something that is on every page in the site, such as a color.

The Find and Replace dialog box (see Figure 17-14) has several unique features that are worth mentioning.

Find In

This drop-down list gives you several options for finding text and code within your site.

- **Current Document** This is a standard search in the currently opened document.
- **Entire Local Site** This allows you to do a site-wide search and replace.

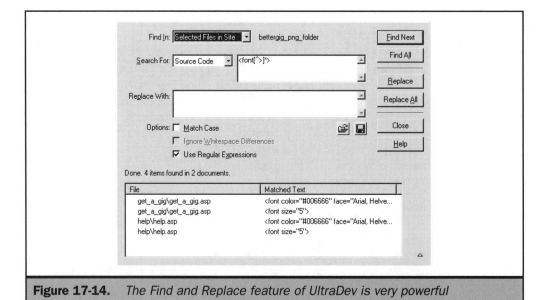

Figure 17-14. *The Find and Replace feature of UltraDev is very powerful*

- **Selected Files in Site**   This allows you to multi-select files in the Site window and restrict your search to certain files.

- **Folder**   This allows you to do searches on any folder on your hard drive. In effect, it turns UltraDev into a powerful search-and-replace tool that you can use outside of UltraDev (see Figure 17-15).

Search For

This is a drop-down list that gives you four search options:

- **Source Code**   Allows you to search through the source code of your page—scripting, server-side code, tags, and actual text all fall under this category. In short, if it's in the document in any form, you can find it with this option.

- **Text**   Narrows the search to the actual text that is viewable on the page. For instance, if you want to search for the word *color*, but you don't want to match the instances of the word in the HTML, then you could use the Text option.

- **Text (Advanced)**   Allows you to refine your search to text that is contained within or outside of certain tags. There are further refinements and several other options that can be accessed by clicking the plus (+) button.

- **Specific Tag**   Allows you to not only search for specific tags, but also to search for attributes within those tags and even set the attributes for a tag site-wide. For example, if you wanted all <td> tags to have a mouseover attribute set to a certain function, you could do it here. Or, if you wanted all <font> tags with a size of 2 to have their size attribute changed to 3 (see Figure 17-16), you could do it with this feature.

Options

The Options for the Find/Replace dialog box are shown as check boxes, and are as follows:

- **Match Case**   This allows you to match only those words that match the case exactly so, for example, *font* wouldn't match *Font*.

Figure 17-15.   *Setting the Find/Replace feature loose on your computer allows you to do complex searches on entire directories or even entire drives on your computer*

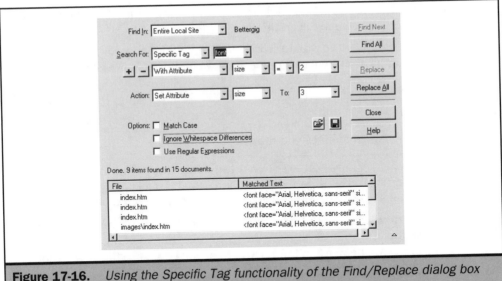

Figure 17-16. *Using the Specific Tag functionality of the Find/Replace dialog box allows you to do site-wide attribute changes*

- **Ignore Whitespace Differences** This allows you to do searches in which spaces, line feeds, and tabs have no effect on the outcome of the search.
- **Use Regular Expressions** If you know how to use Regular Expressions, you can take advantage of the powerful RegExp features of the Find/Replacedialog. For example, to search for all instances of things contained within quotes, you could use the following RegExp:

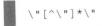

This RegExp searches for a quote, and then gets all characters up to and including the next quote character that it finds. The next RegExp will search for all opening and closing layer tags (see Chapters 20–23 for discussions of Regular Expressions and their uses in UltraDev).

Open and Save Buttons

The Open and Save buttons are the folder and disk icons in the dialog box. If you can't figure out what these buttons have to do with searching and replacing, consider this: a search that consists of complex search criteria may be useful in other sites and can be saved and reopened for reuse. After you have gone through the trouble of defining a search criteria, such as removing all Netscape <layer> tags from the site, you may decide that the search was worth saving so you don't have to type it in again. You can also save a complex RegExp that requires testing and retesting until you get the exact expression that you need.

The search criterion is saved in the Queries folder under the Configuration folder in UltraDev. The file is saved with a .dwr extension and is an XML file that Dreamweaver and UltraDev can translate the next time you want to use the same search criteria.

When you save a query (a find/replace expression with a .dwr extension), you can move these queries from machine to machine and even share them with other people. The files are located in the Queries folder.

Summary

The Site features of UltraDev will make your life easier if you know how to take advantage of them. Whether you are a single developer or a member of a team, proper planning and utilization of the time-saving features of UltraDev will help you deliver a well-organized site in a fraction of the time that it once took.

Chapter 18

Adding Database
Features to Your Site

The primary reason to use an application server such as ASP, JSP, or ColdFusion is to be able to serve live content from a database. While there are other reasons, databases are the key to a successful dynamic site. In this chapter, we're going to add many of the standard types of database functionality that you might use with your own site. We'll build upon the basic structure that was set up for the Bettergig.com Web site, and use the database that was built in Chapter 16.

Defining the Database Connection

Database connections were covered in Chapter 12. If you haven't read that chapter and don't know how to create a connection, now would be a good time to go back and read it. Each server model has its own specific way to connect to a database, so it's important to have a live connection working before proceeding to add live content to the pages.

Make sure the database is created and in the proper location. On the CD–ROM, you will find SQL scripts for creating an IBM DB2 or Microsoft SQL Server database. Instructions for running the scripts are included in the ReadMe files that accompany the databases on the CD. Also included is an Access 97 version of the database. If you are using the Access version, you'll have to place the file in a secure folder on the server. If you are on a Windows NT or 2000 Server and using IIS, the folder has to have IUSR permissions for the local machine. To secure the folder, you have to do one of two things:

- Place the folder the database resides in outside of the site root. For example, if your site is in the folder e:\inetpub\wwwroot\bettergig, then you can put the database in a folder such as e:\databases.

- If the folder has to reside in the site root (such as in a shared environment with a Web host), make sure that the Web server Read permissions are turned off for that folder. Typically a Web host will provide a secure folder (such as a cgi-bin folder) for your databases or scripts.

Create a new connection for the site (if you haven't done so already) by choosing Connections from the Modify menu. If there are already other connections in the Connections folder for the site, you can delete them. You should name the connection connBettergig and test it to make sure that it works before proceeding. Once you have a working connection to the Bettergig database, you can proceed with the tutorials.

 UltraDev 1 users have machine-wide database connections that are usable for all sites. UltraDev 4 allows the migration of all of these connections upon installation to each site that is defined.

The Application.cfm File

ColdFusion users will need to have an Application.cfm page in place before any work can be done with this site. In general, the Application.cfm page will allow you to "turn on" session variables in the site. A typical Application.cfm page will look like this:

```
<cfapplication name="Bettergig"
clientstorage="Registry"
clientmanagement="yes"
sessionmanagement="yes"
applicationtimeout="#CreateTimeSpan(0,1,0,0)#"
sessiontimeout="#CreateTimeSpan(0,0,10,0)#">
```

The <cfapplication> tag is the only requirement for the file. The session-management attribute is the requirement for the Bettergig site: it needs to be set to Yes for session variables to be used. Also, any pages using ColdFusion and UltraDev's user authentication Server Behaviors will need the Application.cfm file defined in this manner. Consult the ColdFusion documentation that came with the ColdFusion server or at the Allaire Website for more information about the Application.cfm page.

The New User Pages

In a Web application, there is typically a page where users can register a username and a password that they will use each time they log in to the site. There is also typically an access level set for the user. This allows the user to see only those pages that have the same access level attached to them. We'll go through a few examples using some of the standard UltraDev Server Behaviors for data access, as well as some of the new Server Behaviors and Live Objects available with UltraDev 4.

There are a couple of standard techniques that you will always see on a page like this, and we'll implement them here:

- Three input fields for Username, Password, and Confirm Password. The Password and Confirm Password fields have to match in order to proceed.

- A search of the database for the Username so that you don't have two identical usernames in the database.

We'll begin by creating a New User page based on the GigTemp template. After creating the new page called new_user.asp (or new_user.jsp or new_user.cfm) in the new_user directory, we'll move to the content editable region and insert a form object by clicking the Insert menu and choosing Form. Inside that form object, we'll insert a table that's four rows by two columns. If the table is inserted properly, it should be within the red outline of the invisible form element. You can double-check by going into Code view and making sure that the <table> tags are within the <form> tags.

Place the items in Table 18-1 into the table on the new_user page.

All that's left to do on the new_user page is to set the Action of the form to point to the welcome_new_user page. This can be set by selecting the form tag in the tag selector in the lower-left corner of the main window (see Figure 18-1) and opening up the Property Inspector for the form. It's a good idea to work with the Property Inspector open at all times; but if it's not open, it can be opened by selecting Properties from the Window menu.

The form Method should be set to POST, and the Action attribute can be left blank for now. The Action attribute can generally be filled in manually or you can click the Browse button (the folder icon) to browse to the file on the hard drive that you want the action set to. In this particular case, our Insert Server Behavior will set its own special action here. Many of the UltraDev Server Behaviors—including the Insert, Update, and Move To behaviors—automatically take care of the form actions with server-side code.

Adding a Validate Form Behavior

The three fields are required fields, so you'll have to add a FormValidation behavior to the Submit button. To add this behavior, you'll have to perform the following steps:

1. Select the form by clicking it in the tag selector or right-clicking the red form outline in the design environment.

2. If the Behaviors palette isn't showing, select it from the Window menu.

3. Click the plus sign (+) in the Behaviors palette.

Text	Form Element
Enter a Username	text field named txtUsername
Enter a Password	text field named txtPassword
Confirm Password	text field named txtConfirm
	Submit button

Table 18-1. *The New_user Page Contains Form Elements to Get the Username and Password*

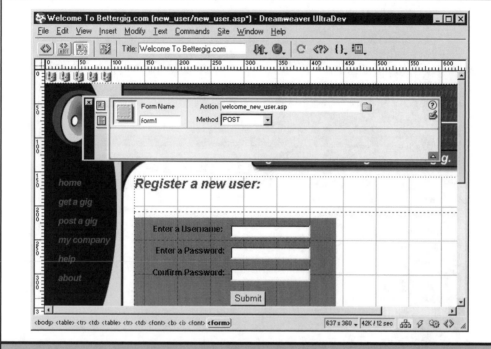

Figure 18-1. *Selecting the form tag in the tag selector allows you to enter form properties in the Property Inspector*

4. Choose Validate Form from the drop-down list.

5. The Validate Form behavior has a checkbox for Required. Check this box for each element in turn (see Figure 18-2).

UltraDev provides some basic form validations, but you can find others on the Macromedia Exchange that provide more functionality, such as checking for length and illegal characters.

Validating your form elements before submitting them to the database can prevent many errors down the line. Some forms will even validate that an address is valid before allowing any database insert. Other forms of validation are for valid numbers, e-mail addresses, ZIP codes, states, or credit card numbers.

Inserting a Custom JavaScript Function

One last validation is required, and you'll probably have to hand-code this one unless you can find a behavior that does this on the Exchange or on a third-party site: you have to validate that the Password and Confirm Password fields match. To do this,

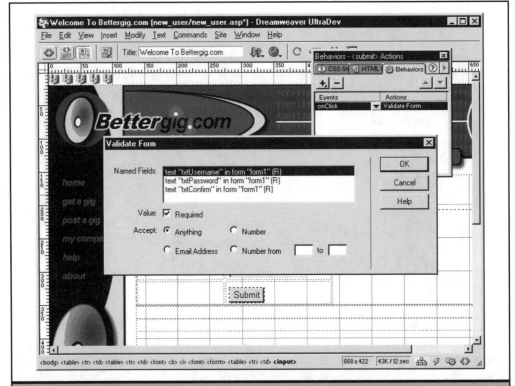

Figure 18-2. *The built-in Validate Form behavior allows you to choose required form elements*

you'll need to insert a little custom JavaScript. It's important that the Password field is accurate. If users entering the password make a mistake the first time they enter the password, they won't be able to return to the site.

To insert JavaScript into your page, you'll have to be in Code view. Since you've already added JavaScript behaviors to the page, there is already a section in the head of the document with JavaScript functions. If this weren't the case, you would have to add the following language declaration inside the head tags:

```
<script language="JavaScript">
<!--
//insert functions here
//-->
</script>
```

The language declaration tells the browser that the next lines will contain JavaScript. This script can be inline (no function declaration) or it can contain functions. If it's inline, it will execute once when the page loads. It's usually a good idea to enclose your scripts inside of functions and call them when needed, such as in the <body> tag onLoad() event.

The next line is an HTML comment tag so that the functions will be invisible to the HTML rendering engine of the browser. After including the functions, a JavaScript comment tag hides an HTML close comment tag. The closing script tag rounds out the section.

In this section, you'll have to type in a function that will allow you to confirm that the password fields match each other. The function will be called from the onSubmit() event of the form object. The function looks like this:

```
function form1_onSubmit() {
if(document.form1.txtPassword.value !=¬
document.form1.txtConfirm.value) {
    alert("The passwords didn't match");
    return false;
    }
return true;
}
```

The function was named form1_onSubmit as a way of describing the functionality of the JavaScript function. The function simply checks to make sure that the values of the two text fields match each other. If they don't, the function returns false to the caller; and if they do, the function returns true.

To call the function, you'll have to edit the form tag to insert an onSubmit() event. There are several ways you can do this:

- Go into Code view and hand-code the event.
- Add a Call JavaScript behavior to the form via the Behaviors palette.
- Right-click (CTRL-click on a Macintosh) on the red form outline in the design window and choose Edit Tag <form>.
- Choose the form tag from the tag selector in the lower-left corner of the design window, right-click (CTRL-click on the Macintosh), and choose Edit Tag (shown in Figure 18-3).

With the tag editor open, change the following event of the <form> tag to reflect the new function:

```
onSubmit="MM_validateForm ('txtUsername','','R','txtPassword','','R', ¬
'txtConfirm','','R'); return document .MM_returnValue && ¬
form1_onSubmit ()"
```

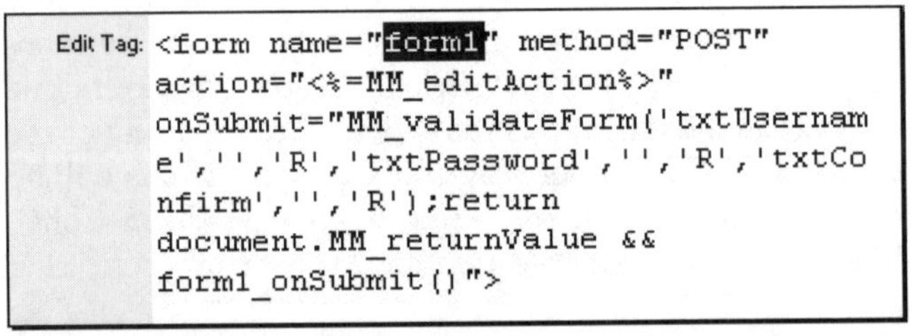

```
Edit Tag: <form name="form1" method="POST"
          action="<%=MM_editAction%>"
          onSubmit="MM_validateForm('txtUsernam
          e','','R','txtPassword','','R','txtCo
          nfirm','','R');return
          document.MM_returnValue &&
          form1_onSubmit()">
```

Figure 18-3. *The tag selector allows you to hand-code your HTML tags individually with the tag editor*

Notice that the function is not called directly, and instead we "return" the function to the onSubmit event. This will allow a false or true value returned from the function to dictate whether or not the form is submitted. If the function returns false, the onSubmit event won't allow the form to be submitted. You can use this technique in your own custom JavaScript functions to validate form fields or test for other conditions.

Adding the Insert Record Server Behavior

Now that the form validation is done and the form is ready to be submitted to the database, you can add an Insert Record Server Behavior to the page. This is accomplished by clicking the plus sign (+) on the Server Behaviors palette and choosing Insert Record from the drop-down list. This will bring up the dialog box shown in Figure 18-4. This dialog box allows you to set up your database insert using the form elements that are available on the page. The following fields need to be filled in.

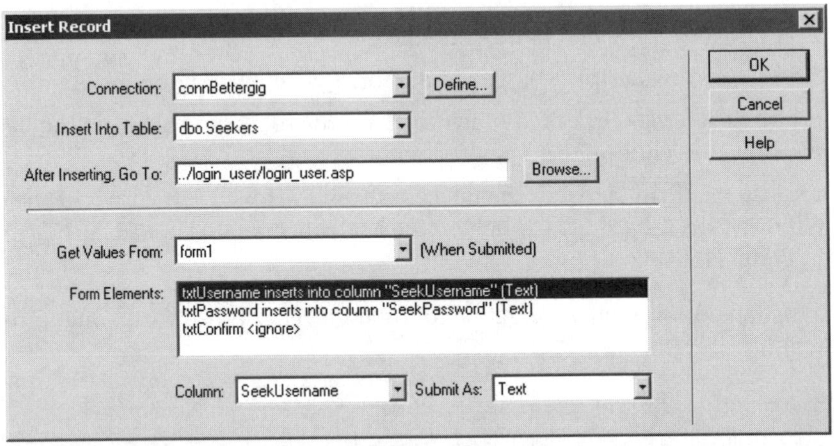

Figure 18-4. *The dialog box for inserting records into a database using the Insert Record Server Behavior*

- **Connection**   This will be the connBettergig connection to the Bettergig database. If no connections are listed, click the Define button to define the connBettergig connection (see Chapter 12 for more information on connections).

- **Insert into Table**   This will be a drop-down list of all tables in the database. Choose the Seekers table for the insert.

- **After Inserting, Go To**   This allows you to redirect the user to another page after the insert. Set this to the login_user page.

- **Get Values From**   Set this to Form1. It should be the only form on the page; but if you have multiple forms, there will be a drop-down list of forms that are available.

- **Form Elements**   The text fields should all be listed here. You have to set these up one by one by selecting the form element and choosing the appropriate column and appropriate data type underneath the text box. txtUsername will insert into the SeekUsername column and txtPassword will insert into the SeekPassword column. Leave the txtConfirm field set to <ignore>.

After completing these steps, you can click the OK button and the Server Behavior will be applied to the page. The Server Behavior will automatically write all of the code to your page to complete the database insert.

Testing for a Duplicate Username

On a standard database insert, you can use the Insert Record Server Behavior from the Server Behaviors palette by itself. This insert action will be a little different, however, because you have to first search the database for the username. If it exists, you'll send the user back to the new_user page to try again. This is accomplished by using the new User Authentication set of Server Behaviors. There is one called Check New Username, which is exactly what is needed.

In order to use this behavior, the form and Insert Server Behaviors need to be applied to the page first. This Server Behavior will check to see that the Insert behavior is in place. If it isn't, you'll see an error message telling you to put an Insert Record behavior on the page first.

The dialog box for the Check New Username (shown in Figure 18-5) prompts you for two parameters:

- **Username Field**   Set this to the txtUsername field. It should show up in the drop-down list of possible fields.

- **If Already Exists, Go To**   Set this to point to the failed_new_user page. If the page hasn't been created yet, you can type it in the box—be sure to create it in the same folder so that the relative path to the page will still work.

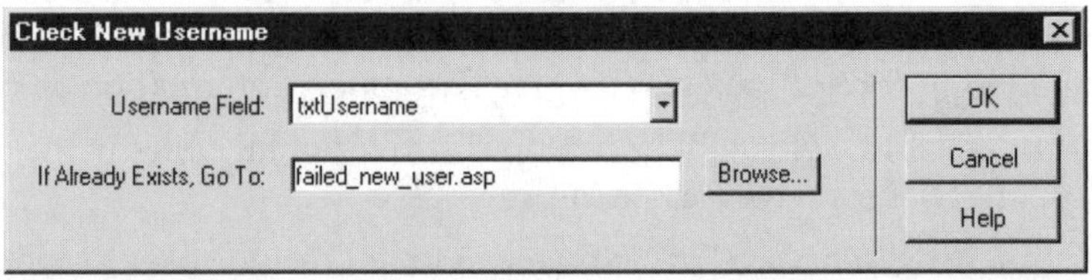

Check New Username

Username Field: txtUsername

If Already Exists, Go To: failed_new_user.asp   Browse...

OK

Cancel

Help

Figure 18-5. *The Check New Username Server Behavior has two parameters*

This Server Behavior automatically creates a recordset that will check your database for the username and redirect the user to a failed page if the username already exists. The recordset doesn't show up as a recordset in the Data Bindings palette; it is specific to this behavior. If you remove the Server Behavior from the page, the recordset will be removed as well. In UltraDev 1, this functionality had to be hand-coded. Chapter 24 will illustrate the same technique of checking the database for a duplicate username by creating your own recordset and hand-coding the functionality.

Creating the failed_new_user and login_user Pages

The failed_new_user page will do nothing but display a message to the user if he has entered a username that already exists. The page should be based on the same template as the other pages to maintain consistency. Place a message on the page: "Username exists. Please go back and choose another." Then put a link on the page using the text "<<<back" to link back to the new_user page. Do this with a bit of JavaScript. Highlight the text that you entered (that is, <<<back) and open up the Properties window. In the Link text field, insert the following script:

```
JavaScript:history.go(-1)
```

This JavaScript command will allow you to return to the previous page using the browser's history. With this method, you can use the page as an all-purpose error page for duplicate usernames (for the job seekers and employers).

Session Variables

Session variables were explained in Chapters 8 to 10, which dealt with the server models; but they play an important part of the Bettergig site, so we'll do a quick refresher. Session variables are available in the three server models that UltraDev supports (ASP, JSP, and ColdFusion) and have similar implementations in each. A session is created when a user requests a page that has a file extension that invokes the server. The server creates a session with a session ID number and keeps track of these numbers internally by storing the information in memory and on the user's machine in a cookie. Session variables can store pertinent information about a user or about the current session. Since the Web is a stateless environment, session variables play a key part in keeping information "alive" as the user accesses various pages in the site. While there are other methods of maintaining state, session variables are the easiest and most widely used method. Typically, users are given an ID number when they log in to the site.

The login_user Page

The login_user page will allow the newly inserted user to officially log in and begin to use the site. A login page will typically serve several purposes:

1. It will check the database for the username/password combination.

2. It will retrieve a unique identifier such as a user ID number for the person who has just logged in and store it in a session variable so that it is available to all pages that the user might go to. In the case of the built-in UltraDev Server Behaviors, the username is the unique identifier.

3. It will retrieve an access group level for users so that they will only be allowed on the pages that their access level is set for. The access level is typically stored in a session variable as well.

Start the page by making sure that it is based on the template that you've been using. Next, insert a three-row, two-column table into the Content editable region on the page. The table will be set up like Table 18-2.

With the form on the page, all you have to do now is to apply another of the new UltraDev 4 Server Behaviors: Log in User. This behavior will retrieve a recordset based on the username and password that is entered on the page, and it will insert the username and access level of the user into session variables. Once this is complete, the user will be redirected to the page they came from.

Any page can have protection on it so that a user has to be logged in to use the page. If users try to access the page without logging in, they'll be directed to the login page. Upon a successful login, users will be redirected to the page that they tried to access the first time. This saves a lot of complex logic to determine where to send a user after logging in.

Text	Form Element
Username	text field named txtUsername
Password	text field named txtPassword
(blank)	Submit button

Table 18-2. *Format for the User Login Table on the login_user Page*

For the purposes of this exercise, we'll create a "one-stop" login page. New users can use the page as well as old users who already have data entered in the database.

To apply the Server Behavior, simply click the plus sign (+) on the Server Behavior palette and choose User Authentication | Log in User. That will bring up the dialog box shown in Figure 18-6.

The parameters for the Server Behavior should be filled in as follows:

- **Get Input from Form**   Drop-down list of all forms on the page (form1, in this case).

- **Username Field**   txtUsername.

- **Password Field**   txtPassword.

- **Validate Using Connection**   The database connection used in the validation (connBettergig, in this case).

- **Table**   The database table in which the user information is stored (Seekers, in this case).

- **Username Column**   SeekUsername.

- **Password Column**   SeekPassword.

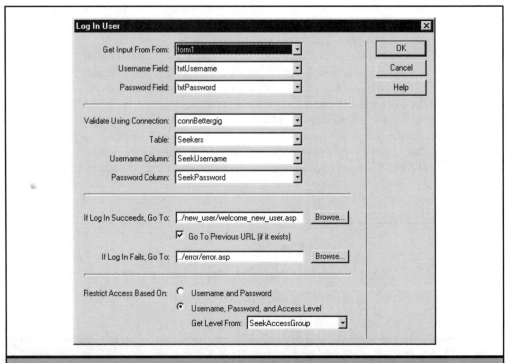

Figure 18-6.   *The Log in User Server Behavior allows the automatic generation of the server-side script to log in a user*

- **If Log in Succeeds, Go To** welcome_new_user page. Click the Browse button to find the page so that you get the correct relative path.
- **Go to Previous URL (If It Exists)** This checkbox should be checked.
- **If Log in Fails, Go To** This should be set to the error page. Again, browse to the page in order to get the correct relative path.
- **Restrict Access Based On** Username, Password, and Access Level.
- **Get Level From** The database column that the Access Level is retrieved from (SeekAccessGroup, in this case).

The User Authentication Server Behaviors were all designed to work hand in hand. By using this behavior on the login_user page, session variables that are set on this page can be retrieved with the Restrict Access to Page Server Behavior on other pages.

Introducing Live Objects

Live Objects are new to UltraDev 4. They reside in the Objects palette in the Live tab and can also be found in the Insert menu under the Live Objects menu item. A Live Object is simply an object that contains server-side code, usually in the form of a Server Behavior. Most of the Live Objects will automatically insert the code necessary to replicate one or more Server Behaviors. For example, the Recordset Navigation Bar will insert First, Previous, Next, and Last links on the page; and it will automatically insert the Move to First, Move to Previous, Move to Next, Move to Last Server Behaviors, as well as the Server Behaviors that show each link depending on the recordset status. This one object effectively adds a table, four hyperlinks, and eight Server Behaviors to the page with one click.

The welcome_new_user Page

The Live Object that will be inserted on the welcome_new_user page will be the Record Update Form object. This object will take the place of a lot of labor-intensive work by allowing you to insert the following into the page:

- An Update Server Behavior
- Form fields to correspond to all database fields that are being updated
- Labels to correspond to the form fields (so that your txtUsername field could have a label that says "Please enter a username," for instance)
- Default values for form fields
- A page to go to after the update takes place

BUILDING
LANGUAGE-SPECIFIC
DATA-DRIVEN SITES

Note *To those who remember the Macromedia program Drumbeat 2000, which UltraDev replaced, the Live Objects form a core functionality that is similar to the Drumbeat Data Form Wizard.*

Before inserting the object, you need to create a recordset. The recordset will retrieve all of the columns that are to be updated so that this form can function as a dual-purpose New User form and a Change Your Personal Information form. The record for the user is created the first time the user accesses the new_user page, but the only entries are the SeekUsername and SeekPassword fields. In addition, if you remember from Chapter 16, in which the database was designed, the SeekAccessGroup column had a default value inserted into it. In the case of the job seekers, the value was Seekers.

Create a new recordset by clicking the plus sign (+) in the Data Bindings palette and choosing Recordset. Name the recordset rsGetSeeker. You'll be writing the SQL statement in Advanced mode. The SQL statement will look like this:

```
SELECT SeekUsername, SeekAddress, SeekCity, SeekEmail, SeekFax,
SeekFirstName, SeekLastName, SeekPhone, SeekState, SeekZip, SeekID
FROM Seekers
WHERE SeekUsername = 'svUsername'
```

The parameter svUsername that is in the SQL statement has to be defined in the Variables box in the Recordset dialog box. The variable should be set up like Table 18-3.

To insert the Update object, position your cursor at the spot on the page where you want the object to be inserted. Then go to the Insert menu and click Live Objects | Record Update Form (see Figure 18-7). This will show the Insert Record Update Form dialog box seen in Figure 18-8. There are quite a few options in this box, and the time saving is enormous. The parameters that you need to include are as follows:

- **Connection** Choose the connBettergig connection for this field. If it's not defined, click the Define button. Connections are covered in Chapter 12.

- **Table to Update** The database table that the form will update.

Server Model	Name	Default Value	Runtime Value
ASP	svUsername	%	Session("MM_Username")
JSP	svUsername	%	session.getValue ("MM_Username")
ColdFusion	svUsername	%	#session.MM_Username#

Table 18-3. *Setting Up the Variable for the SQL Statement in the rsGetSeeker Recordset*

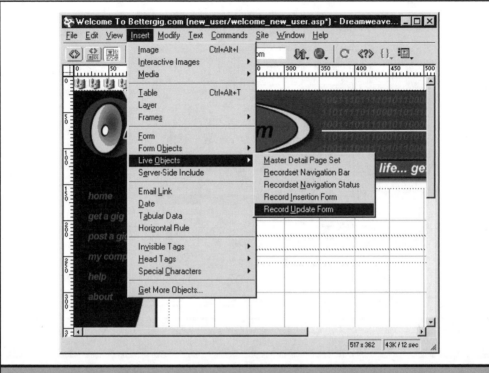

Figure 18-7. *Choosing Record Update Form from the Insert menu*

- **Select Record From** The recordset that is used to get the correct record.

- **Unique Key Column** Usually the Primary Key of the database table. Use the SeekID field.

- **After Updating, Go To** You should use the Browse button to fill in this field with the page that the user will be redirected to. In this case, it's going to be the post_resume page.

- **Form Fields** This is where the fun begins. Column (database column), Labels (descriptive text), Display As (form field), and Submit As (data type) are listed for each form element. These should correspond with each column in the recordset; however, several columns will not be needed. SeekUsername, SeekPassword, SeekAccessGroup, and SeekID should all be removed by clicking the minus (–) sign after highlighting the field. Also, the labels can be adjusted to something that is more user friendly (such as First Name instead of SeekFirstName). All of the fields can be submitted as text.

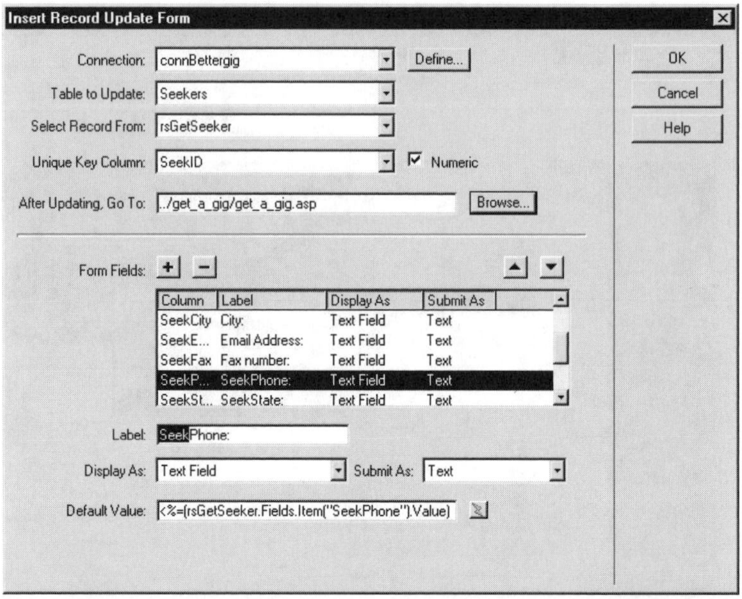

Figure 18-8. *The Insert Record Update Form dialog box*

After changing each form field , setting the labels to something user friendly, and making sure all of the Submit As columns are filled in with Text, click the OK button. This Live Object will insert an Update Server Behavior on the page, as well as a table with the form fields and descriptive labels. At the bottom of the table is a Submit button. In addition, each form field is set as a Dynamic Text Field retrieving the data from the database to be displayed in the form field as the default value. Two hidden fields are added as well: MM_recordid and MM_update. These are fields that the Update Server Behavior needs in order to work properly. The MM_recordid hidden field contains the value of the SeekUserID field of the current record, so that the update will occur on the correct record.

If the table didn't insert into the proper place, you can select it and drop it into the place on the page where you want it to reside. If you move it around, however, you'll need to make sure that the table, including the hidden fields, is within the form tags.

The Insert Record Insertion Form Live Object

The next page to create for the new job seeker is the post_resume page in the get_a_gig folder. On this page, the user will be able to insert the data necessary to complete an online resume. Rather than allowing the user to upload a resume as a file, the Bettergig site allows the user to create a resume using predefined form fields. This will allow for easy searching of the database.

Similar to the Update Record Live Object is the Record Insertion Form Live Object. This object doesn't generally require a predefined recordset, since it is only inserting and not updating data; but in this case, we need to retrieve the SeekID for the job seeker. In the next chapter, we'll illustrate several methods of hand-coding to allow you to keep values such as these in session variables.

Create a new recordset named rsGetSeekID using the connBettergig connection. As always, you should use the Advanced dialog box for the recordset. The SQL statement will look like this:

```
SELECT SeekID
FROM Seekers
WHERE SeekUsername = 'svUsername'
```

After writing your SQL statement, you'll need to define the variable that is used (see Table 18-4).

To insert the Record Insertion form, choose Insert | Live Objects | Record Insertion Form or double-click the icon in the Live folder on the Objects palette. This will bring up the Insert Record Insertion Form dialog box shown in Figure 18-9. You can place your cursor where you want the object to appear; otherwise, it will be inserted at the bottom of the page and you can drag it into position.

The parameters that you need to define for this Live Object are as follows:

- **Connection**   Set this to connBettergig.

- **Insert into Table**   Set this to the Resumes table.

- **After Inserting, Go To**   Set this to the view_resume page (click the Browse button to ensure that your relative path will be accurate).

- **Form Fields**   These fields will be created automatically by the Record Insertion Form object. Set them up as in Table 18-5.

Server Model	Name	Default Value	Runtime Value
ASP	svUsername	%	Session("MM_Username")
JSP	svUsername	%	session.getValue ("MM_Username")
ColdFusion	svUsername	%	#session.MM_Username#

Table 18-4. *Variable Definition for the rsGetSeekID Recordset*

BUILDING
LANGUAGE-SPECIFIC
DATA-DRIVEN SITES

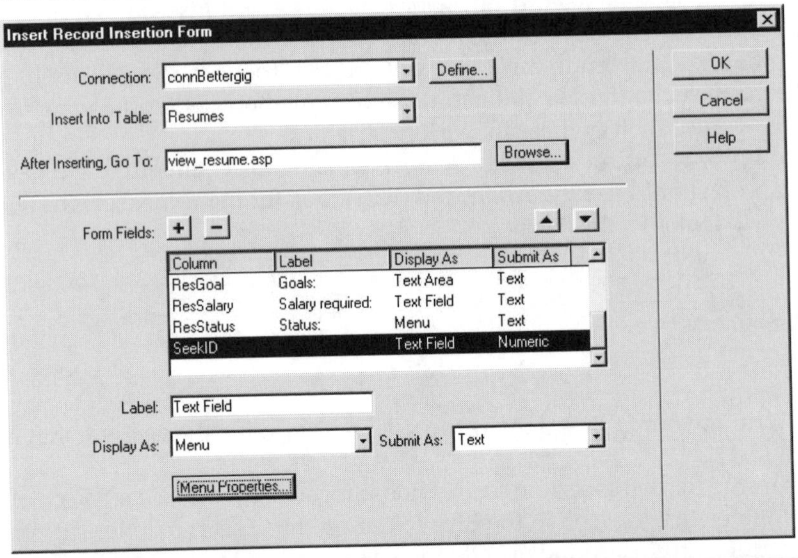

Figure 18-9. The Insert Record Insertion Form dialog box

The ResStatus menu needs to be filled in with a couple of entries: Currently Employed and Currently Available. You can do this by clicking the Menu Properties button. This will bring up the dialog box shown in Figure 18-10, in which you can set the Label and Value options as shown.

Column	Label	Display As	Submit As
ResAvailable	Available	Text Field	Text
ResCitizenship	Citizenship	Text Field	Text
ResContact	Contact	Text Field	Text
ResEducation	Education	Text Area	Text
ResExperience	Experience	Text Area	Text
ResGoal	Goals	Text Area	Text
ResSalary	Salary Requirement	Text Field	Text
ResStatus	Status	Menu	Text
SeekID		Text Field	Numeric

Table 18-5. Form Field Definition for the Record Insertion Form

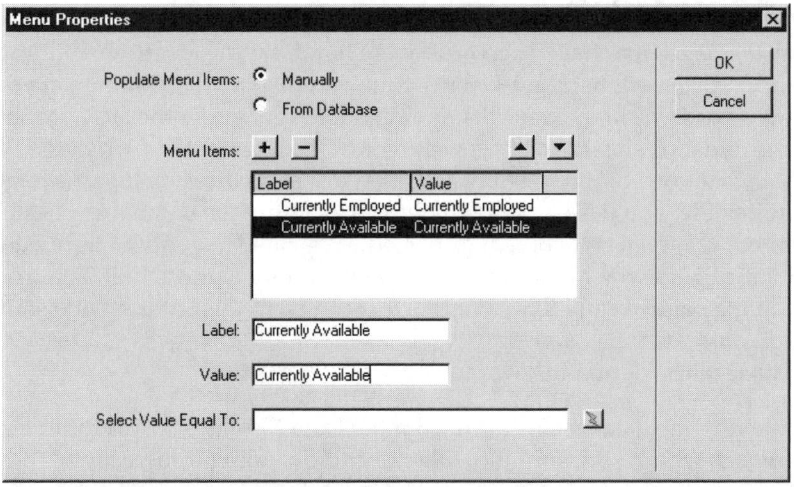

Figure 18-10.   *Setting the menu options for the ResStatus field allows you to specify options*

The SeekID column needs to have a default value added to it by clicking the lightning bolt icon and browsing the SeekID column of the rsGetSeekID recordset. This will ensure that the resume will be added to the database with a reference to the correct user.

Note   *Using the Menu option allows you to set a predefined list of options for the user. These can also come from a recordset, which makes it an easy way to set up a dynamic menu.*

There's going to be one more little change that will have to be hand-coded. The Record Insertion Form object doesn't allow for the use of a hidden form object, but that's what you need to be able to insert the SeekID number. This isn't the sort of data that you want the user to be able to type in and change, so you'll have to go into Code view and simply change the following code from

```
<input type="text" name="SeekID"
```

to

```
<input type="hidden" name="SeekID"
```

This turns the text field into a hidden form element that will be submitted along with all of the text fields and text areas on the page. This will ensure both data integrity and that the resume is identified by the correct SeekID number.

Displaying Data

Until now, the pages that have been built were handling the insertion and updating of data. This next page will handle a Details page and display the resume data that was entered on the post_resume page. Displaying data is generally the easy part of putting together the dynamic site. It involves writing a SQL statement to extract the data from the database that you want to display and then inserting the data into the page. If you are in Design view, you'll see a placeholder representing the data. This placeholder can be moved, dragged, cut, copied, or pasted; it can also have styles applied to it as if it were static text. If you are in Live Data view, you'll see the actual data from the database on the page. Again, this dynamic text can be treated as if it were static text and manipulated the same way.

The data can be inserted in several ways:

- Dragging the database column from the Data Bindings Inspector to a spot on the page where you want it displayed and dropping it there.

- Selecting a column in the Data Bindings Inspector and clicking the Insert button. The dynamic text will be inserted at the last position of the cursor.

- Hand-coding. You can always hand-code your pages, including items that are coming from a data source. You might, for example, want to include a recordset column in a hand-coded server-side script.

One technique that may help you design your pages is to set up placeholders for all of the dynamic content. In a situation in which a designer will design a page and then pass the page to the programmer, UltraDev is a perfect tool. The programmer can simply highlight the static text on the page, select the dynamic item from the Data Bindings Inspector, and click Insert. The dynamic text will replace the static text on the page and retain all of its formatting. For example, if you place the following text on the page

First Name: Jack

Last Name: O'Lantern

while in Design mode, you can later add a recordset to the page named rsGetNames with column names First and Last. Simply highlight "Jack" and insert the First column, and then highlight "O'Lantern" and insert the Last column, and the display will now look like this:

First Name: {rsGetNames.First}

Last Name: {rsGetNames.Last}

Using this method allows the designers to have full control over the design of the pages, including the design of the dynamic content. It also allows the programmers to make the necessary changes to the code without interfering with the design. There is a far greater chance of maintaining design accuracy, and there is also a lot less back-and-forth interaction between the designer and programmer. You can even take it one step further and have the designers lock all regions of the page in a template and allow the insertion of only the dynamic data.

Live Data Mode

Live Data mode has been around since UltraDev1, but it is now more accessible to the designer/programmer with the new Live Data Mode button on the toolbar (shown in Figure 18-11). Live Data gives you the ability to view your page *in the design environment* as if it were a Web page being served by the application server. That gives you the ability to edit and design pages in an environment that is as close to the way the end user will see the page as is possible.

Live Data Settings

Frequently, on a dynamic page you will need to supply parameters to the page in order to view the page properly. In our particular case, the page will assume that a user is already logged in and that the username is stored in the session variable MM_Username. This can be easily simulated with the Live Data settings of UltraDev. What these settings

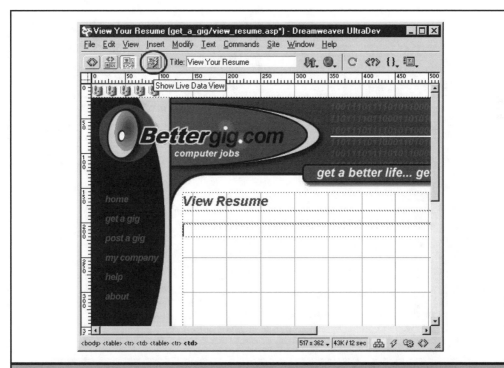

Figure 18-11.   *The new toolbar in UltraDev 4 includes a button for Live Data*

do is allow you to insert some server-side script into the UltraDev environment that will get executed before the page is served to the Live Data server. In the past, you would have to actually insert the code on the page itself temporarily in order to test the page; but with the Live Data settings, you can let UltraDev handle the details.

Go to View | Live Data Settings to see the dialog box shown in Figure 18-12. In this dialog box you are allowed to specify URL variables with a name/value pair, and you can write your own custom initialization script. The settings that you specify here can be saved so that whenever you want to work on the page, the Live Data settings will automatically revert to whatever you previously saved.

The Initialization Script should be valid syntax for whichever application server you are working with. For example, to work in Live Data for the view_resume page that you are about to design, you could insert one of the following initialization scripts, depending upon which server model you are using:

```
<% session("MM_Username") = "jack" %> (ASP)

<% session.putValue("MM_Username", "jack") %> (JSP)

<CFSET session.MM_Username="jack">  (ColdFusion)
```

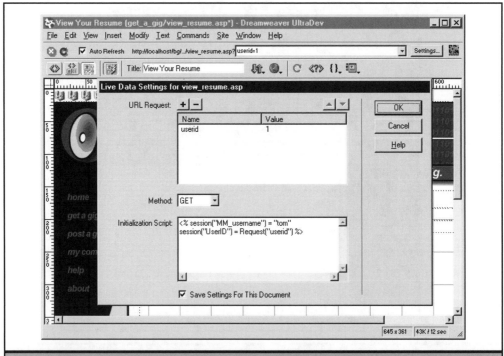

Figure 18-12. *Live Data Settings allow you to run server-side scripts in Live Data mode before your page loads*

Writing the SQL Statement

When you want to display the data from the database, the SQL (Structured Query Language) statement is the key. With the SQL statement, you are able to pick and choose the data that you want to retrieve. Writing good SQL is an art in itself, and it is necessary to learn for a successful dynamic Web site. SQL can be generated by many popular database programs, such as Microsoft Access, Microsoft SQL Server, or IBM DB2. In these programs, there are Query or View builders that take the hassle out of writing SQL by hand.

Simple SQL that retrieves data from one table is relatively easy to write. As you've seen in previous examples in this chapter, and the chapters on database design and SQL, you must use a Select statement to retrieve the values that you want to display. When you're dealing with only one table, it's just a matter of picking the columns from the UltraDev query builder.

When you have complex joins between tables, however, it's necessary to know the language inside and out. The SQL statement for the view_resume page will get its data from two tables that are related by the SeekID number of the end user (the job seeker). The SQL will use an inner join to relate the tables to each other. The SQL is as follows:

```
SELECT Resumes.ResGoal, Resumes.ResEducation,
       Resumes.ResExperience, Resumes.ResCitizenship,
       Resumes.ResAvailable, Resumes.ResStatus,
       Resumes.ResSalary, Resumes.ResContact, Resumes.ResID,
       Seekers.SeekFirstName, Seekers.SeekLastName,
       Seekers.SeekAddress, Seekers.SeekCity,
       Seekers.SeekState, Seekers.SeekZip,
       Seekers.SeekEmail, Seekers.SeekFax, Seekers.SeekPhone
FROM Resumes
INNER JOIN Seekers
ON Resumes.SeekID = Seekers.SeekID
WHERE (Seekers.SeekUsername = 'svUsername') OR
       (Resumes.ResID = VarResID)
```

The variables needed for this statement is shown in the following table:

Server Model	Name	Default Value	Runtime Value
ASP	svUsername	%	Session("MM_Username")
	VarResID	0	Request (ResID)
JSP	svUsername	%	session.getValue ("MM_Username")

Server Model	Name	Default Value	Runtime Value
	VarResID	0	request.get Parameter (ResID)
ColdFusion	svUsername	%	#session.MM_ Username#
	VarResID	0	#ResID#

As you can see, the SQL is drawing its data from two tables: Seekers and Resumes, which are joined on the SeekID column. To further complicate matters, the SeekID is retrieved from the Seekers table by using the session variable that was set up in the previous pages: MM_Username. The session variable needs to be assigned to a special variable inside the UltraDev environment. This variable is named svUsername and is inserted into the SQL statement to take the place of the session variable. This is one of the idiosyncrasies of UltraDev that needs to be adhered to if you want to be able to access the recordset through the Data Bindings palette. Also, a variable named varResID is defined to take the place of an incoming request variable named ResID. The SQL statements will retrieve the resume based on either a resume ID number or a job seeker username value, depending on the situation.

You can see from the SQL statement that we've added the table name as a prefix to each column. This isn't always necessary, but it's a good practice to get into when you start getting into more complex SQL statements. Using this technique allows you to make sure there's no confusion in the columns. In this case, there is a SeekID field in both tables, so this column would have to be referred to with a table name prefix. Another method, as described in Chapter 14, is to assign aliases to the columns.

In any event, now that you have the SQL, you can create the recordset named rsDisplayResume based on the connBettergig connection. After testing it to make sure it works and is error free, click OK, and the recordset will appear in the Data Bindings palette. All of the columns that are going to be displayed are shown in the Data Bindings palette and can now be inserted easily into the page.

To begin inserting the data, you can add a table to the page, or simply begin typing in the content region and use <br> and <p> tags to separate your content. Whichever method you prefer, the technique for getting the data to the page is the same: put your cursor where you want to insert the dynamic text, select the column in the Data Bindings palette, and click the Insert button. The other method is to simply drag the column from the Data Bindings palette and drop it on the page where you want it. If you are viewing the page in Live Data mode, the data from the database will be displayed on the page (see Figure 18-13). If not in Live Data mode, you'll see placeholders for the dynamic data. In either case, the dynamic text can be manipulated in the design environment to allow for text styles and placement.

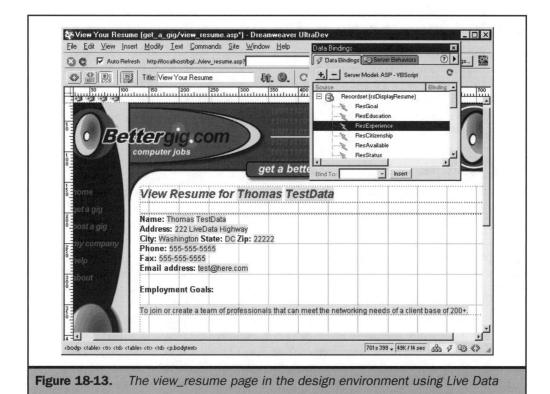

Figure 18-13. *The view_resume page in the design environment using Live Data*

Preserving the Whitespace with HTML
 Tags

After you've added each database column to the page in turn, you will have a
completed page displaying the resume of the logged-in user. Remember, the browser
doesn't recognize line breaks, so you must insert <br> tags wherever there is a line
break in the text. These must be hand-coded and will be different for each server
model. The code to do this is as follows (replace [column] with your own dynamic
data representation):

```
Replace([column],chr(10),"<br>") (VBScript)
[column].replace(/\n/g,"<br>\n") (JavaScript)
[column].replace("\n","<br>\n") (Java)
ParagraphFormat([column]) (ColdFusion)
```

Adding the Company Pages

The Bettergig site has two basic types of users: the job seeker and the company representative. The companies will post jobs that are available, and the job seekers will post their resumes to be viewed. So far in this chapter, the job seeker has been able to insert himself in the database, log in, insert a resume, and view the resume. The next step is to include the functionality for the company representative to post job information for the job seeker to be able to search.

The my_company Pages

Company representatives using the Bettergig.com Web site will have to log in also. Rather than complicate the site with script, we've separated the sections for job seekers and company representatives. They are also separated in the database, with the individual company data being stored in the Employers table. What you'll have to do is to create pages similar to the new_user pages already created. Copying and adapting pages is one of the things that is easy to do in UltraDev. The server-side script code on the pages is recognized as individual Server Behaviors that can be modified.

Start with the new_company_user page. This page will be a direct copy of the new_user page already created. Simply copy the new_user page in the Site window and paste a copy into the my_company folder. Rename the new_user file to new_company_user and open it up. There are two Server Behaviors on this page: Insert Record and Check New Username. Start with the Insert Record Server Behavior. Open up the dialog box by double-clicking the Server Behavior in the Server Behavior palette. This puts the behavior into edit mode, allowing you to make changes to it.

The connection will remain the same, but the Insert into Table parameter will change. Set this to the Employers table.

The next parameter to define is the page to go to after a successful insert. This should be set to the login_company_user page in the login_company_user folder. The login_company_user page will be a direct copy of the login_user page , which you'll adapt as well.

The form elements will also have to be set up again. The txtUsername field will be bound to the EmpUsername field of the Employers table, and the txtPassword field will be bound to the EmpPassword field. Once again, the txtConfirm field should be set to <ignore>.

After making these changes, click the OK button. There may be a red check mark next to the Check New Username Server Behavior at this point. You'll have to make some changes to this one as well. Open it up and make sure the Username field is set to txtUsername. Then change the If Already Exists field to the failed_new_user page in the new_user folder. Browse to the file to keep the relative links correct.

This illustrates one of the key time-saving features of UltraDev: the ability to create similar pages by copying, pasting, and making minor changes to the functionality. The Server Behaviors are predefined blocks of code that have parameters that can change. By double-clicking a Server Behavior and then clicking the OK button, the block of code is rebuilt using the new parameters.

Save the file and open up the welcome_company_user page. If this page doesn't exist yet, create a page with this name based on the template. This page will have similar functionality to the welcome_new_user page for the job seekers, but it will apply to the company representatives. Apply the same steps here that you applied to the welcome_new_user page, but base it on the Employers table. Here are the steps:

1. Create a recordset named rsGetEmployer, and use the following SQL statement:

```
SELECT EmpName, EmpContact, EmpAddress, EmpAddress2, EmpCity,
EmpState, EmpZip, EmpPhone, EmpFax, EmpEmail, EmpID
FROM Employers
WHERE EmpUsername = 'svUsername'
```

2. Add the parameter to the SQL variables declaration, as shown in the following table.

Server Model	Name	Default Value	Runtime Value
ASP	svUsername	%	Session("MM_Username")
JSP	svUsername	%	session.getValue ("MM_Username")
ColdFusion	svUsername	%	#session.MM_Username#

3. Add the Record Update Form Live Object, making sure you tie all of the fields to the proper fields in the database, just as you did for the welcome_new_user page.

4. After updating, go to post_a_gig. You should browse to this page with the browse button to make sure the relative path is correct.

5. Re-create the login_user page for the company. You can do this by simply copying the file and pasting it into the login_company folder and renaming it login_company_user. Double-click on the Log In User behavior and change the fields so that they reference the Employers table instead of the Seekers table. If Log in Succeeds should be set to point to the welcome_company_user page. Then click OK, and the page will be ready to save once again.

Tip *While it might seem wasteful to have almost exact copies of certain pages on the server, remember that we are dealing with server-side code, not HTML pages. If you have to insert server script into a page to differentiate between different users or different situations, the server has to execute more code, creating greater overall strain on the server. It's much better to have extra pages doing simple things than extra code doing more complex things.*

Post a Gig

The company representatives that come to the Bettergig site will have two primary reasons for coming to the site: to post new jobs and to search for a job seeker who might fit into a position with their company. We'll start with the post_a_gig page.

The functionality of this page will be similar to the post_a_resume page with a few small changes. The JobCategory and JobSubCategory fields in the Jobs table are foreign keys to the Category and SubCategory tables. What this means is that the lists of categories and subcategories are actually stored in the other tables to allow for a more dynamic and expandable database. If more categories are added, they only need to be added to the Categories table.

What this means to our post_a_gig page is that we only want the user to be able to choose from the list of categories and subcategories from the database. This is typically accomplished with a drop-down list menu. The difference here is that the lists will be generated dynamically. By doing it in this way, if new categories are added to the database, the Web pages will not need to be updated—all of the information will be coming from the database, and, therefore, it will always be up to date.

Adding the Recordsets to the Page

This page will need three recordsets.

1. rsGetCategories will pull all information from the Categories table. Use a Select statement like this:

   ```
   SELECT * from Categories
   ```

2. rsGetSubCategories will pull all information from the SubCategories table. Use a Select statement like this:

   ```
   SELECT * from SubCategories
   ```

3. rsGetEmpID will get the employer's UserID (the EmpID primary key field) for insertion in the Jobs table. Use a Select statement like this:

   ```
   SELECT EmpID
   FROM Employers
   WHERE EmpUsername = 'svUsername'
   ```

Once again, the variable needs to be set up for the UltraDev environment, as in the following table:

Server Model	Name	Default Value	Runtime Value
ASP	svUsername	%	Session("MM_Username")
JSP	svUsername	%	session.getValue ("MM_Username")
ColdFusion	svUsername	%	#session.MM_Username#

Adding the Record Insertion Form Live Object

The next thing you'll have to do is to insert another Live Object: the Record Insertion Form. This time you'll set up the drop-down menu boxes with the information coming from the two recordsets that have been defined. Start by positioning the cursor at the Content editable region, and then choose the Record Insertion Form from the Insert menu or double-click the object from the Live section of the Objects palette. This will bring up the dialog box shown in Figure 18-14. There is a lot of information associated with this one step, so make sure you follow along closely.

- **Connection** This will once again be the connBettergig connection.
- **Insert into Table** This will be the Jobs table.
- **After Inserting, Go To** Set this up by clicking the Browse button and navigating to the view_all_gigs page
- **Form Fields** These will be a little tricky this time. We'll address them separately.

Setting Up the Form Fields for the Insert

The EmpID column will have no label because it must be converted to a hidden form field the object is placed on the page, as was done earlier for the post_a_resume page. Forget about that part for now and leave it as a Text field. The Submit As field

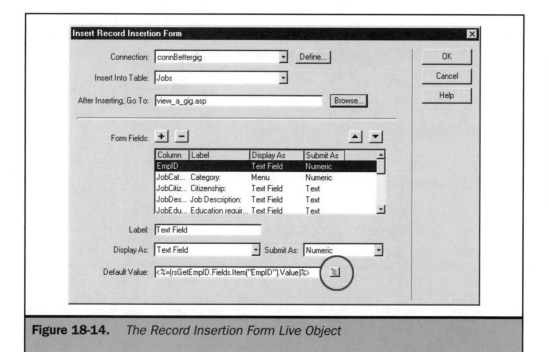

Figure 18-14. *The Record Insertion Form Live Object*

should be set to Numeric, and the Default Value will require a special step. Click the lightning bolt icon (see Figure 18-14) to bring up the Dynamic Data dialog box (see Figure 18-15), and then click the EmpID field in the rsGetEmpID recordset. This will set the value of the form field to the value in the EmpID field based on the record you retrieve by querying the database with the Username contained in the session variable.

Setting Up Dynamic Menu Fields

The JobCategory column and JobSubCategory columns will each have recordsets attached to them. To properly set up these two fields, follow these steps for each of the two fields:

1. Set the Label field to a user-friendly label, such as Job Category and Subcategory.

2. Set the Display As field to Menu.

3. Set the Submit As field to Numeric.

4. Click the Menu Properties button; the dialog box shown in Figure 18-16 will pop up.

5. Click the From Database radio button.

6. Set the Recordset field to rsGetCategories for the JobCategories menu and rsGetSubCategories for the JobSubCategories menu.

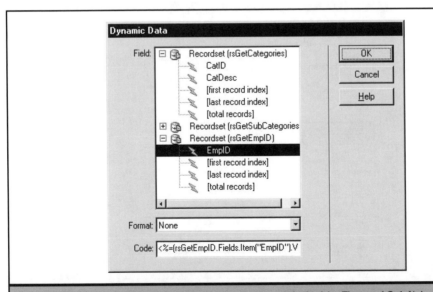

Figure 18-15. *Clicking the lightning bolt icon (circled in Figure 18-14) launches the Dynamic Data dialog box*

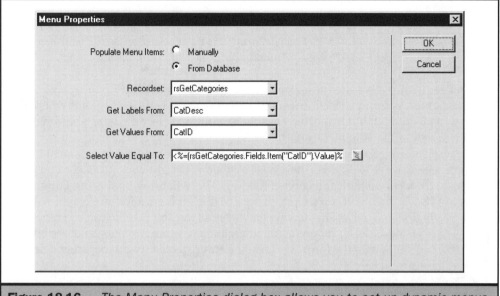

Figure 18-16. *The Menu Properties dialog box allows you to set up dynamic menus from a recordset*

7. Set the Get Labels From field to the CatDesc and SubCatDesc fields, respectively. These will be the actual drop-down items that the end user will choose from.

8. Set the Get Values From to the CatID and SubCatID fields. These will be the values that will be inserted into the Jobs table. By using these foreign keys in the table, you'll be able to get the description fields easily from the Categories and SubCategories tables when you need to display the Job data later.

9. The Select Value Equal To field has the lightening bolt icon once again, but you don't have to click the button, because this is the value of the selected menu item. Just fill in the number 1 in the text field and this will cause the first item in the table to be selected (assuming your tables start their count at 1).

Finishing the Page

That will take care of the dynamic menus in the form, but you'll have one static menu as well: JobStatus. This menu should be set to populate manually. Fill in three menu items by clicking the plus sign (+) in the dialog box and set the labels to Permanent, Contract, and Temp to Perm. The values should be set to 1, 2, and 3. The Select Value Equal To box should once again be set to 1 to select the first item.

The other form fields can all be set to Text Fields, with the exception of the JobID form field—make sure you remove this item, as the database will create this number automatically if it is set up as an Autonumber or Identity column in the database.

One of the mistakes many people make is to try to do an Insert or Update statement with the Primary Key included in the statement. This will usually cause a database error, as the database itself takes care of incrementing this value. When inserting your Insert or Update statement, make sure no Autonumber or Identity columns are chosen.

After setting up all of the form elements in the Insert form and double-checking all items, click the OK button. The form should be inserted exactly at the point where the cursor was positioned. If it is located elsewhere, you can select the table and drag it where you would like it to be inserted.

The next step, of course, is to change that text field into a hidden form element. There are several ways to do this. The easiest method is to right-click (CTRL-click on the Macintosh) the form element and choose Edit Tag. This will bring up the Tag Editor (see Figure 18-17). Then you can simply change Text to Hidden, and the element will be automatically updated in Design view when you close the Tag Editor. You can move the hidden tag from the table, if you prefer, by dragging it to a location outside of the bounds of the table but still within the form tag. Then the empty table row can be safely deleted.

View All Gigs and View a Gig

This page will bring into play a new Live Object called Insert Master Detail Pageset. This new object (new to UltraDev 4, that is) automates the process of creating a Master page containing a list of records that each link to specific Details pages. This is a typical recordset navigation technique that is used on most sites that have dynamic content. For example, when you search for a book on Amazon.com, a list of books that match your search criteria will be displayed, with links to the details of each book upon clicking its title.

Creating the Recordset

For the Master Detail object to work, you must first specify a recordset. The recordset will contain all of the items that you want displayed on the Details page. For the Jobs page, you'll need to have a fairly complex statement. If you recall, the Categories and SubCategories fields are drawn from separate tables. This dramatically decreases the size of the database, but it also increases the complexity of the SQL. However, SQL is a powerful language that is designed specifically for retrieving items from a database. Once again, until you become comfortable with the language, it's a good idea to create SQL statements with a graphical interface, such as the View builder interface that is

```
Edit Tag: <input type="text" name="EmpID"
         value="<%=(rsGetEmpID.Fields.Item("Em
         pID").Value)%>" size="32">
```

Figure 18-17. *The Tag Editor allows quick edits on individual tags, including changing text elements to hidden elements*

included in Microsoft SQL Server (shown in Figure 18-18). Most modern databases have a similar interface that allows you to choose the columns that you want to have displayed, as well as the columns that are needed for the joins.

Create a new recordset named rsGetJobs. The SQL statement needed here is as follows:

```
SELECT Jobs.JobID, Jobs.JobLocation, Jobs.JobStatus, Jobs.JobSalary,
   Jobs.JobEducation, Jobs.JobDescription, Jobs.JobStartDate,
   Jobs.JobTerm, Jobs.JobCitizenship, Employers.EmpName,
   SubCategories.SubCatDesc, Categories.CatDesc
FROM SubCategories
INNER JOIN (Employers
   INNER JOIN (Categories
      INNER JOIN Jobs ON Categories.CatID = Jobs.JobCategory)
   ON Employers.EmpID = Jobs.EmpID)
ON SubCategories.SubCatID = Jobs.JobSubCategory
WHERE (Employers.EmpUsername= 'svUsername')
```

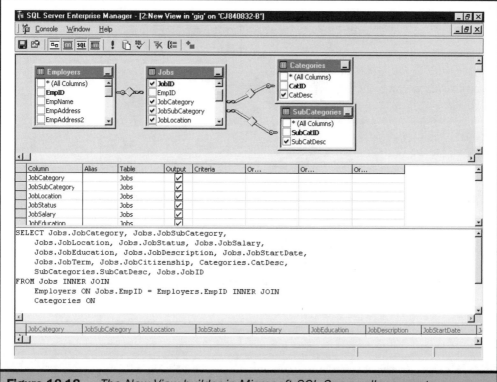

Figure 18-18.   *The New View builder in Microsoft SQL Server allows you to graphically create your SQL statements*

Once again, you need to define the variable needed for the SQL statement. Refer back to Table 18-4 for the variable definition. This SQL statement will retrieve the Jobs and the Categories and SubCategories for each job, and it will only retrieve the jobs that are referenced by the EmpID number of the currently logged-in employer representative.

Adding the Insert Master Detail Live Object

This Live Object, like the others, is accessed either from the Objects palette in the Live panel, or by clicking Insert | Live Objects | Insert Master-Detail Pageset. This will bring up the dialog box shown in Figure 18-19.

When you use this object, there are two pages that are affected—the current page will be the Master page, and the Detail page can be specified from this dialog box. Follow these steps for the view_all_jobs and view_a_job pages:

1. Choose the newly created recordset rsGetJobs.

2. Choose your Master Page Fields. These will be displayed in a table and are only meant to be a summary of the jobs available. Pick the JobID, JobStartDate, and JobDescription from the list of fields and remove the rest.

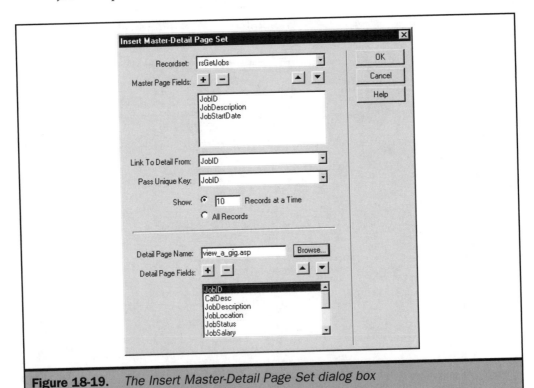

Figure 18-19. *The Insert Master-Detail Page Set dialog box*

3. Set the Link to Detail From attribute to the JobID field.

4. Set the Pass Unique Key to the JobID field.

5. Click the Show *x* Records at a Time radio button and leave it set to the default (10).

6. Browse to the view_a_gig page by clicking the Browse button next to the Detail Page Name field.

7. At Detail Page Fields, click the up and down arrows to reorder the fields in a logical order for display on the page.

8. Click the OK button, and the object will be inserted into this page. In addition, the Detail page will be updated with a table containing all of the fields that were specified.

Caution *If your Preferences are set to have one window open at a time, UltraDev will prompt you to save the page after applying this object. You should click Yes, as the page has to be closed in order for UltraDev to open up the Detail page and insert the recordset and table into that page.*

If you look at Figure 18-20, you'll see that UltraDev has inserted about 16 different Server Behaviors just on the Master page. First, a table is inserted containing column headings and the database columns that were specified. Next, a Repeat Region Server Behavior is applied to the table row containing the dynamic data. Then another Live Object is inserted—the Recordset Navigation Bar. This object holds eight different Server Behaviors by itself, showing First, Previous, Next, and Last links to allow the user to browse through the records. Last, another Live Object is inserted as part of the package—the Recordset Navigation Status display, which shows the typical First to Last of Total Records display.

Tip *When you use a Live Object, you aren't just inserting a bunch of code. The object is actually inserting specific Server Behaviors that can later be edited, changed, or removed from the page. In the case of the Master page, there are 16 separate Server Behaviors that can later be manipulated.*

One last thing to do is to add a <<<back link to the view_a_gig page in the same way that you did on the failed_new_user page. Put the text **<<<back** on the page and set a link equal to the following JavaScript:

```
JavaScript:history.go(-1)
```

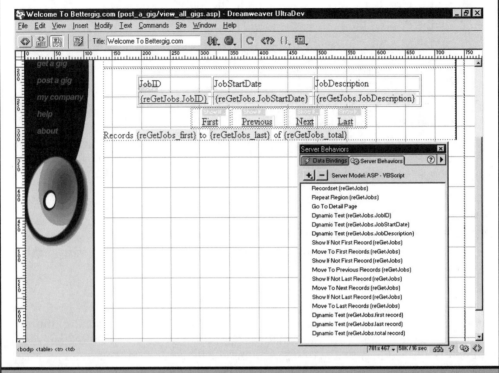

Figure 18-20. *The Master page after inserting the Master-Detail Live Object*

The Repeat Region Server Behavior

You've been dealing with some of the great new features of UltraDev 4 that allow the use of Live Objects, which automate the process of creating data-driven pages. Users of UltraDev1 have become accustomed to using the Repeat Region Server Behavior. This behavior was inserted into the Master page using the Insert Master-Detail Page Set object. It's important to be able to use the Repeat Region in many situations by itself, so we'll go over some of its uses.

When you select dynamic data on the page and apply a Repeat Region, the behavior inserts server-side looping code around your selection. In addition, there are built-in variables that keep track of your loop so that you can show your data in blocks of 5, 10, 20, or whatever value you choose. The key to using the behavior is knowing what is going on beneath the surface.

Repeating HTML Code

When the server reads the page, it will execute code that is within the server tags. In the case of ASP and JSP, these are the <% open tags and %> close tags. For ColdFusion, anything that begins with <CF is a valid ColdFusion tag that will be translated by the server.

A loop can take many forms; but in most cases, it is a for/next loop, a do/while loop, or a while/wend loop. Each language has its own syntax, but the functionality is similar. ColdFusion has looping built into several of its tags, which makes writing a ColdFusion loop much easier than a similar ASP or JSP loop. If the server encounters a loop, whatever is between the loop is repeated for as many times as the loop iterates. For example, the following pseudo-code will display a table with three rows:

```
<table>
<% For I = 1 to 3 %>
    <tr>
        <td>Loop number <% = I %></td>
    </tr>
<% Next %>
</table>
```

When the server code executes, the following table will be output to the browser:

```
<table>
    <tr>
        <td>Loop number 1</td>
    </tr>
    <tr>
        <td>Loop number 2</td>
    </tr>
    <tr>
        <td>Loop number 3</td>
    </tr>
</table>
```

Not only is the code within the loop repeated, but the variable that contains the loop index is also output to the browser. This opens up many possibilities, and the Repeat Region Server Behavior simplifies many of these operations.

Repeat Region on a Table

The most often used Repeat Region is a dynamic table. We'll create an Administrator page in the admin folder named all_seekers and apply the behavior to the page. The steps to apply the Server Behavior to a table are as follows:

1. Create a recordset that returns more than one row of data. For this example, create a recordset named rsSeekers using the following SQL:

   ```
   SELECT SeekFirstName, SeekLastName, SeekEmail FROM Seekers
   ```

2. Insert a table on your page. The table can have one row and as many columns as you have dynamic data to display. Alternatively, you can insert a two-row table and make the first row the column headings. In this example, we'll apply a two-row, three-column table to the page.

3. Drag and drop or insert the dynamic text, text fields, images, checkboxes, or whatever other item you might want repeated into the table cells. For this example, insert the columns SeekFirstName, SeekLastName, and SeekEmail into the second row of the table.

4. Select the table row containing the dynamic data and apply the Repeat Region Server Behavior to the row. The behavior will allow you to specify the number of rows you want repeated or All Records. Choose All Records for this example.

5. The first row will contain the column headings, so you can type in the text for First, Last, and Email in the table cells and give this text a Bold style.

6. You can turn the email address into a hyperlink by applying a link to the rsSeekers.email placeholder. Simply right-click (CTRL-click on the Macintosh) and choose Make Link. Select Filename From should be set to Datasources by clicking the appropriate radio button. Choose the SeekEmail field from the menu. Lastly, type the text **mailto:** in front of the dynamic data and click OK.

The page in the design environment should look like Figure 18-21. If you browse the page at this point, you'll have a list of all job seekers in the Seekers table.

Repeat Region in a Dynamic List

Repeat Regions can be applied to more than just tables. For example, you can place some dynamic text on the page, insert a <br> tag next to it, and apply the Repeat Region Server Behavior to the dynamic text. When you browse it, it will show up as if you typed the data one per line. In other words, the <br> tag is repeated along with the dynamic text.

This technique can also be used with a dynamic list. Lists can be bullets (unordered lists) or numbers (ordered lists), or they can have a graphic as a bullet. Whichever one you choose, you can do it dynamically with a Repeat Region. We'll create another

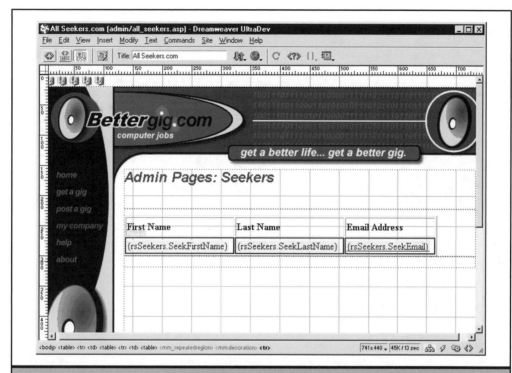

Figure 18-21. *The all_seekers page in the UltraDev design environment after applying a Repeat Region to the table row*

Administrator page in the admin folder named all_companies and apply a Repeat Region to a list. The steps are as follows:

1. Create a recordset named rsEmployers from the Employers table and use the following SQL statement:

```
SELECT EmpName, EmpPhone FROM Employers
```

2. Place some dummy text on the page (to be replaced later).

3. Apply a list to the text by right-clicking (CTRL-click on the Macintosh) on the selected text and choosing List | Unordered List.

4. Drag the EmpName column onto the selected text. It will replace the text.

5. Add a space and then insert the EmpPhone dynamic text right next to it.

6. SHIFT-select both placeholders of the dynamic text and apply a Repeat Region Server Behavior to the page, choosing All Records.

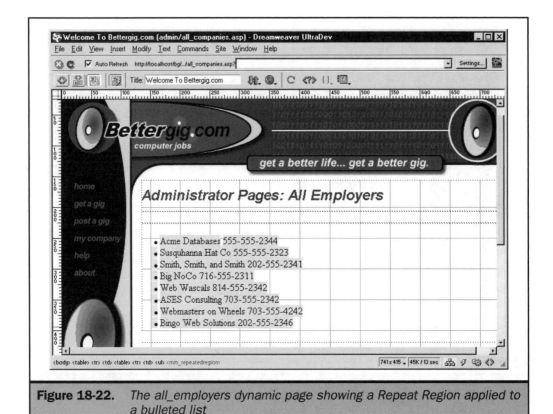

Figure 18-22.   *The all_employers dynamic page showing a Repeat Region applied to a bulleted list*

Figure 18-22 shows the page with Live Data turned on. You can see that the bullets appear in front of each row from the database. If you look at the underlying code, you'll see that the code is broken down like this (pseudo-code):

```
<ul>
<% loop code %>
<li><% recordset columns %></li>
<% end loop code %>
</ul>
```

Just like the dynamic table, the Repeat Region wraps a loop around the line items of the unordered list, allowing you to create a dynamic list. If you had chosen Ordered List from the menu, the bullets would have been replaced by numbers from 1 to however many items are returned from the database.

Repeating a Show/Hide Layer Using Repeat Region

One of the great ways to use a looping construct in a page that's executed on the server is to give unique names to HTML elements. This is done by using the index number of the loop or, in the case of ColdFusion, the internal CurrentRow variable and appending the counter to the end of the HTML element name, like this:

```
<input type="text" name="txtTitle<%=Repeat1__index%>">(ASP or JSP)
<input type="text" name="txtTitle#Recordset.CurrentRow#">(CF)
```

If this code were with a Repeat Region loop, the code that is output would look like this:

```
<input type="text" name="txtTitle1">
<input type="text" name="txtTitle2">
<input type="text" name="txtTitle3">
etc.
```

Obviously, this technique has many uses. One advanced use of it is to name a layer on the page with a dynamic name such as this, and then use the Show/Hide Layers standard UltraDev behavior to allow the generation of a custom layer for each element in the loop. This can be done by hand-coding, but it can also be accomplished with a little ingenuity using the graphical design elements of UltraDev.

Open up the all_jobs file in the admin folder and create a recordset named rsJobs. The SQL statement for the recordset will look like this:

```
SELECT Employers.EmpName, Jobs.JobDescription, Jobs.JobEducation,
       Jobs.JobLocation, Jobs.JobSalary, Jobs.JobStartDate, Jobs.JobID
       FROM Employers
INNER JOIN (Categories
    INNER JOIN Jobs on Categories.CatID = Jobs.JobCategory)
ON Employers.EmpID = Jobs.EmpID
```

This SQL statement will return a list of all jobs with a few selected fields from the table, as well as the Employer name from the Employers table. We'll use the image details.gif for the mouseover to show/hide the layer on the page. The page will display a list of all jobs in "short" form (as in a Master page), and the layer that is being shown/ hidden will contain the information for the individual jobs (as in a Details page). Additionally, a Go To Details Page Server Behavior will be added as well.

 The method shown involves the nesting of Layers, which may not work in some versions of Netscape.

The technique used to get the dynamic show/hide layers to work properly requires careful attention to the correct order of steps:

1. Go to Modify | Convert | Tables to Layers. This will change all tables on the page to layers using <div> tags. This is necessary because you shouldn't have a layer defined inside a table. (The page will have to be detached from the template first.)

2. Insert a new layer on the page by clicking Insert | Layer, and then drag the new layer to a place on the page in the content region. The layer should be sized so that it takes up the left half of the area (see Figure 18-23).

3. Insert a table that's 1 row and 3 columns into the layer at 300 pixels wide with no border. Inside this table you can type in the text for the column heads—**Company Name** and **Location**. These should also be set to Bold text style. The third column can be left blank; it's there for alignment purposes only.

4. Below that table, but inside the same layer, insert another table that is 1 row and 3 columns and set to 90% width with no border.

5. Inside this table, in cell 1 insert the EmpName column, and in cell 2 insert the JobLocation column. In cell 3 insert the image details.gif.

6. Click the mouse anywhere inside the layer and insert another layer. Drag the new layer to the right of the first layer so that the two layers are approximately

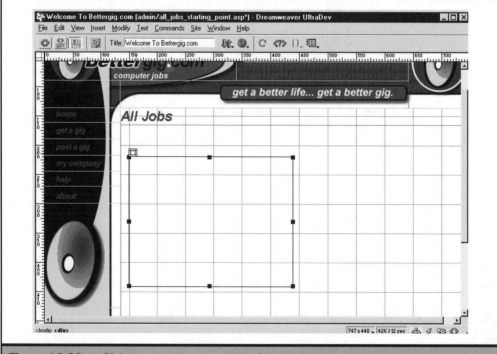

Figure 18-23. *Sizing a new layer on the left half of the content area of the page*

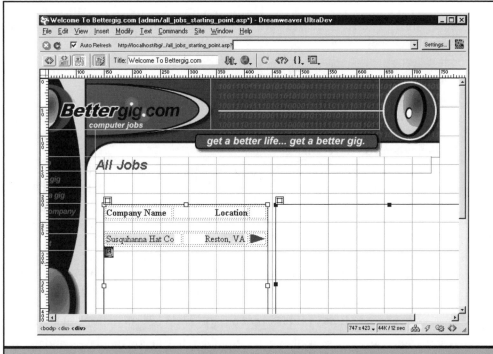

Figure 18-24.   *The all_jobs page through step 6 contains 2 layers next to each other*

the same size (the page up until this point is shown in Figure 18-24). If you look at the code, the <div> tag has been created as a child tag of the first layer that you inserted.

7. SHIFT-select the entire second table (the table with the dynamic data in it) and the new layer tag together. The layer tag should be directly next to or below the table.

8. Apply a Repeat Region to the selected area showing 10 records.

9. Click inside the second layer that's on the right half of the page and insert a table that is two columns and six rows with no border, at 300 pixels wide.

10. Drag the EmpName, JobLocation, JobSalary, JobEducation, JobStartDate, and JobDescription fields to the table cells of column 2 of the table inside the second layer, and place appropriate descriptive labels in column 1 that correspond to the fields.

11. Select the layer once again, and right-click (CTRL-click on the Macintosh) and choose Edit Tag | <div>. Here is where you are going to give the layer a dynamic name.

BUILDING
LANGUAGE-SPECIFIC
DATA-DRIVEN SITES

12. As you open it, the layer id should be highlighted. Change the id attribute to match the code that follows (inside the quotation marks with no spaces) so that it appears like this (see in Figure 18-25):

```
id="LayerDyn<%=Repeat1__index%>" (ASP and JSP)
id="LayerDyn#rsJobs.CurrentRow#" (ColdFusion)
```

13. Open the Properties Inspector for the layer and change its visibility (vis) to hidden. This will cause it to disappear in the design environment. If you need to tweak the positioning later, you can set it back to default and then set it to hidden when you have finished editing.

14. Select the Details.gif image and apply a Show-Hide Layers behavior to it, located in the Behaviors palette. Select the new dynamic layer from the list of layers (it should appear under one of the other layers, as it was created "inside" of that layer). Click the Show button, click OK, and then set the event to onMouseOver in the Behaviors palette.

15. Select the image once again and apply another Show-Hide Layer behavior to it. Select the dynamic layer from the list of layers, click the Hide button this time, click OK, and then set the event of the behavior to the onMouseOut event. The only two events that should be in the palette for the image are onMouseOver and onMouseOut. If any others pop up (as they do occasionally) delete them.

16. Insert a small layer directly above the left table, click inside that layer, and apply the Recordset Navigation Bar Live Object. This object will insert First, Previous, Next, and Last links to the page, allowing you to browse the recordset.

17. Apply a Go To Details Page Server Behavior to the image (details.gif). For the Details page attribute, browse to the view_a_gig page and use the JobID column as the URL parameter.

Tip   *You can also set the background color of the layer, making for a truly dynamic page. By clicking the bgcolor icon in the Property Inspector of the layer, you can use the Color Picker eyedropper to pick a color on your page to apply to the layer. It should be noted for ColdFusion users that whenever you insert a color into a dynamic area of the page, you have to manually edit the code to insert an extra # sign (such as ##009999).*

```
Edit Tag: <div id="LayerDyn<%=Repeat1__index%>"
" style="position:absolute;
width:407px; height:277px; z-index:1;
left: 307px; top: 0px">
```

Figure 18-25.   *The Quick Tag Editor makes it easy to add dynamic attributes to the tags*

If you've followed all of these steps, the page should look something like Figure 18-26. You should now be able to browse the page and mouse over the images in the table to show the details of the jobs. This technique is based on a technique from the award-winning Massimo Foti, whose Dreamweaver extensions have opened up new possibilities for Web designers.

 Caution *The method of applying dynamic layers will sometimes cause UltraDev to crash if you try to move the layer after it has been defined as dynamic. This is a known bug that still exists as of the publication date of this book. For best results, position the layer before applying the dynamic ID attribute.*

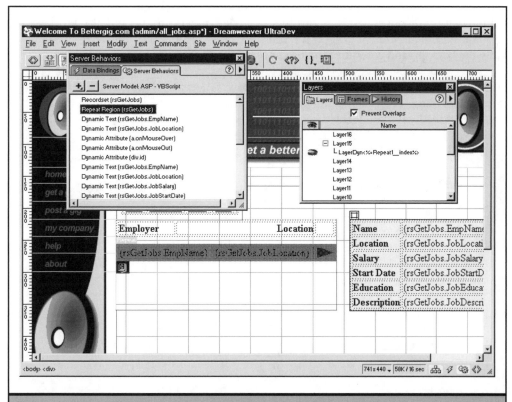

Figure 18-26. *The finished page with dynamic layers*

Alternating Colors in a Repeat Region

One of the most frequently used techniques for a dynamic table is to alternate the colors of the table rows. There's nothing built into UltraDev to take care of this for you; but by doing a little bit of hand-coding, you can accomplish this fairly easily.

As we saw in the Show/Hide example, the index variable can be manipulated to achieve dynamic effects. In that example, you appended the number to a layer name to give each layer a different name. To get the effect of an alternate colored table, you have only two choices. The effect is easy to implement with the Modulus math function, which gives the remainder of an integer division. For example, 3 MOD 2 = 1, because the remainder of 3, divided by 2, is 1. In fact, the modulus of any integer divided by 2 is going to be either 1 or 0, so you can set up a simple if statement to test for the value and set the colors accordingly.

The first step is to make sure that you have two different CSS classes previously defined. You can define new styles by right-clicking (CTRL-clicking on the Macintosh) on the page and choosing CSS Styles > New Style. This technique will also work with the BGCOLOR attribute if you prefer, but the Class attribute will allow you to set not only the background color, but the typeface and style as well.

After your Repeat Region is applied to the page, you can open up the Code view and navigate to the <tr> tag of the repeating row. Alternatively, you can edit the tag by right-clicking (or CTRL-clicking on the Macintosh) the correct <tr> tag in the tag selector in the lower left of the design page. Then you can edit the tag directly. The code is as follows, for all four different languages:

```
VBScript
<tr class = <%If (Repeat1__index MOD 2) Then%>
    "yourclass1"
<%Else%>
    "yourclass2"
<%End If%>>

JavaScript or Java
<tr class = <%if(Repeat1__index % 2 == 1) { %>
    "yourclass1"
<%else%>
    "yourclass2"
<%}%>>

ColdFusion
<tr class = ¬
    ##IIF(CurrentRow MOD 2, DE("yourclass1"),DE("yourclass2#))#">
```

Notice that the ending tag for the <tr> tag is after the server markup tags in the ASP and JSP implementations. Two closing >> tags in a row might look wrong, but the server tags will be stripped out by the server, including all server-side code, leaving just the class name and the closing tag. After the page is browsed, the code will look something like this:

```
<tr class = "yourclass1">
   <td>stuff</td>
</tr>
<tr class = "yourclass2">
   <td>more stuff</td>
</tr>
<tr class = "yourclass1">
   <td>stuff</td>
</tr>
etc.
```

If you apply this code to the table and Repeat Region on the view_all_gigs page, the result will look like Figure 18-27. This technique can be applied in all sorts of different ways. If you desire a checkerboard effect, for example, you can apply a similar technique to a <td> tag instead, using your own counter-variable.

Adding More Administrator Pages

As we've pointed out previously, the new Live Objects that automate the process of developing certain types of dynamic pages is one of the nicest features of UltraDev. You can use this to your advantage while designing your site by creating temporary or Administrator pages for viewing, inserting, and updating your test data. These pages can be as simple or as complex as you desire, but their main purpose is to allow you to have access to the database on the server in a visual environment so that you can look at and manipulate the data.

For example, to have access to the Seekers table on the server, you can open up a new page under the admin folder named update_seekers. On this page, create a recordset named rsSeekers and write a basic Select All statement like this:

```
SELECT * FROM Seekers
```

This statement is the simplest of SQL statements and will return all of the columns in the database. After creating the recordset, position your cursor in the middle of the content area where you want the Update table to be inserted, and click Insert | Live

BUILDING LANGUAGE-SPECIFIC DATA-DRIVEN SITES

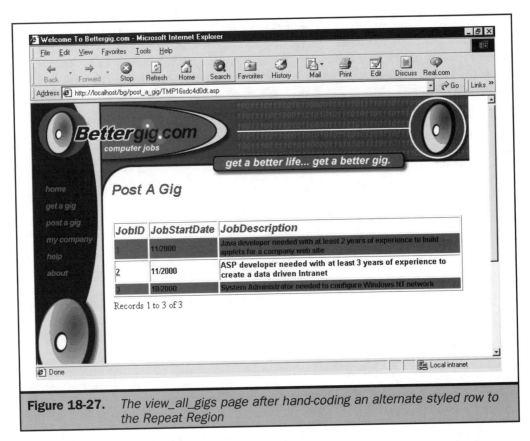

Figure 18-27.   *The view_all_gigs page after hand-coding an alternate styled row to the Repeat Region*

Objects | Record Update Form. The only modification you have to make to the form is to remove the SeekID field from the form. This is to prevent database errors, as the SeekID is the Autonumber field that gets written automatically by the database. Make sure this field is chosen as the key column in the form.

Since the primary purpose of a page like this is to be able to view your database and make updates to it, you can leave all of the default labels in place—these are the actual column names that will make it easier to keep track of things.

After applying the object, you have to apply two more objects: Record Navigation Status and Record Navigation Bar. The Record Navigation Status object will insert the recordset information listing the first record displayed, the last record displayed, and the total records in the recordset. The display will show something like this:

Records 1 to 5 of 50

In the case of an update form, there is only one current record showing at any one time, so the first and last records in the status display will be the same, like this:

Records 1 to 1 of 50

Luckily, this text is editable, as are most objects in UltraDev, so you can change the text to look like this:

Record 1 of 50

The Recordset Navigation Bar can insert either text or images. The text that it will insert, as we've seen when it was automatically inserted along with the Master-Detail Live Object, is this:

First Previous Next Last

If you choose to use images, they will be little arrow icons and will automatically be copied by UltraDev into the folder that the page resides in. These are also completely editable and can be changed for images of your choice.

The finished page, which took about five minutes to put together, looks like Figure 18-28. You can create a page like this for each one of your database tables, if you like. When you are accessing data on a remote server, it is frequently hard to get

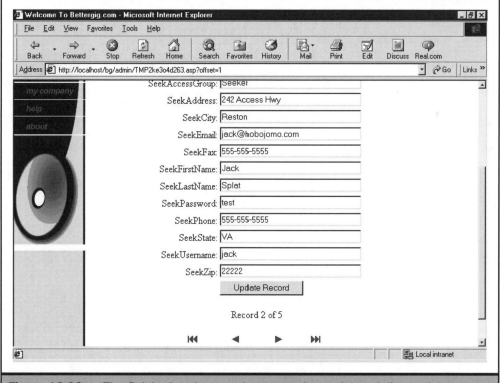

Figure 18-28.   *The finished update_seekers page is a quick-and-dirty update page for the Seekers table in the Bettergig database*

a birds-eye view of the data; but this technique is easily applied and gives you total control over your test data. Later, the pages can be turned into Admin pages with special access levels to allow the system administrator to tweak the data easily.

Summary

UltraDev offers a rich assortment of dynamic features that make creating data driven Web applications easy. UltraDev 4 has added Live Objects to the mix, which speeds up the process of development considerably. Also, the standard Server Behaviors, such as Repeat Region, offer versatile functionality that goes beyond the surface. You're only limited by your imagination, as we showed with the dynamic Show-Hide Layer functionality. In the next chapter, we'll be getting into some more complex database and server features to add more functionality to the Bettergig site.

Chapter 19

Advanced Database Features Using UltraDev

A database exists for the purpose of storing data in some defined manner so that it can be accessed and presented in a meaningful or useful way. The key to a successful database is the organization of the tables within that database. The key to a successful data-driven Web site is being able to retrieve the information that you need from a well-organized database. Furthermore, the key to programming a data-driven site is being able to write the SQL statements needed to retrieve the desired information. SQL is the language that you'll need to use and become proficient in if you want to build a more advanced site, whether you are working in ASP, JSP, or ColdFusion.

In Chapter 18, we examined some of the ways to include dynamic content in a Web site using UltraDev's built-in Live Objects and Server Behaviors. In this chapter, we'll continue to build upon the Bettergig.com site by adding some of the more advanced features of a data-driven site, beginning with a search page.

Search Pages

The ability to search a database for specific information is one of the most popular features of a data-driven site. Search engines such as Yahoo, Google, or Hotbot all use databases that are searchable by using highly optimized search algorithms and indexed tables. While your Web site probably won't require the industrial-strength engines of these search sites, a search page will likely be a desirable addition to your site.

A Basic Search Page

Searching the database can be simple or complex. The simplest search to perform on a database is to find a match for a piece of data in one field of the database. To perform a search like this, the SQL statement needs to retrieve only those rows in which the field contains the search criteria.

The Job Search

A job seeker will either be posting a resume to the site or looking for a job that's been posted. To search for a job, the job seeker will have to search the job description for a keyword and be able to view the jobs that match that keyword. Later, we'll add the ability to search more than one field or more than one keyword.

Open the get_a_gig page in the site. Start the page by inserting a form with a form field and a Submit button within that form. This page will accept a word and then display the results of the search, also allowing for another search by having the form field on the page available for a new search. The text field should be named **searchfield**, and the action of the form should be set to this page (get_a_gig).

Next, you'll need to create the recordset that retrieves the form field and queries the database for a match. Create a new recordset, name it **rsGetAGig**, and write the SQL using the JobDescription field of the Jobs table:

```
SELECT JobDescription, JobID from Jobs WHERE JobDescription LIKE
'%txtSearchfield%'
```

> **Note**   *The Select statement used in a typical search operation uses the Like keyword with wildcard characters. This allows for keyword searches within a database field. The standard wildcard character for "anything" is %. If you put this character before and after your keyword variable, the text contained in the variable can be matched anywhere in the field.*

You'll have to set up a variable in the recordset dialog box, as shown in Table 19-1.

After defining the variable, the SQL statement should be ready to test. With the "dummy" data in the Default Value column, the SQL statement won't return any rows. This is because there is no match in the database within the JobDescription field. As discussed in the last chapter, the Default Value is one of the safeguards that UltraDev adds to the code: it exists to help prevent database errors from occurring if the expected incoming variables are null.

Adding the Data and Repeat Region

After defining your SQL statement, the next step is to put the database fields on the page. This time, the process will be manual using a table and a Repeat Region. Insert a two-row, two-column table on the page and label the cells in the first row **Job ID** and **Description**. In the second row, you are going to insert the corresponding database columns, which are rsGetAGig.JobID and rsGetAGig.JobDescription.

Next, select the table row by using the tag selector in the lower-left corner of the design window or by CTRL-clicking (COMMAND-click on the Macintosh) the two table cells. Next, apply a Repeat Region to the area showing all records. Finally, select the entire table and apply a Show Region If Recordset Is Not Empty Server behavior to the area. This will allow the table to be shown *only* if there are search results.

Server Model	Name	Default Value	Run-Time Value
ASP	txtSearchField	xyz	Request("searchfield")
JSP	txtSearchField	xyz	request.getParameter("searchfield")
ColdFusion	txtSearchField	xyz	#searchfield#

Table 19-1.   *Variables Defined for the rsGetAGig Recordset for the Search Field*

If you save the page and try it out, it should show only the search field and button. If you enter a word that is contained in the description of one of the jobs, the table will be displayed with the ID number and the description for each matching record. But if no matches are found, only the search field will be displayed again. It's also a good idea to include alternate text in the event of an empty search.

Inserting Alternate Text

While there are several ways of doing this—most of which would involve some hand-coding—you can once again include alternate text with UltraDev's built-in Server behaviors. The opposite of the Show Region If Recordset Is Not Empty is the Show Region If Recordset Is Empty Server behavior. The steps are as follows:

1. Type the text **No Matching Records** next to or beneath the table that you inserted.

2. Select the text.

3. Apply the Show Region If Recordset Is Empty Server Behavior.

The page should now look like the page in Figure 19-1. Now, when you browse the page, your text will be visible if there are no records; and if there are records, your table with the results of the search will be visible.

Figure 19-1. *The basic search page includes alternate text for an empty search*

Adding a Link to the Detail Page

The search page as it stands will show the summary of all matches of your search, but the page only shows the job description. To view all information for an item returned from the search, you'll have to link to a Detail page. If you recall from Chapter 18, a Master-Detail page set was built automatically with the Insert Master-Detail Page Set Live Object. You can re-use the view_a_gig page by simply linking to it with the appropriate variable, which in this case is the JobID.

There is a built-in UltraDev Server Behavior (once again) that makes the whole process easy. Simply select the JobID field in the design environment and choose the Go to Detail Page Server Behavior (shown in Figure 19-2).

The required parameters for the behavior are as follows:

- **Link**   This should be filled out automatically to reflect the selected recordset column on the page.

- **Detail Page**   Browse to the view_a_gig page in the post_a_gig folder by clicking the Browse button. This will ensure that the proper relative path to the page is used.

- **Pass URL Parameter**   This should be set to the JobID field of the recordset.

- **Recordset**   This will be the rsGetAGig recordset.

- **Column**   Once again, this should be set to the JobID field.

- **Pass Existing Parameters**   These can be left blank for now.

After clicking OK and saving the file, you can browse the page to search for a job, click the link, and be taken to a Detail page listing all the information about that job.

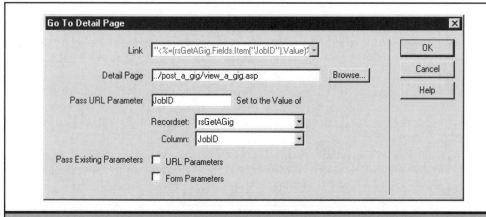

Figure 19-2.   *The Go to Detail Page Server Behavior makes quick work of linking to a Detail page*

Adding Advanced Search Features

Now that the basic search page is working, it's time to add some more advanced search features to the page. A job seeker may want to enter keywords that might be within one of several fields in the database. Rather than have a different form field for each database field, it's possible to include them all in one search.

Combining Fields

While there are certainly many ways to combine your database fields for a search, one of the easiest involves concatenating the fields at the database level. This technique will work in all databases, so those without the benefit of stored procedures will be able to use this technique.

Create a view in your database named getSearchField. If you are using Microsoft Access, *Queries* is the term that is used for Access views, but the functionality is similar. The view can be accessed from the recordset dialog box in UltraDev just as a table can. Use the following SQL in the view:

```
SELECT Categories.CatDesc+' '+
    SubCategories.SubCatDesc+' '+
    Jobs.JobLocation+' '+
    Jobs.JobEducation+' '+
    Jobs.JobDescription
AS SearchField, Jobs.JobID, Employers.EmpName, Categories.CatDesc
FROM SubCategories
INNER JOIN (Employers
    INNER JOIN (Categories
        INNER JOIN Jobs ON Categories.CatID = Jobs.JobCategory)
    ON Employers.EmpID = Jobs.EmpID)
ON SubCategories.SubCatID = Jobs.JobSubCategory
```

The SQL looks complicated, but all it will do is get the fields from the Jobs table that you'll want to search—JobLocation, JobDescription—as well as the related fields from related tables like JobCategory, JobSubCategory, and EmpName. These fields are retrieved through the Inner joins to the related tables based on the foreign keys that are stored in the Jobs table. The query can be written by hand or created with a visual query builder interface in your DBMS. The Microsoft SQL Server view building interface is shown in Figure 19-3.

The visual tools will only take you so far, however, and a little hand-coding of your SQL will yield you a little more flexibility. In this case, you'll want to concatenate the fields into one big field named SearchField. You can also insert a space between each field, although this isn't absolutely necessary with this type of search.

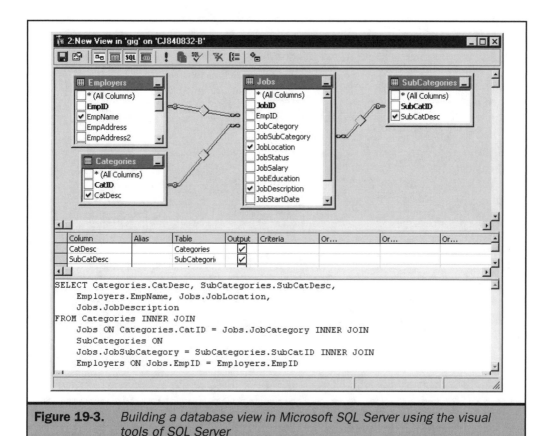

Figure 19-3.   *Building a database view in Microsoft SQL Server using the visual tools of SQL Server*

The fields are concatenated with the plus (+) sign, but your own database may have a different method. The result is that all relevant fields are tacked together, and a few other necessary fields are also retrieved: Jobs.JobID, Employers.EmpName, and Categories. CatDesc. We'll use these in the HTML table that shows the search results.

Modifying the Original Search Page

After creating and saving the view, move back to the get_a_gig page and open up the recordset rsGetAGig. You'll need to change the SQL statement to retrieve data from the new view instead of from the Jobs table. You should be in the Advanced Recordset dialog box and choose the getSearchField view from the Views Database Item at the bottom of the box (see Figure 19-4). The variable declaration will remain the same, but the SQL statement needs to be changed.

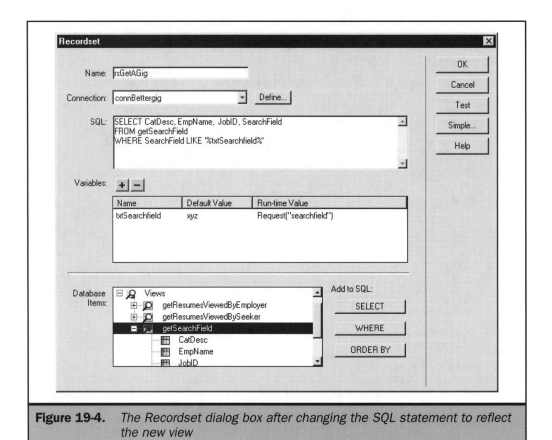

Figure 19-4.   *The Recordset dialog box after changing the SQL statement to reflect the new view*

The SQL should be written as follows:

```
SELECT CatDesc, EmpName, JobID, SearchField
FROM getSearchField
WHERE SearchField LIKE '%txtSearchField%'
```

As you can see, only the table name and the column names changed. The Where clause remains the same.

Modifying recordsets is often a much easier process than creating one from scratch, particularly if the SQL statement is complex. Also, remember that recordsets can be copied from one page to another by right-clicking (CTRL-clicking on the Macintosh) the recordset in the Data Bindings palette, choosing Copy, opening up another page, and choosing Paste.

Notice that you now have four fields in the recordset and that the JobDescription field no longer exists. You'll have to modify the page slightly to accommodate the new fields, but there is a simple method of doing this that will help speed up the process. The steps are as follows:

1. Select the table that the Repeat Region has been applied to.

2. Open the Property Inspector for that table.

3. Change the Cols field from 2 to 3. This will add a blank column to the table. Notice that this new column is also within the Repeat Region.

4. Add a heading to the newly created third column, **Employer Name**.

5. Drop the EmpName column into the empty cell beneath the heading.

6. Select the rsGetAGig.JobDescription in the second column and delete it.

7. Move to the Data Bindings palette and click the CatDesc field.

8. Click the Insert button on the Data Bindings palette to insert this field into the newly vacated empty cell in the second column of the table.

By making these few simple modifications to the page, you now have a more sophisticated search page that actually searches five separate fields for the keyword and returns the JobID, employer name, and category description from the database for the matched records. Also, the Go to Detail behavior still works, since you are using the same JobID field.

As you can see, modifications to existing pages are easily accomplished with UltraDev and can be huge timesavers after you get the hang of it. It's not always necessary to start from scratch when you want to create a new page.

Adding Multiple Search Words

Sophisticated search engines allow you to enter many different combinations of search criteria. While it's beyond the scope of this book to go into detail about the different methods, you should be aware of what you might need and possible approaches to the problem.

Obviously, the most basic requirement is to allow for multiple words in the search. It is impossible to predict how the user will enter the data, however. You can specify the requirements on the page, such as "Enter your search words separated by commas—phrases can be enclosed in quotes." As you can imagine, these two simple requirements can drastically increase the complexity of the code contained in the page.

There are basically two ways to approach the problem:

- Add server-side code to the page to handle the different situations.
- Build a stored procedure within the database to handle the tasks.

Using Server-Side Code

Hand-coding requires a knowledge of the server language that you are working with. The task of creating a dynamic SQL query is fairly straightforward, but it requires string manipulation and knowledge of SQL as well. Also, UltraDev has strict rules governing its recordsets; and if you change the way that the SQL is created by adding server-side conditonal logic into the SQL, the recordset will cease to work in the Data Bindings palette. As long as you already have your recordset columns on the page where you want them, this isn't a problem.

What you'll have to do is remove the Where clause from the SQL statement while you are in Code view on the page, not from the recordset dialog box. The remaining SQL statement will then look like this:

```
SELECT CatDesc, EmpName, JobID, SearchField
FROM getSearchField
```

The next thing to do is to add a block of code to the page to parse the text field into three possible situations:

- One word or a group of words is entered.
- A group of words is entered inside of quotes.
- A group of words is entered separated by commas.

The first option will use the standard Where clause that was previously created. The second option will require the quotes to be stripped off before using the standard Where clause that was previously created. The third option requires that the words be separated. For instance, if the job seeker enters the words **web,asp,vbscript**, the words need to be added to the Where clause like this:

```
WHERE SearchField LIKE '%asp%' AND SearchField LIKE '%web%' AND
SearchField LIKE '%vbscript%'
```

The difficulty lies in the fact that there is no way of knowing how many words will be entered. You can write a short script to take care of the three situations. This pseudo-code illustrates the functionality that the script will accomplish:

```
Define SQLstr to hold the 'where' clause of the SQL statement
myField holds the incoming form field data
IF myField has quotes
     remove the quotes
     Build SQLstr as the Where clause using the
       phrase that had quotes around it
ELSE IF myField has commas
     separate the parts of myField
```

```
       construct a Where clause to allow for all of the substrings
          in myField
ELSE
       use myField as it stands and construct the Where clause
END OF IF STATEMENTS
Execute the SQL adding the Where clause to it
```

Following is the code for all four languages that should be inserted right before the recordset is created:

VBScript version

```
Dim SQLstr
Dim myField
myField = rsGetAGig__txtSearchField
If instr(myField,chr(34)) Then
   myField= Replace(myField,chr(34),"")
SQLstr = " WHERE SearchField LIKE '%"
SQLstr = SQLstr + replace(myField, "'", "''") + "%'"
ElseIf instr(myField,",") Then
    Dim splitField
    SQLstr = " WHERE"
    splitField = split(myField,",")
    for i = 0 to ubound(splitField)
        SQLstr = SQLstr & " SearchField LIKE '%"
        SQLstr = SQLstr & replace(splitField(i), "'", "''") & "%'"
        if i < ubound(splitField) Then SQLstr = SQLstr & " AND "
        Next
Else
    SQLstr = " WHERE SearchField LIKE '%"
    SQLstr = SQLstr & Replace(myField, "'", "''") & "%'"
End if
%>
```

JavaScript version

```
var SQLstr;
var myField = rsGetAGig__txtSearchField;
if (myField.indexOf('"')!= -1) {
   myField= myField.replace(/"/g,'');
   SQLstr = " WHERE SearchField LIKE '%"
   SQLstr = SQLstr + myField.replace(/'/g, "''") + "%'"
}else if (myField.indexOf(',')!= -1) {
   var splitField = myField.split(",");
   SQLstr = " WHERE";
   for (var i = 0; i < splitField.length;i++){
```

```
        SQLstr = SQLstr + " SearchField LIKE '%";
        SQLstr = SQLstr + splitField[i].replace(/'/g, "''") + "%'";
        if (i < splitField.length-1) SQLstr = SQLstr + " AND ";
    }
}else{
    SQLstr = " WHERE SearchField LIKE '%"
    SQLstr = SQLstr + myField.replace(/'/g, "''") + "%'"
}
%>
```

ColdFusion Version

```
<cfset myField = rsGetAGig__txtSearchField>
<cfif (find("'",myField))>
  <cfset myField= Replace(myField,"'","","all")>
  <cfset SQLstr = " WHERE SearchField LIKE '%#myField#%'">
<cfelseif (find(',',myField))>
  <cfset SQLstr = " WHERE">
  <CFLOOP INDEX="splitField" LIST="#myField#">
    <cfset SQLstr = SQLstr & " SearchField LIKE '%">
    <cfset SQLstr = SQLstr & splitField & "%'">
    <cfif splitField NEQ ListLast(myField)>
      <cfset SQLstr = SQLstr & " AND ">
    </cfif>
  </CFLOOP>
<cfelse>
  <cfset SQLstr = " WHERE SearchField LIKE '%#myfield#%'">
</cfif>
```

Java version

```
String SQLstr;
String myField = rsGetAGig__txtSearchField;
if(myField.indexOf("'")!= -1) {
   myField = myField.replace("'",' ').trim();//space inserted
   //and then removed because the replace method doesn't work
   //with null values
   SQLstr = " WHERE SearchField LIKE '%";
   SQLstr = SQLstr + myField + "%'";
}else if (myField.indexOf(',') != -1){
   SQLstr = " WHERE ";
   java.util.StringTokenizer tokens = new
      java.util.StringTokenizer(myField,",");//one line!
   String[] splitField = new String[tokens.countTokens()];
   for (int i=0; tokens.hasMoreTokens(); i++) {
```

```
        splitField[i] = tokens.nextToken();
        SQLstr = SQLstr + " SearchField LIKE '%";
        SQLstr = SQLstr + splitField[i] + "%'";
        if(tokens.hasMoreTokens()) SQLstr = SQLstr + " AND ";
        }
}else{
    SQLstr = " WHERE SearchField LIKE '%";
    SQLstr = SQLstr + myField + "%'";
}
%>
```

After inserting the script, you also have to change the UltraDev-generated SQL statement to reflect the change. What you are going to be doing is removing the Where clause from the UltraDev SQL and inserting the SQLstr to take its place. Your new SQL should look like this for ASP and JSP:

```
"SELECT SearchField, JobID, EmpName, CatDesc FROM getSearchField"¬
+ SQLstr
```

ColdFusion users can insert the variable directly into the SQL, like this:

```
"SELECT SearchField, JobID, EmpName, CatDesc FROM ¬
getSearchField #PreserveSingleQuotes(SQLstr)#"
```

> **Tip**
> *When hand-coding, it's a good idea to get all of your Server Behavior and Data Bindings work out of the way first. Also, if you need the Data Bindings functionality again, you can do this simply by removing the SQLstr variable from the end of the SQL statement. All of the UltraDev functionality will return when the SQL is recognizable to the program once again.*

You'll notice that after you add the variable to the SQL statement, the recordset no longer shows up inside the Data Bindings Inspector, and you'll see red checkmarks next to several items in the Server Behaviors palette. This is normal and merely indicates that UltraDev no longer recognizes the items as the items that it generated. When you begin hand-coding, the Data Bindings palette and Server Behaviors palette can be closed they are useless at this point.

> **Tip**
> *If you attempt to edit a Server Behavior with a red checkmark in it, you should make sure that the red checkmark isn't there because you changed the code manually. By reediting the Server Behavior, the red checkmark will disappear, but so will your hand-coded script!*

Hand-coding your page is always an option when you want to add more functionality to the page, but it also forces you to put your programming logic in the page. In many cases, it is preferable to place your logic in the database. That's where stored procedures come in.

Using a Stored Procedure

Stored procedures allow for more complex database transactions and are available for most of the top database systems, including Oracle, IBM's DB2, and Microsoft SQL Server. A stored procedure allows you to create sets of commands inside your database that execute faster and are capable of much more complex combinations of commands that would be impossible to accomplish with a standard SQL statement from within a Web page. Also, the ability to make batches of commands and transactions allows for more secure transactions to the database. For example, in an online transaction, a stored procedure could execute multiple-order updates, account debiting, and accounting all within one stored procedure.

Additionally, the stored procedures are compiled, allowing for quicker execution times within the RDBMS. They also allow for the complex business logic of the site to be confined to the database, where the highly optimized database engine can handle the task. Many programmers would argue that all business logic should be confined to the database by defining the parameters in your Web application and sending them to the stored procedure to process. The stored procedure would process the parameters, execute whatever commands might be contained within, and then send back to the application any return values that are defined.

A stored procedure to conduct a basic search of the jobs table could be written as follows. Note that this is a Microsoft SQL Server stored procedure, and your own RDBMS might have slightly different syntax:

```
CREATE PROCEDURE spSearchJobs
    @SQLstr varchar(255) = "xyz"
AS
SELECT SearchField, JobID, EmpName, CatDesc
FROM getSearchField
WHERE SearchField LIKE '%' + @SQLstr + '%'
```

This stored procedure can be saved with the name spSearchJobs (we add the *sp* prefix to all of our stored procedures). Notice also that it is calling the getSearchField view that was created earlier. Later, you can incorporate the view directly into the stored procedure for more speed and efficiency, or turn it into a separate stored procedure that you can call from this stored procedure.

Tip	*Another advantage of stored procedures is that you can call one stored procedure from within another.*

To allow the Web page to execute the stored procedure, you'll have to create a new search page similar to the basic search page created earlier. The page should have the text field named searchfield and a Submit button, with the action of the <form> tag pointing to the page itself. There also should be a two-row, three-column table inserted to receive the values that will be returned by the stored procedure.

Next, you'll have to add a Command object to the page from the Data Bindings palette. This is applied much like the recordset and accepts these parameters:

- **Name**   cmdGetAGig
- **Connection**   connBettergig
- **Type**   Stored Procedure
- **Return Recordset Named**   rsGetAGig
- **SQL**   dbo.spSearchJobs
- **Variables**   Should be set up as in Table 19-2

Name	Type	Direction	Size	Default Value
@SQLstr	VarChar	in	255	xyz

Table 19-2.   *Variable Defined for the spGetAGig Command*

Additionally, the run-time values need to be set up to reflect the server model that you are working with. Refer to Table 19-1 for the run-time values for this attribute. The Command dialog box is shown in Figure 19-5. After clicking the OK button, the Command will show up in the Data Bindings palette just like a recordset (shown in Figure 19-6), and the fields can be inserted into the page in exactly the same manner. Repeat Regions can be applied as well.

You should now be able to apply a table to the page, insert the stored-procedure return columns, and apply a Repeat Region to the page to complete the simple search page.

Tip *Using stored procedures also allows for greater security within the database. While users of Microsoft Access might enjoy the power of being able to access the actual production tables of the database, it's generally not good practice to give your end user access to these tables. Using a stored procedure allows you to give the user permission to access the table only through the carefully constructed stored procedure rather than the table itself.*

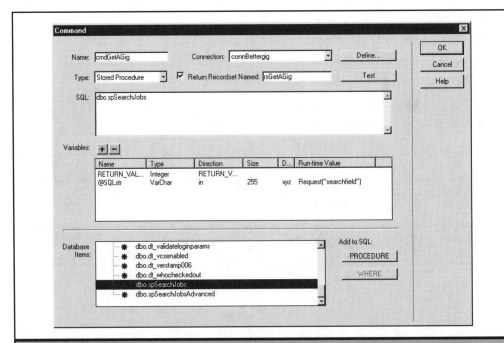

Figure 19-5. *The Command Server Behavior allows stored procedures (as well as Insert, Update, and Delete commands) to be inserted into a Web page*

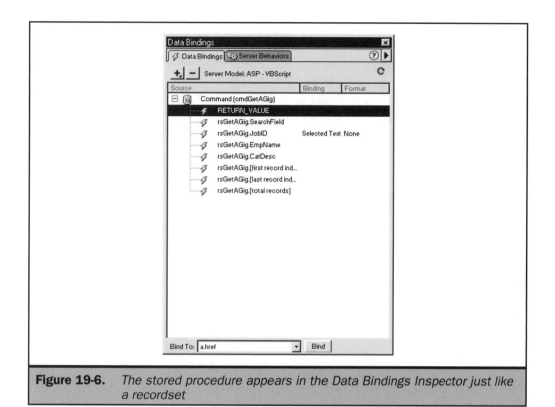

Figure 19-6. *The stored procedure appears in the Data Bindings Inspector just like a recordset*

To add the complex search functionality to the stored procedure, you need to have more than just a basic knowledge of SQL. SQL is capable of complex programming logic. There are looping and conditional statements associated with it as in VBScript, JavaScript, CFML, or Java. To implement a more complex stored procedure for searching the database, you could modify the stored procedure that was already written or write a new stored procedure such as the following:

```
CREATE PROCEDURE spSearchJobsAdvanced
    --set the incoming parameter
@SQLstr varchar(255) = "xyz"
 AS
    --then declare some variables.
Declare @temp varchar(255)
```

```
Declare @searchstring varchar(255)
    --We are going to allow 4 search variables.
Declare @searchstring1 varchar(255)
Declare @searchstring2 varchar(255)
Declare @searchstring3 varchar(255)
Declare @searchstring4 varchar(255)
    --set the default values of the search variables
Select @searchstring1 = '%'
Select @searchstring2 = '%'
Select @searchstring3 = '%'
Select @searchstring4 = '%'
    --declare a counter for the number of criterion
Declare @counter int
Select @counter = 0
    --@index will hold the current comma position
Declare @index int
    --set the initial value of the @temp variable to the
    -- entire incoming @SQLstr parameter
Select @temp = @SQLstr
    --strip off any quotes and replace with spaces, then trim
    -- the spaces.  SQL doesn't allow empty strings.
Select @temp = rtrim(ltrim(Replace(@temp,char(34)," ")))
--check for a null string
if @temp is null RETURN
--begin a loop. The @temp variable will have search strings
-- removed one at a time
WHILE @temp is not null
BEGIN
--look for comma
Select @index = CHARINDEX(',', @temp)
if @index = 0
--if no comma, then the whole string is used.
BEGIN
    SELECT @searchstring = ltrim(rtrim(@temp))
    SELECT @temp = null
END
else
--if there's a comma, separate the first part from the second part
BEGIN
    SELECT @searchstring = ltrim(rtrim(LEFT(@temp, @index-1)))
     --the new searchstring
    SELECT @temp = RIGHT(@temp,LEN(@temp) - @index)
```

```
      -- the rest
END
    SELECT @counter = @counter + 1
--set the variables depending on what position they were in.  For
-- example, a string like 'asp,web,vbscript' has 3 substrings
-- so the @searchstring4 would always contain the default '%'
if @counter = 1 Select @searchstring1 = '%' + @searchstring + '%'
if @counter = 2 Select @searchstring2 = '%' + @searchstring + '%'
if @counter = 3 Select @searchstring3 = '%' + @searchstring + '%'
if @counter = 4 Select @searchstring4 = '%' + @searchstring + '%'
END
--the parsing of the search parameters is finished.  Get the data
-- from the getSearchField view that was created earlier
Select SearchField, JobID, EmpName, CatDesc
FROM getSearchField
WHERE SearchField LIKE  @searchstring1
AND SearchField LIKE @searchstring2
AND SearchField LIKE @searchstring3
AND SearchField LIKE @searchstring4
```

This stored procedure can be applied in the same manner as the simple stored procedure that was built previously, as it accepts only one parameter and returns the same fields. In fact, if you are modifying the existing stored procedure, it isn't necessary to change the page at all. However, now the new stored procedure is much more flexible, and the functionality remains similar to the multiple-search criteria server-side script approach.

 As shown, the stored procedure was modified to make the Web application more flexible, but the Web application had no changes to it. This is one of the advantages of stored procedures, as they allow you to move the logic into the database and out of the Web application. It also illustrates the "black box" approach—hiding the details of the functionality from the application.

Adding the my_company and find_a_seeker Pages

The my_company and find_a_seeker pages will allow the company user to have access to the various resumes that are available. The my_company page will be a set of simple links to the various pages that are available to the employer, including the find_a_seeker page, which will be a list of resumes available. You should set up the my_company page with links to all of the pages that are available to the employer. You could also create a search page similar to the get_a_gig page that was created earlier that searches resumes instead of jobs. The my_company page should have a Restrict Access to Page Server behavior on it that only allows employers to access the page. This behavior was described in the last chapter.

The find_a_seeker page—also containing the Restrict Access to Page Server behavior—will be a simple list of all resumes. Clicking a link will take you to the view_resume page that has already been created. To create this list, follow these steps:

1. Apply a recordset named rsGetResumes to the page. The SQL should read as follows:

   ```
   SELECT ResID, ResGoal FROM Resumes
   ```

2. Insert a two-row, two-column table on the page.

3. Add column headings and insert the two database columns into the table.

4. Add a Repeat Region to the second row showing ten records.

5. Add a Recordset Navigation Bar Live Object to the page

6. Add a Go to Detail Page Server behavior to the view_resume page using the ResID column as the URL parameter.

Note   *If in doubt as to how to apply any of these steps, see the previous chapter, in which the various Server behaviors were explained in detail.*

Adding a Resumes Viewed Page

Every time a potential employer views a resume, the employer's ID number (EmpID), as well as the resume ID number (ResID), will be stored in another table that was created just for this purpose. The table name is ResumesViewed and is a *linking* table because it contains foreign keys from the Employers table and the Resumes table that effectively link the two tables together when the fields have something in common. In the case of the ResumesViewed table, the fact that the employer has viewed the resume is the common thread between the two tables. Each time the resume is viewed, it will cause a line to be added to this table storing the ResID, EmpID, and ResumesViewedID fields.

You can add functionality like this by placing an Insert command on the view_resume page. This is not the Insert Server Behavior that was used when form fields were involved. Rather, the Insert command is accessed through the Command Server Behavior by using the drop-down menu (see Figure 19-7). This method of applying an insert gives you a little more flexibility with your Insert statement. With the Insert Server Behavior you are limited to form fields.

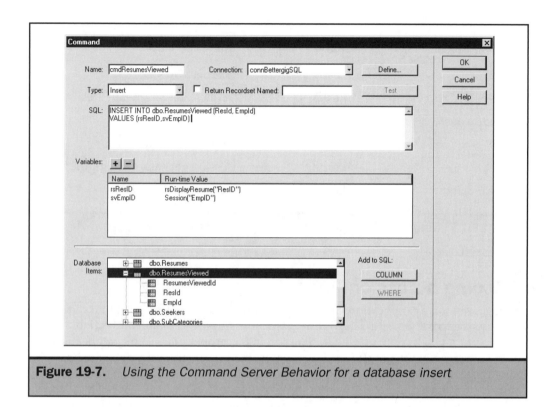

Figure 19-7. *Using the Command Server Behavior for a database insert*

Set up the insert by using the following parameters:

- **Name** cmdResumesViewed
- **Connection** connBettergig
- **Type** Insert
- **SQL** INSERT INTO ResumesViewed (ResID,EmpID) VALUES (rqResID,svEmpID)
- **Variables** As shown in Table 19-3

The session variable for EmpID hasn't been set up yet, but it can be hand-coded on the welcome_company_user page that the company users will see when they log in.

Note   *ColdFusion users should use the standard recordset dialog box to write the SQL to handle the insert to the database.*

Server Model	Name	Run-Time Value
ASP	rqResID	Request("ResID")
JSP	rqResID	request.getParameter("ResID")
ColdFusion	rqResID	#ResID#
ASP	svEmpID	Session("svEmpID")
JSP	svEmpID	session.getValue("svEmpID")
ColdFusion	svEmpID	#Session.svEmpID#

Table 19-3. *Setting Up Variables for the Insert Command*

Hand-Coding a Session Variable

Adding a session or application variable declaration is an easy process, but it requires basic knowledge of server-side scripting. Depending upon the data your variable is going to hold, you have to put the declaration in the proper place in the application. For the purposes of the EmpID session variable, the EmpID from the database has to be there. There is a place in the application where that occurs, and that is on the welcome_company_user page immediately after the recordset rsGetEmployer has been called.

When hand-coding inside the UltraDev environment, it's usually a good idea to separate your code from the UltraDev-generated code. That way you ensure that your hand-coding won't get written over by UltraDev. The reasoning behind this is simple: UltraDev has specific patterns of code that it searches for when editing a Server Behavior that it has inserted on the page. In most cases, the pattern begins at the start of a given script block and ends at the end of the block. For example, in a script block for a Server Behavior, you have an opening tag, the script, and then the closing tag. If you insert some extra script inside the tags, you run the risk that UltraDev will not be able to recognize its own Server Behavior anymore or, if it does, that it might strip off the code you inserted. This is not true in every case; but, in general, you should separate your code by enclosing it in its own script tags.

After the rsGetEmployer recordset is declared, insert the following line:

```
<%Session("svEmpID") = rsGetEmployer("EmpID")%> (ASP)
<%session.putValue("svEmpID",rsGetEmployer.getInt("EmpID"))%> (JSP)
<CFSET Session.svEmpId = rsGetEmployer.EmpID> (ColdFusion)
```

Adding Conditional Logic

The view_resume page will be accessible by the job seeker and by the employer. The ResumesViewed table will be updated only when the employer views the page. This is accomplished by adding conditional logic to the page. You saw it earlier with the Show Region Server Behavior. This behavior works very well for showing and hiding things that are going to be seen on the Web page. In this particular case, however, the item that you need to hide is a section of server-side code on the page before the <body> tags that performs the database insert. This functionality will have to be hand-coded.

Once again, the server-side script can be enclosed in its own script tags to ensure that the UltraDev-generated script isn't tampered with. This can be done by first finding the code for the Insert command and then applying your conditional code around it. In general, when you have a condition, there is a Begin condition tag and an End condition tag. Next you'll find the sample conditional code that you can use around the Insert command:

VBScript Version

```
<%If (session("svEmpID")<> "") Then%>
<%
''
''insert code
''
%>
<%End If%>
```

JavaScript Version

```
<%if(String(Session("svEmpID"))!="undefined") {%>
<%
//
//insert code
//
%>
<%}%>
```

ColdFusion Version

```
<CFIF IsDefinded(Session.svEmpID")>
<!---
---insert code
--->
</CFIF>
```

Java Version

```
<%if(session.getValue("svEmpID")!=null) {%>
<%
//
//insert code
//
%>
<%}%>
```

In ASP, there will be slight performance degradation by having the server-side tags opening and closing, but the loss will be minimal, and probably not even discernable. The important thing to remember about using this method is that it will allow the Server Behaviors to remain separate and functional within UltraDev. When your page is finished, you can remove the extraneous tags if you feel that it is necessary. JSP pages are compiled into servlets (as explained in Chapter 9), so the extra tags don't affect the page performance at all. ColdFusion, of course, is entirely made up of tags, so there is no performance penalty here.

Adding a resumes_viewed Page to the Admin Section

There are several ways to use the data in the ResumesViewed table. For example, job seekers can check how many times their resumes are viewed. Also, the employer could get a feel for how many times other employers have looked at a particular resume. For the site administrator, the table can supply general summary data for the site. You'll add this functionality to the resume_viewed page in the Admin subfolder.

Using Count(*)

SQL has aggregate functions that allow you to examine data in your database as groups of data rather than individual pieces of data. A Sum function, for example, will return the sum of all items in a column. A Min or Max function will return the lowest and highest values in the table.

The Count function allows you to get counts of your data, depending upon conditions that you set in the SQL statement. If you wanted to get a count of how many times the employers actually viewed the resumes, you could write a SQL statement like this:

```
SELECT COUNT(ResumesViewed.ResId) AS ResumeByEmployer,
    Employers.EmpName
FROM ResumesViewed INNER JOIN
    Employers ON
    ResumesViewed.EmpId = Employers.EmpID
GROUP BY Employers.EmpName
```

This SQL statement counts the number of times each employer viewed resumes. This statement doesn't separate the resumes by individual seeker, but rather gives the total count of how many times a specific employer viewed *any* resume. The Count is given the alias ResumeByEmployer so that you can reference the number on your Web page. The ResumesViewed table contained only the EmpID number, but by using an Inner join in the statement you can get the employers name as well; this gives the data more meaning to the end user. When the statement is run, the result might be something like Table 19-4.

The SQL statement could be copied and pasted as is into the UltraDev query builder, or you can create a view named getResumesViewedByEmployer out of the statement and then access it with a SQL statement inside of the UltraDev environment like this:

```
Select ResumesByEmployer, EmpName FROM getResumesViewedByEmployer
```

ResumesByEmployer	EmpName
8	Acme Databases
21	Smith, Smith, and Smith Enterprises
7	Susquehanna Hat Co.

Table 19-4. *Sample Count of How Many Times an Employer Viewed a Resume*

The latter method is preferable; but whichever you choose, the result is that you should create a recordset on the page named rsGetResumesViewedByEmployer. After creating this recordset, you can insert a table on the page, add the column headings and column information as you've done before, and apply a Repeat Region to the row containing the data. When browsing the page, the results of the SQL statement will be shown.

Another count that you'll want on this page is the resumes viewed by job seeker. This count will show how many times each individual resume was viewed. It could also be used on a page specific to job seekers to allow them to see how many times the resume was viewed. For now, however, you can insert it on this Admin page.

The SQL statement should read as follows:

```
SELECT COUNT(ResumesViewed.ResId) AS ResumesCount,
    Seekers.SeekFirstName + ' ' + Seekers.SeekLastName as FullName
FROM Resumes INNER JOIN
    ResumesViewed ON
    Resumes.ResID = ResumesViewed.ResId INNER JOIN
    Seekers ON Resumes.SeekID = Seekers.SeekID
GROUP BY ResumesViewed.ResID, Seekers.SeekLastName,
    Seekers.SeekFirstName
```

The statement is similar to the getResumesViewedByEmployer statement; however, this one retrieves information about the job seeker. To do this, you need an Inner join to the Resumes table, which, in turn, needs to be joined to the Seekers table. Also, the SeekFirstName and SeekLastName are combined—with a space inserted between them—to form the FullName alias. Upon running this query, you might have results like that found in Table 19-5.

Once again, you can create a view named getResumesViewedBySeeker and access it with a simple SQL statement from within UltraDev, like this:

```
SELECT FullName, ResumesCount FROM getResumesViewedBySeeker
```

Create a recordset named rsGetResumesViewedBySeeker using this statement and again, apply the table, column headings, columns, and Repeat Region to the page. Now the page should have two tables on it that give accurate counts containing data pertaining to both the job seeker and the employer.

FullName	ResumesCount
Jack Splat	8
Thomas Testdata	10
Jack Springer	5
Biff Bopper	1

Table 19-5.   *Counting the Resumes Viewed for Each Job Seeker*

Adding the Error Page

An error page can be as simple or as complex as you want to make it, but its primary purpose is to alert the user to an error condition. In this site, the error page is a one-stop place where a user is redirected if an error occurs on a page.

One error condition you'll want to catch is the attempt to access a page without the proper authorization. You'll want the user to have the chance to log in properly and be taken back to the page he attempted to access. This is accomplished fairly easily with the built-in User Authentication Server Behaviors—simply redirect the user to the login page from the Restrict Access to Page Server Behavior. If you recall, we set this parameter in all cases to this Error page instead.

When a user encounters an error condition, you may want to log the error so that the errors can later be examined. Also, several pages in the site will be accessible by different types of users—administrators, job seekers, and employers. As these different groups all have their own login pages, you'll want them to login on the appropriate page.

The Restrict Access to Page behavior will append a querystring variable of accessdenied to the end of the URL when it redirects the user to the error page. This accessdenied variable contains the relative location of the page that the error occurred on. By picking up this variable, you can append it to the proper link to redirect the user to the appropriate page. For example, the view_a_gig page can be accessed by all three groups, and there is no way of knowing which group the person belongs to if he hasn't logged in yet. You can simply set up a link for each login page and put the appropriate text on the page:

Are you a Job Seeker? Sign in or Register now.

Are you an Employer? Sign in or Register now.

The job seeker will be redirected to the login_user page in the login_user directory, and the employer will be redirected to the login_company_user page in the login_company_user directory. Make the link by highlighting the words "Sign in" and then right-clicking (CTRL-clicking on the Macintosh) and choosing Make Link. Browse to the page that you are setting the link to.

You'll have to manually code the querystring at the end of the link by placing your cursor at the end of the link in the URL field of the Make Link dialogue box and placing the following server-side code:

?<%=Request("query_string")%> (ASP)

?<%=request.getParameter("query_string")%> (JSP)

?<CFOUTPUT>#cgi.query_string#</CFOUTPUT> (ColdFusion)

Next, highlight the word "Register" in each line and set the link to the appropriate registration page. In the case of the job seeker it will be the new_user page in the new_user directory, and in the case of the employer it will be the new_company_user in the my_company directory.

After doing this, whenever a user encounters an error that is the result of not being logged in, he will be redirected to this error page, at which time he can choose to login properly or register if he is a new user. After a successful login, he will be redirected back to the page on which the error originally occurred.

By appending a querystring variable for other types of error conditions, you can catch those variables on this error page and write the code to apply the appropriate actions depending on what type of error it is.

Summary

In the last chapter, the Server Behaviors and Data Bindings palettes were introduced; in this chapter, we've taken the functionality a little further with more advanced concepts, including stored procedures, commands, hand-coding, and aggregate queries using the Count keyword. There is certainly a lot more that could be covered to add more functionality to the site, but this was only meant as a starting point.

In the next few chapters, the extensibility framework of UltraDev will be examined to show you how to add your own features to the program, and how to turn your own snippets of code into Objects, Commands, Server Formats, and Server Behaviors.

The
Complete
Reference

Part V

Getting The Most Out of UltraDev

The Complete Reference

Chapter 20

Extending UltraDev

One of the most exciting features of UltraDev is the ability to add your own features to it, or *extend* it. UltraDev and Dreamweaver are built around a document object model (DOM), much like a fourth-generation browser. Although UltraDev is referenced throughout the chapter, many of the techniques described work in Dreamweaver as well. UltraDev is, in fact, built upon a combination of a subset of the Netscape Navigator 4 DOM and a subset of the World Wide Web Consortium (W3C) DOM. The rendering engine of Dreamweaver and UltraDev is based on the Netscape DOM, so the extensions conform more closely to the syntax and specifications of that DOM.

The principles behind the DOM have their basis in object-oriented programming (OOP). In short, everything in your document is an object, from an image or form item, to comments and tags. The document itself is an object and is the root level of the DOM. Everything in the document can be accessed through the document object.

The extensions are written in HTML and JavaScript, with the ability also to write somewhat more complex extensions in C or C++. For example, when you click the Table object in UltraDev, the pop-up interface that appears is an HTML form, with a JavaScript include file that does the dirty work of putting the code together and inserting it into the document where you want it. The idea that you can extend an HTML tool with HTML itself is ingenious—it allows Web developers with HTML and JavaScript experience to add features to the tool to make it more productive in their own environment. The UltraDev on your desktop will be very different from the UltraDev on another's desktop, because you will likely have added the features that make working with UltraDev easier for you.

Understanding Extensions

To access the extensibility features of UltraDev, you need to be fairly proficient in JavaScript. Several good JavaScript books are available, and having a good one handy at all times is wise. Also, many of the extensibility features rely on regular expressions, a part of JavaScript that is not well documented. Information on regular expressions, also known as *Regexes,* or *RegExps,* can be found in Perl resources as well, because the syntax is very similar. Chapters 21 and 22 discuss Regexes and their implementation in UltraDev in detail. After you are comfortable with Regexes, you will be able to write complex Server Behaviors and other extensions where document manipulation is important.

All the extensions to UltraDev reside in the Configuration folder at the root of the UltraDev folder. If you look inside the folder, you'll see folders for Commands, Objects, Floaters, Inspectors, Menus, Server Behaviors, and Translators, among others. The files in these folders correspond directly to the different areas of UltraDev that are extensible. For example, every item on the Commands menu of UltraDev has a corresponding HTML file in the Configuration | Commands folder. Every object in the Objects folder has corresponding files in the Configuration | Objects folder. By modifying these files or creating your own, you can effectively change the functionality of UltraDev. Chapter 21 demonstrates how to build several objects.

Note *See the section "Configuration Folders," later in the chapter, for a breakdown of the different folders contained within. Many of these folders and their corresponding extensions will be explained in detail in Chapter 23.*

Adding features to UltraDev is valuable, but the best part of it is that your HTML and server-side script is "live" in the code window while you work on your page. "Repeat Region" is a perfect example of this. This Server Behavior consists of some very sophisticated JavaScript to get the Behavior to work with the page, but the results are astounding. When you apply the Behavior and switch to "Live Data" (SHIFT-CTRL-R), the page is rendered in "real time," giving you not only a chance to "preview" the page, but also the ability to edit the page in a form that only exists in concept.

To explain further, when a user requests your page, the server fetches the page— if it has the proper file extension (.jsp, .asp, or .cfm)—and executes the code, sending only HTML and client-side scripts to the browser. UltraDev, however, is executing your server code on the fly, showing you the results of your server code as if it were the result of an HTTP request. The page you are editing inside of the UltraDev environment in Live Data view is a rendition of how your page will look in a browser, but it doesn't actually exist in that form. UltraDev goes one step further than other Web-development tools by letting you edit this "ghost" page in a visual environment as if it were your final product.

Dreamweaver was designed with extensibility in mind. Because UltraDev is based on Dreamweaver's architecture, you can create and apply similar extensions to UltraDev. As mentioned earlier, UltraDev has a DOM similar to a browser. The DOM is described in detail in the "Extending Dreamweaver and UltraDev" document included in the Help menu of UltraDev, and also on the UltraDev CD-ROM as a printable PDF document. You can also get a bound version from Macromedia for a small fee. The UltraDev application programming interface (API) has over 400 JavaScript functions that are not accessible by the DOM of a standard browser, however, because UltraDev relies on *selection*, which is not a necessity in a browser. The ability to *select* areas of HTML, objects, and script, and apply commands or Behaviors to the selection, is what makes UltraDev a powerful HTML-authoring environment.

Extensions are essentially *code that is inserted into the page.* Unlike a text editor or a text-based HTML editor, such as Homesite or BBEdit, the HTML tags are *rendered* into actual objects that you can see and manipulate by moving, dragging, assigning attributes, or changing the code. When you drop an image on the page, for instance, you can go back and click the image to be presented with a Property Inspector that shows you the attributes that go along with the image. If you happen to change some of the code in HTML source view, those changes are reflected on the screen visually, as well as in the attributes of the Inspector. These are all things that you have to consider when you are writing your own extensions to UltraDev. An object extension, such as a table, has an associated Property Inspector. In addition, when you are writing Server Behaviors, you must consider the four different server-side languages that are part of UltraDev. You don't *have* to write all four versions, but you can if you want the extension to be usable by anyone with UltraDev.

The Extension Interface

Most extensions have an *interface* for receiving attributes from the user. This interface can be designed inside of the UltraDev environment, because it is just an HTML form. Most of the standard rules of HTML apply, and you can use standard HTML form elements to accept input from the user. There are several ways to go about designing the interface. Generally, it is recommended to start with a basic table and add your attributes to it, as shown in Figure 20-1.

One thing to think about when you are designing your interface is that your text fields and other form fields should have meaningful names. When you are writing your code to manipulate the data that you retrieve from the interface, a text field named firstRowColor is certainly more readable than textfield2. Other considerations also exist. You might think that your extension looks great in purple, but Macromedia has strict guidelines that you should follow to remain 100-percent compatible with UltraDev:

- Don't use font or background colors. Use the standard UltraDev colors that are picked by default.

- Don't use font styles.

- Your company or personal logo can be in the interface, but it should be on the bottom. Alternatively, you can put an About button on the interface and link it to an HTML page or another tab in your interface.

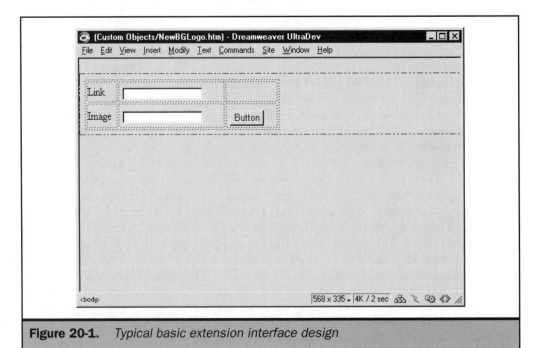

Figure 20-1.   *Typical basic extension interface design*

- You can include a brief help text on the bottom of the interface itself, with the color set to #D3D3D3.
- Extensions should have a Help button.

These are just a few of the guidelines. A full list can be found in the file ui_guidelines.html under . . \Macromedia\Extension Manager\Help\.

> **Tip** *To get the visual look of your interface, you can design it in the UltraDev environment and then edit it in Homesite, BBEdit, or your text editor of choice to clean up the code. Make sure to remove all styles, colors, and fonts that may have been added erroneously to the page during the design process.*

In addition to the HTML elements, your interface can include all the JavaScript functions that are used in the execution of the extension, or it can have a line at the top, such as the following, to import the JavaScript functions as an include file:

```
<script src="myextension.js"></script>
```

This file should have the same name as your HTML file, except with a .js extension. This JavaScript file should contain only the localized functions that are necessary for your particular extension. Any shared functions can be placed in a file in the Shared folder. When you have your interface file ready, it can be saved into the appropriate folder under Configuration.

Most of the hard work of writing extensions is hand-coding JavaScript into the .js file for manipulating the document, which can better be done in Homesite, BBEdit, or your editor of choice. The JavaScript code that is contained in this file has a few basic functions:

- Gets the attributes from the form that was submitted (the interface)
- Gets pertinent information from the document being edited, such as the current selection or the insertion point
- Puts the user-defined attributes into a string with the HTML and script that is to be inserted into the document
- Inserts the resulting string into the user's document

Selections and Offsets

Sometimes extension writing is a fairly simple procedure, but other times it may require some very complex document and string manipulation to accomplish, as in the case of Server Behaviors. The same principles apply to all extensions, though, from the basic objects to the complex Server Behaviors. Depending on what your extension is doing, it could work with either a *selection* or an *insertion point*. A *selection* is a highlighted area on the page. An *insertion point,* which is a specified point in your document, is either where the cursor is located or any point within the document. Here is an example that retrieves the highlighted code or object from a page using the getSelection() method of Dreamweaver, which is a function from the UltraDev API for getting a selection:

```
var theSelection = dreamweaver.getSelection();
```

This function will return an array of two values that represent the beginning of the selection and the end of the selection as *offsets* from the beginning of the document. To check whether an actual selection is made, or whether you are simply dealing with an insertion point, you make a test to see whether the two values match—meaning nothing is selected. You make a test with a block like this:

```
if (theSelection[0] == theSelection[1]) {
    //we have an insertion point, not a selection
    }else{
    //we have a selection
    };
```

This function can be used both ways—and can be used to display an error message if the extension requires a selection and the user hasn't selected anything. You can then manipulate the document yourself by using the powerful function getDocumentDom(), which returns the contents of the document in object form:

```
var theDom = getDocumentDom('document');
```

The object that is returned, theDom, can be used to get the actual selection in text format by first getting the documentElement property of the document node (theDom). After you have that, you use the outerHTML property of the documentElement to get the actual text of the entire document:

```
var theDom = getDocumentDom('document');
var theSelection = theDom.getSelection();
var theEntireDocument = theDom.documentElement.outerHTML;
var theSelectedText = theEntireDocument.substring(theSelection[0], theSelection[1]);
```

Now, the variable theSelectedText contains the actual text that is highlighted in the document window. If this happens to be an object such as an image, the variable will contain the entire object, including tags and attributes. You can start to see that this becomes a very powerful tool for inserting things into your document, or for editing things that are already in your document. Highlighting an image, for example, will put the contents of the entire HTML code block for rendering that image into the variable, which can then be manipulated, altered, or given Behaviors.

Tip *Another way to highlight a block of HTML on the page is to click the tag name in the lower-left corner of the document window. This highlights the corresponding code in the HTML source window, and the corresponding object in the design window.*

You can also get the text before the selection or the text after the selection by using the selection and the offsets to the selection. Added to the previous code, the following lines of code will return the two blocks of text around the selection:

```
var beforeTheSelectedText = theEntireDocument.substring(0, theSelection[0]);
var afterTheSelectedText = theEntireDocument.substring(theSelection[1]);
```

The first example (before selection) starts at the zero position on the page and gets all text up to the beginning of the selection. The second line gets all text starting at the point where the selection ends. This gives you three parts now—before the selection, the selection, and after the selection. You could easily take these three parts of the page and put them back together or manipulate the text in one or more of the parts. Suppose you want to make the selection a link. You could do that with a simple <a href> tag around the selection, like this:

```
theSelection = ' <a href="http://www.myhomepage.com">' + ¬
theSelectedText + '</a>';
```

Notice that the preceding just concatenated the string with the opening tag, the selection, and the closing tag. Now, the theSelection variable holds the original selection wrapped in a link. To write it back to the page, you have to concatenate the strings together like this:

```
var theDom = getDocumentDom('document');
theDom.outerHTML = beforeTheSelectedText + theSelection + ¬
afterTheSelectedText;
```

Now your updated page contains a link around the text that you had selected.

Nodes

Nodes are essential to the understanding of the DOM, both in browsers and in UltraDev extensions, and are required for some of the complex HTML manipulation within UltraDev. Every tag in the document is a node. Nodes have many properties that can be used by the developer to build extensions. The properties are accessed through standard *dot* notation, as in myNode.property. The terminology that will be used may be more familiar to those comfortable with the Netscape DOM, which is quite different from the DOM that Internet Explorer programmers are used to. When building extensions, you'll be accessing objects and their properties as you would when working with the Netscape browser.

The following are the four basic types of nodes, which can be checked with the nodeType property:

- **DOCUMENT_NODE** The document-level node that enables you to have access to all parts of the document
- **ELEMENT_NODE** A node for an HTML tag, such as <table>
- **COMMENT_NODE** An HTML comment surrounded by <!- ->
- **TEXT_NODE** A block of text that is on the page

To better understand nodes, examine the following:

```
<table>
    <tr>
        <td>First</td>
        <td>Last</td>
        <!--this is a comment node-->
    </tr>
</table>
```

The <table> tag is the outermost node in the example. It is an ELEMENT_NODE type node, and contains nodes within, called *child nodes*, accessible through the childNodes property of the table node. The one item in the childNodes array is the <tr> node. That node has a childNodes array as well, with three items in it—two <td> tag pairs and a COMMENT-NODE type node. Nodes also have parents, accessible through the parentNode property. The parentNode of <tr> is the <table> node. Not seen here is the parent of the <table>, the <body> node. Parent to the <body> node is the <html> node, which is the DOCUMENT-NODE nodeType.

You've already seen the outerHTML property of the document node—this was the entire document, including the tags that made up the node. Another property is the innerHTML property, which retrieves what is *between* the tags. This property is useful for getting text and properties that are contained within a tag. Another handy property of a node is the tagName property. The tagName property of the <table> tag is table, which you could use in a situation in which you are looking for a particular node, like this:

```
for (i=0; i<someNodes.length; i++) {
    if(someNodes[i].tagName == "table") {
        //found a table tag--do some stuff to it
        };
    };
```

You can use this method to your advantage if you are trying to insert some code into a specific tag, such as adding a JavaScript rollover Behavior to an <image> tag, or putting some server-side code into a repeat-region table tag to alternate colored rows. Or, you could write your own custom tag, such as <TM:MYTAG>, put it into the Custom Tags folder, and then do a check for whether or not myNode.tagName is equal to TM:MYTAG. Another way to find a tag is to use the function findTag(tagName), located in the DOM.js file.

 Inserting a custom tag of your own creation is a quick and dirty way to recognize your own code in a page, especially during the debugging phase of your extension writing. Wrapping the code with the tag enables you to find the node easily by using the findTag(tagName) function.

Dot Notation

Accessing properties of the DOM or objects in the DOM is done with standard *dot* notation. The root of the "tree" is the document, and all objects can be accessed through it. The objects that you will be accessing in your extension interface will be predominantly form items, such as text fields (or edit boxes), check boxes, radio buttons, and drop-down select boxes. Getting to these is easy through the document root. Start with document.formname to get the form, and then access your form element through its name, like this:

```
document.formname.elementname
```

Depending on what kind of element it is, different properties will be associated with it. A check box will have a "checked" property; a text field will have a "text" property. The code looks like this:

```
var isCheckboxChecked = document.myForm.myCheckbox.checked;
var myText = document.myForm.myTextfield.text;
```

Dot notation can be pretty complicated, but after you are able to follow the logic of it, it will be easy to get the properties of any object. The following example is a little more complex. Suppose you have a select box in an HTML form that will access a list of recordsets available to the page. After the user has made a selection, you now will be able to retrieve it. You start with a select box on the form named selectRecordset. You can use dot notation to retrieve the text. To illustrate the complexity, the following shows the entire statement on one line, using dot notation:

```
var myRecordset = document.forms[0].selectRecordset.options[document.forms[0].¬
selectRecordset.selectedIndex].text;
```

You start with "document" and get to the "forms" array next. Because you have only one form on the page, you access the first element in the array, which has a zero index—forms[0]. If you knew the name of the form, you could have used that in its place, but forms[0] is a good general-purpose way of getting the form object on a page. Next, you access the name of the element in the form, selectRecordset. The options of the select box are numbered from 0 to however many recordsets are on the page, so you want to pick the option that is selected. No "selected option" property exists, but there is a selectedIndex property. Because you need the actual text and not the index, you will access the DOM again with document.forms[0].selectRecordset.selectedIndex to get your [index] number. Now, you have the selected option value from the box, and all that remains is to get the text of that option. You do that with the "text" property.

You could organize this into more easily readable lines, as follows (note that the following code retrieves the same text property):

```
var theForm = document.forms[0];
var theSelectBox = theForm.selectRecordset;
var theIndex = theSelectBox.selectedIndex;
var theOption = theSelectBox.options[theIndex];
var theText = theOption.text;
```

By accessing the individual objects and properties in a hierarchical fashion, the code is far more readable. In any event, you can see how the hierarchical approach is implemented in the DOM. You can access the properties, methods, and events of any particular object by using dot notation.

Note   *As you are writing your extensions and testing them, you will find that you have to reload the extensions into the UltraDev environment for your changes to be recognized. This can be done in one of two ways: you can restart the program, or you can CTRL-click the title bar of the Objects floater. This will bring up the standard Object menu with one key command at the bottom that's new: Reload Extensions (see Figure 20-2). This feature is undocumented and unsupported, because not all extensions are reloaded this way.*

The UltraDev API Methods

The DOM also has methods. Methods can be considered built-in functions of the DOM. To access the methods of the DOM, you use dot notation as well:

```
theNode.theMethod();
```

getElementsByTagName(tagName)

Given the name of the tag, the method simply retrieves the tag that you are searching for. You can call this method with a node, or with the entire DOM. If you are searching for all images on the page, you would call it like this:

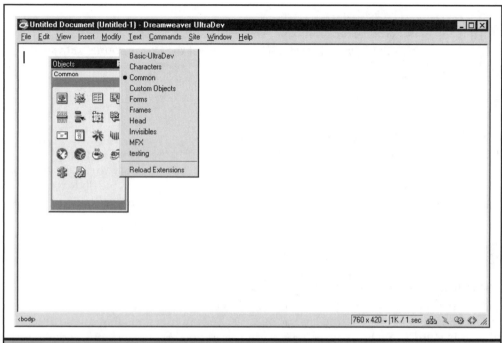

Figure 20-2. *Reloading the extensions by CTRL-clicking the title bar*

```
var myImageNodeList = ¬
dreamweaver.getDocumentDom().getElementsByTagName("img");
```

or

```
var theDom = dreamweaver.getDocumentDom();
var myImageNodeList = theDom.getElementsByTagName("img");
```

hasChildNodes()
This method returns true or false. Use it to determine whether any child nodes are within the node that you are calling it from, as in the following:

```
if (myNode.hasChildNodes()) {
    //do this
};
```

getAttribute(attrName)

Use this method if you need to find any given attribute of a node. If your node (myNode) contains the following text, then you can get the image source path with myNode.getAttribute("src"):

```
<img src="myImage" height=30 width=40>
```

setAttribute(attrName, attrValue)

This method does the opposite of getAttribute and returns no value. You supply the attribute name and the value you want the attribute to have, and setAttribute will write the HTML to your page for you. For example, if you have a table node named myTable, and you want to set the width to 50% with a click, put the following line in a command:

```
myTable.setAttribute("width","50%");
```

removeAttribute(attrName)

This method removes a given attribute as well as its value from a node.

As earlier mentioned, UltraDev has over 300 built-in functions that can be used to your benefit. You'll be exploring more of these as you build extensions in the next few chapters.

Shared Folder Functions

You don't need to reinvent the wheel when writing your extensions, so it's always a good idea to reuse whatever you can. In addition to the standard methods of the DOM, hundreds of functions are available in the Shared folder under Configuration—some are well documented and some aren't. After you learn your way around the shared folder, you'll be writing extensions much more quickly. Certain repetitive tasks are streamlined by using the appropriate function. The following sections take a look at a few of them.

findObject(objName, parentObj)

This function (located in .. \Shared\MM\Scripts\CMN\UI.js) will be one of your most-used functions. It replaces a lot of repetitive DOM accesses. When the OK button is clicked in your extension, your JavaScript needs to fetch the values from the form that was just submitted. Suppose that you have a text field in your interface named recordset and a drop-down box named myOptionsBox. You could use

```
var recordsetName = document.forms[0].recordset.selectedIndex;
var myOptions = document.forms[0].myOptionsBox.options[document.forms[0].¬
myOptionsBox.selectedIndex].text;
```

or use the findObject function like this:

```
var recordsetName = findObject("recordset").value;
var myOptions = ¬
findObject("myOptionsBox").options[findObject("myOptionsBox").¬
selectedIndex].text;
```

The first method uses the standard DOM methods of retrieving the object's properties, whereas the second method uses the findObject function and is a little easier to read. The findObject function returns the actual object that you are looking for, with all of the properties intact. We generally prefer using the findObject function, but will illustrate both methods in the extensions we will be building in the following chapters.

Note   *You may notice that UltraDev actually inserts a similar findObject() function in your HTML pages as a function of some of the built-in Behaviors. This function performs similar actions within the confines of the browser.*

getAllObjectTags(tagName)

This function (located in . . \Shared\MM\Scripts\CMN\docInfo.js) returns an array of all tags of the same type as the tagName attribute that you send to the function. For example, if you are looking for all tables on a page, you would call this function and assign the resulting array to a variable, such as the following:

```
var myTableTagArray = getAllObjectTags("table");
```

getSelectedObject()

This is a simple function (located in . . \Shared\MM\Scripts\CMN\docInfo.js) that returns the object that is currently selected in the document, like this:

```
var theObject = getSelectedObject();
```

If you take a look at the actual function, it is pretty basic, and illustrates another method of accessing an object. The entire function consists of two lines:

```
var currSel = dreamweaver.getSelection();
return dreamweaver.offsetsToNode(currSel[0],currSel[1]);
```

The first line gets the selection in the document made by the user, and the second line uses a built-in DOM method, offsetsToNode. This method converts the two offsets from the beginning of the document into the *node* that the selected code is contained within. In the following example,

```
<table>
    <tr>
        <td>Hello</td>
    </tr>
</table>
```

if you highlight Hello in the document and pass the *offsets* (the number of characters into the document to the first character of the selection, and the number of characters into the document to the first character after the selection) to the offsetsToNode built-in function, you are returned the object that contains the <td> tag set. You can test this using the following:

```
var test = getSelectedObject();
alert(test.outerHTML);
```

If you run this little script in an extension, an alert box pops up with <td>Hello</td> in it, as shown in Figure 20-3. So, while Hello is the selection, the selected object is the <td> node. This also illustrates your best method of debugging

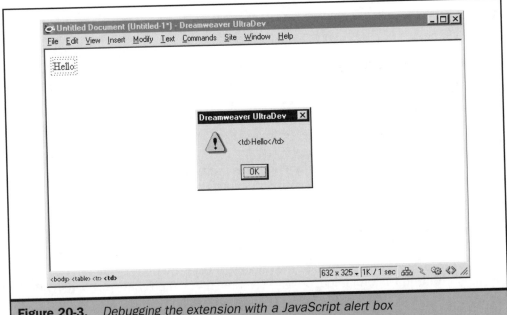

Figure 20-3. *Debugging the extension with a JavaScript alert box*

your extensions—alert boxes. Dreamweaver has no built-in debugger, and no JavaScript debugger will work with extensions within the Dreamweaver environment, so you are left with using alerts to check your work.

createUniqueName(tagName,tagString,arrToSearch)

You use this function (located in ..\Shared\MM\Scripts\CMN\docInfo.js) if you are adding a tag for an object on the page and want the object to have a default name that is unique. Suppose your object inserts a check box on the page, but you want it to have a name such as checkbox2 if a checkbox1 already exists on the page. This function will do that for you.

The tagName variable is your tag that is being searched for. The tagString variable is the name that you want to use, such as "checkbox" to return checkbox1 as your name. This name can be anything, and doesn't have to match the default name for the tag in question. The arrToSearch variable is an optional array of elements to do the search in. If no array is given, the whole document is searched by default.

selectionInsideTag(tagName)

This function (located in ..\Shared\MM\Scripts\CMN\docInfo.js) returns true or false, depending on whether or not the currently selected text is within a particular tag. Suppose your extension depends on the selection being within a table cell. You could access this function as follows:

```
if (selectionInsideTag("td")) {
    //it is!  do something with it
    } else {
    //it's not.  Error condition
    };
```

findTag(tagName)

This function (located in ..\Shared\MM\Scripts\CMN\DOM.js) returns a node containing the object of a specific tag for which you are looking. You can also pass it a startNode variable as the second element in the tagName array. This is an optional variable, and if it isn't given, the function will search the entire document.

Note

The findTag function is a recursive function and is a good example of the recursion technique. Recursion enables you to traverse through a tree and its nodes without leaving the function. Basically, you start with your root node and examine it; if you don't find what you are looking for in the root node, you move through the child nodes successively by calling the function again within the function itself for each child node. This causes the function to continue looping until all nodes are searched, or until it finds a match.

For example, if you want to remove all bold tags from the document, you can do so like this:

```
function stripBolds(){
var boldTag = findTag("b");  //get the tag
var insideBold = boldTag.innerHTML;  //get what's inside the tag
boldTag.outerHTML = insideBold;  //set the outside equal to the inside
//effectively stripping off the tag
if(findTag("b")) stripBolds() //more recursion -- if there's another bold
//do the function again
}
```

nodeList(startNode)

This function (located in . . \Shared\MM\Scripts\CMN\DOM.js) returns an array of all nodes that are within a node passed to the function. If, for example, you pass it the node consisting of the following text,

```
<table><tr><td>hello</td></tr></table>
```

the result returned will be a three-element array with the <table> node, the <tr> node, and the <td> node.

isInsideTag(tag, tagNames)

This function (located in . . \Shared\MM\Scripts\CMN\DOM.js) is passed two parameters: the tag name you are searching for, and the list of tags in which to search for it. The tagNames variable is a comma-separated list of tags that you want to check for the existence of a specific tag name. For instance, if you want to see whether there is a <b> tag within any heading tags, you can call the function like this:

```
if (isInsideTag("b","h1,h2,h3,h4,h5,h6")) {
    //it is--do something
    } else {
    //it isn't--do something else
    };
```

browseFile(fieldToStoreURL)

With this function (located in . . \Shared\MM\Scripts\CMN\file.js), you pass a textfield name into the fieldToStoreURL variable. Typically, you invoke this function with a button or an image of a small folder next to the text field that you want to store the filename in (see Figure 20-4) and call it in the onClick event of that button or image

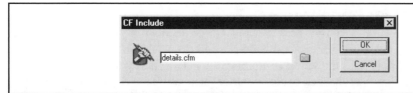

Figure 20-5. *The CF Include extension by Massimo Foti uses the browseFile function called from the onClick event of the folder image (an image field)*

field. It brings up the Select File dialog box (see Figure 20-5) and inserts the result into the text field.

```
myFile = browseFile("myTextField") //bring up the file dialog and
//save the filename in the "myFile" variable
```

Figure 20-4. *The Select File dialog box is called when you use the browseFile function*

checkForFormTag(formItemStr)

This function (located in . . \Shared\MM\Scripts\CMN\form.js) is handy if you happen to be inserting a form element, such as a special-purpose text field or check box that you've designed. Simply pass the string containing the HTML that you are putting on the page, and the function will check to see whether the text will be contained within a form tag after it gets inserted. It does this by checking the currently selected text and checking up the tree until it finds a form tag. If there is no form tag, the function will put a form tag around your text and make sure it has a unique name. If your selection is contained within a layer, the function will only search within the layer, because you can have more than one form tag on a page with layers.

 When referring to layers in the UltraDev environment, the term generally refers to <div>, <span>, <layer>, *and* <ilayer> *tags.*

For example, if you are inserting a custom textfield object that you designed, and you want to make sure it is inside of a form tag, you can do it like this:

```
var textfieldToInsert = myTextfield.outerHTML; //get the HTML from the
//code you are inserting
checkForFormTag(textfieldTextToInsert); //wrap it with a form tag if it's
//not inside of a form
```

isLayer(obj)

When passed an object (node), this function (located in . . \Shared\MM\Scripts\ CMN\form.js) indicates whether or not the given object is a layer, by checking for all possible layer tags—<layer>, <ilayer>, <div>, and <span>.

insertIntoDocument(textStr, bBlockTag)

This function (located in . . \Shared\MM\Scripts\CMN\form.js) inserts a string of text into a document, plain and simple. The text can be anything—HTML, text, or JavaScript. Simply pass the text you want inserted at the insertion point to the function through the textStr variable, and set the bBlockTag to "true" if the text you are inserting is a block-level tag, such as a layer, table, heading, or form. The reason for setting the bBlockTag to true is that the function will close off any open block-level tag before inserting the code, such as if there is an open <p> tag. The function will generate a closing </p> tag in front of your code and reopen it after your code that is inserted. This function is generally used in extensions other than objects. There is a built-in function called objectTag() that is used in objects that will automatically insert your text.

badChars(theStr)

Pass any string to this function (located in . . \Shared\MM\Scripts\CMN\string.js) and it will tell you whether the string contains one of the following bad characters:

```
~!@#$%^&*()_+|`-=\{}[]:";'<>,./?
```

The function returns "true" if any of these characters are in the string.

getParam(tagStr, param)

This function (located in .. \Shared\MM\Scripts\CMN\string.js) returns the value of any named parameter from a string passed to it. In the example <cfquery name="recordset1">, tagStr is equal to <cfquery name="recordset1"> and "name" is the parameter. The function will return an array with "recordset1" being element [0] in the array. Suppose you pass the following string,

```
<TD><IMG SRC="trans.gif" Align="left" Width="1" Height="1"></TD>
<TD><IMG SRC="trans.gif" Align="left" Width="89" Height="1"> </TD>
```

using this expression,

```
var myWidthArray = getParam(theString, "Width");
```

the function would return "1" as myWidthArray[0] and "89" as myWidthArray[1].

quote(textStr, quoteType)

This function (located in .. \Shared\MM\Scripts\CMN\string.js) simply wraps the textStr variable that is passed to the function in single or double quotes, depending on the value of quoteType. Use 1 for single quotes and 2 for double quotes.

stripSpaces(theStr)

This function (located in .. \Shared\MM\Scripts\CMN\string.js) strips the leading and trailing spaces from a string that is passed to it.

These are just some of the functions available. As you develop extensions and rework existing extensions, you will find yourself doing some tasks over and over. The functions contained within the Shared folder will greatly enhance your workflow. Also, as you write functions that you might need to reuse, you can package them with your extensions and place your own folder in the Shared folder.

In addition to extending the environment by giving yourself more commands, Behaviors, objects, and so forth, you can change the menus within the UltraDev environment. This takes a little knowledge of XML, but it's not much different from the standard HTML that you are accustomed to using. At the most basic level, UltraDev automatically places certain things in the menus as you put files into the Configuration folder. If you put the file My Server Behavior.htm into the ServerBehaviors folder, the next time you open up UltraDev, you will have a new Behavior in the menu.

> **Note** *All the menu files are written in XML (eXtensible Markup Language). In addition, the MXI files that are required to package an extension are written in XML. It is not truly valid XML and can't be displayed in a dedicated XML editor, but rather is a limited version of XML that UltraDev uses and understands. The UltraDev derivation uses special characters ('<>"&) that have to be substituted in real XML.*

As a matter of practice, you won't always want to rely on UltraDev to put the extensions in the menus. It's usually better to specify where you want your item to appear. You can also add commands to your contextual menus, and add submenus where needed. Suppose you have a set of extensions for adding text formatting to your pages. Your extensions might consist of formats or phrases that your company uses on a day-to-day basis. You might decide that the best place to put these is in a submenu on the contextual menu for the document. That way, your much-needed commands are only a right-click away. By manipulating the menus.xml file, you can customize the UltraDev interface itself by changing the menus and menu items.

Configuration Folders

If you open up the UltraDev program directory, the Configuration folder contained within holds all of the menu items—Commands, Behaviors, Server Behaviors, and other extensions to the UltraDev environment. The files are contained within individual folders whose names correspond to their menu items. There are also several folders that don't have a corresponding visible menu in the UltraDev environment but contain files that are necessary internally for the operation of the program. The following is a description of some of those folders:

- **Behaviors** Contains actions that your objects can take, which usually are JavaScript functions that respond to different events on an HTML page. The files in this folder correspond to the menu items in the Behaviors floater.

- **BrowserProfiles** Contains the information needed by UltraDev to verify that a given browser can handle the various tags, properties, methods, and events that are on the page. If you choose the command Check Target Browsers from the File menu, the command will use data from these files to determine whether or not your page meets the requirements of a given browser. Any page with server-side code will be parsed and executed before it is checked against the target browser.

- **Commands** Includes the actions that you can apply to your page when you choose an item from the Commands menu on the standard UltraDev menu bar. Typically, a command also has a corresponding menu item in contextual menus for ease of use. Additionally, many commands can be called by other extensions, and perform a wide variety of tasks that make them perhaps the most flexible extension available.

■ **Connections** Includes the physical connections that you have defined within UltraDev. These connections are listed in the connections.xml file. This file has the information about each and every connection that you've made in UltraDev. This comes in handy if you switch machines, for example, or do a system reinstallation. You can copy this file to the new Connections directory, and all of your connections will show up in the program.

■ **DataSources** Contains the files that appear in your Data Bindings palette. The file DataSources.xml contains the information for the Data Bindings menu. You could, for example, decide on a different approach for how your page connects to your database, and write a new extension called NewRecordset to handle it.

■ **Dictionaries** Contains the spelling-check features of UltraDev, accessible through the Text menu. You can download new dictionaries from the Macromedia site, or make your own. The Personal.dat file includes any personal words that you may have added to the dictionary. You can examine this file in Wordpad, BBEdit, or any text editor of choice. If you move to another machine and use the spelling-check feature a lot, you may want to copy this file to your new machine.

■ **Encodings** Contains the information for various document character encodings, as shown in the Document Encoding drop-down box in the Page Properties dialog box under the Modify menu. There are several character encodings available by default. These are listed in the EncodingMenu.xml file. If you want to add your own encoding format, you should also change this file to reflect your new encoding file.

■ **Extensions** By its very name, you would think that this is where UltraDev extensions reside. It is, in fact, the repository for the MXI files (files with an .mxi file extension) that accompany any extensions that you have installed. These MXI files are actually XML files that contain instructions to the Extension Manager for installing an extension into UltraDev or Dreamweaver.

■ **Floaters** Stores your custom floaters, if you decide to implement them. UltraDev comes with only one JavaScript floater installed—the Welcome floater—but you are free to add more if you like. These are discussed in Chapter 23.

■ **Inspectors** Contains the Inspectors, or Property Inspectors, which are the little attribute sheets that pop up at the bottom of the screen when you make a selection in the document. The Inspector's job is to find all the attributes of the selected object or Behavior and display them so that the user can edit them. Typically, when writing an extension, you also write an Inspector to go with it. These are discussed in Chapter 23.

■ **JDBCDrivers** If you're a JSP programmer and use custom classes for your JDBC database drivers, this is where you can put them to have UltraDev recognize them. Copy your JAR or ZIP files to this folder, and UltraDev will recognize them. Additionally, you may have to edit the Connections.xml file to get your JSP drivers to be recognized.

■ **JSExtensions** By its name, you might think that this is where your JavaScript extensions go—it's not. This is where the various DLLs (shared libraries) from C-level extensions reside. The name JSExtensions relates to the fact that these shared libraries give you more JavaScript functionality in your extension writing. You can create extensions in C that interact with JavaScript extensions and the UltraDev API.

■ **Menus** Contains the main UltraDev menu, menus.xml, as well as a backup copy. Although you can manually edit the menus.xml file, it is much better to write your changes to the file as an extension in an MXI file so that the changes can be easily uninstalled.

■ **Objects** Includes the objects that reside in your Objects floater. The folder is organized into subfolders, each of which has a corresponding tab in the Objects floater. If you put object files into these subfolders, they will appear in your object floater. These are discussed in the next chapter.

■ **Plugins** The UnsupportedPlugins.txt file contains a list of plug-ins that are not supported by Dreamweaver. You can place plug-ins that you use into this folder.

■ **Queries** Stores your Find/Replace patterns when saved. You may have noticed a little disk icon in the Find/Replace dialog box. When you click this icon, your search pattern is saved into this folder for reuse.

■ **ServerBehaviors** Contains the complex server-side scripts that turn UltraDev into a database-aware development environment. Server Behaviors are typically the hardest of the extensions to write. The main folder has three subfolders, one for each of the server languages—JSP, ASP, and ColdFusion. These are discussed in Chapter 22.

■ **ServerFormats** Contains the various formats for displaying different types of data in UltraDev, depending on which server format you happen to be using. These formats are accessible through Dynamic Data | Format. You can edit the ServerFormats.xml file to add more menu items to the menu, and edit the Formats.xml file to add new formats to the mix.

■ **ServerModels** Includes the files that define some of the functions common to the specific server model that you happen to be working on. If you want to add a new server model, such as PHP, you have to define the various standard UltraDev functions in this folder, such as findAllRepeatedRegionNames() and findAllRecordsetNames().

■ **Shared** Contains a wealth of functions and general information in the form of fully commented JavaScript for use by extension developers to add to the functionality of UltraDev.

■ **SiteCache**   Stores information about links in your site. The folder is empty until you define your sites. You are prompted "Would you like to create a cache file for this site?" when you create a site. The results of the cache reside in this folder.

■ **Startup**   Scripts that need to run as UltraDev starts up are placed in this folder.

■ **Templates**   Contains the empty template files for your use as a Web developer. You can place skeleton HTML, ASP, JSP, CF, or whatever files you use frequently into this folder, which will save you time in development. When you want to create a new file, choose File | New From Template, and a list of the files in this folder will be presented. For example, suppose you have a recordset that is used on several pages in your site. You could define it on a page, and then save the page into this folder. Every time you start a new page with that recordset on it, you can create it from this template. The file default.htm is the standard start file for all new pages. You can modify this particular file for your own use, as well.

■ **ThirdPartyTags**   Stores tags other than the standard HTML tags. You'll find files for ASP, CF, JSP, and other third-party tags in here. These can be edited, or new files can be added. If UltraDev comes across a tag that it doesn't understand, it looks in this folder for a match.

■ **Translators**   Contains translators that will translate a file and insert it into a page. Translators can be used for Include files or any other sort of file that you want to be able to edit in the UltraDev environment. Note also that the Live Data files reside in this folder.

Additional Configuration Folders for UltraDev 4

UltraDev 4 introduced several new items to the Configuration folder that correspond to the new features of UltraDev 4, such as JavaBeans, a client-side debugger, and Flash Objects. In keeping with tradition, many of the new features are extensible and can be customized to your needs.

■ **Classes**   UltraDev 4 adds JavaBeans to the arsenal, and enables you to add your class files to this folder.

■ **Debugger**   Contains the new JavaScript debugger and its parts.

■ **Flash Objects**   As Macromedia continues to integrate its product lines, some of the features of its successful products make their way into other products. This folder includes objects created in Flash that can be used in UltraDev.

■ **Generator**   Includes the files for Generator, Macromedia's high-end program for integrating dynamic graphics into a site, which is tightly integrated with UltraDev.

- **ExtensionData** Includes XML files that the new Server Behaviors use. The extension developer can modify these or create his own. Also, when you create a new Server Behavior with the new Behavior builder, the resulting XML files are placed in this folder. The Participants subfolder contains the essential data.

- **Reports** UltraDev 4 has an extensible site-reporting architecture that allows you to create your own reports based on whichever criteria you establish. HTML/JavaScript report extensions can be stored in this folder.

- **SourceControl** UltraDev 4 introduces the ability to use the program with WebDAV and SourceSafe. The data is stored in this folder.

- **Reference** UltraDev 4 has a new set of integrated reference books in HTML format. You can create your own reference books that conform to the standard defined in the extensibility documents and place them in here.

As you can see, all parts of UltraDev are open for customization. The API is laid out in such a way as to simplify the process of writing your own objects, commands, Behaviors, and whatever else you may require. The 400-page "Extending Dreamweaver and UltraDev" document contains technical information on the techniques and methods of extension writing. This document has been expanded to over 600 pages for UltraDev 4. Also, the help files in the Extension Manager folder give the ground rules for writing "official" extensions that can be packaged and submitted to Macromedia for approval, or posted on the Exchange for Dreamweaver or UltraDev.

The best way to start writing extensions, though, is to dive right in and write one. At some point, the Library items won't give you all the functionality you need, and you'll want to create a custom extension to insert some code on the page. Extensions give you the power to add user-defined attributes to a block of code easily, and go back and edit those attributes if necessary. The easiest extension to start with is the object—so the next chapter begins by showing you how to write Object extensions.

Chapter 21

Objects

Objects are simply snippets of HTML and script that are written to the Web page as a predetermined string of code. They usually represent "visual" elements of HTML, such as images, form fields, tables, and other "physical" things that a user can see on the page. Objects are also the most basic of extensions that you can write yourself.

Objects reside in the Objects folder under Configuration. If you look inside this folder, you'll see other subfolders—Characters, Common, Forms, Frames, Head, and Invisibles. These folders appear in the corresponding tabs of the Objects palette in UltraDev. In addition, UltraDev 4 adds the following new objects to the mix: Live Objects, Special, and Tools. If you add your own folder inside of the Objects folder, you effectively add a new tab to the Objects palette. If you plan to write Object extensions, it's a good idea to separate them from the standard extensions by putting your own folder in here.

Objects have three corresponding files:

- **HTML file**   Contains the user interface and the form to get any attributes from the user.

- **JS file**   Contains the functions that do the work to create your object. The JS file is optional, because you can include your JavaScript in the HTML file. In general, if the JavaScript occupies more than a few lines, it could be included as a separate file.

- **GIF file**   An 18 × 18–pixel GIF image that will be the icon in the Objects palette. If the GIF file is missing, UltraDev gives your object a generic icon.

Standard icons (files with the .ico extension) are 16 × 16, so converting them into a GIF file using a dedicated icon editor such as Microangelo is a snap. UltraDev Object GIF files will even work fine at 16 × 16. You can create one in any good image-editing program as well.

These files all have the same name—the name of the object—each with its own respective file extension. For example, a Table object will have Table.htm, Table.js, and Table.gif files associated with it.

Modifying an Object

You'll start by modifying a simple object, before you dive in and create a new one. Begin by copying the Table.htm, Table.js, and Table.gif files from the Common folder to a new folder under Objects, named Custom Objects, and then start up UltraDev. If you click the subtitle bar under the Objects title bar in the floater, you should find your new Custom Objects tab in the menu. Click it, and the Table object should now be on the menu.

Start with a very basic change—you'll wrap the table with a layer automatically so that it can be dragged around on the screen in true WYSIWYG fashion. To do this, you need to add one function to the JS file—objectInsertLayer().

Open the Table.js file in HomeSite, BBEdit, or any text editor of choice; add the following function to the file; and then save it:

```
function objectInsertLayer() {
    return "TRUE";
};
```

After the file is saved, it is ready for use; but if you have UltraDev open, it won't change until you "reload" your extensions.

Note   *You can reload the extensions in UltraDev by restarting the program or by CTRL–clicking the subtitle bar of the Object menu and clicking the menu item Reload Extensions. This is an unsupported feature, because it doesn't work with all extensions, but it is a great timesaver for some extension work.*

Click the Table object in the palette and "draw" a table onto your page by clicking anywhere on the page, and holding the button down as you move the mouse downward and to the right. When you release the mouse button, your table should be there, wrapped in a layer. If you desire to change the sizes of the layer or the table, you can click the handles of the layer or table and resize it so that they match, or differ, as your need dictates. Now, you can move the table around on the page by clicking and holding on the little drag handle in the upper-left corner of the layer box. This trick works with most objects, and it approximates the WYSIWYG approach of desktop publishing programs that is lacking from most Web design software. Some UltraDev users have made entire palettes of these objects.

Caution   *UltraDev recognizes the table and the layer as two separate objects. They can easily become separated, because they are not actually combined as one unit. But, with this example, you can see how easy it is to make a significant change in the functionality of an object.*

Now that you've had exposure to the power of extensibility, you're ready to delve into the world of objects.

Object Files

An object file is built as a basic HTML page. The most basic form of object is raw HTML that you may insert into your file. If you have some code that you want to put into your page, and it's something that's used frequently, you can put the code into its own

HTML page, package and save it as an object, and then it will be available for use any time you need it. These kinds of objects are known as *simple objects,* because they require no user interaction or user-defined attributes of any kind. They are simply inserted as is into the open document at the insertion point. These could also be saved as Library items, but are more easily transferable as objects from site to site and from computer to computer. In addition, you can go beyond the basic functionality of a Library item when you include user-defined attributes.

> **Caution** *It's better to always avoid using <head>, <body>, <meta>, or other similar tags that are considered standard in a well-formed HTML file within an object file that uses the "simple" object form (no objectTag() function). Also, you should always put the string of code you want to insert inside a single pair of <html> tags. If not, UltraDev may add spurious or redundant <meta> and <style> tags to the document where the object is inserted.*

Suppose you have a company logo and tagline that are included in various places within your pages. Use the Bettergig.com site logo from the CD-ROM as an example. You could insert an image, navigate to the correct file on your hard drive, and then insert your tagline—a procedure that may be repeated as many times as is required. However, if the procedure is something that you may need to do frequently, it would be to your advantage to make it into an object. This will certainly speed up the process of design.

You are now going to create this simple extension, using the BGigLogo.gif file on the CD-ROM. Create a new site called TestExtensions in a folder named TestExtensions under your root, and then place the BGigLogo.gif file into that folder. Open your text editor of choice, and enter the following HTML code onto a blank page:

```
<html>
<a href="http://www.bettergig.com">
<img src="BGLogo.GIF" align="center" hspace=5
alt="Get a better life. . .get a better gig!"></a>
<b> Get a better life. . .get a better gig!</b><br>
This site and its contents &copy;2000 by Bettergig.com
</html>
```

Now, save the file under the Custom Objects folder, inside the Objects folder, as BGLogo.htm. Reload your extensions, and the new extension should be ready for use. Go ahead and click the generic icon. The logo with the tagline should appear on your page (see Figure 21-1). This technique will work with any HTML that you need to insert into a page. It will always insert the object at the cursor insertion point. This might be a good time to include an icon with the object, because you are going to build a few more. At this point, copy the BGLogo.gif file from the CD-ROM to the Custom Objects folder, and reload your extensions. Now, the generic icon should be replaced with a custom icon to match your extension.

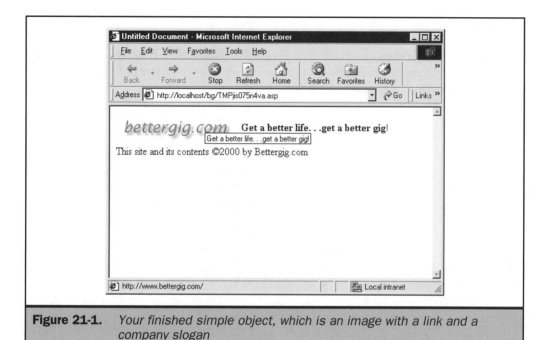

Figure 21-1.   *Your finished simple object, which is an image with a link and a company slogan*

The objectTag() Function

Suppose you want to make more complex objects. This is where the objectTag() function comes into play. Your simple objects can be expanded to create more complex entities with user-defined attributes. The way that most of the objects in UltraDev work is that the HTML file contains form elements that the user is able to fill out with the various attributes that the object requires. For instance, in the Table object, you are prompted for rows, columns, cell padding, cell spacing, width, border, and percent/pixels. These text fields are all form elements in the HTML file, Table.htm. The JS file then takes these user- defined attributes and formats them in such a way as to create a string of HTML code that represents an HTML table. After the formatting is complete, the objectTag() function returns the string to UltraDev that contains the complete table, which is then inserted into the source and rendered by UltraDev to the page visually.

GETTING THE MOST
OUT OF ULTRADEV

Note   *In UltraDev, a fine line sometimes exists between a Library item and an object. Generally speaking, items such as those in the example you just completed are fine as Library items. They become object material only when you need to reuse them frequently throughout your Web site development or apply any user-defined attributes to them.*

The objectTag() function is built into the Dreamweaver and UltraDev DOM and is called when an object is selected, if it exists. If the function doesn't exist, the entire HTML file is inserted into the document, as it was earlier with the simple object. It is wise to take advantage of the simple object whenever you don't have any user-defined attributes to be concerned with. If you do have user-defined attributes, create a JS file and include the objectTag() function, along with whichever other functions are necessary to format your attributes properly for the final page. The way to include the JS file in the object is to place an include line into the HTML file, like this:

```
<script language = "javascript"¬
src="Table.js"></script>
```

You may also include any other files that you may need. Many useful functions are available in the Shared directory in the Configuration folder. This Shared directory is also where you should put your own often-used functions within your own folder that you have named. By Macromedia's standards, an extension stored in the root folders under Configuration should only have one of each of the three file types mentioned—JS, HTM, and GIF. For example, the BGLogo extension could have BGLogo.htm, BGLogo.js, and BGLogo.gif. Anything else should be placed in the Shared directory. This is where things such as company logos, JS files of shared functions, images, or temporary directories should go. Then, you can reference your file in an object like this:

```
<script language = "javascript"¬
src="../../Shared/Bettergig/BGFiles/Functions.js">
```

Using the objectTag() Function in the Company Logo Example

To demonstrate a few of the principles previously discussed, you now are going to build another object. You'll build the company logo–generating object, but this time you'll use the objectTag() function to put it on the page. When you previously built the simple object, the actual HTML from the object file was written to the page. That's fine when a predefined piece of code is being inserted on the page. But, in the case in which you are receiving input or attributes from the Web developer, you need to do a little string manipulation to put the user-defined attributes together with the HTML.

Create a new HTML file named NewBGLogo.htm. Begin by inserting a script declaration in the head section referencing your JS file:

```
<html>
<head>
<script language = "javascript" src="NewBGLogo.js"></script>
</head>
<body>
</body>
</html>
```

This enables you to use functions in a NewBGLogo.js file in your object. Save the file in the Custom Objects folder. Now, you need to create the NewBGLogo.js file. This can be done in any text editor, such as BBEdit on the Mac or HomeSite on the PC. Start with a blank page and insert the following function:

```
function objectTag() {
    var tag = '';
    tag ='<a href="http://www.bettergig.com">';
    tag += '<img src="BGigLogo.GIF" align="center" hspace=5 ';
    tag += 'alt=" Get a better life. . .get a better gig!" ></a>\n';
    tag += '<b> Get a better life. . .get a better gig!</b><br>\n';
    tag += 'This site and its contents &copy;2000 by Bettergig.com';
    return tag;
    }
```

Save the file as NewBGLogo.js in the Custom Objects folder, and then reload your extensions or restart UltraDev.

This object does exactly the same thing that your original simple object does—insert the code at the cursor insertion point. What is different, however, is that the code that you want to put on the page is actually now built as a string, and then returned by the objectTag() function to UltraDev. If you apply the object to the page, you'll see the same object as before. Also notice that when you use this approach, you have to make sure your spaces are in all the right places. A space is inserted after the alternate text declaration (to allow for other image attributes to be inserted), and a space is inserted after the hspace declaration, because you are adding the next line *immediately* after this line. Newline characters (\n) also are placed into the text to break up your source code. These will not affect how end users see the page when they browse, but it will make your source code easier to read.

This approach is very powerful, because you now can get parameters from the user and add them to the string to make the object more functional. In the UltraDev environment, open the file NewBGLogo.htm that you just created. To do this, you should first define a new site as Custom Objects with the Custom Objects folder as the root of the site. You can leave the Server Model and Server Access pages blank. Now, open the file. Your page will be blank. Add a table with two rows and three columns (see Figure 21-2) with the following attributes applied to the objects:

- Text field named txtLink
- Text field named txtImage
- Button named browse

This provides a way for the developer to put his or her own image into the object without hard-coding the name of the image into the object. The link will be user defined, as well.

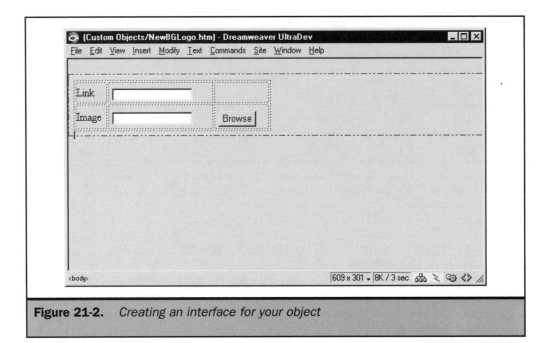

Figure 21-2.   *Creating an interface for your object*

Now save the file. If you reload your extensions and click your NewBGLogo file, the dialog box will be invoked. It doesn't do anything yet, because you haven't added any functionality to it, but you can see that UltraDev has added the OK and Cancel buttons to the form. These will be on every object. You can add a third button, Help, simply by adding a displayHelp() function. UltraDev will automatically add a Help button if it sees this function.

Now examine how to get the parameters from a form. You'll be accessing the form elements with the findObject() function, as described in Chapter 20. The txtLink field will be a standard text field HTML object, getting text from the user. The txtImage field will get its value from a filename that you designate by browsing files with the Browse button. You want to invoke a function of the onClick method of the button to bring up a dialog box that will fetch the filename of an image on your hard drive. There's a built-in function that does this—browseFile(fieldToStoreURL)—and it will take a text field object as the parameter. This function resides in the File.js file in the \Shared\MM\Scripts\Cmn directory. To get the text field object, you'll use the findObject(objName) function, described in Chapter 20. This resides in the UI.js file. You'll have to set up these shared files as include files to be able to access the functions. At this time, add the following lines after the other script-declaration line in the NewBGLogo.htm file:

```
<script language = "javascript"¬
src="..\..\Shared\MM\Scripts\Cmn\UI.js"></script>
<script language = "javascript"¬
src="..\..\Shared\MM\Scripts\Cmn\file.js"></script>
```

This will set the references to the shared files that contain the functions. The browseFile function takes as a parameter the name of a form field in your form. You'll use txtImage. To access the function, you need to set an onClick event for your button, like this:

```
<input type="button" name="browse" value="Browse"
onClick="browseFile(findObject('txtImage'))">
```

This enables the user to browse the hard drive for a file, and insert the result into the Image text field in the NewBGLogo object. Then, you need to initialize the user interface by inserting a function into your JS file called initializeUI(). This function is used in most extensions that contain a user interface of some sort.

```
function initializeUI() {
findObject("txtLink").focus(); //sets the focus in the link field
findObject("txtLink").select(); //sets insertion point in the link field
}
```

You then invoke the function by referencing it in the <body> tag's onLoad event in the HTM file:

```
<body onLoad="initializeUI()">
```

Note   *Putting a function in the onLoad event of the <body> tag of an extension is directing the extension to call this function first as the object is being applied to the page.*

Go ahead and save the object and then try to use it. At this point, when you click the Browse button, the Select File dialog box should pop up and ask you to select a file. If the file you choose doesn't reside in your Web folder, the function will ask you whether you want to copy it there. After you indicate that you would like to copy the selected filename, it will be copied in your text field, ready to be inserted into your object.

All that needs to be done now is to take the information that the user has entered in the two form fields and insert it into the tag string. You'll use the findObject() function to get the values in this way, inserted at the beginning of the objectTag() function:

```
var theImage = findObject("txtImage").value;
var theLink = findObject("txtLink").value;
```

As noted earlier, you could have used dot notation to access the document node also, as in the following:

```
var theImage = document.forms[0].txtImage.value;
var theLink = document.forms[0].txtLink.value;
```

Both ways are valid, but you should get into the habit of doing one or the other to maintain consistency in your extensions. We prefer to use the findObject() function to keep things consistent and readable. Once you have the values of the text fields assigned to variables, it will be very easy to manipulate your string of HTML. Simply remove the hard-coded values for the link and image source, and replace them with your variable names. We use plus signs (+) to put our string together. Your final objectTag() function looks like this:

```
function objectTag() {
    var tag = '';
    tag='<a href="' + theLink + '">';
    tag+='<img src="' + theImage + '" align="center" hspace=5 ';
    tag+='alt=" Get a better life. . .get a better gig!" ></a>\n';
    tag+='<b> Get a better life. . .get a better gig!</b><br>\n';
    tag+='This site and its contents &copy;2000 by Bettergig.com';
    return tag;
}
```

This example also demonstrates that you can include quotes in your strings by using single quotes around the string. If you need to include actual single quotes in the string, you surround your string, including the single quotes, with double quotes. JavaScript is flexible in that it allows both single and double quotes to surround a string. The other possibility is to use an escape code—a backslash (\)—to include double quotes in the string, as in this line:

```
tag = "\"Hello,\" said John"
```

Building a Table Object with Alternating Row Colors

Now you are going to create a more complex object. You'll take the standard Table object and add an option to put rows into it that alternate in color. At first, this object is going to work with a standard table (no dynamic data or repeated regions). Later, you'll add the functionality to make it work with dynamic data in all three server models—ASP, JSP, and ColdFusion.

Copy the Table.htm, Table.js, and Table.gif files to the Custom Objects folder and name them CustomTable.htm, CustomTable.js, and CustomTable.gif, respectively. The first step is to open the HTM file inside the UltraDev environment and add two rows to it. You can do this by going to the Table Inspector and incrementing the Rows by two, or right-clicking the table and choosing Insert Rows or Columns and selecting Rows and typing **2**. On these two new rows, you have to eliminate the middle row divider by right-clicking inside the middle cell of each row and choosing Table | Increase Column Span. That accomplished, you'll add your new form fields— two list menus and two buttons. The attributes for these two rows should be set as follows:

- Row 1:
  - **Caption**   Even Rows
  - **Listmenu**   Named evenStyle
  - **Button**   Named browseEven with a label of "New"

- Row 2:
  - **Caption**   Odd Rows
  - **Listmenu**   Named oddStyle
  - **Button**   Named browseOdd with a label of "New"

In addition, the two listmenus should have the *list values* attribute set to "**no styles defined**" and the *initially selected* attribute set to "**no styles defined**" as well.

When you've finished, the table should look like the table in Figure 21-3. Save it, and open it in your text editor. You're going to add some functionality to the buttons. Begin by adding the following text (in bold) to the browseEven and browseOdd buttons, respectively:

```
<input type="button" name="browseEven" value="New"¬
onClick="getMoreStyles('evenStyle')">

<input type="button" name="browseOdd" value="New"¬
onClick="getMoreStyles('oddStyle')">
```

Note   *You can also use an image button in place of the standard button for extensions such as these.*

You also have to change the reference to your JS file by changing the reference line to the following:

```
<script language = "javascript"¬
src="CustomTable.js"></script>
```

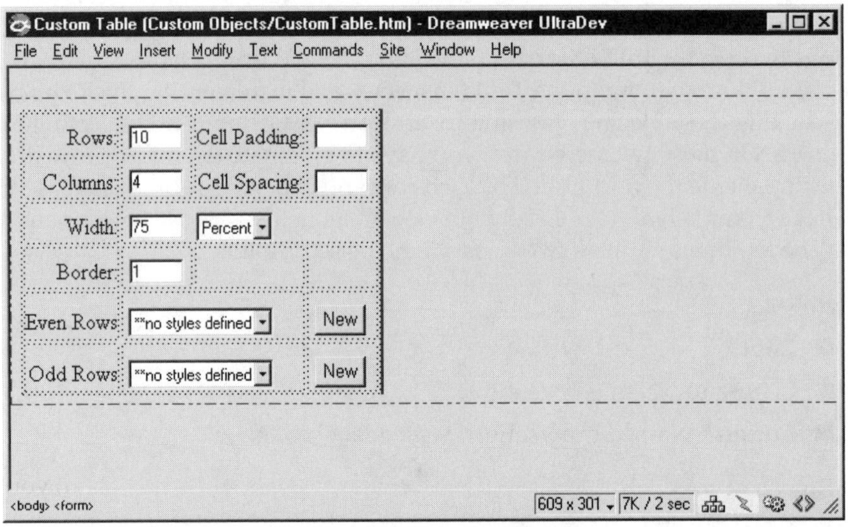

Figure 21-3. Your new Table object with select boxes for styles and buttons for defining new styles

Notice the comment right below the script reference that says "Remove the following SCRIPT tag if you are modifying this file for your own use." You can safely delete these lines, which reference the UltraDev help file for the Table object. In fact, the line is passing a displayHelp() function into your object, which, as you may remember, will cause UltraDev to put a Help button on your form. You'll create your own later.

For now, you'll add a function to populate the select boxes. This is a general function that you can use in your own extensions. It takes two parameters—the select box name and an array of strings to insert into the box:

```
function populateSelect(theSelectbox,theArray){
    var theSelect;
    theSelect = findObject(theSelectbox); //gets the object
    theSelect.options.length = 0;          //initializes options to 0
    //and also removes any current entries from the select box
    for (var i=0; i<theArray.length; i++){//loop through the array
        theSelect.options[i] = new Option(theArray[i]);//set the options
    }
    theSelect.selectedIndex = 0;           //set the selected index to 0
}
```

You'll be calling this function from the initializeUI() function, which is called on the onLoad event of the <body> tag. You'll add the following lines to the beginning of the initializeUI() function:

```
var theStyles = new Array();  //declare a new array
//the following line gets all styles on the page
theStyles = dreamweaver.cssStylePalette.getStyles();
if(theStyles.length > 0) {
//if there are any styles, we want to populate both select boxes
    populateSelect("evenStyle",theStyles);
    populateSelect("oddStyle",theStyles);
    }
```

Recall the onClick() function that you attached to the buttons; you're going to write that function now. The function is going to enable you to create a new style using the built-in Dreamweaver Style definition dialog box. When the style is created, you'll populate your select box again with the new information. To do this, you need the select box name, the one parameter that is passed to the function:

```
function getMoreStyles(theStyleSelect) {
    var theStyles = new Array();
    dreamweaver.cssStylePalette.newStyle();
//this invokes the CSS dialog box
    theStyles = dreamweaver.cssStylePalette.getStyles();
//get all styles available to the page
    populateSelect(theStyleSelect,theStyles);
//populate the select box with the styles
    }
```

If you save the file now and reload your extensions or restart UltraDev, the New buttons (refer to Figure 21-3) should work. When you click one, the Style definition dialog box opens, and you then can define a style and name it. After you've done that, the style should appear in the select box.

 When you build your own extensions, you should include error-handling routines to prevent users from entering "bad" attributes. This discussion has been kept simple to outline the basic principles of extension building, but error handling is important and should be attached to any form field that allows a user to input information.

You'll add these variable definitions to the beginning of the CustomTable.js file. The two chosen styles will be put into a two-element array, so that when you loop to create the table, you can also loop through the array:

```
var rowColor = new Array();
var TempIndex = findObject("oddStyle").selectedIndex;
rowColor[0] = findObject("oddStyle").options[TempIndex].text;
TempIndex = findObject("evenStyle").selectedIndex;
rowColor[1] = findObject("evenStyle").options[TempIndex].text;
```

Now that you have two styles to work with, you simply need to put the sections of code within the code to have UltraDev automatically generate a new table with rows that alternate in color. To do this, locate the table row definition line, which looks like this:

```
tableRow = "<"+"tr>" + tableRow + "<"+"/tr>";
```

You'll get rid of this line. You'll change it to reflect your alternate table rows, and then insert it into the function that follows it, until it reads like this:

```
for(i=0; i<Rows; i++) {
    newRow = '<tr class="' + rowColor[i%2] + '">'
    newRow += (tableRow + "<" + "/tr>");
    tableContent += newRow;
    }
```

Here, the JavaScript MOD function (%) is used to get the remainder of a division between i and 2. This will either be 1 or 0, so that your rowColor array will alternate. The string builds up table row after table row until it has finished. All that remains now is to save it and try it on a page (see Figure 21-4).

Adding Server-Side Code to the Object

Because UltraDev can handle server-side code as well, you can add some to your table. Generally speaking, it is best to put your server-side code into a Server Behavior, a procedure that is addressed in Chapter 22. In the meantime, give your alternating colored rows Table object the capability to work with a standard Repeated Region. Remember, the Repeated Region Server Behavior works well if you use a one-row table and apply the Server Behavior to the cells in the row. You now are going to insert some server-side code into the Table object itself to handle the changing of styles. In addition, you'll make it work with all three server models. You accomplish that by using a built-in function to determine the server language and place it into the serverLanguage variable in your variable declaration section:

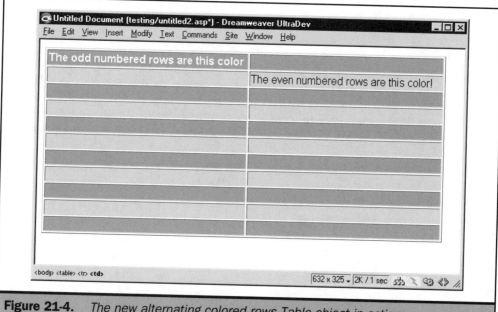

Figure 21-4.   *The new alternating colored rows Table object in action*

```
var theDom = getDocumentDOM();
var serverLanguage = theDom.serverModel.getServerLanguage();
```

Note	*Putting your server-side code into an object has advantages and disadvantages. The advantage is that it's easy to implement. The disadvantage is that you can't "remove" it, as you can a dedicated Server Behavior. Luckily, UltraDev has built-in Property Inspectors for any custom server code—click the "gold shield" icon on the page, and your custom code will pop up in an Inspector.*

Now, you have to decide what code to use. For the ASP model using VBScript, you'll use the following to replace a <tr> tag:

```
<tr class= ¬
<%If (Repeat1__numRows Mod 2) Then%>
(substitute odd rowColor)
<%Else%>
(substitute even rowColor)
```

```
<%End If%>
>
```

This code manipulates the HTML on the server side by putting it within an If/Then/Else block of code. You send only one of the style class names to the browser through each iteration of the loop. You use the UltraDev Repeated Region variable Repeat1__numRows to get your row color. It's similar in concept to the standard table that you just constructed, but the server does it on-the-fly. Here's the JavaScript code for the ASP model:

```
<tr class=
<%if(Repeat1__numRows % 2 == 1) {
//(substitute odd rowColor)
<%}else{%>
//(substitute even rowColor)
<%}%>
>
```

Note *The term "JavaScript" also is used when referring to the server-side ASP JScript code. It is more correct to refer to it as "JScript," but the Dreamweaver API recognizes the term "JavaScript."*

The principle is the same, but the syntax is a little different. Luckily for you, the Java version for JSP is the same as the JavaScript version. All that remains is a ColdFusion version (this should be on one line):

```
<tr class=
#IIF(CurrentRow MOD 2, DE(substitute odd rowColor)¬
DE(substitute even rowColor))#>
```

The principle is the same for the ColdFusion version, but you use the CurrentRow variable that's built into the ColdFusion server. The Repeated Region Server Behavior in ColdFusion doesn't have a loop attached to it—it uses the built-in power of the CFOUTPUT tag on the server side to iterate through the loops.

First, you need to put a check box into your interface to allow you to check whether the user is using a Repeat Region in the table. The interface has two free cells— cells three and four in row four. Put the caption "Repeated region?" in cell three and a checkbox in cell four, with the name "repeatRegion" and with a checked value of 1. Initial state should be "unchecked."

Tip   *Checkboxes are a handy way to implement an optional feature in an extension. By checking the box, the user is in effect adding additional code to the extension.*

Next, you'll initialize some variables at the beginning of the objectTag section. Place the following code somewhere at the beginning of the function:

```
var theDom = dw.getDocumentDOM();
var serverLanguage = theDom.serverModel.getServerLanguage();
var RepeatRegion = findObject("repeatRegion").checked;
//is it checked?
var serverLangIndex = 0;
//initialize your index for server languages
if(RepeatRegion == false) {
    serverLangIndex = 0;
    //if not checked (false), this is a static table
}else{
    if(serverLanguage == "VBScript") serverLangIndex = 1;
    if(serverLanguage == "Cold Fusion") serverLangIndex = 2;
    if(serverLanguage == "Java" || serverLanguage == "JavaScript")
serverLangIndex = 3;
    }
```

Now, build an array of <tr> tags for the different server models:

```
var tableRowTags = new Array();
tableRowTags[1]='<tr class=<%If (Repeat1__numRows Mod 2) Then%>"';
tableRowTags[1] += (rowColor[0] +  '"<%Else%>"');
tableRowTags[1] += (rowColor[1] + '"<%End If%>>');
//VBScript version

tableRowTags[2] = '<tr class=#IIF(CurrentRow MOD 2, DE("';
tableRowTags[2] += (rowColor[0] + '",DE("');
tableRowTags[2] += (rowColor[1] + '"))#>');   //ColdFusion version

tableRowTags[3] = '<tr class=<%if(Repeat1__numRows % 2 == 1) {%>"';
tableRowTags[3] += (rowColor[0] + '"<%}else{%>"');
tableRowTags[3] += (rowColor[1] + '"<%}%>>');
//JavaScript and Java version
```

Finally, add the code that will build the table rows "dynamically" with the Repeated Region Server Behavior, while at the same time leaving the ability to use a static-type table with alternate-style rows. You'll change the table row concatenation routine as follows (the new code is in bold):

```
for (i=0; i< Rows; i++){
    if (serverLangIndex) {
        newRow = tableRowTags[serverLangIndex]:
        newRow += tableRow + "<" + "/tr>";
    }else{
        newRow = '<tr class="' + rowColor[i % 2] +'">';
        newRow += (tableRow + "<"+"/tr>");
    }
    tableContent += newRow;
}
```

If you save the file and reload your extensions, the table will now work with a Repeat Region. Generally, when working with a Repeated Region, you use a one- row table and then select the cells to apply the repeat to. If you happen to choose a two- or three-row table, the colors will repeat every second or third row, as can be expected. By adding the preceding few simple lines to a standard object, you will completely shape and remodel the table into a more flexible object. In this object, server-side code was also added for three server models using about 20 lines of JavaScript code.

Implementing all the server models in your extensions isn't necessary. However, if you know how to program for one model, inserting extra code for the other server models isn't that much more difficult. The hard work is writing the functions and building the algorithms that do the work; but after that is done, you simply plug in the code. If you only choose to work with one server model, however, it is still a good idea to check for which server model being used and throw an alert if the user happens to be working with a server model that your extension doesn't support. If you have an ASP object, for instance, you can check for the server model; and if it's not ASP, display an error message that says "This object only works in ASP."

Display Help

Building a help file is something you might want to consider if your extension is complex or requires any special instructions. The help file can be a basic HTML page with instructions, or a complex series of pages with images and hyperlinks. However you decide to do it, the basic method for displaying a help file is with the displayHelp() function. This is a function that UltraDev will look for when a user accesses your extension. If the function exists in your extension file in any form, the extension interface will have a Help button below the Cancel and OK buttons.

At its most basic level, the displayHelp() function can just flash an alert box like this:

```
function displayHelp() {
    var alertText = "Choose two styles from the drop-down lists\n"
    alertText += "or click the 'New' button to create new styles."
    alert(alertText);
}
```

At a more advanced level, you can use the built-in browseDocument(path) function of UltraDev, which causes your default browser to pop up with the Web page that is passed to the function. You can call the function like this:

```
dreamweaver.browseDocument(myHelpPage);
```

Note   *Keep in mind that you have to pass the entire path to the function; otherwise, UltraDev won't know where to find it.*

Another built-in function, getConfigurationPath(), enables you to find the path of the UltraDev program on the hard drive. This works on both the Mac and in Windows. The getConfigurationPath() function will return the full path to the Configuration folder. It's called like this:

```
var pathToConfig = dw.getConfigurationPath();
```

After you have that information, you can append the location of your help file to it, like this:

```
var fullPath = pathToConfig + "/Shared/MyFolder/Helpdocs/CustomTable.htm";
```

The full displayHelp() function for the CustomTable object would look like this:

```
function displayHelp() {
    var pathToConfig = dw.getConfigurationPath();
    var fullPath = pathToConfig +¬
"/Shared/MyFolder/Helpdocs/CustomTable.htm"
    dreamweaver.browseDocument(fullPath);
    }
```

Instead of putting a help file into the shared folder, you could have it on the Web somewhere, and just point to your Web site using the full path of the file, like this:

```
dreamweaver.browseDocument("http://www.mysite.com/help/CustomTable.htm");
```

Now that you've added some server-side functionality to an already existing object, you'll build one from scratch, using some ASP code.

 ## Creating a Server Object

In this section, you will build an object that will display the last access date of the page to the user. You'll need to use the File System object of ASP to do it, and you'll write a VBScript and a JavaScript version of the object. This object could also have been written as a Server Behavior.

> **Tip** *Generally speaking, if your code fits into one code block and resides inside the <body> tag, you can use an object instead of a Server Behavior.*

The following is the VBScript code that you are going to use:

```
<%
DateFile = Server.MapPath("\DateFile.txt")
On Error Resume Next
Set TM_fs = Server.CreateObject("Scripting.FileSystemObject")
Set a = TM_fs.OpenTextFile(DateFile, 1, 0, 0)
LastDate = a.ReadLine
InStream.Close
Application("lastAccessDate")= LastDate
LastDate = Month(Now) & "/" & Day(Now) & "/" & Year(Now)
LastDate = LastDate & " " & Time
set b = TM_fs.CreateTextFile (DateFile, 1, 0)
b.WriteLine LastDate
b.Close
%>
This page was last viewed on
<% Response.Write(Application("lastAccessDate"))%>
```

As you've already read, you now simply need to build the code into a string that will be returned to the UltraDev environment and then be inserted into the page. Server-side code has a few additional caveats. For one, you need to make sure that the language declaration is at the top of the page. Also, because UltraDev handles several server models, you need to make sure that you are currently in the correct language for the object. You accomplish this in much the same way that you did in the CustomTable object. However, in this case, you'll flash an alert box if the user is in a JSP or ColdFusion site, or doesn't have a server model declared. Your code skeleton, before you add the return object to it, is as follows:

```
<html>
<head>
<title>Insert Last Access Date</title>
<meta http-equiv="Content-Type" content="text/html;¬
charset=iso-8859-1">
<script language = "javascript"¬
src="../Shared/MM/Scripts/CMN/docInfo.js"></SCRIPT>
<script language = "javascript"¬
src="../Shared/MM/Scripts/CMN/DOM.js"></SCRIPT>
<script language="javascript">
//--------------        API FUNCTIONS     --------------
function insertLanguageDeclaration() {
var theDom = dw.getDocumentDOM();
var serverLanguage = theDom.serverModel.getServerLanguage();
if (serverLanguage != "CFML") {
    var htmlNode = theDom.getElementsByTagName("html")[0];
    var preHeadCode=htmlNode.outerHTML;
    var pattern = new RegExp('<%@LANGUAGE=[^%]*%>');
    var theNode = pattern.exec(preHeadCode);
    if(theNode == null) {
        theNode = "<%@LANGUAGE=" + serverLanguage.toUpperCase() +¬
        "%>\n";
        EndSection = preHeadCode;
    }else{
        EndSection = RegExp.rightContext;
    };
    htmlNode.outerHTML =  theNode + EndSection;
}
return serverLanguage;
}

function objectTag() {
var serverLanguage = insertLanguageDeclaration();
var tag = "";
var myScriptObject = "";
if(serverLanguage=="VBScript") {
    myScriptObject = new VBScriptObject();
}else if(serverLanguage=="JavaScript") {
    myScriptObject = new JavaScriptObject();
}else{
    alert("Object not compatible with Server Model");
return"";
```

```
}
tag = myScriptObject.text;
return tag;
}
</script></head><body></body></html>
```

Caution *A good rule when designing Web pages is to test your code in all the various browsers that you are targeting. The same rule applies to testing the code that your extensions will produce.*

Note that two shared folders are included that contain some functions you'll be using. After the script declaration and function assignments, the objectTag() function begins by assigning your server language to a variable by calling the insertLanguage Declaration() function. This function gets the HTML node (the entire document) and puts the outerHTML into the variable preHeadNode. After you have the entire document in a string, you can do a search for the language declaration line. You do this by using regular expressions, or RegExes. Regular expressions will be addressed in greater detail in Chapter 22. The following two lines do the search and then assign the result to a variable:

```
var pattern = new RegExp('<%@LANGUAGE=[^%]*%>');
var theNode = pattern.exec(preHeadCode);
```

The *pattern* variable is your RegEx expression. You create the expression with the RegExp constructor. The variable consists of the code that you are searching for, and both a special negated-character class, [^%], which represents any character up to but not including the percent sign, and a special repetition character, *, which represents zero or more of the previous character. The combination of the two, [^%]*, means "zero or more of any character up to but not including %." You end the string with a %>, which is the closing ASP bracket. Your resulting expression is looking for <%@LANGUAGE= and any characters up to and including %>. The next line executes the pattern against the preHeadCode string with the exec method of RegExp, which in effect searches the entire document for the occurrence of your language declaration.

When you execute RegExp, you can access various attributes of the string that were searched for a match. The variable, theNode, now contains the matched string, if there was a match, or nothing at all, if there was no match. The rightContext contains everything to the right of the match, and the leftContext contains everything to the left of the match. At this point, check whether the string is null. If it is null, you'll assign the language declaration to the string with the following line:

```
theNode = "<%@LANGUAGE=" + serverLanguage.toUpperCase() + "%>\n";
```

Next, you'll assign the preHeadCode contents to the variable EndSection. This variable contains the entire document, which is now going to be the "end section" of code when you concatenate the string. If it isn't null and there *is* a match, you'll assign RegExp.rightContext to the EndSection variable. Then, you just put the two sections together and put it back into the DOM with the following line:

```
htmlNode.outerHTML =  theNode + EndSection;
```

The document at this point includes the language declaration.

Using Objects in Your Object

Note that you have two functions yet to create—VBScriptObject() and JavaScriptObject(). These two functions are going to build up the string of code for your objectTag() function. By doing it in this way, you have the flexibility to add other server models easily simply by adding another block of code to the object. You will be calling the variables a little differently, though. You'll *instantiate* each variable as an object, and assign the new instance of the object to the myScriptObject variable that you already created. By using JavaScript's built-in object-oriented functionality, you have greater flexibility with your code. While not a "true" OOP language, because it doesn't have a well-defined "class" notion, the functionality can be easily simulated.

The way in which you instantiate a class in JavaScript is to define a function and reference the function itself within the function as "this." The function is called the *constructor* and doesn't return any value. To call it, you will use the keyword new, which creates an *instance* of the object. After that point, you can access the public properties of the object. You're giving it only one property—text. However, you could have a name property, a type property, a language property, or even a favoriteFood property. As you build more complex extensions, you may create more complex classes with their own properties and methods. The classes you build are only limited by what you store in the object. Chapter 22 looks at the ssClasses.js file, which contains the Server Behavior classes that you will use to create Server Behaviors.

Object-Oriented Programming in UltraDev

OOP is, at its root, a concept in programming that you can apply to virtually any program that you may want to build. You have to think of an object in terms of a physical thing. You can think of it as a black box. In a black box, you know what the box does, and you know how to interface with it, but you don't have to know the details of how it works. Consider a VCR, for example. All VCRs have a place to insert the tape. They have a Play button; Record button; and buttons for Rewind, Fast Forward, On, and Off. All VCRs aren't the same, but they are all derived from the same basic principles, which is called the *class* in programming terms. This class describes the various properties, methods, and events of the object.

To implement the VCR class in JavaScript, you would put it in a function, like this:

```
function VCR(theName) {
     this.name = theName;
     this.buttons = new Array();
     this.speeds = new Array();
     this.manufacturer = "";
     this.color = "";
     this.state = false; //on or off
     }
```

The function describes the *properties* that the object has. Then, when you want to create the object *instance* in a program, you call it with the new keyword, like this:

```
var myVCR = new VCR("Panasonic");
```

After defining the object, you can give it any properties that it may need. You can now define the properties by referring to the object by the name of this instance— myVCR:

```
myVCR.buttons[0] = "Stop"
myVCR.buttons[1] = "Play"
myVCR.buttons[2] = "Rewind"
myVCR.buttons[3] = "On/off"
```

Your VCR only has four buttons. You can access the length of the Buttons property of the object like this:

```
var howManyButtons = myVCR.buttons.length
```

And, you can access the names of these buttons by looping through the array, like this:

```
for(i=0;i<howManyButtons;i++) {
     alert (myVCR.buttons[i]);
     }
```

You can give your objects methods by defining a *prototype*, like this:

```
VCR.prototype.play = VCR_Play
function VCR_Play(Tape_Is_Inserted) {
     if (Tape_Is_Inserted) {
          alert("Now playing the tape")
     }else{
```

```
            return false;
        }
        return true;
    }
```

Now, the play() method can be called by referencing the object, like this:

```
myVCR.play(true);
```

This code passes a "true" to the object, indicating that a tape is inside the machine. The play() method will then flash the alert box saying that the tape is playing. The play() method only takes one *parameter*—a true or false value indicating whether or not the tape is in the machine.

This is a working JavaScript object. What use is this? Well, actually, you probably don't have use for a VCR in a program, but this just shows the versatility of the approach. By defining an object, giving it properties and methods, and making those attributes known to other programmers, the object can be implemented in programs for whatever functionality the program demands. The play() method works in all objects of the VCR class. As a programmer, you don't have to know how it does it—you just know that it is passed a true or false value, and that it will play the tape if it is sent a true value. The function is *encapsulated* as a black box.

You could implement another VCR object with 20 buttons, and it would be a completely different object, but it would be based on the same class and have the same methods of the previous myVCR object instance. They are both members of the VCR class, but they have different properties that distinguish them. The methods remain consistent—they both have a play() method that can be accessed. If the VCR program is rewritten, other programs that rely on the VCR class will still work if the rules are kept intact, and the play() method still has the same attributes.

The VBScriptObject() Class

The following is the VBScriptObject() class, which you can insert above the objectTag() function:

```
function VBScriptObject() {
tag = '\n<%';
tag += '\nDateFile = Server.MapPath("\DateFile.txt")';
tag += '\nOn Error Resume Next';
tag += '\nSet TM_fs = Server.CreateObject("Scripting.FileSystemObject")';
tag += '\nSet a = TM_fs.OpenTextFile(DateFile, 1, 0, 0)';
tag += '\nLastDate = a.ReadLine';
tag += '\nInStream.Close';
tag += '\nApplication("lastAccessDate")= LastDate';
tag += '\nLastDate = Month(Now) & "/" & Day(Now) & "/" & Year(Now)';
```

```
    tag += '\nLastDate = LastDate & " " & Time';
    tag += '\nset b = TM_fs.CreateTextFile (DateFile, 1, 0)';
    tag += '\nb.WriteLine LastDate';
    tag += '\nb.Close';
    tag += '\n%>';
    tag += '\nThis page was last viewed on';
    tag += '\n<%';
    tag += '\nResponse.Write(Application("lastAccessDate"))';
    tag += '\n%>';
    this.text = tag;
    }
```

This function's sole purpose is to build the string of code that you want to insert. You assign the tag variable to the text property of the object. Notice that you stop and start the ASP tags around the phrase "This page last viewed on," because the ASP code is hidden on the page. This one line will be inserted into the document as if the user had typed it into the design window. By doing it like this, instead of by using a Response.Write statement, the user is allowed to view the phrase in design mode.

You are calling your objects VBScriptObject and JavaScriptObject in this example, but these are just names—you could have called them anything. If you give your objects and methods names that are descriptive, the code will be easier to maintain.

The JavaScriptObject() Class

Next, you'll create a JavaScript class for use with an ASP JavaScript site:

```
function JavaScriptObject() {
tag += '\nsPath = Server.mapPath("DateFile.txt");';
tag += '\nApplication.Lock();';
tag += '\nvar TM_fs = Server.CreateObject("Scripting.FileSystemObject");';
tag += '\nif (!TM_fs.FileExists(sPath)) {';
tag += '\n   TM_fs.CreateTextFile(sPath);';
tag += '\n   DateFile = TM_fs.OpenTextFile(sPath,2);';
tag += '\n   DateFile.Writeline(0);';
tag += '\n   DateFile.Close()';
tag += '\n   }';
tag += '\nvar DateTime = TM_fs.OpenTextFile(sPath,1);';
tag += '\nLastDate = (String(DateTime.ReadLine()));';
tag += '\nDateTime.Close();';
tag += '\nApplication("lastAccessDate") = LastDate;';
tag += '\nLastDate = todayStr() + " " + nowStr();';
tag += '\nDateFile = TM_fs.OpenTextFile(sPath,2);';
tag += '\nDateFile.Writeline(LastDate);';
tag += '\nDateFile.Close();';
```

```
tag += '\nApplication.Unlock();';
tag += '\nTM_fs = null;';
tag += '\nDateFile = null';
tag += '\nfunction nowStr() {';
tag += '\n  //returns the current system time as a string.';
tag += '\n  var now = new Date()';
tag += '\n  newHours = hours = now.getHours()';
tag += '\n  if (hours==0) newHours = 12';
tag += '\n  minutes = now.getMinutes()';
tag += '\n  seconds = now.getSeconds()';
tag += '\n  timeStr = "" + ((hours > 12) ? hours - 12 : hours)';
tag += '\n  timeStr  += ((minutes < 10) ? ":0" : ":") + minutes';
tag += '\n  timeStr  += ((seconds < 10) ? ":0" : ":") + seconds';
tag += '\n  timeStr  += (newHours >= 12) ? " PM" : " AM"';
tag += '\nreturn timeStr';
tag += '\n}';
tag += '\nfunction todayStr() {';
tag += '\n//returns the current system date as a string.';
tag += '\nvar anydate = new Date()';
tag += '\nvar year = anydate.getYear()';
tag += '\nyear = year + 1900 * (year<2000)';
tag += '\n    return anydate.getMonth()+1+"/"+anydate.getDate()+"/"+ year';
tag += '\n}';
tag += '\n%>';
tag += '\n This page was last accessed on ';
tag += '\n <% Response.Write(Application("lastAccessDate"))';
tag += '\n%>';
this.text = tag;
}
```

Your final JavaScript routine, shown in the preceding, is a little more complex only because JavaScript doesn't have the built-in date and time manipulation that VBScript has. Regardless, the final functionality will be the same.

One final option is included in case the server language is not JavaScript or VBScript. This code is inserted intentionally at the end of the function as a fail-safe. If there is no language match, the program will drop down to this block of code, which will alert the user that the object doesn't work with the current server configuration.

 Tip

The "trickling down method" is one way to approach this type of coding. You check your code as it makes its way through a series of If/Then/Else statements; and if it doesn't find a match, it ends up on a default condition.

All that remains after you've instantiated your VBScriptObject() is to assign it to a variable so that the objectTag() function will return the result to UltraDev. The text property of the scriptObject contains the complete script to be inserted. At this point, the language is inconsequential.

If you save the object now in your Custom Objects folder and restart UltraDev, you can apply the object to the page (see Figure 21-5). You'll see the text "This page last viewed on" surrounded by two ASP tags. You can apply text styles to the object, if you wish, by selecting a style and bringing up your CSS Styles floater. Build a style and apply it to the selection. If you preview the page in a browser, the first time you view it, the date won't be filled in, because this is the first access of the page. Close the browser, reopen it, and view it a second time. The date and time should appear on the page (see Figure 21-6).

Adding a ColdFusion Version

Now that you have a nice framework already set up, you are ready to add the ColdFusion version of the code. At this point, two steps are required:

1. Create a ColdFusionObject() class constructor.

2. Insert the two lines necessary to instantiate the constructor.

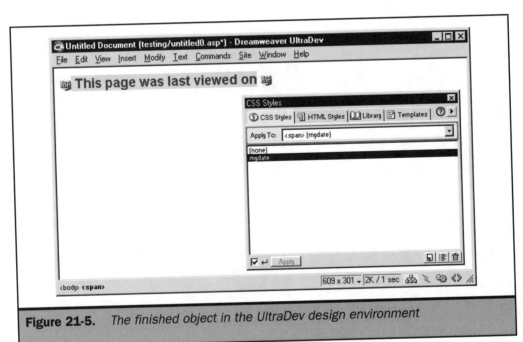

Figure 21-5. The finished object in the UltraDev design environment

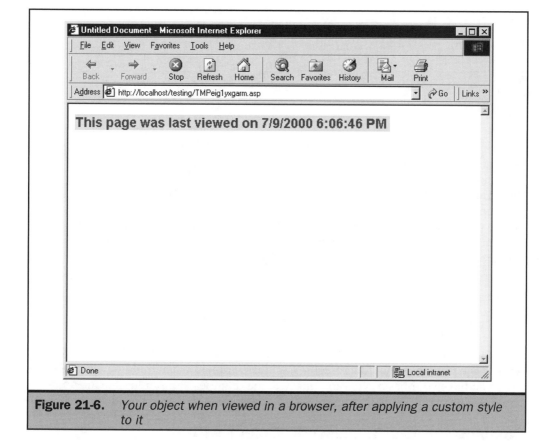

Figure 21-6. *Your object when viewed in a browser, after applying a custom style to it*

To create the constructor, use the following code:

```
function ColdFusionObject() {
var tag='<CFSET LastAccessDate="">';
tag += '\n<CFSET FILENAME=#getdirectoryfrompath(gettemplatepath())#
& "DateFile.txt">';
tag += '\n<CFIF #FileExists(filename)is "Yes">';
tag += '\n<CFFILE ACTION="read" FILE="#filename#"';
tag += 'VARIABLE="LastAccessDate">';
tag += '\n</CFIF>';
tag += '\nThis page was last viewed on ';
```

```
tag += '<CFOUTPUT>#LastAccessDate#</CFOUTPUT>';
tag += '\n<CFFILE ACTION="write" FILE="filename"';
tag += 'OUTPUT="#DateFormat(Now(),"mm/dd/yy")#
#TimeFormat(Now(),"hh:mm:ss tt")#">';
this.text = tag;
}
```

ColdFusion is a tag-based language that includes a lot more functionality already built into the server. File manipulation is straightforward in ColdFusion, so you can create an object with similar functionality to the ASP object with only a few lines of code. The one thing that you are doing differently is to find the path to the current page, because the CFFILE tag needs a path for the file to be read/written. You do that by using the two built-in ColdFusion functions GetDirectoryFromPath() and GetTemplatePath(). Now, you'll instantiate the object in your objectTag() function body, right after the test for the JavaScript object:

```
}else if(serverLanguage=="Cfml") {
    myScriptObject = new ColdFusionObject();
```

That's all there is to it. Now the object works for ColdFusion as well. These are some of the principles that Macromedia engineers applied when building UltraDev. After you have your basic extension finished, making the extension usable in another server language isn't difficult. You could just as easily add JSP or PHP code to the object.

Combine the LastAccessDate Object with the NewBGLogo File

Take the object-building process one step further and combine the LastAccessDate object with your Bettergig logo object. Copy these lines from the NewBGLogo.htm file:

```
tag ='<a href="http://www.bettergig.com">';
tag += '<img src="BGigLogo.GIF" align="center" hspace=5 ';
tag += 'alt="Get a better GIG!" ></a>\n';
tag += '<b>Get a better GIG!</b><br>\n';
tag += 'This site and its contents &copy;2000 by Bettergig.com';
```

Next, paste the lines right into the LastAccessDate object above these two lines:

```
tag = myScriptObject.text;
return tag;
```

A few alterations have to be made. Change tag = in the first line to tag +=. Also, insert a <br> tag after the copyright line, like this:

```
tag += 'This site and its contents &copy;2000 by Bettergig.com<br>';
```

Now, save the new object as LogoWithDate.htm and you have a brand new logo object that displays the last access date of the page.

Creating a User Login Form

You'll conclude this chapter with a standard Username/Password type of form that can either be dropped into any existing page or be the foundation around which you can create a new page. It will have the standard features that you might expect from a UserLogin form:

- A Username field
- A Password field
- A Submit button
- A "remember me" checkbox named "chkRemember"
- A registration page link

You'll put the whole thing in a layer, so that it can exist on another page that already has a form. After you finish, it will be ready for a typical UserLogin application and will be able to coexist with the Server Behavior that you will be building in the next chapter.

Up to now, you've been building the interfaces in UltraDev, to take advantage of the great HTML formatting capabilities of the program. When you do your actual coding, however, you can use a program such as HomeSite or BBEdit (which comes bundled with UltraDev). Figure 21-7 shows your UserLogin form in the HomeSite environment. When you're working on an extension such as this, at some point, it's a good idea to switch to a coding environment so that things can be copied and pasted into your extensions more easily, although UltraDev 4 has a much-improved coding environment.

For the next exercise, you can either build your own form to look like the form in Figure 21-7, or copy the UserLogin.htm file from the CD-ROM. You're going to turn the code into a string so that it can be returned in the objectTag() function.

Open a new, blank file and name it "UserLoginForm.js." In it, copy and paste the entire code block from the UserLogin.htm file, from the beginning <div> tag to the closing </div> tag.

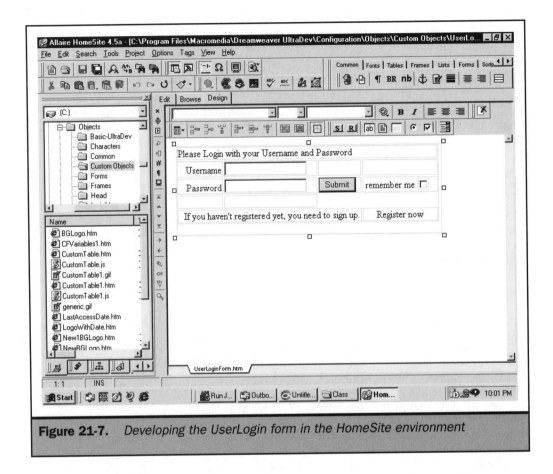

Figure 21-7. Developing the UserLogin form in the HomeSite environment

Now, you're going to turn it into a string variable. Put the objectTag() function block around the entire table and start to put your opening and closing single quotes around each line. By doing it in this way, you ensure that your indenting and formatting stay the same—you're simply wrapping it up neatly into one string. As Figure 21-8 shows, you have single quotes around the individual lines and a + sign to concatenate the string. You leave all the spacing in the string, so that when the object is applied, it will be nicely formatted. By using the single quotes around the code, all of your double quotes around the parameters in the code are left intact. There is one apostrophe in the following line that needs to have a backslash placed in front of it as an escape code:

```
'If you haven\'t registered yet, you need to sign up.</td>'+
```

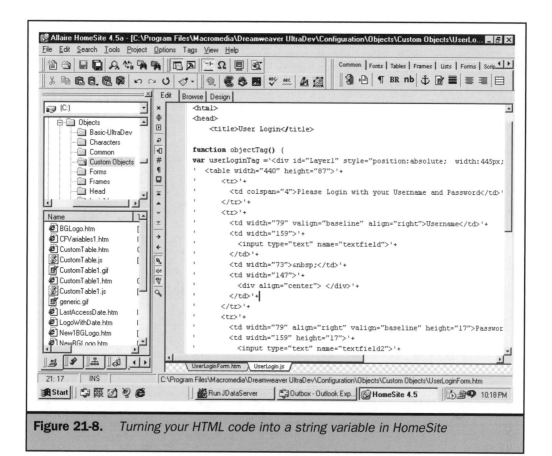

Figure 21-8. *Turning your HTML code into a string variable in HomeSite*

The attributes that you want to get from the user in this particular form are an *action* page for the form to be submitted to, and a *registration* page for a link. Where do these come from? You have to build a second form to act as the user interface—the user won't see the one you just built. It's strictly run-time code, applied as an entire string. When a user wants to apply the object, the user will be presented with a form that prompts for the action and registration pages. You'll create a new form, name it "UserLoginForm.htm," and save it in the Custom Objects folder. At the beginning of the file, you have to declare your include files, so do that first as follows:

```
<script language = "javascript"
src="UserLoginForm.js"></script>
```

```
<script language = "javascript"
src="..Shared/MM/Scripts/CMN/docInfo.js"></script>
<script language = "javascript"
src="..Shared/MM/Scripts/CMN/DOM.js"></script>
```

That form will require two text fields and two buttons. Set it up as shown in Table 21-1.

Set up the onClick events of both buttons in the HTML file, like this:

```
<input type="button" name="btnAction" value="Browse"
onClick="browseFile(findObject('actionPage'))">

<input type="button" name="btnReg" value="Browse"
onClick="browseFile(findObject('regPage'))">
```

Now, you have to define the initializeUI function in the JS file.

```
initializeUI() {
findObject("actionPage").focus();//sets focus on textfield
findObject("actionPage").select();//sets insertion point
}
```

Labels	Text Fields	Buttons
Action page	Text field named "actionPage"	Button named "btnAction" with no action
Registration page	Text field named "regPage"	Button named "btnReg" with no action

Table 21-1. *Setting Up the User Login Form Interface*

In your objectTag() function, you must now retrieve the values of the two text fields. The functionality for getting the filename information is supplied by the browseFile() function once again, so you simply need to pull the names out of the box:

```
var strActionPage= findObject("actionPage").value;//get the
value of the textfield
var strRegPage= findObject("regPage").value;//get the value
of the textfield
//change this line:
'   <form name="UserLoginForm" action="">'+
//to
'   <form name="UserLoginForm" action="' + strActionPage + '">'+
//change this line:
'       <div align="center">Register Now </div>'+
//to
'       <div align="center"><a href="' + strRegPage + '">Register Now </a></div>'+
//turn Register Now into a hot link
```

This User Login object can be used in conjunction with the Log In User Server Behavior that is included with UltraDev 4, or the User Login Server Behavior that is included on the CD-ROM, which works with UltraDev 1 or UltraDev 4.

Summary

This chapter has covered some of the basic parts of extension writing. Objects are the most popular extension to start with because of their visual nature—you can see your results almost instantly. They're also the easiest of the extensions to work with. You've also applied some OOP techniques in the formation of the extension files to prepare for the object-oriented approach that is found in some of the shared Macromedia files that the Server Behaviors use. The next chapter treks through the world of Server Behaviors, the extensions that separate UltraDev from Dreamweaver.

Chapter 22

Building Server Behavior Extensions

To begin a discussion on UltraDev extensions, you must focus on the area that separates UltraDev from its baby brother, Dreamweaver, and that is Server Behaviors. Server Behaviors differ from regular behaviors in their implementation. Typically, the server markup will go above the <html> tag, although many of the Server Behaviors can insert code directly into the body of the document or even around an area of selected text.

The Server Behaviors have built-in intelligence to enable scripts that are inserted to be positioned relative to other Server Behaviors on the page, and to allow them to be edited by double-clicking them in the Server Behavior palette. This is no small feat, as they also remember the various user-defined attributes they contain, such as recordset information, variable values, and page references. In addition, they have the ability to be removed as a unit, which is remarkable considering that some Server Behaviors contain several blocks of code or are interspersed with HTML and text. These are the steps that UltraDev follows when a Server Behavior is applied to a page:

1. Select the Server Behavior from the menu.

2. The Server Behavior first checks to see whether it can be applied. (For instance, does it need a recordset?) If not, it aborts.

3. If the page meets the requirements of the Server Behavior, the behavior builds a list of all Server Behaviors of that type and, if necessary, generates unique names for variables and attributes (for instance, Repeat1, Repeat2, and so on). If not, it aborts.

4. It takes all the user-defined attributes and inserts them into a mask string. The mask is nothing more than the final code that will be inserted into the page, with masks holding the place of the actual attributes (for instance, ##rsname## or @@rsname@@ could hold the place of the actual recordset name that will be used).

5. After the replacements are made in the string, the code is inserted according to *weight*. A description of weights can be found in Table 22-1.

Weight Description	Inserted Where?
0–99 (numbered weights)	Above the <html> tag, relative to any other Server Behavior that has a numbered weight attached to it. A recordset has a weight of 50, so a behavior that executes after a recordset will be between 51 and 99.

Table 22-1. *The Weights Available to the Server Behavior Programmer*

Weight Description	Inserted Where?
aboveHTML+*nn*	Identical to the preceding, where *nn* is the weight number. This is new in UltraDev 4. Numbered weights not including this prefix are automatically given the prefix in the SSRecord.
belowHTML+*nn*	Inserts weighted code below the closing </html> tag, where *nn* is a relative weight between 0 and 99. This was also added in UltraDev 4.
beforeNode	Before the selected node.
afterNode	After the selected node.
replaceNode	Replaces the node with the Server Behavior.
beforeSelection	If there's a selection on the page, inserted before; otherwise, inserted at the insertion point.
afterSelection	If there's a selection on the page, inserted after; otherwise, inserted at the insertion point.
replaceSelection	Replaces the current selection or inserted at the insertion point.
afterDocument	Inserted after the closing </html> tag. This weight was used in UltraDev 1 and is converted to belowHTML for backward compatibility.
nodeAttribute+attribname	Sets the attribute for attribname for the node given.
nodeAttribute	Inserts a chunk of code into the tag after the tag name.

Table 22-1. *The Weights Available to the Server Behavior Programmer* (continued)

6. After it's inserted, UltraDev will do another search through the document for Server Behaviors to repopulate the list in the Server Behavior floater.

7. The new Server Behavior should appear in the list.

There are several ways to build a Server Behavior extension. This chapter will cover those methods, beginning with the foundation of Server Behaviors as they were implemented in UltraDev 1, and moving on to the Server Behavior Builder that was introduced in UltraDev 4. Last, the XML format of the new Server Behavior extensions will be covered briefly. Once you know the foundation, creating complex Server Behaviors either by hand or with the new Server Behavior Builder will be much easier.

If you've used the Server Behavior Builder, you might wonder why you would want to create a Server Behavior by hand. There are several reasons for this:

- The Server Behavior Builder uses a combination of HTML/JavaScript/XML, and is a shortcut to creating Server Behaviors. However, it still follows the same principles as the hand-coded behaviors.

- You can't create Server Behaviors with the Builder that include partial or incomplete sections of script, which is often necessary in more complex extensions.

- The Builder doesn't organize the behaviors—they exist on one big list, which soon becomes cumbersome.

- The HTML interfaces that are created with the Builder are limited.

- It is difficult to create behaviors that use more than one server model.

- Server Behaviors are often used in conjunction with more complex data sources, commands, and server formats. These extensions don't use the XML format as of this writing.

- Knowing what each of the functions actually does allows you to insert your own custom code into the Server Behaviors created by the Builder.

We'll start with building a couple of simple Server Behaviors by hand-coding the functions that are necessary for the extension. If you are only interested in using the Server Behavior Builder, you can skip ahead to that portion of this chapter, because hand-coding Server Behaviors is not a project to be taken lightly.

Steps for Building a Server Behavior Extension

Unlike objects, which we covered in the previous chapter, Server Behaviors have several functions that must be included in writing the extension. These functions take care of the housekeeping involved in the creation of an instance of a Server Behavior on your page. Following is the basic framework required to write the extension:

1. You need the final code that you want to use. This should be fully tested code. While you're debugging the Server Behavior, you don't want to worry about whether the final code works. After you have a working block of code, you are ready to start building the Server Behavior.

2. Create the actual HTML file that will act as the user interface for the behavior. This is pretty straightforward and consistent for all extensions. User interfaces have been covered in Chapters 20 and 21.

3. Add your include file references to the document. Server Behaviors use a standard set of JavaScript files from the Shared directory.

4. Set some other global variables that are needed for the behavior, including the code *weight*.

5. Include the initializeUI() function. This will set up the user interface if it requires any information, such as recordsets.

6. Add a search string at the top of the file. This will be a simple unique string that is found in your code. It acts as a "scout" for the behavior. When you apply any edits to your document, UltraDev will look for the search string in your document; and if it doesn't find it, it won't even bother to check for an instance of the behavior.

7. Write the pattern and mask variables for your code (which we'll refer to as the PATT and MASK variables). The PATT variable is a regular expression pattern used to find the code in the document, and the MASK variable is your actual code to be inserted, with "masks" in place of your user-defined attributes.

8. Write function skeletons for the five required Server Behaviors functions, and any other functions you may need:

   ■ **canApplyServerBehavior()**   Checks to make sure that the page has the necessary ingredients for the Server Behavior. If you're editing an existing instance of a Server Behavior, the function takes an SSRecord object as an argument.

   ■ **findServerBehaviors()**   Returns an array of SSRecord object instances on the page.

   ■ **applyServerBehavior()**   Does the work of inserting the behavior onto the page. If you're editing an existing instance of a Server Behavior, the function takes an SSRecord as an argument.

   ■ **inspectServerBehavior()**   Takes an SSRecord as an argument and updates the behavior's user interface to reflect the parameters of the behavior.

   ■ **deleteServerBehavior()**   Takes an SSRecord as an argument and deletes the SB from the page.

9. Implement each of the required functions in turn and any supporting functions. As you're writing the functions, you should test them along the way, making sure each part does what it's supposed to do up to that point. This one step is 90 percent of your work!

10. Implement the analyzeServerBehavior function, if needed. This function performs a couple of tasks: making sure the node is, in fact, an instance of your behavior, and setting certain properties in the SSRecord (including the incomplete property, the selectedNode property, the title property, and the participants property).

11. Implement, if needed, copyServerBehavior and pasteServerBehavior. These are only necessary if you want your user to be able to copy and paste the behaviors into the same document or another document.

> **Note** *These are intended as basic guidelines; and, as is the case with even good rules, there are times when you will break them and implement a Server Behavior a little differently.*

As you can see, it's quite a bit more complex than putting an object into your document. We'll go through a complete Server Behavior example step by step to illustrate how a simple Server Behavior can be implemented.

Your Final Code—The First Step

You'll begin at the end—with the code that you want the Server Behavior to insert in the page. Our exercise will involve a relatively simple behavior to go along with the login object we created in the previous chapter—a User Login Server Behavior. This is a slightly different behavior than the Log In User Server Behavior that comes standard with UltraDev 4, as it will set a session variable equal to the UserID number of the user in the database. This version is a typical implementation of a user login script:

1. User comes to the login page and is presented with a form for username and password.

2. User clicks the Submit button and is taken to the check-in page. This is the page where the Server Behavior will be applied.

3. If the user has entered the correct username and password, he is assigned session variables for his user ID and access group level and redirected to the success page.

4. The user is sent to the failed page if the information isn't correct.

> **Note** *There are many different ways to implement a user login application. We've chosen the three-page approach—login form, success page, failed page—because it is reliable and the logic behind it is easy to understand. Once you build this Server Behavior it will be easy to adapt it to your own design.*

We'll show you the code for all three server models (ASP, JSP, and ColdFusion) and all four languages (ASP VBScript, ASP JavaScript, ColdFusion, and JSP), but you only have to implement one of these if you prefer. The functions will remain the same. This

Server Behavior will assume that the user has already defined a recordset/query with the following attributes:

- A table with fields for Username, Password, UserID, and AccessGroup.
- A select query similar to the following:

```
SELECT txtUsername, txtPassword, txtAccessGroup, intUserID
FROM Login
WHERE txtUsername = 'TM_username'
AND txtPassword = 'TM_password'
```

Your variables in the Recordset dialog box will be as shown in Tables 22-2, 22-3, and 22-4 (note the differences between the different server models).

Name	Default Value	Run-Time Value
TM_username	testvalue	Request.Form("username")
TM_password	testpass	Request.Form("password")

Table 22-2. *ASP Variables Defined in the Recordset Definition Dialog Box*

Name	Default Value	Run-Time Value
TM_username	testvalue	#Form.username#
TM_password	testpass	#Form.password#

Table 22-3. *ColdFusion Variables Defined in the Recordset Definition Dialog Box*

Name	Default Value	Run-Time Value
TM_username	testvalue	request.getParameter ("username")
TM_password	testpass	request.getParameter ("password")

Table 22-4. *JSP Variables Defined in the Recordset Definition Dialog Box*

The variable names were chosen because they will be unique to your Server Behavior. This technique is important in UltraDev extensions and even more important for Server Behaviors. Server Behaviors are located in the document by finding *patterns*; so if you make parts of the behavior unique, there is less chance of another Server Behavior finding yours by mistake.

Giving your variables unique names is one way to make sure that your code doesn't get interpreted by another behavior as one of its participants. You'll notice that Macromedia uses specific naming conventions in the naming of the built-in variables, such as Repeat1__numRows and MM_offset.

This is your final code that you'll base your Server Behavior on in all four languages.

ASP VBScript Code Listing

```
<%
If Recordset1.BOF or Recordset1.EOF Then
     Response.Redirect("failed.asp")
Else
     Session("TM_userid") = Recordset1("UserID")
     Session("TM_accessGroup") = Recordset1("AccessGroup")
     Response.Redirect("success.asp")
End if
%>
```

ASP JavaScript (JScript) Code Listing

```
<%
if (Recordset1.bof || Recordset1.eof) {
     Response.Redirect("failed.asp");
}else{
     Session("TM_userid") = Recordset1("UserID");
     Session("TM_accessGroup") = Recordset1("AccessGroup");
     Response.Redirect("success.asp");
}
%>
```

ColdFusion Code Listing

```
<CFIF Recordset1.RecordCount is 0>
     <CFLOCATION URL="failed.cfm">
<CFELSE>
```

```
        <CFSET Session.TM_userid = Recordset1.UserID>
        <CFSET Session.TM_accessGroup = Recordset1.accessGroup>
        <CFLOCATION URL="success.cfm">
</CFIF>
```

JSP Code Listing

```
<%
if(Recordset1_isEmpty) {
    response.sendRedirect("failed.jsp");
}else{
    session.putValue("TM_userid",Recordset1.getString("UserID"));
    session.putValue("TM_accessGroup",Recordset1.getString ¬
("AccessGroup"));
    response.sendRedirect("success.jsp");
}
%>
```

> **Note**   *The code listings that follow will work with any or all of the server languages without any change to the behavior. You can include all of them or any one of them by using the PATT and MASK variables that reference your server language. In other words, if you are developing a VBScript extension, use only the PATT and MASK variables for VBScript.*

The code implementation is almost identical for each of the server languages, with the appropriate syntax changes for each language. Since the recordset is designed to take as input a username and password from a login form, there will be only one match in the database. Your Server Behavior simply checks to see if any rows were returned. If not, the login will fail and the user will be redirected to the *failed* page. If the user was successful, he will be redirected to the *success* page.

> **Note**   *To implement the login form page, you can use the user login form object that we built in Chapter 21 or create one manually.*

Now that the design of the final functionality is in place and the code is implemented, the Server Behavior can be written.

Create the HTML File—the Interface

To create your interface, you have to decide which attributes are going to be user defined and build an HTML form to get these attributes from the user. In this example, you will need a redirect page for a failed login, a redirect page for a successful login, and a recordset from which to get the user information. We'll assume that the form names are username and password and the columns in the database are txtUsername, txtPassword, and intUserID. Build this form in UltraDev just like you did the others. When finished, the code will look like this, and the form should look something like the form in Figure 22-1.

```
<html>
<head>
<title>Login Server Behavior</title>
<meta http-equiv="Content-Type" content="text/html; ¬
 charset=iso-8859-1">
</head>
<body onLoad="initializeUI()">
<form name="form1" method="post" action="">
  <table>
    <tr align="center">
      <td valign="baseline" colspan="3">User Login ¬
Server Behavior</td>
    </tr>
    <tr>
      <td valign="baseline" align="right">Success page</td>
      <td>
        <input type="text" name="txtSuccess">
      </td>
      <td>
        <input type="button" name="btnSuccess" value="Browse"¬
onClick="browseFile(findObject('txtSuccess'))">
      </td>
    </tr>
    <tr>
      <td valign="baseline" align="right">Failed page</td>
      <td>
        <input type="text" name="txtFailed">
      </td>
      <td>
        <input type="button" name="btnFailed" value="Browse" ¬
onClick="browseFile(findObject('txtFailed'))">
      </td>
    </tr>
    <tr>
      <td valign="baseline" align="right">Recordset</td>
      <td>
```

```
      <select name="theRecordset">
        <option>**no recordsets found**</option>
      </select>
    </td>
    <td> </td>
  </tr>
  </table>
</form>
</body>
</html>
```

Add Your Include Files

The next step is to attach a list of all of the common functions that make up a Server Behavior. These functions are for string manipulation, user interface controls, file manipulation, and the Server Behavior API. The files are all fully commented, so you

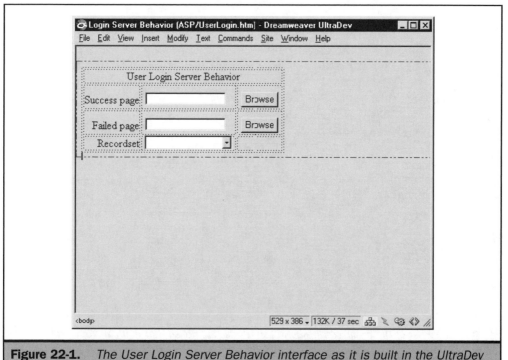

Figure 22-1.   *The User Login Server Behavior interface as it is built in the UltraDev environment*

may go through them to better understand the files and all the functions contained within. In fact, we consider all the files in the Shared folder to be required reading for the extension developer.

```
<script language="javascript" ¬
src="../../Shared/MM/Scripts/CMN/UI.js"></script>
<!--contains the "findObject()" function-->
<script language="javascript" ¬
src="../../Shared/MM/Scripts/CMN/string.js"></script>
<!--general string handling-->
<script language="javascript" ¬
src="../../Shared/MM/Scripts/CMN/DOM.js"></script>
<!--functions for working with the DOM and nodes-->
<script language="javascript" ¬
src="../../Shared/MM/Scripts/CMN/file.js"></script>
<!--filename manipulation and helper functions, like ¬
"browseFile()"-->
<script language="javascript" ¬
src="../../Shared/MM/Scripts/Class/ListControlClass.js">
</script>
<!--useful class for implementing a listbox in your interface-->
<script language="javascript" ¬
src="../../Shared/UltraDev/Scripts/ssClasses.js">
</script>
<!--this one's a MUST for Server Behaviors-- ¬
the SSRecord class is within-->
<script language="javascript" ¬
src="../../Shared/UltraDev/Scripts/ssDocManager.js">
</script>
<!--various functions for Server Behaviors like ¬
"getServerData()"-->
<script language="javascript" ¬
src="../../Shared/UltraDev/Scripts/ssCmnElements.js">
</script>
<!--more necessary Server Behavior functions, like ¬
"findAllRecordsetNames()"-->
```

Tip   *Keep a list of these shared files handy in a separate file so that you can copy and paste the necessary code into your extensions. As you write Server Behaviors, you'll find that you will use this list in every Server Behavior.*

Define Global Variables and Implement the initializeUI() Function

The initializeUI() function will take care of setting up your interface for any user-defined attributes you may need. This is where you will put your functions to populate select boxes with lists of recordsets or columns from recordsets that are on the page. Any variables that you may want available throughout your Server Behavior should also be defined in a global variables section at the start of your page directly below your include file declarations:

```
<script language="JavaScript">
<!--
/////////////////////////////////////
//Start global variable section here
/////////////////////////////////////
var LIST_RS
var theFailedPage = findObject("txtFailed").value;
var theSuccessPage = findObject("txtSuccess").value;
var MODEL_IS_CF = (dw.getDocumentDOM().serverModel.getServerName()¬
  == "ColdFusion");
var MODEL_IS_ASP =
(dw.getDocumentDOM().serverModel.getServerName()¬
  == "ASP");
var WGHT_AspUserLogin = 51; //right after the recordset
var WGHT_JspUserLogin = WGHT_AspUserLogin;
var WGHT_CfmlUserLogin = WGHT_AspUserLogin;
```

MODEL_IS_CF and MODEL_IS_ASP are Boolean variables that are handy to have even if you don't employ a different version of your extension, since some things are specific to the different server models. You can do a check in your extension to see if the variable is true, and if it is, take the appropriate action. In this particular behavior, both are needed because there are some ColdFusion-specific things that don't apply to ASP and JSP, and some ASP things that don't apply to JSP and ColdFusion. You also assign the code *weight*, which is a relational order that the SSEdits class uses to insert the code into the document. The recordset has a weight of 50, so you'll give this one 51 to be applied right after the recordset.

```
/////////////////////////////
//Start  functions
/////////////////////////////
function initializeUI() {
  LIST_RS = new ListControl("theRecordset");
```

```
var rsNames = findAllRecordsetNames();
if (rsNames) LIST_RS.setAll(rsNames,rsNames);
}
//^^^^insert the rest of your functions above this line^^^^
//-->
</script>
```

The first thing this function will do is build a recordset menu. LIST_RS uses the list Control class in the ListControlClass.js file. Read the comments in the file to become familiar with all the properties, methods, and events of this class. This class makes it easy to work with list controls. You don't use the "var" keyword because you set up LIST_RS as a global variable earlier.

You can put this file into one of your Server Behaviors folders (ASP, JSP, or ColdFusion), and it should appear on the Server Behavior menu after closing down and restarting UltraDev. When you choose it, if there are any recordsets on the page, they will appear in the drop-down box. In addition, if you click the Browse buttons, you will invoke the File Open dialog box. The results of the File Open dialog box will automatically be placed into the text fields, which, in turn, will be stored in global variables that you can use throughout the extension. The extension still doesn't do anything, but you'll find that if you test your extensions piece by piece there will be far fewer debugging headaches. If you've reached this stage and the interface works, you can go on to the next step.

The Search String—Finding the Behavior in Your Document

The next thing you want to add is a search string to the very top of the file. It should be the first line in the file. UltraDev will take the search string and look for it in your document each time you make an edit. UltraDev actually goes through the list of *all* search strings to determine whether the behaviors are on the page. The search string can be something short, but preferably something that's unique to your behavior to make the search more efficient. If the search string is found in the document, the findServerBehaviors function is called to determine if the behavior is *actually* on the page.

Caution *Be careful when you create the search string. Frequently, when you are coding your behavior, you will change the code that is used in the behavior and the search string will no longer match. If the search string doesn't appear somewhere in your code, the Server Behavior won't be found by the findServerBehaviors function.*

The search string works like a quick glance, skimming through the document to see if the document warrants the attention of the more powerful findServerBehaviors function. You may want to use a variable in your extensions that will be unique to that extension only and use this in the search string:

```
<!--Search:"TM_accessGroup"-->
```

Now whenever the string "TM_accessGroup" is found in a document, the findServerBehaviors function in this extension will be called. This is one of the reasons for using the variable prefix TM_. You should have your own variable prefix for your own extensions.

The search string shouldn't be too complicated, as it's only intended to do a quick search, but it also shouldn't be something too common that will be found in many behaviors.

 Don't use HTML comments in your search string. The UltraDev interpreter will pick up your comment as a literal comment in your Server Behavior, and the search string will never execute.

Building Your PATT and MASK Variables

This subject could warrant an entire chapter or even a book by itself. The MASK variables are the easier to implement of the two. A *mask* is simply the final code that you want on the page, with the user-defined attributes "masked" out with unique characters surrounding them, such as @@ or ##. The MASK can be pulled out and replaced with the attributes. The PATT variables, on the other hand, use complex regular expressions to enable the detection of the block of code in the document.

Regular Expressions Explained

Regular expressions (also known as a regex or RegExp) are a part of many popular languages, such as Perl, JavaScript, VBScript, and ColdFusion, to name but a few. A regular expression is an object that contains patterns of characters that are to be matched in a string or a document. JavaScript has a built-in RegExp object that has several well-defined properties, methods, and events. A RegExp can be defined either as a string or as a set of characters within the slash (/) characters, as in the following line:

```
var thePattern = /this\s*is\s*a\s*pattern/;
```

If the pattern is defined like a string, wrapped in quotes, you must use double backslashes for the escape sequence, like this:

```
var thePattern = "this\\s*is\\s*a\\s*pattern";
```

The patterns themselves represent the text you are searching for. If you wanted to find your name, for instance, you could simply use the name literally, like this:

```
var thePattern = /Tom/;
```

But if you wanted to find any instance of Tom, Tommy, or Thomas, you could use a RegExp like this:

```
var thePattern = /Tom|Tommy|Thomas/;
```

The pipe (|) character acts as an "or" in the expression, as in "Tom or Tommy or Thomas." You might also want to find any name that begins with the letter T, like this:

```
var thePattern = /T\w+/;
```

This expression uses the *character class* \w, which stands for a letter, underscore, or number character, and the + directive, which means "one or more of the previous character." In this case, \w+ means "one or more letter/number characters up to a non-letter/number character." This expression will continue to match a word beginning with T until a non-letter/number character is found. There are several character classes in the RegExp object, notably:

- [....] Any characters contained within brackets (for example, [abc] will match any a, b, or c character)
- [^...] Any characters *not* in the brackets (for example, [^123] will match any character that's not 1, 2, or 3)
- . Any character that's not a newline (\n) character
- \d Any digit character
- \D Any non-digit character
- \s Any whitespace character (space, tab, newline)
- \S Any non-whitespace character
- \W Any non-letter, non-underscore, or non-numeral character

In addition, the * directive means "zero or more of the previous character." A useful combination is \s*, which means "zero or more of any whitespace character." This allows for the fact that a user might insert spaces or carriage returns in the code, which would make the match for your code fail if you used only a space or carriage return character in your pattern, because it's not an exact match.

Additionally, there are certain characters that require an escape character:

```
/ \ . * + ? | ( ) [ ] { }
```

These are used within the RegExp object as classes and directives; so to use the literal characters, you have to "escape" the character, like this:

```
var thePattern = /What\s*is\s*2\s*\+\s*2\?/gi
```

This string is searching for "What is 2 + 2?" It will also find "What is 2+2?," or even

"What

is

2+2?"

We've also introduced the global identifier (g) and the case-insensitive identifier (i). The global simply means that *all* occurrences of a match will be returned, and the case-insensitive identifier will match regardless of case.

Another concept is *grouping*. When you put parts of your expression within parentheses, the RegExp remembers the string that is matched within the parentheses. You could say the following:

```
var thePattern = '(.*)\\.ActiveConnection\\s*\\=\\s*\\"(.*)\\";';
```

The (.*) in the first part of the expression matches "zero or more characters up to the next character in the expression." What you're searching for in this example is the recordset name (the first set of parentheses) and the connection string (the second set of parentheses). You would have a match with the following:

```
Recordset1.ActiveConnection = "dsn=Bookstore";
```

When a match is completed, an array is returned. The zero element (thePattern[0]) contains the entire matched string. The first element (thePattern[1]) will contain what is in the first set of parentheses (Recordset1), and the second element (thePattern[2]) will contain the match from the second set of parentheses (dsn=Bookstore). This is information that is useful as you match your patterns to the document.

Caution   *The .* pattern is used frequently in regular expressions, but doesn't always return the desired match. It's known as a "greedy" expression because it sometimes matches more than you expect. It's always better to use a less greedy negated class. A negated class for the pattern defined in the preceding example would be [^.]*, which means "any and all characters up to but not including the first . (period character)."*

The PATT and MASK Strings in Your Server Behavior

For this particular extension, your user-defined attributes are the failed login page, the success page, and the recordset name. These will be contained in the global variables you set, so it's a simple matter of using JavaScript's RegExp replace method to put your attributes into the final string to be inserted, like this:

```
chunk = chunk.replace(/##rsname##/g,theRecordset);
```

The "g" stands for "global," which means that all instances of the MASK will be replaced. Your MASK variable strings are built up just like the object strings you did in the previous chapter—line by line. The MASKS are then substituted for the user-defined attributes. The mask characters that are used are typically ## or @@, which are inserted around an identifying name for the variable. The following shows the MASK code for each of the four server languages you'll be implementing. As stated earlier, you can implement one or more of these in your own code without changing the format of the Server Behavior.

ASP VBScript MASK String

```
var MASK_AspVbUserLogin = '\n<%\n'+
'If ##rsname##.BOF or ##rsname##.EOF Then\n'+
'    Response.Redirect("##failed##")\n'+
'Else\n'+
'    Session("TM_userid") = ##rsname##("UserID")\n'+
'    Session("TM_accessGroup") = ##rsname##("AccessGroup")\n'+
'    Response.Redirect("##success##")\n'+

'End if\n'+
'%>\n';
```

> **Note**
>
> *Notice how the code is formatted to correspond roughly with the finished code. That makes it easier to debug a faulty MASK or PATT variable. You'll find that frequently you'll have to go through your PATT variables one character at a time to ensure accuracy. The strings should be built using line-feed characters, spaces, and plus signs to concatenate the string.*

ASP VBScript PATT String

```
var PATT_AspVbUserLogin = '(<%\\s*'+
'If\\s*)(.*)(\\.BOF\\s*or\\s*)(.*)(\\.EOF\\s*Then\\s*'+
```

```
'Response\\.Redirect\\(\\")(.*)(\\"\\)\\s*'+
'Else\\s*'+
'Session\\(\\"TM\\_userid\\"\\)\\s*=\\s*)(.*)(\\(\\"UserID\\"\\))'+
'\\s*Session\\(\\"TM\\_accessGroup\\"\\)\\s*=\\s*)(.*)'+
'(\\(\\"AccessGroup\\"\\)\\s*'+
'Response\\.Redirect\\(\\")(.*)(\\"\\)\\s*'+
'End\\s*if\\s*%>)';
```

ASP JavaScript MASK String

```
var MASK_AspJsUserLogin = '\n<%\n'+
'if (##rsname##.bof || ##rsname##.eof) {\n'+
'     Response.Redirect("##failed##");\n'+
'}else{\n'+
'     Session("TM_userid") = ##rsname##("UserID");\n'+
'     Session("TM_accessGroup") = ##rsname##("AccessGroup");\n'+
'     Response.Redirect("##success##");\n'+
'}\n%>';
```

ASP JavaScript PATT String

```
var PATT_AspJsUserLogin = '(<%\\s*'+
'if\\s*\\()(.*)(\\.bof\\s*\\|\\|\\s*)(.*)(\\.eof\\)\\s*\\{\\s*'+
'     Response\\.Redirect\\(\\")(.*)(\\"\\);\\s*\\'+
'}else\\{\\s*'+
'     Session\\(\\"TM\\_userid\\"\\)\\s*=\\s*)(.*)'+
'(\\(\\"UserID\\"\\);\\s*'+
'     Session\\(\\"TM\\_accessGroup\\"\\)\\s*=\\s*)(.*)'+
'(\\(\\"AccessGroup\\"\\);\\s*'+
'     Response\\.Redirect\\(\\")(.*)(\\"\\);\\s*'+
'\\}\\s*%>)'
```

ColdFusion MASK String

```
var MASK_CfmlUserLogin =
'\n<CFIF ##rsname##.RecordCount is 0>\n'+
'     <CFLOCATION URL="##failed##">\n'+
'<CFELSE>\n'+
'     <CFSET Session.TM_userid = ##rsname##.UserID>\n'+
```

```
'        <CFSET Session.TM_accessGroup = ##rsname##.accessGroup>\n'+
'        <CFLOCATION URL="##success##">\n'+
'</CFIF>\n';
```

ColdFusion PATT String

```
var PATT_CfmlUserLogin =
'(<CFIF\\s*)(.*)(\\.RecordCount\\s*is\\s*0>)\\s*'+
'<CFLOCATION\\s*URL=\\")(.*)(\\">)\\s*'+
'<CFELSE>\\s*'+
'<CFSET\\s*Session\\.TM\\_userid\\s*=\\s*)(.*)(\\.UserID>)\\s*'+
'<CFSET\\s*Session\\.TM\\_accessGroup\\s*=\\s*)(.*)'+
'(\\.accessGroup>)\\s*'+
'<CFLOCATION\\s*URL=\\")(.*)(\\">)\\s*'+
'<\\/CFIF>\\s*)';
```

JSP MASK String

```
var MASK_JspUserLogin =
'\n<% if(##rsname##_isEmpty) {\n'+
'    response.sendRedirect("##failed##");\n'+
'}else{\n'+
'
session.putValue("TM_userid",##rsname##.getString("UserID"));\n'+
'    session.putValue("TM_accessGroup",##rsname##.getString'+
'("AccessGroup"));\n'+
'    response.sendRedirect("##success##");\n'+
'}\n %>';
```

JSP PATT String

```
var PATT_JspUserLogin =
'(<%\\s*if\\()(.*)(\\_isEmpty\\)\\s*'+
'\\{\\s*response\\.sendRedirect\\(\\")(.*)(\\"\\);\\s*'+
'\\}else\\{\\s*session\\.putValue\\(\\"TM\\_userid\\"\\,)(.*)'+
'(\\.getString\\(\\"UserID\\"\\)\\);\\s*'+
'session\\.putValue\\(\\"TM\\_accessGroup\\"\\,)(.*)'+
'(\\.getString\\(\\"AccessGroup\\"\\)\\);\\s*'+
'response\\.sendRedirect\\(\\")(.*)(\\"\\);\\s*'+
'\\}\\s*%>)';
```

Your MASK variable looks pretty basic compared to the pattern variables, which are fairly complex regular expressions . You utilized RegExps briefly in Chapter 21, but here is where their utility and functionality are maximized. The patterns contain all of the code that has to be matched on the page. The methods you use in a RegExp are match(), exec(), test(), search(), and replace().

What a RegExp will enable you to do is compare the RegExp to the actual page, with the results of the search returned in various forms:

- A complete matched string
- Groupings of attributes that you need to retrieve, in an array and also with individual variable names ($1, $2, $3 . . .)
- A *leftContext* and *rightContext*, for finding the areas before and after the match
- An array of all matches if using the match() method

When building the patterns, you have to decide what is going to be a literal string in your code that will be matched, what will be variable, and what will be grouped for retrieval. This should be done line by line for the final code that is used. Let's take a look at this line of code as an example:

```
<%
If Recordset1.EOF Then Response.Redirect("failed.asp")
%>
```

The recordset name and the failed page will be variables that can change and be inserted by the user. We'll start with those variables by making them grouping objects like this:

```
<%
If (.+).EOF Then Response.Redirect("(.+)")
%>
```

The next thing you need to do is to escape any special characters, which are characters that have a special meaning to the RegExp object. In this line of code, the following characters need to be escaped by a double backslash: parenthesis, period, space, newline, and quote. Now the line looks like this:

```
<%\\s*
If\\s*(.+)\\.EOF\\s*Then\\s*Response\\.Redirect\\(\\"(.+)\\"\\)
\\s*%>
```

> One misplaced character in a regular expression can cause the whole match to fail and cause the Server Behavior to be unrecognizable to UltraDev.

It's undeniable that the code is starting to look a little confusing. The literal parentheses are escaped by the double backslash while the grouping parentheses aren't. Also, the newline characters and the space characters are grouped together with \\s*, which will pick up zero or more of any whitespace character. This grouping is handy if a user decides to add blank lines or remove spaces from a behavior after it's applied to the page. The next thing you want to do is to group the items together that *aren't* variable. That way, you can take the strings apart after they are matched, and put them back together with the new attributes. Your code now looks like this after going through and grouping all of the ungrouped code:

```
(<%\\s*
If\\s*)(.+)(\\.EOF\\s*Then
\\s*Response\\.Redirect\\(\\)"(.+)(\\"\\)
\\s*%>)
```

Now all you have to do is assign it to a variable and make the string more readable by separating the lines and putting single quotes around each line:

```
var myPattern = '(<%\\s*'+
'If\\s*)(.+)(\\.EOF\\s*Then'+
'\\s*Response\\.Redirect\\(\\)"(.+)(\\"\\)'+
'\\s*%>)';
```

At this point, if you perform a match on a string of code (theDocument, in the following example), you'll have a grouping of all elements that you need to examine. We'll create the RegExp object from the pattern and then perform an exec on the object using the string, theDocument:

```
var theRegex = new RegExp(myPattern,"i");//make a RegExp object
var newChunk = theRegex.exec(theDocument);
```

After doing this, you can examine the different elements of the match. The variable, theRegex, is an array consisting of every member of your grouping. Table 22-5 shows the content of each element.

Now you can appreciate how powerful it is. This information can be used to take the document apart, replace the user-defined attributes such as recordset name, and then put the document back together again. The better your pattern is, the more versatile your behavior becomes. Why do we do it this way?

Element	What the Element Contains	Variable Name
theRegex[0]	Entire matched string from theDocument	$0
theRegex[1]	<%\nIf	$1
theRegex[2]	Recordset1	$2
theRegex[3]	.eof Then Response.Redirect("	$3
theRegex[4]	failed.asp	$4
theRegex[5]	")\n%>	$5
RegExp.rightContext	Everything in theDocument after the match	n/a
RegExp.leftContext	Everything in theDocument before the match	n/a

Table 22-5.   *The Contents of the RegExp Object After a Match*

Let's say, for example, that there is a <table> tag in the Server Behavior. You could match it with a RegExp like this:

```
var thePattern = /<table>/gi;
```

What happens when the user edits the table, though? Let's say a user makes the table wider and puts a style on it. Now the match doesn't work anymore, and the Server Behavior won't show up in the Server Behavior inspector because the table tag looks like this:

```
<table class="mystyle" width="50%">
```

When you build your pattern variables, it's a good idea to make the patterns as flexible as possible so that if the document is edited, the UltraDev environment will still be able to pick out the Server Behaviors. So, if the pattern were written like this instead,

```
var thePattern = /<table[^>]*>/gi;
```

the match would still occur, because you are matching "<table and everything up to and including the > character." This could be advantageous when you want to edit a Server Behavior—the match can be pulled apart from the user-defined attributes and put back together with the new attributes without sacrificing any changes the user may have made in the document along the way. This way, changes made by a user through hand-coding aren't at risk of being overwritten by reapplying an extension. Obviously, this depends on how well the patterns are written.

Write the Function Skeletons

Put the following function skeletons into your Server Behavior:

```
function canApplyServerBehavior() {
return true;
}
function findServerBehaviors() {
return Array();
}
function applyServerBehaviors(ssRec) {
return"";
}
function inspectServerBehavior(ssRec) {
}
function deleteServerBehavior(ssRec) {
}
function analyzeServerBehavior(ssRec) {
}
function buildSSRecord(node) {
return ssRec;
}
function buildSSEdits(priorRec,newRec) {
return editList;
}
function displayHelp() {
alert("Enter your Recordset name, failed Login page and Success page");
}
```

These are all the functions you'll need to complete the Server Behavior. In addition to the five functions mentioned earlier, you've also built a skeleton for the buildSSRecord function, which will give you an instance of the SSRecord class, and the buildSSEdits function, which will actually insert the code into the document. Also, the displayHelp function will add a help button to your interface, and allow you to attach a help file or use the alert box that you start with here; and the analyzeServerBehavior function, which you'll use to make sure all your parameters are still in the code.

Implementing canApplyServerBehavior()

This function checks to see whether the document has the necessary elements to allow the inclusion of the Server Behavior. The function could be used to make sure there is only one instance of itself on the page, or it could be used to check for an instance of a recordset on the page. We'll do both of those checks here. The function is passed an SSRecord if you're editing an existing behavior, and nothing if it's a new instance. It returns false if the behavior can't be applied to the page for one reason or another. A typical implementation of this function is as follows:

```
function canApplyServerBehavior(oldSSRec) {
  var errMsg = "";
  if((findServerBehaviors().length==1) && (oldSSRec==null)) {
  //if there is already an instance on the page
    errMsg = "Only one LOGIN can appear on a page\n";
    }
  if (findAllRecordsetNames().length == 0) {
  //if there are no recordsets
    errMsg += "You must have a recordset defined\n";
  }
  if (errMsg) alert(errMsg); //popup error message
  return (errMsg == "");      //return false if error message
}
```

Here, you are calling the findServerBehaviors function from this behavior itself, and checking to see whether there is already an instance on the page. If there is, you also check to see whether the function was passed an existing ssRec—the "oldSSRec" variable—which means that you're editing an existing behavior. The error message becomes active if you have an instance on the page *and* you are working with a new instance of the behavior. Then you check for the existence of a recordset on the page. If either or both of the error messages are assigned, you display an alert box. The last statement evaluates to true if there is no error message and false if there is. If the function returns false, all further operations within the behavior cease. You can try it out now on a blank page, and it should show an error message if there aren't any recordsets on the page.

 It is a good idea to get in the habit of frequently testing your extensions while you are developing them. By placing alert boxes in key spots in your code, you can make sure that the functions are receiving and returning the correct parameters.

Implementing the findServerBehaviors() Function

This function is called whenever a user edits the document in some way and the search string at the top of the document is found in the document. This function will locate all instances of the behavior in the current document and return an array of SSRecord objects that contain these instances. Your User Login behavior can only have one instance, but now you'll use a standard function that can be reused for other Server Behaviors with more than one instance allowed. The function is as follows:

```
function findServerBehaviors() {
  var i, ssRec, ssRecList = new Array();
  var dom = dw.getDocumentDOM();
  if (MODEL_IS_CF) {//CF needs special handling
//because the nodes aren't "locked"
      var nodes = dom.getElementsByTagName("CFIF");
  }else{
      var nodes = findLockedScriptNodes(dom);
  }
  for (i=0; i<nodes.length; i++) {
      tagStr=(MODEL_IS_CF)?nodes[i].outerHTML:unescape(nodes[i].orig);
```

The unescape() method takes the incoming node and gets the *untranslated* value of that node. All ASP and JSP tags are translated and locked by UltraDev, so you have to perform this step. You also could have checked for the existence of the ORIG attribute, which is a string that contains the untranlated source code within the locked tags in UltraDev. For ColdFusion, this step is skipped and the actual outerHTML of the node is read. Next, you use your RegExp PATT variable to match the text of the node:

```
if (tagStr.match(getServerData("PATT","userlogin"))) {
```

The function getServerData returns "PATT_AspVbUserLogin" if the server model is ASP/VB, "PATT_AspJsUserLogin" in ASP/JS, "PATT_CfmlUserLogin" in ColdFusion, and "PATT_JspUserLogin" in JSP. The match method of the RegExp object will match the string variable tagStr against your RegExp pattern variable.

```
        ssRec = buildSSRecord(nodes[i]);
        if (ssRec) ssRecList.push(ssRec); //add record to the array
    }
  }
  return ssRecList; //empty means there are none here yet
}
```

You'll notice two ColdFusion-specific lines in the function. These can stay in or come out if you're not using ColdFusion. They'll come in handy if you decide to implement CF versions of your extensions. Since ColdFusion is a tag-based language,

Use Built-in Functions to Make Server Behaviors Reusable

When dealing with Server Behaviors, it's better to implement the code in a general way so that all server models may reuse it. For example, one function that's available is getServerData(theType, theID). The variables you'll use in the creation of a Server Behavior follow a standard of TYPE_*ServernameVariablename* (for example, PATT_AspMyVariable or MASK_CfmlMyVariable. This way you don't have to use the actual variable names in your code—you can use the function that will return the correct variable. You could have the following:

```
var MASK_AspVbRedirect = 'Response.Redirect("##mypage##")';
var MASK_AspJsRedirect = 'Response.Redirect("##mypage##")';
var MASK_CfmlRedirect = '<CFLOCATION URL="##mypage##">';
var MASK_JspRedirct = 'response.sendRedirect("##mypage##")';
```

Instead of referencing the specific mask variable in your code, you reference it through the function by the type of variable and the name, like this:

```
theCodeChunk = getServerData("mask","redirect");
```

The variable theCodeChunk now contains the correct code for the server model that is in use.

the server markup tags will be different for every behavior. In ASP and JSP, there are hidden MM:BEGINLOCK and MM:ENDLOCK XML tags around any server-side code that are *translated* by UltraDev while the page is being viewed in design mode. These hidden tags make it easy to isolate and retrieve the blocks of code. We'll be discussing these special XML tags in more detail in Chapter 23.

If an instance of the code is found on the page, the buildSSRecord function is called to set the parameters of a new SSRecord object, thereby creating a new instance of the Server Behavior. If not, the function returns an empty array. We'll move on to the applyServerBehavior function next, since SSRecord won't get called until there is actually an instance of the extension on the page.

Implementing the applyServerBehavior() Function

The applyServerBehavior is responsible for doing the actual insertion of your code in the page. It does this intelligently by *weight*, as mentioned earlier. The function does several things:

■ It gathers user-defined attributes—in this case, a recordset and two redirect pages from the user interface.

■ It checks to make sure the attributes entered by the user are acceptable.

- It takes the MASK string that you defined earlier and inserts the attributes into the string.

- It implements the SSEdits class to perform the actual insertion of the code into the document.

- It differentiates between an "edited" Server Behavior and a new one.

- It returns an error message if something went wrong.

The first thing the function will do is to grab the attributes from the form that was submitted and put the results into variables. It also has to check to make sure that the data is good. If the user is supposed to enter an integer, for example, and he uses a word instead, you have to throw an error and give control back to the interface or abort the process. Since your Server Behavior takes three attributes—recordset name, failed page, and success page—you have to make sure that all three have been provided. After verifying the information, you send it to the buildSSEdits function. Here is your completed applyServerBehaviors function:

```
function applyServerBehavior(priorRec) {
var editList;
var errMsg = "";
var theRSname = LIST_RS.getValue(); //get recordset
theFailedPage = findObject("txtFailed").value;//get the failed page
theSuccessPage = findObject("txtSuccess").value;//get the success page
if(theFailedPage==""||theSuccessPage==""||theRSname==""){//verify input
   errMsg = 'All fields are required for this behavior';
} else {
   editList = buildSSEdits(priorRec,theRSname,theFailedPage,
theSuccessPage);
   editList.insert();
}
return errMsg;
}
```

As in the case of the SSRecord class in findServerBehaviors, there is a class in UltraDev that makes the insertion of the code easy: the SSEdits class. This class is located in the ssClasses.js file. The SSEdits class has two methods that are used to insert the code: insert() and add(). The insert() method executes the actual insertion of the code into the page after the buildSSEdits function has been called. The add() method is used to apply an edit. The add() method itself has five possible parameters:

- **text**   This is the text string that is going to be inserted; if it's an empty string, it effectively deletes the behavior from the page.

- **priorNode**   If an existing node is being edited, it will be passed to the add() method; otherwise, a false or empty string is passed.

- **weight**   This is the attribute that shows the SSEdits class where the code is to be inserted. Weights were discussed earlier in the chapter.

- **relativeNode**   An optional attribute that you use when assigning one of the "relative" node weights (afterNode, beforeNode, or replaceNode)

- **dontStripCfoutput**   Another optional attribute used in the ColdFusion server model to tell the SSEdit class not to strip off CFOUTPUT tags from the behavior.

You have two possible ways of applying a Server Behavior: add a new behavior and edit an existing behavior. Generally, the buildSSEdits function is called from the applyServerBehavior function, as it was in this example. This function will put to use the pattern strings that were built earlier. When the user edits an existing Server Behavior, this function has the *prior node* passed to it (the existing behavior node). It takes it apart with the RegExp object, makes the appropriate changes to it, and then returns the newly built string to the applyServerBehavior function. The buildSSEdits function in this example is as follows:

```
function buildSSEdits(priorRec,rsName,failedPage,successPage){
var editList = new SSEdits();//create a new object
if (priorRec){ // we are editing an existing record
    var priorNode = priorRec.participants[0];
    var chunk = priorNode.outerHTML;
    var pattern = getServerData("PATT","UserLogin");
    var theRegex = new RegExp(pattern,"i");
    var newChunk = theRegex.exec(chunk);
    chunk="";
    newChunk[0]="";
    if(MODEL_IS_ASP) {
    newChunk[2]=newChunk[4]=newChunk[8]=newChunk[10]=rsName;
    newChunk[6]=failedPage;
    newChunk[12]=successPage;
}else{//CF or JSP
    newChunk[2]=newChunk[6]=newChunk[8]=rsName;
    newChunk[4]=failedPage;
    newChunk[10]=successPage;
    }
    for (i=1;i<newChunk.length;i++) chunk +=newChunk[i];
    editList.add(chunk, priorNode, "replaceNode");
```

```
}else{ // we are inserting a new record
    chunk = getServerData("mask","UserLogin");
    chunk = chunk.replace(/##rsname##/g,rsName);
    chunk = chunk.replace(/##failed##/g,failedPage);
    chunk = chunk.replace(/##success##/g,successPage);
    editList.add(chunk, "", getServerData("WGHT","UserLogin"));
}
return editList;
}
```

The buildSSEdits function has passed to it a prior SSRecord, providing there is one (in other words, if the function is editing an existing record), a new SSRecord that was defined in the applyServerBehavior function, the failed page, and the success page. As you build your own Server Behaviors, you'll want to keep in mind that any user-defined attributes ought to be passed to this function in some way. They can be passed directly or as members of an array.

Once a couple of variables have been defined and you get the outerHTML of the prior node, you grab the pattern variable for the current server model and execute a RegExp. After this is done, the variable array newChunk is holding all of the information needed to put the string together with the new attributes. All of your groupings in the pattern—the areas surrounded by parentheses—are numbered and easily taken apart to be rebuilt.

After the match is executed, the string is put back together with the new attributes. You've assigned the new attributes to their respective positions in the array. The recordset, which shows up three or four times in the code, depending on the server model, is assigned in one line, in this way:

```
newChunk[2]=newChunk[4]=newChunk[8]=newChunk[10]=rsName;
```

Then the add() method of the SSEdits class is called to mark the node for an add back into the document. In this case, you use a replaceNode weight because the new, improved node is replacing the original node.

The other case in the buildSSEdits function is when the user is adding a new instance of the Server Behavior. In that case, you get the MASK string directly and perform simple replacements of the attributes before applying the add() method and returning to the applyServerBehavior function. You do the replacements one at a time like this:

```
chunk = chunk.replace(/##rsname##/g,newRec.rs);
```

The "g" in the expression means a global replacement—that is, every occurrence of the mask will get replaced with the parameter. If you were to leave off the "g," only the first occurrence would have been replaced. When control returns to applyServerBehavior, the only thing left to do is to apply the edits using the SSEdits class method insert(), which will execute any add method that is pending.

The SSRecord Class

When we spoke of classes and objects earlier in Chapter 21, we were only scratching the surface in preparation for the SSRecord. The SSRecord is a full-fledged class with public and private properties, methods, and events. We'll use the analogy of a box. If you think of the SSRecord class as a blueprint describing how the box is built, the SSRecord *instance* is the actual box that you build. Inside the box is all of the information about your Server Behavior. This box can be passed from function to function and retain all of the properties that it contains.

Just as you can build more than one box from the blueprints, you can also have more than one instance of an SSRecord on any given page. Each instance will contain all properties of that particular instance and keep it separate from other Server Behavior instances—even behaviors of the same type. Type is one of the properties of the SSRecord. Some of the others are

- **title** Title used in your behavior. This is what actually shows up in your Server Behavior floater.

- **selectedNode** Pointer to the node of the Server Behavior. This causes the behavior to be highlighted in Code view and on the page if you select it from the Server Behaviors floater.

- **incomplete** A Boolean flag that can be set to check whether something is missing from your behavior. If it's set, a little red exclamation point shows up next to your title in the floater.

- **participants** An array of pointers to all of the nodes that are members of your Server Behavior. In many cases this will only be one.

- **weights** The weights that are assigned to the various participants of your behavior. They coincide with the participants property (for example, participants[0] uses weight[0], participants[1] uses weight[1], and so on).

To declare a new instance of an SSRecord, you use the *new* keyword, as in the following:

```
var mySSRecord = new SSRecord();.
```

After creating the object, you attach the properties that belong to it. In addition, you can add your own properties. For example, if you have a recordset name that you want to become part of the behavior, reference it by using dot notation: *mySSRecord.rsname*. Or if your Server Behavior has a foo property, you can reference it using mySSRecord.foo. By referencing the property in this way, the property is placed "inside the box" so that it goes with the SSRecord wherever it goes.

The function is passed the node that is a participant in the Server Behavior. The first thing to do is to get the outerHTML of the node (or the "unescaped" HTML if it's an ASP or JSP node). Then you ensure that you have the right one by using the match() method of the RegExp object. When you use match, anything contained within parentheses in the pattern is returned as a token variable. In this case, if there are tokens in the match and there are more than two, you know you found the correct node:

```
function buildSSRecord(node) {
    var ssRec = null, tokens, tagStr;
    var dom = dw.getDocumentDOM();
    tagStr=(MODEL_IS_CF)?node.outerHTML:unescape(node.orig);
    tokens = tagStr.match(RegExp(getServerData("patt","UserLogin")));
    // make sure we have the right one
    if (tokens && tokens.length > 2){
// construct a new SSRecord
    ssRec = new SSRecord();
    ssRec.participants.push(node);
    ssRec.weights.push(""); //leave it blank for now
```

The participants array will contain the node and any other nodes in the Server Behavior. Next, you set the selected node property so that when a user selects this behavior in the Server Behaviors palette, the block of code will be highlighted in the HTML source view:

```
ssRec.selectedNode = node;
ssRec.success = (MODEL_IS_ASP)?tokens[12]:tokens[10];//success page
ssRec.failed = (MODEL_IS_ASP)?tokens[6]:tokens[4];//failed page
ssRec.rs   = tokens[2];//recordset name
```

You have set the user-defined attributes of the SSRecord—success page, failed page, and recordset name. Notice that the tokens work out differently for JSP, ASP, and ColdFusion. In ASP, there are two extra tokens, so you have to make sure that the right token is going into the SSRecord. Next, the title of the behavior is set. The title property will be the caption the user sees in the Server Behavior palette. It's a good idea to include an element that is user defined in the title, so it will be recognizable to the user, especially if the user can put more than one of the Server Behaviors on the page. In this case, the recordset name is put in parentheses:

```
    //set title
    ssRec.title = "UserLogin(" + ssRec.rs + ")";
    //incomplete if recordset not defined
    ssRec.incomplete = (!recordsetNameIsValid(ssRec.rs));
    }
return ssRec;
}
```

After the title, the incomplete property is set if the recordset name isn't valid. You use a function from one of your included shared files called recordsetNameIsValid to check whether the name is a valid one. After that's finished, all that is left is to return the SSRecord to the calling function.

The ssRec that is returned to the findServerBehaviors function now contains all of the properties of a specific instance of the code contained in the behavior. It also contains information about where it is in the document. If there is no recordset on the page or if there is a problem of some kind with the recordset (maybe a user modified the code), the incomplete flag is set. It also has a title, which will appear in the Server Behavior floater.

inspectServerBehavior

This function is called when a user double-clicks the Server Behavior instance in the Server Behavior palette. An SSRecord containing the information about that Server Behavior is passed to the function. The function then pulls out any values that it needs to populate the dialog box. The dialog box of that behavior is then brought up and contains all values that the user had entered when the behavior was first applied to the page. The user can then edit the attributes of the behavior, after which the applyServerBehavior function is called again—this time with a priorRecord variable containing the SSRecord of the behavior *before* the edits were made. It's up to the SSEdits class to determine which attributes are new and which are original.

This function's sole purpose is to populate the user interface with values from the behavior, so the following would be the implementation for this behavior:

```
function inspectServerBehavior(ssRec) {
findObject("txtSuccess").value = ssRec.success;
findObject("txtFailed").value = ssRec.failed;
LIST_RS.pickValue(ssRec.rs);
}
```

You use the findObject function to put the values of the success page and the failed page back into the text fields of the interface. Then you use the pickValue() method of the ListControlClass to choose the correct recordset name and display it in the select box.

The List Control Class is a special class that's available in the ListControlClass.js file under the Shared/MM/Scripts/Classes directory. It allows the UltraDev extension developer to more easily implement list boxes and select boxes. The file is well documented, and used throughout the extensions on the CD and within UltraDev itself.

Cleaning Up—analyzeServerBehavior

The behavior is basically complete at this point. The analyzeServerBehavior function can be added to it if you care to do some last-minute checks. In this particular behavior example, you conducted your checks in the buildSSRecord function; but you could have done that here as well. We'll demonstrate its use by putting in a final check for the three attributes—recordset, failed page, and success page:

```
function analyzeServerBehavior(ssRec) {
if (!ssRec.failed || !ssRec.success || ¬
!recordsetNameIsValid(ssRec.rs)) {
    ssRec.incomplete = true;
    }
}
```

This function is checking to see whether the failed page, the success page, and the recordset name are all in place. If they aren't, the incomplete flag of the SSRecord is set to true. You can try out the functionality by applying the behavior to the page and then going back to the page in HTML source view and deleting one of the items. If you look at the Server Behavior palette, there should be a red checkmark next to the item name at this point. If you were to bring up the user interface again by double-clicking the Server Behavior in the Server Behavior palette, one of the fields would be blank. But if you enter the attribute into the box and then click OK, the behavior will be complete again.

deleteServerBehavior

In many cases, the deleteServerBehavior function is the easiest to write. Generally, in the simpler behaviors, it's merely a matter of calling the del() method of the SSRecord class, and the behavior will be deleted. This function is called when a user clicks the minus (–) button on the Server Behavior floater. Here's how the deleteServerBehavior function is implemented for the User Login behavior:

```
function deleteServerBehavior(ssRec) {
    ssRec.del();
    return true;
    }
```

The del() method takes two optional Boolean parameters. The first, preserveLinkContent, can be set to true if the behavior has link nodes and you want to preserve the text of the links like this:

```
<a href="http://www.mypage.com?id=<%=someVariable%>">View details</a>
```

In this case, after the del() method is called, "View details" would be left on the page, but the link would be deleted. The second parameter is preserveBetweenLocks. This will remove the code wrapping the original selection, but leave the selection in place. For example, Repeated Region uses this, because it "wraps" your selection with the Server Behavior. In the preceding example, you didn't have to use the two optional parameters, so you called the method with no parameters.

In certain cases in which your behavior might be too complex to fit within the confines of a node, the del() method can't be used. In these cases, you may use whatever method is at your disposal to remove the Server Behavior from the page. Using regular expressions and pattern matching would be one way.

Other Functions

There are a couple of other functions that weren't used in this behavior, but are available to the writer of Server Behaviors. They are the copyServerBehavior and pasteServerBehavior functions. Their names alone should indicate the functionality they provide. In this particular case, there is usually only one "login" checkpoint in a site, so there wouldn't be a need to copy and paste the Server Behavior onto another page. What you will now do, however, is build another Server Behavior where a copy/paste methodology would come in handy—an access level behavior. This behavior will tie in nicely with the User Login behavior and the Login Form object from Chapter 21. It is similar to the Restrict Access to Page Server Behavior that came with UltraDev 4. It differs in that it uses a user ID primary key from the database in a session variable instead of a username, making it easier to use in some cases when you need to keep track of a user ID number throughout the site.

The User Login Framework

The basic premise of the user login extensions that are being built in this chapter is this: a user comes to the Web site and is asked to log in. He logs in using his username and password, and is given access to only those pages on the site for which he has been given an access privilege. For example, if you have a site where a user pays a subscription fee for access to certain parts of the site, you can give him a *permission* level that corresponds to the permission level on those certain pages. This is accomplished by granting access rights to each user, and then performing a check at the beginning of each page to verify that the user is allowed to see the page based on his access level or group.

The database that contains the information about the user—username, password, and user ID—also contains information about the user's access group. You'll use this as the basis on which to build the next Server Behavior.

We've chosen a model in which the user is a member of a single access group— Web user, customer, premium customer, employee, or administrator. The pages that can be visited, on the other hand, can have various levels of permitted access. For example, a page that displays a news story about your company might be viewable by all access groups, whereas a page that displays personal information about your employees will only have administrator access rights associated with it. We'll address the multiple permitted accesses with a list of *comma-separated values*. These are easily searched in all of the languages. So, in our news story example, the access-level list would be

```
webuser, customer, premium customer, employee, administrator
```

The behavior will apply an access group check at the top of each page to which it's applied. The basic structure of the code is as follows:

1. A user requests the page, either by a link or by some other means.

2. The page checks to see whether the user is logged in by checking the UserID session variable that was set in the User Login Server Behavior, and sends him to the login page if not.

3. The page will then check the user's access level against the access level of the page. If the user doesn't have permission to view the page, he'll be redirected to a "no access permission" page.

4. If the user passes those tests, the page will be displayed.

By implementing the group levels in this way, you have great flexibility with your pages and your access group names, which can be anything—you're not confined to a list of available access groups. The variable user-defined attributes will be the login page name, the access denied page, and the list of access groups for the page. Let's have a look at the code:

ASP VBScript Code Listing

```
<%
If Session("TM_userID") <> "" Then
    Dim TM_groupsAllowed
    TM_groupsAllowed = "admin,customer"
    If InStr(TM_groupsAllowed,Session("TM_accessgroup")) = 0 Then
        Response.Redirect("denied.asp")
    End If
Else
    Response.Redirect("login.asp")
End if
%>
```

ASP JavaScript Code Listing

```
<%
if(Session("TM_userID")!= null) {
    var TM_groupsAllowed = "admin,customer";
    if(TM_groupsAllowed.indexOf(Session("TM_accessGroup"))==-1){
        Response.Redirect("denied.asp");
    }
}else{
    Response.Redirect("login.asp")
}
%>
```

JSP Code Listing

```
<%
if(session.getValue("TM_userid")!= null) {
    String TM_groupsAllowed = "admin,customer";
    String TM_accessGroup = (String)(session.getAttribute("TM_accessGroup"));
    if((TM_groupsAllowed.indexOf(TM_accessGroup))== -1) {
        response.sendRedirect("denied.jsp");
    }
}else{
    response.sendRedirect("LoginFormJSP.jsp");
}
%>
```

ColdFusion Code Listing

```
<CFIF IsDefined("Session.TM_userID")>
    <CFSET TM_groupsAllowed="admin,customer">
    <CFIF Not (Listfind(TM_groupsAllowed,Session.TM_accessgroup))>
        <CFLOCATION URL="denied.cfm">
    </CFIF>
<CFELSE>
    <CFLOCATION URL="login.cfm">
</CFIF>
```

The functionality of the code is virtually identical in all server models, using the appropriate syntax in each to search the string of access groups for the particular access group of the user. First, you'll build the user interface and step through it, function by function again—sequentially this time. Any differences from the User Login Server Behavior will be explained. Many of the functions will only require small changes. Your basic user interface code, along with the search string at the top and the include file declarations, looks like this:

```
<!--search:"TM_groupsAllowed"-->
<html>
<head>
<title>User Access Server Behavior</title>

<script language="javascript" ¬
src="../../Shared/MM/Scripts/CMN/UI.js"></script>
<script language="javascript" ¬
src="../../Shared/MM/Scripts/CMN/string.js"></script>
<script language="javascript" ¬
src="../../Shared/MM/Scripts/CMN/DOM.js"></script>
<script language="javascript" ¬
src="../../Shared/MM/Scripts/CMN/file.js"></script>
<script language="javascript" ¬
src="../../Shared/MM/Scripts/Class/ListControlClass.js">
</script>
<script language="javascript" ¬
src="../../Shared/UltraDev/Scripts/ssClasses.js"></script>
<script language="javascript" ¬
src="../../Shared/UltraDev/Scripts/ssDocManager.js"></script>
<script language="javascript" ¬
src="../../Shared/UltraDev/Scripts/ssCmnElements.js"></script>
```

```
<SCRIPT LANGUAGE="JavaScript">
<!--

//^^^^insert the rest of your functions above the closing ¬
script tag^^^^
//-->
</script>
</head>
<body onLoad="initializeUI()">
<form name="form1" method="post" action="">
  <table>
    <tr align="center">
      <td valign="baseline" colspan="3">User Access ¬
Server Behavior</td>
    </tr>
    <tr>
      <td valign="baseline" align="right">Access Groups ¬
(comma separated list)</td>
      <td colspan=2>
        <input type="text" size="40" name="txtAccessGroups">
      </td>
    </tr>
    <tr>
      <td valign="baseline" align="right">Denied page</td>
      <td>
        <input type="text" name="txtDenied">
      </td>
      <td>
        <input type="button" name="btnDenied" value="Browse" ¬
onClick="browseFile(findObject('txtDenied'))">
      </td>
    </tr>
    <tr>
      <td valign="baseline" align="right">Failed page</td>
      <td>
        <input type="text" name="txtFailed">
      </td>
      <td>
        <input type="button" name="btnFailed" value="Browse" ¬
onClick="browseFile(findObject('txtFailed'))">
      </td>
```

```
      </tr>
    </table>
  </form>
  </body>
  </html>
```

The interface takes three values as input: the list of comma-separated access groups, the denied page, and the failed page. Next, you set up the global variables:

```
//start Global variable section here
var theFailedPage = findObject("txtFailed").value;
var theDeniedPage = findObject("txtDenied").value;
var theAcccessGroups = findObject("txtAccessGroups").value;
var MODEL_IS_CF = (dw.getDocumentDOM().serverModel.getServerName()
 == "Cold Fusion");
```

Then you build the pattern and mask variables and assign them. Once again, all three server models are provided for you, but you only need to use the ones that you intend to apply:

ASP VBScript MASK and PATT Variables

```
var MASK_AspVbUserAccess =
'\n<% If Session("TM_userID") <> "" Then\n'+
'      Dim TM_groupsAllowed \n'+
'      TM_groupsAllowed = "##accessgroups##"\n'+
'      If Instr(TM_groupsAllowed,Session("TM_accessgroup")) = 0 Then\n'+
'          Response.Redirect("##denied##")\n'+
'      End If\n'+
'Else\n'+
'      Response.Redirect("##failed##")\n'+
'End if\n %>';

var PATT_AspVbUserAccess = '(<%\\s*If\\s*Session\\(\\"TM\\_userID\\"\\)\\s*<>\\s*'+
'\\"\\"\\s*Then\\s*'+
'Dim\\s*TM\\_groupsAllowed\\s*'+
'TM\\_groupsAllowed\\s*=\\s*\\")(.*)(\\"\\s*'+
'If\\s*Instr\\(TM\\_groupsAllowed\\,'+
'Session\\(\\"TM\\_accessgroup\\"\\)\\)\\s*\\=\\s*0\\s*Then\\s*'+
'Response\\.Redirect\\(\\")(.*)(\\"\\)\\s*'+
'End\\s*If\\s*'+
```

```
'Else\\s*'+
'Response\\.Redirect\\(\\")(.*)(\\"\\)\\s*'+
'End\\s*if\\s*%>)';
```

ASP JavaScript MASK and PATT Variables

```
var MASK_AspJsUserAccess=
'\n<% if(Session("TM_userID")!= null) {\n'+
'       var TM_groupsAllowed = "##accessgroups##";\n'+
'       if(TM_groupsAllowed.indexOf(Session("TM_accessGroup"))==-1){\n'+
'           Response.Redirect("##denied##");\n'+
'       }\n'+
'}else{\n'+
'       Response.Redirect("##failed##")\n'+
'}\n %>';


var PATT_AspJsUserAccess = '(<%\\s*if\\(Session\\('+
'\\"TM\\_userID\\"\\)!= \\s*null\\)\\s*\\{\\s*'+
'var\\s*TM\\_groupsAllowed\\s*=\\s*\\")(.*)(\\";\\s*'+
'if\\(TM\\_groupsAllowed\\.indexOf\\(Session\\'+
'(\\"TM\\_accessGroup\\"\\)==\\-1\\)\\)\\{\\s*'+
'Response\\.Redirect\\(\\")(.*)(\\"\\);\\s*\\}\\s*'+
'\\}else\\{\\s*'+
'Response\\.Redirect\\(\\")(.*)(\\"\\)\\s*'+
'\\}\\s*%>)';
```

ColdFusion MASK and PATT Variables

```
var MASK_CfmlUserAccess = '\n<CFIF IsDefined("Session.TM_userID")>\n'+
'       <CFSET TM_groupsAllowed ="##accessgroups##">'+
'       <CFIF Not (Listfind(TM_groupsAllowed,'+
'Session.TM_accessgroup))>\n'+
'           <CFLOCATION URL="##denied##">\n'+
'       </CFIF>\n'+
'<CFELSE>\n'+
'       <CFLOCATION URL="##failed##">\n'+
'</CFIF>\n';


var PATT_CfmlUserAccess = '(<CFIF\\s*IsDefined\\(\\"Session\\.TM\\_userID\\"\\)>\\s*'+
'<cfset\\s*TM\\_groupsAllowed\\s*\\=\\")(.*)(\\">\\s*'+
```

```
'<CFIF\\s*not\\s*\\(Listfind\\(TM\\_groupsAllowed\\s*\\,'+
'Session\\.TM\\_accessgroup\\)\\)\\)>\\s*'+
'<CFLOCATION\\s*URL=\\")(.*)(\\">\\s*'+
'<\\/CFIF>\\s*'+
'<CFELSE>\\s*'+
'<CFLOCATION\\s*URL=\\")(.*)(\\">\\s*'+
'<\\/CFIF>)';
```

JSP MASK and PATT Variables

```
var MASK_JspUserAccess=
'<%\nif(session.getValue("TM_userid")!= null) {\n'+
'        String TM_groupsAllowed = "##accessgroups##";\n'+
'        String TM_accessGroup = '+
'String)(session.getAttribute("TM_accessGroup"));\n'+
'        if((TM_groupsAllowed.indexOf(TM_accessGroup))== -1) {\n'+
'            response.sendRedirect("##denied##");\n'+
'            }\n'+
'}else{\n'+
'        response.sendRedirect("##failed##");\n'+
'}\n%>';

var PATT_JspUserAccess = '(<%\\s*if\\(session\\.getValue\\(\\"TM\\_userid\\"\\)!='+
'\\s*null\\)\\s*\\{\\s*'+
'String\\s*TM\\_groupsAllowed\\s*=\\s*\\")(.*)(";\\s*'+
'String\\s*TM\\_accessGroup\\s*=\\s*\\(String\\)\\(('+
'session\\.getAttribute\\(\\"TM\\_accessGroup\\"\\)\\);\\s*'+
'if\\(\\(TM\\_groupsAllowed\\.indexOf\\(TM\\_accessGroup\\)'+
'\\)==\\s*\\-1\\)\\s*\\{\\s*'+
'response\\.sendRedirect\\(\\")(.*)(\\"\\);\\s*'+
'\\}\\s*\\}else\\{\\s*'+
'response\\.sendRedirect\\(\\")(.*)(\\"\\);\\s*'+
'\\}\\s*%>)';
```

The weight string assignments are next. Notice you give this behavior a weight of 1 so it will come before all other behaviors:

```
var WGHT_AspUserAccess = "1";
var WGHT_JspUserAccess = WGHT_AspUserAccess;
var WGHT_CfmlUserAccess = WGHT_AspUserAccess;
```

You then implement the initializeUI() function, which doesn't have much to do in this extension since there aren't any list boxes or recordsets:

```
//Start functions

function initializeUI() {
findObject("txtAccessGroups").focus(); //set focus on textbox
findObject("txtAccessGroups").select(); //set insertion point
}
```

Next comes the canApplyServerBehavior() function. The only thing you need to check is that there isn't already an instance of the behavior on the page:

```
function canApplyServerBehavior(oldSSRec) {
    var errMsg = "";
    if((findServerBehaviors().length==1) && (oldSSRec==null)) {
        errMsg = "Only one UserAccess Server Behavior on a page\n";
    }
    if (errMsg) alert(errMsg); //popup error message
    return (errMsg == "");      //return false if error message
}
```

Note

You'll notice that most of the functions in the Server Behaviors can be used over and over again. Once you get a basic framework down, it's simply a matter of adapting it to the code that you want to use for a new behavior.

Now the findServerBehaviors function is declared. This function is actually identical to the findServerBehavior function in the User Login Server Behavior:

```
function findServerBehaviors() {
    var i, ssRec, ssRecList = new Array();
    var dom = dw.getDocumentDOM();
    if (MODEL_IS_CF) {
        var nodes = dom.getElementsByTagName("CFIF");
    }else{
        var nodes = findLockedScriptNodes(dom);
    }
    for (i=0; i<nodes.length; i++) {
        tagStr = ¬
(MODEL_IS_CF)?nodes[i].outerHTML:unescape(nodes[i].orig);
        if (tagStr.match(getServerData("patt","useraccess"))) {
        ssRec = buildSSRecord(nodes[i]);
        if (ssRec) ssRecList.push(ssRec); //add record to the array
```

```
        }
    }
    return ssRecList; //empty means there are none here yet
}
```

The applyServerBehavior function is next. The only changes you made to this function from the User Login behavior are the names of the text fields:

```
function applyServerBehavior(priorRec) {
    var editList;
    var errMsg="";
    theFailedPage=findObject("txtFailed").value;
    //get the failed page
    theDeniedPage=findObject("txtDenied").value;
    //get the success page
    theAccessGroups=findObject("txtAccessGroups").value;
    if(theAccessGroups==""||theFailedPage==""||theDeniedPage==""){
        errMsg='All fields are required for this behavior';
    }else{
        editList = buildSSEdits(priorRec,theAccessGroups, ¬
theFailedPage,theDeniedPage);
        editList.insert();
    }
    return errMsg;
}
```

In the applyServerBehavior function, you are retrieving the values of the text fields, making sure that they are all there, and then sending the values along with a prior SSRecord, if there is one, to the buildSSEdits function. After that, the insert() method of the SSEdits class is called. Here is the buildSSEdits function:

```
function buildSSEdits(priorRec,accessGroups,failedPage,deniedPage){
    var editList = new SSEdits();
    if (priorRec){ // we are editing an existing record
        var priorNode = priorRec.participants[0];
        var chunk = priorNode.outerHTML;
        var pattern = getServerData("PATT","UserAccess");
        var theRegex = new RegExp(pattern,"i");
        var newChunk = theRegex.exec(chunk);
        chunk="";
```

```
            newChunk[0]="";
            newChunk[2]=accessGroups;
            newChunk[4]=deniedPage;
            newChunk[6]=failedPage;
            for (i=1;i<newChunk.length;i++) chunk +=newChunk[i];
                editList.add(chunk, priorNode, "replaceNode");
        }else{ // we are inserting a new record
            chunk = getServerData("mask","UserAccess");
            chunk = chunk.replace(/##accessgroups##/g,accessGroups);
            chunk = chunk.replace(/##failed##/g,failedPage);
            chunk = chunk.replace(/##denied##/g,deniedPage);
            editList.add(chunk, "", getServerData("WGHT","UserAccess"));
        }
    return editList;
}
```

The processes in the buildSSEdits function are the same here as in your UserLogin behavior. First, if there is a prior record, the instance of the Server Behavior is pulled out of the document and taken apart. The new attributes are put in the correct places in the string, and the string is given to the add() method of the SSEdits class. If you are building a new Server Behavior, the MASK string is brought into the chunk variable, and the attributes are put into the string in the appropriate places and sent to the add() method.

Next, you have the buildSSRecord function, which will set all the attributes of the behavior to an instance of an SSRecord object:

```
function buildSSRecord(node) {
    var ssRec = null, tokens, tagStr;
    var dom = dw.getDocumentDOM();
    tagStr=(MODEL_IS_CF)?node.outerHTML:unescape(node.orig);
    tokens =
tagStr.match(RegExp(getServerData("PATT","UserAccess")));
    if (tokens && tokens.length > 6){
        // construct a new SSRecord
        ssRec = new SSRecord();
        ssRec.participants.push(node);
        ssRec.weights.push("");
        ssRec.selectedNode = node;
        ssRec.denied = tokens[4];//success page
        ssRec.failed = tokens[6];//failed page
        ssRec.accessGroups = tokens[2];//group list
        //set title
        ssRec.title = "UserAccess(" + ssRec.accessGroups + ")";
```

```
        }
    return ssRec;
    }
```

Again, this looks very similar to the User Login Server Behavior example at the beginning of the chapter. The only differences are the names of the properties of the SSRecord. Here, you are using a denied property and an accessGroups property. In addition, the accessGroups property is used in the title of the object, so that the user can look at the Server Behaviors floater at a glance and tell what the access level is on the page. This is done by enclosing the ssRec.accessGroups property in parenthesis and concatenating it with the UserAccess title.

Just a few more functions to go, and the UserAccess behavior will be complete. In the event of an edit of the Server Behavior, the inspectServerBehavior function will populate the text fields in the user interface with the values from the SSRecord object:

```
function inspectServerBehavior(ssRec) {
    findObject("txtDenied").value = ssRec.denied;
    findObject("txtFailed").value = ssRec.failed;
    findObject("txtAccessGroups").value = ssRec.accessGroups;
}
```

In the event that the user clicks the minus button (–) in the Server Behaviors floater, the delete function will be called:

```
function deleteServerBehavior(ssRec) {
    ssRec.del(false);
    return true;
}
```

Finally, the analyzeServerBehavior function will do a little housekeeping at the end to make sure all the attributes are present. If not, it sets a flag that will cause a red checkmark to be displayed in the Server Behaviors floater:

```
function analyzeServerBehavior(ssRec) {
    if (!ssRec.failed || !ssRec.denied || !ssRec.accessGroups) {
    ssRec.incomplete = true;
    }
}
```

> | Tip |
>
> *The analyzeServerBehavior function serves double duty. It can also be used to mark as "deleted" nodes that were found as possible matches for your behavior if they don't match certain criteria you establish. The behavior doesn't get deleted from the page; but, instead, it is prevented from appearing in the floater as a member of your Server Behavior family.*

Now it's time to implement the two functions that are the subject of this example: copyServerBehavior and pasteServerBehavior. Again, these will come in handy for this particular extension, since you will want to put this one, or one like it, on every page in your site. If UltraDev sees these two functions in the extension, the Copy and Paste contextual menu items will become activated and you'll be able to copy and paste the extension from page to page.

Here's the copyServerBehavior function for your User Access behavior:

```
function copyServerBehavior(ssRec) {
    var tagStr;
    ssRec.parts = new Array();
    beginLock = getMyBeginLock(ssRec.participants[0]);
    if (beginLock) {
        tagStr = unescape(beginLock.getAttribute("ORIG"));
    }else{
        tagStr = ssRec.participants[i].outerHTML;
    }
    ssRec.parts.push(String(tagStr));
    return (ssRec.parts.length > 0);
}
```

As you can see, the SSRecord object of the behavior is passed to the function. This happens internally through the Server Behavior API. If a user right-clicks the Server Behavior instance in the floater, and then clicks Copy, UltraDev will pass the SSRecord object to this function for manipulation. The function gets the actual text (the outerHTML) of the object and places it in the SSRecord object to be passed to the pasteServerBehavior function. Note that if there is more than one participant, you will want to implement a loop here. The return value is true if the length of the string is greater than zero. If this function returns true, the Paste menu item in the Server Behavior floater becomes active.

And now, here's the pasteServerBehavior function:

```
function pasteServerBehavior(ssRec) {
    var tagStr, chunk, editList = new SSEdits();
    chunk = ssRec.parts[0];
    if(findServerBehaviors().length !=0){
        alert("No more than one User Access behavior on a page")
```

```
}else{
editList.add(chunk, "", ssRec.weights[0]);
editList.insert(true);
}
}
```

Similar to the copy function, the SSRecord object is passed to the pasteServerBehavior function. That function now contains the "parts" array. The array in this particular implementation only has one element, so you'll access it with the zero index. Next, call the findServerBehaviors function to see if there are any User Access behaviors already on the page. If an instance already exists on the page, an alert is flashed to the user and the function ends without pasting the behavior into the document. If not, a new SSEdits object is created, and the "chunk" variable, which is the text of the Server Behavior instance, is passed to the add() method, which in turn calls the insert() method to actually do the pasting of the behavior into the document.

Tip   *The Server Behavior Builder in UltraDev 4 doesn't include the copy and paste functions in the Server Behaviors it builds. These can be inserted manually.*

Where Do You Keep Your Server Behaviors?

You might be wondering how to keep track of Server Behaviors after they start to accumulate. The Server Behavior palette will become cluttered in no time if the behaviors are kept in the main ServerBehaviors folder. The Server Behavior Builder will put the behaviors that it creates at the root level of the ServerBehaviors folder, making it even more cluttered. Let's take a look at how the folder is organized and where you can put your files, which can also apply to the files made with the Server Behavior Builder.

Inside the main Server Behaviors folder are three other folders—one for each server model (ASP, JSP, and Cold Fusion). In a Macromedia extension, the extension will typically be saved as an .htm file in the main folder. Together with the HTML files in some of the larger extensions are JS files for the functions. The two behaviors you just completed were fairly short, so they were just saved as a unit. However, you could have removed all the JavaScript and placed it in its own file. In addition to the JS file, some extensions have a special JS file just for the PATT and MASK variables, as these can get fairly lengthy for some of the complex extensions. The extensions, however, must reside in the *individual server model folders* in order for the Server Behavior floater to be able to see them. This can be accomplished by placing the main HTML file in the root Server Behaviors directory, and then placing an HTML file with the same name in each of the server model folders the extension works with. This HTML file, however, will only have three lines:

```
<!-- Search:"TM_groupsAllowed"-->
<!-- #include virtual="../UserAccess.htm" -->
<title>User Access Level</title>
```

UltraDev will see this file and put it in the Server Behaviors floater. When a user double-clicks the item on the menu to access the behavior, the actual file at the root level is included using a server-side include statement. This allows you to use the same relative paths in your Server Behavior file as you would if you were to put the file directly into the ASP folder, for instance.

That doesn't solve the organization problem of the menu, however. Fortunately, UltraDev is smart enough to give a new menu item to each folder that resides in the three Server Model folders under the Server Behavior root. Just as you did in the Objects chapter, you can create a Custom Extension folder, or call it by any name you choose, and put it in the ASP, JSP, or Cold Fusion folder for your own use. You can then either put your extension into this folder or put the short pointer file in there and put your extension in the root ServerBehaviors folder, so it can be accessed more easily by other commands, objects, and behaviors you might write. If you do that, however, you have to make sure that the relative path in your include line is correct:

```
<!-- #include virtual="../../UserAccess.htm" -->
```

instead of

```
<!-- #include virtual="../UserAccess.htm" -->
```

In additon, any references to JavaScript that include files will need to be changed as well in your main HTML Server Behavior file. These references are usually at the top of the file and should be changed to reflect the new location of the HTML file. For example, if you are moving the file into a subfolder, you would have to append ../ to the beginning of each include path, as in the previous examples.

Note *Another way to change the menus is to write commands in the MXI file that are used to create a packaged extension. These commands allow you to put your extensions virtually anywhere and point the menu items to the appropriate file. MXI files will be discussed in Chapter 23.*

Where Do You Go from Here?

Now that you've completed your second Server Behavior, you can see the pattern evolving. You can use similar techniques to build Server Behaviors for any application. Some of the functions are completely transportable to other Server Behaviors, while others will require extensive modification to be reusable. The PATT and MASK variables can be used in Property Inspectors or Translators to allow those extensions to find instances of your Server Behavior.

In any case, the basic framework is in place. You should now be able to use the Server Behavior API to build a behavior that will insert any sort of server markup into your documents. If these two objects don't match your needs, you can add to them or rewrite them to suit your own applications.

Using the UltraDev Server Behavior Builder

UltraDev 4 introduced a Server Behavior Builder that takes the hard work out of building simple Server Behaviors. Also, there is an entirely new architecture in place using XML group and participant files. These files are located in the ExtensionData folder. After you create a Server Behavior using the Builder, a group XML file for the extension and participant XML files for each of the participants are created. In addition, there is an HTML interface file that is placed in the ServerBehaviors folder under the correct server model subfolder.

Of course, the best way to learn how to use the Server Behavior Builder is by actually creating a Server Behavior.

Creating a Server Behavior with the Builder

Frequently, when you are accessing dynamic text, such as a database column, there will be a need to replace instances of the text with another character, word, or HTML tag. For example, when retrieving text from a database that has a line-feed character, the text will be displayed on the HTML page as one long string; however, HTML text must be formatted with <br> tags. Or assume you need to replace a certain word or token in the text with the user's name, current time, current date, or some other dynamic data. You are now able to build an extremely simple Server Behavior that can address all of these situations.

Creating the Code for the Server Behavior

As with the hand-coded Server Behaviors, the most important thing to remember is that the code you use to create the Server Behavior should work properly before even beginning the creation process. Also, there are limitations with the Server Behavior Builder that you should be aware of before starting:

- The code blocks have to be completely enclosed by tags. For example, you can't insert text or code after a closing tag.

- You can't have an unclosed tag as part of a participant. For example, you can't have a <table> open tag in one participant and a </table> close tag in another.

- You can wrap a selection with a balanced tag pair, but you can't enclose a selection within a set of server-side tags.

■ You can't edit the user selection in any way within the confines of the Builder. For example, if you want to enclose a dynamic database column with a server-side function, it can't be done with the Builder.

Experimentation with the Builder will enable you to develop solutions for some of the functionality you may want to achieve, but there are also some things that just can't be done.

Trial and error is the best method for trying out the functionality of the new Server Behavior Builder. Many features aren't in place, and the functionality is limited; but with a little ingenuity, you can create workarounds for the inherent limitations of the Builder.

The code you will be dealing with for this particular extension will, of course, vary from server model to server model. The Java code is a little more complex but accomplishes the same thing and will be inserted in the Server Behavior Builder in exactly the same way as the others. The code is as follows:

VBScript

```
<%=Replace((RecordsetName.Fields.Item("column").Value),replacethis, ¬
withthis)%>
```

JavaScript

```
<%
var columnname = RecordsetName.Fields.Item("columnname").Value;
var ToReplace = replacethis;
var ReplaceWith = withthis;
var i = columnname.indexOf(ToReplace);
while (i != -1)  {
    columnname= columnname.substr(0,i) + ReplaceWith + ¬
columnname.substr(i + ToReplace.length,columnname.length);
    i = columnname.indexOf(ToReplace,i);
}
Response.Write(columnname);
%>
```

JSP

```
<%
String columnname;  //if using this SB more than once on a page
```

```
String ToReplace;    //you should declare the variables in a
String ReplaceWith; //separate script block
int TM_i;           //
columnname = rsDisplayResume.getString("RESEDUCATION");
ToReplace = "\n";
ReplaceWith = "<br>";
TM_i = columnname.indexOf(ToReplace);
while (TM_i  != -1)             {
    columnname=columnname.substring(0,TM_i )+ReplaceWith+ ¬
columnname.substring(TM_i+ToReplace.length(),columnname.length());
    TM_i=columnname.indexOf(ToReplace,TM_i );
}
out.println(columnname);
%>
```

ColdFusion

```
#Replace(RecordsetName. Column, replacethis, withthis,"All")#
</CFOUTPUT>
```

Giving the Server Behavior a Name

The Server Behavior Builder is accessed from the Server Behavior palette by clicking the plus sign (+) on the Server Behavior palette and then clicking New Server Behavior. This will show the New Server Behavior dialog box, shown in Figure 22-2. In this dialog box you are given options for

- **Server Model**   This can be ASP/JavaScript, ASP/VBScript, ColdFusion, or JSP.
- **Name**   This is the name of the Server Behavior.
- **Option: Copy Existing Server Behavior**   Select this check box to start creating your extension from an already existing Server Behavior.
- **Behavior to Copy**   This drop-down list lists all available Server Behaviors that you can copy from.

You'll name this new Server Behavior as Dynamic Text with Replace and then choose your server model. The Copy Existing Server Behavior option can be left unselected. Upon completion of the naming process, click the OK button.

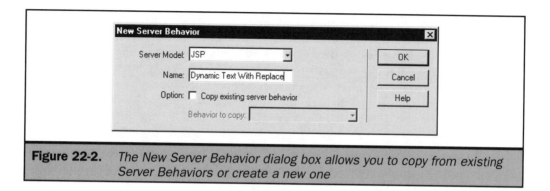

Figure 22-2. The New Server Behavior dialog box allows you to copy from existing Server Behaviors or create a new one

Adding the Code Block to the Builder

After clicking OK in the Server Behavior Builder, you will see the dialog box shown in Figure 22-3. There are several steps to follow here.

1. Click the plus sign (+) to insert a new code block. This will default to the Server Behavior name appended with _block1. This is fine for now; but later, when you develop more complex extensions, you can choose more meaningful names.

2. You should copy and paste your code block into the Code Block box.

3. Starting with the first parameter in the code block, highlight the parameter (in this case, RecordsetName).

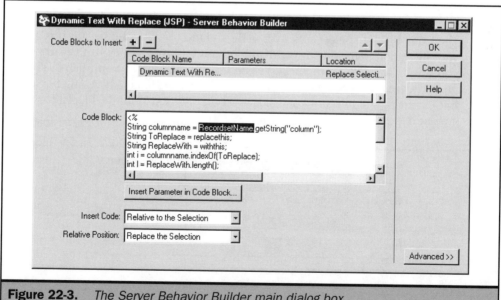

Figure 22-3. The Server Behavior Builder main dialog box

4. Click the Insert Parameter in Code Block button (see Figure 22-4). Choose a name to identify the parameter, such as Recordset Name. This is the name that will appear in the Server Behavior interface when you apply the behavior to the page. If the parameter appears more than once in the code block, you will be prompted to replace all occurrences. You should always say yes to this. The parameter name is inserted into the code block surrounded by @@ to identify it as a parameter. This is how the Server Behavior Builder transforms your code block into a MASK variable.

5. Follow steps 3 and 4 for each of the other three parameters that are in this behavior: column, replacethis, and withthis. The names you choose should be Column Name, String to Replace, and Replace With.

6. The Insert Code drop-down box has several options. For this Server Behavior, choose Relative to the Selection.

7. The Relative Position drop-down box also has several options that vary according to which position you choose for the Insert Code box. For this Server Behavior, choose Replace the Selection.

8. Click the Advanced button. This will extend the dialog box with some advanced features (as shown in Figure 22-5).

9. The Server Behavior Title box shows you the title that will actually appear in the Server Behavior inspector. The parameters that you inserted into the behavior are listed to the right of the Server Behavior name in parentheses. You can leave these here, or if there is a long list of them, only put the parameters in here that will give your Server Behavior title some meaning when you see the title in the Server Behavior inspector. For this particular behavior, leave this set to the default.

10. The Code Block to Select box is set to the default (No Selection). This box gives you the option to have your code highlighted in the design environment when you select the behavior in the Server Behavior palette. To accomplish this, you must choose your code block from the drop-down list of blocks available. For this extension, there is only one block—Dynamic Text With Re_block1 (or similar depending on the name you gave it).

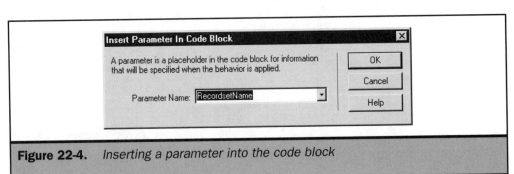

Figure 22-4. *Inserting a parameter into the code block*

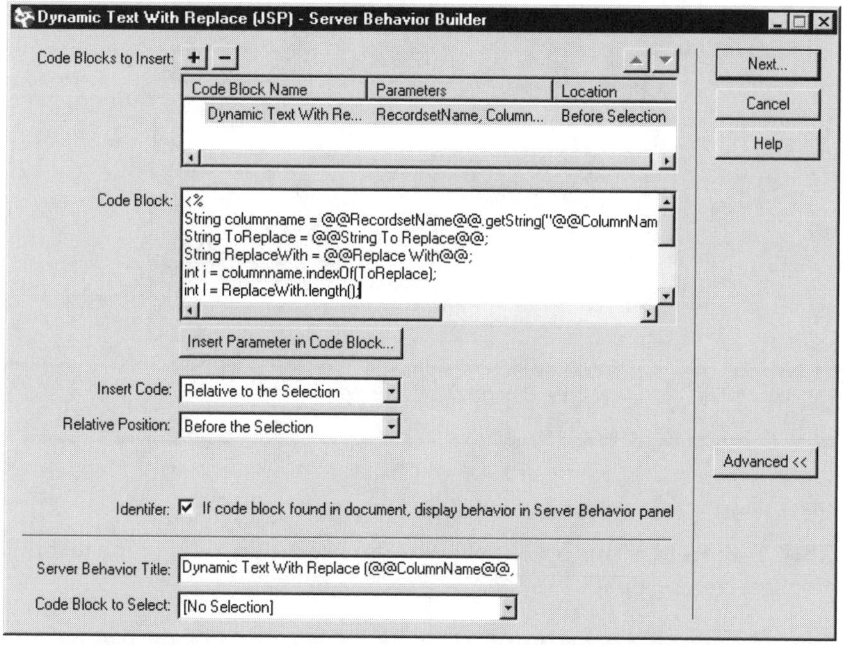

Figure 22-5. *Clicking the Advanced button gives you more options*

11. Make sure the Identifier box is selected. This ensures that the block is highlighted in the design environment based on the choice you made in step 10.

After completing these steps, you can click the Next button to take you to the next dialog box.

Creating the HTML Interface for Your Server Behavior

Upon clicking Next in the Server Behavior Builder, you are taken to the Generate Behavior Dialog Box dialog box, shown in Figure 22-6. This dialog box allows you to choose from the following types of interface controls for your HTML interface for the Server Behavior:

- **Dynamic Text Field** This will place a lightning bolt button next to your text field so that a dynamic text item can be chosen.
- **Recordset Field Menu** This gives you a list of columns in your recordsets.
- **Recordset Menu** This allows you to choose from a list of recordsets on the page.

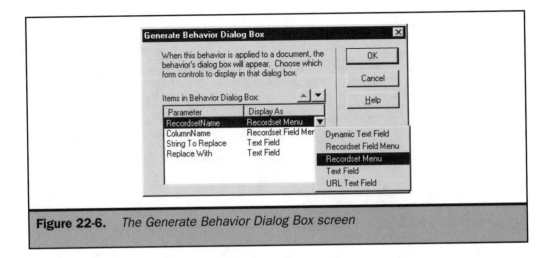

Figure 22-6.   *The Generate Behavior Dialog Box screen*

- ■ **Text Field**   This is a plain text field.
- ■ **URL Text Field**   This option places a Browse button next to the text field so you can choose a path to a file.

For this behavior, choose Recordset Menu for the Recordset Name parameter, Recordset Field Menu for the Column Name parameter, and Text Fields for the two remaining parameters—String to Replace and Replace With. The up and down arrows allow you to position the fields on the interface in the order you choose. Figure 22-6 shows that the list is as follows: Recordset Name is first, followed by Column Name, String to Replace, and Replace With. This order follows the logical order of the Server Behavior.

After clicking the OK button, you now have a new Server Behavior that can be applied to any page you choose. The behavior appears in the Server Behavior palette at the bottom of the list of behaviors.

Using the Server Behavior

This behavior can now be applied. Notice that because you chose Recordset Menu for the interface, the behavior actually prohibits you from putting the behavior on the page if you don't have a recordset defined already. The auto-generated interfaces have basic validation only, and any other validation you might want to do on the field would have to be hand-coded. For example, if you wanted to restrict a file field in a URL text field to a certain type of file, such as GIF, you could place the input validation into the HTML file. In addition, if any fields are left blank, the behavior can still be applied, which can generate errors on your final page. You should make sure you insert the proper validation in your HTML file in the canApplyServerBehavior(sbObj) function.

If you have a page with a recordset on it, apply the behavior and select one of the columns. The view_a_gig page has several columns with line breaks in them that were hand-coded in Chapter 18. Now that you have a Server Behavior to perform the work, this functionality need not be hand-coded anymore. If you apply the behavior to the page (shown in Figure 22-7), you can use the following parameters (note that this is a VBScript example):

- **Recordset Name** rsDisplayResume
- **Recordset Column** ResExperience
- **String to Replace** Chr(10)
- **Replace With** "<br>"

The Server Behavior will appear in the Server Behavior palette along with the parameters. Figure 22-8 shows the page with three instances of the behavior. Notice that in the behavior, you must use quotes around the string if you are working with literal text. This enables you to use the behavior with any combination of possible literal or variable strings. A partial list of possible uses of the Server Behavior is shown in Table 22-6.

String to Replace	Replace With	Language
chr(10)	" " & chr(10)	VBScript
"[nametoken]"	Recordset("firstname")	VBScript or JavaScript
"[timetoken]"	TimeFormat(Now())	ColdFusion
"\n"	"</td></tr><td><tr>"	JavaScript or Java
"\n"	"</li><li>"	JavaScript or Java
"*"	'<img src="images/bullet.gif">'	JavaScript
"[name]"	session.getValue ("firstname")	Java

Table 22-6.   *Possible Values for the Dynamic Text with Replace Server Behavior*

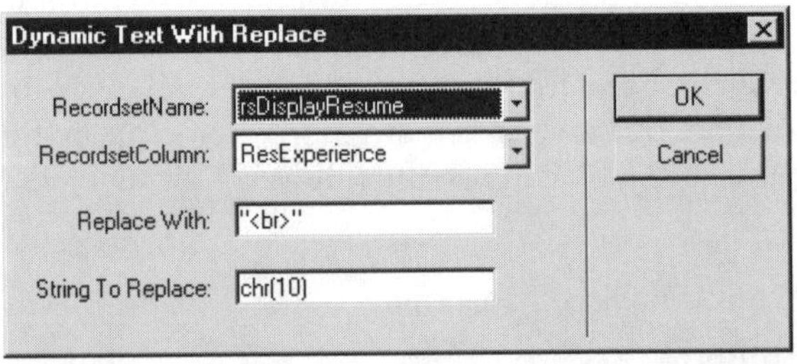

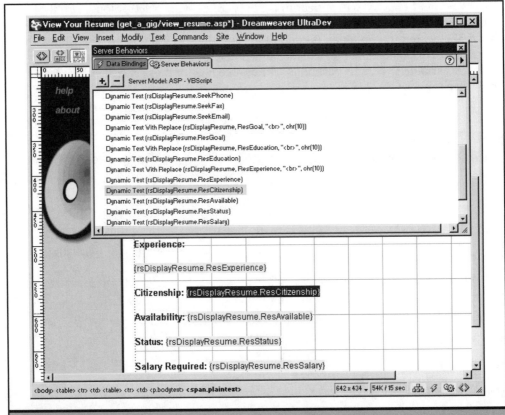

Figure 22-7. *Applying the newly created Server Behavior to the page*

Figure 22-8. *The view_a_gig page with three instances of the Server Behavior applied to it*

Creating a Server Behavior with More Than One Participant

Using the Server Behavior Builder allows you to quickly build complex Server Behaviors with as many code blocks as you may need. In many cases, there are conditions that must be met before certain parts of your page are displayed. UltraDev comes with a Show Region behavior that deals with recordsets; but, frequently, you may need to check for other conditions, such as the value of a session variable, a cookie, or whether two different values match each other. This is easy with the Server Behavior Builder because you can choose to insert a block of code before the selection and a block of code after the selection. In a situation such as this, the first block would be the IF statement, and the second block would be the END IF block. Your first block might look like this:

```
<%if (session("User")<>"Tom) then %>(VBScript)
<%if (session("User")!="Tom) {%>(JavaScript)
<%if (session.getValue("User")!="Tom"){%>(Java)
```

and the second block might look like this:

```
<%End If%>(VBScript)
<%}%>   (Java and JavaScript)
```

   To create a Server Behavior such as this, you'll use the same methods as outlined in the preceding example, except that you would add a second participant and give the Relative Position drop-down box a value of After the Selection.

   A ColdFusion user can use the special Relative Position choice of Wrap Around Selection for this example. Any time you have a tag that has a corresponding close tag, you may use this option. The ColdFusion example is as follows:

```
<cfif (session.user NEQ "Tom")></cfif>
```

   Using a balanced set of tags like this will cause UltraDev to insert the beginning <cfif> tag before the selection and the ending </cfif> tag after the selection. However, in the previous VBScript, JavaScript, and Java examples, the code blocks are completely separate tag blocks, so they aren't able to use this special Wrap Around Selection feature. One of the limitations of the feature is that it can only be used once in a Server Behavior. You cannot, for example, insert a <td></td> in one block and a <tr></tr> in another block and expect them to both wrap around the selection. Doing so will actually cause the page to write the selection out twice—once with a <td> pair wrapped around it and once with a <tr> pair wrapped around it.

Copying an Existing Server Behavior

One of the most remarkable features of the new Server Behavior Builder is the ability to copy existing Server Behaviors, and change them in some way to allow you to create new Server Behaviors that have similar or more advanced functionality. One obvious application of this would be to develop a Nesting Repeat Region based on the standard Repeat Region behavior. This Server Behavior is useful only to JSP and ASP, however, since ColdFusion users have this functionality built into the <CFQUERY> tag.

To build this Server Behavior, you must first understand how the nesting will occur. In this example, the first recordset created returns a list of U.S. states. The outer Repeat Region will cycle through the list of states. Inside that Repeat Region exists a second recordset that retrieves names based on the current column value of the state column in the first recordset.

This second recordset will get called each time as the outer Repeat Region cycles through the loop. After the second recordset is executed, the inner loop begins, cycling through the results of the second recordset. After that loop ends, the outer loop continues. This cycle continues until all the results of the first recordset have been repeated.

 This is just one of many nesting techniques and should be used sparingly, but works well with large databases where it is prudent to retrieve only a few records at a time. Other techniques involve the recordset requery or movefirst methods, filtering, or data shaping, and are beyond the scope of this exercise.

A New Recordset Server Behavior

The limitation of the Recordset Server Behavior that comes with UltraDev 4 is that it is defined in the same place for every instance—it has a weight of aboveHTML+50. This means that when you insert a recordset, it is positioned relative to other Server Behaviors above the HTML tag. To create a new version that has a position in the body of the document, you can copy the existing recordset. Here are the steps to accomplish this:

1. Create a new Server Behavior by clicking the plus sign (+) in the Server Behavior palette and selecting New Server Behavior.

2. Choose the Server Model, fill in the name RecordsetForNesting, and select the Copy Existing Server Behavior option.

3. Choose Recordset from the list of drop-down Server Behaviors and click OK. This will bring you to the Server Behavior Builder interface that you've worked with previously. All of the existing participants (four in all) are listed in the interface. The only things you'll be changing about the participants are the relative positions.

4. The first participant is the connection include statement. This can remain the same.

5. The second participant is the variable declaration code block. This participant needs to have the Insert Code parameter set to Relative to the Selection, and the Relative Position set to Before the Selection. This allows the variable to be set up with a new value upon each iteration of the loop.

6. The third participant in the behavior is RecordsetForNesting_main. This participant needs to have the Insert Code parameter set to Relative to the Selection, and the Relative Position set to Before the Selection.

7. The fourth and last participant is the recordset close command, which needs no modification.

8. Add a comment to the main code block, such as "Recordset for nested repeats," using the comment syntax of the language you are working with. This ensures that the original Recordset Server Behavior isn't going to interfere with the new recordset.

Caution *The important thing to realize when you make a copy of an existing Server Behavior is that you must make a change to the code—even if it's just a comment—to ensure that UltraDev does not confuse your Server Behavior with the original Server Behavior.*

That's all there is to it. Now you have a recordset that can be inserted anywhere in the body of your document. Obviously, there are other changes that can be made to the recordset as well, but such things can be experimented with later.

Creating the Nested Repeat Server Behavior

The preceding procedures will be used to create the Nested Repeat Server Behavior as well. First, create a new Server Behavior and choose to copy an existing Server Behavior. This time you'll select the repeatedRegion Server Behavior from the list. Once again, change the Relative Position of the Nested Repeat_init block to Before Selection, as you'll want this inside the outer loop.

Add a comment line to the begin and end code blocks to ensure that the original Repeat Region Server Behavior doesn't find this behavior and cause an error condition to occur. Sometimes the comment lines won't affect the behavior but may still cause an error, in which case you can change a variable name to make sure that your participant won't be found by another extension. In the case of the Repeat Region, we've found that the pattern in the original Repeat Region Server Behavior is greedy and actually finds this behavior as a Repeat Region even if a comment is inserted. You can change all references to the variable @@loopName@@_ _numRows from numRows to num1Rows to make sure that the code won't be found and this Server Behavior will be unique.

After you finish these steps and save the behavior, you can apply the Nested Repeat as you would the standard Repeat Region, but it's not ready yet. If you try it inside a regular Repeat Region, you will still get an error message that says you can't nest Repeat Regions. Since the behavior was copied from the existing one, you must remove the check that prevents applying nested regions. This is where the knowledge of Server Behaviors that you acquired in the first part of this chapter is going to pay off. You must know where to find the various functions that contain the functionality of the behavior.

 A nested repeat region could also be efficiently coded by hand and turned into a Server Behavior.

Editing the Builder-Generated Files by Hand

The Server Behaviors generated by the Server Behavior Builder are stored in the same place as the standard Server Behaviors—in the ServerBehaviors folder. The HTML interfaces are usually stored in the subfolder of the server model in which you built the behavior. In other words, if you built an ASP extension, the interface will be in the ASP folder.

If you build a new behavior in the Builder that is not based on an existing behavior, all the functions will be contained in this interface file. In the case of the Nested Region behavior, however, many of the functions are located in the Repeated Region.js file that is located in the main ServerBehaviors folder. This is because the Builder only provides the most basic functionality to your Server Behavior. To add better validation; better interface controls like color pickers, radio buttons, or checkboxes; and functions like copyServerBehavior or pasteServerBehavior, you must do so by hand-coding.

The best method for approaching a situation like this is to make a copy of the Repeated Region.js file and name it Repeated RegionNew.js, and then change the reference to it in the Nested Region.htm file, like this:

```
<script src="../Repeated RegionNew.js"></script>
```

This way, if any Macromedia updates are installed to UltraDev, you won't have to worry that your file will be written over. Also, you won't have to worry about changing the functionality of the existing Repeat Region Server Behavior.

If you went through the first part of the chapter that dealt with hand-coding a Server Behavior, you might remember the canApplyServerBehavior function. This is where most of the validation occurs when you attempt to add a Server Behavior to the page. In this particular case, there is a line that performs the check to see whether the repeat is inside another repeat. The following line should be commented out:

```
//var errMsg - checkForInvalidSelection();
```

That's all there is to it. By commenting out that one line you can now apply a nested Repeat Region.

There's one more change you may want to make. As you may recall, you had to move the init block from the position it was in (aboveHTML+51) to Before Selection. This was done to allow the region to work inside another region. The one problem that emerges is that it also causes all of the "move to" Server Behaviors to cease functioning for that region. (This is another reason you didn't modify the original Repeat Region file!) That's perfectly fine for this behavior, however, since you will always want *all* records returned from this inner loop. You simply have to remove the option to choose anything other than all records by removing the choice from the HTML interface.

First, remove the HTML table rows that contain the choice for all records and the text field for selecting the number of records. All that should remain on the interface is the rsName <select> box and its label.

Next, edit the Repeated RegionNew.js file to remove the references to these interface items. Once again, the knowledge of hand-coded Server Behaviors is going to come in handy. You need to edit the applyServerBehavior function, the inspectServerBehavior function, and the initializeUI() function.

 It's usually a good idea when making edits to your extension files to comment out the sections you are removing rather than actually deleting them. This is just in case you may have made a mistake and have to put the code back in. You can do this by commenting each line with a double slash (//) or use a block comment around a large section that spans several lines /*code here*/.

Starting with the applyServerBehavior function, you need to comment out or delete the section that begins with the following line:

```
if (RADIOS.count.getSelectedIndex() == RADIO_value)"
```

Remove everything up to and including the following line:

```
} else { //all
```

Next, keep the following two lines:

```
paramObj.numRows = -1;
paramObj.MM_subType = "all";
```

Then remove the next closing bracket. This effectively removes the part of the code that retrieves the information from the user interface about the Repeat count.

Next, edit the inspectServerBehavior function. This function, if you recall from the earlier section about hand-coding Server Behaviors, populates the HTML user interface with the values that already exist in the Server Behavior when a user makes an edit on the Server Behavior. This function has one line that will remain—the rest can be commented out or deleted. The following line should be left intact:

```
rsName.inspectServerBehavior(sbObj)
```

This line uses one of the new Server Behavior controls to populate the recordset drop-down list in the interface. These controls are located in the Configuration\Shared\Controls\Scripts folder and can be used in your own extensions.

One last edit to the initializeUI() function will finish off the extension. Again, there is one line that should be left in this function:

```
rsName.initializeUI();
```

The other lines can be commented out. You might notice that there is a function named updateUI that contains references to the radio buttons that were removed. This function will never get called, since you removed all references to it. You can leave it intact.

Applying the New Nested Region Behavior to the Page

Create a page called all_companies_by_state in the admin folder of the Bettergig site to test out these new Server Behaviors. To apply the new behavior to the page, you must follow these steps:

1. Insert a two-row, two-column table into the content region of the page.

2. Apply a standard recordset to the page named rsGetStates, using a SQL statement to retrieve the column information for the outer loop. The statement in this case is

   ```
   SELECT Distinct EmpState from Employers
   ```

3. Drag and drop the newly created dynamic column EmpState to the first column of the first row. You can set the style of this text to Bold for emphasis.

4. Select both rows of the table. You can do this easily by positioning your cursor in the second row, second column; holding down the mouse button; and dragging the mouse across the table, as shown in Figure 22-9. Apply a standard Repeat Region to the area, choosing to show three records at a time.

5. In the second cell of the first row, position your cursor and insert a RecordsetForNesting Server Behavior. Create a recordset named rsGetNames, using the EmpState column from the first recordset as a parameter. The variable in the recordset should have a run-time value of rsGetStates("EmpState"). The SQL should look something like this:

   ```
   SELECT EmpName, EmpContact FROM Employers
   WHERE EmpState = 'myVariable'
   ```

6. In the second row of the table, insert the EmpName column into the first cell of the row and the EmpContact column into the second cell of the table.

7. Select the second row of the table and apply the Nested Region Server Behavior you just created. Make sure you choose the correct recordset from the drop-down box (rsGetNames).

8. Somewhere below the table, you can insert the Recordset Navigation Bar object.

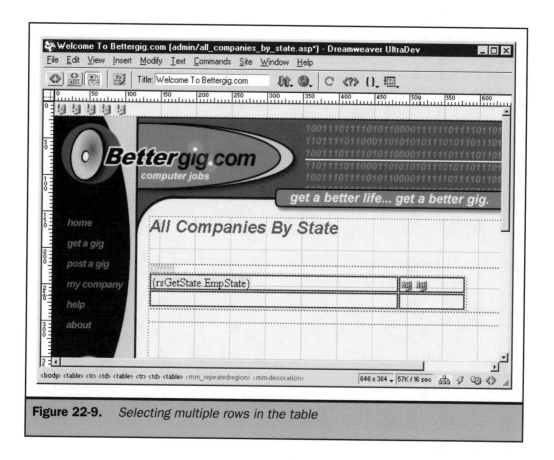

Figure 22-9.   *Selecting multiple rows in the table*

After applying these steps, you should be able to browse the page and cycle through the records for the states. The nested repeat should show the employers for each state.

Creating a Translator for the Nested Region

You may have noticed that the newly created Nested Region Server Behavior doesn't show the nice little Repeat tab any more. Because the Server Behavior is now a completely new entity, the translators for the standard Repeat Region won't work with the new Nested Repeat. You can create a new translator participant for the Nested Repeat by looking at the XML files that are part of the new XML architecture of UltraDev 4.

Translators are the extensions that take care of translating the code that is inserted into the page into a user-friendly viewable item. Translators are discussed in greater detail in Chapter 23.

The ExtensionData Folder

All the XML files for the Server Behavior extensions created by the Server Behavior Builder are stored in the ExtensionData folder. Typically, there is a main *Group* file and then a *Participant* file for each of the code blocks that were created. The Group file contains general information about the Participant files. The Group file for the Nested Repeat Server Behavior looks like this:

```
<group name="NestedRepeat" serverBehavior="NestedRepeat.htm"
dataSource="Recordset.htm">
        <groupParticipants selectParticipant="NestedRepeat_begin">
                <groupParticipant name="NestedRepeat_init2" partType="member" />
                <groupParticipant name="NestedRepeat_begin" />
                <groupParticipant name="NestedRepeat_end2" />
        </groupParticipants>
        <title>NestedRepeat</title>
</group>
```

As you can see, the XML tags are pretty easy to understand. The name attribute gives the name of the Server Behavior, and the serverBehavior attribute shows the actual Server Behavior file. Then, the <groupParticipants> tag contains the selectParticpant attribute, which is the name of the participant that causes the code to become selected in the design environment when the user selects the Server Behavior in the Server Behavior palette. The <groupParticipant> tags are child tags of the <groupParticipants> tag, and list the names of the various participants of the extension. The names are equal to the XML participant files minus the .xml file extension.

Group Participants

Each of the participant files contain a single code block. It could be a set of server tags, HTML tags, or an attribute of a tag. If the Server Behavior was built with the Server Behavior Builder, you'll have one participant file for each code block or attribute that you assigned in the Builder. If you look at the NestedRepeat_begin participant file generated for the NestedRepeat, you'll see the main requirements:

```
<participant name="NestedRepeat_begin">
        <implementation serverModel="ASP/VBScript">
                <quickSearch><![CDATA[__num1Rows]]></quickSearch>
                <insertText location="beforeSelection"><![CDATA[
<% 'Begin Nested Repeat
While ((@@loopName@@__num1Rows <> 0) AND (NOT @@rsName@@.EOF))
%>
]]></insertText>
                <searchPatterns whereToSearch="directive">
                        <searchPattern paramNames="loopName,rsName" ¬
limitSearch="all">
<![CDATA[/<%\s*'Begin\s*Nested\s*Repeat\s*While\s*\(\(((.*) ¬
```

```
__num1Rows\s*<>\s*0\)\s*AND\s*\(NOT\s*(.*)\.EOF\)\)\s*%>/i]]>
</searchPattern>
            </searchPatterns>
        </implementation>
</participant>
```

Depending on which server model you implemented, your own file may look a little different, but the tags will be the same. The main tag is the <participant> tag, which gives the name of the participant. Beneath that is the <implementation> tag, which lists the name of the server model for which the participant is used. If you have implemented a Server Behavior with more than one server model, you might have multiple <implementation> tags in this one document.

The <quickSearch> tag acts like a quick glance through the document to find an instance of your behavior. In the manually created Server Behaviors, you used a Search String comment tag at the top of the Server Behavior file to act as your quick search. If UltraDev doesn't find the <quickSearch> string in the document, it knows that a more thorough search for the Server Behavior is not required.

Next, the <insertText> tag contains the code that is being inserted, and tells UltraDev where to put the code. The code contains the variables you've defined and is similar to the MASK variables you built earlier in the chapter. With the knowledge of how the MASK variables work, you can create these <insertText> tags manually as well.

The <searchPattern> tags contain information about the regular expression pattern used to find the code in the user's document. This is similar to the PATT variables discussed earlier in the chapter. Again, with the knowledge of how these PATT variables are built, you can build your own from scratch or modify the patterns created by the Builder to make them more efficient and more powerful. See the box Tweaking the SBB-Generated Patterns for more. The <searchPattern> tag also contains a list of the parameters that were defined in the Builder. The <searchPattern> tag is contained within a <searchPatterns> tag, allowing the use of several pattern blocks to be used by defining separate <searchPattern> tags for each one.

Tweaking the SBB-Generated Patterns

One of the time-saving features of the Server Behavior Builder is the fact that it generates all of the regular expressions that your Server Behavior needs. This saves time in the long run, but you also have to be aware of the pitfalls.

The expression that is generated is a strict translation of your code into a regular expression, with no room for code modifications by the end user. For example, if you have a Server Behavior that consists of the following code:

```
<table>
    <tr>
```

```
            <td><%=Session("Firstname")%></td>
        </tr>
    </table>
```

the regular expression that will be generated looks like this:

```
/<table>\s*<tr>\s*<td>\s*<%=Session\("(.*)"\)%>[^\0]*<\/td>[^\0]
* ¬
<\/tr>[^\0]*<\/table>/I
```

The problem with the pattern is that as soon as someone modifies the table on the page, the code will look completely different, like this:

```
<table width="157">
    <tr>
        <td height="131"><%=Session("Firstname")%></td>
    </tr>
</table>
```

The pattern doesn't work any more and the Server Behavior doesn't show up in the palette. By changing the generated pattern inside of the XML participant files, you can change the pattern so that it is more receptive to change, as in the following pattern, which will match both pieces of code:

```
/<table[^>]*>\s*<tr[^>]*>\s*<td[^>]*>\s*<%=Session\("(.*)"\)%> ¬
[^\0]*<\/td>[^\0]*<\/tr>[^\0]*<\/table>/I
```

By simply modifying the <table>, <tr>, and <td> tags with a [^>]* pattern to reflect "anything or everything up to the > character," you have made the pattern much more flexible in the UltraDev environment.

Translator Participants

To go along with the new XML format for Server Behaviors, translators also can be written using XML. The translator participants are located in the ExtensionData>MM>Translations folder. These can be created from scratch for your own Server Behaviors, allowing you to place a user-friendly representation of your code in the design environment instead of the gold script shield that accompanies a generic script. For the Nested Repeat Server Behavior, you'll want a translator that works in a similar fashion to the Repeat Region translator, allowing a light, gray-colored Repeat tab to be displayed around the region. In the Nested Repeat behavior, the tab should say Nested Repeat instead of Repeat.

To create the Translator participant files for the Nested Repeat Server Behavior, you can cheat a little and use the RepeatedRegion_Start and RepeatedRegion_End files as starting points or create them from scratch. The translator participants must have unique names that are different from the names of the Server Behavior participants. This is set in the <participant> tag in the top of the file. This should be set to the name of the file, excluding the .xml extension.

The following is the XML code for the NestedRegion_Start participant for ASP/VBScript. The search patterns will be different for the ASP/JavaScript and the JSP versions:

```
<implementation serverModel="ASP/VBScript">
    <translator>
        <searchPatterns>
            <searchPattern paramNames="loopName,rsName">
<![CDATA[/<%\s*'Begin\s*Nested\s*Repeat\s*While\s*\(\((.*) ¬
__num1Rows\s*<>\s*0\)\s*AND\s*\(NOT\s*(.*)\.EOF\)\)\s*%>/i]]>
            </searchPattern>
            <searchPattern requiredLocation="trailing">
<![CDATA[/<%\s*'end\s*nested\s*repeat\s*(.*)__index=.*__index\+1 ¬
\s*.*__num1Rows=.*__num1Rows-1\s*(.*)\.MoveNext\(\)\s*Wend\s*%>/i]]>
            </searchPattern>
        </searchPatterns>
        <translations>
            <translation whereToSearch="directive" ¬
            translationType="tabbed region start">
                <openTag>TM_NESTED_REPEAT</openTag>
                <attributes>
                    <attribute>NAME="@@loopName@@"</attribute>
                    <attribute>SOURCE="@@rsName@@"</attribute>
                </attributes>
                <display>Nested Repeat</display>
            </translation>
        </translations>
    </translator>
</implementation>
```

The first <searchPattern> tag is similar to the same tag in the Server Behavior participant files. The regular expression defined in this tag will be identical to the expression defined in the Server Behavior participant file. In fact, you can copy/paste the <searchPattern> tag from the NestedRepeat_begin.xml file.

The second <searchPattern> tag in this participant is actually the same pattern that is in the RepeatRegion_end participant. Therefore, it follows that you can copy/paste the pattern from the NestedRepeat_end participant and use it here. The added attribute requiredLocation="trailing" tells the translator that this participant is the end of the translation and that it is a required participant.

> *When creating translator participant files for your own Server Behaviors, it is easier to copy the Server Behavior <searchPattern> tags verbatim from the Server Behavior XML participant files.*

Next are the <translation> tags, enclosed within a pair of <translations> tags. The whereToSearch attribute tells the translator where the search patterns might be located. A whereToSearch attribute of Directive implies that it is in a section of server-side script. The whereToSearch attribute could contain a tag name here as well. For example, if you had a special type of table you wanted to translate, you could use an attribute of whereToSearch="table". The translationType indicates the type of translator this is. Here, it's a tabbed region start type. Other possible types are dynamic data, dynamic image, dynamic source, tabbed region end, and custom.

The <opentag> tag is an optional tag that will actually allow you to place a tag with values into the translated source code of the document. This is explained further in Chapter 23. The Repeat Region file has an <opentag> value of MM_REPEATED-REGION. Since this is a Nested Region, you can write your own open tag in its place—TM_NESTED_REPEAT.

The <opentag> tag can have attributes that usually correspond to the variables defined by the user for the Server Behavior. In this case, the values were for loopName and rsName. These values can come in handy when creating Property Inspectors for your Server Behavior.

Next is the <display> tag. This is where you place the actual text the user sees in the design environment. In the case of the standard Repeat Region translator, there is a variable MM.LABEL_RepeatTabbedOutlineLabel. That variable contains the value "Repeat." You can put a variable or literal value in the display tag. In this case, use the literal value "Nested Repeat." This will cause the tab in the design environment to show the Nested Repeat label.

After completing the changes and saving this file, you can do the same thing for the NestedRegion_End file. The participant patterns should be copied from the NestedRepeat_end and NestedRepeat_begin Server Behavior participant files. The code is as follows:

```
<implementation serverModel="ASP/VBScript">
    <translator>
        <searchPatterns>
            <searchPattern paramNames="loopName,rsName" ¬
            limitSearch="all">
<![CDATA[/<%\s*'end\s*nested\s*repeat\s*(.*)__index=.*__index\+1 ¬
\s*.*__num1Rows=.*__num1Rows-1\s*(.*)\.MoveNext\(\)\s*Wend\s*%>/i]]> ¬
```

```
        </searchPattern>
        <searchPattern requiredLocation="leading">
<![CDATA[/<%\s*'Begin\s*Nested\s*Repeat\s*While\s*\(\(((.*)__num1Rows ¬
\s*<>\s*0\)\s*AND\s*\(NOT\s*(.*)\.EOF\)\)\)\s*%>/i]]>
        </searchPattern>
    </searchPatterns>
    <translations>
        <translation whereToSearch="directive" ¬
         translationType="tabbed region end">
            <closeTag>TM_NESTED_REPEAT</closeTag>
        </translation>
    </translations>
  </translator>
</implementation>
```

Notice that in the NestedRegion_End file, there is a <closetag> to correspond with the <opentag> from the NestedRegion_Start file. Also, the <searchPattern> tag has a requiredLocation="leading" to correspond to the pattern for the NestedRepeat_begin participant.

If you save these files and look at the all_companies_by_state page that you created earlier, it should appear as in Figure 22-10, with a tabbed outline that says Nested Repeat instead of the gold shield icons that had little significance in the design environment.

The Server Behavior Helper Functions

The creation of Server Behaviors has been simplified with UltraDev 4. Much of the hand-coding has been replaced by automatic functionality of the Server Behavior Builder. If you have a piece of code that can't be built with the Builder, however, you can still take advantage of the helper or shortcut functions that were introduced in UltraDev 4. The requirement for using the helper functions is that your group and participant files are written in XML and stored in the ExtensionData folder.

findSBs()

This function is called from the findServerBehaviors function. If you recall from the first part of this chapter, the findServerBehaviors function was responsible for finding all instances of your Server Behavior on a given page. The function is called like this:

```
findServerBehaviors() {
    paramObj = new Object();
    sbArray= findSBs();
    rsName.findServerBehaviors(paramObj);
```

```
    return sbArray;
}
```

The rsName.findServerBehaviors call is a special method of the RecordsetMenu class that can be found in the Configuration\Shared\Controls\Scripts folder. These special control classes also take much of the work out of building Server Behaviors. A thorough knowledge of these classes is necessary if you want to make changes to an auto-generated Server Behavior.

applySB()

This helper function is called after the user has defined any attributes the Server Behavior requires. If the user is editing an existing Server Behavior, the parameter

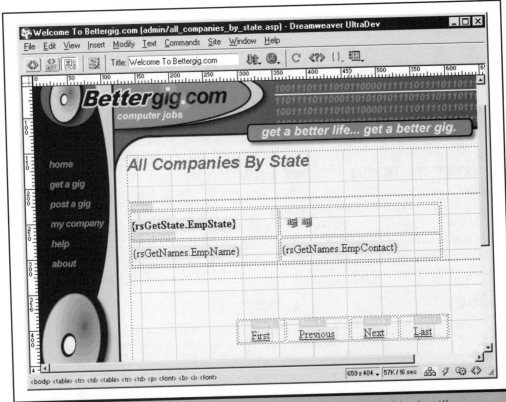

Figure 22-10. *The Nested Repeat Server Behavior now has a tabbed outline translator that displays the words "Nested Repeat" in the tab*

sbObj is passed to the function. For example, if the behavior requires a recordset, the function might look like this:

```
function applyServerBehavior(sbObj) {
    paramObj = new Object();
    paramObj.rs = myRecordset;
    applySB(paramObj,sbObj);
}
```

deleteSB()

The deleteServerBehavior function is called when the user selects the Server Behavior in the Server Behavior palette and clicks the minus (–) sign to delete the Server Behavior. The deleteSB() function is called from within the deleteServerBehavior function. If there are any special rules for the removal of the participants, the rules are given in the <delete> tag of the participant. The following example shows a basic implementation:

```
function deleteServerBehavior(sbObj) {
    deleteSB(sbObj);
}
```

Summary

In this chapter, you've learned how to create Server Behaviors in several ways. Server Behaviors can be hand-coded in HTML and JavaScript, or you can create XML participant files for the Server Behavior. In addition, the new Server Behavior Builder has removed a lot of the tedious work in building basic Server Behaviors. The Builder was introduced in UltraDev 4 and has some limitations, but promises to be an outstanding feature in years to come. For a full explanation of the new Server Behavior XML format, you should read the extensibility documentation that comes with UltraDev 4.

In the next chapter, you'll build other types of extensions, including translators, inspectors, and commands.

Chapter 23

Other Extensions

UltraDev extensibility begins with objects and culminates with Server Behaviors; but there are quite a few other extension types in between, some of which will be discussed briefly in this chapter. Because UltraDev differs from its baby brother, Dreamweaver, in its use of databases, this chapter focuses primarily on live data-related extensions.

Commands

Commands are perhaps the most powerful of the extensions, because they can perform powerful document and site manipulation, and can be called from any other extension. Some of them appear on the Commands menu of UltraDev and include such things as Clean Up HTML and Add/Remove Netscape Resize Fix. A command can add code to a page or manipulate code that's already on the page. Sometimes, a fine line separates commands, objects, behaviors, and Server Behaviors; but no matter what you decide to do with your code, it's a good idea to know all the possibilities that are available to you.

A Command file is similar to the HTML files that you created for objects and Server Behaviors, but differs in a few respects. For one, not every command has a corresponding menu item. If you look inside the Commands folder, you'll see quite a few commands that don't appear on the Commands menu. To keep the command from appearing on the menu, simply put the following as the first line in your command file:

```
<!-- MENU-LOCATION=NONE -->
```

There are a few ways you can use commands to enhance your other extensions. You can invoke a command with a dw.runCommand() function call or with the dw.popupCommand() function call.

This is done for many reasons. Commands are more versatile than some of the other extensions, for example, Inspectors. A Property Inspector must reside in a small interface to conform to the pre-defined size of an Inspector. Frequently, you will have to invoke a command to display a larger interface for editing some code or attributes. If you look at the Asp.js file in the Inspectors folder, for instance, you'll notice the launchASPEditDialog() function, which gets the selected object and then calls the dw.popupCommand("EditContent") to invoke a code editor for the ASP code block that was selected by the user. You can do this in your own Property Inspectors, as well.

As always, looking at existing code is a great way to learn how to apply the techniques to your own programming. The existing Command files offer a wealth of information.

The following syntax presents a very basic command, to show you how to manipulate the document. This command simply wraps any selected text or object with comment tags, so that you can freely comment your HTML without leaving the design environment. You can also choose to "comment out" some text or an object while designing your site, which is useful for debugging.

```
<html>
<head>
<title>MakeComment</title>
<script language="javascript">
<!--
function makeComment() {
var openTag = '<!--\n'
var closeTag = '\n-->';
// Get Selected text and wrap with comment tags
    var dom = dw.getDocumentDOM(); //get the DOM
    var sel = dom.getSelection(); //get the selected text or object
    var wrapthis = dom.documentElement.outerHTML.substring(sel[0], sel[1]);
    wrapthis = openTag + wrapthis + closeTag; //wrap the selected text
    dw.getDocumentDOM().insertHTML(wrapthis); //insert into the document
    window.close();
      }
// -->
</script>
</head>
<body onLoad="makeComment()">
</body>
</html>
```

The code is fairly simple. First, it declares two variables for your opening and closing comment tags. Then, it declares the makeComment() function, which is called from the body onLoad event of the extension. The makeComment() function simply gets the document DOM, and then it acquires the selected text by using the offsets that were returned by the getSelection method of the DOM and getting the outerHTML property. Then, all that is left to do is to wrap the opening and closing comment tags around the selection, and insert the entire string back into the document.

At this point, if you save the extension in the Commands folder with the name MakeComment.htm and restart UltraDev, you can apply it by making a selection on the page and then choosing MakeComment from the Commands menu. When you do this, any selected text or object will be collapsed into a comment tag. How are you going to "uncomment" the item now? You'll write another command, StripCommentTags, to do this. Here is the code for that command:

```html
<html>
<head>
<title>StripCommentTags</title>
<script language="javascript">
<!--
function stripComment() {
    // Get Selected comment and strip comment tags
    var doc = dw.getDocumentDOM(); //get the DOM
    var sel = doc.getSelection(); //get the selection
    var theNode = dw.offsetsToNode(sel[0],sel[1]);
    if(theNode.nodeType==Node.COMMENT_NODE) {
        sel=theNode.data;
        dw.getDocumentDOM().insertHTML(sel);
    }
    window.close();
}
// -->
</script>
</head>
<body onLoad="stripComment()">
</body>
</html>
```

This command works in a similar fashion to the MakeComment command. However, after getting the selection, the command first checks to see whether the selected node is a comment node. If it is a comment, it gets the *data* property of the node. The data property contains the area that's inside the tags in *comment* nodes and *text* nodes. It's similar to the innerHTML property of the *element* nodes. After getting the data property, you then write the HTML to the document without the comment tags.

These techniques can be used to add server-side code, as well. You could easily modify the MakeComment command to insert any of the server markup listed in Table 23-1, or to insert code before and after the selected text simply by changing the openTag and closeTag variables.

Another feature worth mentioning about Command files is the ability to define on-the-fly the buttons for the interface—making them contextual depending upon conditions that you can set up programmatically. One good example of this technique is the Add/Remove Netscape Resize Fix command. In that command, the button

openTag	closeTag
<% =	%>
<%Response.Write("	")%>
<cfoutput>	</cfoutput>
<%try{	}catch(java.lang.Exception e){;}%>
<%If Session("Username")<>"" Then %>	<%End If%>
<cfif IsDefined("Session.Username")>	</cfif>
<%if(MM_offset != 0)%>	<%}%>

Table 23-1. *Possible Opening and Closing Tags for a Modified Command Extension*

shown in the interface depends upon whether or not the user has already applied the command to the page. If the command has been applied, the user is shown the Remove button; whereas if the command hasn't been applied yet, the user is shown the Add button. You could easily adapt your MakeComment/StripComment commands to share one single interface by using this technique. A comment command that illustrates this idea is included in the CD–ROM.

Translators

Translators are the extensions that convert your HTML into a viewable object in the design environment. When you insert some server markup in the body of an HTML document, for instance, you don't want the design environment to show the actual code. To get a clean representation of the code, you can write a Translator to accomplish this. For example, when you drag a recordset column from the Data Bindings Inspector to the page that you are editing, what you see is a representation of the actual code that's inserted. Typical placeholders for recordset columns are shown in Figure 23-1. The code that is underlying the translated code for one column is this:

```
<%=(Recordset1.Fields.Item("Title").Value%> (ASP)

<cfoutput>#Recordset1.Title#</cfoutput> (ColdFusion)

<% =(((Recordset1_data = Recordset1.getObject("Title")== null ||¬
Recordset1.wasNull()))?"":Recordset1_data) %> (JSP)
```

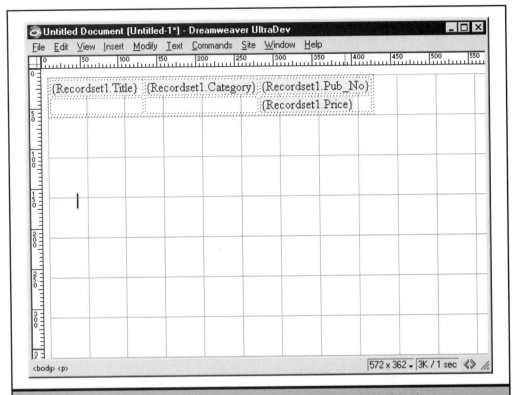

Figure 23-1. *Translated recordset columns show "placeholders" in the design environment*

UltraDev does this by catching the code before it is sent to the design environment and translating it into something that's more user friendly. The code, of course, has to be matched in the document before it can be translated. In the case of ASP and JSP, UltraDev does this by *locking* the server markup that is underlying in special MM:BEGINLOCK and MM:ENDLOCK pairs. These tags are XML tags that are read internally by UltraDev and translated into the proper display text while you are viewing it. The Translators only show up in the design environment, allowing you to edit the underlying HTML by viewing the source in HTML source view. In the case of ColdFusion, UltraDev merely has to look for the specific CF tag, which in many cases doesn't have the locking XML tags around it.

What does this underlying XML look like? An easy way to see the tags is to edit one of the three primary Translators: ASP.htm, JSP.htm, or ColdFusion.htm. A line in the file lets you write a text file to your C drive if you're on Windows, or to your desktop if you're on a Macintosh. Find the following line:

```
var debugTranslator = false;
```

and change the attribute to true. After doing this, you can open up any document in UltraDev and be able to view the AfterTranslation.txt file that contains the entire document translated with all XML tags intact. This is helpful for the extension developer because you can actually see the locked tags and their attributes.

Another trick to allow you to view the entire document with the hidden XML tags intact is to follow these steps:

1. Go to Preferences | Preview in Browser.

2. Uncheck the Preview Using Application Server option.

3. Close the Preferences dialog box.

4. Preview the page in your browser by clicking F12 or choosing File | Preview in Browser.

5. Use the View Source command of the browser, and you should be able to see the entire translated document, with all invisible tags.

Tip   *Another good way to view the invisible XML tags that surround server markup while debugging an extension is to place an alert box somewhere in your extension where you are able to isolate a node to work on it, such as in a findServerBehaviors function. Simply put an alert box in the code that reads "alert(node.outerHTML)," and you will be able to see the invisible information when you make an edit on the page or apply the extension.*

If you open a blank document and insert the LastAccessDate object that you built in Chapter 21, you can open the AfterTranslation.txt document and take a look. This is what the VBScript version looks like:

```
<MM:BeginLock translatorClass="MM_ASPSCRIPT" type="language"
depFiles="" orig="%3C%25@LANGUAGE=VBSCRIPT%25%3E" >
<MM_SCRIPT_LANGUAGE NAME=VBSCRIPT><MM:EndLock>
<html>
<head>
<title>Untitled Document</title>
<meta http-equiv="Content-Type" content="text/html; charset=iso-8859-1">
</head>
<body bgcolor="#FFFFFF">
```

```
<div id="Layer1" style="position: absolute; left: 8px; top: 11px;
width: 504px; height: 19px; z-index: 1">
<MM:BeginLock translatorClass="MM_ASPSCRIPT" type="script"
depFiles="" orig="%3C%25"
DateFile = Server.MapPath(%22DateFile.txt%22)
On Error Resume Next
Set TM_fs = Server.CreateObject(%22Scripting.FileSystemObject%22)
Set a = TM_fs.OpenTextFile(DateFile, 1, 0, 0)
LastDate = a.ReadLine
InStream.Close
Application(%22lastAccessDate%22)= LastDate
LastDate = Month(Now) & %22/%22 & Day(Now) & %22/%22 & Year(Now)
LastDate = LastDate & %22 %22 & Time
set b = TM_fs.CreateTextFile (DateFile, 1, 0)
b.WriteLine LastDate
b.Close%25%3E" ><MM_ASPSCRIPT><MM:EndLock>
This page was last accessed on <MM:BeginLock
translatorClass="MM_ASPSCRIPT" type="script" depFiles="" orig="%3C%25
Response.Write(Application(%22lastAccessDate%22))
%25%3E" ><MM_ASPSCRIPT><MM:EndLock></div>
</body>
</html>
```

The first thing you'll notice is that locks are placed around each script block on the page. If you look at the locks placed around the LastAccessDate object on the page, you'll notice the following attributes:

- translatorClass="MM_ASPSCRIPT"
- type="script"
- depFiles=""
- orig="%3C%25"

The translator class is the descriptive name of the class that is being translated, and is a unique identifier for the locked node. In the case of generic scripts, this attribute would be either MM_ASPSCRIPT or MM_JSPSCRIPT. The generic ColdFusion tags aren't locked, because it is a tag-based language and the tags can be translated easily without putting locks around them. The type attribute is another descriptive phrase that will help you locate a specific locked region. You might notice that the language declaration at the top of the file has a type attribute of "language", whereas the LastAccessDate object has a generic type of "script". When you write your own Translators, you can apply a descriptive type if you so desire, or the Translator type can simply be the name of the tag that is being translated.

The third attribute is depFiles, which stands for "dependent files" and contains a comma-separated list of file paths that the translated source depends on, as in the case of a server-side include Translator.

The last attribute is the *orig* attribute, which appeared in the Server Behaviors built in the last chapter. This attribute contains the entire untranslated content of the object, with the following four characters being URL encoded into hexadecimal values: quote "(%22), less than < (%3C), greater than > (%3E), and percent sign % (%25). Recall from Chapter 22 that you used this line to get the unescaped content of the locked node:

```
tagStr = unescape(node.outerHTML)
```

After calling the unescape method, the hex-encoded values are returned to their original state. You can reverse the process by calling the escape(string) method, which will insert the hex-encoded values in place of the actual string.

Translators are called when any of the following happens:

- Opening a file
- Switching to the document window after editing the HTML source
- Changing the properties of an object
- Inserting an object
- Refreshing the document after changing it in another application
- Applying a template to the document
- Pasting or dragging content into the document window
- Saving changes to a dependent file
- Invoking a command, behavior, Server Behavior, or other extension that changes innerHTML, outerHTML, or data property
- Changing the document through the Modify menu commands Convert Tables to Layers, Convert Layers to Tables, and Translate
- Changing a tag in the Quick Tag editor

Translators are called before the DOM is created; therefore, if you are writing your own Translator, you have to manipulate the document as one large string of text instead of relying on methods of the DOM.

You are going to write an ASP Translator to translate the code from the LastAccessDate object when it is inserted and show the following text in its place:

{Last Access Date Object}

You may recall a small workaround that was performed when building the object in Chapter 21. This workaround enabled the user to see the object on the screen instead of the little gold ASP shield that otherwise would be there if the entire object were written as one script block. Because you're going to translate the code into something user friendly in the document window at this point, you'll change the object to reflect the following:

Old Code

```
tag += '\n%>';
tag += '\n This page was last accessed on ';
tag += '\n <% Response.Write(Application("lastAccessDate"))';
```

New Code

```
tag += '\n Response.Write("This page was last accessed on ")¬
 & Application("lastAccessDate"))';
```

Notice that you are simply removing the close tag from the previous block and including the text portion in the Response.Write statement. This is the VBScript version, but the JavaScript version will be similar. After making the changes, the object will show the generic gold ASP shield on the page. Your Translator will turn this gold shield into a placeholder with a lightly shaded aqua-blue color, which denotes a block of translated content.

To begin your LastAccessDate Translator, you'll create a new HTML file named LAD_Translator_ASP.htm and save it in the Translators folder. The initial block of code for the file is as follows:

```
<html>
<head>
<title>ASP Last Access Date Translator</title>
<meta http-equiv="Content-Type" content="text/html; charset="">
<script language="JavaScript">
```

A Translator has two required functions: getTranslatorInfo() and translateMarkup(). The following sections describe the functions as you implement them for the Last Access Date Translator.

getTranslatorInfo( )

The getTranslatorInfo() function takes no arguments and returns an array of strings that describe the Translator. The function, with comments, is as follows:

```
function getTranslatorInfo(){
returnArray = new Array( 7 )
returnArray[0] = "LAD_translator_ASP"      //The translator Class
returnArray[1] = "Last Access Date Translator ASP"  // The title
returnArray[2] = "1"      // The number of extensions
returnArray[3] = "asp"    // The first extension
returnArray[4] = "1"      // The number of expressions
returnArray[5] = "TM\_fs\.OpenTextFile" // Regular Expression
returnArray[6] = "byExpression";  // run default
return returnArray
}
```

The zero element in the array is the *class* of the Translator, which is a unique identifier for the Translator; it may contain only alphanumeric characters, underscores, or hyphens, but no spaces. The second element, which is the number one element, is the *title* of the Translator. This can be a descriptive phrase of up to 40 characters, and it can include spaces. The third element is the *number of file extensions* that the Translator will translate. In this case, there's only one, .asp. The next element is the beginning of the file extension list. Again, there's only one extension for this Translator, so the list is only one element long. That element contains the text of the file extension—"asp". The next element contains the number of regular expressions that could be in the document before the Translator will act on the content. In this case, there's only one, once again, so the next element contains the regular expression that will be searched for.

> **Tip**
>
> *To make a Translator that works for more than just ASP files, you can increase the extension count in the array, and then list the extensions that the Translator will work with in the following array members.*

The last element is the *runDefault* attribute, which specifies how the Translator gets called. The possible values are allFiles, noFiles, byExtension, and byExpression. If you specify byExtension, the Translator will act on the file that has the file extension specified . If you specify byExpression, the Translator works on documents that contain a match for the regular expression.

Tip *In UltraDev 1, these settings can be overridden in the Preferences menu, under the Translation category. This feature was discarded in UltraDev 4.*

translateMarkup()

The translateMarkup() function is passed three parameters: docName, siteRoot, and docContent. The docName parameter is the document path for the current document. The siteRoot parameter is the path of the current site, or is null if the current document isn't contained within a site. The third parameter, docContent, is the content of the entire document. This is the string that you'll be concerned with in this Translator. The function has to search the document for an instance of the tag or block of code that you want to translate, and match it up with the appropriate display text, as well as put a lock around it to identify it as "your" code. The translateMarkup() function for the LastAccessDate Translator is as follows:

```
function translateMarkup(docName, siteRoot, inStr) {
var outStr = "";
pattLockStart = '<MM:BeginLock translatorClass="MM_ASPSCRIPT"
type="script" depFiles=""';
pattLockEnd = '<MM:EndLock>';
var lockEnd = 0;
for (;;) {
    lockStart=inStr.indexOf(pattLockStart,lockEnd);
    if (lockStart < 0) break; // no more locked code blocks - we're done.
    outStr += inStr.substring(lockEnd,lockStart);
    lockEnd = inStr.indexOf(pattLockEnd,lockStart) +
pattLockEnd.length
    tag = inStr.substring(lockStart,lockEnd)
    outStr += translateTag(tag);
    }
outStr += inStr.substring(lockEnd);
    return outStr;
}
```

The docContent string has been named *inStr* in this function, to make the code more readable. This function has an inStr, which is the entire document as it is passed to the function, and an outStr—which will be the document that you reassemble by looking at each locked block of code to see if it is one of yours. The variable pattLockStart is the opening lock that is on a generic ASP text, and pattLockEnd is the pattern for the end lock. You'll match these against the document and mark the positions when you find a match, removing the content before the match and adding it to the outStr variable. When you've found a match, the tag is sent to another function— translateTag, in this example—which is doing the work of testing the string for a match with your code. If the translateTag function doesn't find a match, it returns the original content to the calling statement. Here's your translateTag function:

```
function translateTag(tag) {
// translate this locked node if it is ours.
// If not return the original to the caller.
var retTag = "";
var pattOrigStart = ' orig="';
var pattOrigEnd = '"';
var reDynamicStart = /TM\_fs\.OpenTextFile/;
origStart = tag.indexOf(pattOrigStart) + pattOrigStart.length;
if (origStart < 0) return tag; // no orig tag in this locked block
origEnd = tag.indexOf(pattOrigEnd,origStart);
orig = tag.substring(origStart,origEnd);
orig = unescape(orig);
dynamicStart = orig.search(reDynamicStart);
if (dynamicStart < 0) return tag; //returns the tag if
// this locked code block is not a Last Access Date Object
var displayText = "";
if (orig.indexOf("TM_fs.OpenTextFile") >= 0) {
displayText = "{Last Access Date Object}";
} // The following lines will
// check to see if we found our dynamic sources here.
// If we did not, copy tag to retTag
if (displayText.length > 0) {
retTag = '<MM:BeginLock translatorClass="MM_ASPSCRIPT"¬
type="script" depFiles="" orig="' +
escape(orig) + '" ><TM_DYNAMIC_CONTENT><MM:DECORATION ¬
HILITECOLOR="Dyn Untranslated Color">' +
displayText +
'</MM:DECORATION></TM_DYNAMIC_CONTENT><MM:EndLock>';
} else {
retTag = tag;}
return retTag;
}
```

This function simply checks the incoming code for an instance of the code "TM_fs.OpenTextFile", which is unique to your Last Access Date extension. If the code is in the block, you perform some manipulation on it to grab the *orig* attribute. The orig attribute is the complete code content of the script, to which you add your own XML lock tags around it to denote it as a block of code unique to the Last Access Date extension. If the code doesn't contain "TM_fs.OpenTextFile", you simply return the original code to the caller.

Next, you set the displayText variable, which will be the placeholder for the tag in the design environment. That variable is contained in another XML tag pair:

```
<MM:DECORATION HILITECOLOR="Dyn Untranslated Color">
{Last Access Date Object}
</MM:DECORATION>
```

The MM:DECORATION pair sets the color of the text as the default color for dynamic data placeholders. This color can be changed by going to Preferences | HTML Colors and scrolling down the Tag Specific list until you find MM:DECORATION. If you've ever wondered what this tag is, now you know. Again, all of these XML tags are used by UltraDev internally to assist the developer with displaying, translating, and keeping track of the actual code that is written by UltraDev or by the user.

Finishing Of the Translator

All that's left now is the closing code for the HTML file, and then you will have finished. This code closes the <script>, <head>, and <html> tags:

```
</script>
</head>
</html>
```

Debugging a Translator can be something of a nightmare, because certain errors will cause the Translator to fail without providing an error message. In these cases, you can turn the Translator into a command and then run the command as a *Mimic Translator*. The Dreamweaver and UltraDev Extensibility documents outline the process, in the "Finding Bugs in Your Translator" section.

UltraDev 4 introduced a new translator architecture that is based on XML (and was described in Chapter 23). You can find out about the new architecture in the UltraDev extensibility documents, included in the Help section of UltraDev.

Translators don't generally exist as extensions by themselves, but rather are the finishing touch to an extension that inserts server markup into the body of the document.

Tip   *If you write an extension that displays a gold ASP, JSP, or ColdFusion shield in the design environment, it's a good candidate for a Translator.*

Inspectors

Inspectors—or Property Inspectors, as they are also known—are the floaters that display the properties of an object or behavior that is selected in the design environment. Many of the built-in Inspectors are written in C, such as the Table

Inspector; but you can also write these in JavaScript. Like Translators, Inspectors usually don't exist as units by themselves, but rather complement an existing extension by providing a user interface for editing the attributes of a selected extension.

 A Property Inspector is the only floater that isn't dockable. Also, its size is fixed, unlike the other floaters.

The Interface of a Property Inspector

The Inspector interface is built just like the interfaces for the other extensions, such as objects and Server Behaviors. The interface, however, must conform to certain Macromedia standards. The Property Inspectors appear when you choose Windows | Properties. You'll notice that the narrow box that appears doesn't have a lot of room for attributes. Most Property Inspectors call commands with the various buttons that appear on the Inspector. The standard ASP Inspector, shown in Figure 23-2, consists entirely of just one button, Edit. By clicking the button, a code window is invoked by the EditContent command. Other Inspectors are more complicated, and contain many attributes and commands within the confines of the Inspector—as in the Table Inspector, shown in Figure 23-3.

Since the real estate of the Property Inspector box is so scarce, many Inspectors are written using layers rather than tables. This allows for more precise placement of your attribute fields within the confines of the Inspector. The interface can be designed in the UltraDev environment. Use the Layer object from the Common Objects tab to precisely place your layers in the interface, and then place your text and form elements in the layers. The Layer floater can then be used to select individual layers as you are working with the extension.

The Property Inspector has two states: expanded and collapsed. The fully expanded Inspector measures 87 pixels high by 482 pixels wide. A Property Inspector is collapsed by clicking the little arrow in its lower-right corner.

You are going to build a custom Property Inspector for the User Access Level Server Behavior that you built in Chapter 22. Your goal is to be able to show the attributes that were assigned when you created the behavior, but have them appear within the confines of an Inspector. The Property Inspector works a little differently

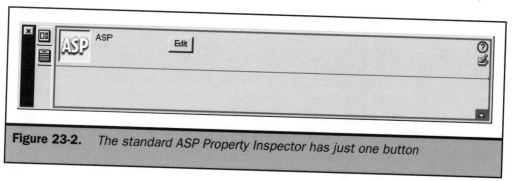

Figure 23-2. *The standard ASP Property Inspector has just one button*

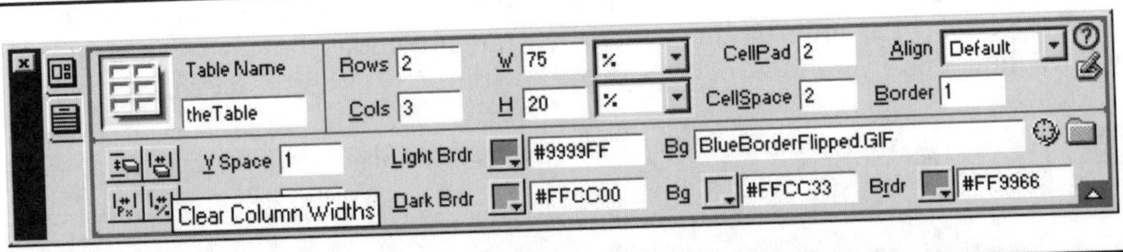

Figure 23-3. The Table Inspector is overflowing with attributes and buttons

than the typical extension interface—it has no OK button to click to save your changes. When you make a change in the Property Inspector, it's immediate, so you have to code it accordingly. The remainder of this section goes through the code for the Property Inspector step by step for the ASP/JSP Inspector, and notes any differences for the ColdFusion Inspector as well.

The following code is the interface code. Pay particular attention to the function that calls on the onBlur event of the form objects. Because you are dealing with an Inspector, the changes in the document occur on-the-fly as you are entering information in the Inspector. Also, notice the layers used. You may choose to use tables for your own Inspectors; but as your Inspectors get more and more complex, layers make it easier to fit everything into the small space of the Inspector.

```html
<html>
<head>
<title>User Access Group Inspector</title>
<script language="javascript" src="_pi_common.js"></script>
<script src="../Shared/UltraDev/Scripts/ssDocManager.js"></script>
<script src="../Shared/UltraDev/Scripts/ssClasses.js"></script>
<meta http-equiv="Content-Type" content="text/html; ¬
charset=iso-8859-1">
</head>
<body>
<div id="lyrEdit" style="position:absolute; left:373px;
top:51px; width:180px; height:25px; z-index:7">Code:
<input type="button" name="Button" value="Edit"
onClick="launchEditDialog()">
</div>
```

```html
<form name="form1" method="post" action="">
<div id="labelAccess" style="position:absolute; left:148px;
top:4px; width:139px; height:15px; z-index:6">Access Groups:
</div>

<div id="lyrAccess" style="position:absolute; left:148px;
top:13px; width:139px; height:32px;  z-index:3">
<input type="text" name="txtAccessGroups" onBlur="setAttributes()">
</div>

<div id="labelDenied" style="position:absolute; left:287px;
top:4px; width:76px; height:15px;
z-index:1">Denied page: </div>

<div id="labelFailed" style="position:absolute; left:287px;
top:27px; width:82px; height:19px;
z-index:2">Failed page: </div>

<div id="lyrDenied" style="position:absolute; left:350px;
top:-6px; width:149px; height:32px;  z-index:3">
<input type="text" name="txtDenied" size="18"
onBlur="setAttributes()">
<input type="image" border="0" name="btnDenied"
src="browsefolder.gif"
width="15" height="13" onClick="browseFile(THE_DENIED);
setAttributes()"></div>

<div id="lyrFailed" style="position:absolute; left:350px;
top:13px; width:160px; height:32px;  z-index:4">
<input type="text" name="txtFailed" size="18"
onBlur="setAttributes()">
<input type="image" border="0" name="btnFailed"
src="browsefolder.gif" width="15" height="13"
onClick="browseFile(THE_FAILED);setAttributes()">
</div>
<div id="lyrTitle" style="position:absolute; left:23px; top:6px;
width:105px; height:60px; z-index:5">User Access Server Behavior
</div>
</form>
</body>
</html>
```

After placing the form elements in the UltraDev environment inside of layers, you need to do a little bit of manipulation of the code to get the elements to appear properly. The best way to do this is by trial and error, or by using a *tracing image*. Tracing images come in handy for building Web sites, but also for laying out your extension interfaces. A tracing image can be chosen by going to the View menu and then clicking Tracing Image>Load. The Tracing Image interface is shown in Figure 23-4. This should be an image of an Inspector that you can use to model your own Inspector. Just save the image as a JPG at the size of 482 × 87 pixels, and set the transparency to about 20 to 30 percent. After loading the image, you need to set the X and Y positions by going to the Tracing Image | Adjust Position menu item and setting the position to X-0 and Y-0. Then, you can use it as a guide for positioning your layers and elements. Figure 23-5 shows an Inspector being designed over a tracing image.

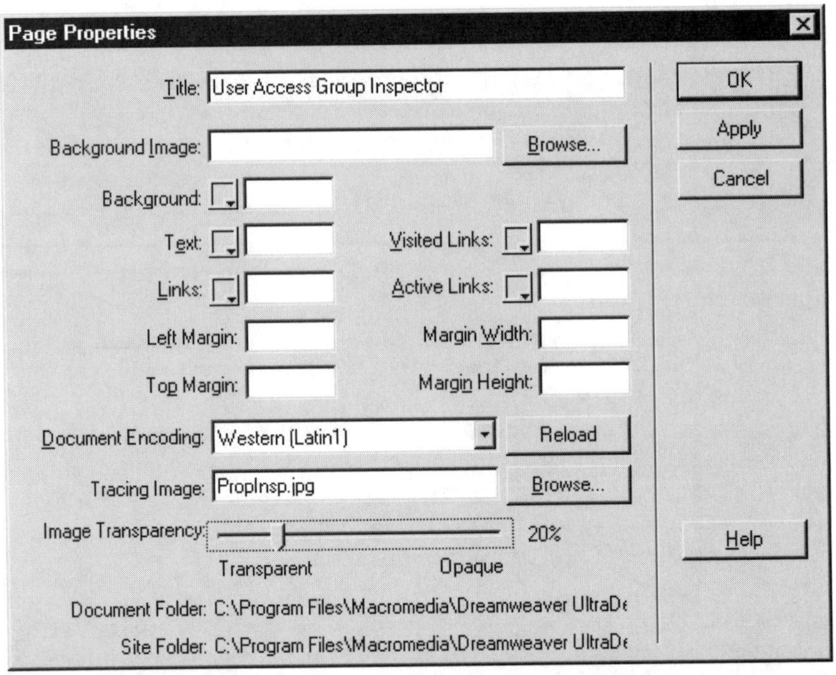

Figure 23-4. *The Tracing Image interface—note that you can set the transparency of the image; 20 to 30 percent is usually good*

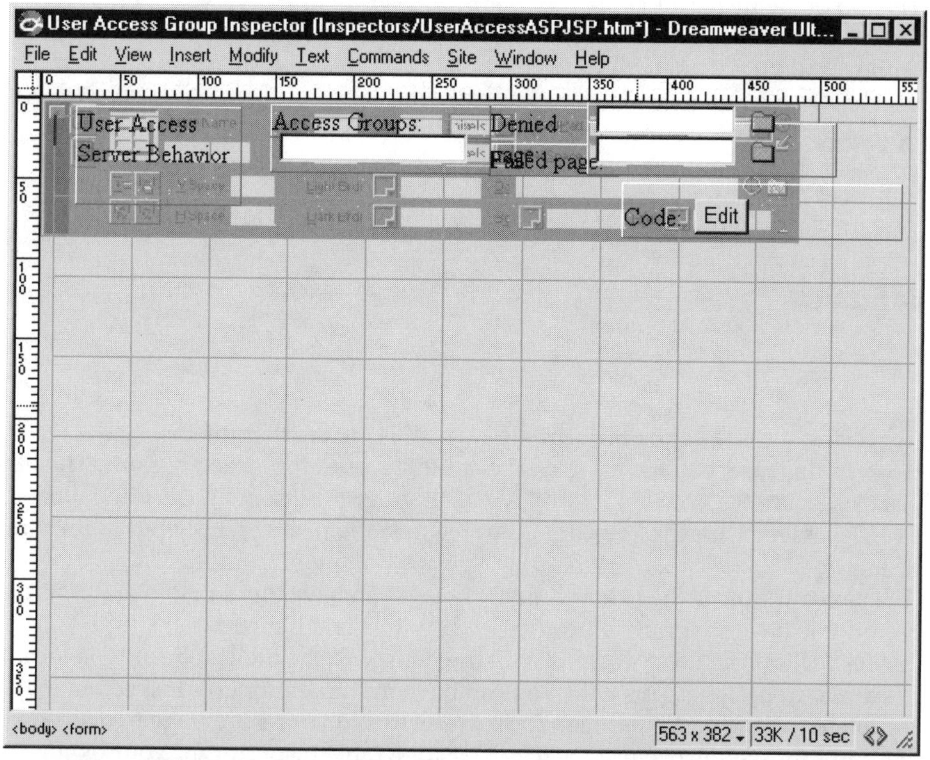

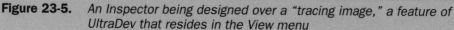

Figure 23-5. An Inspector being designed over a "tracing image," a feature of UltraDev that resides in the View menu

Tracing images are great time savers when you have to design a Web page or an interface that has to conform to certain standards of size or positioning.

Remember to take the tracing image off before you save the Inspector; otherwise, the image will become part of the extension!

There are two mandatory functions in the Property Inspector: inspectSelection and canInspectSelection. In addition, you can specify a displayHelp() function in your Inspector, as in all extensions, and the Help dialog box that you choose will be displayed when the user clicks the little question mark on the top-right corner of the Inspector.

The top of the Inspector contains the attribute string as the very first line. All Inspectors must have this string or they won't work. Place this line as the very first in the file:

ASP/JSP

```
<!-- tag:*LOCKED*, priority:5,selection:exact,hline,vline-->
```

ColdFusion

```
<!-- tag:cfif, priority:5,selection:exact,hline,vline-->
```

The string starts with the tag attribute, which is the tag that the Inspector is to be used for. In this case, you have a special class that's used for locked regions. The other special classes are *COMMENT* and *ASP*, although ASP is deprecated in favor of the LOCKED class for UltraDev. For the ColdFusion version, you simply put in the name of the tag.

The next attribute is the priority. Because tags can have more than one Property Inspector, you have to specify a priority level, with 1 being the lowest and 10 being the highest. UltraDev always begins with the item with the highest priority level and moves down from there. This way, you can have multiple Property Inspectors that can be called for one particular tag. You can use this to your advantage to override the built-in Property Inspectors, such as a custom Table Inspector for your own custom table.

Next is the selection attribute. This can be set to either exact or within, depending on whether the selection can be within the tag or must be exactly contained in the tag. The hline and vline attributes refer to the actual Inspector interface. Referring to Figure 23-2, which shows the standard ASP Inspector, the horizontal line going through the center of the interface is the hline attribute. If you don't specify it, the line won't be there. The vline attribute generally divides the title of the Inspector from the attributes. Referring to Figure 23-3, to vline attribute appears to the left of the Table Name attribute, separating it from the other attributes. By clicking the little arrow at the bottom-right corner of the Inspector, you can collapse the Inspector up to the hline. Generally, you put the main attributes in the top half of the Inspector, and any secondary attributes in the lower half.

You'll also use an include file that contains the PATT and MASK strings for the UserAccess Server Behavior. These strings will enable you to do the same sort of document manipulation that you did in the Server Behavior. The strings are copied verbatim from the behavior and placed in a blank JS file in the Inspectors folder. The include line inserted at the top of your Inspector HTML file is as follows:

```
<script language="javascript" SRC="UserAccess.js"></script>
```

> **Tip**
> *You can make better use of shared components by separating all of your JavaScript from your HTML files when you build extensions. The examples shown have been including the code in one file for simplicity; but if you separate them, you can use the functions and global variables from other extensions simply by including the file.*

The next thing in the HTML file is the global variable declaration. You insert this code right after the include file declarations:

```
<script language="javascript">
//Global variables
var THE_DENIED = findObject("txtDenied");
var THE_FAILED = findObject("txtFailed");
var THE_ACCESSGROUPS = findObject("txtAccessGroups");
var LANG_IS_JAVASCRIPT = ¬
(dw.getDocumentDOM().serverModel.getServerLanguage()=="JavaScript");
```

The canInspectSelection() Function

The canInspectSelection() function does the job of telling UltraDev whether or not the current selection is a valid candidate to display the Inspector. The function does whatever is required to determine this. In the case of your custom-built Server Behaviors, your nodes contain unique strings that won't be in any other Server Behavior—variables with a TM_ prefix. Your canInspectSelection() function will contain a simple search for the variable name TM_groupsAllowed:

```
function canInspectSelection(){
var theObj = getSelectedObj();
if (theObj.outerHTML.indexOf("TM_groupsAllowed")>0) return true;
return false;
}
```

> **Tip**
> *A unique property, variable name, or function name in an extension will make it much easier to find your code in the document.*

If the currently selected node contains the string "TM_groupsAllowed", then the function returns true and the Inspector is displayed. If not, the function will return false.

The inspectSelection() Function

The inspectSelection() function is called after the canInspectSelection() function returns a true value to UltraDev. This function has to take the selection apart and separate the static code from the user-defined attributes, and then display the attributes in the user interface. It's similar to the way you built the Server Behavior to display the attributes in the interface, except that Inspectors do it on-the-fly and don't have to wait for the user to click the OK button. Here is the inspectSelection function:

ASP/JSP

```
function inspectSelection() {
var theObj = getSelectedObj();
var theContent = theObj.outerHTML;
var theArray = getQuotedAttributes(theContent)
THE_DENIED.value=(!LANG_IS_JAVASCRIPT)?theArray[4]:theArray[3];
THE_FAILED.value = (!LANG_IS_JAVASCRIPT)?theArray[5]:theArray[4];
THE_ACCESSGROUPS.value = (!LANG_IS_JAVASCRIPT)?theArray[2]:theArray[1];
}
```

ColdFusion

```
function inspectSelection() {
var theObj = getSelectedObj();
var theContent = theObj.outerHTML;
var theArray = getQuotedAttributes(theContent)
THE_DENIED.value=theArray[2]
THE_FAILED.value = theArray[3]
THE_ACCESSGROUPS.value = theArray[1]
}
```

First, you get the selected object and then get the outerHTML property, which will be the underlying code. You then pass the code through another function, getQuotedAttributes, which is a custom function that will pull any attribute out of the string that is in quotes and return an array of the attributes. After getting all the attributes, you put the correct attributes into the text fields to be displayed in the interface. The ASP/JSP version has the name of the denied page, failed page, and accessgroups variable coming from different elements of the array, because the VBScript version has one extra set of quotes in the original MASK string. Here is your getQuotedAttributes function, which will traverse a string and pick out anything in quotes and place it in an array:

```
function getQuotedAttributes(theContent) {
var thePattern = '[^\\"]\\"([^\\"]*)\\"';
var theReturnArray = new Array();
var i=0;
do {
    var theRegex =  new RegExp(thePattern);
    var theAttributes = theRegex.exec(theContent);
    if(theAttributes){
        theReturnArray[i++] = theAttributes[1];
        //contains the string inside the quotes
        theContent = RegExp.rightContext
        }
    }
    while (theAttributes)
return theReturnArray;
}
```

Notice the use of the regular expression in the function. This expression simply gets all characters up to the first quote, throws them away, and then moves to the set of characters after the quote. It stores these characters up to the next quote in the RegExp object, and then grabs the quote and throws it away. Then, it stores the string (contained in theAttributes[1] at this point) in theReturnArray, before removing that section from the original string and repeating the process until the string is completely searched.

Other Custom Support Functions

The function that does the work of updating the code in the document is setAttributes(), your custom code-insertion routine for this Inspector. The function is as follows:

```
function setAttributes(){
var newChunk = new Array();
var theObj = getSelectedObj();
var theContent = theObj.outerHTML;
var pattern = getServerData("PATT","UserAccess");
var theRegex = new RegExp(pattern,"i");
newChunk = theRegex.exec(theContent);
if(newChunk){
    theContent="";
    newChunk[2]=THE_ACCESSGROUPS.value;
    newChunk[4]=THE_DENIED.value;
    newChunk[6]=THE_FAILED.value;
    for (i=1;i<newChunk.length;i++) theContent +=newChunk[i];
```

```
var myVars = new SSEdits();
myVars.add(theContent,null,"replaceSelection");
myVars.insert();
    }
}
```

This function is a simplified version of the buildSSEdits function that you wrote for the Server Behavior, and is virtually identical. One of the main differences is that you are getting your attributes from the text fields directly instead of having the attributes passed into the function. Another major difference is that, because an Inspector only works with code that is already on the page, you don't have to implement the SSEdits class for inserting a new record—only for updating the existing behavior by using a "replaceSelection" weight in the add() method of SSEdits. You simply grab the values from the text fields and rebuild the code string that was taken apart by the regular expression. Then, you apply the insert. This function is called from the onBlur event of each form element in the Inspector. This way, you're assured that the code will be changed every time the user makes an edit in the Inspector.

There's only one function left, launchEditDialog(), which will be called from the Edit button on your interface. This function will call the editContents function that resides in the MM.dll file and is a C-shared DLL that can be accessed through JavaScript in the UltraDev environment. The function will allow the editing of the script and place the result in a return string that you can reinsert into the database. Again, notice the differences in the ASP/JSP and ColdFusion version. The CF version is not concerned about the locked node.

ASP/JSP

```
function launchEditDialog(){
var theObj = getSelectedObj();
origAttr = theObj.getAttribute("ORIG");
aspStr = unescape( origAttr );
MM.editContents=aspStr;
dw.popupCommand("EditContent");
if (MM.retVal == "OK"){
    //update the node in the dom.
    curSelection = dreamweaver.getSelection();
    dw.editLockedRegions(curSelection);
    theObj.setAttribute("ORIG",escape(MM.editContents));
    }
}
```

ColdFusion

```
function launchEditDialog(){
var theObj = getSelectedObj();
var theContent = theObj.outerHTML;
MM.editContents=theContent;
dw.popupCommand("EditContent");
if (MM.retVal == "OK"){
    //update the selection in the dom.
    var myVars = new SSEdits();
    myVars.add(MM.editContents,null,"replaceSelection");
    myVars.insert();
    }
}
```

If you put this file in the Inspectors folder and restart UltraDev, the Inspector should show itself whenever you select the UserAccess Server Behavior in the floater. Figure 23-6 shows the completed interface for the User Access Server Behavior.

Inspectors can be written for objects, Server Behaviors, behaviors, or data sources. Although Inspectors are often unnecessary for Server Behaviors, implementing an Inspector gives your extension a final touch, and gives the user an easy way to view and change the attributes of an extension.

Floaters

A custom floater is another form of extension that gives UltraDev and Dreamweaver a unique way to interact with the user. You can use a floater to incorporate special functionality of your own design into the UltraDev environment. A floater could be described as a "Property Inspector on steroids." The restrictions of Inspectors don't apply to floaters, so you can add as much functionality as you need in the floater

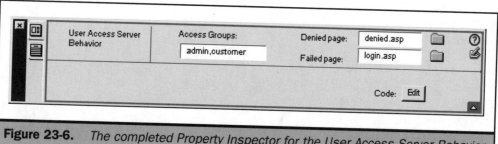

Figure 23-6. *The completed Property Inspector for the User Access Server Behavior*

interface. One typical use is to add a pop-up window and attach it to a button in a Property Inspector to "spread out" the Inspector and give it more functionality.

Floaters don't pop up automatically when dropped into a folder, as do the other extensions, however. They have to be invoked by a function call either through a menu item or a button on another extension. You can invoke a floater by calling dw.setFloaterVisibility(floatername,true) or dw.toggleFloater(floatername). The easiest way to do this is by adding a line to the menus.xml file, like this:

```
<menuitem name="MyFloater" enabled="true"
command="dw.toggleFloater('MyFloater')"
id="DWContext_Text_MyFloater" />
```

A menu item like this can be placed anywhere, but a good place for a floater is in the Window menu on the main menu bar for UltraDev. Floaters can also be put in the contextual menu—usually, if it's something that deserves its own floater, it's probably something that you want just a right-click away. The menu item in the preceding code has an ID name that hints that it might be under the DWContext_Text menu, which is the main document contextual menu. The Menus.xml file is discussed a little later.

Now you are going to build a simple floater that will display the currently selected tag's HTML in an interface that will enable you to make changes in the HTML and have the changes reflected immediately. It will be like having a mini-HTML source viewer viewable perpetually.

Begin by creating a new HTML file. Call it QuickHTMLView.htm and save it in the Floaters folder. Place this code in the document as the interface:

```
<html>
<head>
<title>Quick HTML Editor</title>
<script language="JavaScript">
    //^^your code goes here^^
updateCode(){
}
</script>
</head>
<body>
<form name="theForm">
<textarea name="theCode" cols="45" rows="20"
onBlur="updateCode()"></textarea>
</form>
</body>
</html>
```

Now, you need to edit the menus.xml file in the DWMenu_Window section. Open the menus.xml file in your text editor and use the *find* command to search for the following text, which will display all the menu items that are currently in the Window menu in UltraDev: <menu name="_Window" id="DWMenu_Window">. Place the following line at the bottom of the menu before the closing </menu> for that particular menu:

```
<menuitem name="Quick HTML Editor" enabled="true" ¬
command="dw.toggleFloater('QuickHTMLEditor')" ¬
checked="dw.getFloaterVisibility('QuickHTMLEditor')" ¬
id="DWContext_Text_QuickHTML" />
```

> **Caution** *Always make a backup of a menu file before you edit. If you make a change that you can't undo, the program may become unusable and you may have to reinstall. By backing up the menu file, you eliminate this risk.*

The checked attribute shows your floater on the menu with a checkmark next to the name if it is active in the design environment. After editing the menu in this way, you can close UltraDev and restart it, and the Quick HTML Editor menu item should appear. If you click it, the floater should pop up, ready for your text to be input. At this point, the functionality isn't built in yet, but it's now a working floater that can be used by itself or docked with the other floaters.

You've already put the function body for the updateCode() function in the file, so fill that in first:

```
function updateCode(){
var theDOM = dw.getDocumentDOM();
if(theDOM){
    var offsets = theDOM.getSelection();
    var theCode = document.theForm.theCode.value;
    theNode = theDOM.offsetsToNode(offsets[0],offsets[1]);
    if(theCode=="" && theNode!=null) {
        theCode = theDOM.documentElement.outerHTML;
    }
    var theContent = theNode.outerHTML;
    if(theContent){
        theNode.outerHTML = theCode;
    }else{
        theDOM.documentElement.outerHTML= theCode;
    }
}
```

GETTING THE MOST
OUT OF ULTRADEV

As you can see, there's nothing here that hasn't already been covered. First, you check to see whether the DOM exists, and if it doesn't, you don't even bother to go into the function. This happens if the user doesn't have any documents open. If the DOM exists, you obtain the currently selected code with the getSelection() method of the DOM and then get the current value of the text field (theCode) of the interface. If these two items aren't empty, you set the outerHTML of the node to whatever is in the text field. If one of these is empty, that means no element is currently selected, so the outerHTML of the documentElement is displayed instead.

Half of the battle is won—the text from the floater is now being written back to the document. The next step is to get the code from the document and update the floater. You'll do this with one of the built-in floater functions, selectionChanged(). This is one of those processor-intensive functions that should be used only when necessary, because UltraDev is constantly checking the selection and calling this function on any change. You'll use it here, because you want the code to be updated as it changes. Here's the function:

```
function selectionChanged(){
var theDOM = dw.getDocumentDOM();
if(theDOM) {
    var offsets = theDOM.getSelection();
    theNode = theDOM.offsetsToNode(offsets[0],offsets[1]);
    var theContent = theNode.outerHTML;
    if(theContent){
        document.theForm.theCode.value = theContent;
    }else{
    document.theForm.theCode.value=theDOM.documentElement.outerHTML
        }
    }
}
```

This function does the opposite of the updateCode() function—it takes whatever is in the currently selected node and displays the outerHTML of that node. If you save this file and restart UltraDev, you now have a mini-editor that will have as its content whatever happens to be under the cursor as the currently selected node. If there's no selection, the entire document will show up in the window.

Tip   *A bug in Dreamweaver 3 and UltraDev 1 causes the little question mark icon to be unusable for the displayHelp function. If you want to include a help file for your floater, you have to display an image button and call the function from that button.*

Now the floater will display the currently selected node and allow you to update the document from the floater. Like all floaters, this one can be toggled on and off, and can be docked with another floater or set of floaters. Figure 23-7 shows the completed floater docked and in use.

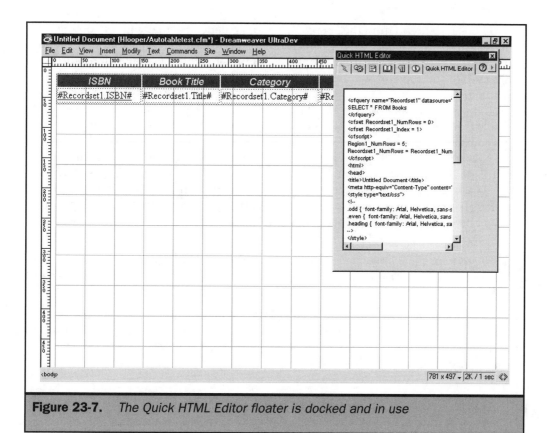

Figure 23-7.   *The Quick HTML Editor floater is docked and in use*

Data Sources

Data sources are the variables, recordsets, and database commands that return data to a Web page to be displayed. A session or application variable would be considered a data source, as well as a column in a recordset. Data sources are found in the Data Bindings palette, alongside the Server Behaviors palette in a default installation of UltraDev.

The palette has a plus (+) and a minus (-) button just like the Server Behaviors palette, but the menu entries in this palette don't "do" anything to the page. A data source can be put on the page to display data, as you did when you dropped database columns into the design environment, but it doesn't perform any action.

Data sources are extensible, too, like most features of UltraDev. You are free to modify and add to the Data Bindings palette by designing your own data sources or modifying existing data sources.

Data sources are also accessible by choosing Dynamic Elements | Dynamic Text from the Server Behaviors menu. Indeed, this is the only way to edit a data source, because you can't double-click a data source from the Data Bindings palette to edit it.

If you choose the menu from the Server Behaviors palette, it actually gives you the underlying code to the data source, which can be modified or given a *format*. The data source format is chosen from a predefined list of possible formats that include such things as date and time formatting, money formatting, and other forms of number formatting.

You'll now build an example of a data source using a type of variable that isn't available from the stock Data Bindings palette—a Local variable. A data source can get pretty complex, interacting with Server Behaviors and Translators. On the CD-ROM, you'll notice that the extension comes packaged along with an icon, a command, a Server Behavior, and a Translator. This discussion will just go over the basics of an actual data source implementation without the accompanying Server Behavior and Translator, but you are free to examine the other files to discover the underlying functionality. This is the ASP version of the data source.

By writing a corresponding Server Behavior for a data source, you can give it extra functionality, such as the ability to apply data formats from the Server Behavior palette.

To begin, the Data Source requires an HTML file that will reside in the DataSources folder in one of the subfolders, depending upon which server model you are working with. This one will be an ASP Data Source, so you'll need to create a LocalVariable.htm file in the ASP directory. The file will start with this code:

```
<html>
<head>
<script src="helper.js"></script>
<script src ="../../Shared/MM/Scripts/CMN/string.js"></script>
<script src ="../../Shared/UltraDev/Scripts/ssDocManager.js">
</script>
<script language="javascript">
//The rest of the functions will go here
</script>
<title>Local Variable</title>
</head>
</html>
```

When a user first hits the plus sign to add a data source, the addDynamicSource() function is called. Your implementation of that function is as follows, beginning with two global variables of your images for the Data Bindings palette:

```
var local_filename = "LOC_D.gif"
var datasourceleaf_filename = "DSL_D.gif"
function addDynamicSource()
{
    if (!MMNotes.open(dw.getSiteRoot(),true)) {
        alert(MM.MSG_DesignNotesOff);
        return;
    }
MM.retVal = "";
MM.localContents = "";
dw.popupCommand("Local Variable");
if (MM.retVal == "OK") {
    var theResponse = MM.localContents;
    if (theResponse.length) {
        var siteURL = dw.getSiteRoot();
        if (siteURL.length){
            addValueToNote(siteURL,"localCount","local",theResponse);
        }else{
            alert(MM.MSG_DefineSite);
        }
    }else{
        alert(MM.MSG_Definelocal);
        }
    }
}
```

The function basically pops up a command that grabs the name of the local variable
that the user defines and stores it in a special array in the site design notes, after it has
checked for the existence of the notes. It stores the information about the data source
in the notes so that other pages can retrieve it. The command that you are calling is
just a basic HTML interface that retrieves the user's input of a variable name and
returns it to this function. This is the code for the Command file, which you can name
LocalVariables.htm and store in the Commands folder:

```
<!-- MENU-LOCATION=NONE -->
<html>
<head>
<title>Local Variable</title>
<script src="Local Variable.js"></script>
<script src="../Shared/MM/Scripts/CMN/localText.js"></script>
<SCRIPT SRC="../Shared/MM/Scripts/CMN/displayHelp.js"></script>
<script language="javascript">
```

```
function commandButtons(){
  return new Array(BTN_OK,"okClicked()",BTN_Cancel,"window.close()");
}
function okClicked(){
  var nameObj = document.forms[0].theName;
  if (nameObj.value) {
    MM.localContents = nameObj.value;
    MM.retVal = "OK";
    window.close();
  } else {
    alert("Please fill in a name or cancel");
  }
}
</script>
</head>
<body>
<form>
    <table border="0">
      <tr>
        <td align="right" valign="baseline" nowrap>Name:</td>
        <td valign="baseline" nowrap>
          <input name="theName" type="text" style="width:150px">
        </td>
      </tr>
    </table>
</form>
</body>
</html>
```

After getting the data source, UltraDev empties the Data Bindings palette and calls the findDynamicSources() function in each file in the DataSources folder. If the function finds a data source, UltraDev then calls the generateDynamicSourceBindings() function in that file to rebuild the palette from scratch. Those two functions for your Local variable data source, which should be placed into the LocalVariables.htm Data Source file that you created, are as follows:

```
function findDynamicSources() {
var DSL = new Array();
var siteURL = dw.getSiteRoot()
if (siteURL.length){
    var LBindingsArray = new Array();
    getValuesFromNote(siteURL,LBindingsArray,"local","localCount");
    if (LBindingsArray.length > 0) {
        DSL.push(new ObjectInfo("Local Variables", ¬
```

```
            local_filename, false))
        }
    }
    return DSL;
}

function generateDynamicSourceBindings(elementName) {
    var BindingsArray = new Array();
    var outArray;
    var siteURL = dw.getSiteRoot();
    if (elementName != "local")
        elementName = "local"
    if (siteURL.length){
    getValuesFromNote(siteURL,BindingsArray,elementName,"localCount");
    outArray = GenerateObjectInfoForSourceBindings(BindingsArray,¬
     datasourceleaf_filename);
    }
    return outArray;
}
```

The first function finds the values of the data sources from the site notes and adds them to the array that it returns to UltraDev. The function then creates a new objectInfo object for this particular data source, to which it adds the title of the data source, the image filename that gets displayed in the palette, and an "allow delete" flag. Then, the bindings are added to the palette by the call to the generateDynamicSourceBindings function.

Caution   *Data sources are perhaps the most complex extension type, and require complex interactions among commands, Server Behaviors, Translators, data formats, and the data source itself. Building one shouldn't be taken lightly!*

Next is the generateDynamicDataRef function, which actually builds the string that gets inserted into the document. In this case, you are simply placing <%= and %> around the variable name. This is the ASP equivalent of Response.Write, which is used quite often as shorthand in the body of a Web page. If this were a ColdFusion data source, you would add <cfoutput>#{*variable name*}#</cfoutput> around the variable name.

```
function generateDynamicDataRef(elementName,bindingName) {
    retStr = "<%=" + bindingName + "%>";
    return retStr;
}
```

Next is the inspectDynamicDataRef function, which simply returns the source (which is "Local" in this case) and binding (the variable name):

```
function inspectDynamicDataRef(expression)
{
var retArray = new Array();
// Quickly reject if the expression doesn't contain "<%="
var exprIndex = expression.indexOf("<%=");
if (exprIndex != -1){
    if(expression.indexOf(".")==-1||expression.indexOf('"')==-1){
    //if no dot or no quotes, must be local
        var found = expression.search(/<%=\s*(\w+)\s*%>/i)
        if (found != -1){
            retArray[0] = "Local";
            retArray[1] = RegExp.$1;
            }
        }
    }
return retArray;
}
```

Finally, the deleteDynamicSource() function is defined, which is called when a user clicks the minus (-) button on the Data Sources floater:

```
function deleteDynamicSource(sourceName,bindingName){
var siteURL = dw.getSiteRoot();
if (siteURL.length){
    deleteValueFromNote(siteURL,"localCount","Local",bindingName);
    }
}
```

The preceding code gives you a working data source for a Local variable type. Any additional functionality, such as the use of server formats and having the data source show up in the Server Behaviors palette as a Dynamic Text item, has to be coded separately into a Server Behavior. In addition, to get the data source to show up on the page as a viewable entity, you have to write a Translator to do this. These extensions have been included on the CD-ROM for those of you who want to probe deeper into data sources.

Server Formats

Server formats are special extensions that you can apply to dynamic text elements, such as the Session and Application variables, and recordset columns. You can apply a server format by double-clicking a data source in the Server Behaviors palette. Typical formats include currency formatting, date and time formatting, upper- and lowercase formatting, and other standard text formatting. When you apply the server format to the element on the page, the extension takes care of stripping off the server tags, adding the special formatting, and then putting the tags back on. In addition, if any special functions are required for the formatting, the extension inserts the appropriate code into the head of the document.

> **Tip** *Server formats are easy to write and often offer the best method for doing some "last minute" text formatting for database fields, variables, and other data sources.*

As with other areas of UltraDev, you can extend or write your own server formats. These extensions are built a little differently than some of the other extensions. You must insert a RegExp pattern right into the menu file. Like the regular expressions that are used in Server Behaviors, this expression is used by UltraDev to match the format in the code on your page.

There are three folders within the Server Formats folder that correspond with the three server models that work with UltraDev—ASP, JSP, and ColdFusion. Each of these folders has a corresponding Formats.xml menu file as well, which is the menu where your changes will go.

The extensions are fairly consistent. You can easily take an existing server format and change it to reflect the new format that you want to implement. You'll find that most of the server formats contain three basic functions: formatDynamicDataRef, applyFormat(), and deleteFormat(). In addition, some of the formats will write a function to the head of the user's document. In those cases, a fourth function will build a string that contains the text of the function.

You now are going to build an ASP version of a Preserve Whitespace server format. The ColdFusion and JSP versions can be built using identical techniques. This is a format that can be applied to a database field that may contain new lines and tabs that don't translate to HTML. The format will take care of replacing these instances with <br> tags and strings of nonbreaking spaces in place of the tab character.

The HTML File for Preserve Whitespace

The first thing to do, of course, is to create an HTML file named PreserveWhitespace.htm and save it in the ASP folder under Server Formats. The file should contain the following text:

```
<!-- MENU-LOCATION=NONE -->
<html>
<head>
<title>PreserveWhitespace</title>
<script language="javascript" ¬
src="../../Shared/UltraDev/scripts/ssCmnElements.js">
</script>
```

```
<script language="javascript" ¬
src="../../Shared/UltraDev/scripts/ssClasses.js">
</script>
<script language="javascript" ¬
src="../../Shared/MM/Scripts/CMN/dom.js"></script>
<script language="javascript" ¬
src="../../Shared/UltraDev/scripts/ssDocManager.js">
</script>
<script language="javascript" src="FormatsSupport.js"></script>
<script language="javascript" src="PreserveWhitespace.js"></script>
</head>
<body>
</body>
</html>
```

Some of the standard include files are listed here, as well as a new one,
FormatsSupport.js, which contains some necessary support functions for the server
format that you are creating. A PreserveWhitespace.js file that will contain all the
functions for this particular server format is referenced as well.

Creating the New Format

All of the main functions are going to be housed in the JS file, so go ahead and create
that now. The code that you include will remove all line-feed characters and replace
them with a line feed and a <br> tag. You could do a simple "replace" of the line feed
with a <br> tag, but the line-feed character creates better HTML formatting when you
view the source of the output page. In addition to the line feed, you're replacing the tab
character (chr(9)) with a series of five nonbreaking spaces. Here's the VBScript code for
the function:

```
<SCRIPT RUNAT=SERVER LANGUAGE=VBSCRIPT>
function PreserveWhitespace(str)
tabStr = chr(160)&chr(160)&chr(160)&chr(160)&chr(160)
str = Replace(str,chr(10),chr(10)&"<br>")
str = Replace(str,chr(9),tabStr)
PreserveWhitespace = str
End Function
</SCRIPT>
```

Because the function is enclosed with its own language declaration, the function
will run on a site that is defined for JavaScript as well. The preceding code has to be
built into a string and inserted into the head of the document. Because the code exists
as a generic function that can be used by a data source in the body of the document,

you don't have to worry about the *weights* of a Server Behavior—it can fall anywhere within the head and still function properly. The following function builds the string and returns the complete string to the caller:

```
function getWholeJSFormatFunc() {
    strRet  = '<SCRIPT RUNAT=SERVER LANGUAGE=VBSCRIPT>\n';
    strRet += 'function PreserveWhitespace(str)        \n';
    strRet += 'tabStr =chr(160)&chr(160)&chr(160)&chr(160)&chr(160)\n';
    strRet += 'str = Replace(str,chr(10),chr(10)&"<BR>")\n';
    strRet += 'str = Replace(str,chr(9),tabStr)\n';
    strRet += 'PreserveWhitespace = str\n';
    strRet += 'End Function\n';
    strRet += '</SCRIPT>\n';
    return strRet;
}
```

The formatDynamicDataRef Function Implementation

Next, you'll define a global variable that is used to name the Server Format within the extension:

```
var formatFunc = "PreserveWhitespace";
```

The following function will be called by UltraDev if the user chooses the Preserve Whitespace format from the Data Bindings palette or the Dynamic Text Server Behavior:

```
function formatDynamicDataRef(str, format){
var ret = str;
var iStart = getIndexOfEqualsForResponseWrite(str);
if (iStart > -1){
    var iEnd = str.indexOf("%>", iStart+1);
    if (iEnd > -1){
ret = str.substring(0, iStart+1) + " " + formatFunc + "(";
ret +=  + str.substring(iStart+1, iEnd) + ") " + str.substr(iEnd);
    }else{
        alert("No ASP end tag");
        }
    }else{
        alert("No equals sign");
        }
return ret;
}
```

The dynamic text, or data source, that the format is being applied to is passed to the function in the str variable. The second argument, format, is the JavaScript object that describes the format that's being applied.

The function marks the open and close tags for the dynamic data passed into the str variable and remembers the index location, and then inserts the function name along with opening and closing parentheses. The function is also doing some preliminary error checking by making sure that there is an equals sign and a closing ASP tag.

The applyFormat() Function

Next, you'll implement the function that does the work of inserting the function into the head of the document. You'll find that this function is almost identical in all server formats that require a function in the head. You simply use the DOM to insert the code directly before the <html> tag:

```
function applyFormat(){
if (getFunctionVersion(formatFunc, null) == -1){
    var currSel = dw.getSelection();
    var htmlNode = dw.getDocumentDOM().documentElement;
    var oldHtmlOffsets = dw.nodeToOffsets(htmlNode);
    var wholeFunc = getWholeJSFormatFunc();
    insertBeforeHTMLTag(wholeFunc);
    htmlNode = dreamweaver.getDocumentDOM().documentElement;
    var newHtmlOffsets = dw.nodeToOffsets(htmlNode);
    var delta = newHtmlOffsets[1] - oldHtmlOffsets[1];
    dw.setSelection(currSel[0]+delta, currSel[1]+delta);
    }
}
```

The deleteFormat() Function

The deleteFormat() function does the exact opposite of the applyFormat() function. It goes into the DOM and removes the function that was added. The first thing that it does, however, is to check to make sure that no other data sources are on the page that might need the function to remain—if so, it merely exits, leaving the function intact:

```
function deleteFormat(){
if ((numFormatFunctionInvokations(formatFunc, 1) < 1) && ¬
(getFunctionVersion(formatFunc, null) > -1)){
    var currSel = dw.getSelection();
    var htmlNode = dw.getDocumentDOM().documentElement;
    var oldHtmlOffsets = dw.nodeToOffsets(htmlNode);
    deleteWholeScriptContainingFunction(formatFunc);
    htmlNode = dreamweaver.getDocumentDOM().documentElement;
```

```
var newHtmlOffsets = dw.nodeToOffsets(htmlNode);
var delta = newHtmlOffsets[1] - oldHtmlOffsets[1];
dw.setSelection(currSel[0]+delta, currSel[1]+delta);
}
}
```

The only thing unusual about this function is the call to a shared function from the FormatsSupport.js file—deleteWholeScriptContainingFunction. The name says it all: it does the job of deleting the function in question.

Editing the Formats.xml File

The last thing that needs to be done to create a working server format is to add a menu entry to the Formats.xml file that is in the same folder as the extension. Each subfolder under Server Formats (ASP, JSP, and ColdFusion) has its own Formats.xml file. The following lines need to be added after the last </menu> tag but before the closing </format> tag:

```
<menu name = "New Formats" ¬
id="DWMenu_ServerFormatDef_ASP_2_NewFormats">
<format file="PreserveWhitespace" title="Preserve Whitespace"¬
expression="<%\s*=\s*PreserveWhitespace\([^%]*%>" ¬
id="DWMenu_ServerFormatDef_ASP_2_PRES_WHITE" />
</menu>
```

Caution   *Never edit a menu file without first making a backup of the file.*

Notice the use of the <format> tag. The <format> tag is actually a JavaScript object that will contain information about the server format needed by UltraDev to apply the format. The tag includes the following standard attributes:

- A file attribute, which is the title of the file used in the format (your PreserveWhitespace.htm file)

- A title attribute for how it is displayed in the menu

- An expression attribute, which is the RegExp that actually takes care of locating the format in the document after it's been applied

- An ID attribute, which must be a unique ID name

These are the required attributes, but you can also include other information about the server format here as well, and then access it through dot notation in the formatDynamicDataRef function. For instance, if you have a server format that displays a certain number of characters in a data source, you could have a numChars attribute and access it by using format.numChars in the function.

Packaging Extensions

As previously mentioned, menus generally should not be edited directly; but if they are edited, they must be edited very carefully. How do you make changes to a menu without physically changing one? By using an extension *package*. UltraDev comes with the Extension Manager that also includes a built-in packager for extensions.

 With UltraDev 1, the Packager isn't installed by default. You have to specify that you want it installed by doing a custom installation and checking Developer Tools when you install the Package Manager. The Packager resides in the Extension Manager folder. If it's not there, you'll have to reinstall the Extension Manager.

The process of creating a package is started by writing a Macromedia eXtension Information (MXI) file with all the information about your extension. The MXI file is in a limited XML format. It's not *true* eXtensible Markup Language, and as such shouldn't be edited in a dedicated XML editor; instead, it's a subset of XML that is recognized by the UltraDev API. To write your MXI file, you can use the template that's included in the UltraDev package, or you can modify an existing MXI file.

When you install a third-party extension, the MXI files are unpacked to the Extensions folder under Configuration. These files don't have an editor associated with them, but they can be opened in Notepad or BBEdit, or any text editor. Make sure you save as plain text after you make your changes to the file.

Tip *Windows users can assign a new contextual menu item named Edit for the Extension Manager by going to the standard Windows folder menu item View | Folder Options, clicking the Edit button, and assigning a new Edit action by browsing to the Notepad or Wordpad application.*

The next section goes through the process of creating the MXI file and packaging an extension by using the Access Group behavior that you created in Chapter 22.

Main Tag

The main tag of the MXI file is the <macromedia-extension> tag. This tag specifies the name, version, type, and the optional attribute of requires-restart. In addition, if you submit the extension to the Macromedia UltraDev Exchange, Macromedia will insert an ID number into this tag. The ID number should not be edited, however.

```
<macromedia-extension
    name="User Access Level"
    version="1.0.0"
    type="ServerBehavior"
    requires-restart="true" >
```

The name should be a unique name, and is usually the same as the title that you give to the extension in the HTML file of that extension. The version number consists of three digits representing the main version number, the revision number, and the minor revision number. For example, if you begin with 1.0.0 and submit the extension to Macromedia, and you are asked to make small changes in the extension, you should number the next version 1.0.1, and so on.

The type attribute should be one of the extension types recognized by UltraDev. A list of available types is shown in Table 23-2. The requires-restart attribute is optional and should be used if your extension requires UltraDev to be restarted after the extension is installed.

Products and Authors Tags

The next tag is the <products> tag, which consists of the names of the programs that the extension will work with. Some commands, objects, behaviors, and other extensions might work with Dreamweaver in addition to UltraDev, but the Server Behaviors and other server-related extensions should be defined as UltraDev only by specifying them in this tag. If you specify the version attribute as 1, the extension will install into versions greater than 1; and if you specify version 4, the extension won't install to UltraDev 1. By the same token, if you specify Dreamweaver 3, the extension will install to Dreamweaver 3 and 4, and UltraDev 1 and 4.

```
<products>
    <product name="UltraDev" version="1" primary="true"/>
</products>
```

Next is the <author name> tag, which you can use to identify the extension as written by you, or you can put a company name in here:

```
<author  name="Thomas Muck"> </author>
```

object	command	behavior (or action)	translator	dictionary
browserProfile	encoding	floater	propertyInspector	jsExtension
query	template	thirdPartyTags	plugin	report
suite	dataSource	serverFormat	serverBehavior	serverModel

Table 23-2.   *Legal UltraDev Extension Types*

Description of the Extension

The next required tag is the description of the extension, using a <description> tag. Inside this tag is a CDATA attribute that sets off the start of your description data. The description should indicate the basic functionality and usage of the extension. The text of the description can contain HTML limited to <br> tags and   characters:

```
<description>
<![CDATA[
This behavior allows you to set access levels on a page, and <br>
redirect the user to a "failed" page if the person isn't logged<br>
on and to a "denied" page if the person doesn't have the proper<br>
permissions for the page.  Works in JSP, ASP, and ColdFusion.
]]>
</description>
```

If your extension description is complex, make liberal use of <br> and   in your description—spaces, tabs, and newlines are ignored when the description is displayed in the Package Manager.

After the description of the extension is the <UI-Access> tag, in which you describe how the extension is accessed and applied to the Web page. The <UI-Access> tag also has the CDATA directive, and has the same HTML restrictions as the <description> tag:

```
<UI-Access>
<![CDATA[
You can run this behavior by choosing:<br>
ServerBehaviors>UltraDev: The Complete Reference>User Access Level
]]>
</UI-Access>
```

Putting Your Files into the Extension Package

Before you package your extension, you should copy all the files to a staging area, which can be a central folder for all of your extension packages, or a folder that mimics the directory structure of the UltraDev Configuration folder. Macromedia advises against packaging the extensions directly from within the UltraDev environment. You can try to keep a folder that has all of your extension packages in separate subfolders within a main extension package staging area. The child tag of the <files> tag is the <file name> tag, in which you actually give the name of each file that is to be included in the extension package. By keeping the MXI file within this same staging area folder, you can keep your packaging paths simple for the <file name> tag. All the server models are included in the code, but you can use the line that corresponds to the version that you are using, as follows:

```
<files>
<file name="asp/UserAccess.htm" ¬
destination="$dreamweaver/configuration/ServerBehaviors/ASP/">
</file>
<file name="jsp/UserAccess.htm" ¬
destination="$dreamweaver/configuration/ServerBehaviors/JSP/">
</file>
<file name="ColdFusion/UserAccess.htm" ¬
destination="$dreamweaver/configuration/ServerBehaviors/
ColdFusion/"></file>
<file name="UserAccessASPJSP.htm" ¬
destination="$dreamweaver/configuration/inspectors/" ></file>
<file name="UserAccessCF.htm" ¬
destination="$dreamweaver/configuration/inspectors/" ></file>
<file name="UserAccess.htm" ¬
destination="$dreamweaver/configuration/ServerBehaviors"></file>
<file name="UserAccess.js" ¬
destination="$dreamweaver/configuration/ServerBehaviors"></file>
/>
```

Tip   *The filename always has to be a relative path to the file from the MXI file. By using a staging area, you can eliminate the complex use of paths in your filenames.*

The filename is given, and must be listed as a relative path to the MXI file. The destination is also given as a path, with the path referencing the UltraDev root folder by using a $dreamweaver directive. This is a built-in variable that refers to the program that is receiving the installation, and can be used for both Dreamweaver and UltraDev, although you can also use $ultradev also. The only other options at the present time are $fireworks for a Fireworks extension and $flash for a Flash extension.

Changing the UltraDev Menus

Next are the configuration changes. These are the additions to the various menus within UltraDev. In fact, you can build an extension that is nothing but menu changes. Suppose you want the Paste As Text command to be accessible from the contextual menu to conform to your work habits. You could edit the menus.xml file by hand, or you could create an MXI file with the menu change spelled out in a <configuration-changes> tag. This way, the changes can be undone simply by removing the extension from UltraDev. This is just a better way to handle your menus so that the changes you make to the menu can be documented and undone if needed.

The <configuration-changes> tag for this particular extension is as follows (once again, you need only use the code for the server model that you are working with):

```
<configuration-changes>
 <server-behavior-changes servermodel="ASP">
  <menu-insert appendTo="DWMenu_ServerBehaviors_ASP_2">
   <menu name="User Login" id="TMMenu_ServerBehaviors_Login_ASP">
   </menu>
  </menu-insert>
  <menu-insert appendTo="TMMenu_ServerBehaviors_Login_ASP">
   <menuitem file="UserAccess.htm" ¬
 id="TMMenu_ServerBehaviors_Login_ASP_UserAccess" />
  </menu-insert>
 </server-behavior-changes>
 <server-behavior-changes servermodel="JSP">
  <menu-insert appendTo="DWMenu_ServerBehaviors_JSP_1">
   <menu name="User Login" id="TMMenu_ServerBehaviors_Login_JSP">
   </menu>
  </menu-insert>
  <menu-insert appendTo="TMMenu_ServerBehaviors_Login_JSP">
   <menuitem file="UserAccess.htm" ¬
 id="TMMenu_ServerBehaviors_Login_JSP_UserAccess" />
  </menu-insert>
 </server-behavior-changes>
 <server-behavior-changes servermodel="ColdFusion">
  <menu-insert appendTo="DWMenu_ServerBehaviors_CF_4">
   <menu name="User Login" id="TMMenu_ServerBehaviors_Login_CF">
   </menu>
  </menu-insert>
  <menu-insert appendTo="TMMenu_ServerBehaviors_Login_CF">
   <menuitem file="UserAccess.htm" ¬
 id="TMMenu_ServerBehaviors_Login_CF_UserAccess" />
  </menu-insert>
 </server-behavior-changes>
</configuration-changes>
```

Notice the ID attribute that is added to the menu items. The ID should be something unique to your extension. Macromedia recommends adding a unique prefix to the beginning of the menu item. For instance, the preceding code adds a menu item to the DWMenu_ServerBehaviors_ASP_2 menu. The new ID is given a unique prefix ("TM") and a unique suffix ("Login_ASP"). The final ID is TMMenu_ServerBehaviors_Login_ASP, and will be unique to this Server Behavior.

This is necessary to avoid conflicts with other extensions written by yourself or other people.

Wrapping Up the Package

After completing all of the required tags, you must close out the main tag:

```
</macromedia-extension>
```

Now that you have an MXI file for the extension, you can open it in the Macromedia Extension Manager. On a PC, right-click the MXI file and click Open with Macromedia Extension Manager; on a Mac, open the Extension Manager and click File | Open. Newer versions of the Extension Manager will open if you double-click the MXI file. Next, you are prompted for Extension to Package (see Figure 23-8) and the filename to Save Package As. After this process is completed, you can install the extension in any machine by using the MXP file that is the result of the packaging operation. The MXP file contains all the files of your extension, as well as the MXI file to tell UltraDev where to put the files and what changes to make to the UltraDev menus. When the extension is installed, the MXI file is installed to the Extensions folder under Configuration, so that the Extension Manager can keep track of which extensions are installed.

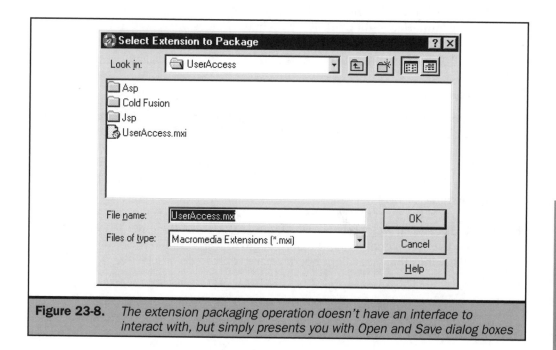

Figure 23-8. *The extension packaging operation doesn't have an interface to interact with, but simply presents you with Open and Save dialog boxes*

The Extension Manager has gone through many changes since it was created. Older versions of the Manager also contained a separate Packager program. You should read the help files that came with the version on your computer, and check the Macromedia Web site for the newest version.

Packaged extensions can be submitted to the Macromedia Exchange and shared with other users. The submission process is outlined on the Macromedia Exchange Web site, at www.macromedia.com/exchange. In addition to the submission, there is also an option for a Macromedia seal of approval, which verifies that the extension has been tested for bugs and compatibility issues by the Macromedia Quality Assurance engineers, and is a good indication that the extension is safe to install. Whether you choose to submit your extension to the Exchange or not, you should package your extensions. Packaging the extensions offers these advantages:

- It allows you to keep track of installed extensions more easily.
- Uninstalling an extension is much easier, since all extension files are removed at once.
- Changes to the menu files are reversible when the extension is uninstalled.
- Transporting the extension is easier, because all of the individual files contained in the extension are in one package.
- Extensions can be "turned off" by unchecking the package in the Extension Manager interface—they still show up in the Extension Manager, but are inactive in UltraDev.

Summary

This chapter and the preceding few chapters have gone over many of the extension types available to UltraDev. You've built objects, Server Behaviors, Translators, commands, and a few other extension types as well. These chapters have only scratched the surface. Many other extension types are available, including the ability to create extensions in C. Once you've mastered extensibility, a whole world of new options opens up for you as a Web developer.

If you can add the tools that you need to UltraDev, you can be more productive in your day-to-day Web development. Also, if you are aware of the inner workings of UltraDev, and know its limitations, you also begin to learn how to push the program to accomplish things that you might not have been able to do otherwise.

The
Complete
Reference

Chapter 24

The UltraDev Shopping Cart: UltraDev Gets E-Commerce Ability

The buzzword on everybody's lips these days is "e-commerce." You can't turn on the radio or television without hearing about it being promoted by companies talking about their Web sites. Everybody's doing it. What exactly is it? What is an e-store?

Simply put, when you buy something from a Web site, you are conducting an electronic-commerce, or *e-commerce*, transaction. It could be as simple as buying a book from Amazon.com or sending some flowers with 1800flowers.com. These Web sites are considered *e-stores* because they provide a *virtual* storefront where you may buy goods or services. The only difference is that you can sit in the comfort of your own home while you shop.

The e-store has to operate under the same principles as a regular store. It has to be able to provide merchandise, keep inventories, conduct transactions, and ship merchandise to the customers. Of course, many of these things are often outsourced to other companies. For instance, a third party could take care of your credit card transactions, and the actual inventory could come from somewhere else—even your own hard drive, if you are selling software.

Typically, an e-store is based on a shopping cart model. A shopping cart is usually nothing more than a cookie, variable structure, or database that stores the items a user has chosen. When UltraDev was first released, there was a lot of clamor for a shopping cart. The product that UltraDev was replacing, Drumbeat 2000, had e-commerce capability built into the program. Many people looked at UltraDev as a downgrade rather than an upgrade, because of its lack of basic e-commerce functionality. Luckily, Rick Crawford, formerly of Elemental Software and creator of the Drumbeat shopping cart, decided to fill the need. His company, PowerClimb, built the UltraDev Shopping Cart, which is available for free from the Macromedia Web site, and also from the PowerClimb Web site at www.powerclimb.com.

The UltraDev Shopping Cart

The UltraDev Shopping Cart was developed as a limited shopping cart model. It was never intended to be a complete e-store solution—just a shopping cart that can be built upon. Whereas Drumbeat 2000 boasted a complete e-store with credit card transactions through CyberCash, the UltraDev Shopping Cart is a more basic foundation on which to develop an e-store.

A *shopping cart* is simply a place where data can be stored while a transaction is happening. Just like a real shopping cart in a store, it holds the items for you until you check out. The typical shopping scenario involves a person going to a Web site, choosing items to buy from the site, adding items to a shopping cart, and then checking out. The UltraDev Shopping Cart automates the process of getting the product information from the database and storing it in the temporary cart on the user's machine in preparation for the transaction. In addition, the cart contents are maintained for a predefined length of time, so that if the user decides to leave and then come back, his or her cart will still contain the same merchandise. The UltraDev Shopping Cart doesn't have much functionality beyond that, but that alone is a considerable time-saver.

At the time of this writing, the UltraDev Shopping Cart is available as a 1.1 version for ASP, and as a 1.2 beta version for JSP and ColdFusion from the PowerClimb site. There are also CyberCash and Authorize.Net back-end settlement behaviors available from the PowerClimb site, which simplify sending credit card data to these two companies. Other behaviors for credit card integration have been promised as well, and may be available by the time you read this.

The Cart Data Source

The cart is implemented as a data source, similar to a recordset. When you choose the UltraDev Shopping Cart from the Data Sources palette, a dialog box pops up (see Figure 24-1) allowing you to specify the fields that you want in your cart. Five fields are set up by default: ProductID, Quantity, Name, Price, and Total. These will most likely correspond to fields in your database, but the UltraDev Shopping Cart doesn't require that a database be used. It could be used, for example, to print out an order rather than create an online order. For those people who don't have the online capabilities for e-commerce, but still want to implement an e-store, the UltraDev Shopping Cart can still be used.

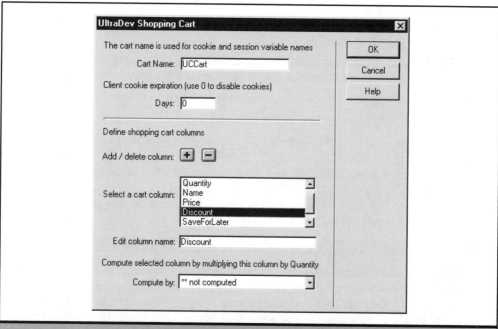

Figure 24-1.   *The UltraDev Shopping Cart data source, listing the default fields that are available for the cart, and allowing additional fields to be entered*

The UltraDev Shopping Cart can also be used to drive an e-mail-based order system. You can copy the cart contents to the body of an e-mail and have the e-mail sent to you to process. Using this method, you don't need a database.

In addition to the cart columns, the UltraDev Shopping Cart data source includes three additional values that you can use in your pages: number of items, total quantity of items, and total price. Notice that you can manipulate the cart columns and the other cart variables on the page just as you would do with recordset columns or other data sources. You can drag them from the Data Bindings palette and drop them on the page, and even assign server formats to them.

Although this discussion refers to the cart columns as "columns," they are not to be confused with database columns. The term relates to the internal structure that is used. If your cart is thought of as a table, the "columns" are the internal units for each item (such as name, price, and quantity), and the individual line items are the "rows."

The cart needs to reside on each page that requires any cart interaction. Typically, you'll have the following pages in your e-commerce site:

- A Products page (or series of pages) that lists all products with brief descriptions
- A products detail page, built dynamically for each product, that lists complete details of the product
- A Cart page, which you typically link to on all of your pages with a View Cart graphic, displaying to the user the items that are currently in the cart
- An Order Confirmation page, where the user confirms the order before committing to it

The way you apply the cart to your site is to choose it from the Data Bindings palette or Server Behaviors palette and give it the attributes you need—cart name, cookie expiration (in days), columns, and compute by, which you can use to apply computations to a specific field. After you define a cart on one page, the other pages in your site that use the cart will have to have the *identical cart on each page.* You can accomplish this in either of two ways:

- Create identical carts, with all of the same attributes for each page.
- Copy the cart by right-clicking the cart in the Data Bindings or Server Behaviors palette (CTRL-click on the Macintosh) and choosing Copy (see Figure 24-2). Then, go to the page that you want the cart applied to and right-click inside the Data Bindings palette again (or anywhere on the page) and choose Paste from the contextual menu. A perfect replica of the cart you just created will be placed on that page.

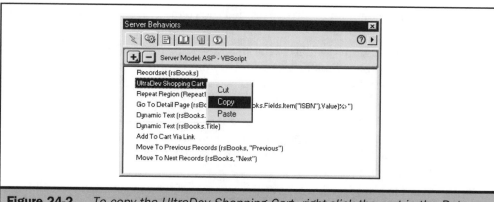

Figure 24-2.   *To copy the UltraDev Shopping Cart, right-click the cart in the Data Bindings or Server Behaviors palette and click Copy*

The Cart Server Behaviors

In addition to the data source that is the "actual" cart, you can apply to a page Server Behaviors (see Figure 24-3) that will do several different things. Here is a basic rundown of the cart Server Behaviors:

- **Add to Cart Via Form**   Adds an item (or items) to the cart by using a form and a Submit button. You can use this Server Behavior if you need to populate a list, for example, and have the user choose an item on the list; or it can be used when the user is allowed to manually insert text into a form field.

- **Add to Cart Via Link**   Does the same thing as the Add to Cart Via Form Server Behavior, but will send only the unique product ID number to the next page in a URL variable. Typically, you would use this method if you already

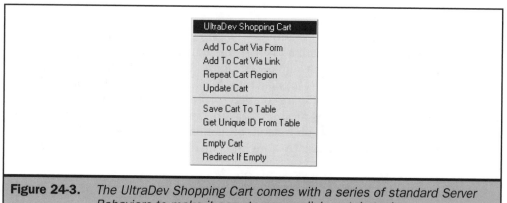

Figure 24-3.   *The UltraDev Shopping Cart comes with a series of standard Server Behaviors to make it easy to accomplish certain tasks*

have all of the information that is needed (no color or size decisions to make) or if you are implementing a Detail page with a list of items.

■ **Repeat Cart Region** Similar to the standard Repeated Region that you can apply to data from a database, except that you use this with the cart only. The standard Repeated Region won't work with the cart. Use the Repeat Cart Region instead. Typically, you would use this on your View Cart page, displaying everything in the cart.

■ **Update Cart** For use on a page where you might be changing quantities, or changing items. You need to have a form and a text field (or other form field) on the page.

■ **Save Cart to Table** Used to save the contents of the cart to a database table. Frequently, you'll want to also submit the data to a credit card company or online commerce server, so keep that in mind when you are ready to save the cart data.

■ **Get Unique ID from Table** Gets a specified column from the database and increments the number by 1 to use as a unique ID number. Typically, this is used with an "autonumber" style of column, as in Microsoft Access.

■ **Empty Cart** Empties the cart of its contents. Actually, it destroys the cart cookie and re-creates it as a new cart.

■ **Redirect If Empty** Used on a Cart Display page to redirect the user to another page if there isn't anything in the cart. Again, this is an optional behavior, and can be used to provide a more elegant method of displaying an empty cart by having a specific EmptyCart page to go to.

That was just a short introduction to the cart. What better way to learn how to use the cart than to build a complete site using it, which you'll do next.

The Site

This section goes through the typical implementation of a small e-commerce site. Aside from the shopping cart, you'll add an e-store database that contains product information, customer information, and order information. You'll also implement a login system and a customer insert/update form for keeping track of customers. The site will be for a typical online software company, called Acme Databases, that offers downloadable software as well as product software on CD-ROM. In addition, it offers hardcopy documentation such as books and/or manuals. As you can see, this example introduces a few twists to the typical e-store implementation, but the fundamentals are the same:

■ CD-ROMs and books need shipping costs added in.

■ Downloads won't have shipping costs.

- Downloads need page protection to prevent unauthorized downloads.
- CD-ROMs and books need variable quantities, whereas downloads will always be set to one.

As you build the site, you'll be using the UltraDev Shopping Cart, which can be downloaded from the Macromedia Exchange at www.macromedia.com/exchange/ultradev, or from the creators of the cart, PowerClimb, at www.powerclimb.com. PowerClimb has additional information about the cart available on its site, as well as the latest updates that may be available.

Also, the tutorial is kept as generic as possible, so that no matter which database or server model (ASP, JSP, or ColdFusion) you're using, you'll be able to follow along. Any language-specific features will be noted and the methods for each of the server languages will be shown.

Because this is a generic example and a small-scale example, the site is implemented without stored procedures. If you have access to a database that allows for the use of stored procedures, you should consider using them.

The Database for the Acme Databases Site

The first thing to do when building a site is to determine and develop a database plan, so you'll do that now. The plan for the site is to sell online software (databases), CD-ROMs, and documentation in the form of books. You are going to need several tables for this database, which are listed in Table 24-1.

Table Name	Description
Customers	Names, addresses, and personal information about the customers
Products	List of all available products with detailed information
Orders	List of order information to keep track of individual orders
OrderDetails	Line items of individual orders
ShippingMethods	Types of shipping and cost for each
PaymentMethods	Types of payments accepted
Payments	List of all payments made
MyCompanyInfo	Information about the company

Table 24-1.   *Database Used for the Sample Acme Databases E-Store*

Customers Table

The title of the Customers table is a bit of a misnomer, because the entries in the table are not actual customers until they buy something. People will be assigned a customer ID when they sign-up to shop at the online store. Certain information is going to be "required" at the time of sign-up, but not all information. When the customer places an actual order, he or she will have to fill in the missing blanks of information. For example, a customer's address won't be considered to be required while he or she shops; but after the order is placed, the information is needed for shipping or contacting the customer. You'll implement this by having a "sign-up" form with minimal requirements, and then by implementing an "orders" form that requires more complete information.

The column information for the Customers table is shown in Table 24-2. The Size column is a general gauge of the length of the field, but is not a hard-and-fast rule.

Name	Type	Size	Special Characteristics
CustomerID	Autonumber or identity	4	Primary key
CompanyName	Text	50	
ContactFirstName	Text	30	
ContactLastName	Text	50	
BillingAddress	Text	255	
City	Text	50	
StateOrProvince	Text	20	
PostalCode	Text	20	
Country	Text	50	
ContactTitle	Text	50	
PhoneNumber	Text	30	
FaxNumber	Text	30	
Username	Text	20	
Password	Text	20	
AccessGroup	Text	20	

Table 24-2.   *Customers Table for the Acme Databases Web Site*

As in the database you created in Chapter 16, the columns listed are generic and will apply to Microsoft Access. You should adapt the column types to your own RDBMS system—for further information consult Chapter 16. A Microsoft Access version of the database, as well as Microsoft SQL Server and IBM DB2 scripts, are included on the CD ROM.

Products Table

The Products table will contain information about the individual products that the store will be selling. In addition to product name and description, the table will have a column named Download that is a simple *bit* column—that is, it can hold either a 1 or a 0. This acts as a flag to determine whether the product is a download or not. If it is, a few other columns will apply to the product: DownloadLink and DownloadCount. The DownloadLink column will contain a physical location in the Web site of the product that can be downloaded. The DownloadCount column will contain a running tally of the number of downloads that the file has received, and will be updated by incrementing the value every time a particular file is downloaded. There is also a column for Weight, which will obviously be 0 for a download, but will contain a weight for a physical item. ProductID will be the primary key for the table, and will contain an autonumber or identity column to make that part of the data entry automatic—every item that gets added to the database will have an ID number assigned to it.

The column information for the Products table is shown in Table 24-3.

Name	Type	Size	Special Characteristics
ProductID	Autonumber or identity	4	Primary key
ProductName	Text	50	
UnitPrice	Money	8	
Description	Text	255	
Download	Bit or Boolean	1	
Weight	Number (int)	4	
DownloadLink	Text	50	
DownloadCount	Number (int)	4	

Table 24-3.   *The Products Table for the Acme Databases Web Site*

Orders Table

The Orders table will contain one entry for each order placed. The table is not the place for specific order details, such as which items are on the order. You'll implement an Order Details table specifically for that. The table will, however, hold shipping information (because it frequently differs from the billing information), freight charges, and shipping information. The primary key is the OrderID column and will be an autonumber or identity column. The CustomerID is a foreign key to the Customers table, and the ShippingMethodId is a foreign key to the ShippingMethods table.

The payment information isn't stored in this table because you're going to consider the Payment as a complete entity that is independent of the physical Order that is placed. They conceivably could have been grouped into the same table, but the rules of database design dictate that you should separate entities whenever possible.

The chart in Figure 24-4 shows that the Orders table sits in the center of the chart. The whole concept of an e-store revolves around a customer placing an order. In your

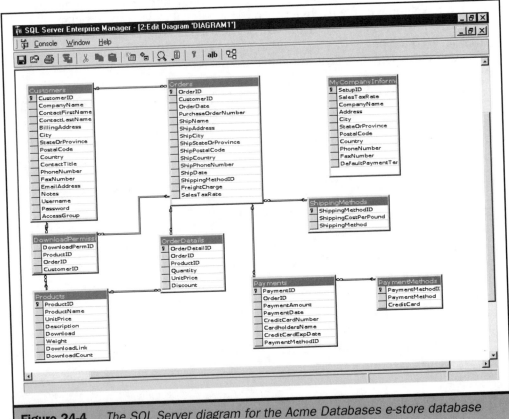

Figure 24-4.   The SQL Server diagram for the Acme Databases e-store database showing the relationships between the tables

case, and in the case of any e-store, the order is the key component of the transaction. It holds links to the customer who made the order, the products on the order (via the Order Details table), the method of shipping that order, and the payment made on the order. By accessing one row in the Orders table, you can—through SQL statements—find all the information that relates to that order to create an invoice.

The column information for the Orders table is shown in Table 24-4.

OrderDetails Table

The OrderDetails table will contain line-item information for the orders that are placed. The OrderDetailID will be the primary key for the table and will contain a unique

Name	Type	Size	Special Characteristics
OrderID	Autonumber or identity	4	Primary key.
CustomerID	Number (int)	4	Foreign key to Customers.
OrderDate	Text	30	This could be date/time, but text is used for complete compatibility.
PurchaseOrderNumber	Text	30	
ShipName	Text	50	
ShipAddress	Text	255	
ShipCity	Text	50	
ShipStateOrProvince	Text	50	
ShipPostalCode	Text	20	
ShipCountry	Text	50	
ShipPhoneNumber	Text	30	
ShipDate	Text	30	
ShippingMethodID	Number (int)	4	
FreightCharge	Money	8	
SalesTaxRate	Number (float)	8	

Table 24-4.   *Orders Table for the Acme Databases Web Site*

identifier for that particular transaction. For instance, a typical order might contain three items. Each item would be contained in one row in this table, and each would reference the OrderID through the foreign key contained in the table.

Other columns in the table will be UnitPrice, Quantity, and Discount. The UnitPrice will come from the Products table, but is kept separately in this table so that it can be modified on an individual-order basis. For instance, a customer could call up and ask to receive a special price on an item because he can find it somewhere else for a cheaper price. You don't want to change the unit price of the item itself, but you can change it on this one particular order by noting it in the Discount column. The ProductID field references the product, and is a foreign key to the Products table. The Quantity column indicates the number of orders for a particular item and is used to calculate the line item price and the shipping weight. These calculated fields aren't stored in the database, but are implemented in your application.

The column information for the OrderDetails table is shown in Table 24-5.

ShippingMethods Table

This table will hold the information about the different shipping methods that are available. The primary key will be the ShippingMethodID and will be an autonumber or identity column. There are also columns for ShippingMethod, which is a descriptive name of the method, and ShippingCostPerPound, which can be used in shipping calculations for your Orders table.

The column information for the ShippingMethods table is shown in Table 24-6.

Name	Type	Size	Special Characteristics
OrderDetailID	Number (int)	4	Primary key
OrderID	Number (int)	4	Foreign key to Orders
ProductID	Number (int)	4	Foreign key to Products
Quantity	Number (int)	4	
UnitPrice	Money	8	
Discount	Number (float)	8	

Table 24-5. *The OrderDetails Table for the Acme Databases Web Site*

Name	Type	Size	Special Characteristics
ShippingMethodID	Autonumber or identity	4	Primary key
ShippingMethod	Text	20	
ShippingCostPerPound	Number (int)	4	

Table 24-6.   *The ShippingMethods Table for the Acme Databases Web Site*

PaymentMethods Table

This table will contain information about the various payment methods that are available. The PaymentMethodID will be an autonumber or identity column that will act as the primary key for the table. The name of the payment method will be kept in the PaymentMethod column and is just a simple descriptive name for the method. The CreditCard column is a bit datatype and contains either a 1 or a 0 as a flag for whether or not the payment method is a credit card. The bit datatypes are handy for quick-and-dirty "yes/no" types of problems, such as "Is the payment method a credit card?" Among other things, a payment method could be a check, money order, or a company account.

The column information for the PaymentMethods table is shown in Table 24-7.

Payments Table

This table will contain information about all the payments that are made. If a person orders something online, and makes the purchase with a credit card, details of the transaction will be contained in one row of this table. It could be considered a

Name	Type	Size	Special Characteristics
PaymentMethodID	Autonumber or identity	4	Primary key
PaymentMethod	Text	50	
CreditCard	Bit	1	

Table 24-7.   *The PaymentMethods Table for the Acme Databases Web Site*

"monetary transactions" table, since the table will detail each and every transaction that is made, with one row for each transaction.

The PaymentsID column will be an autonumber or identity column, and it will be the primary key for the table. OrderID is a foreign key to the Orders table, and will reference a specific order number from that table. The PaymentAmount column will contain the amount of payment, which would be equal to the computed values of the unit price for each item purchased, multiplied by the quantity of that item, with sales tax, shipping, and any discounts also figured into the mix. PaymentDate will contain the actual date that the payment was made, which should also correspond to the date of the purchase, unless you are implementing some sort of payment schedule or other method of payment. If a person were to pay by check, for instance, the PaymentDate would be different from the OrderDate contained in the Orders table.

Other columns in the table deal with the credit card number, card holder's name, and expiration date, along with the PaymentMethodID—which will be a foreign key to the PaymentMethod table. The reasoning behind keeping the methods in a separate table is to prevent faulty information from being entered. Typically, the payment method will be a radio button or select list on a form so that only one method can be chosen, and it will correspond to a list of choices on the Web page.

The column information for the Payments table is shown in Table 24-8.

Name	Type	Size	Special Characteristics
PaymentID	Autonumber or identity	4	Primary key
OrderID	Number (int)	4	Foreign key to the Orders table
PaymentAmount	Money	8	
PaymentDate	Text	30	
CreditCardNumber	Text	30	
CardHoldersName	Text	50	
CreditCardExpDate	Date/time	4	
PaymentMethodID	Number (int)	4	

Table 24-8. *The Payments Table for the Acme Databases Web Site*

MyCompanyInfo Table

The MyCompanyInfo table will be the only unrelated table in the database. It is there simply to keep the Acme Databases company information in one place. This can be used for invoices, e-mail messages, Web pages, or wherever you might need to insert your company data. The information stored in here is simply the name, address, phone and fax numbers, and so forth.

One column in this table needs a little explanation. The column DefaultPaymentTerms is a 255-character column that contains the payment terms for the company. This can be a short descriptive paragraph detailing payment terms, so that it only needs to be updated in this one place for the site, invoices, e-mail messages, and so forth. You may also add things to this table that might be pertinent to your own company, such as a standard disclaimer whose wording might change, or the information for various contact people, such as technical support, customer service, or the sales department.

The column information for the MyCompanyInfo table is shown in Table 24-9.

Name	Type	Size	Special Characteristics
SetupID	Autonumber or identity	4	Primary key
SalesTaxRate	Number (float)	8	
CompanyName	Text	50	
Address	Text	255	
City	Text	50	
StateOrProvince	Text	20	
PostalCode	Text	20	
Country	Text	50	
PhoneNumber	Text	30	
FaxNumber	Text	30	
DefaultPaymentTerms	Text	255	

Table 24-9.   *The MyCompanyInformation Table for the Acme Databases Web Site*

The Database Structure and Other General Database Issues

In the tables previously listed, RDBMS-specific syntax wasn't given, but instead we have focused on the general data types and lengths. For instance, the PhoneNumber column is listed as text/30, but could just as easily be stored as a number. Generally, it is logical to store fields that need to be calculated in some way as a number, and other numeric fields that don't have to have any calculations performed on them as text, varchars, or strings. For instance, a phone number will never be added, subtracted, multiplied, or divided in any way, so there's no need to store it as a number. Also, text fields tend to reduce database errors in these cases, if the person were to enter a letter instead of a number.

A price, on the other hand, should be stored as a special *money* field. Computers often have errors in rounding when it comes to floating-point (noninteger) values, and database manufacturers have taken this into account when implementing special *money* data types.

Autonumber or identity columns are used in this example for all of the primary keys, but this was merely a choice of convenience. In the real world, special algorithms to determine a unique identifier would be better suited for an e-store. You could choose to use a combination of the person's name with a 16-digit random number, or a timestamp, or an RDBMS-specific globally unique identifier. After building the tables, make sure you identify the foreign key constraints for the tables to maintain referential integrity. This is done differently depending on your database. Make sure you know your RDBMS inside and out to be able to implement primary and foreign key constraints. In Access and SQL Server, it's simply a matter of building a diagram of the database and connecting the primary and foreign keys together (refer to Figure 24-4 for the SQL Server diagram). You can read the AcmeDatabases.sql SQL scripts included on the CD ROM to look at the SQL programming needed to create tables that implement primary and foreign keys.

Implement the Connection

After the database is in place, tested, and ready to run, you'll want to deploy the database to the proper Web folder (if it's a file-based database) or create it on the server (if it's a server-based database), and create your connection to the database. This might be an ODBC data source, which means you'll have to have the DSN set up on the remote server by the server administrator. If you're using a DSN-less or OLE DB connection, you'll need to find the correct path to the database. For a JDBC connection, make sure you have all the details you'll need, such as the driver type and URL, and that the class path for these drivers is accessible to both UltraDev and to the JSP application server.

If you haven't done so already, now is a good time to create the site folder within UltraDev and create the connection by going to Modify | Connections and inserting a new connection named connAcmeDatabases (see Figure 24-5). If you are using UltraDev 4, the connection information will be stored in the Connections folder.

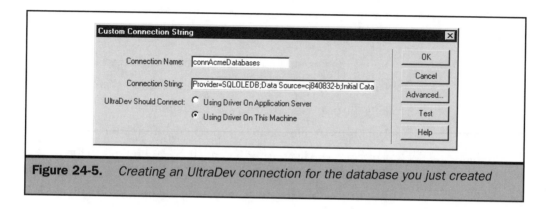

Figure 24-5.   *Creating an UltraDev connection for the database you just created*

The Site Tree for Acme Databases

The home page of the Acme Databases site will be called simply home.asp, home.cfm, or home.jsp, depending on the server model you're working with. It's a good idea to create blank pages for all pages in the site before starting on the site, so Table 24-10 shows a list of the page names and their purpose in the site. The page names serve double-duty as the filenames (with the appropriate extension: .asp, .jsp, or .cfm) and the titles. The items with asterisks (*) are the pages that contain an actual Cart on the page. You can create a blank page by right-clicking in the Site Files window and choosing New File. You can name them in the Site Files window, and also apply a title to the page by going to the Modify menu and clicking Page Properties The first item in the menu that pops up is for Title (see Figure 24-6). UltraDev 4 users have the page title in front of them in the design environment and no longer need to modify it through the Page Properties dialog box.

Implementing the Template

Templates make site creation much easier because they enable you to reuse certain parts of your pages that repeat from page to page. In the case of your sample e-store, the name of the company, Acme Databases, will be at the top of each page, and the links to the main pages will be implemented as a table at the top of the page. If you decide to use a different link style or implement a different logo at some point, you only have to change it on the template page, and then let UltraDev automatically update the pages that are served by the template.

To implement the logo and links section, you'll have to create a two-row, one-column table and stretch it to 90 percent of the browser width. To center the table on the page, go to the Properties floater and click the *center* icon. You have six links for this site, so you need to have six cells in the second row of the table. You can do this easily by positioning the cursor in the second row, right-clicking, and then clicking Table | Decrease Column Span over and over until you have six cells in the row (see Figure 24-7).

Page	Description
Home	Your home page, with a Login form for registered users.
Success	Pass-through page to verify users and redirect them.
Cart*	Lets the user view the cart and its contents.
AboutUs	Details the Acme Databases company information.
Products*	The complete list of products available, with links to the Details page for each product.
Details*	Lists individual products with more detailed information for each.
CheckOut*	The page on which users enter personal information.
CheckOut1*	Presents the confirmation of the user's order and totals for shipping and sales tax.
CheckOut2*	The page on which users actually supply the order information, such as shipping addresses, and so on.
CheckOut3	Allows payment for the order with a credit card.
SignUp	The page on which users enter their personal information the first time they log in to the site.
SignUp1	The page that records the new username and password.
ThankYou	A "thank you" page to signify a successful order.
Download	Any files that have been paid for can be downloaded from this page—links to DownloadCount.
DownloadCount	Counts the number of downloads and redirects the user to the actual download.
EmptyCart	If a user chooses to View Cart and the cart is empty, the user is redirected to this page.
Error	An all-purpose Error page for failed logins, access levels, and unfulfilled orders.

Table 24-10. *The Acme Databases Site and All of Its Pages*

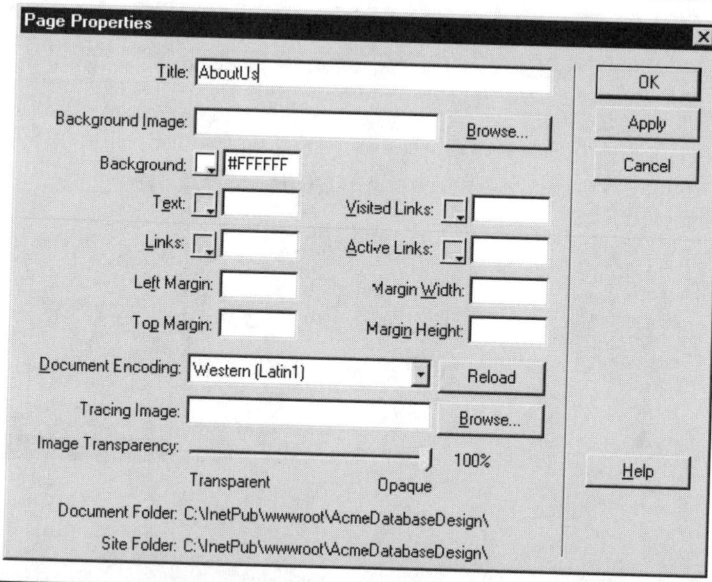

Figure 24-6. *Putting a title on a page using the Page Properties dialog box*

After you have the columns, it's simply a matter of setting the text for each of the links—Home, Products, Download, Sign Up, View Cart, About Us. After setting the text, you can set the links to point to each of the corresponding blank pages in the site by highlighting the text and going to the Properties palette and clicking the folder icon (see Figure 24-8) to bring up the link dialog box. Now, you can point the link to the proper file.

> **Tip**
>
> *By creating blank files for each page in your site when you begin your site, you are able to set up the navigation system to the site before any actual functionality is in place. This makes it easier to keep track of the flow of your site as you work on the functionality, and allows you to test each page as you go.*

After creating your logo and your links, you need to create an editable region. You can do this by first setting your cursor under the table you just created. Then, you'll need to go to the Modify menu and choose Templates | New Editable Region. A dialog box will ask for a name, which you'll simply call **BelowLinks**. After clicking OK, the body of the document below the link section you created will be completely editable

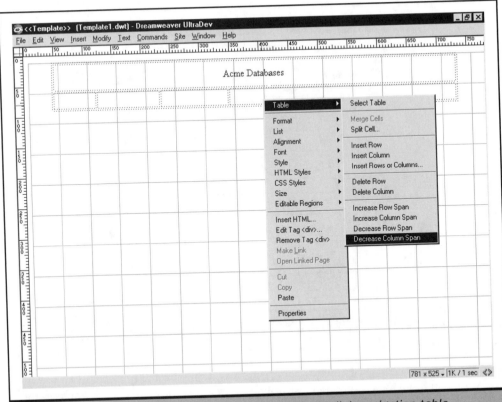

Figure 24-7. *Adding cells to one row of a table for the link navigation table*

on your pages, while the area above—the logo and links—will be locked to prevent it from being edited. Then, you can go to the Modify menu again and choose Templates | Update Pages to apply the template to all pages in the site.

Obviously, this is a very simple design for the e-store, but the purpose of this exercise is to build the shopping cart functionality. The design concepts are kept to a minimum in this chapter.

Last, it's important in a template to define an editable region in the head to allow for behaviors to be written without a problem. The template will have an editable region defined for the <title> tag by default. You should add a new editable region directly below this editable region, like this:

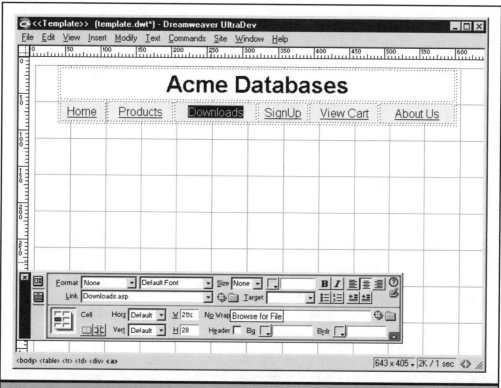

Figure 24-8.   *The Properties palette has a folder icon to allow you to set a link to a page in your site or a URL somewhere else*

```
<!-- #BeginEditable "head content" -->
<!--head stuff-->
<!-- #EndEditable -->
```

By inserting an editable region for the head content, the client-side behaviors won't run into the obstacle of a locked region.

Implementing the AboutUs Page

The AboutUs page is a typical page that you might find in an e-store that contains information about the company. For your Acme Databases site, you'll be drawing the information from the database using the MyCompanyInformation table. You could just as easily hand-code the information in the Web page itself, but you want the information to be maintainable by someone other than the Web designer. By putting the information in the database, if any information changes, someone from the company can update the information directly in the database or from a Web form instead of going back to the Web designer.

When designing a site for a client, it's a good idea to leave as much of the site maintenance as possible in the hands of the client. This prevents service calls to update the Web site and allows the client to perform trivial tasks such as updating a contact name or address.

You'll create a recordset on the page by accessing Recordset from the Data Bindings palette and creating a new recordset. Name the recordset rsMyCompany and select the CompanyName, Address, City, StateOrProvince, PostalCode, Country, PhoneNumber, FaxNumber, and DefaultPaymentTerms. This can be done quite easily if you are in the Simple recordset dialog box by choosing the connection connAcmeDatabases and then picking the table MyCompanyInformation. Instead of choosing All columns, choose Selected columns and then CTRL-click each column (COMMAND-click on the Macintosh) to highlight the columns you want. The Advanced recordset is similar, but you'll have to click the Select button once for each column that you choose (see Figure 24-9). After testing the connection by clicking the Test button, click OK and the recordset will appear on the page.

The Recordset dialog box defaults to the Simple version when you start up UltraDev for the first time. By clicking the Advanced button, you can access the Advanced version of the dialog box, which allows the editing of SQL statements by hand. When in the Advanced dialog box, the Advanced button turns into a Simple button to get back to the Simple dialog box.

The SQL statement for the rsMyCompany recordset is as follows:

```
SELECT CompanyName, Address, City, StateOrProvince, PostalCode,
Country, PhoneNumber, FaxNumber, DefaultPaymentTerms
FROM MyCompanyInformation
```

Next, insert some text on the page under the links to give a short description of the company:

We are a fictitious database design company that sells complete databases as well as database structures. The databases are downloadable. We also sell printed documentation that can be purchased online.

You can browse the Products page and click on an item to view the details, or simply add it to your cart. The Cart page allows you to change the quantities of the items or remove items completely from the cart.

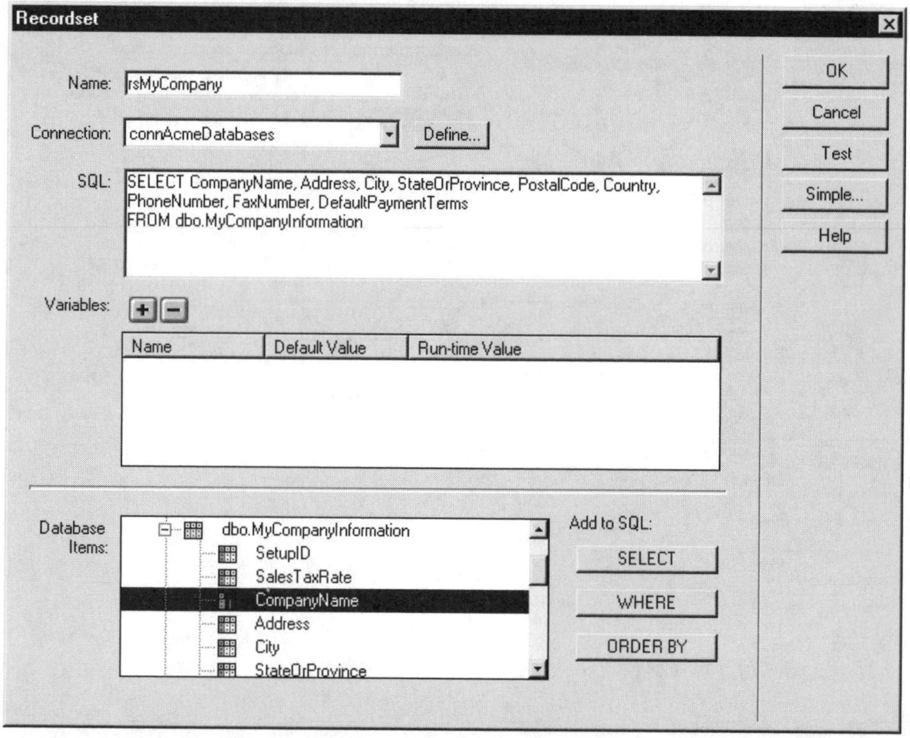

Figure 24-9.   *Write your own SQL statements by hand or click the buttons for Select when highlighting each column in turn*

If you aren't yet a member, you can sign up and choose a username and password for access to the order forms.

You'll make a link to the SignUp page on the words "sign up" by highlighting the text, going to Modify | Make Link, and choosing the SignUp page from the list of pages. This duplicates the link at the top, but sometimes a link in the context of a paragraph of text will be more likely to catch the user's attention.

Next, insert a two-column, six-row table on the page and make it borderless. The first column will contain the following values: Company Name, Address, (blank), (blank), Phone, and Fax. This column should be right-justified, which you can do by selecting each of the cells in the first column, and then going to the Properties floater and choosing the icon for right-justification (see Figure 24-10). You'll also make the entire first column bold by clicking the B icon in the Properties floater.

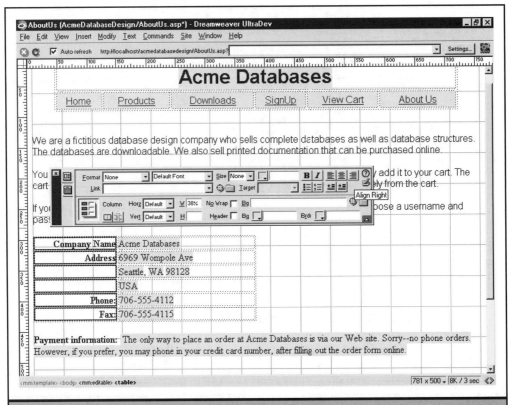

Figure 24-10. *Adding the company information to the table in Live Data mode and setting the justification property for the first column to align right*

In the second column, drag the database columns from the Data Bindings Inspector to the cells one by one. Company Name and Address will go in the first two cells. In cell three, put the City, then put a comma and a space, then drop the StateOrProvince column next to it, then insert one more space, and then put the PostalCode. This way, all three columns will be in the one cell of the table. Cell four will contain the Country column, cell five will have the PhoneNumber, and cell six will contain the FaxNumber column. If you are working in Live Data mode, which is often preferable when doing your page design, you'll see the actual values from the database in the table (refer to Figure 24-10). Live Data mode is also preferable for this type of work because it doesn't crowd the table with the recordset column placeholders, like {rsMyCompany. StateOrProvince}. Live Data mode will show the actual State from the database (WA in this case), which takes up considerably less room.

Right below the table, put some text—**Payment Information**—and make that bold as well. Next to that text, drag the column for DefaultPaymentTerms. This will complete the AboutUs page.

Implementing the Home Page

The Home page in the site will also serve as a user login page. You can use the Login object you developed in Chapter 21 (also on the CD-ROM) or build a login form from scratch. The main items that you need on the form are as follows:

- A text field named username
- A text field named password
- A form that has its Action attribute set to the Success page and method of Post
- A Submit button that has its action set to Submit form
- A Register Now link set to the SignUp page, with appropriate text, such as "If you haven't registered yet, you need to sign up"
- A checkbox with the name chkRemember and the value of 1

You need to place some code on the page to implement the Remember Me feature of the Login form. Part of this will have to be hand-coded, but part of it can be done with some built-in UltraDev features and the built-in Server Behaviors.

Steps to Implement the Remember Me Feature of the Login Page for ASP

1. Create three Request.Cookie data sources by going to the Data Bindings palette and clicking the plus sign (+) to create a new data source.
2. Choose Request Variable from the list. The Request Variable dialog box should pop up (see Figure 24-11).
3. Choose Request.Cookie from the list and give it a name of **ckUsername**.
4. Follow steps 1–3 two more times and create Request.Cookie data sources for **ckPassword** and **ckRememberMe**.
5. Go to the Server Behaviors menu and choose Dynamic Elements | Dynamic Text Field.
6. Set the username text field to the Cookies.ckUsername by clicking the lightening-bolt icon that signifies a dynamic data source and choosing the ckUsername cookie from the list.
7. Follow steps 5 and 6 for the Dynamic Elements | Dynamic Text password text field.

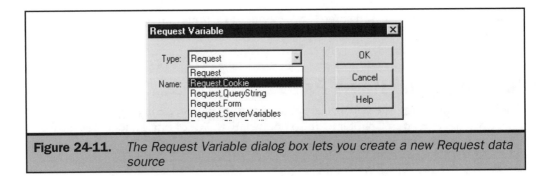

Figure 24-11.   *The Request Variable dialog box lets you create a new Request data source*

8. Go to the Server Behaviors menu and choose Dynamic Elements | Dynamic Check Box.

9. Set the Check If property to Cookies.ckRememberMe (see Figure 24-12).

10. Set the Equal To property to 1.

If you are using JSP or ColdFusion, the use of cookies requires hand-coding. Cookies are only implemented in ASP. UltraDev 4 introduced cookies in ColdFusion, but you still need to hand-code a CFIF statement around the cookie.

Steps to Implement the Remember Me Feature of the Login Page for ColdFusion

1. Set the Username text field code to look like this:

```
<input type="text" name="username"
value="<CFIF IsDefined("cookie.ckUsername")>
    <CFOUTPUT>#cookie.ckUsername#</CFOUTPUT>
</CFIF>">
```

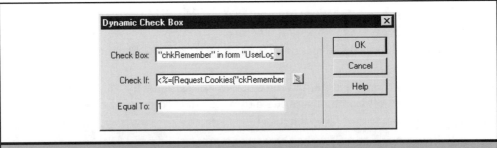

Figure 24-12.   *The Dynamic Check Box dialog box lets you choose a data source for the checkbox on the page*

2. Set the Password text field code to look like this:

```
<input type="text" name="password"
value="<CFIF IsDefined("cookie.ckPassword")>
    <CFOUTPUT>#cookie.ckPassword#</CFOUTPUT>
</CFIF>">
```

3. Set the chkRemember checkbox code to look like this:

```
<input type="checkbox" name="chkRemember" value="1"
<CFIF (IsDefined("cookie.ckRememberMe"))> checked
</CFIF>>
```

Steps to Implement the Remember Me Feature of the Login Page for JSP

1. First, you need a custom code block to get the values of any cookies that are already defined. This is a little more elaborate in JSP because you can't get a cookie by name without looping through the entire cookie object:

```
<%
boolean RememberMe = true;
String strUsername="";
String strPassword="";
Cookie[] cookies = request.getCookies();
for (int i=0; i<cookies.length; i++) {
    Cookie thisCookie = cookies[i];
    if(thisCookie.getName().equals("ckRemember") &&
      (thisCookie.getValue()==null)) {
        RememberMe = false;
        }
    if(thisCookie.getName().equals("ckUsername")) {
      strUsername = thisCookie.getValue();
      }
    if(thisCookie.getName().equals("ckPassword")) {
    strPassword = thisCookie.getValue();
    break;
  }
}
if (RememberMe != true) {
    strUsername="";
  strPassword="";
}
%>
```

2. Insert the variable strUsername that you declared in the preceding function to the value of the username form element:

```
<input type="text" name="username" value="<%=strUsername%>">
```

3. Insert the variable strPassword that you declared in the preceding function to the value of the password form element:

```
<input type="text" name="password" value="<%=strPassword%>">
```

4. Check the RememberMe variable that was defined in the preceding function for a true value, and if it's true, type **checked** for the checkbox state:

```
<input type="checkbox" name="chkRemember" value="1"
<%if(RememberMe==true){%>checked <%}%>>
```

These steps will set the values of the form elements to the appropriate values based on data that's stored in the cookies. The first time that a user visits this page, a cookie will not be stored yet. If the user checks the Remember Me box on the form, you'll have some code implemented on the action page (which was set to the Success page earlier) to set the values of the cookie so that the next time the user comes back, he or she will have the information already filled in.

The Success Page

The Success page will be a "pass-through" page that simply checks the username and password for the user who has just attempted to log in. This page will contain a recordset to verify the username and password for the user, and a User Login Server Behavior that you created in Chapter 22. If you didn't create that Server Behavior, it's available on the CD-ROM. Simply double-click the MXP file to install it to UltraDev. This Server Behavior is used rather than the built-in UltraDev 4 Log in User Server Behavior so that users of UltraDev 1 won't be left behind, and also because the implementation won't interfere with the description of the site functionality.

The recordset will have a name of rsGetUserID and will use the same connection—connAcmeDatabases. Recall from Chapter 22 that the Server Behavior will check the username and password against the values stored in the database and send the user to a Success page if the user supplies a valid username/password combination. If the user does not supply a valid username/password combination, he or she is redirected to an Error page. Successful logins will also have session variables set to the UserID column and the AccessGroup column of the database. Each succeeding page will have a User Access Server Behavior applied to it with the following attributes:

- Access Groups: web, admin
- Denied page: Error.asp (or Error.jsp or Error.cfm)
- Failed page: Error.asp (or Error.jsp or Error.cfm)

Once again, the User Access Server Behavior that you created in Chapter 22 is used rather than the built-in Restrict Access to Page Server Behavior that is new to UltraDev version 4. The User Access Server Behavior is also available on the CD-ROM.

To create the recordset, you'll need to use the Advanced recordset creation dialog box. You may notice that the Customers table doesn't have a UserID column. You can use an alias for your database column CustomerID to create the UserID field by using the *as* keyword. First, you'll need to create a SQL statement that looks like this:

```
Select CustomerID as UserID, AccessGroup
FROM Customers
WHERE Username = 'TM_username' AND Password = 'TM_password'
```

In the Variable declaration box, you'll set up your two variables (TM_username and TM_password) to accept the incoming form variables. This will differ in the three server models, so use the appropriate values from Table 24-11.

Now, you need to add the custom User Login Server Behavior (see Figure 24-13). You'll assign the Success page as the Products page to which the user will be taken upon a successful login. The Failed page property of the Server Behavior will be your Error page. The recordset will be the rsGetUserID that you've just set up.

There's only one more thing to do on this page, and that's to set the cookies if the user has chosen Remember Me from the home page. There are no built-in behaviors that will do this for you, so you'll have to add a bit of hand-coding. This code will be placed right after the language declaration at the top of the page in HTML source view, and will differ in the three server models. The code will check for the value of the checkbox; and if it is checked, it will set the three cookies for the user.

Name	Default Value	Run-Time Value	Server
TM_username	%	Request("username")	ASP
	%	request.getParameter("username")	JSP
	%	#username#	CF
TM_password	%	Request("password")	ASP
	%	request.getParameter("password")	JSP
	%	#password#	CF

Table 24-11. *Variable Declaration for the rsGetUserID Recordset for All Three Server Models*

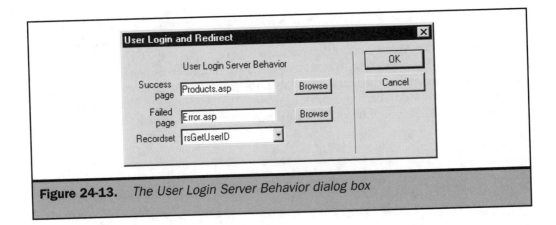

Figure 24-13. *The User Login Server Behavior dialog box*

VBScript Cookie Code for ASP Pages

```
<%
If Request.Form("chkRemember") = "checkbox" Then
     Response.Cookies("ckUsername") = Request("username")
     Response.Cookies("ckPassword") = Request("password")
     Response.Cookies("ckRememberMe") = "1"
     Response.Cookies("ckUsername").expires = Date + 30
     Response.Cookies("ckPassword").expires = Date + 30
     Response.Cookies("ckRememberMe").expires = Date + 30
Else
     Response.Cookies("ckUsername") = ""
     Response.Cookies("ckPassword") = ""
     Response.Cookies("ckRememberMe") = ""
End If
%>
```

JavaScript Cookie Code for ASP Pages

```
<%
if (Request.Form("chkRemember") == "1") {
     Response.Cookies("ckUsername") = Request("username")
     Response.Cookies("ckPassword") = Request("password")
     Response.Cookies("ckRememberMe") = "1"
     var expdate = new Date();
     expdate.setTime (expdate.getTime() + (30 * 24 * 60 * 60 * 1000));
     var newExpdate = parseInt (expdate.getMonth()+1)+'/'+ ¬
     expdate.getDate() + '/' + expdate.getFullYear();
```

```
        Response.Cookies("ckUsername").expires = newExpdate;
        Response.Cookies("ckPassword").expires = newExpdate;
        Response.Cookies("ckRememberMe").expires = newExpdate;
    }else{
        Response.Cookies("ckUsername") = ""
        Response.Cookies("ckPassword") = ""
        Response.Cookies("ckRememberMe") = ""
    }
%>
```

ColdFusion Cookie Code

```
<CFIF IsDefined("form.chkRemember")>
    <CFCOOKIE name = "ckUsername"
        Value="#username#" Expires="30">
    <CFCOOKIE name = "ckPassword"
        Value="#password#" Expires="30">
    <CFCOOKIE name = "ckRememberMe" Value="1" Expires="30">
<CFELSE>
    <CFCOOKIE name = "ckUsername" Expires="Now">
    <CFCOOKIE name = "ckPassword" Expires="Now">
    <CFCOOKIE name = "ckRememberMe" Expires="Now">
</CFIF>
```

| Note |

*ColdFusion users will have to change the line on the page that reads
<cflocation url="products.cfm"> to <CFHEADER NAME = "refresh"
VALUE="0; URL=products.cfm"> This is because in ColdFusion you can't
have a <CFLOCATION> tag on the same page as a <CFCOOKIE> tag.*

Java Cookie Code

```
<%
int RememberMe=0;
Cookie ckRemember = new Cookie("ckRemember", ¬
((request.getParameter("chkRemember")!=null)?request.getParameter ¬
("chkRemember"):""));
Cookie ckUsername = new Cookie("ckUsername", ¬
((request.getParameter("username")!=null)?request.getParameter ¬
("username"):""));
```

```
Cookie ckPassword = new Cookie("ckPassword", ¬
((request.getParameter("password")!=null)?request.getParameter ¬
("password"):""));
response.addCookie(ckRemember);
response.addCookie(ckUsername);
response.addCookie(ckPassword);
if(request.getParameter("chkRemember")!="1"){
     RememberMe = 24*60*60*30;
     }
ckRemember.setMaxAge(RememberMe);
ckUsername.setMaxAge(RememberMe);
ckPassword.setMaxAge(RememberMe);
%>
```

Implementing the Products Page and Detail Page

The Products page will contain the first instance of the cart on your site. This page will also contain a complete list of products available to the customer. Here, the user will be able to select a product to add to the cart, or select a link to view the product in greater detail. The Detail page will have the cart added to it as well. The user will be able to add items to the cart from both pages, and will be redirected to the Cart page upon adding an item to the cart.

 When working with the cart, it is important to realize that the cart is stored as a cookie on the client machine. If you decide at some point to change the functionality of the cart during the testing phase—adding or deleting columns, for instance—the cookie on your test machine should be located and deleted manually. The cookie can be located by searching the folder where your temporary internet files are located for your particular machine. This is especially true for JSP, where a minor inconstancy can cause the page to crash. You could alternatively write a custom page specifically to kill the cart when needed.

The Products Page

To start the Products page, first make sure the page is attached to the template. If you've been following along, it should already be attached. If not, you can attach it by going to the Modify menu and clicking Templates | Apply Template to Page. Next, add a User Access Server Behavior to the page (from the CD-ROM). The Server Behavior will have an Access Group attribute of "web, admin" and have the two redirect pages set to the Error page (as described earlier).

Next, you'll have to create a recordset on the page. Name this one rsProducts and use the same connAcmeDatabases connection that you already created. The select statement will get the ProductID, ProductName, Weight, and UnitPrice from the database with the following SQL statement:

```
SELECT ProductID, ProductName, UnitPrice, Weight
FROM Products
```

You will need to add a table to the page that is two rows by three columns. In the first row, put the following table headings—**Add to Cart**, **Product Name**, and **Price**. In the second row, enter the text **Add to Cart** in the first cell, drag the recordset column ProductName to the second cell, and then drag the recordset column UnitPrice to the third cell.

Before you go any further, you need to add the Shopping Cart to the page. To do so, go to the Data Bindings palette and choose the UltraDev Shopping Cart from the list of available items. This brings up the dialog box shown in Figure 24-14. Set the Client Cookie Expiration to 30 days. The default is 0, which effectively disables cookies. Also, you are going to add two columns to the cart, named Weight and Total Weight, by clicking the plus sign (+) for each added column. TotalWeight will have to have the value computed by multiplying the Weight column by the Quantity column. This calculation is built into the Shopping Cart by selecting Compute By | Weight from the drop-down list on the Shopping Cart.

As you may recall, the identical Shopping Cart has to appear on each page that uses the Shopping Cart. This can be done by copying and pasting a Shopping Cart from one page to another page, or by giving the Shopping Cart the identical attributes.

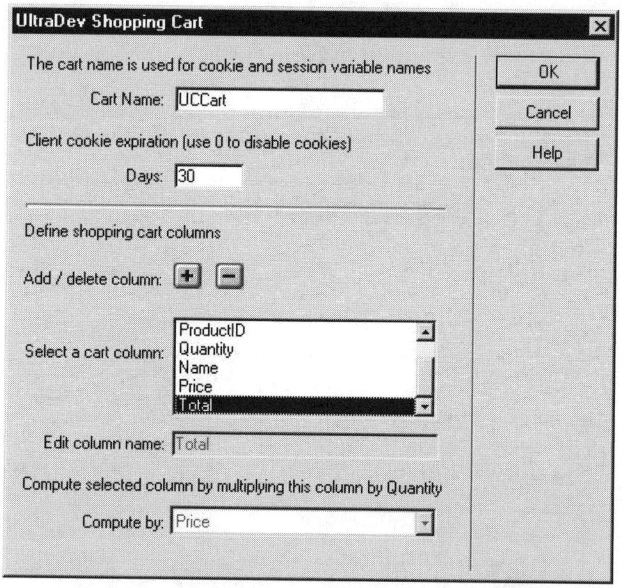

Figure 24-14. *The UltraDev Shopping Cart dialog box lets you define the attributes and add columns if necessary*

Next, you need to apply the Server Behavior Add to Cart Via Link to the text "Add to Cart" that you placed in the first cell of row two. After choosing the Server Behavior from the Server Behaviors menu, the dialog box in Figure 24-15 will pop up. This box has quite a few parameters to fill in, which are described here:

- **Link**   Set to the "Add to Cart" text.
- **Cart Columns**   Go through each one of these settings one by one. For the cart columns ProductID, Name, Weight, and Price, click the Recset Col radio button and then choose the correct column in the recordset from the drop-down list box. For the cart column Quantity, click the Literal radio button and enter a value of **1**. This will add one item to the cart when the link is clicked.
- **Recordset**   Set to rsProducts.
- **Index Column**   Set to the primary key of the table, which is ProductID in this case.
- **Go To URL**   Set to the Cart page in your Acme Databases example, but you could set it back to the current page, if you like. By setting it to the Cart page, the user is able to see the updated cart each time he or she adds something to it.

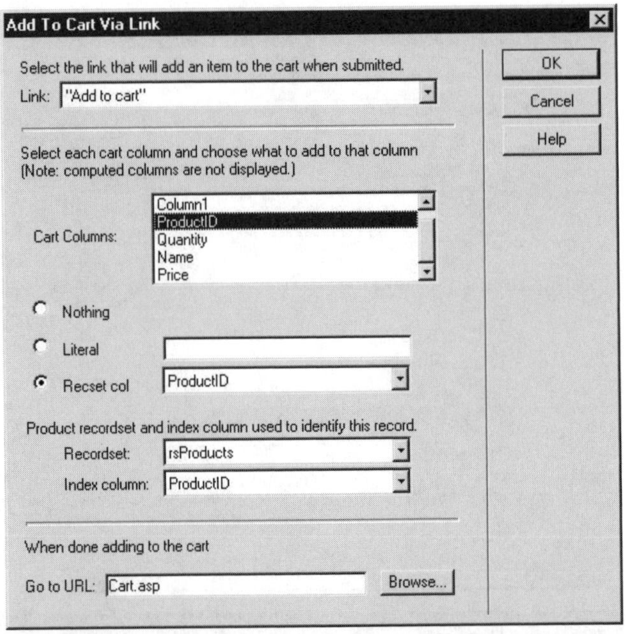

Figure 24-15.   *The Add to Cart Via Link Server Behavior has several attributes that need to be filled in*

Next, you can apply the Repeated Region Server Behavior to row two of your table. Row one contains column headings, so if you apply the repeat just to the second row, you create a dynamic table with column headings. Select the three cells by CTRL-clicking (COMMAND-click on the Macintosh) or by dragging the mouse across the three cells. Choose the Repeated Region Server Behavior from the Server Behaviors menu and choose All Records. This will cause the table to display all the products in the Products table.

Next, you can make the display a little prettier by adding a server format to the UnitPrice column. You can do this by double-clicking the Dynamic Text (rsProducts.UnitPrice) from the Server Behaviors palette and then choosing Currency–Default from the Format drop-down box (see Figure 24-16).

The one last item for the Products page is to set the link to the Detail page, which you can do by selecting the ProductName dynamic text on the page (in the second cell of row two in your table) and then choosing Server Behavior Go to Detail Page. This Server Behavior opens the dialog box shown in Figure 24-17. The parameters should be set as follows:

- **Link** Should already be set to the correct database column if you highlighted the correct text when you chose this Server Behavior.
- **Detail Page** Point to your Detail page by clicking Browse and browsing to it.
- **Pass URL Parameter** Set to ProductID.
- **Recordset** Set the drop-down list to rsProducts.

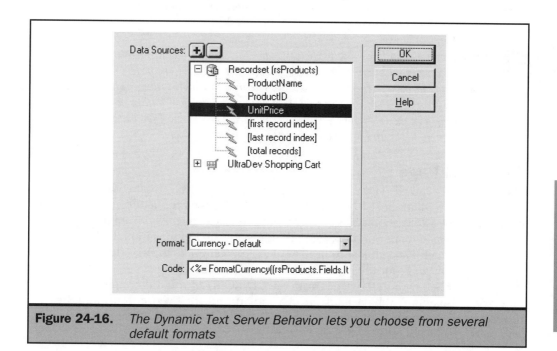

Figure 24-16. *The Dynamic Text Server Behavior lets you choose from several default formats*

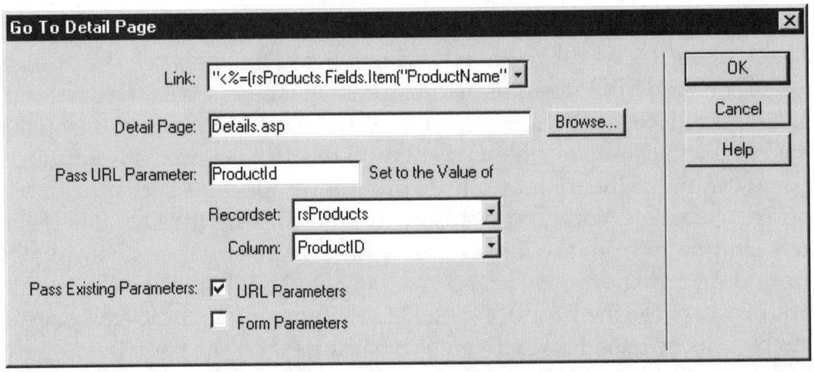

Figure 24-17.   *The Go to Detail Page Server Behavior dialog box*

- ■ **Column**   Set the drop-down list to ProductID.
- ■ **Pass Existing Parameters**   Uncheck both checkboxes

That should do it for the Products page. If you've done everything correctly, you should be able to browse the page at this point and see a list of all the products in the database. The two links won't work yet, though, because you haven't implemented the Cart page or the Detail page yet.

Note   *Keep in mind when browsing to the pages in this site that you are dealing with a Web application, and the entry point for that application is the Home page. Attempting to access another page in the application without first logging in from the home page will cause an error. You can prevent this by either logging in each time or setting up Live Data scripts in the Live Data Settings dialog box. The "Using Live Data Settings" box explains how to set up Live Data scripts.*

The Detail Page

This page will be linked via the Products page, so it doesn't really exist without it. The Products page contains links to each of the products, and the ProductID is passed to this page so that the information about a particular product can be pulled from the database.

Open the Detail page and make sure that it is attached to the template. If it isn't, go to the Modify menu and choose Templates | Apply Template to Page. This will give you the logo and links for the rest of the site at the top of the page. Next, add a User Access Server Behavior to the page (from the CD-ROM) as you did on the last page. The Server Behavior will have an Access Group attribute of "web, admin" and the two redirect pages set to the Error page.

Using Live Data Settings

When you have a Web application such as this one, frequently there are special prerequisites to viewing the page. For instance, on most of the pages in this site, there are session variables defined for TM_userid and TM_accessGroup. In addition, pages such as the Detail page require a URL parameter in order for the recordset to work properly. One way around the problem is always to enter the application from the entry point—the Home page in this instance. Another way is to set up your Live Data Settings properly.

Go to the View menu and choose Live Data Settings. You'll be presented with the dialog box shown in Figure 24-18. This is the Live Data Settings dialog box and it allows you to set up any incoming request variable that your page might need. It also allows your page to execute short scripts before the page is loaded. These settings work with Live Data view and also when you click F12 to preview the page in a browser. If you were to try to preview the Products page from within UltraDev, it would take you directly to the Error page unless your Live Data settings are defined, because you haven't logged in yet.

For most of the pages in this site, you'll need to define two session variables for the User Access Server Behavior: TM_userid and TM_accessGroup. These should be declared using the language that your site uses. If you've decided to use a different method of user authentication, make sure that you declare the proper variables for your particular solution.

The following script blocks define the session variables for the User Access Server Behavior that is included on the CD ROM and will allow you to view your pages in Live Data view or use the Preview in Browser command:

```
<% session("TM_userid")="1"
session("TM_accessGroup")="web" %> (VBScript)


<% session("TM_userid")="1";
session("TM_accessGroup")="web"%> (JavaScript)


<% session.setAttribute("TM_userid","1");
session.setAttribute("TM_accessGroup","web"); %> (JSP)


<cfset session.TM_userid="1">
<cfset session TM_accessGroup="web"> (ColdFusion)
```

You can use the Live Data Settings dialog box to define any script blocks that you want executed before the page loads, and also to pass any request variables to the page that might be needed for the page to execute properly.

Next, you'll need to add a recordset to the page. This recordset will return just one row from the Products table. You do that by passing the ProductID to this page from the link on the Products page. If you happen to pass a ProductID of 5, the product with the ProductID of 5 will be returned to the page to be displayed. If there isn't a ProductID, the page won't work. Create a new recordset named **rsProductDetails** using the same connection that you've been using throughout the site (connAcmeDatabases). The SQL statement will look like this:

```
SELECT ProductName, UnitPrice, Description, Weight, ProductID
FROM Products
WHERE ProductID = TM_productID
```

You'll have to add a variable with the attributes shown in Table 24-12.

If you've been working with Live Data, viewing the page in design mode can be a problem, since the productID isn't being passed to the page from the Products page while in design mode . You can get around this problem by setting a URL Request in the Live Data Settings, shown in Figure 24-18. Setting up your Live Data settings is explained in the Using Live Data Settings box. Click the plus sign (+) to add a URL Request variable and give it a name of ProductID and a value of **1**.

Next, you need to add the Shopping Cart to the page. The sure-fire method to get the same cart on the page that you have on the Products page is to follow these steps:

1. Open the Products page.
2. Copy the UltraDev Shopping Cart from the Data Bindings palette by right-clicking (CTRL-clicking on the Macintosh) and choosing Copy from the contextual menu.
3. Close the page and open the Detail page.
4. Go to the Data Bindings palette, right-click, and choose Paste from the contextual menu.

Alternatively, you can add the cart from the menu and just make sure that you give it the exact same attributes that you gave it on the previous page. This procedure is error prone, however, and the preferred method is to copy/paste.

Name	Default Value	Run-Time Value	Server
TM_productID	0	Request("ProductID")	ASP
		request.getParameter("ProductID")	JSP
		#productID#	CF

Table 24-12. *Variable to Be Used in the rsProductDetails Recordset*

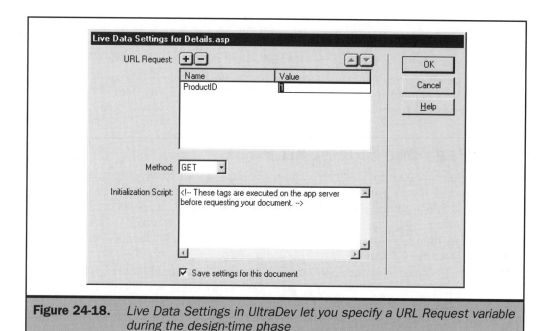

Figure 24-18.   *Live Data Settings in UltraDev let you specify a URL Request variable during the design-time phase*

Next, you'll add a table to the page to display the product details. Because you're pulling five columns from the database, you'll insert a table with five rows and two columns, and with no border. The first column will contain the values Product ID, Product Name, Price, Weight, and Description. Make these descriptive labels bold and right-justify them. Then, you'll have to drag each item in turn from the Data Bindings palette to the table—the ProductID will go next to the Product ID label, the ProductName next to the Product Name label, and so on. If you are working in Live Data, the actual data from the database will be seen on the page at this point. If not, you'll see the recordset column placeholders, such as {rsProductDetails.ProductID}.

Once again, the Price column should have a currency format applied to it. Do this by double-clicking the Dynamic Text (rsProductDetails.UnitPrice) item in the Server Behaviors palette and then choosing the Currency – Default format from the list, as was shown previously in Figure 24-16.

You need to add just one more Server Behavior, and the Detail page will be complete. Apply the Add to Cart Via Link Server Behavior to this page now by choosing the Server Behavior from the Server Behaviors menu under the UltraDev Shopping Cart submenu. Once again, make sure the recordset is set to rsProductDetails, and that all cart columns correspond to the proper recordset columns. Also, the Quantity column should be set to the Literal value of 1, because one click will add the item one time to the cart. And, again, the Go to URL attribute should be set to the Cart page. Aside from the recordset name, all the attributes should be identical to the way you applied this Server Behavior to the Products page.

If you've applied everything correctly and added the request variable to the Live Data Settings dialog box, you should be able to browse the page to test it. Also, if you open the Products page and browse it, you will be able to click any item in the page and have the Detail page show the product details for the item you clicked.

The Cart Page and EmptyCart Page

Up to this point, you've applied the UltraDev Shopping Cart to two pages, but the actual Cart page hasn't been created yet. This is the page that users will see when they choose View Cart from the menu. The cart contents are kept in a cookie on the user's machine for the time that you specify when you create the cart, which was 30 days in this case. Any time the user comes back to the site within that 30 days, the cart contents will have been retained and can be displayed on the Cart page.

Open the Cart page and make sure that it is attached to the template you have created. If it isn't attached, you'll have to go to the Modify menu and choose Templates | Apply Template to Page. Next, add a User Access Server Behavior to the page (from the CD-ROM) as you have been doing on each page. The Server Behavior will have an Access Group attribute of "web, admin" and the two redirect pages set to the Error page.

Next, you need to add the cart to the page. Do this in the same manner that you did it for the Detail page: copy and paste the cart from the Products page. Although you may be able to add the cart through the Data Bindings palette by giving it the same attributes, it's much safer to copy and paste the working cart from another page. Remember that the cart has to be *identical* in order for the pages to work correctly.

This page will have several elements that you haven't encountered yet. You'll use some existing Server Behaviors that you're familiar with, but you'll also be doing a little hand-coding. Remember that the UltraDev Shopping Cart is only a cart, and any business logic has to be added on a case-by-case basis. Also, you are going to want to add shipping costs into the cart contents. One other feature that you'll be implementing is a Remove checkbox in the cart itself. The cart comes with a Quantity field that can be changed, and an Update Cart Server Behavior, but does not include an easy way to remove an item from the cart.

Start the page by adding a Form object to the page. You can do this by going to the Insert menu and clicking Form. This will add the <form> tags to the page, and you'll see a red outline where the form exists on the page. Place the cursor inside this red outline and go back to the Insert menu. This time, insert a Table object, with five rows and six columns. If you did this correctly, the form outline should expand and the table should reside inside the form tags. If you did not do it correctly, you'll have to go into the HTML source view and place the opening <form> tag around the <table> tags. You can do this by selecting the entire opening <form> tag (<form name="form1"

method="post" action="">) and either cutting and pasting to a spot right above the table tag, or dragging and dropping right above the <table> tag. The closing <form> tag (</form>) then has to be placed right after the closing <table> tag (</table>). Another method is to select the entire table and drag and drop the table to a spot inside the form. Whichever method you choose, the end result is that the table is entirely within the form.

Tip *The easiest method of inserting an object into a form is to make sure that your cursor is inside the form and then choose the object from the Insert menu.*

After the table is on the page, you can fill in the first row, which will act as a table heading. The values for the heading are as follows: ID, Quantity, Product Name, Remove, Price, and Total. After filling in the heading information, select the six cells and apply a bold style to them.

Row two will contain the cart contents. Open the Data Bindings palette and expand the UltraDev Shopping Cart. The columns should all be listed in the palette. Drag the ProductID to row two, cell one. Drag the Name column to row two, cell three (skip cell two for now). Drag the cart Price column to row two, cell five (skip cell four for now). The cart Total should be dragged to row two, cell six.

Tip *Data sources from the Data Bindings palette can be dragged onto the page or they can be inserted by positioning your cursor on the page where you want the item to appear, selecting the item from the palette, and then clicking the Insert button on the palette.*

In the second row, you skipped the Quantity column. In this cell, you are going to insert a text field and name it txtQuantity in the Properties floater. Give it a Char Width of 6. Then, go to the Server Behaviors menu once again and choose Dynamic Elements | Dynamic Text Field. The dialog box will prompt you for the text field name, which should be txtQuantity, and then you can set the value by clicking the lightening-bolt button, which will bring up the Dynamic Data dialog box. Expand the Shopping Cart data source and choose the Quantity column.

Next, to apply the Repeat Cart Region, select the entire second row of the table containing the cart items, and then go to the Server Behaviors palette and choose UltraDev Shopping Cart. Choose the menu item Repeat Cart Region. This is similar to the Repeated Region Server Behavior that you used previously with recordsets, but this Server Behavior only applies to the Shopping Cart.

You may have noticed that you also skipped the Remove column, located in row two, cell four. You'll insert a checkbox in this cell and name it chkRemove. Here, you are going to add a little bit of hand-coding to make the checkbox automatically remove the cart item from the page. This code is going to differ for all four server languages, so each one is listed here. Go into HTML source view (Code view) and locate the checkbox input tag. After the Value attribute and before the closing > tag, insert an onClick event for the checkbox, as follows:

 Caution *The next code(s) should be placed all on one line in Code view.*

VBScript

```
onClick="document.form1.txtQuantity<%If UCCart1.GetItemCount()>1 ¬
Then Response.Write("[" & UCCart1__i & "]")%>.value=0,submit()"
```

JavaScript

```
onClick="document.form1.txtQuantity<%if (UCCart1.GetItemCount()>1) ¬
{Response.Write('[' + UCCart1__i + ']')}%>.value=0,submit()"
```

Java

```
onClick="document.form1.txtQuantity<%if ((int)(uc_getItemCount( ¬
session))>1) {out.print("[" + UCCart1__i + "]");}%>.value=0,submit()"
```

ColdFusion

```
onClick="document.form1.txtQuantity ¬
<CFIF #ArrayLen(Session.UCCart1[1])# gt 1> ¬
<CFOUTPUT>'[' & #UCCart1__i# & ']'</CFOUTPUT> </CFIF>.value=0,submit()"
```

This code for the checkbox will simply test the loop to see whether there is more than one item in it. If there is more than one item, the text field named txtQuantity will be an array. If there is only one item in the cart, txtQuantity stands by itself as a text field—it isn't part of an array. Then, the code will write out the brackets and the item number if it happens to be a member of an array. In other words, if there is one item in the cart, you use txtQuantity by itself. If there is more than one item, then you use txtQuantity[UCCart1__i]. After writing the correct text field name, you set the value to 0 and then submit the form, which will perform an update to the cart.

Note *If the elements have the same name when using HTML form elements, they will automatically be placed into an array. You can use this to your advantage in certain circumstances by looping through the array of items to retrieve the values. In this particular case, however, our code is complicated by the fact that there may be only one element (checkbox); and if there is only one element, the array is never formed.*

In the last three rows, skip to column five and insert the following text:

- Row three, cell five   **Subtotal**
- Row four, cell five   **Shipping**
- Row five, cell five   **Total Price**

Then, in row three, cell six, drag the cart sum(Total) data source. After you've completed this, you can right-click (CTRL-click on the Macintosh) in the empty cells and choose Table | Increase Column Span until all the empty cells in the last three rows are gone. Take a look at Figure 24-19 as a guide for how the table will look when you have finished.

You've probably noticed the form on the page; you also need a Submit button and an action page. You'll add a Submit button now, making sure that the button is placed inside the <form> tags, and then add the Update Cart Server Behavior, which will

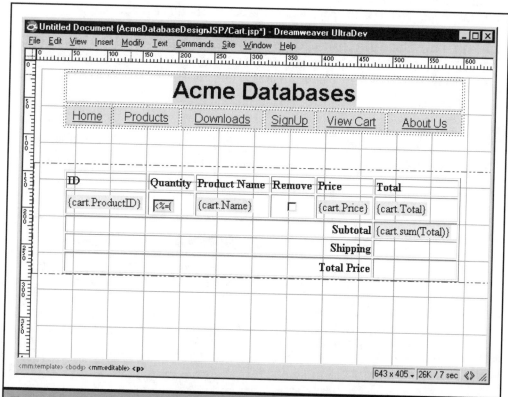

Figure 24-19.   *The Shopping Cart display is a simple table with the Colspan attributes modified in the last three rows*

enable you to set the action page. The Server Behavior is located in the Server Behaviors palette under the UltraDev Shopping Cart menu item. After clicking the menu item, you are presented with the dialog box shown in Figure 24-20. The Go to URL dialog box acts as the "Action." If you were to look at the actual code, the form action is actually set to the Update function of the Server Behavior. That function will redirect the user to the page listed in the Go to URL box. In this case, you'll set the box to this page itself (the Cart page), and set the form element to the txtQuantity element.

Next, you'll apply an Empty Cart Server Behavior. To do so, go to the Server Behavior palette, choose the UltraDev Shopping Cart menu item, and then choose Empty Cart. The dialog box asks you for a link, which you should make Empty cart, and a Go to URL dialog box, which you should set to the current page (the Cart page), as well. The Empty Cart dialog box is shown in Figure 24-21.

One thing that you have to do is to redirect the user to a different page if the cart is empty. There is a Server Behavior specifically for this task: Redirect If Cart Empty. To apply this Server Behavior, you just need to choose it from the Server Behaviors menu and then choose a page to redirect the user to. You've set up an EmptyCart page as part of your site, so this is the page where the behavior will be pointed.

Adding the Calculations for Shipping Weight and Total Price

All that's left on the Cart page is to add in the shipping weight and then total up the cart. To do that, you have to do a little hand-coding once again. All four server languages will have different code, so all of the code will be listed.

Whenever you are inserting your own server-side script, it is a good idea to create your own script tags, so that you don't interfere with the recognition of the UltraDev-generated script.

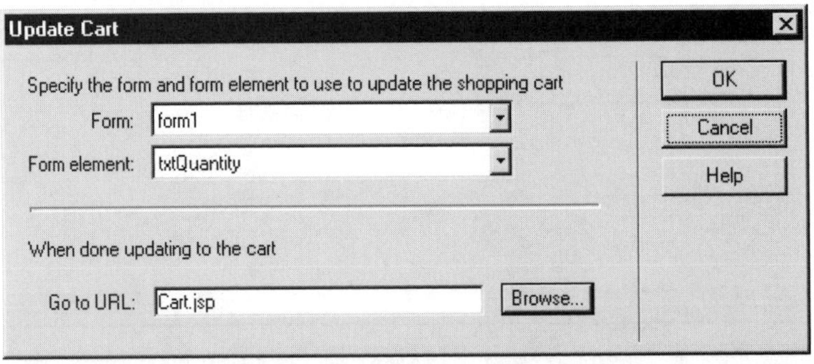

Figure 24-20. *The Update Cart Server Behavior enables you to set a page to go to after the cart is updated*

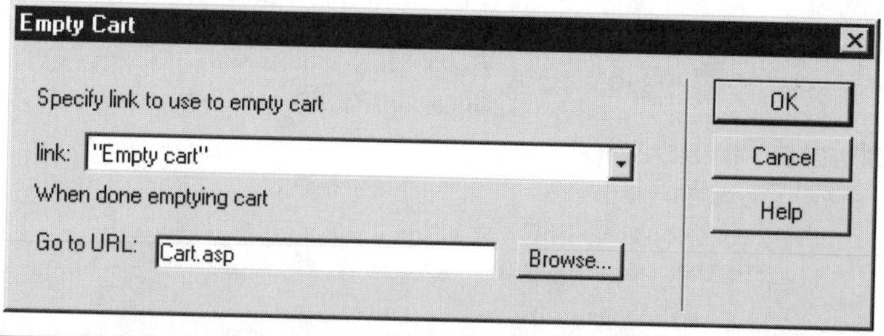

Figure 24-21.   *The Empty Cart dialog box has two attributes: Link and Go To URL*

The shipping weight total is stored in the cart on a line-by-line basis; recall that you use the quantity multiplied by the line-item weight to come up with the TotalWeight column. This data is stored in the cart itself, which makes it easy for you to keep track of a total shipping weight for each line item. There is even a sum(TotalWeight) data source in the Data Bindings Inspector for the cart. This is a sum of all the line items of weight for the cart. All you have to do is to figure out a price per pound and multiply that number by the total.

Drag the sum(TotalWeight) data source to the empty cell that is set up for the Standard Shipping amount. Since this is just the weight, your hand-coding will take care of the calculation for the shipping cost. For this example, you're going to charge $4.00 per pound for standard shipping, so you merely need to insert the calculation into the cell. The ColdFusion version will need the *evaluate* function added to it.

VBScript and JavaScript

```
<%=(UCCart1.GetColumnTotal("TotalWeight")*4)%>
```

Java

```
<%=((uc_getColumnTotal(session,"TotalWeight"))*4)%>
```

ColdFusion

```
<cfoutput>#evaluate(UCCart_SUM_TotalWeight*4)#</cfoutput>
```

The Total column will have to have one more hand-coded calculation for the Total Price in the last cell of the last column. You'll add the shipping cost to the subtotal. You can do this by copying and pasting the code from the subtotal and the shipping total to the Total Price cell in your table and inserting a plus (+) sign between them. This is what the final code will look like in the Total Price cell:

VBScript and JavaScript

```
<%(UCCart1.GetColumnTotal("Total")+
UCCart1.GetColumnTotal("TotalWeight")*4)%>
```

Java

```
<%=((uc_getColumnTotal(session,"Total"))+
((uc_getColumnTotal(session,"TotalWeight"))*4))%>
```

ColdFusion

```
<CFOUTPUT>
#evaluate(UCCart_SUM_Total + UCCart_Sum_TotalWeight * 4)#
</CFOUTPUT>
```

One final touch is required to format the cells that contain monetary values. You must apply a currency format to the individual price cells by selecting the individual script blocks and applying Server Format | Currency | Default to the highlighted item. You should do this for each of the monetary values on the page. To get the decimal points to line up, you need to select all the items, right-click, select Properties, and then click the Align Right button on the Properties floater. With right justification, the decimal points should all line up nicely.

The JSP version of the Web site won't be able to use the currency format built into UltraDev for the cart columns, so it will have to be hand-coded. The "Format Currency for JSP" box explains the process.

Last, you need to link to the CheckOut page. Type the text **Proceed to Check out** below the cart and set a link to the CheckOut page. To accomplish this, highlight the text "Check out," right-click, and select Make Link. This opens the Select File dialog box, which allows you to set the link to the CheckOut page.

Format Currency for JSP

If you are following along for JSP, you know that all variables must be properly typed in Java. The built-in UltraDev currency formats don't work with the UltraDev Shopping Cart, because the formats of the variables aren't supported by the functions. You can create your own functions, however, by hand-coding them into the document. The two functions that we've written to take care of the cart currency format follow:

```
<%!
public String DoStringCurrency(String myNumber)
{
    String myString = "";
    int myNumberConverted= ¬
((int)(Float.valueOf(myNumber).floatValue()*100 + .5));
    myString = String.valueOf((float)myNumberConverted/100);
    if(myString.length() - myString.indexOf(".") == 2) {
        myString = myString + "0";
        }
    return "$" + myString;
}
%>
<%!
public String DoFloatCurrency(float myNumber)
{
    String myString = "";
    int myNumberConverted = ((int)(myNumber * 100 + .5));
    myString = String.valueOf((float)myNumberConverted/100);
    if(myString.length() - myString.indexOf(".") == 2) {
        myString = myString + "0";
        }
    return "$" + myString;
}
%>
```

The first function accepts a string and returns a string to the caller. The second function accepts a floating-point number and returns a string to the caller. These functions can be pasted above the <html> tag in the document. The following line of code illustrates the method of applying the function to the cart column:

Was:

```
<%= (uc_getColumnValue(session,"Price",UCCart1__i)) %>
```

After Applying Format:

```
<%= DoStringCurrency(uc_getColumnValue(session,"Price",UCCart1__i)) %>
```

The two cart line items Unit Price and Total will need the DoStringCurrency() function applied to them, and the three calculated fields (Sub Total, Shipping, and Total Price) will need DoFloatCurrency() applied to them.

The EmptyCart Page

This page, once again, should be based on the template you created. If it isn't, you have to go to the Modify menu and click Templates | Apply Template to Page.

On the EmptyCart page, you'll simply put a statement that says "Your Cart is empty. Back to Products." The word "Products" will have a link set to the Products page. To accomplish this, highlight the text "Products," right-click, and select Make Link. This opens the Select File dialog box, which enables you to set the link to the Products page.

Implementing the CheckOut Pages

The CheckOut pages will also be based on the template you created. If you open the page and find that the template isn't attached to it, you have to go to the Modify menu and click Templates | Apply Template to Page. These pages will be similar insofar as they will contain a form for the user to provide information to be entered into the database.

The CheckOut Page

The scenario at this point is this: the user has chosen some items to buy, and has clicked the link to Proceed to Checkout. At this point, you need to gather the user information, the order information, the shipping information, and the type of transaction—whether it's a credit card transaction or a "bill me" transaction. You'll implement it in a fashion similar to the "wizard" metaphor that you've seen in programs before. Start the page by adding a User Access Server Behavior to the page (from the CD-ROM) as you have been doing on each page. The Server Behavior will have an Access Group attribute of "web, admin" and the two redirect pages set to the Error page.

The next step is to get the user data. The user will need to have personal data stored in the database. The first thing to do is to get the user's personal data from the database, if it already exists, and place it into various predetermined form fields on the page. Then, the user can either choose to accept what is there (if he or she is a past customer), or enter new information if the information in the database is inaccurate or incomplete. Start by placing a recordset on the page:

1. Create a new recordset by choosing Recordset from the Data Bindings palette. Name it **rsCustomer**.

2. Choose the connAcmeDatabases connection from the drop-down list.

3. Create a SQL statement based on the Customers table, and use the majority of the columns. The SQL statement will look like this:

```
SELECT CustomerID, CompanyName, ContactFirstName, ContactLastName,
    BillingAddress, City, StateOrProvince, PostalCode, Country,
    ContactTitle, PhoneNumber, FaxNumber, EmailAddress, Notes
FROM Customers
WHERE CustomerID = TM_customerID
```

4. The TM_customerID variable that takes the value of the incoming session variable storing the UserID needs to be defined in the Variables box, as shown in Table 24-13.

5. Click the Test button to verify the connection. If you used a default value of 0, and there are no users with that CustomerID, no rows will be returned from the test box.

6. Click the OK button to apply the recordset to the page.

Name	Default Value	Run-Time Value	Server Model
TM_customerID	0	Session("TM_userid")	ASP
		#Session.TM_userid#	ColdFusion
		session.getValue("TM_userid")	JSP

Table 24-13.   *Variable Used in the CheckOut Page to Get the Correct User from the Database*

The recordset doesn't update the Username or Password values—that should be saved for a separate Change Your Username and Password screen. The CheckOut page should stick to the task at hand—the transaction. Also, the AccessGroups column in the database table is a column that is set by an administrator and should never be accessed by the user. The CustomerID is the primary key for the table and, as such, should never be changed, but it is retrieved here to match up with the session variable.

The next step is to build the update form. This could be implemented with a Record Update Form Live Object in UltraDev 4, but the manual process will be outlined here. (The automated process is covered in Chapter 18.) Note that you are updating rather than inserting—even if it is a new user—because the user already has a customer record in the table with a username, password, user ID, and access level at the very least. If this is a return visit, the customer's information will be displayed in the form fields so that the info can either be updated or the user can click the next button to proceed.

Place a table that's 14 rows by 2 columns on the page under the main links. In this table, you'll put the field names in the left column and form fields in the right column. These labels and text fields will correspond to the columns you retrieved in your preceding select statement—Company Name, Contact First Name, Contact Last Name, Billing Address, City, State or Province, Postal Code, Country, Contact Title, Phone Number, Fax Number, Email Address, and Notes. Each form field should be given a name that relates to the column it addresses. This example uses the identical names of the recordset columns to name the form fields, but some programmers prefer to use a "txt" or "frm" prefix on the names.

After building the form, you need to add an Update Server Behavior to the page. This is one of the standard UltraDev Server Behaviors located in the Server Behaviors menu. After the Server Behavior is applied, it will prompt for the following items (shown in Figure 24-22):

- **Connection**   The database connection.
- **Table to Update**   The Customers table in the database.
- **Select Record From**   The recordset applied to the page—rsCustomer, in this example.
- **Unique Key Column**   Your CustomerID column.
- **Get Value from Form**   The name of the form.
- **Form Elements**   A list of all the elements. You should check this list to make sure that all the elements are getting updated as they should. Also, make sure any form fields that don't update a column are set to <ignore>. There shouldn't be any on this page.
- **When Done Updating**   The URL to go to after the update is complete. Set this to **CheckOut1**.

After applying the Update Server Behavior, the screen should look like Figure 24-23. The form fields are all bound to the database columns in the code, so that when a user

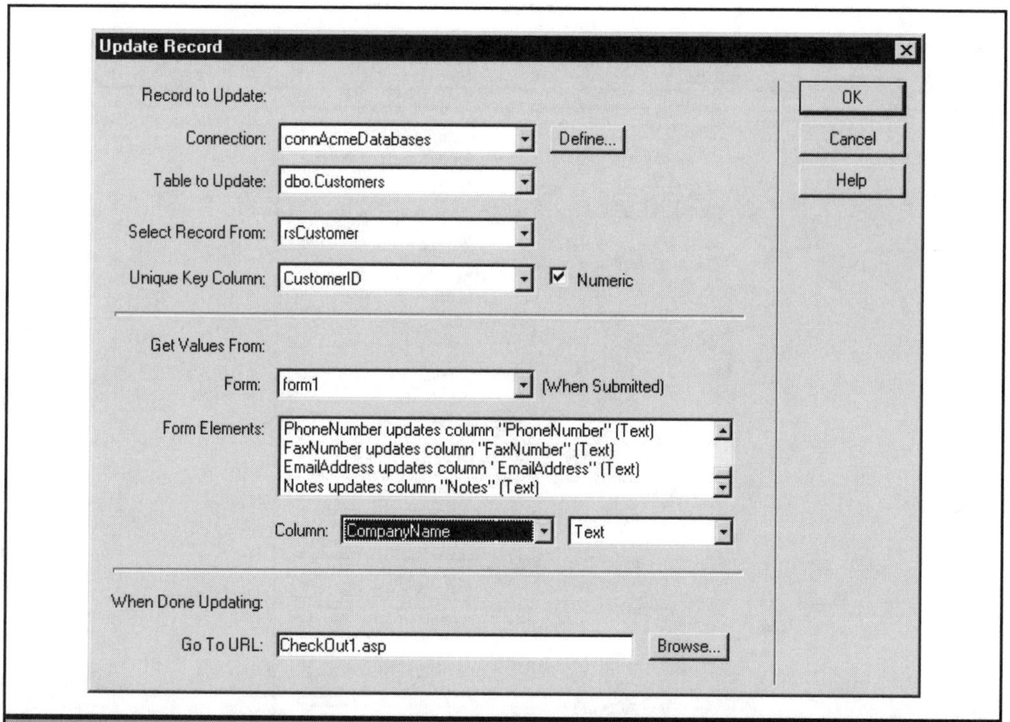

Figure 24-22.   *The UltraDev Update Server Behavior dialog box*

presses the Submit button, the database is updated and the user is taken to the next page. In this way, the user's information is stored in the database immediately upon submitting it. The transaction can still be canceled after this point, but the user's personal information is still inserted into the database. In this way, it's different from the traditional wizard that writes all the data to the database at the end of the transaction.

One final detail is to add a button to the page to submit the form and send the user to the next page. You'll leave the button as a submit-type button and change the Label to read Proceed to Checkout >>>. The greater-than signs signify that the process is moving forward, as in a wizard.

Caution   *In a true wizard, the database isn't written to until the final OK button is clicked. The current example implements a basic scenario for a small-scale e-store, and the user's information is stored before the order is committed. In a real-world situation, you might want to keep all of your transactions to the database until the end, and then write them with a stored procedure with the ability to* roll back *in case one of the transactions failed.*

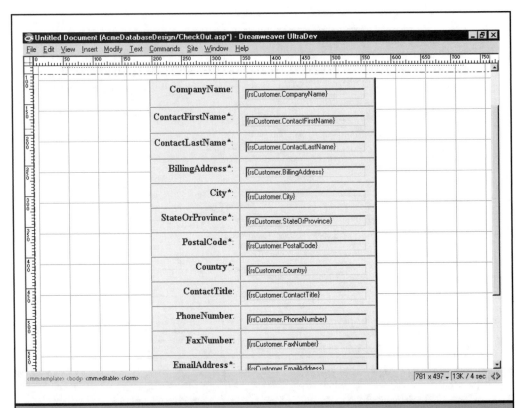

Figure 24-23.   *The Update Server Behavior has been applied to the page. The dynamic items are highlighted to show them as dynamic*

The CheckOut1 Page

Next, you'll implement the CheckOut1 page, which will be the second in a series of four CheckOut pages. Start the page by adding a User Access Server Behavior to the page (from the CD-ROM) as you have been doing on each page. Also, make sure the page is attached to the template that you've been using throughout this exercise.

Next, copy and paste the cart from one of the other pages. This ensures that the identical cart structure will get transposed to this page. You can copy it from any of the pages that have the cart on it—Products, Details, and Cart pages. The cart should be identical on each page. Then you'll need to insert a table on the page to hold the cart's contents. Since this CheckOut page acts as a confirmation of the items being purchased, the cart contents will have to be displayed in such a way that they are not editable. By the time the user has decided to check out, the cart contents are set. Any changes will have to be made by going back to the Cart page to remove items or increase quantities, or to the Products page to add items.

You'll need to add a recordset to the page to get the current user information. Call it **rsGetUser** and use the UserID stored in your session variable to get the information. The recordset will be based on the same connection that you've been using for the entire site: connAcmeDatabases. Your Select statement will look like this:

```
SELECT CustomerID, CompanyName, ContactFirstName, ContactLastName,
BillingAddress, City, StateOrProvince, PostalCode, Country,
ContactTitle, PhoneNumber, FaxNumber, EmailAddress, Notes
FROM Customers WHERE CustomerID = svUserID
```

The statement is simple, and just brings the columns that you need for the order to the page based on the CustomerID. You'll also need to declare a variable to hold the session variable information: svUserID. The values to enter in the Advanced recordset declaration box are listed in Table 24-14.

Next, you'll insert a seven-row, five-column table to display the cart contents. The steps to display the contents are almost identical to those for the Cart page, although there won't be any form items here to allow changes to the contents, and you will be adding sales tax:

1. Insert the column headings in the first row: **Product Name**, **Quantity**, **Total Weight**, **Price**, and **Total Price**.

2. Make the column headings bold and right-justified by applying the commands from the Properties floater.

3. Drag the Name, Quantity, TotalWeight, Price, and TotalPrice columns from the cart to the corresponding columns in row two, and right-justify those as well.

4. Apply a Repeat Cart Region to row two.

5. Row three should contain the text **Totals:** in the first column.

6. Drag sum(Quantity) from the cart in the Data Bindings palette to row three, cell two. This is the total quantity of items.

7. Drag sum(Total) from the cart in the Data Bindings palette to row three, cell five. This is the subtotal of all the line items before any calculations are done on them.

8. Drag sum(TotalWeight) from the cart in the Data Bindings palette to row four, cell three. This is the total weight of all items in the cart.

9. In the next cell, cell four, in row four, insert the text **x $4.00/lb** as an identifier that you're multiplying the weight by $4.00 per pound.

Name	Default Value	Run-Time Value	Server Language
svUserID	0	Session("TM_userid")	ASP
		session.getValue("TM_userid")	JSP
		#Session.TM_userid#	ColdFusion

Table 24-14. *Setting Up the svUserID Variable to Hold the Session Variable Containing the UserID*

10. Insert the custom code block from the following listings. This code can go anywhere on the page, but it's helpful to put it close to the cart display—right before the Repeat Cart Region Server Behavior in Code view. In the code, you're going to declare five new variables to take care of the business logic of the site:

- **UCCart1_subTotal** Uses the sum(Total) from the cart
- **UCCart1_shippingCost** Uses the sum(TotalWeight) * 4
- **UCCart1_totalPlusShipping** Uses the subtotal plus the shipping cost
- **UCCart1_salesTax** Uses a figure of 4.5% for Virginia residents, which it checks for
- **UCCart1_grandTotal** The total of all costs

ASP VBScript

```
<%
Dim UCCart1_subTotal
Dim UCCart1_shippingCost
Dim UCCart1_totalPlusShipping
Dim UCCart1_salesTax
Dim UCCart1_salesTaxRate
Dim UCCart1_grandTotal
UCCart1_subTotal = UCCart1.GetColumnTotal("Total")
UCCart1_shippingCost = UCCart1.GetColumnTotal("TotalWeight") * 4
UCCart1_totalPlusShipping = UCCart1_subTotal+UCCart1_shippingCost
UCCart1_salesTax = 0
UCCart1_salesTaxRate = 0
If Lcase(rsGetUser.Fields.Item("StateOrProvince").Value)="va" Then
   UCCart1_salesTaxRate = 0.045
   UCCart1_salesTax=UCCart1_salesTaxRate * UCCart1_totalPlusShipping
```

```
End if
UCCart1_grandTotal = UCCart1_totalPlusShipping + UCCart1_salesTax
Session("uccartOrderDate") = Now()
Session("grandTotal") = UCCart1_grandTotal
%>
```

ASP JavaScript

```
<%
var UCCart1_subTotal = UCCart1.GetColumnTotal("Total");
var UCCart1_shippingCost = UCCart1.GetColumnTotal("TotalWeight") * 4;
var UCCart1_totalPlusShipping = UCCart1_subTotal+UCCart1_shippingCost;
var UCCart1_salesTax = 0;
var UCCart1_salesTaxRate = 0;
if((rsGetUser.Fields.Item("StateOrProvince").Value).toLower=="va"){
  UCCart1_salesTaxRate = 0.045;
  UCCart1_salesTax=UCCart1_salesTaxRate*UCCart1_totalPlusShipping;
}
var UCCart1_grandTotal=UCCart1_totalPlusShipping+UCCart1_salesTax;
Session("uccartOrderDate") = new Date();
Session("grandTotal") = UCCart1_grandTotal
%>
```

Java

```
<%
float UCCart1_subTotal = uc_getColumnTotal(session,"Total");
float UCCart1_shippingCost = ¬
uc_getColumnTotal(session,"TotalWeight") * 4;
float UCCart1_totalPlusShipping = ¬
UCCart1_subTotal+UCCart1_shippingCost;
float UCCart1_salesTax = 0;
float UCCart1_salesTaxRate = 0;
if ((rsGetUser.getString("StateOrProvince")).toLowerCase()=="va"){
  UCCart1_salesTaxRate = 0.045f;
  UCCart1_salesTax=UCCart1_salesTaxRate*UCCart1_totalPlusShipping;
}
float UCCart1_grandTotal =
UCCart1_totalPlusShipping + UCCart1_salesTax;
```

```java
String uccartOrderDate = new Date().toString();
if(session.getAttribute("uccartOrderDate")==null)
session.setAttribute("uccartOrderDate", uccartOrderDate);
session.setAttribute("grandTotal",String.valueOf(UCCart1_grandTotal));
//**Note: The java package "java.util.Date" must be included to use
//the date constructor.  Make sure the following line is at the top
//of your JSP page:
//import="java.util.*" or import="java.util.Date"
//alternatively, the import attribute can contain a comma-separated
//list of class packages:
//import="java.sql.*,java.util.Date", or the method can be addressed
//directly, like this:  new java.util.Date().toString()
%>
```

Caution   *The ColdFusion code has to be inserted on the page at a specific point after all of the UCCart variables have already been declared, which is directly after the row in which the variable UCCart_SUM_TotalWeight is used.*

ColdFusion

```coldfusion
<cfscript>
UCCart1_shippingCost = UCCart1_SUM_TotalWeight * 4;
UCCart1_totalPlusShipping = UCCart1_SUM_Total+UCCart1_shippingCost;
UCCart1_salesTax = 0;
UCCart1_salesTaxRate = 0;
If (Lcase(rsGetUser.StateOrProvince) eq "va"){
  UCCart1_salesTaxRate = 0.045;
  UCCart1_salesTax=UCCart1_salesTaxRate*UCCart1_totalPlusShipping;
}
UCCart1_grandTotal = UCCart1_totalPlusShipping + UCCart1_salesTax;
session.uccartOrderDate = DateFormat(Now()) & " " & TimeFormat(Now())
session.grandTotal = UCCart1_grandTotal;
</cfscript>
<!---**Note that when you use "Now()" in ColdFusion, a special
formatted string is returned in the format of:
{ts '2000-10-01 11:45:28'}
You can format this better yourself by using:
DateFormat(now(),"mm/dd/yyyy") &" "& TimeFormat(now(),"hh:mm:ss")

--->
```

The business logic for the page is defined in one single script block. You can see that it will be easy to add additional logic to the block if necessary, or strip out the logic that you don't need. With the variables containing the values you need for the rest of the cart display, it's simply a matter of displaying the values on the page now. The session variable uccartOrderDate will be used as a unique identifier later to retrieve your order from the database. The session variable grandTotal will contain the total of the shopping cart plus shipping and plus tax.

Continue with the steps to display the cart contents:

11. Use the UCCart1_shippingCost variable in row four, cell five, for the total shipping cost. The code is **<%=UCCart1_shippingCost%>** for ASP and JSP, and **<CFOUTPUT>#UCCart1_shippingCost#</CFOUTPUT>** for ColdFusion.

12. Put the text **Subtotal** in row five, cell four, as a label.

13. Use the UCCart1_totalPlusShipping variable in row five, cell five, for the total plus shipping cost. The code is **<%=UCCart1_totalPlusShipping%>** for ASP and JSP, and **<CFOUTPUT>#UCCart1_totalPlusShipping#</CFOUTPUT>** for ColdFusion.

14. Put the text **Virginia residents add 4.5% sales tax** in row six, cell four, as a label. You can then right-click and select Table | Increase Column Span to eliminate the empty cells in the row.

15. Use the UCCart1_salesTax variable in row six, cell five, for the sales tax cost. The code is **<%=UCCart1_salesTax%>** for ASP and JSP, and **<CFOUTPUT >#UCCart1_salesTax#</CFOUTPUT>** for ColdFusion.

16. Put the text **Grand Total** in row seven, cell four, as a label.

17. Use the UCCart1_grandTotal variable in row seven, cell five, for the grand total of the cart. The code is **<%=UCCart1_grandTotal%>** for ASP and JSP, and **<CFOUTPUT >#UCCart1_grandTotal#</CFOUTPUT>** for ColdFusion.

18. Apply server formats of Currency | Default to all of the monetary columns. When you've finished, the page should look like the page in Figure 24-24. Once again, JSP users will have to use the custom functions described earlier rather than the UltraDev-supplied server formats.

Next, you'll add a few buttons, which will be placed in another table. First, add a form below the main cart display. Then, inside the form, add a table of two columns and one row to allow the buttons to be placed in the table cells for easy alignment on the page. Name the left button **shop** and add the text **Continue to Shop**. Name the right button **checkout** and add the text **Proceed to Checkout>>>**. The left shop button will be a *button*-type button, while the checkout button will be a *submit*-type button.

On the left button, you're going to have to put a little custom client-side JavaScript to get the button to act as a link to the Products page. Right-click the button and choose

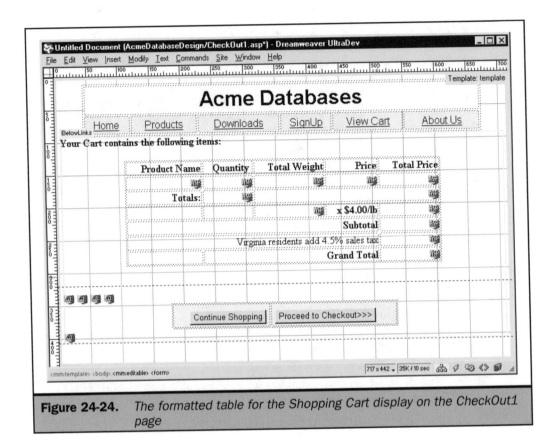

Figure 24-24. *The formatted table for the Shopping Cart display on the CheckOut1 page*

Edit Tag <input> from the list. This will allow you to insert the following code before the closing tag:

```
onClick='javascript:document.location.href="Products.asp"'>
```

Obviously, you'll have to substitute the page name of your own Products page here. This will create a link back to the Products page without causing the form data to be submitted. The buttons must be inside the form. Look at the code in Code view and make sure the checkout button is contained within the <form> tags.

Implementing Hidden Form Fields for the Database Insert

You are going to create the order in the database now with some hidden form fields and an Insert Server Behavior. One of the problems that you have to deal with when creating an order is that you need a unique order number. If your database is generating autonumbers or has an incrementing identity column, you have to add the order to the page, retrieve that order's unique order number, and then insert the cart into the

OrderDetails page. The OrderDetails page will have one row added for each row in the cart, and it will reference the Customers table using the CustomerID field, and the Orders table using the OrderID field.

One method of retrieving that autonumber or identity column is to generate a timestamp and insert it into the database. Then, you can retrieve that timestamp with a Select statement and get the unique order number. Obviously, if you have a high-traffic site, you could conceivably have two orders placed at precisely the same time. You'll eliminate the risks by using the timestamp in combination with the UserID variable that's stored in a session variable. You'll store the timestamp in a session variable as well.

Tip   *If you are using a database that supports stored procedures, you can usually retrieve an identity column using a return value. In Microsoft SQL Server, you can use Select @@identity inside a stored procedure to return the value.*

You'll insert four hidden form fields within the form that's already on the page. You can do this by putting your cursor within the form, and going to the Insert menu and clicking Form Object | Hidden Field. Do this five times. Then, you can double-click each of the hidden field gold-shield icons (see Figure 24-25), and assign

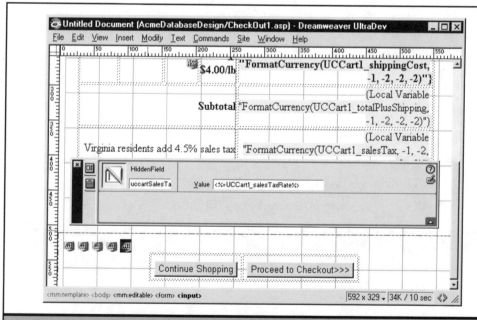

Figure 24-25.   *The hidden form fields can be renamed and have their values set from the Property Inspector*

Name	Value (ASP)
uccartShipping	`<%=UCCart1_shippingCost%>`
uccartOrderDate	`<%=Session("uccartOrderDate")%>`
uccartSalesTaxRate	`<%=UCCart1_salesTaxRate%>`
uccartCustID	`<%= Session("TM_userID")%>`

Table 24-15.   *ASP Hidden Form Field Names and Values*

new names and values to the hidden fields. The names and values are listed in Tables 24-15, 24-16, and 24-17 for ASP, JSP, and ColdFusion, respectively.

> **Tip**   *Another method of assigning values to hidden form elements is to drag a data source to the gold shield that represents the form element and drop it onto the selected shield.*

Next, you'll assign an Insert RecordServer Behavior to the page to insert the four form fields previously defined. The Insert Record Server Behavior will bind the form fields to the database columns in the Insert SQL statement, and will allow a redirect to another page after the insert takes place. The dialog box for the Insert Record Server Behavior is shown in Figure 24-26.

Name	Value (JSP)
uccartShipping	`<%=UCCart1_shippingCost%>`
uccartOrderDate	`<%=session.getAttribute("uccartOrderDate")%>`
uccartSalesTaxRate	`<%=UCCart1_salesTaxRate%>`
uccartCustID	`<%= session.getValue("TM_userid")%>`

Table 24-16.   *JSP Hidden Form Field Names and Values*

Name	Value (ColdFusion)
uccartShipping	<CFOUTPUT>#UCCart1_shippingCost#</CFOUTPUT>
uccartOrderDate	<CFOUTPUT >#Session.uccartOrderDate#</CFOUTPUT>
uccartSalesTaxRate	<CFOUTPUT>#UCCart1_salesTaxRate#</CFOUTPUT>
uccartCustID	<CFOUTPUT>#Session.TM_userID#</CFOUTPUT>

Table 24-17.   *ColdFusion Hidden Form Field Names and Values*

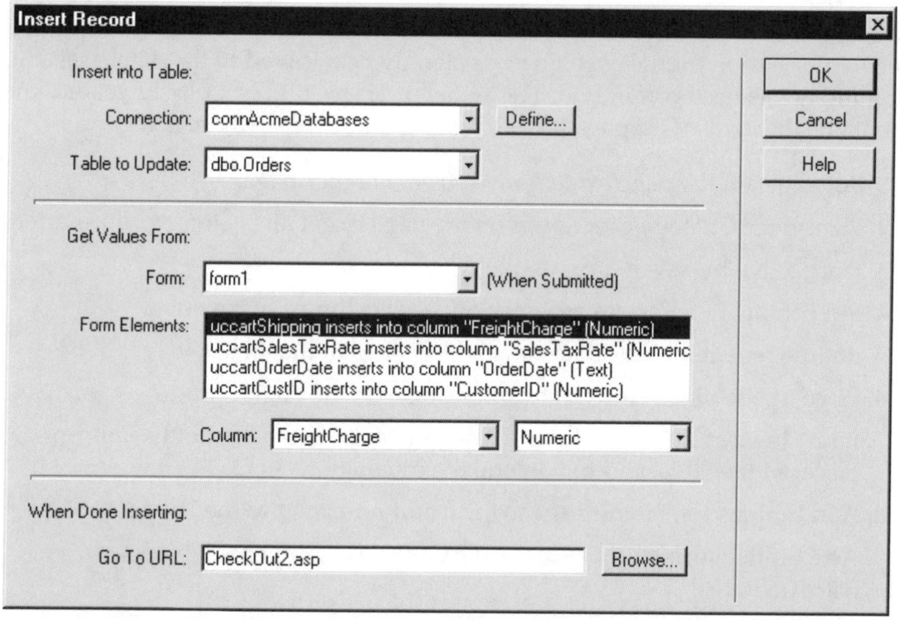

Figure 24-26.   *The Insert Record Server Behavior enables you to insert the hidden form fields into the database*

The steps necessary to use the Insert Record Server Behavior are as follows:

1. The Connection drop-down box should point to the connAcmeDatabases connection.

2. Choose the Orders table from the Table to Update drop-down box.

3. The Form drop-down box should be set to the form on the page that contains the hidden form elements. That should be the only form on the page.

4. The Form Elements box has a list of the form elements and corresponding columns are listed below in the Column drop-down box. You need to go through these one by one and make sure the form element and column match up. The Column drop-down boxes list the individual columns and data type. Note that your OrderDate column is going to be text, not a date type, because you want an exact match when you search for it.

5. Finally, the Go to URL box should contain the **CheckOut2** page.

That does it for the CheckOut1 page. If the customer has reached this point, the personal information for the customer has already been saved to the database, and the order number has been committed. The actual order hasn't been placed yet and the cart still contains the items. This page has a lot going on, so here's a quick recap:

1. Put a cart on the page by copying it from another page.

2. Place the rsCustomer recordset on the page to get all customer information.

3. Place a five-by-seven table on the page.

4. Put column headings in row one, and cart columns in row two.

5. Put the remaining cart data sources for totals in the table.

6. Place a code block with the business logic on the page.

7. Insert the variables that were defined in the code block into the appropriate places in the table, and hand-code the calculations in Code view.

8. Add buttons for submitting the form and returning to the Products page.

9. Add hidden forms for CustomerID, OrderDate, FreightCharges, and SalesTaxRate.

10. Assign the Insert Server Behavior.

The CheckOut2 Page

This is the next page in your series of CheckOut pages. This page will gather any shipping information that is necessary. It will also store the cart contents in the database and destroy the cart after the contents are saved to the database. Start the page by adding a User Access Server Behavior to the page (from the CD-ROM) as you have been doing on each page. Also, make sure that the page is attached to the template that you've been using.

First, you need to define a recordset that uses the session variables for the CustomerID and the OrderDate. Create a new recordset named **rsGetOrderNo**. It will be based on the same connection that you've been using—connAcmeDatabases. The Select statement will look like this:

```
SELECT OrderID, OrderDate, FreightCharge, SalesTaxRate
FROM Orders
WHERE OrderDate = 'TM_orderDate' AND CustomerID = TM_userid
```

Notice that the TM_orderDate variable has single quotes around it, whereas the TM_userid variable doesn't. The reason is that you're dealing with text and numeric variables, and the variable type has to be defined correctly in the query or the query won't work. By the same token, the Default Value column should contain a % for the string variable TM_orderDate, and a 0 for the numeric variable TM_userid.

You need to define the two variables for the query, as listed in Table 24-18.

Next, you'll add a 2-column, 13-row table to act as the form for the user input. You'll add the captions in column one and the form elements in column two. The form elements, once again, will have identical names as the database columns. The captions in column one will be as follows: Customer ID, Order Date, Ship Name, Ship Address, Ship City, Ship State or Province, Ship Postal Code, Ship Country, Ship Phone Number, Approximate Ship Date, Freight Charge, and Sales Tax Rate.

Name	Default Value	Run-Time Value	Server Model
TM_orderDate	%	Session("uccartOrderDate")	ASP
		session.getValue("uccartOrderDate")	JSP
		#Session.uccartOrderDate#	ColdFusion
TM_userid	0	Session("TM_userid")	ASP
		session.getValue("TM_userid")	JSP
		#Session.TM_userid #	ColdFusion

Table 24-18. *Variables for the rsGetOrderNo Recordset*

Column two will contain form elements, but not all text fields. The Customer ID is already set, so it will be displayed as text, as will the Order Date, Freight Charge, and Sales Tax Rate. The CustomerID field will contain the session variable TM_userid in the cell. Also, the ShipDate column will have some code that estimates the shipping date. These columns will be placed into hidden form fields, as well, so that the rows in the database will get updated. The easiest way to do this is to insert a hidden form element into the table cell where you would normally put the text field. Then, open the Data Bindings Inspector and expand the recordset entry so that the columns are showing. Drag each column from the recordset to the hidden form element (the hidden form element shows up as a gold shield in design view). When you drop the column on the hidden form element, the server markup code that gets the data from the database is placed into the value field of the hidden element—which is exactly where you want it. Alternatively, you can open the Properties Inspector for each hidden element in turn and type in the server markup that is needed.

The CustomerID field should have a hidden form field set to the session variable TM_userid. The code that appears in the cell, as well as in the value property of the hidden form element, is this:

ASP

```
<%=Session("TM_userid")%>
```

JSP

```
<%=session.getValue("TM_userid");%>
```

ColdFusion

```
<CFOUTPUT>#Session.TM_userid#</CFOUTPUT>
```

All the other captions should have text fields positioned in column two of the table. The form fields should then be named by opening the Properties Inspector for each field in turn and changing the name to match the name of the database column that it will update. You'll have to name the text fields and the hidden form elements as well.

The one column that you'll do a little differently is the Approximate Ship Date. That caption should be positioned next to a hidden form field named ShipDate, to correspond to the database column. In that field, you'll insert some code to give an approximate date to the user. You want to add seven to the current date, to indicate that the product will ship in approximately one week. The code is listed here:

VBScript

```
<%=Date() + 7%>
```

JavaScript

```
<%var todayDate = new Date();
todayDate=Math.floor(todayDate.getMilliseconds()+7*24*60*60*1000);
var shipDate = new Date();
shipDate.setMilliseconds(todayDate);
Response.Write(parseInt(shipDate.getMonth()+1)+'/'+ ¬
shipDate.getDate() + '/' + shipDate.getFullYear());
%>
```

Java

```
<%
Date todayDate = new Date();
long dateMilliseconds = todayDate.getTime() + 7*24*60*60*1000;
Date shipDate = new Date();
shipDate.setTime(dateMilliseconds);
String shipDateStr = Integer.toString(shipDate.getMonth()+1)+'/';
shipDateStr += Integer.toString(shipDate.getDate())+'/';
shipDateStr += Integer.toString(shipDate.getYear()+1900);
out.print(shipDateStr);
//**Note: The java package "java.util.Date" must be included to use
//the date constructor.  Make sure the following line is at the top
//of your JSP page:
//import="java.util.*" or import="java.util.Date"
//alternatively, the import attribute can contain a comma-separated
//list of class packages:
//import="java.sql.*,java.util.Date"
%>
```

ColdFusion

```
<CFOUTPUT>
#DateFormat(DateAdd("d","7",Now()),"MM/DD/YY")#
</CFOUTPUT>
```

This code can go into the Value attribute of the hidden form element. You might prefer to split the code into a separate code block so that the Value attribute just contains a simple write statement. That's perfectly fine, although this technique works well. The only thing that gets written to the user's browser is the outcome of the code—which will be the current date plus seven days. In this way, a hidden form element can contain a computed value. As you can see from the code, working with dates in Java or JavaScript is not as easy as working with VBScript or ColdFusion. The result is the same, however.

Tip   *For the purposes of this exercise, which demonstrates a dynamically calculated hidden form field value, server-side scripting is used to add a week to the date. In actual practice, a SQL DateAdd function will do this nicely if your RDBMS supports it.*

For every table cell that has a hidden form element, you should duplicate the code in the hidden element's Value attribute as text so that you can display the results on the page as well. The following example shows a table cell in JSP demonstrating the technique:

```
<td>
     <input type="hidden" name="OrderDate"
value="<%=session.getAttribute("uccartOrderDate")%>">
<%=session.getAttribute("uccartOrderDate")%>
</td>
```

You can see that the Value of the hidden element is set to the session variable uccartOrderDate. The session variable is read one more time to display the text in the table cell.

Next, put a submit button in the bottom cell of the table. The label should read **Continue to Checkout>>>**. If you haven't already put a form on the page, do so now. The form should encompass all of the form elements.

Next, you'll add an Update Record Server Behavior. You'll apply this in the same manner that you did on the Customers page. The attributes are as follows:

- **Connection** connAcmeDatabases
- **Table to Update** Orders
- **Select Record From** rsGetOrderNo
- **Unique Key Column** OrderID
- **Get Values from Form** Form1
- **Form Elements** Each should correspond to the column in the database that matches the name, if you've set them up this way; make sure that each column gets updated by the correct form element by going through these one by one.

- **Column**   Variable type should be checked for each column to make sure that the text and numeric values are appropriate; also, note that OrderDate is stored as a text type.
- **Go To URL**   Leave blank—you'll set the URL in another Server Behavior later.

Saving the Cart to the Database

The last thing you need to do to this page is to put a Server Behavior on the page that will save the cart and the order information to the database table OrderDetails. You could do this manually using the UltraDev Server Behaviors, but there is a Server Behavior built into the cart that will do this: Save Cart to Table (see Figure 24-27).

 There is a bug is some versions of the UltraDev Shopping Cart that causes the Save Cart to Table Server Behavior to generate an error in UltraDev 4. There is a patch available on the CD-Rom that fixes the Server Behavior. You should only apply the patch if you get the error message that getEnclosingTokenForSQLType is not defined:

The Save Cart to Table Server Behavior will take the cart contents and allow you to map the columns in the cart to columns in the database. Then, when your page performs an update or insert to another table, this Server Behavior will insert the cart contents to the Order Details table that you have established. The steps are as follows:

1. Set the connection to **connAcmeDatabases**.
2. Set the table to the **OrderDetails** table.
3. Go through each column in turn and bind it to a database column, with the exception of the Weight, Name, TotalWeight, and Total columns.
4. Set the Unique ID Destination Column to --**OrderID** and check the box for Numeric.
5. Click the lightening-bolt icon to get the Unique ID value, which will contain the OrderID column from the rsGetOrderNo recordset. The code that is generated may have to be tweaked for your own implementation.
6. Use the Browse button to browse to the CheckOut3 page for the Go to URL box. On this page, you will be asked to pay for the order.

Note that the Weight, Name, TotalWeight, and Total columns are not saved to the database. The items are in the cart so that a Cart Display page can show the contents of the cart with the details of the products, without another trip to the database. The weights and names are stored in the Products table of the database and do not need to be stored in the OrderDetails table. That would add redundant data to the database. Also, the totals shouldn't be stored, because they are calculated fields. One rule of database design, you may remember, is that calculated fields shouldn't be stored in the database, because they depend on another column for their result. If someone were to change the Unit Price of an item, the total price would then be inaccurate. You may decide to forego these rules in your own database design for convenience, but the rules are implemented here.

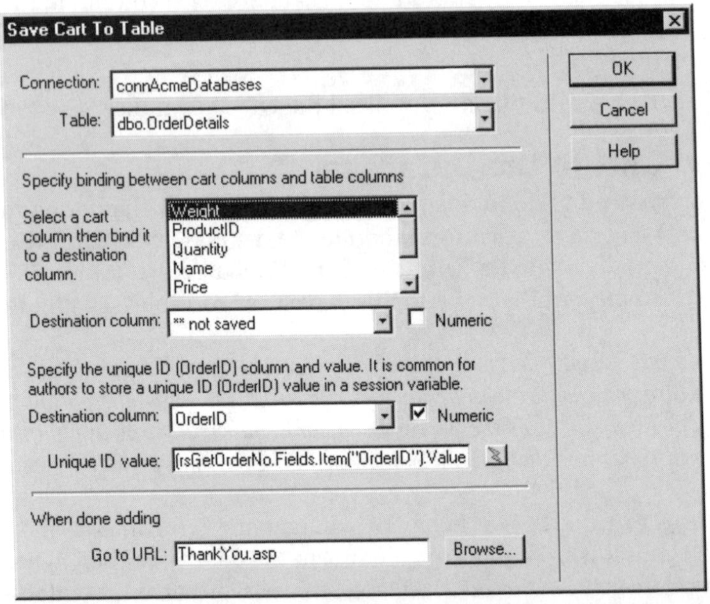

Figure 24-27.   The Save Cart to Table Server Behavior allows you to save the line items of the cart to the Order Details table in your database

Paying for the Order

Start the CheckOut3 page by adding a User Access Server Behavior to the page (from the CD-ROM) as you have been doing on each page. Also, make sure that the template is attached to the page. If it is not, go to the Modify menu and click Templates | Apply Template to Page.

There are many methods for accepting credit cards on your e-commerce site. Most small Web sites will have the e-commerce functionality implemented by a third party. Generally, you need to provide a form that posts the following transaction information to the service:

- Amount of transaction
- Invoice number
- Credit card type
- Credit card number

- Expiration date
- Name on card
- Account name
- Account number

The session variable that is holding the total cost of the order (grandTotal) can be placed in a hidden form field, as well as your account name and number for the transaction. The user should fill out the credit card information. Typically, the credit card type will be in a drop-down box.

You'll implement the transaction as a simple insert to the database, but the steps are similar to submitting the form to an online transaction company. You are asking the user to fill out the credit card information on a form, whereupon the form is submitted after it's been completed.

You'll insert a six-row, two-column table on the page and place descriptors in the first column of the table—Credit Card Type, Name on Card, Card Number, Expiration Date, Grand Total, and Commit Transaction. The second column should have the following: a drop-down box in row one; text fields in rows two, three, and four; two hidden form elements in row five; and a submit button in row six. Put a form tag around the whole thing and then name the form elements one at a time by using the Property Inspector. These will be named according to the column names in the Payments table of the database. The PaymentAmount column will be bound to one of the hidden elements, which will contain the value of the session variable named grandTotal. Do this either by dragging the session variable from the Data Bindings palette to the hidden form element or by typing into the Property Inspector the appropriate code for the session variable. The other hidden form element will contain the value of the session variable named uccartOrderDate.

Next you'll create a recordset to get the payment types for the drop-down list. Create a new recordset named rsPaymentTypes and use the following SQL statement:

```
Select PaymentMethodID, PaymentMethod, CreditCard
FROM PaymentMethods
```

Next, you assign the result to the drop-down box. The way to do this is to choose Dynamic Elements | Dynamic List/Menu from the Server Behaviors menu and simply bind the database columns (see Figure 24-28). The Label should be bound to the PaymentMethod column, and the Value should be bound to the PaymentMethodID column. Last, the Select Value Equal To attribute will be bound to the PaymentMethod column as well.

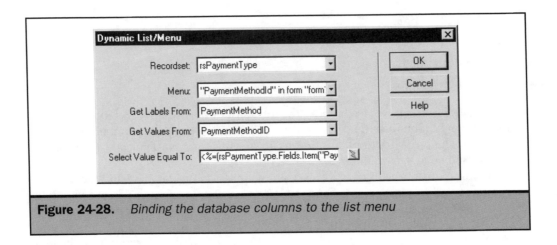

Figure 24-28.   *Binding the database columns to the list menu*

Tip   *In actual practice, a recordset like this can be placed at the application level and called once when the application starts. Declare it in the Global.asa, Global.jsa, or Application.cfm file and use conditional logic so that the database is accessed only once when the application starts (on restart). A recordset that feeds a drop-down box should be a read-only, forward-only cursor.*

Next, you'll put an Insert Record Server Behavior on the page. Use the same connection once again (connAcmeDatabases) and use the Payments table. Make sure the form elements are bound to the correct columns and that the data type is correct. You'll have to go through the columns one by one to make sure that all are accounted for. Last, set the Go to URL attribute to the ThankYou page.

That completes the transaction. The order information is stored in the database, as well as the customer's information and the payment information. There are still a few other loose ends that need to be tied up.

The ThankYou Page

Once again, you'll have to make sure that the template is attached. If it's not attached, go to the Modify menu and click Templates | Apply Template to Page. The User Access Server Behavior doesn't have to be applied here—because it's only a page thanking the user for the order, there isn't anything that requires server-side script. This page should be an HTML page, so make sure it's saved with an .htm file extension. Place a "thank you" message on the page. The links at the top of the page should give users enough options to find their way out of the site. Chances are good, though, that the users will be using the Download link if they ordered any downloadable merchandise. You can make the choice clearer by adding some text and a link to the Download page:

If you've ordered downloadable merchandise, proceed to the Download page.

Any page on your site that doesn't require server-side scripting should be made into a plain HTML page wherever possible to conserve precious server resources.

The Download Pages

Recall that you are offering file downloads on the Acme Databases site as part of the products list. After users purchase software, you must have a way for them to retrieve their downloads. You'll do this by going directly to the OrderDetails table in the database and pulling out the information about purchases. When a user reaches the Download page, the user's CustomerID is stored in a session variable. That's all you need to make the connection between the Customer, the Orders table, the OrderDetails table, and the Products table.

Start the page by adding a User Access Server Behavior to the page (from the CD-ROM) as we have been doing on each page. Also, make sure the page is attached to the template that we've been using for each page. If not, you'll need to go to Modify | Templates | Apply Template to Page and apply the template.

The download information (link, name, and download count) is stored in the Products table. The ProductID values are stored in the OrderDetails table that will enable you to retrieve the product information. To retrieve only the download information for the current customer, you go to the Orders table to match the OrderID and match the CustomerID. The SQL statement will look like this:

```
SELECT OrderDetails.ProductID, Products.ProductName,
   Products.DownloadLink, Products.DownloadCount
FROM OrderDetails
INNER JOIN Products ON
   OrderDetails.ProductID = Products.ProductID
INNER JOIN Orders ON
   OrderDetails.OrderID = Orders.OrderID
WHERE (Orders.CustomerID = TM_userid)
GROUP BY OrderDetails.ProductID,
   Products.ProductName,
   Products.DownloadLink,
   Products.DownloadCount
HAVING (NOT (Products.DownloadLink = N''))
```

This SQL statement accomplishes the task. This is the Microsoft SQL Server version of the query. It may be slightly different for your own RDBMS. The statement will retrieve only those download links that the user has specifically paid for and has an OrderID for.

Create a recordset named **rsDownloads** and type the preceding query into the Advanced recordset creation SQL box. Something this complex can't be built by using the limited "wizard" in the SQL builder. Luckily, if you are using tools such as

Microsoft Access, Microsoft SQL Server, or IBM's DB2, they include query-building tools that make the task of building complex queries much less painful. The key is to retrieve *only* the records that you need.

 Using autonumber or other incremental primary key values poses a security risk and shouldn't be used in an advanced site where security is a concern. The art of creating unique identifiers varies from RDBMS to RDBMS and from application server to application server, and is beyond the scope of this book. Autonumbers are perfectly acceptable for noncritical data, however.

You'll also need to create a variable to accept the session variable TM_userid as the filter for the database. The values for the variable are shown in Table 24-19.

Next, insert a two-row, three-column table on the page and put the labels for the table on row one. The labels will be Product ID, Product Purchased, and Download Count. In row two, put the rsDownloads.ProductID in cell one, ProductName in cell two, and DownloadCount in cell three.

To create the link for the download, select the ProductName text, right-click, and select Make Link. The link will be the DownloadCount page. Before closing the box, you need to add two parameters to the link (see Figure 24-29). By clicking the Parameters button, you can add a parameter named Link that comes from the data source for the DownloadLink column, and a parameter named File that will contain the data source for the ProductID column.

Next, you'll add a Repeated Region behavior to the second row that contains the column information. Set the Repeated Region to show all records by clicking the All radio button.

That does it for the Download page. Half of the battle is won now. You've added a link to the DownloadCount page where the actual download will occur, and you've eliminated some of the security risks by passing the download link to the user from the database. In an actual site, you would likely include one more layer of security to

Name	Default Value	Run-Time Value	Server Language
TM_userid	0	Session("TM_userid")	ASP
		session.getValue("TM_userid")	JSP
		#Session.TM_userid#	ColdFusion

Table 24-19.   *The Session Variable TM_userid Is Used to Filter the Recordset*

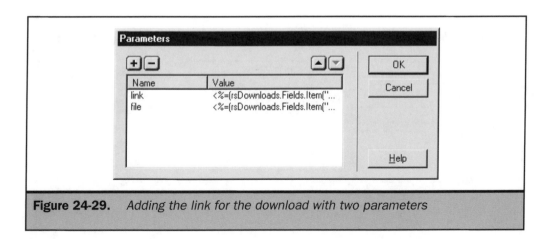

Figure 24-29.   *Adding the link for the download with two parameters*

prevent unauthorized downloads. This is something that would be determined at the site level, depending on the server model.

The DownloadCount Page

This page will accept the download link from the Download page and redirect the user to the actual file on the server. Start the page by adding a User Access Server Behavior to the page (from the CD-ROM) as you have been doing on each page.

Also, a value in the database in the DownloadCount column will be incremented. This is accomplished by inserting a command on the page if you are using ASP, a prepared statement if you're using JSP, or an update query if you are using ColdFusion. Note that in ColdFusion, you can write the SQL in a standard Recordset dialog box.

You can insert a command by opening the Server Behaviors palette and clicking Command (see Figure 24-30) or by clicking Prepared in JSP. The command will have the attributes listed in Table 24-20. The values listed in the table need to be entered into the UltraDev Command or Prepared Server Behavior dialog box to perform an update command. ColdFusion users will add the values to the Recordset creation dialog box.

Next, you'll need to add a redirect statement that points to the file that is to be downloaded. This was passed from the previous page in the Link QueryString variable, so you can add this bit of code to the page to take care of the redirect:

ASP VBScript

```
<%
If Request("Link") <> "" Then Response.Redirect(Request("Link"))
%>
```

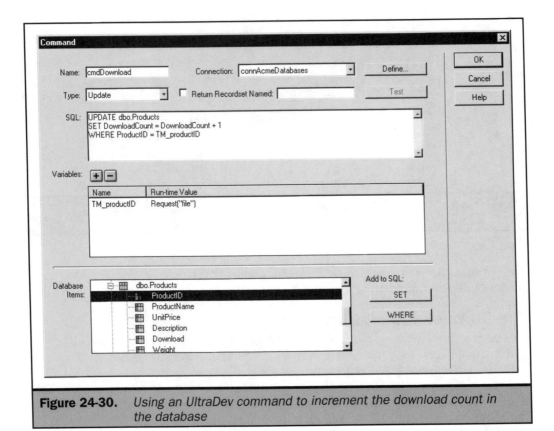

Figure 24-30. *Using an UltraDev command to increment the download count in the database*

ASP JavaScript

```
<%
if(Request("Link")!=null) Response.Redirect(Request("Link"));
%>
```

JSP

```
<%
if (request.getParameter("Link")!=null) {
   response.sendRedirect(request.getParameter("Link"));
   }
%>
```

Attribute	Value
Name	cmdDownload
Connection	connAcmeDatabases
Type	Update
SQL	UPDATE Products SET DownloadCount = DownloadCount + 1 WHERE ProductID = TM_productID
Variables: Name	TM_ProductID
Run-time Value (ASP)	Request("file")
Run-time Value (JSP)	request.getParameter("file")
Run-time Value (ColdFusion)	#URL.file#

Table 24-20.   *Values for the cmdDownload Update Command*

ColdFusion

```
<CFIF IsDefined("url.Link")>
    <CFIF url.Link NEQ "">
        <CFLOCATION url="#url.Link#">
    </CFIF>
</CFIF>
```

Last, you'll put a line of text on the page to act as an error statement if the URL variable wasn't passed for one reason or another:

There was an error. Try again or contact Customer Service.

The Error Page

You'll implement an Error page that will serve as a universal Error page to which all errors will be redirected. Put some generic text on the page, such as "There was an error." As your site gets more complex, you can customize your Error pages to specific problems that the user might encounter. One method is to redirect a user to an Error page and include a query string variable (or URL variable for the ColdFusion users). You could pass an error variable named error with a value that consists of a predetermined error number, as in Error.asp?error=3. In pseudocode, the error page would look like this:

```
If Request(error) is 1
     Display "You need to log in"
If Request(error) is 2
     Display "You need a valid password"
If Request(error) is 3
     Display "There was a database error"
```

Another method is to pass the actual error text to the error page, as in the following statement:

```
Response.Redirect("Error.asp?error=Failed%20login")
```

On the error page you could then display the incoming QueryString variable on the page, as in

```
There was an error: <%=Request("error")%>
```

The SignUp and Signup1 Pages

You'll implement a basic SignUp page that asks the user to choose a username and password, and then allows them to shop on the site. This page should once again be attached to the template, but it won't have the User Access Server Behavior on it. Since the user will be registering for the first time, there won't be a unique CustomerID yet.

Several things need to happen when the user signs in for the first time:

1. The user enters a username, which must be unique: it must not exist in the database.
2. The user enters a password, which should be entered twice for confirmation.
3. The username and password are inserted into the database and a CustomerID is issued to the user.
4. The login screen is bypassed and the cookie is set on the user's machine for the site.

The first step, of course, is to create the form. First, insert a form on the page and then insert a four-row, two-column table inside the form and put the following captions in column one: **Enter a Username**, **Enter a Password**, and **Confirm Password**. Insert text fields in column two to correspond to the captions named username, password, and passwordConfirm. The two password text fields should be "password"-type boxes by checking the radio button in the Property Inspector of each form field for "password."

Insert a submit button in the last row. Make sure that the form tags are around the entire table by examining it in Code view.

Next, you need to edit the form tag, which can be done in any one of three ways:

- By opening the HTML source view (or Code view) and directly editing the code
- By right-clicking (CTRL-clicking on the Macintosh) the broken red line that makes up the "form" in design view and choosing "edit tag <form>"
- By right-clicking the <form> tag button on the bottom left of the design window and choosing "edit tag <form>"

Create an onSubmit() event by placing the following code into the <form> tag:

```
onSubmit="return form1_onSubmit()"
```

Next, you have to create the form1_onSubmit() function that's called in the event. In the head of the document, place this client-side JavaScript:

```
<script language="JavaScript">
<!--
function form1_onSubmit() {
if (document.form1.password.value != ¬
document.form1.passwordConfirm.value) {
    alert("The passwords must match.");
    return false;
    }
return true;
}
//-->
</script>
```

The preceding function merely confirms that the password values match. In actual practice, you'll want to validate all form fields in your site, including the username field on this page.

Next, set the Action of the form by using the Property Inspector of the form and browsing to the SignUp1 page, which you'll create next.

The SignUp1 Page

The SignUp1 page will be a pass-through page. The page will open a recordset to check the database for username values and insert the username and password if the username is unique. You did this in Chapter 18 with the Check New Username Server Behavior, but now you'll do it manually. The first thing to do is to make sure that this page is *not* attached to the template. Since it's just a pass-through page, you don't want any extra weight (code) attached to the page. In fact, the page doesn't need any HTML code whatsoever, so feel free to remove it in HTML source view. Also, you don't want the User Access Server Behavior on the page either, because it's the user's first visit.

Next, you'll put a recordset on the page and set it to the connAcmeDatabases connection that you've been using throughout the site. The name of the recordset should be **rsDoesCustomerExist**. Your SQL statement will be as follows:

```
SELECT Username, Password
FROM Customers
WHERE Username = 'TM_username'
```

The variable will be set to take the place of the incoming form variable, as shown in Table 24-21.

The next few steps will require a little hand-coding and a little trickery. If you followed the Server Behavior chapter, you know that UltraDev inserts the server-side code with a *weight* attached to it. Each Server Behavior has a specified weight that allows UltraDev to insert the code in relation to other weighted code blocks. For instance, a recordset has a weight of 50, and a typical User Login Server Behavior has a weight of 51 so that it executes directly after the recordset creation. In some cases, however, the weight of the Server Behavior might not be appropriate. Or, if the weights match exactly, the Server Behaviors have to be applied in the correct order. Also, sometimes when you go back to edit a Server Behavior, it will move to a position out of the order that it was in originally if it had the same weight as another Server Behavior.

The point of this is that you want to put a recordset and an insert command on the page together. The command will depend on the recordset being executed first, so you have to make sure the recordset is placed on the page first, and that it remains that way after applying the command.

This discussion refers to the ASP Server Behavior command; but in JSP, you use a Prepared Server Behavior, and in ColdFusion, you use a standard recordset and insert an Insert statement in the Query dialog box.

Name	Default Value	Run-Time Value	Server
TM_username	%	Request("username")	ASP
	%	request.getParameter("username")	JSP
	%	#username#	CF

Table 24-21. *The Variable for Username Is Set Up in the Recordset Creation Dialog Box*

Apply a command (or Prepared Server Behavior for JSP, or query for CF) to the page and set it to Insert. The values should be applied as shown in Table 24-22.

Take a look at the Code view and make sure that the code block that this insert command resides in is placed after the recordset. If it isn't, you'll have to cut and paste it to a place below the recordset.

Next, you'll add a little hand-coding to allow the insert command to take place *only* if the recordset doesn't return any rows. Insert the following code immediately above the insert command, but within the same code block:

ASP VBScript

```
If rsDoesCustomerExist.eof AND rsDoesCustomerExist.bof Then
```

Attribute	Value
Name	cmdGetUsers
Connection	connAcmeDatabases
Type	Insert
SQL	INSERT INTO Customers (Username,Password)VALUES ('TM_username', 'TM_password')
Variables: Name	TM_username
Run-time Value (ASP)	Request("username")
Run-time Value (JSP)	request.getParameter("username")
Run-time Value (ColdFusion)	#username#
Name	TM_password
Run-time Value (ASP)	Request("password")
Run-time Value (JSP)	request.getParameter("password")
Run-time Value (ColdFusion)	#password#

Table 24-22.   *Parameters for the Insert Command/Prepared/Query*

ASP JavaScript

```
if(rsDoesCustomerExist.eof && rsDoesCustomerExist.bof) {
```

Java

```
if(rsDoesCustomerExist_isEmpty) {
```

ColdFusion

```
<CFIF rsDoesCustomerExist.RecordCount EQ 0>
```

The code above the insert command effectively creates the opening of an If/Then/Else statement. Then, after the insert command code, but within the same block once again, insert this code, which will end the conditional region:

ASP VBScript

```
Response.Redirect("Success.asp?username=" & Request("username") & ¬
"&password=" & Request("password"))
Else
Response.Redirect("Error.asp")
End If
```

ASP JavaScript

```
Response.Redirect("Success.asp?username=" + Request("username") + ¬
"&password=" + Request("password"));
}else{
Response.Redirect("Error.asp");
}
```

Java

```
response.sendRedirect("Success.jsp?username=" + ¬
(String)request.getParameter("username") + ¬
"&password=" + (String)request.getParameter("password"));
}else{
```

```
response.sendRedirect("Error.jsp");
}
```

ColdFusion

```
<CFLOCATION ¬
url="Success.cfm?username=#username#&password=#password#">
<CFELSE>
<CFLOCATION url="Error.cfm">
</CFIF>
```

The preceding code will cause the user to be redirected to the Success page if the username was unique, and to the Error page if the username already exists in the database. The Success page, as you may recall, set up the cookies and the session variables for the CustomerID and AccessGroups. That page used the incoming form variables named username and password. From this page, you are sending QueryString or URL variables instead. The query is set up so that it will work with both. This is a technique that is used in many of the built-in Server Behaviors that rely

---

A Few Notes About Scaling the Site

The site as it stands is a good starting point for a small-scale e-store. Keep in mind, however, that certain techniques were used to keep the site small and simple. When scaling to a larger or more secure site, there are several things to consider.

- Databases such as Microsoft SQL Server, IBM's DB2, and Oracle8i have stored procedures that allow the use of transactions. Stored procedures should be used to allow the use of multiple queries, multiple inserts, and return values.

- Business functionality should be moved to components on the server. In ASP, these could be COM components; in JSP, you can use Enterprise JavaBeans (EJBs); and in ColdFusion, you can use custom tags. Another option would be to move more functionality into the database as stored procedures.

- The download links should be secured in such a way as to prevent unauthorized use. One method is to dynamically apply AccessGroup levels to the page as the actual filenames. In other words, if a user has "zipcode.mdb" privileges, he'll be able to download the zipcode.mdb file.

Also, the files should be stored in a directory that doesn't have READ access. In addition, the files should be downloaded by sending a binary stream to the browser instead of being linked to.

- Anything that is subject to privacy issues, such as credit card numbers, shouldn't be stored in a database; or if they are, they should be encrypted. User IDs, usernames, passwords, and other private pieces of data shouldn't be left open for hackers to access. Security issues are beyond the scope of this book.

- The current cart is only configured as a cookie. If the user leaves the site and then comes back to the site from another machine, the cart contents won't be there. You could implement another database table to accommodate "active" carts.

on a form variable being submitted the first time a page is hit, and QueryString variables upon subsequent hits.

Summary

This chapter has gone through a complete implementation of a sample small e-store using the UltraDev Shopping Cart. You've built the store from the ground up, including the database design, site design, page implementation, and shopping cart functionality. As you can see, building an e-store is no trivial task, and even the most basic e-commerce site is going to require a lot of work. It was this chapter's intent to better illustrate the process of developing basic e-commerce capability with UltraDev on any Web site.

A Few Last Words

UltraDev is a program that deals with a multitude of different technologies. To become proficient in the use of UltraDev, you'll need to be proficient in HTML, JavaScript, SQL, graphics, database design, and one of the four server technologies that UltraDev can be used with. We've tried to present the material in such a way as to give the user a complete picture of what is possible with the program.

The Complete Reference

Appendix A

What's on the CD

821

The CD-ROM that comes with the book contains the major examples presented in the book, as well as the multimedia tutorial. The CD-ROM is broken down into directories that correspond to the chapters in the book.

Chapter 16 contains an Access database that is covered in the tutorial in the chapter. This database is necessary to complete the exercises in Chapters 18 and 19. Also included are the sample data in CSV format for each table, and SQL scripts to generate the database for Microsoft SQL Server and IBM DB2. If you have another database type, you can use the information in the chapter to build your own database and import the sample data.

Chapters 18 and 19 contain the completed Web sites that correspond to the exercises in the chapters. The sites are complete for all four server languages covered and work with UltraDev 4. Also included is a bare-bones site so that you can build the site from the starting point of Chapter 18. The template has been applied to the pages, so that all that's needed is the addition of server-side functionality.

Chapters 20–23 contain all the code necessary to complete the extensions that are built in the chapters, as well as the completed extensions. The ReadMe file in each folder will give any necessary instructions.

Chapter 24 contains the completed e-store that is built in the chapter in all four server languages; it also includes UD1 and UD4 versions of the sample store. The database that is needed for the chapter is included as an Access 97 version. Also included are the raw sample data in CSV format and SQL scripts needed to generate the databases for Microsoft SQL Server and IBM DB2.

Additional information can be found in the ReadMe files that accompany each folder.

The multimedia tutorial has a setup program. You should run the setup program and install it onto your computer.

If you find a problem with any of the software, please write to us and let us know. Updates, when available, will be posted at www.basic-ultradev.com.

Appendix B

Resources

W e've attempted to provide a broad overview of the knowledge base that relates to Dreamweaver UltraDev. If you require further research, the Web offers a vast collection of resources. Also, we've listed a few other books out there that relate to the topics covered in this book.

Web Sites

The following are a few useful links.

UltraDev Links

- **www.basic-ultradev.com**   Our site; any updates to the software on the CD will be available here

- **www.dreamweaverfever.com** /   Drew McLellan's site of Dreamweaver and UltraDev extensions and tutorials

- **http://www.udzone.com**   UltraDev extensions and community site run by George Petrov and Waldo Smeets

- **www.macromedia.com/support/ultradev**   Macromedia's UltraDev Support Site

- **www.magicbeat.com**   UltraDev and related topics from Jag Sidhu's Web development site, featuring popular mailing lists

- **www.projectseven.com**   Al Sparber's Dreamweaver and UltraDev tutorials, extensions, and design packs

- **www.macromedia.com/support/dreamweaver/extend/form/**   Macromedia's UltraDev and Dreamweaver extensibility newsgroup

- **www.ultradevextensions.com**   Wayne Lambright's UltraDev tutorials and portal site for UltraDev users

- **www.hiran.desilva.com/ultradev**   Ultradev Cookbook with tutorials by Hiran de Silva

- **www.massimocorner.com**   Massimo Foti's corner of the Web has tons of extensions for Dreamweaver and UltraDev

- **http://jjooee.media3.net/udtmp**   Joe Milicevic's UltraDev extensions, including the original Server Behavior builder

- **www.charon.co.uk**   UltraDev demos and extensions from Julian Roberts

- **http://ultradeviant.co.uk**   Owen Palmer's tutorials and extensions

- **www.princeton.edu/~rcurtis/ultradev/index.htm**   UltraDev and shopping cart tutorials

Asp Links

- www.4guysfromrolla.com
- www.asp101.com
- www.asphole.com
- www.asptoday.com

JSP Links

- **www.allaire.com/jrun**   Main site for Allaire's JRun application server
- **www.allaire.com/developer**   Allaire developer page
- **www-4.ibm.com/software/webservers/index.html**   Main link for IBM's Websphere application server
- **http://java.sun.com/products/jsp/**   Information from Sun Microsystems about JSP
- **www.unifyewave.com/**   Application server from Unify, who also offers extensions for UltraDev

DOM Links

- **www.w3.org/TR/REC-DOM-Level-1/level-one-core.html**   w3c document and technical details about the DOM
- **http://developer.netscape.com**   Many useful documents dealing with HTML and JavaScript

ColdFusion Links

- **www.houseoffusion.com/**   Excellent mailing lists and tutorials
- **www.forta.com/cf/**   Ben Forta, author of the most popular ColdFusion books, has this informative site
- **http://forums.allaire.com/DevConf/index.cfm**   Allaire's support forums
- **www.sys-con.com/coldfusion/**   Official site of *Cold Fusion Developer's Journal* magazine
- **www.cfvault.com/**   News, articles, and links
- **www.defusion.com/**   News, articles, and links
- **www.forta.com/cf/isp/list.cfm**   A list of ColdFusion Web hosts from Ben Forta's site

Database Links

- **www.microsoft.com/sql/**   Microsoft SQL Server home page
- **www.oracle.com/ip/deploy/database/index.html**   Home page for Oracle's line of database products
- **www.mysql.com**   Official home page for MySQL
- **www.postgresql.org/index.html**   Home page for PostgreSQL
- **www-4.ibm.com/software/data/db2/**   IBM DB2 information

Recommended Reading

The Coldfusion 4.0 Web Application Construction Kit
by Ben Forta, Nate Weiss (Contributor), David E. Crawford (Contributor)
Paperback; 1001 pages; 3rd edition (December 23, 1998)
Macmillan Publishing Company
ISBN: 078971809X

Advanced Cold Fusion 4 Application Development
by Ben Forta, Nate Weiss (Contributor), and Gerry Libertelli (Contributor)
Paperback; 730 pages (November 1, 1998)
Macmillan Publishing Company
ISBN: 0789718103

Core Servlets and JavaServer Pages (JSP)
by Marty Hall
Paperback; 608 pages; 1st edition (May 26, 2000)
Prentice-Hall PTR/Sun Microsystems Press
ISBN: 0130893404

Professional JSP : Using JavaServer Pages, Servlets, EJB, JNDI, JDBC, XML, XSLT, and WML
by Karl Avedal, Danny Ayers, et. al.
Paperback; 897 pages; 1st edition (January 15, 2000)
Wrox Press Inc.
ISBN: 1861003625

Instant ASP Scripts
by Greg Buczek
Paperback; 800 pages; Book & CD-ROM edition (July 16, 1999)
Osborne McGraw-Hill
ISBN: 0071352058

Professional Active Server Pages 3.0
by Alex Homer, David Sussman, et. al.
Paperback; 1277 pages; 3rd edition (September 1999)
Wrox Press Inc.
ISBN: 1861002610

Fireworks 3 Bible
by Joseph W. Lowery with Simon White
Paperback; 895 pages (July 15, 2000)
IDG Books Worldwide
ISBN: 0764534750

JavaScript Bible, 3rd Edition
by Danny Goodman and Brendan Eich
Paperback; 1,015 pages; 3rd edition (March 1998)
IDG Books Worldwide
ISBN: 0764531883

JavaScript: The Definitive Guide
by David Flanagan
Paperback; 776 pages; 3rd edition (June 1998)
O'Reilly & Associates
ISBN: 1565923928

Dynamic HTML: The Definitive Reference
by Danny Goodman
Paperback; 1,073 pages (August 1998)
O'Reilly & Associates
ISBN: 1565924940

Mastering Regular Expressions
by Jeffrey E. Friedl
Paperback; 368 pages (January 1997)
O'Reilly & Associates
ISBN: 1565922573

Sams Teach Yourself SQL in 10 Minutes
by Ben Forta
Paperback; 208 pages (August 1999)
Macmillan Computer Publishing
ISBN: 0672316641

SQL Server 2000 Web Application Developer's Guide
by Craig Utley
608 pages (November 2000)
Osborne Media Group
ISBN: 0-07-212619-1

Professional SQL Server 7.0 Programming
by Rob Vieira
Mass Market Paperback; 1,138 pages; 1st edition (1999)
Wrox Press Inc.
ISBN: 1861002319

Access 2000: The Complete Reference
by Virginia Andersen
Paperback; 1,319 pages; Book & CD-ROM edition (May 1999)
Osborne McGraw-Hill
ISBN: 0078825121

Index

INTERNATIONAL CONTACT INFORMATION

AUSTRALIA
McGraw-Hill Book Company Australia Pty. Ltd.
TEL +61-2-9417-9899
FAX +61-2-9417-5687
http://www.mcgraw-hill.com.au
books-it_sydney@mcgraw-hill.com

CANADA
McGraw-Hill Ryerson Ltd.
TEL +905-430-5000
FAX +905-430-5020
http://www.mcgrawhill.ca

GREECE, MIDDLE EAST,
NORTHERN AFRICA
McGraw-Hill Hellas
TEL +30-1-656-0990-3-4
FAX +30-1-654-5525

MEXICO (Also serving Latin America)
McGraw-Hill Interamericana Editores S.A. de C.V.
TEL +525-117-1583
FAX +525-117-1589
http://www.mcgraw-hill.com.mx
fernando_castellanos@mcgraw-hill.com

SINGAPORE (Serving Asia)
McGraw-Hill Book Company
TEL +65-863-1580
FAX +65-862-3354
http://www.mcgraw-hill.com.sg
mghasia@mcgraw-hill.com

SOUTH AFRICA
McGraw-Hill South Africa
TEL +27-11-622-7512
FAX +27-11-622-9045
robyn_swanepoel@mcgraw-hill.com

UNITED KINGDOM & EUROPE
(Excluding Southern Europe)
McGraw-Hill Publishing Company
TEL +44-1-628-502500
FAX +44-1-628-770224
http://www.mcgraw-hill.co.uk
computing_neurope@mcgraw-hill.com

ALL OTHER INQUIRIES Contact:
Osborne/McGraw-Hill
TEL +1-510-549-6600
FAX +1-510-883-7600
http://www.osborne.com
omg_international@mcgraw-hill.com

WARNING: BEFORE OPENING THE DISC PACKAGE, CAREFULLY READ THE TERMS AND CONDITIONS OF THE FOLLOWING COPYRIGHT STATEMENT AND LIMITED CD-ROM WARRANTY.

Copyright Statement

This software is protected by both United States copyright law and international copyright treaty provision. Except as noted in the contents of the CD-ROM, you must treat this software just like a book. However, you may copy it into a computer to be used and you may make archival copies of the software for the sole purpose of backing up the software and protecting your investment from loss. By saying, "just like a book," The McGraw-Hill Companies, Inc. ("Osborne/McGraw-Hill") means, for example, that this software may be used by any number of people and may be freely moved from one computer location to another, so long as there is no possibility of its being used at one location or on one computer while it is being used at another. Just as a book cannot be read by two different people in two different places at the same time, neither can the software be used by two different people in two different places at the same time.

Limited Warranty

Osborne/McGraw-Hill warrants the physical compact disc enclosed herein to be free of defects in materials and workmanship for a period of sixty days from the purchase date. If you live in the U.S. and the CD included in your book has defects in materials or workmanship, please call McGraw-Hill at 1-800-217-0059, 9 A.M. to 5 P.M., Monday through Friday, Eastern Standard Time, and McGraw-Hill will replace the defective disc. If you live outside the U.S., please contact your local McGraw-Hill office. You can find contact information for most offices on the International Contact Information page immediately following the index of this book, or send an e-mail to omg_international@mcgraw-hill.com.

The entire and exclusive liability and remedy for breach of this Limited Warranty shall be limited to replacement of the defective disc, and shall not include or extend to any claim for or right to cover any other damages, including but not limited to, loss of profit, data, or use of the software, or special incidental, or consequential damages or other similar claims, even if Osborne/McGraw-Hill has been specifically advised of the possibility of such damages. In no event will Osborne/McGraw-Hill's liability for any damages to you or any other person ever exceed the lower of the suggested list price or actual price paid for the license to use the software, regardless of any form of the claim.

OSBORNE/McGRAW-HILL SPECIFICALLY DISCLAIMS ALL OTHER WARRANTIES, EXPRESS OR IMPLIED, INCLUDING BUT NOT LIMITED TO, ANY IMPLIED WARRANTY OF MERCHANTABILITY OR FITNESS FOR A PARTICULAR PURPOSE. Specifically, Osborne/McGraw-Hill makes no representation or warranty that the software is fit for any particular purpose, and any implied warranty of merchantability is limited to the sixty-day duration of the Limited Warranty covering the physical disc only (and not the software), and is otherwise expressly and specifically disclaimed.

This limited warranty gives you specific legal rights; you may have others which may vary from state to state. Some states do not allow the exclusion of incidental or consequential damages, or the limitation on how long an implied warranty lasts, so some of the above may not apply to you.

This agreement constitutes the entire agreement between the parties relating to use of the Product. The terms of any purchase order shall have no effect on the terms of this Agreement. Failure of Osborne/McGraw-Hill to insist at any time on strict compliance with this Agreement shall not constitute a waiver of any rights under this Agreement. This Agreement shall be construed and governed in accordance with the laws of New York. If any provision of this Agreement is held to be contrary to law, that provision will be enforced to the maximum extent permissible, and the remaining provisions will remain in force and effect.

NO TECHNICAL SUPPORT IS PROVIDED WITH THIS CD-ROM.

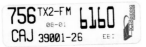